Grief After Suicide

THE SERIES IN DEATH, DYING, AND BEREAVEMENT
ROBERT NEIMEYER, CONSULTING EDITOR

FORMERLY THE **SERIES IN DEATH EDUCATION, AGING, AND HEALTH CARE**
HANNELORE WASS, CONSULTING EDITOR

Grief After Suicide

*Understanding the Consequences
and Caring for the Survivors*

Edited by
John R. Jordan
John L. McIntosh

Routledge
Taylor & Francis Group
New York   London

Routledge
Taylor & Francis Group
270 Madison Avenue
New York, NY 10016

Routledge
Taylor & Francis Group
27 Church Road
Hove, East Sussex BN3 2FA

© 2011 by Taylor and Francis Group, LLC
Routledge is an imprint of Taylor & Francis Group, an Informa business

Printed in the United States of America on acid-free paper
10 9 8 7 6 5 4 3

International Standard Book Number: 978-0-415-99355-5 (Hardback)

Library of Congress Cataloging-in-Publication Data

Jordan, John R.
    Grief after suicide : understanding the consequences and caring for the
survivors / John R. Jordan and John L. McIntosh.
        p. cm.
    Includes bibliographical references and index.
    ISBN 978-0-415-99355-5 (hardcover : alk. paper)
    1. Grief--Psychological aspects. 2. Suicide--Psychological aspects. 3.
Bereavement--Psychological aspects. 4. Suicide--United States. 5. Grief--United
States. I. McIntosh, John L. II. Title.

HV6545.J66 2010
362.28'3--dc22   2010015911

**Visit the Taylor & Francis Web site at
http://www.taylorandfrancis.com**

**and the Routledge Web site at
http://www.routledgementalhealth.com**

This book is dedicated to people everywhere who have lost a loved one to suicide. We hope that it helps in the growing effort to make the journey of survivors a healing one.

CONTENTS

SECTION 1   THE IMPACT OF SUICIDE

SECTION 4   PROMISING PROGRAMS OF SUPPORT FOR SURVIVORS: INTERNATIONAL PROGRAMS

SECTION 5   CONCLUSIONS

SERIES EDITOR'S FOREWORD

Grief After Suicide is a volume written for two readerships: for every thoughtful clinician who welcomes an empirically informed orientation to the daunting terrain of suicide survivorship, and for every researcher who seeks to make a practical contribution to the growing knowledge base concerning the tragic aftermath of self-destruction. Both readers will be satisfied by what they find in this substantial compendium, the clinician by the book's innumerable scientifically grounded and therapeutically astute insights into assessment issues and treatment strategies for working with the suicide bereaved, and the researcher by the sweeping and integrative review of decades of theoretical and empirical advances. As a piece of clinical scholarship that aims to bridge the sometimes distant domains of research and practice, this volume is a masterpiece.

And so it should be, in a sense, as it represents the culmination of the careers of two eminent clinical scholars, John R. (Jack) Jordan and John L. McIntosh. Each brings the wisdom of a long and deep engagement in suicidology to the authorship and editorship of this volume, a joint *gravitas* that informs their discussion of controversial questions such as whether suicide bereavement differs, and in what respect, from other forms of loss—particularly those under traumatic conditions. Likewise, countless hours of working alongside survivors to rebuild their shattered lives leavens the editors' review of therapeutic issues and procedures, guiding them as they sift the most reliable of research findings for "news you can use" as a practicing clinician confronted by the distress and disorientation that is nearly always the emotional aftermath of a loved one's fatal and tragic decision to choose dying over living. Moreover, beyond their own meaty contributions to the material between these covers, the editors have recruited a veritable *Who's Who* of researchers and therapists active in the area, who collectively address in probing but readable terms nearly every facet of the topic the reader could imagine, while minimizing the risk of redundancy. Thus, whether the reader is seeking information on the incidence, risk factors, coping challenges, family dynamics, or prospects for positive outcomes associated with suicide survivorship, or is hoping for research-substantiated guidance in working with grieving parents, spouses, children, adolescents, families, groups, or even organizations following the elective death of a member, he or she will not be disappointed.

As if this were not enough for one volume, the editors have included 18 brief chapters outlining the leading programs offering tailored services to suicide survivors, both in the United States and abroad. In an important sense, then, the book is more than an authoritative review of a broad-ranging field of scholarship, and more than a clinical handbook for dealing with the immediate and long-term challenges faced by clients touched by this life-altering loss. It is also a virtual blueprint for progressive programs to address a pressing social need that transcends national boundaries, calling for creative local solutions to a global problem.

Finally, the editors close the book—and in a sense close the circle—by considering thoroughly the sorts of methodological and substantive issues that should inform future research efforts if they are to be even more clinically useful in their yield. The consistent focus on bridging research and practice that weaves like a leitmotif through the pages of this volume is as clearly in evidence in the book's closing chapters as it is in those devoted to the exploration of practice strategies stemming from different contemporary models (whether the dual process model of coping with bereavement or approaches to meaning reconstruction). It is this integrative thrust of the writing that marshals the disparate collection of the topical chapters into an integrative whole, and makes the volume in general a compelling read.

In short, *Grief After Suicide* easily nominates itself as the most comprehensively conceived, critically informed, and clinically useful book of its kind on the contemporary scene, and it is likely to retain this status for many years. Perhaps it is not too much to hope that the cogent scientific information and clinical wisdom distilled, integrated, and illustrated in frequent case studies in this volume will greatly benefit or perhaps even save the lives of many suicide survivors who might themselves otherwise succumb to despair. It is a certainty that it will greatly enrich and orient the professional lives of many of the therapists and interventionists who attempt to help them.

Robert A. Neimeyer, PhD
Series Editor

FOREWORD

This rich offering presents a wondrous cornucopia of perspectives, specific theories, systematic research evidence, as well as hard won clinical experience regarding survivors of suicide. Inclusive it is, but not *all*-inclusive: selectivity both keen and wise has been employed by the editors—no surprise given their invaluable past contributions and leadership roles in suicidology. Their approach reminds one of the anecdote told of Arnold Toynbee who, following his public lecture at Oxford on religion, was approached by the mythical little old lady who sweetly asked him if one didn't always have to have an open mind on such matters. Toynbee is said to have replied "Yes, but not so open that my brains fall out."

This collection represents more than an update, a reference source, a milestone, though it obviously qualifies as all of these. It also deliberately constructs a launching platform with guidance for future research and for survivor service programs. Its vision is broad enough to deal sensitively with the legacy of postsuicide psychological, professional, and legal complexities bequeathed on therapists. Comprehensive, scholarly, often tough-minded, it buries—except for predictable Lazarus-like returns—many of our simplisms. It includes quite recent research, some not yet published, and has a strong integrative thrust where feasible. It represents a model of respectful forthright disagreement between major conceptual stances and disparate readings of evidence. Amidst a literature awash with methodological misdemeanors, felonies, and capital crimes, the authors here, in general, happily chose to extract and accent the best and predominant findings rather than scold and howl at the moon over shortcomings. Proper humility and caution about our current knowledge base is repeatedly evidenced in such phrases as "dearth of studies," "few studies," "not scientifically established," "tentative findings," and "relatively little controlled studies."

At a substantive level the authors highlight many significant veins of ore. To mention but a few, one recognizes a more multilayered contextualism, an intensified recognition that no survivor is an island. Survivors are placed in surviving families, with heightened accent on the power of postsuicide family dynamics, family members' asynchronies of coping styles and pacing that go well beyond matters of blaming or silencing. The role of peers is extended and dissected well beyond the customary focus on adolescents. A longstanding neglect of the reverberations on survivors within the workplace organizations that are so central a part of our existence is corrected. (Intriguingly, the one organizational context previously scoped and analyzed has been the mental health setting, pinpointing the swirling, oft destructive reactions of the "failed" therapist's colleagues.) The survivor's immediate social milieu has long been in our focus. But the picture now has become far more transactional, moving beyond one-dimensional images of social shunning or awkward avoidance to parallel, interactive concepts of survivor "self-stigmatization" and self-isolation. Beyond the immediate community context, the potency of broader cultural variables, doctrines (religious and otherwise), the *meanings* ascribed to suicide, the plethora of culturally assumed or assigned motivations of suicide (including benevolence), the availability or exclusion of redemptive ritual ... all receive richer recognition or freshened analysis. And along with it, realization of the conflicting crosscurrents *within* societal domains rather than prior implicit assumptions of a single or even primary set of attitudes, values, and beliefs.

Amidst suicidology's general well-differentiated approach to survivor groups, e.g., by age (children, adolescents, adults), kin relationship (widows, widowers, siblings, parents of adolescents), degree of involvement/intimacy (friends, acquaintances), or special functions (therapists), we begin to see in these pages emerging allusions to the reactions of old if not elderly parents to their adult children's suicides, and—what may well await us in mounting numbers—adult offsprings' responses to their aging parents' suicides. Coming from a different sector entirely, we find suggestion that in considering survivor reactions (and services), perhaps we best first attend to a metric of survivor attachment to the deceased.

Joining trends in the psychological and psychiatric literature, more and more we find stress not just on the substantial percentage of survivors appearing at least as recovered as the nonsuicide bereaved, or even assessed as "within normal limits" on a set of measures, but emphasis upon and detailing of specific mechanisms of survivor coping and resilience, as well as multiple pathways to eventual adaptation. Heavy weight is assigned to the role of cognitive processes, the survivor's construction of meaning, and a coherent narrative of the suicide that promotes an acceptable, nondestructive, self-esteem–supporting understanding of the suicide and its relation to the survivor's life. Beyond that, as a relative latecomer to our formal literature, we find references to posttraumatic growth (with the savvy recognition this does not exclude the co-existence of suffering or damage).

Those systematic conceptual and empirical components of the book are, in welcome supplementation, followed by opportunities to learn of and from an array of descriptions of intervention programs for survivors. They represent well the current, ever evolving, expanding state-of-the-field of programs for survivors of suicide. They also represent our proud legacy from the seeds sown by an initial lonely band of survivor pioneers, who in a context of deep personal grief pitted their creativity, dedication, persistence, and resilience against powerful tides of ignorance, stigma, and avoidance. This section of the book represents must reading for any individual or organization seeking to initiate or expand services to survivors of suicide.

Suicide survivors here are variously defined, ranging from family members to a far wider set of those seriously affected by the suicide. The described programs for them range from national to local; from government to private foundations to a single individual's efforts; from low cost to free; and from services set in schools, coroners' offices, workplaces, places of worship, hospices, senior centers, or funeral homes. They involve face-to-face contact or telephone or Internet connection, and are freestanding or a component of broader organizations. Services are provided by professionals or lay survivors, or jointly; are targeted for any and all survivors or for specific age, gender, religious, ethnic, subcultural or indigenous groups; are provided one-on-one, or for families, extended families, or exclusively in groups; involve immediate proactive outreach orientations or require survivor initiative; are located in urban vs. rural settings; and may be open-ended or time-limited.

Such services often make available a burgeoning set of written materials for survivors—pamphlets, brochures, workbooks, books, newsletters, and so forth—as well as richly informative Web sites. Some include participation in the training of police, fire, and other first responders in immediate contact with survivors, or in the education of mental health professionals or clergy. At another level, we have graduated to the point of generating directories of suicide survivor services, quasi-accreditation of survivor programs, training manuals, segments of national and international conferences exclusively devoted to survivor issues, and the creation of formal, response plans vis-à-vis suicides in institutional settings. Truly a creative, productive ferment! How proud Shneidman would be!

Yet for all the progress of aid to survivors visible in and beyond the programs presented, there are gaps, blind spots, indeed possible sources of self-defeat also apparent, e.g., with a few admirable exceptions, too little outreach, *early* outreach, to those survivors who can accept it; too little attention to the *obstacles* survivors encounter in obtaining care. But above all we must be concerned about the lack of evaluation—oft unblinking indifference to objective evaluation—of the effectiveness of our services to survivors. We can only go so far in this realm carried by the virtues of our empathy and good intentions. Perhaps we can comfort ourselves for a while longer considering this period of invention as our "thousand flowers blooming" stage. But surely we must be working toward a point when we will have differentiated systematic intervention research-based best practice guidelines for our various forms of ameliorative work with suicide survivors.

It is said that generals are always planning for the preceding war, and intelligence agencies are always planning how to prevent their prior fiascos. Perhaps understandably: as a distinguished physicist once put it, "Prediction is very difficult, especially about the future." But we do soon need to be thinking through the implications for survivors, for instance, of increasingly enhanced and easily available suicide "technologies," physician-assisted suicides or what hospital associations much prefer to call "managed deaths," ever-briefer psychiatric hospitalizations of the suicidal, aging populations, the downside of diminishing stigma surrounding suicide, and the unique problems of serving the immediate comrades and far-flung family members of suicides in the armed services. Past performance suggests we will. Meanwhile, this book's editors and contributors have produced a document that will simultaneously energize, refine, and direct the future efforts of investigators, teachers, agency program leaders, mental health professionals, and lay volunteers alike in preventing the ugly arithmetic of adding the warping of suicide survivor lives to the life already tragically ended.

Albert C. Cain

ACKNOWLEDGMENTS

For my part, this book has depended on the help of many people who have supported and inspired me in writing it. I think of myself as only a "distant" survivor of suicide loss (a great-uncle, Arthur Spencer). Arthur's death was a sad experience for me, but it was not a life-transforming one. Instead, my clients who are suicide survivors have taught me almost everything that I know about the journey of despair and resilience that survivors walk. Therefore, I must first thank my clients for the gift of allowing me to share their journey with them—the knowledge that I have gained from walking that journey with so many people has led directly to this book, as well as the motivation to create it. Second, I thank the many, many students and trainees who have attended workshops that I have given over the years on grief counseling, traumatic loss, and suicide prevention and postvention. Although it may seem that students learn from their teacher, in truth the process is quite reciprocal and many of my ideas have been formulated and refined in the process of interacting with trainees around the world. Third, I express my gratitude toward my children, Kate and John, who deserve special thanks. Being a parent to them has taught me (sometimes unwillingly and certainly imperfectly) patience, persistence, and forgiveness—qualities that have helped me to complete this book. Their chosen paths of service to others continue to inspire and make both their mother and me very proud. Last, this book literally would not exist without the forbearance, patience, willingness to carry more than her share of the family load, and unending support of my wife, Mary Ruby. I am deeply grateful for all that she has given to me over the years of our marriage, including the time and space to allow this book to come to fruition.

—John R. Jordan

There have been no suicides in my family of which I am aware, but my contact with survivors began when among the first individuals associated with suicidology I met were two survivors, Stephanie Weber and Adina Wrobleski. Their sharing of their loss and the dearth of information and research about this topic raised my awareness and recognition of the importance of suicide survivorship. I extend special thanks to the many survivors who have taught me so much about suicide bereavement, sharing their experiences and providing information. In particular, I thank Adina Wrobleski, Stephanie Weber, Karen Dunne-Maxim, Edward Dunne, Iris and Jack Bolton, Betsy Ross, Michelle Linn-Gust, Frank Campbell and the LOSS Team from the Baton Rouge Crisis Intervention Center, Frank Jones, Judy Meade, and the many others who have played an important role. I also thank my family, specifically my wife Charleen, my children Shawn and Kim, Kim's husband, Paul and son Ethan (who was born during the writing of this book), and my parents, Donald and Marietta, for their support and love. In addition I thank my institution, Indiana University South Bend, for its support of my efforts across the years, and my colleagues in the Department of Psychology and Academic Affairs. Finally, I acknowledge the role of my mentor, John Santos, Professor Emeritus of the University of Notre Dame, for the support and encouragement he has provided both early in my graduate years and throughout my career.

—John L. McIntosh

EDITORS

John R. (Jack) Jordan, PhD, FT, is a licensed psychologist in private practice in Wellesley, Massachusetts, and Pawtucket, Rhode Island, where he specializes in working with loss and bereavement. He is the founder and, until 2007, was the director of the Family Loss Project, a research and clinical practice providing services for bereaved families. Dr. Jordan has specialized in work with survivors of suicide and other losses for more than 30 years. As a Fellow in Thanatology from the Association for Death Education and Counseling (ADEC), he maintains an active practice in grief counseling for individuals and couples. He has run support groups for bereaved parents, young widows and widowers, and suicide survivors, with the latter running for more than 13 years.

Dr. Jordan is the Clinical Consultant for Grief Support Services of the Samaritans in Boston, where he is helping to develop innovative outreach and support programs for suicide survivors. He is also the Professional Advisor to the Survivor Council of the American Foundation for Suicide Prevention (AFSP), and a former board member of AFSP (New England Affiliate) and ADEC. In 2006, Dr. Jordan was invited to become a member of the International Workgroup on Death, Dying, and Bereavement, and was the recipient of the ADEC 2006 Research Recognition Award. He has been involved in several research projects on the needs of people grieving after a suicide, and in 2004 received research funding from AFSP to investigate the support needs of survivors after a suicide.

Dr. Jordan has provided training nationally and internationally for therapists, healthcare professionals, and clergy through PESI Healthcare/CMI Education, the American Foundation for Suicide Prevention, and as an independent speaker. He has also helped to organize and lead many healing workshops for suicide survivors. His clinical and research articles in the areas of bereavement after suicide, support group models, the integration of research and practice in thanatology, and loss in family and larger social systems have been published in numerous professional journals, including *Omega, Death Studies, Suicide and Life-Threatening Behavior, Psychiatric Annals, Crisis, Grief Matters,* and *Family Process.* Dr. Jordan is the co-author, with Bob Baugher, of *After Suicide Loss: Coping with Your Grief* (Baugher and Jordan, 2004), a book on suicide bereavement for surviving friends and family.

Photo courtesy Indiana University

John L. McIntosh, PhD, is Associate Vice Chancellor for Academic Affairs and Professor of Psychology at Indiana University (IU) South Bend. He has previously authored, co-authored, or co-edited six books on suicide, including *Elder Suicide: Research, Theory and Treatment* (American Psychological Association, 1994) and *Suicide and Its Aftermath: Understanding and Counseling the Survivors* (W. W. Norton, 1987). Dr. McIntosh has contributed many chapters and articles to books and professional journals and made numerous professional presentations and keynote addresses at professional conferences. He also serves on the editorial boards of *Suicide and Life-Threatening Behavior, Gerontology and Geriatrics Education,* and *Crisis: The Journal of Crisis Intervention and Suicide Prevention,* as well as on the Editorial Advisory Board of *Advancing Suicide Prevention* magazine. Dr. McIntosh is a past president of the American Association of Suicidology (AAS), the 1990 recipient of the association's prestigious Edwin Shneidman Award (awarded to a person below the age of 40 for scholarly contributions in research to the field of suicidology), and the 1999 recipient of the Roger Tierney Award for Service. Dr. McIntosh's work has been reported in newspapers and magazines across the country, including the *Wall Street Journal, Washington Post, New York Times, USA Today, Boston Globe, Chicago Tribune,* and *Newsweek.* He also appeared on *The Phil Donahue Show* (1986) and *The Oprah Winfrey Show* (1989) to discuss suicide in the elderly.

Dr. McIntosh has been recognized by his campus and university for his research and teaching. He is a recipient of IU South Bend's Distinguished Teaching Award, the Eldon F. Lundquist Faculty Fellow, and the Distinguished Research Award, as well as an Indiana University all-university President's Award for Distinguished Teaching.

CONTRIBUTORS

Margaret Nelson Agee, PhD
Senior Lecturer
School of Counseling,
   Human Services and
   Social Work
University of Auckland
Auckland, New Zealand

Rosalie S. Aldrich, PhD
Adjunct Professor, Department of
   Communication
Honors Program
Indiana State University
Terre Haute, IN

Karl Andriessen, M Suicidology
Coordinator
Suicide Prevention Program
Flemish Mental Health Centers
Gent, Belgium

LaRita Archibald
Founder and Director
HEARTBEAT Survivors After
   Suicide, Inc.
Colorado Springs, CO

Karyl Chastain Beal, MEd, CT
Founder and Administrator
Parents of Suicide–Friends &
   Families of Suicides
   Internet Community, and
   the International Suicide
   Memorial Wall
Columbia, TN

**Susan Beaton, Graduate
Diploma Psychology**
National Advisor on
   Suicide Prevention
Lifelines Australia
Canberra, Australia

Lawrence Berkowitz, EdD
Director
Riverside Trauma Center
Needham, MA

Iris M. Bolton, MA
Director Emeritus
LINK Counseling Center
Atlanta, GA

Emily Bullitt, BA
Samaritans
Boston and Framingham, MA

Peter Bycroft, MS
Adjunct Professor
Faculty of Arts and Social
    Sciences, University of the
    Sunshine Coast
Queensland, Australia

**Frank R. Campbell, PhD,
LCSW, CT**
Senior Consultant
Campbell & Associates
    Consulting, LLC
Past President
American Association of
    Suicidology
Baton Rouge, LA

Julie Cerel, PhD
Assistant Professor and Licensed
    Psychologist
College of Social Work, University
    of Kentucky
Lexington, KY

Amy Chow, PhD, RSW, FT
Assistant Professor, Department
    of Social Work and Social
    Administration, University of
    Hong Kong
Hong Kong, SAR, China

Kari Dyregrov, PhD
Senior Researcher
Norwegian Institute of Public
    Health (Suicide Research Team)
Oslo, Norway
Research Leader, Center for Crisis
    Psychology
Bergen, Norway

Norman L. Farberow, PhD
Founder
Los Angeles Suicide Prevention
    Center (now Didi Hirsch
    Suicide Prevention Center) and
    International Association for
    Suicide Prevention
Past President
American Association of Suicidology
Los Angeles, CA

William Feigelman, PhD
Professor of Sociology Emeritus
Nassau Community College
Garden City, NY

Jill Fisher, M Suicidology
National Coordinator
Standby Response Service, United
    Synergies Ltd.
Queensland, Australia

Stephanie Gantt, MA
Research Assistant
Department of Psychiatry and
    Behavioral Sciences, School of
    Medicine, Emory University
Atlanta, GA

Onja Grad, PhD
Clinical Psychologist and
    Psychotherapist
University Psychiatric Hospital
Medical Professor
University of Ljubljana
Ljubljana, Slovenia

Nina Gutin, PhD
Co-Chair, Clinician-Survivor
    Task Force
American Association of Suicidology
Private Practice
Pasadena, CA

Joanne L. Harpel, JD, MPhil
Director of Survivor Initiatives
American Foundation for Suicide
  Prevention
New York, NY

**Jill Harrington-Lamorie,
MSW, LSW, ACSW**
Director of Professional Education
Tragedy Assistance Program for
  Survivors (TAPS)
Washington, DC

Roberta Hurtig, MA
Executive Director
Samaritans
Boston and Framingham, MA

Nadine J. Kaslow, PhD
Professor, Vice Chair for Faculty
  Development, and Chief
  Psychologist
Department of Psychiatry and
  Behavioral Sciences, School of
  Medicine, Emory University
Atlanta, GA

Kim Kates, BA
Director of Grief Support Services
Samaritans
Boston and Framingham, MA

Marilyn Koenig
Co-Founder & Executive Director
Friends for Survival, Inc.
Sacramento, CA

Michelle Linn-Gust, PhD
President-Elect
American Association of
  Suicidology
Washington, DC

Doreen S. Marshall, PhD, LPC
Associate Professor and Chair,
  Counseling Department
Argosy University
Private Practice
Atlanta, GA

James McCauley, LICSW
Assistant Director
Riverside Trauma Center
Needham, MA

Vanessa L. McGann, PhD
Co-Chair, Clinician-Survivor
  Task Force
American Association of Suicidology
Private Practice
New York, NY

Jannette McMenamy, PhD
Associate Professor of Behavioral
  Sciences
Fitchburg State College
Fitchburg, MA

**Ann M. Mitchell, PhD, RN,
FAAN**
Associate Professor of Nursing
  and Psychiatry
Department of Health and
  Community Systems, School
  of Nursing
Department of Psychiatry, School
  of Medicine
University of Pittsburgh
Pittsburgh, PA

Lyn Morris, MFT
Director
Didi Hirsch Suicide Prevention
  Center
Los Angeles, CA

Robert A. Neimeyer, PhD
Professor, Department of
    Psychology
University of Memphis
Memphis, TN

Miesha Rhodes, LMSW
Project Coordinator, Department
    of Psychiatry and Behavioral
    Sciences, School of Medicine
Emory University
Atlanta, GA

Rev. Charles T. Rubey, MSW, LCSW
Loving Outreach to Survivors
    of Suicide (LOSS) Program,
    Catholic Charities of Chicago
Chicago, IL

Kim Ruocco, MSW, LSW
Director of Suicide Education and
    Support
Tragedy Assistance Program
    for Survivors (TAPS)
Washington, DC

Tara C. Samples, MS
Graduate Student, Department of
    Clinical Psychology
Fielding Graduate University
Santa Barbara, CA

Diana C. Sands, PhD
Director
Bereaved by Suicide Service
Sydney, Australia

Donna Schuurman, EdD, FT
Executive Director
The Dougy Center for Grieving
    Children and Families
Portland, OR

Madelyn Schwartz, MA, ABS
Senior Deputy
Thurston County Coroner's Office
Olympia, WA

Nancy Boyd Webb, PhD, LICSW, RPT-S
Distinguished Professor of Social
    Work Emerita
Fordham University
Private Practice
Amesbury, MA

Susan Wesner, MSN, RN
Clinical Nurse Specialist,
    General Adult Clinic, Western
    Psychiatric Institute and Clinic
University of Pittsburgh Medical
    Center
Pittsburgh, PA

Paul Yip, PhD
Director
Hong Kong Jockey Club Centre
    for Suicide Research and
    Prevention
Professor, Department of
    Social Work and Social
    Administration
University of Hong Kong
Hong Kong, SAR, China

INTRODUCTION

Suicide is a critical public health issue. Each year, nearly a million individuals worldwide take their own lives (WHO, 2009), with more than 33,000 Americans dying by suicide (McIntosh, 2009). These deaths leave in their wakes persons who are known as survivors of suicide or the bereaved by suicide. Although it has long been known that suicide can leave devastation in its wake (Cain, 1972), until recently suicide survivors have received relatively little attention in suicidology compared to the focus on understanding and treating suicidal individuals. We believe that the time has come for this to change. As Shneidman noted years ago, work with those bereaved by suicide is a direct form of prevention with a population at risk for suicide themselves, as well as many other mental health and social problems (Shneidman, 1972). This volume demonstrates the considerable empirical evidence substantiating the idea that intervention with suicide survivors is not just the correct thing to do ethically, it is clinically the necessary thing to do, given the potential psychiatric morbidity and even mortality that can follow for suicide survivors.

The suicide bereaved must not only attempt to cope with the death of someone close to them, but must do so in a likely context of shame, stigma, guilt, blame, and confusion about the responsibility for the death, all of which are frequently associated with bereavement after this type of death. Although no reliable determination of the number of suicide survivors exists, even by cautious estimates the numbers are substantial. For instance, in the United States alone, there are conservatively at least 4.6 million living individuals who have lost someone to death by suicide (McIntosh, 2009). These survivors represent mothers, fathers, siblings, grandparents, uncles, aunts, spouses, extended family members, fiancés, partners, friends, coworkers, classmates, teachers, therapists, neighbors, and the many others with whom those who die by suicide had significant relationships. The impact of suicide loss ranges from mild to devastating, depending on many factors. For some, it can literally be life transforming.

Given the enormous impact that suicide can have on individuals, families, and communities, it is surprising and disheartening that in more than 20 years only two major books (Dunne, McIntosh, Dunne-Maxim, 1987; Mishara, 1995) have attempted to summarize the literature on the experience of losing someone to suicide. This lack of attention is the reason that we felt an urgent need to write this book. Although it reaches back to the very beginnings of the literature on grief after suicide, the present volume primarily focuses on the body of knowledge that has accumulated since the publication of Dunne, McIntosh, and Dunne-Maxim's (1987) seminal compilation on the impact of suicide. Our over-arching goal is to bring the field "up to date" on what we do (and do not) know about the experience of bereavement after suicide, and to address the various approaches that have been developed and are emerging to assist those who are bereaved by suicide.

The book provides new approaches to understanding the survivor experience as well as the definition of the term suicide survivor. A new perspective on suicide bereavement within the larger context of the general grief and bereavement research and theory is offered. Current evidence about bereavement following suicide is presented both generally as well as with respect to special populations of survivors. Although similarities between suicide and other bereavement circumstances are noted, the differences are detailed in particular, including those for which evidence already exists and those still to be empirically demonstrated. The full body of knowledge is brought to bear in characterizing suicide bereavement. Thus, the merit of research-based evidence is reviewed and applied to further our understanding and assistance efforts, but additionally, the highly valuable evidence that emerges from clinical practice and case studies, as well as personal accounts of survivors, are incorporated. This volume's goals are to establish not only what is known about suicide survivors and postvention efforts to assist them, but also to draw attention to vital information that is not known but would help us to better understand and assist survivors of suicide. Recommendations for future research and postvention goals for the future are also thoroughly addressed.

The book is organized into five distinct sections. Section 1 is concerned with what we know about the general impact of suicide on survivors. Chapter 1 provides a conceptual framework and rationale for the study of suicide bereavement, and offers a new operational definition of survivorship that we hope will allow research and clinical intervention to advance significantly. Chapter 2 addresses a long-standing debate within the literature (including between the two of us) regarding whether bereavement after suicide is the same as or different from bereavement after other types of losses. We provide a new and we hope more nuanced conceptual framework for answering this important theoretical and practical question.

Following these initial chapters, the first section of the book concludes with three chapters focused on the primary knowledge about suicide grief within particular subpopulations of survivors. Chapter 3 reviews the body of literature involving adults as survivors of suicide while Chapter 4 conveys the same information with respect to the impact of suicide on children and adolescents. Both chapters include a significant focus on the kinship relations of survivors and their deceased loved ones and how those relationships affect bereavement. Chapter 5 considers the often under recognized impact on caregivers of the suicide death of a patient or client.

Section 2 focuses on what we know about helping survivors after a suicide happens. Chapter 6 is based on the premise that intervention programs should be grounded in the empirically established needs of the people who are to be served. It provides an overview of the empirical literature on what survivors tell us has been helpful to them in their efforts to cope, as well as unpublished data from a new study on this subject. Chapter 7 suggests guidelines for mental health providers after the suicide of a client, with practical suggestions to assist both the clinician as well as other survivors of the client's death.

The remaining six chapters of this section focus on various special approaches, settings, and populations with respect to helping after a suicide. These include postvention for organizations (e.g., schools, workplaces; Chapter 8), and grief counseling (primarily individual therapy) for adults (Chapter 9) and for child or adolescent survivors of suicide (Chapter 10). Different approaches to intervention with suicide survivors are also highlighted in Chapter 11 (a narrative or constructivist approach), Chapter 12 (an overview of group work with survivors), and Chapter 13 (a description of family techniques with suicide survivors). Chapter 13 also addresses special issues involved in providing culturally sensitive postvention services.

Sections 3 and 4 are organized around invited descriptions of what we consider promising suicide survivor support programs within the United States (Section 3) and internationally (Section 4). The "minichapters" in these sections describe innovative and model programs, including their histories and methods, as well as lessons learned during their development. In addition to a diversity of support and therapy approaches, several highly creative programs for special groups of survivors are detailed. Many of the programs are pioneers in the survivor movement. Resources and activities for and about survivors provided by national organizations in the United States devoted to suicide prevention are also included.

The book concludes in Section 5 with two chapters that look to the future of understanding and helping suicide survivors over the next decade. Chapter 33 considers the various methodological issues and problems associated with suicide bereavement research, as well as the value associated with combining the complementary bodies of knowledge derived from empirical research and qualitative, clinical, and anecdotal evidence. In addition, research priorities are described for future investigations that would enhance understanding of survivors and guide the therapeutic efforts that aim to assist their healing. Chapter 34 provides a call to action with respect to community and programmatic support that we believe need to be developed over the next 10 years for survivors. As Chapter 33 conveys an agenda for research, Chapter 34 proposes common elements of support infrastructure for survivors that we believe need to be developed for suicide survivors around the world.

☐ References

Cain, A. C. (Ed.). (1972). *Survivors of suicide*. Springfield, IL: Charles C Thomas.

Dunne, E. J., McIntosh, J. L., & Dunne-Maxim, K. (Eds.). (1987). *Suicide and its aftermath: Understanding and counseling the survivors*. New York: W. W. Norton.

McIntosh, J. L. (2009, April 25). *U.S.A. suicide: 2006 official final data*. Washington, DC: American Association of Suicidology. Retrieved from http://www.suicidology.org/c/document_library/get_file?folderId=228&name=DLFE-142.pdf

Mishara, B. L. (Ed.). (1995). *The impact of suicide*. New York: Springer.

Shneidman, E. S. (1972). Foreword. In A. C. Cain (Ed.), *Survivors of suicide* (pp. ix-xi). Springfield, IL: Charles C Thomas.

World Health Organization. (2009). *Mental health: Suicide prevention* (SUPRE). Retrieved from http://www.who.int/mental_health/prevention/suicide/suicideprevent/en/index.html

SECTION 1

The Impact of Suicide

Suicide Bereavement: Why Study Survivors of Suicide Loss?

John R. Jordan and John L. McIntosh

The personal narratives of many suicide survivors testify to the reality that the death of a loved one to suicide can be an enormously difficult experience, one that may have life-transforming effects on the mourner (Alexander, 1991; Jackson, 2004; Stimming & Stimming, 1999; Wrobleski, 2002). Empirical and clinical study of survivors also offers considerable support for this intuitive understanding that the loss of a loved one to suicide may be a particularly difficult form of bereavement (de Groot, De Keijser, & Neeleman, 2006; Jordan, 2001, 2008, 2009; Knieper, 1999). Nonetheless, the question of whether mourning after suicide is different—and, if so, whether the differences are quantitative or qualitative in nature (or both)—remains a challenge to be resolved (McIntosh, 2003). The answers to these questions have important implications for how we think about the impact of suicide on survivors and how we develop support services that might ameliorate some of the suffering of those left behind (Jordan, 2001; McIntosh, 2003). Beyond that, there are important definitional issues about survivorship that suicidology and thanatology have yet to address satisfactorily. These issues include determining (a) who is considered a survivor, (b) how many survivors there are, and (c) what the relationship is between exposure to suicide and the experience of becoming a survivor. Our goals for this opening chapter are twofold: to offer a framework for addressing questions (a) and (b) and to make the case for why specialized study of suicide bereavement is needed. In Chapter 2, we address the debate within the literature about whether bereavement after suicide may differ from bereavement after other modes of death—and, if so, in what ways. We also offer a conceptual framework for thinking about the differences and commonalities in bereavement after suicide and after other types of losses. In Chapters 3 through 5, we provide comprehensive reviews of the literature that address the actual impact of suicide on adults, children, and families, and on clinicians who work with suicidal patients.

☐ The Definition of Suicide Survivorship

Who Is a Survivor?

The question of what constitutes survivorship is both conceptual and empirical. Perhaps surprisingly, the conceptual specification of who is a suicide survivor has never really been addressed, let alone agreed upon by writers in the field (Andriessen, 2009; Cerel, Padgett, Conwell, & Reed, 2009; McIntosh, 2003).[1] Most survivor research studies simply define exposure to a suicide as the criteria for participation, and/or they study the immediate kin of the deceased—or, in the case of adolescents, the close friends of the deceased. Nonetheless, we believe that these definitions are, respectively, too broad or too narrow to denote who should be regarded as a potential suicide survivor. The reality is that we simply do not know how many people in a social network are negatively affected by a given suicide because the literature has made two simplistic assumptions: (a) that all suicides are more or less the same in their impact and (b) that the degree

---

[1] The phrase *suicide survivor* itself has presented problems within suicidology (Seager, 2004) and among the general public because the term could logically refer either to someone who has attempted suicide and survived the attempt or to someone who is surviving the death of a loved one to suicide (as in "Mr. Jones is survived by his wife and children."). However, within suicidology and the survivor community in the United States, the meaning of a suicide survivor as someone who is grieving after the suicide of another person appears to have come into wide usage, and we will continue with that convention in this book (McIntosh, 2003).

of impact is largely a function of the degree of kinship closeness to the deceased. We believe that the time has come to develop a more inclusive and empirically based foundation for defining survivorship.

For example, consider the hypothetical suicide of a middle-aged man, a Mr. Smith. He is deeply involved in his small-town community as a son, husband, father, brother, professional person, volunteer soccer coach for his children's teams, deacon in his church, and longtime resident of his town. Although it is obvious that Mr. Smith's wife and children are likely considered survivors, there are many others in his social network who might also be significantly and quite negatively affected by his death. To name but a few, there are his parents, siblings, and extended family members; his colleagues and clients at work; his neighbors; the children and parents of the teams he has coached; his fellow church members; and his current friends not only from the town but from earlier in his life (e.g., a college roommate or a former girlfriend). Although not all of these people will necessarily be significantly affected by Mr. Smith's death, it seems plausible that any one of them might, in fact, be a candidate for a problematic bereavement experience after his suicide.

Contrast Mr. Smith's death with the suicide death of a Mr. Jones. He is an elderly homeless man who has suffered from mental illness most of his adult life. He has been reclusive for many years, having only sporadic contact with a small number of other homeless people and with social agency workers. He has only one living sister, with whom he has not had contact for many years. It seems plausible, in the case of Mr. Jones's death, that there are far fewer people for whom his death will deal a severe and lasting psychological blow.

Defining Survivorship

As shown in the two examples offered previously, *survivorship* might be defined by at least three dimensions. The previously mentioned and most common one is kinship proximity—and, certainly, the family members of either Mr. Smith or Mr. Jones are at risk for having a difficult response to these deaths. Empirical evidence supports the idea that kinship proximity is directly related to the severity of impact of a suicide (Cleiren, Diekstra, Kerkhof, & van der Wal, 1994; Mitchell, Kim, Prigerson, & Mortimer-Stephens, 2004). However, if Mr. Jones's sister has not had contact with him for many years and is dealing with her own medical or financial problems, she may actually have very little response to her brother's death, despite the closeness of her formal kinship relationship with Mr. Jones. Thus, kinship proximity may not always be a marker of survivorship.

A second and more inclusive criterion for survivorship would be those people who have (or have had) a close psychological association with or attachment to the deceased, regardless of their kinship status. The circle of potential survivors grows larger when this definition is used. For Mr. Smith, a larger circle of individuals—for example, his close friends, the children whom he has coached, and a former college roommate with whom he had been very close—might all experience high levels of grief and distress at his passing. Even for Mr. Jones, the circle of potential survivors might be larger than first assumed. For example, an agency social worker who has known and worked with him periodically for many years might find herself feeling surprisingly sad and guilty after her client's suicide. The impact of suicide on professionals who may have worked with the deceased, and the potential for these professionals to also become survivors, has been largely ignored in the mental health field (Campbell, 2006; see Chapter 5 for more information on this topic). A definition of survivorship that includes those who are more closely psychologically involved with the deceased has also received empirical support as an important predictor of grief intensity and distress (Brent, Perper, Moritz, Liotus, et al., 1993; Mitchell et al., 2004; Reed, 1993; Reed & Greenwald, 1991; J. Zhang, Tong, & Zhou, 2005).

A third definition of survivorship would include those who are greatly distressed after the suicide, regardless of their kinship relationship with or psychological closeness to the deceased. For example, the parent of one of the children coached by Mr. Smith who has known him only casually might feel quite angry with Mr. Smith's "betrayal" of the children through the suicide and the bad role model that this parent believes has been set for them. Another example is a homeless person who has never met Mr. Jones but who has been depressed and struggling with his own suicidal feelings—he may hear the news of the suicide on the street and decide to take his own life. Yet another example is someone who feels psychologically responsible for causing, or failing to prevent, the suicide—for example, the engineer of a subway train that strikes and kills a young person who had jumped into the train's path may experience haunting guilt and trauma symptoms after the death, regardless of his obvious innocence in the death.

A General Definition of Survivorship

We draw on all three of these criteria to propose a more precise answer to the question "Who is a survivor?"

A *suicide survivor* is someone who experiences a high level of self-perceived psychological, physical, and/or social distress for a considerable length of time after exposure to the suicide of another person.

Note that embedded in this definition is an important distinction between exposure to a suicide and survivorship. Thus, only a subset of people who are exposed to a suicide will go on to become survivors. The obvious questions of what constitutes a "high" level of distress and a "considerable" length of time are important and, ultimately, empirical questions that can be answered by good research to establish the normative distribution of distress in social networks affected by suicides. The recent effort in thanatology to create a new diagnostic category called complicated grief (CG)—more recently referred to as *prolonged grief disorder* (PGD; Lichtenthal, Cruess, & Prigerson, 2004; Prigerson et al., 2009; Prigerson & Maciejewski, 2005)—is one possible (but certainly not the only) starting point for this endeavor. For example, people who meet symptom criteria for this new disorder after a suicide could be operationally considered survivors for research purposes. Note also that in our proposed definition, the distress can be self-perceived (e.g., the person reports feeling very guilty), observed by others (e.g., the person acts in very angry ways), or identified by more formal measurement (e.g., grief or depression symptom measures). However, we believe that a key element of the definition of survivorship must include self-definition, regardless of any attempts to "objectively" define this term. Survivorship frequently carries with it a number of negative (and perhaps some positive) consequences that transcend simple grief or psychiatric symptoms to include longer term changes in self-identity and life narrative as a result of the death (Feigelman, Jordan, & Gorman, 2009; Stimming & Stimming, 1999; see Chapter 11 for more discussion of the impact of suicide on meaning making and post-traumatic growth processes in survivors). Thus, we would be hard put to define as a survivor someone who did not personally feel that his or her life had been significantly affected by the death.

The time criterion for survivorship is more difficult to define because, in our experience, many people in the deceased person's social network are initially upset and grieving after a suicide but will not necessarily show a lasting negative impact. Although the 6-month duration requirement for the PGD diagnosis is one possible criterion, our personal experience with survivors suggests that this may be too short a time period and is, therefore, likely to produce too many "false positives." A 1-year duration criterion might better describe those who are significantly affected and who are likely to have lasting effects from the suicide. Again, this is ultimately an empirical question that is best answered by solid research on (a) the types and duration of various bereavement trajectories after a suicide and (b) their relative frequencies in the general population of those exposed to suicide.

We are not suggesting that the PGD criteria are the only—or necessarily the best—specific standard to use in defining survivorship. The hallmark of PGD is yearning for the deceased, a characteristic that is most likely to occur in someone who was psychologically close or attached to the deceased but not necessarily in someone who is very affected without much previous relationship with the deceased (e.g., the subway engineer). We believe that responsibility rests with survivors, clinicians, and researchers to collaboratively develop—and, when necessary, adapt—an operational definition of survivorship that suits the goals of the particular project at hand.

Advantages of This Definition

We believe that the general definition of survivorship offered here has several advantages. First, it allows for the possibility that any person, regardless of their social relationship to the deceased, may be significantly distressed after the suicide and may, thus, become a survivor. This corrects what we believe to be a major error in most previous studies of survivorship: the assumption that kinship or psychological proximity is the defining criteria for survivorship. It seems very likely that the highest proportion of survivors will, in fact, be found in those who are either biologically related to and/or psychologically attached to the deceased. Nonetheless, to assume that these individuals are the only people who need to be considered as possible survivors misses an entire group who may be affected by a suicide but are not typically considered in research studies or for clinical services. In theory, this group could include individuals who did not even personally know the deceased but who can identify with him or her—for example, an adolescent who identifies with the music and lifestyle of a rock star who dies by suicide. We believe that our definition paves the way for research into suicide's potentially widespread ripple effects in social networks (such as Mr. Smith's community) that have, to the best of our knowledge, never been studied except for the peers of adolescents who died by suicide (Brent et al., 1992, 1994; Brent, Perper, Mortiz, Allman et al., 1993; Cerel, Jordan, & Duberstein, 2008).

Second, this definition can be operationalized in a way that allows research on the numbers of survivors to proceed in a more standardized fashion. For example, the use of the proposed criteria for PGD (mentioned earlier) would be one operational way of defining survivorship and empirically studying how many people in the network of the deceased have become survivors after the suicide. Other ways of operationally defining a high level of distress for a considerable period of time can also be developed as suits the needs of the research study or clinical service of interest.

Last, although broad enough to include the more commonly used definitions of survivorship (*exposure, kinship proximity,* and *perceived closeness*), this definition draws an important distinction between simple exposure to suicide and actual survivorship. We believe this is important because only some people who are exposed to a suicide will be significantly negatively affected for a considerable period of time, and identifying those who are at greatest risk will be a key element of prevention efforts to reduce the harmful effects of suicide. It is likely that the risk profile for survivorship will share much in common with the risk factors for the development of post-traumatic stress disorder (PTSD) after other types of traumatic experiences (King, Vogt, & King, 2004) or for CG responses after other types of loss experiences (Hansson & Stroebe, 2007; Reed, 1998; Stroebe, Folkman, Hansson, & Schut, 2006). Nonetheless, certain factors may uniquely contribute to risk after suicide that help differentiate this pattern of bereavement from other types of traumatic events (Callahan, 2000; Jordan, 2001; Melhem et al., 2004a; Range, 1998; Sveen & Walby, 2008). This issue of distinctive factors that may be associated with suicide bereavement is discussed further in Chapter 2. Here, we make the point that it is crucial for purposes of conceptual understanding and for clinical intervention that we learn more about who will likely have the most difficult bereavement trajectories among those exposed to suicide—something that our proposed definition of survivorship should help clarify and facilitate. This also fits with a growing recognition in thanatology that the most distressed mourners after any type of loss are also those who are most in need of—and the most likely to benefit from—organized, professionally based bereavement interventions (Currier, Neimeyer, & Berman, 2008; Jordan & McMenamy, 2004; Jordan & Neimeyer, 2003; B. Zhang, El-Jawahri, & Prigerson, 2006).

☐ The Impact of Survivorship

Exposure Versus Survivorship: How Many Survivors Are There?

Previous reports of the number of survivors have generally failed to define criteria for survivorship, making an evidence-based answer to this question very difficult to develop (McIntosh, 2003). Instead, most authors seem simply to have used "guesstimates" of the number of survivors. For example, Shneidman (1972) suggested that for every suicide, there are at least six survivors, or approximately 200,000 new survivors per year at current U.S. suicide rates. This figure has now been so widely quoted that it is sometimes repeated as an established fact when, in reality, it was only an educated guess by a pioneer in the field. In similar fashion, Wrobleski (2002) offered an estimate of 10 survivors for every suicide. To the best of our knowledge, no one has ever operationally defined survivorship and then conducted epidemiological research to obtain accurate estimates of the true number of people who are significantly affected within a social network after a suicide. This type of study is urgently needed and would greatly advance the field of survivor studies (Cerel et al., 2009; Jordan & McMenamy, 2004; McIntosh, 2003; see Chapter 33 for our proposed research agenda for survivor studies).

In the absence of this type of investigation, however, are there data about the number of people who are simply exposed to the suicide of someone they know? A study by Crosby and Sacks (2002) helps answer this question. Extrapolating from the sample in their well-designed telephone survey of U.S. households, these researchers calculated that approximately 7% of the U.S. population was acquainted with someone who died by suicide in the previous year. This equals about 1 in every 14 people or approximately 21 million people at current U.S. population levels. More surprisingly, slightly more than 1% of the respondents reported that they had a family member who had died by suicide in the last year. In this study, the authors allowed the term "family member" to include not only immediate kin (e.g., a sibling or child—slightly more than 3% of the sample) but also more distant kin (e.g., a cousin—slightly less than 14% of the sample). At current U.S. population levels, this means that approximately 3.3 million people in the United States reported that they had lost a family member to suicide within the last year. The remainder of the respondents reported that they were an acquaintance of the deceased (e.g., a friend or neighbor—about 80.4% of the sample). Extrapolating from the number of suicides in the U.S. in 1993 (31,102) and the percentage of people reporting exposure to a suicide in 1994, the year the data were collected, Crosby and Sacks estimated that for every suicide about 425 people knew about—and, therefore, were exposed to some degree to—the suicide. Taken together, these figures suggest that there is a startlingly high rate of exposure to suicide in the United States. Following our proposed definition of survivorship, even if only a small percentage of those exposed to a suicide are significantly and negatively affected for a considerable period of time—for example, 1 in 30—this would translate, on average, to about 14 people who become profoundly affected survivors after every suicide, or almost 450,000 new survivors every year in the United States. We believe that these numbers on widespread exposure imply that previous estimates of the numbers of survivors in the United States are quite likely a significant underestimate of the true number of people affected by suicide. As we discuss in the section that follows, it also appears that exposure carries risk with it, including the risk of future suicidality in the person exposed.

Risk Associated With Exposure to Suicide

Chapters 3 through 5 of this book provide comprehensive reviews of the impact of suicide on those left behind. Therefore, we will only briefly note here that considerable and compelling evidence now shows that exposure to suicide carries with it the risk for a number of adverse sequelae. Perhaps the most disturbing of these risks is the elevated likelihood for suicide in a person exposed to the suicide of another individual. For example, on the basis of univariate data analysis,[2] Crosby and Sacks (2002) reported that people in their sample who knew someone who had died by suicide within the last year were 1.6 times more likely to have suicidal ideation, 2.9 times more likely to have suicidal plans, and 3.7 times more likely to have made a suicide attempt. Hedstrom, Liu, and Nordvik (2008) found that men in Sweden who were exposed to a suicide within their family and in the workplace were, respectively, 8.3 and 3.5 times more likely to die by suicide than those not exposed (the workplace effect was limited to workplace settings of fewer than 100 persons, probably reflecting the importance of psychological propinquity in contributing to suicide). These authors note that although the risk of exposure to the suicide of a family member is higher, the likelihood of exposure to suicide through the workplace is much greater because of the larger number of people with whom one typically interacts in the workplace. Likewise, de Leo and Heller (2008) examined four large datasets, three of them multinational, and found compelling evidence showing that exposure to the suicide of non–family members also increases the risk of suicidal behavior and death by suicide in those exposed, particularly in young people. Similarly, in a series of large sample studies of the national health registries in Denmark, Agerbo, Qin, and colleagues documented the increased risk of death by suicide among people who have

---

[2] The odds ratios did not achieve statistical significance on multivariate analysis but remained greater than 1 for the presence of all three categories: ideation, plans, and attempts.

lost an immediate family member to suicide (Agerbo, 2003, 2005; Agerbo, Nordentoft, & Mortensen, 2002; Qin, Agerbo, & Mortensen, 2002). Note that the elevated risk also holds true for individuals who lose a spouse to suicide—as much as a 46-fold increase for men losing a spouse to suicide (Agerbo, 2005). This evidence strongly suggests that the hazard for survivors is not simply a function of shared genetics among blood relatives, but also involves psychological and/or role modeling effects on those exposed to a suicide. Moreover, although losing a child or spouse to any cause of death increases the risk of suicide, losing a spouse or child specifically to suicide carries an even greater risk than death from other causes (Agerbo, 2003; Qin & Mortensen, 2003). This elevated risk is also present for kin of family members who exhibit suicidal ideation, have made a suicide attempt, and/or have been hospitalized for psychiatric illness. A large number of additional studies have also documented that a family history of suicidal behavior or suicidal completion is associated with an elevated risk of suicide in the individual exposed to this behavior, particularly when coupled with a history of sexual abuse and/or impulsive aggression (Brent, Bridge, Johnson, & Connolly, 1998; Brent & Mann, 2006; Cheng, Chen, Chen, & Jenkins, 2000; Goodwin, Beautrais, & Fergusson, 2004; Mann et al., 2005; Melhem et al., 2007; Pfeffer, Normandin, & Kakuma, 1998; Qin et al., 2002; Roy & Janal, 2005; Trémeau et al., 2005; Tsuchiya, Agerbo, & Mortensen, 2005).

Beyond the elevated risk for suicide, there is also evidence of other negative psychological, physical, and social consequences of exposure to suicide (see Jordan, 2001; McIntosh, 1996, 1999, 2003; see also Chapters 2 through 5 for reviews). For example, researchers have found that people who lose a close relative to suicide demonstrate greater rates of psychiatric disorder themselves (Kessing, Agerbo, & Mortensen, 2003; Tsuchiya et al., 2005). The literature suggests that survivors may be particularly vulnerable to an increased incidence of complicated or traumatic grief (Bailley, Kral, & Dunham, 1999; Barrett & Scott, 1990; Clarke & Wrigley, 2004; de Groot et al., 2006; Dyregrov, Nordanger, & Dyregrov, 2003; Melhem et al., 2004b; Mitchell et al., 2004); depression (including suicidal ideation; Brent et al., 1994, 1998; Brent, Moritz, Bridge, Perper, & Canobbio, 1996; Crosby & Sacks, 2002; Mitchell, Kim, Prigerson, & Mortimer, 2005; Murphy, Tapper, Johnson, & Lohan, 2003; J. Zhang et al., 2005); and PTSD (Brent et al., 1995; Murphy, Johnson, Chung, & Beaton, 2003). These effects appear to be strongest in the familial relatives of those who died by suicide but are also seen in nonfamilial peer survivors, particularly in adolescents (Brent et al., 1996; Cerel, Roberts, & Nilsen, 2005; Poijula, Dyregrov, Wahlberg, & Jokelainen, 2001). Data also support the contention that survivors experience more stigma and less social support after the loss of someone to suicide than after other types of losses (Cleiren, Grad, Zavasnik, & Diekstra, 1996; Farberow, Gallagher-Thompson, Gilewski, & Thompson, 1992; Harwood, Hawton, Hope, & Jacoby, 2002).

Taken together, these studies offer evidence that exposure to suicide is frequently associated with many negative sequelae, the most important of which is an elevated risk for subsequent suicide in the person exposed. But is this true only of bereavement after suicide, or is this simply a consequence of bereavement of any type? In the next chapter, we explore the question of whether bereavement after suicide is "different" and "worse" than bereavement after other types of losses.

☐ References

Agerbo, E. (2003). Risk of suicide and spouse's psychiatric illness or suicide: Nested case-control study. *BMJ: British Medical Journal, 327,* 1025–1026.

Agerbo, E. (2005). Midlife suicide risk, partner's psychiatric illness, spouse and child bereavement by suicide or other modes of death: A gender specific study. *Journal of Epidemiology & Community Health, 59,* 407–412.

Agerbo, E., Nordentoft, M., & Mortensen, P. B. (2002). Familial, psychiatric, and socioeconomic risk factors for suicide in young people: Nested case-control study. *BMJ: British Medical Journal, 325,* 74–77.

Alexander, V. (1991). Grief after suicide: Giving voice to the loss. *Journal of Geriatric Psychiatry, 24,* 277–291.

Andriessen, K. (2009). Can postvention be prevention? *Crisis: The Journal of Crisis Intervention and Suicide Prevention, 30,* 43–47.

Bailley, S. E., Kral, M. J., & Dunham, K. (1999). Survivors of suicide do grieve differently: Empirical support for a common sense proposition. *Suicide and Life-Threatening Behavior, 29,* 256–271.

Barrett, T. W., & Scott, T. B. (1990). Suicide bereavement and recovery patterns compared with nonsuicide bereavement patterns. *Suicide and Life-Threatening Behavior, 20,* 1–15.

Brent, D. A., Bridge, J., Johnson, B. A., & Connolly, J. (1998). Suicidal behavior runs in families: A controlled family study of adolescent suicide victims. In R. J. Kosky, H. S. Eshkevari, R. D. Goldney, & R. Hassan (Eds.), *Suicide prevention: The global context* (pp. 51–65). New York, NY: Plenum Press.

Brent, D. A., & Mann, J. J. (2006). Familial pathways to suicidal behavior: Understanding and preventing suicide among adolescents. *New England Journal of Medicine, 355,* 2719–2721.

Brent, D. A., Moritz, G., Bridge, J., Perper, J., & Canobbio, R. (1996). Long-term impact of exposure to suicide: A three-year controlled follow-up. *Journal of the American Academy of Child & Adolescent Psychiatry, 35,* 646–653.

Brent, D. A., Perper, J., Moritz, G., Allman, C., Friend, A., Schweers, J., … Harrington, K. (1992). Psychiatric effects of exposure to suicide among the friends and acquaintances of adolescent suicide victims. *Journal of the American Academy of Child & Adolescent Psychiatry, 31,* 629–640.

Brent, D. A., Perper, J. A., Mortiz, G., Allman, C., Schweers, J., Roth, C., … Liotus, L. (1993). Psychiatric sequelae to the loss of an adolescent peer to suicide. *Journal of the American Academy of Child & Adolescent Psychiatry, 32,* 509–517.

Brent, D. A., Perper, J. A., Moritz, G., Liotus, L., Schweers, J., Roth, C., … Allman, C. (1993). Psychiatric impact of the loss of an adolescent sibling to suicide. *Journal of Affective Disorders, 28,* 249–256.

Brent, D. A., Perper, J. A., Moritz, G., Liotus, L., Schweers, J., & Canobbio, R. (1994). Major depression or uncomplicated bereavement? A follow-up of youth exposed to suicide. *Journal of the American Academy of Child & Adolescent Psychiatry, 33,* 231–239.

Brent, D. A., Perper, J. A., Moritz, G., Liotus, L., Richardson, D., Canobbio, R., … Roth, C. (1995). Posttraumatic stress disorder in peers of adolescent suicide victims: Predisposing factors and phenomenology. *Journal of the American Academy of Child & Adolescent Psychiatry, 34,* 209–215.

Callahan, J. (2000). Predictors and correlates of bereavement in suicide support group participants. *Suicide and Life-Threatening Behavior, 30,* 104–124.

Campbell, F. R. (2006). Aftermath of suicide: The clinician's role. In R. I. Simon & R. E. Hales (Eds.), *The American Psychiatric Publishing textbook of suicide assessment and management* (pp. 459–476): Arlington, VA: American Psychiatric Publishing.

Cerel, J., Jordan, J. R., & Duberstein, P. R. (2008). The impact of suicide on the family. *Crisis: The Journal of Crisis Intervention and Suicide Prevention, 29,* 38–44.

Cerel, J., Padgett, J. H., Conwell, Y., & Reed, G. A., Jr. (2009). A call for research: The need to better understand the impact of support groups for suicide survivors. *Suicide and Life-Threatening Behavior, 39,* 269–281.

Cerel, J., Roberts, T. A., & Nilsen, W. J. (2005). Peer suicidal behavior and adolescent risk behavior. *Journal of Nervous and Mental Disease, 193,* 237–243.

Cheng, A. T. A., Chen, T. H. H., Chen, C.-C., & Jenkins, R. (2000). Psychosocial and psychiatric risk factors for suicide: Case-control psychological autopsy study. *British Journal of Psychiatry, 177,* 360–365.

Clarke, C. S., & Wrigley, M. (2004). Suicide-related bereavement and psychiatric morbidity in the elderly. *Irish Journal of Psychological Medicine, 21,* 22–24.

Cleiren, M. P. H. D., Diekstra, R. F. W., Kerkhof, A. J. F. M., & van der Wal, J. (1994). Mode of death and kinship in bereavement: Focusing on "who" rather than "how." *Crisis: The Journal of Crisis Intervention and Suicide Prevention, 15,* 22–36.

Cleiren, M. P. H. D., Grad, O., Zavasnik, A., & Diekstra, R. F. W. (1996). Psychosocial impact of bereavement after suicide and fatal traffic accident: A comparative two-country study. *Acta Psychiatrica Scandinavica, 94,* 37–44.

Crosby, A. E., & Sacks, J. J. (2002). Exposure to suicide: Incidence and association with suicidal ideation and behavior: United States, 1994. *Suicide and Life-Threatening Behavior, 32,* 321–328.

Currier, J. M., Neimeyer, R. A., & Berman, J. S. (2008). The effectiveness of psychotherapeutic interventions for bereaved persons: A comprehensive quantitative review. *Psychological Bulletin, 134,* 648–661.

de Groot, M. H., De Keijser, J., & Neeleman, J. (2006). Grief shortly after suicide and natural death: A comparative study among spouses and first-degree relatives. *Suicide and Life-Threatening Behavior, 36*, 418–431.

de Leo, D., & Heller, T. (2008). Social modeling in the transmission of suicidality. *Crisis: The Journal of Crisis Intervention and Suicide Prevention, 29*, 11–19.

Dyregrov, K., Nordanger, D., & Dyregrov, A. (2003). Predictors of psychosocial distress after suicide, SIDS and accidents. *Death Studies, 27*, 143–165.

Farberow, N. L., Gallagher-Thompson, D., Gilewski, M., & Thompson, L. (1992). The role of social supports in the bereavement process of surviving spouses of suicide and natural deaths. *Suicide and Life-Threatening Behavior, 22*, 107–124.

Feigelman, W., Jordan, J. R., & Gorman, B. S. (2009). Personal growth after suicide loss: Cross-sectional findings suggest growth after loss may be associated with better mental health among survivors. *Omega: Journal of Death and Dying, 59*, 181–202.

Goodwin, R. D., Beautrais, A. L., & Fergusson, D. M. (2004). Familial transmission of suicidal ideation and suicide attempts: Evidence from a general population sample. *Psychiatry Research, 126*, 159–165.

Hansson, R. O., & Stroebe, M. S. (2007). *Bereavement in late life: Coping, adaptation, and developmental influences*. Washington, DC: American Psychological Association.

Harwood, D., Hawton, K., Hope, T., & Jacoby, R. (2002). The grief experiences and needs of bereaved relatives and friends of older people dying through suicide: A descriptive and case-control study. *Journal of Affective Disorders, 72*, 185–194.

Hedstrom, P., Liu, K.-Y., & Nordvik, M. K. (2008). Interaction domains and suicide: A population-based panel study of suicides in Stockholm, 1991–1999. *Social Forces, 87*, 713–740.

Jackson, V. (2004). Surviving my sister's suicide: A journey through grief. In F. Walsh & M. McGoldrick (Eds.), *Living beyond loss: Death in the family* (2nd ed.; pp. 401–406). New York, NY: Norton.

Jordan, J. (2009). After suicide: Clinical work with survivors. *Grief Matters: The Australian Journal of Grief and Bereavement, 12*, 4–9.

Jordan, J. (2001). Is suicide bereavement different? A reassessment of the literature. *Suicide and Life-Threatening Behavior, 31*, 91–102.

Jordan, J. (2008). Bereavement after suicide. *Psychiatric Annals, 38*, 679–685.

Jordan, J., & McMenamy, J. (2004). Interventions for suicide survivors: A review of the literature. *Suicide and Life-Threatening Behavior, 34*, 337–349.

Jordan, J., & Neimeyer, R. A. (2003). Does grief counseling work? *Death Studies, 27*, 765–786.

Kessing, L. V., Agerbo, E., & Mortensen, P. B. (2003). Does the impact of major stressful life events on the risk of developing depression change throughout life? *Psychological Medicine, 33*, 1177–1184.

King, D. W., Vogt, D. S., & King, L. A. (2004). Risk and resilience factors in the etiology of chronic posttraumatic stress disorder. In B. T. Litz (Ed.), *Early intervention for trauma and traumatic loss* (pp. 34–64). New York, NY: Guilford.

Knieper, A. J. (1999). The suicide survivor's grief and recovery. *Suicide and Life-Threatening Behavior, 29*, 353–364.

Lichtenthal, W. G., Cruess, D. G., & Prigerson, H. G. (2004). A case for establishing complicated grief as a distinct mental disorder in DSM-V. *Clinical Psychology Review, 24,* 637–662.

Mann, J. J., Bortinger, J., Oquendo, M. A., Currier, D., Li, S., & Brent, D. A. (2005). Family history of suicidal behavior and mood disorders in probands with mood disorders. *American Journal of Psychiatry, 162,* 1672–1679.

McIntosh, J. L. (1996). Survivors of suicide: A comprehensive bibliography update, 1986–1995. *Omega: Journal of Death and Dying, 33,* 147–175.

McIntosh, J. L. (1999). Research on survivors of suicide. In Mary Stimming & Maureen Stimming (Eds.), *Before their time: Adult children's experiences of parental suicide* (pp. 157–180). Philadelphia, PA: Temple University Press.

McIntosh, J. L. (2003). Suicide survivors: The aftermath of suicide and suicidal behavior. In C. D. Bryant (Ed.), *Handbook of death & dying, Vol. 1* (pp. 339–350). Thousand Oaks, CA: Sage.

Melhem, N. M., Brent, D. A., Ziegler, M., Iyengar, S., Kolko, D., Oquendo, M., … Stanley, J. J. (2007). Familial pathways to early-onset suicidal behavior: Familial and individual antecedents of suicidal behavior. *American Journal of Psychiatry, 164,* 1364–1370.

Melhem, N. M., Day, N., Shear, M. K., Day, R., Reynolds, III, C. F., & Brent, D. (2004a). Predictors of complicated grief among adolescents exposed to a peer's suicide. *Journal of Loss & Trauma, 9,* 21–34.

Melhem, N. M., Day, N., Shear, M. K., Day, R., Reynolds, III, C. F., & Brent, D. (2004b). Traumatic grief among adolescents exposed to a peer's suicide. *American Journal of Psychiatry, 161,* 1411–1416.

Mitchell, A. M., Kim, Y., Prigerson, H. G., & Mortimer, M. K. (2005). Complicated grief and suicidal ideation in adult survivors of suicide. *Suicide and Life-Threatening Behavior, 35,* 498–506.

Mitchell, A. M., Kim, Y., Prigerson, H. G., & Mortimer-Stephens, M. (2004). Complicated grief in survivors of suicide. *Crisis: The Journal of Crisis Intervention and Suicide Prevention, 25,* 12–18.

Murphy, S. A., Johnson, L. C., Chung, I.-J., & Beaton, R. D. (2003). The prevalence of PTSD following the violent death of a child and predictors of change 5 years later. *Journal of Traumatic Stress, 16,* 17–25.

Murphy, S. A., Tapper, V. J., Johnson, L. C., & Lohan, J. (2003). Suicide ideation among parents bereaved by the violent deaths of their children. *Issues in Mental Health Nursing, 24,* 5–25.

Pfeffer, C. R., Normandin, L., & Kakuma, T. (1998). Suicidal children grow up: Relations between family psychopathology and adolescents' lifetime suicidal behavior. *Journal of Nervous and Mental Disease, 186,* 269–275.

Poijula, S., Dyregrov, A., Wahlberg, K.-E., & Jokelainen, J. (2001). Reactions to adolescent suicide and crisis intervention in three secondary schools. *International Journal of Emergency Mental Health, 3,* 97–106.

Prigerson, H. G., Horowitz, M. J., Jacobs, S. C., Parkes, C. M., Aslan, M., Goodkin, K., … Maciejewski, P. K. (2009). Prolonged grief disorder: Psychometric validation of criteria proposed for *DSM-V* and *ICD-11.* [Electronic version]. *PLoS Med 6(8),* e1000121. doi:10.1371/journal .pmed.1000121

Prigerson, H. G., & Maciejewski, P. K. (2005). A call for sound empirical testing and evaluation of criteria for complicated grief proposed for DSM-V. *Omega: Journal of Death and Dying, 52*, 9–19.

Qin, P., Agerbo, E., & Mortensen, P. B. (2002). Suicide risk in relation to family history of completed suicide and psychiatric disorders: A nested case-control study based on longitudinal registers. *Lancet, 360*, 1126–1130.

Qin, P., & Mortensen, P. B. (2003). The impact of parental status on the risk of completed suicide. *Archives of General Psychiatry, 60*, 797–802.

Range, L. M. (1998). When a loss is due to suicide: Unique aspects of bereavement. In J. H. Harvey (Ed.), *Perspectives on loss: A sourcebook* (pp. 213–220). Philadelphia: Brunner/Mazel.

Reed, M. D. (1993). Sudden death and bereavement outcomes: The impact of resources on grief symptomatology and detachment. *Suicide and Life-Threatening Behavior, 23*, 204–220.

Reed, M. D. (1998). Predicting grief symptomatology among the suddenly bereaved. *Suicide and Life-Threatening Behavior, 28*, 285–301.

Reed, M. D., & Greenwald, J. Y. (1991). Survivor-victim status, attachment, and sudden death bereavement. *Suicide and Life-Threatening Behavior, 21*, 385–401.

Roy, A., & Janal, M. (2005). Family history of suicide, female sex, and childhood trauma: Separate or interacting risk factors for attempts at suicide? *Acta Psychiatrica Scandinavica, 112*, 367–371.

Seager, P. (2004). Is it too late to turn back the clock? *Crisis: The Journal of Crisis Intervention and Suicide Prevention, 25*, 93–94.

Shneidman, E. (1972). Foreword. In A. C. Cain (Ed.), *Survivors of suicide* (pp. ix–xi). Oxford: Charles C Thomas.

Stimming, M., & Stimming, M. (1999). *Before their time: Adult children's experiences of parental suicide*. Philadelphia, PA: Temple University Press.

Stroebe, M. S., Folkman, S., Hansson, R. O., & Schut, H. (2006). The prediction of bereavement outcome: Development of an integrative risk factor framework. *Social Science & Medicine, 63*, 2440–2451.

Sveen, C.-A., & Walby, F. A. (2008). Suicide survivors' mental health and grief reactions: A systematic review of controlled studies. *Suicide and Life-Threatening Behavior, 38*, 13–29.

Trémeau, F., Staner, L., Duval, F., Corrêa, H., Crocq, M.-A., Darreye, A., … Macher, J.-P. (2005). Suicide attempts and family history of suicide in three psychiatric populations. *Suicide and Life-Threatening Behavior, 35*, 702–713.

Tsuchiya, K. J., Agerbo, E., & Mortensen, P. B. (2005). Parental death and bipolar disorder: A robust association was found in early maternal suicide. *Journal of Affective Disorders, 86*, 151–159.

Wrobleski, A. (2002). *Suicide: Survivors: A guide for those left behind* (3rd ed.). Minneapolis, MN: SAVE: Suicide Awareness Voices of Education.

Zhang, B., El-Jawahri, A., & Prigerson, H. G. (2006). Update on bereavement research: Evidence-based guidelines for the diagnosis and treatment of complicated bereavement. *Journal of Palliative Medicine, 9*, 1188–1203.

Zhang, J., Tong, H. Q., & Zhou, L. (2005). The effect of bereavement due to suicide on survivors' depression: A study of Chinese samples. *Omega: Journal of Death and Dying, 51*, 217–227.

CHAPTER 2

Is Suicide Bereavement Different? A Framework for Rethinking the Question

John R. Jordan and John L. McIntosh

In the epilogue to his book *Man's Concern About Death,* Toynbee (1968) suggested that

> There are always two parties to a death; the person who dies and the sur-
> vivors who are bereaved.... the sting of death is less sharp for the person
> who dies than it is for the bereaved survivor.... There are two parties to the
> suffering that death inflicts; and in the apportionment of this suffering,
> the survivor takes the brunt." (pp. 269, 271)

Toynbee's look at death considered death in the general sense—not specifically that resulting from a suicide. This chapter presents evidence that addresses the experience of suffering by those bereaved by suicide.

Before proceeding to bereavement following suicide, some brief comments are necessary that can place suicide grief into the larger context of bereavement in general. As in general bereavement, there is no single manner in which all individuals respond to or are affected by the death of a significant other to suicide. Some people will respond mildly, whereas others will experience severe grief and sorrow, often producing what is now referred to as *complicated grief* (CG) or *prolonged grief disorder* (PGD; Prigerson et al., 2009; Prigerson & Maciejewski, 2005; Prigerson, Vanderwerker, & Maciejewski, 2008). Moreover, just as has been concluded for grief in general, it seems likely that the majority of people who are exposed to the suicide of someone close to them are unlikely to experience pathological levels of distress associated with their loss, but most will likely experience suffering in the immediate time period after the death of their loved one (Maciejewski, Zhang, Block, & Prigerson, 2007; Ott, Lueger, Kelber, & Prigerson, 2007; see Chapter 3 for a full review). Recall, however, that in Chapter 1, we made an important distinction between simple exposure to suicide and the experience of becoming a *survivor*, who we defined as someone "who experiences a high level of self-perceived psychological, physical, and/or social distress for a considerable length of time after exposure to the suicide of another person" (see Chapter 1, "A General Definition of Survivorship"). The salient question for this chapter concerns whether people who are exposed to suicide are more likely to be affected deeply and negatively by the death than people who have lost a loved one to other modes of death.

☐ Is Suicide Bereavement Different?

For many people, particularly many suicide survivors, the answer to the question "Is suicide bereavement different?" seems obvious: "Yes." This view is clearly buttressed by some of the empirical research that has shown differences between suicide bereavement and other types of loss (Bailley, Kral, & Dunham, 1999; de Groot, De Keijser, & Neeleman, 2006). Yet, as this review reveals, not all studies of this issue have found differences in suicide bereavement when compared with other modes of death (Sveen & Walby, 2008). Of the studies that have found few or no differences, most have compared suicide survivors specifically with other sudden and/or violent-death survivors, such as those individuals who have survived the accidental death or homicide of someone close to them (Cleiren, Grad, Zavasnik, & Diekstra, 1996; Dyregrov, Nordanger, & Dyregrov, 2003; Murphy, Johnson, Wu, Fan, & Lohan, 2003; Range & Niss, 1990; van der Wal, 1989). Thus, the findings that might answer this question are complex and contradictory, and we ourselves have puzzled over—and even disagreed about—the interpretation of the literature on this question (Jordan, 2001; McIntosh, 1999, 2003).

Why Does This Question Matter?

In one very real sense, the question about differences in bereavement (or the contention that one type of loss is worse than another) does not matter. For the individual who has lost someone important to suicide, the question is irrelevant—it is merely an academic exercise that has nothing to do with the deep emotional pain that they are experiencing. Knowing that the grief after suicide is not so different from the grief after an accidental or even a cancer death may do nothing to reduce that pain.

In another sense, however, the question has real importance, considering that the answer has genuine implications for how we understand the journey of survivors and how we go about offering help to those who must walk that journey. Consider this practical question: Should suicide survivors attend support groups that are homogeneous with regard to cause of death, or does that affinity not matter in terms of receiving benefit from group participation? The first author has spoken with clients who found enormous help by attending the Compassionate Friends, a self-help organization for parents bereaved from any cause of death of a child. Yet he has also heard from people who have felt profoundly alienated by a lack of understanding from members of general bereavement support groups (they were told "It's not fair—my child wanted to live, but yours didn't!") or apparently unknowing clinicians (three sessions into the therapy and not long after the suicide, a therapist told a survivor, "You're dwelling on this too much"). These examples illustrate our point: To answer this and many similar questions, we need to address the question of whether suicide bereavement is different, in what ways, and the implications of any differences for intervention with survivors. Equally relevant questions include "Should clinicians expect grief to take longer after a suicide? Is the intense and prolonged rumination about the responsibility for and preventability of the death normal after suicide but abnormal after other types of death? What are the best ways to specifically help suicide survivors?" The answers to all of these questions depend on addressing the crucial issue of whether, and in what ways, suicide bereavement is different. Presently, the research data give us very little guidance regarding how to answer these important questions (Jordan & McMenamy, 2004).

Whether bereavement following a death by suicide differs from other bereavement is answered by examining existing information regarding bereavement following suicide, including its commonalities with other modes of death as well as its differences from death by other causes. The primary emphasis here is on evidence-based information but—particularly in the preresearch period—the general conclusions about suicide bereavement as outlined in these early works are also noted. In addition, because the various reviews of the literature have, in some cases, produced different conclusions by their authors, a review of the reviews will also be presented.

Literature Regarding Suicide Bereavement Differences

Historically, within the field of suicidology, the problems of suicide survivors have received comparatively little attention. The first focused consideration of the sequelae of suicide was the pioneering 1972 book edited by Albert Cain, *Surviving Suicide* (Cain, 1972). This book provided a number of chapters on various issues in the aftermath of suicide, but—as Cain noted in his introduction—almost no research investigations had been conducted, and the chapters in the book represented a good deal of conjecture and extrapolation from psychoanalytic theory and clinical cases. Cain described nine reactions among suicide survivors: reality distortion, tortured object-relations, guilt, disturbed self-concept, impotent rage, search for meaning, identification with the suicide, depression and self-destructiveness, and incomplete mourning. These features might be considered the early components of what Dunne and Dunne-Maxim, 15 years later, would call the *survivor syndrome* (1987, p. xiv). As he further discussed suicide bereavement, Cain noted some other features that later research and personal accounts would echo. These included anniversary reactions, preoccupation with suicide and involvement in prevention efforts, and feelings of shame, stigma, and abandonment.

In what can be considered the first comprehensive review of the survivor literature, Calhoun, Selby, and Selby (1982) analyzed the results of the research on suicide bereavement. It should be noted that not a single study that Calhoun and colleagues reviewed included a control or comparison group of survivors of deaths other than suicide. However, Calhoun and colleagues did provide an extensive view of a wide range of reactions found among suicide survivors that mirrored those identified by Cain (1972): affective responses (e.g., anger or relief), cognitive responses (e.g., guilt, shock), behavioral changes (e.g., sleep difficulties), physical or health problems, and family interactions (e.g., positive or negative effects on communication). Features of the survivor syndrome that were added to Cain's list included the reactions of relief, shock, and disbelief; health problems as well as more physician visits and increased mortality; and possible negative family system effects. Calhoun et al. were willing to suggest three "cautious generalizations" (p. 417) about the possible aspects of suicide survivorship that were unique. These three features were "search for an understanding of the death" (p. 417), greater feelings of guilt, and "the lower levels of social support" likely to be received by suicide survivors (p. 417).

Ness and Pfeffer (1990) conducted a comprehensive review of the literature specifically to address the question "Is bereavement after suicide different?" They examined the research evidence for such variables as differences in the grieving process; the social adjustment of survivors and the social response of others to survivors; the possibility of increased mortality in survivors, particularly from suicide; and the family backgrounds of survivors. Ness and Pfeffer noted that their conclusions needed to be tentative due to the poor methodology used in most of the research on survivors, including selection biases; small samples sizes; and, most important, frequent lack of comparison or control groups of survivors of other types of deaths. Nonetheless, they concluded that, in general, "The data suggest that there are differences between bereavement due to suicide and bereavement due to other types of death" (p. 283). Specifically, they concluded that (a) the bereavement after suicide is usually characterized by shock followed by an intense need to make sense of the reasons for the death; (b) exposure to the suicide of a family member did appear to increase the risk of suicide in the survivor; and (c) the social attitudes toward survivors of others in the community were more negative than after other types of losses.

Van der Wal (1989) reviewed the studies available at the time and concluded that although it was likely that qualitative differences were present in the experience of grief after suicide, little evidence showed that the course of bereavement was any more severe or prolonged than after other types of losses. Likewise, Clark and Goldney (2000) agreed that there was little evidence of quantitative differences in the bereavement experience of suicide survivors but enumerated a number of themes that were common for survivors. These themes included feelings of shock and disbelief; horror; a need to make sense of the death and answer the question "Why?"; guilt, blame, and rejection; feelings of stigmatization and social isolation; and anger and regret at the wasted life of the deceased. Also mirroring this theme of qualitative differences, Range (1998) described a number of the same aspects of bereavement after suicide, including stigmatization, a feeling of being misunderstood or blamed for the death by others, a search for meaning after the suicide, and a need to conceal the cause of death from others. All of these reviewers were echoed by Jordan's (2001) proposal that suicide bereavement was different, in part, in the thematic content of the grief.

In contradiction to these other reviews—and drawing on data from a well-designed longitudinal study comparing survivors of loss due to long-term illness, traffic fatality, and suicide (as well as other studies)—Cleiren and colleagues concluded that kinship relationship to the deceased was much more important in predicting poor outcome than was the mode of death (Cleiren, 1993; Cleiren & Diekstra, 1995; Cleiren, Diekstra, Kerkhof, & van der Wal, 1994).

McIntosh (1993) published a review of the research investigations that had included some form of comparison or control group. From Calhoun and colleagues' (1982) time to the early 1990s, McIntosh identified only 14 studies that compared the suicide bereaved to those individuals who have survived different modes of death. McIntosh believed that six general conclusions could be drawn from the study results:

1. Bereavement reaction to suicide is generally nonpathological.

2. More similarities than differences are observed between suicide survivors and the survivors of other modes of death, particularly compared with survivors of accidental death

3. It seems quite possible that there are a small number of grief reactions or aspects of grieving that may differ, or are even unique, for suicide survivors and that these unique reactions—along with the larger number of more universal grief reactions—may constitute a nonpathological but definable "survivor syndrome"; however, these precise differences and unique characteristics are not yet fully apparent.

4. The course of suicide survivorship may differ from that of other survivors over time.

5. However, despite the assertion in Conclusion 4, by some time after the second year, differences in grief seem minimal or indistinguishable across survivor groups.

6. Also, despite the assertion in Conclusion 4, the kinship relation of the survivor to the suicide, the precise closeness and quality of the relationship, and the time that has passed since the suicide seem to be important factors in bereavement.

Perhaps the most controversial of McIntosh's conclusions has been the implication of few differences between survivors of suicide and other types of death. Although the research evidence at this time still offers general support for this research-based conclusion (Sveen & Walby, 2008), this is not to say that there are no differences in the bereavement process or reactions of survivors of suicide as compared with loss from other modes of death. Oddly, McIntosh's Conclusion 3 seems to have been overlooked in these same considerations—that is, it seems likely that there are differences in suicide grief, but only research investigations in recent years have begun to provide clear or sufficient evidence for them (Sveen & Walby, 2008). As noted in Chapter 33, well-controlled and longitudinal studies are required to sufficiently demonstrate the degree and type of differences between bereavement experiences. In fact, anecdotal evidence, personal accounts, and clinical experience strongly suggest potential differences (see McIntosh, 1999, for some consideration of this issue). These forms of evidence, however, are not as strong as well-designed studies in demonstrating to the larger scientific community that differences exist.

Although McIntosh's analysis of information about survivors focused on traditionally defined, research-based, and thus primarily quantitative evidence, those who have considered the literature and brought more sensitivity to qualitative evidence have disagreed with McIntosh's conclusions, particularly about bereavement differences. A major reason to re-evaluate conclusions such as those of McIntosh is that survivors and those who assist with their healing would benefit from the identification of common features of suicide bereavement. From this perspective and a belief that the evidence is compelling enough in some areas, Jordan (2001) specifically identified qualitative or "thematic" aspects of suicide bereavement that he believed differentiate it from that associated with other modes of death. These themes were that suicide survivors experienced (a) a greater struggle to find meaning in the loss of the loved one (*meaning making*); (b) greater feelings of guilt, responsibility, and blame; and (c) greater feelings of rejection and abandonment by, and anger toward, the deceased. In addition to these thematic aspects of suicide grief, Jordan also noted the social network and family system effects typically associated with suicide loss. More specifically, Jordan argued that suicide survivors are viewed more negatively by others in their social networks, that suicide survivors are more likely to experience feelings of isolation and stigma, and that awareness of the stigmatization by others affects their own behavior (e.g., avoiding others and lying about the cause of death). Finally, Jordan and others have suggested that family systems are negatively affected by the suicide death of a member (Cerel, Jordan, & Duberstein, 2008; Jordan, 2001). This may reveal itself in the form of disruptions of family interactions as well as an increased risk for suicide among family members (see also Chapter 1).

Among other authors who disagreed with McIntosh (1993) were Ellenbogen and Gratton (2001), who objected not so much to specific features of bereavement but to the general focus on bereavement group differences. These authors believe that the emphasis on group differences ignores the variety of individual differences among suicide survivors. When research tries to look collectively at suicide survivors—or compares this group to other collective groups who have lost someone to a death by another mode—individual differences are hidden. In addition, by performing cause-of-death group comparisons, researchers may miss the differences existing among subgroups of suicide survivors. For example, suicide survivors who had some forewarning of the death (e.g., their loved one had made previous suicide attempts) may have a considerably different reaction than survivors who were completely "blindsided" by the death, a point also made by Clark and Goldney (2000).

In the most recent and most rigorous review of studies of suicide survivors that included a comparison group, Sveen and Walby (2008) conducted a qualitative analysis of the results from 41 studies. The interpretation of the results for each variable considered was determined largely by the number of studies that found or failed to find group differences between suicide survivors and nonsurvivors on each particular reaction. Because this was a qualitative analysis, the authors did not specify an explicit cutoff percentage of studies needed for the conclusion to be drawn that there were, in fact, meaningful differences for suicide survivors. However, it appears that for the authors to reach this conclusion about a given variable, a great majority of studies that measured that variable had to have found significantly greater level of distress or pathology for suicide survivors.

The Sveen and Walby (2008) analysis categorized measured outcomes of the studies into mental health variables and grief reactions. The authors identified only a small number of studies that found differences between suicide survivors and other loss survivors on mental health variables. The authors concluded that it has not been established that there are any significant differences between suicide survivors and those who have survived a death by other modes on most mental health variables. This is a conclusion with which we agree, with the possible exception of suicidality in survivors. The specific mental health measures for which no significant differences were observed included overall general mental health indices, depression, suicidal ideation, symptoms of post-traumatic stress disorder (PTSD), and anxiety. Sveen and Walby did note, however, that only one study with limited statistical power examined the variable of suicide attempts; thus, Sveen and Walby concluded that no inferences could be drawn about this particular variable. They also noted, as have we in Chapter 1, that (a) there is considerable evidence from other non-bereavement-related research and (b) exposure to suicide does carry an elevated risk of suicide attempt and suicide completion in survivors.

Sveen and Walby's (2008) findings about mental health variables are consistent with McIntosh's (1993) contention that bereavement following suicide is no more pathological in terms of producing mental health problems than that following other causes of death. However, when discussing whether there are mental health differences between suicide bereavement and other types of losses, it is important to note that the proposed new diagnostic category for PGD (Prigerson et al., 2008, 2009) has not been well studied with regard to its prevalence in suicide survivors. To the best of our knowledge, only two published studies have examined this issue, finding that feelings of responsibility for the death and closeness of kinship relationship to the deceased predicted CG or PGD in survivors (Melhem et al., 2004; Mitchell, Kim, Prigerson, & Mortimer-Stephens, 2004).

In contrast to the examination of mental health variables, Sveen and Walby's (2008) analysis did reveal support for some significant differences between suicide survivors and other loss survivors for a limited number of grief variables. When looking at overall levels of grief distress, studies that used a generic measure of grief did not generally find differences for suicide survivors, although the authors found that studies using the more generic grief measures tended to be done with older widows and widowers, for whom the cause of death may be less salient an issue. However, in studies that used a suicide-specific measure of grief, the findings revealed higher levels of overall grief distress among suicide survivors than among survivors of other causes of death. They reached similar conclusions for specific feelings of rejection, shame, or stigma; for concealment that the cause of the death was suicide; and for blaming with respect to the death. Interestingly, conclusions of no differences between survivors of suicide and other causes of death were drawn for feelings of anger, loneliness, relief, acceptance, and shock.

There was also a group of grief variables that was somewhat ambiguous as to whether differences exist. More specifically, the findings for variables such as searching for an explanation for the death, social support, family functioning and adjustment, and guilt/responsibility were not decisive enough to conclude that there were definitely differences, particularly when compared with other sudden-death survivors. For example, Sveen and Walby reported that guilt was measured 15 times in 14 different studies, with six of the studies finding more guilt for suicide survivors, one study finding more guilt for accidental-death survivors, and the rest of the studies finding no differences. Three out of four studies found higher levels for a similar variable labeled "responsibility for the death" for suicide survivors, and, as noted previously, the variable of "blaming" did consistently find higher levels of this variable in suicide survivors. The authors concluded that "There is no clear answer to the question of whether suicide survivors experience a higher level of guilt/responsibility than other survivors" (p. 24).

The example of findings about guilt/responsibility/blaming exemplifies some important points about the Sveen and Walby (2008) article and its conclusions. Although it is true that many studies examined by these authors in this valuable review did not find differences on grief variables, typically there were also at least some studies that did find differences between suicide survivors' and others' losses on almost all variables. Moreover, those studies that did find differences almost always found more grief distress in the suicide survivors than in the nonsuicide survivors. This finding suggests a general trend toward suicide survivors reporting greater grief distress in the research literature. Further, virtually the only exceptions to this trend occurred when comparisons were made with survivors of accidental or homicide death—also forms of sudden and usually violent death. Thus, although Sveen and Walby generally conclude that differences for suicide survivors failed to be established on a number of variables, it is equally valid to say that many individual studies did find differences between suicide survivors and other types of loss survivors. Moreover, almost all of the studies that did find differences between causes of death showed greater distress for either suicide survivors or for all sudden, traumatic-death survivors compared with natural-death survivors. In the final section of this chapter, we offer a template for understanding this emerging empirical finding of similarities between survivors of all sudden and violent death, including suicide.

Note also that most of the reviewers whom we have cited previously have identified serious methodological problems that limited their ability to draw firm conclusions about the question of whether suicide bereavement is different from that of other losses (Clark & Goldney, 2000; Jordan, 2001; McIntosh, 1999, 2003; Ness & Pfeffer, 1990; Range, 1998; see Chapter 33 for our recommendations to improve future research in survivor studies). Likewise, Sveen and Walby (2008) identified a variety of limitations and methodological issues associated with the body of studies that they considered in their review. For example, they found that whether differences were observed was related to the type of methodology used in the investigation. Studies using interview methods of data collection were more likely to find differences between suicide bereavement and other types of losses than were those studies that used only "objective," paper-and-pencil self-report measures. As an example, the variable of self-reported social support was measured 27 times in 17 studies, and it was found that suicide survivors reported less social support in 15 of those 27 measurements. However, in all six of the studies that measured social support through interview methods, the suicide survivors reported less social support than did survivors of other types of losses. Likewise, studies that used a measure specific to suicide (i.e., the Grief Experience Questionnaire; Barrett & Scott, 1990) were also more likely to report differences that indicated more distress for suicide survivors. Lastly, Sveen and Walby also noted that suicide survivors are most likely not a homogeneous group, varying in part as a result of the trajectory toward suicide by the deceased and the circumstances of the death. For example, their findings of no excessive shock in suicide survivors compared with survivors of other losses may reflect the fact that some (but not all) suicides are anticipated, mitigating the impact of shock for this subset of survivors and instead producing a relief effect (Clark & Goldney, 2000; Jordan, 2001). Likewise, it is not surprising that accidental-death survivors—who, by definition, have no forewarning of the death—may experience more shock and disbelief than some (but not all) suicide survivors.

☐ Possible Common Themes/Reactions/ Features of Suicide Bereavement

At this point, we have summarized a number of the reviews that have compared bereavement after suicide with other types of losses, ranging from natural death or illness to sudden, unexpected deaths (e.g., heart attack), accidental deaths, and/or homicide. In addition, several literature reviews that have summarized the research on the impact of suicide have been noted (Clark & Goldney, 2000; Cleiren & Diekstra, 1995; Henley, 1984; Jordan, 2001; McIntosh, 1993, 1999, 2003; Ness & Pfeffer, 1990; Range, 1998; van der Wal, 1989). Although the body of current research-based evidence remains inadequate to provide strong evidence of clear and consistent differences or unique features associated with suicide bereavement as compared with bereavement from other causes of death, we believe that the evidence is relatively convincing regarding a small number of reactions and aspects of bereavement after suicide. In line with the review by Sveen and Walby (2008) with regard to mental health variables, and based on the available body of information, we do not believe that there is any convincing evidence for a discrete "survivor's syndrome." The term *syndrome* most often connotes a definable and distinct set of symptoms that are pathological, and, as noted, there is insufficient evidence that suicide grief is any more pathological than grief from other modes of death, particularly other sudden, unexpected, and violent forms of death. In place of the concept of "syndrome," we prefer the idea of common features of suicide bereavement in the sense that these issues frequently (although not always) occur after suicide. Another way of saying this is Jordan's (2001) conceptualization of prominent themes in the subjective experience of survivors. Thus, on the basis of the available research, clinical experience, and personal accounts of survivors, the features discussed in the section that follows represent the likely candidates as common features of suicide bereavement—that is, we believe that many (but not all) suicide survivors will manifest many (but not all) of these themes, reactions, and features.

Features Supported by the Existing Research Evidence

1. Abandonment and rejection—feelings such as "my dead loved one chose to leave me" or "they purposely abandoned me" (e.g., Bailley et al., 1999; Harwood, Hawton, Hope, & Jacoby, 2002; Reed, 1998).

2. Shame and stigma—as noted, often found to be more prominent for suicide survivors and among Sveen and Walby's (2008) supported items (Cleiren et al., 1996; Cvinar, 2005; Farberow, Gallagher-Thompson, Gilewski, & Thompson, 1992; Harwood et al., 2002; Range, 1998; Range & Calhoun, 1990; Séguin, Lesage, & Kiely, 1995; Thompson & Range, 1992), but some studies suggest that this may be true of other traumatic loss survivors as well (Feigelman, Gorman, & Jordan, 2009).

3. Concealment of the cause of death as suicide—probably related to the feelings of shame and stigma and/or the wish to protect the memory of the deceased (Range, 1998).

4. Blaming—This reaction might be related to possible feelings of anger. Survivors may feel that someone was in fact "responsible" for the death, but it might be noted that blaming others casts the focus away from oneself. In some cases, blaming can become scapegoating, with blame attributed to one person and anger directed toward them (e.g., Ross, 1997). The focus of blame can be toward therapists and mental health professionals (see Chapter 5) as well as family members, friends, and colleagues.

5. Increased self-destructiveness or suicidality—Chapter 1 reviews the considerable evidence that both family and nonfamily exposure to suicide elevates the risk for suicide in the survivor. This is usually attributed to a combination of shared genetics (in the case of family members), the sharing of environments and stressors with the deceased, and role-modeling effects associated with the suicide.

Features Not Currently Supported by Sufficient Research Evidence But Supported by Clinical Experience and Survivors' Anecdotal Accounts

1. Guilt—Guilt can be felt regarding what one did, did not do, imagined one might have done, and so forth. Another way in which this feature has been characterized is an obsession with thoughts of "What if...?" and "If only..." (Bailley et al., 1999; Cleiren, 1993; Range, 1998).

2. Anger—Angry feelings may exist toward the deceased, oneself, or others (Cerel, Fristad, Weller, & Weller, 1999; Gyulay, 1989; Wrobleski & McIntosh, 1987). The Latin root of the word *suicide* literally means "self-murder," and the reactions of many (though not all) suicide survivors resemble the intense anger of homicide survivors toward the perpetrator. This anger may, of course, be made more complicated after suicide, considering that the "perpetrator" is also the "victim."

3. Search for explanation/desire to understand why—The focus here for survivors is on the question "Why?" Empirical studies have not yet supported this common clinical and personal observation specifically about suicide, perhaps because this may be true for many kinds of sudden, violent, and seemingly inexplicable and traumatic deaths (e.g., accidents, homicides, sudden infant death syndrome [SIDS] deaths; Currier, Holland, Coleman, & Neimeyer, 2008; Currier, Holland, & Neimeyer, 2006; Holland, Currier, & Neimeyer, 2006; Kauffman, 2002; Keesee, Currier, & Neimeyer, 2008). Moreover, not all suicide survivors are equally likely to exhibit this problem. As we note in here and in Chapter 33, the variability of survivors and subgroups of survivors has not been adequately addressed in current research or conceptualization of suicide bereavement. There may be a number of moderator variables that differentiate among survivors. Findings of "no differences" may be more a reflection of the diversity of survivors such that actual differences are neutralized when these survivors are

combined into a single group for analysis. The issue of a need to "make meaning" is but one of many responses to which this point applies.

4. Relief—Relationships and daily interactions with suicidal and depressed individuals are often associated with troubled and disruptive lives. With their death, the disruption and problems diminish or disappear. Such an experience may well lead to feelings both of relief and of guilt for feeling relieved (Clark & Goldney, 2000; Jordan, 2001). In addition, relief may occur in the case of survivors who perceive that their loved one's psychological pain is now over and they no longer must bear that pain.

5. Shock and disbelief—As with any unexpected, sudden event that cannot be undone, the fact of the death may seem unreal, may be difficult to understand, and may produce feelings of numbness. As will be noted in the section "Different in What Way? Toward a Resolution of the Question," such shock and disbelief is more likely a characteristic of most or all sudden and unexpected deaths—not simply suicide.

6. Family system effects/social support issues/social isolation—In the aftermath of the death, families might become splintered and more troubled as a result of the loss, might become closer, or might experience a complex combination of both. Some survivors also may experience a kind of social ambiguity about the norms of interaction, both within the family and with people in the larger social network. Other people in the lives of survivors may feel uncertainty regarding what to do for or say to them and may feel discomfort in interacting with survivors following a suicide death. Reflecting their own uncertainty and discomfort, these individuals may not provide the various forms of social support often provided after a death, instead avoiding contact with survivors. Another possible source of lessened social support after suicide may be that feelings of guilt, shame, and stigma on the part of survivors may result in their avoiding others and the rituals that might provide the opportunity for support from others. See Cerel, Jordan, and Duberstein (2008) as well as Dyregrov and Dyregrov (2008) for recent reviews of these issues.

7. Activism, obsession with the phenomenon of suicide, and involvement with prevention efforts—This set of related reactions can be viewed either negatively or positively. As Cain (1972) noted, a focus on suicide and its prevention may take on an obsessional quality that is unhealthy (e.g., one outcome could be that the person is completely defined by their role as a victim or "survivor"). However, more often,

this response has been viewed as a positive outcome or result. It has been seen as a form of therapeutic activism that enhances meaning making and feelings of re-empowerment in the face of the massive assault on self-esteem and self-efficacy that suicide may entail. It can also add to the sense of being able to make something good or redemptive come out of the tragedy of the death while also helping to prevent future suicides (Begley & Quayle, 2007; Ness & Pfeffer, 1990; Range, 1998). It can also be viewed as a way to demonstrate that the individual is a "survivor" in the positive sense of that word.

☐ Different in What Way? Toward a Resolution of the Question

Previous commentaries on the question about differences between suicide bereavement and other losses (including our own contributions) have tended to address the question "Is suicide bereavement different?" as if it could be answered with a simple "yes" or "no." However, recent research and theoretical advances in thanatology have led us toward what we believe is a more nuanced and satisfying way to address this issue. In short, we propose that the correct answer to the question should be "It all depends on what aspect of the bereavement experience is being studied." Figure 2.1 illustrates this concept.

As Figure 2.1 illustrates, some aspects of bereavement are nearly universal, regardless of the mode of death. For example, feelings of sorrow at the loss and the yearning to have the loved one return are extremely common in almost all bereavement situations, including, of course, after suicide (Balk, Wogrin, Thornton, & Meagher, 2007; Hansson & Stroebe, 2007; Rando, 1993; Stroebe, Hansson, Schut, & Stroebe, 2008). We might call these the normative and universal aspects of the grief response. On the other hand, the grief responses and resulting processes associated with both unexpected and sudden death—as well as with sudden, violent death—are perceived as nonnormative (i.e., not universal) in most societies. For instance, there may be some elements of bereavement after sudden deaths (e.g., a myocardial infarction) that are a result of the rapidity of the death and lack of psychological preparedness of the mourner. The loss of a loved one to most illnesses allows for some degree of psychological preparation for what life will be like without the loved one, sometimes called *anticipatory mourning* (Rando, 2000). Conversely, the loss of a loved one in a sudden manner may lead to a heightened experience of shock and a sense of unreality about the loss, along with a more prolonged period of reality testing in which confrontation with the

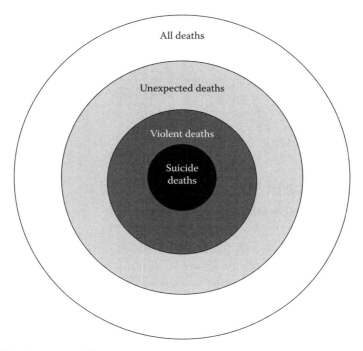

FIGURE 2.1 Aspects of bereavement related to mode of death.

implications of the death can take place. There is empirical support for the idea that unexpected losses tend to increase distress in mourners and lend themselves to more complicated grieving pathways (Miyabayashi & Yasuda, 2007). This might be termed the "shock element" of sudden bereavement.

Additionally, there is growing evidence that the sudden and violent death of a loved one—whether to accident, natural disaster, homicide, or suicide—carries with it an even greater risk of a complicated bereavement trajectory. In addition to the almost always sudden and unexpected nature of the death, violent deaths appear to elevate the potential for depression, PTSD, and other anxiety symptoms as well as for CG or PGD (Armour, 2006; Currier, Holland, Coleman, & Neimeyer, 2006; Green et al., 2001; Murphy et al., 1999; Murphy, Johnson, Chung, & Beaton, 2003; Rynearson, 2001, 2006). Several aspects of violent death may contribute to this increased distress among mourners. These aspects include the horror associated with the physical aspect of dying in a violent manner and the resulting mutilation of the body; an empathic anguish in the mourner when contemplating the physical and psychological suffering of the loved one just prior to that person's death; and the hazard created by direct exposure to the death scene, which is likely to contribute to the development of PTSD. A special case of this exposure might be seen in the case of the individual who discovers the body of an individual who died by suicide (Andress & Corey, 1978). We might call these the "horrifying aspects" of sudden, violent death.

Of equal importance are the attributions made by the mourner about the responsibility for and preventability of a violent death that are generally not present when a loved one dies from an illness, even a sudden one. Traumatic losses appear to present a much greater challenge to the assumptive world of the survivor (Kauffman, 2002). They require considerable time and psychological effort to "make meaning" of the death or, alternatively, to come to terms with the perceived senselessness of the event (Currier, Holland, Coleman, & Neimeyer, 2006; Currier, Holland, & Neimeyer, 2006, 2009; Holland et al., 2006; Neimeyer, 2002, 2005; Neimeyer, Prigerson, & Davies, 2002). When the mourner believes that someone must have been responsible for the death and, by implication, that it could have been prevented, this perception often creates a powerful psychological need to punish that "someone" and obtain justice (Rynearson, 2001). Note that this "someone" can include the bereaved individual, in which case the experience of grief is likely to be dominated by guilt and self-recrimination rather than by fury at another. Violent deaths may also shatter the perception of personal invulnerability that many people take for granted, wherein the common expectation is that loved ones will die of old age and illness, not by violence. The challenge created by violent death to the assumptive world of the mourner can be referred to as the *cognitive destabilization component* of violent loss, an experience that shakes the things that the mourner has taken for granted about their personal world. This experience can include the mourner's relationships with significant others, their "script" for an expected future, and their own identity (see Chapter 11 for more about the impact of suicide on the assumptive world of survivors and a meaning-making or narrative approach to suicide bereavement).

When viewed from this layered framework, the question "Is suicide bereavement different?" can be seen from a new and more complex perspective. More specifically, bereavement after a suicide can be understood to contain elements from all four types of losses represented in Figure 2.1. Surely, sorrow and yearning are as common in the experience of suicide survivors as in other types of loss—for regardless of the mode of death, the individual is still gone forever, and the mourners must confront and adjust to this irreversible change in their life space. Beyond that, as noted previously, suicide may or may not be experienced as an unexpected death. A number of researchers (Cleiren, 1993; Maple,

Plummer, Edwards, & Minichiello, 2007; Reed, 1993, 1998) have observed that many survivors have been on "suicide watch" with the deceased for a period of time before the death, often after a period of mental illness or prior suicide attempts. In these instances, the suicide death was feared but not completely unexpected. However, to the extent that the suicide was unanticipated, it seems likely that survivors will experience much of the shock and disbelief that are characteristic of mourning after any type of unexpected death (see, e.g., Tall, Kõlves, Sisask, & Värnik, 2008, with respect to survivors of suicides by alcohol abusers). Lastly, at least in the United States, most suicides are carried out with firearms, hanging, or other relatively violent methods. This fact means that the attendant trauma reactions that accompany violent deaths are likely to be present to at least some degree, particularly in those who witness the suicide or find the body (Andress & Corey, 1978; Brent et al., 1993; Callahan, 2000).

We can summarize this thinking by stating that there seem to be elements of the response after unexpected deaths and after sudden violent deaths that are likely to be more or less universal, whether the cause of death is an accident, a homicide, or a suicide. When compared "head to head," these different modes of death will not generally show unique responses for suicide survivors. This appears to fit well with the trend in many of the comparison studies cited previously, where, for example, suicide deaths produced similar levels of grief distress as accidental deaths or homicides (Feigelman, Jordan, & Gorman, 2009; Murphy, Johnson, & Lohan, 2003; Murphy, Johnson, Wu et al., 2003; Sveen & Walby, 2008) but more distress than natural deaths. Generally speaking, it appears that suicide bereavement is most different from mourning after death from natural causes; is somewhat different from other sudden, unexpected deaths; and is most similar to loss after other types of sudden and violent causes. It is also important to note that suicides are not all the same; thus, the impact on survivors is not always the same.

It must be re-emphasized that the individual course and intensity of grief and bereavement experiences are complex and are affected by many potential variables, only one of which is the mode of death. Application of the general bereavement research framework developed by Stroebe and colleagues (Stroebe, Folkman, Hansson, & Schut, 2006) to suicide-loss studies would represent a major step forward in this field. The authors argue for the study of the interaction of multiple variables rather than that of single, independent factors. In addition, their model recognizes several categories of variables, including both risk factors and protective factors in bereavement outcome. Among the variables mentioned by Stroebe et al. (2006) that may be relevant to suicide bereavement in particular are stressors such as the sudden, unanticipated, violent, traumatic, and stigmatizing nature often present in suicide loss; the relationship of the bereaved to the deceased, both in quality as well as kinship or type of relationship; coping resources, social support, participation, and availability of intervention programs such as therapy or support groups; family dynamics; culture, race, and ethnicity; the personality of the bereaved individual; the coping history and methods of the survivor; and the gender and age of the bereaved.

☐ Conclusion

Many questions remain unanswered or inadequately answered regarding suicide bereavement as compared with the bereavement associated with other modes of death. It is clear that more research and clinical attention are needed with respect to suicide bereavement. Greater attention to the issues and individuals affected in the aftermath of suicide will increase our understanding of suicide bereavement and, most importantly, lead to more effective intervention to assist survivors' efforts to confront and heal from their loss. Our goal in this chapter, coupled with that in Chapter 1, has been to provide a framework for understanding the remainder of this book. We have addressed the questions of the definition of a survivor, the risks of becoming a survivor, and the issue of whether—and in what ways—bereavement after suicide differs from other types of losses. In the next three chapters of this book, we examine the details of the research on the impact of suicide on adults (Chapter 3), children (Chapter 4), and clinicians (Chapter 5).

☐ References

Andress, V. R., & Corey, D. M. (1978). Survivor-victims: Who discovers or witnesses suicide? *Psychological Reports, 42,* 759–764.

Armour, M. (2006). Violent death: Understanding the context of traumatic and stigmatized grief. *Journal of Human Behavior in the Social Environment, 14,* 53–90.

Bailley, S. E., Kral, M. J., & Dunham, K. (1999). Survivors of suicide do grieve differently: Empirical support for a common sense proposition. *Suicide and Life-Threatening Behavior, 29,* 256–271.

Balk, D., Wogrin, C., Thornton, G., & Meagher, D. (Eds.). (2007). *Handbook of thanatology: The essential body of knowledge for the study of death, dying, and bereavement.* New York, NY: Routledge/Taylor & Francis Group.

Barrett, T., & Scott, T. (1989). Development of the Grief Experience Questionnaire. *Suicide and Life-Threatening Behavior, 19,* 201–215.

Begley, M., & Quayle, E. (2007). The lived experience of adults bereaved by suicide: A phenomenological study. *Crisis: The Journal of Crisis Intervention and Suicide Prevention, 28,* 26–34.

Brent, D. A., Perper, J. A., Moritz, G., Friend, A., Schweers, J., Allman, C., … Balach, L. (1993). Adolescent witnesses to a peer suicide. *Journal of the American Academy of Child & Adolescent Psychiatry, 32,* 1184–1188.

Cain, A. C. (Ed.). (1972). *Survivors of suicide.* Springfield, IL: Charles C Thomas.

Calhoun, L. G., Selby, J. W., & Selby, L. E. (1982). The psychological aftermath of suicide: An analysis of current evidence. *Clinical Psychology Review, 2,* 409–420.

Callahan, J. (2000). Predictors and correlates of bereavement in suicide support group participants. *Suicide and Life-Threatening Behavior, 30,* 104–124.

Cerel, J., Fristad, M. A., Weller, E. B., & Weller, R. A. (1999). Suicide-bereaved children and adolescents: A controlled longitudinal examination. *Journal of the American Academy of Child & Adolescent Psychiatry, 38,* 672–679.

Cerel, J., Jordan, J. R., & Duberstein, P. R. (2008). The impact of suicide on the family. *Crisis: The Journal of Crisis Intervention and Suicide Prevention, 29,* 38–44.

Clark, S. E., & Goldney, R. D. (2000). The impact of suicide on relatives and friends. In K. Hawton & K. van Heeringen (Eds.), *The international handbook of suicide and attempted suicide* (pp. 467–484). New York, NY: Wiley & Sons.

Cleiren, M. P. H. D. (1993). *Bereavement and adaptation: A comparative study of the aftermath of death.* Washington, DC: Hemisphere Publishing.

Cleiren, M. P. H. D., & Diekstra, R. F. W. (1995). After the loss: Bereavement after suicide and other types of death. In B. L. Mishara (Ed.), *The impact of suicide* (pp. 7–39): New York, NY: Springer.

Cleiren, M. P. H. D., Diekstra, R. F. W., Kerkhof, A. J. F. M., & van der Wal, J. (1994). Mode of death and kinship in bereavement: Focusing on "who" rather than "how." *Crisis: The Journal of Crisis Intervention and Suicide Prevention, 15,* 22–36.

Cleiren, M. P. H. D., Grad, O., Zavasnik, A., & Diekstra, R. F. W. (1996). Psychosocial impact of bereavement after suicide and fatal traffic accident: A comparative two-country study. *Acta Psychiatrica Scandinavica, 94,* 37–44.

Currier, J. M., Holland, J. M., Coleman, R. A., & Neimeyer, R. A. (Eds.). (2006). *Bereavement following violent death: An assault on life and meaning.* Amityville, NY: Baywood.

Currier, J. M., Holland, J. M., Coleman, R. A., & Neimeyer, R. A. (2008). Bereavement following violent death: An assault on life and meaning. In R. G. Stevenson & G. R. Cox (Eds.), *Perspectives on violence and violent death* (pp. 177–202): Amityville, NY: Baywood.

Currier, J. M., Holland, J. M., & Neimeyer, R. A. (2006). Sense-making, grief, and the experience of violent loss: Toward a mediational model. *Death Studies, 30,* 403–428.

Currier, J. M., Holland, J. M., & Neimeyer, R. A. (2009). Assumptive worldviews and problematic reactions to bereavement. *Journal of Loss & Trauma, 14,* 181–195.

Cvinar, J. G. (2005). Do suicide survivors suffer social stigma? A review of the literature. *Perspectives in Psychiatric Care, 41,* 14–21.

de Groot, M. H., De Keijser, J., & Neeleman, J. (2006). Grief shortly after suicide and natural death: A comparative study among spouses and first-degree relatives. *Suicide and Life-Threatening Behavior, 36,* 418–431.

Dunne, E. J., & Dunne-Maxim, K. (1987). Preface. In E. J. Dunne, J. L. McIntosh, & K. Dunne-Maxim (Eds.), *Suicide and its aftermath: Understanding and counseling the survivors* (pp. xi–xvi). New York, NY: Norton.

Dyregrov, K., & Dyregrov, A. (2008). *Effective grief and bereavement support: The role of family , friends, colleagues, schools, and support professionals.* Philadelphia, PA: Jessica Kingsley Publishers.

Dyregrov, K., Nordanger, D., & Dyregrov, A. (2003). Predictors of psychosocial distress after suicide, SIDS and accidents. *Death Studies, 27,* 143–165.

Ellenbogen, S., & Gratton, F. (2001). Do they suffer more? Reflections on research comparing suicide survivors to other survivors. *Suicide and Life-Threatening Behavior, 31,* 83–90.

Farberow, N. L., Gallagher-Thompson, D., Gilewski, M., & Thompson, L. (1992). The role of social supports in the bereavement process of surviving spouses of suicide and natural deaths. *Suicide and Life-Threatening Behavior, 22,* 107–124.

Feigelman, W., Gorman, B. S., & Jordan, J. R. (2009). Stigmatization and suicide bereavement. *Death Studies, 33,* 591–508.

Feigelman, W., Jordan, J., & Gorman, B. S. (2009). How they died, time since loss, and bereavement outcomes. *Omega: Journal of Death and Dying, 58,* 251–273.

Green, B. L., Krupnick, J. L., Stockton, P., Goodman, L., Corcoran, C., & Petty, R. (2001). Psychological outcomes associated with traumatic loss in a sample of young women. *American Behavioral Scientist, 44,* 817–837.

Gyulay, J.-E. (1989). What suicide leaves behind. *Issues in Comprehensive Pediatric Nursing, 12,* 103–118.

Hansson, R. O., & Stroebe, M. S. (2007). *Bereavement in late life: Coping, adaptation, and developmental influences.* Washington, DC: American Psychological Association.

Harwood, D., Hawton, K., Hope, T., & Jacoby, R. (2002). The grief experiences and needs of bereaved relatives and friends of older people dying through suicide: A descriptive and case-control study. *Journal of Affective Disorders, 72,* 185–194.

Henley, S. H. (1984). Bereavement following suicide: A review of the literature. *Current Psychological Research & Reviews, 3,* 53–61.

Holland, J. M., Currier, J. M., & Neimeyer, R. A. (2006). Meaning reconstruction in the first two years of bereavement: The role of sense-making and benefit-finding. *Omega: Journal of Death and Dying, 53,* 175–191.

Jordan, J. (2001). Is suicide bereavement different? A reassessment of the literature. *Suicide and Life-Threatening Behavior, 31,* 91–102.

Jordan, J., & McMenamy, J. (2004). Interventions for suicide survivors: A review of the literature. *Suicide and Life-Threatening Behavior, 34,* 337–349.

Kauffman, J. (2002). *Loss of the assumptive world: A theory of traumatic loss*: New York, NY: Brunner-Routledge.

Keesee, N. J., Currier, J. M., & Neimeyer, R. A. (2008). Predictors of grief follow-ing the death of one's child: The contribution of finding meaning. *Journal of Clinical Psychology, 64,* 1145–1163.

Maciejewski, P. K., Zhang, B., Block, S. D., & Prigerson, H. G. (2007). An empiri-cal examination of the stage theory of grief. *JAMA: Journal of the American Medical Association, 297,* 716–723.

Maple, M., Plummer, D., Edwards, H., & Minichiello, V. (2007). The effects of preparedness for suicide following the death of a young adult child. *Suicide and Life-Threatening Behavior, 37,* 127–134.

McIntosh, J. L. (1993). Control group studies of suicide survivors: A review and critique. *Suicide and Life-Threatening Behavior, 23,* 146–161.

McIntosh, J. L. (1999). Research on survivors of suicide. In M. Stimming & M. Stimming (Eds.), *Before their time: Adult children's experiences of parental suicide* (pp. 157–180). Philadelphia, PA: Temple University Press.

McIntosh, J. L. (2003). Suicide survivors: The aftermath of suicide and suicidal behavior. In C. D. Bryant (Ed.), *Handbook of death & dying, Vol. 1* (pp. 339–350). Thousand Oaks, CA: Sage Publications.

Melhem, N. M., Day, N., Shear, M. K., Day, R., Reynolds III, C. F., & Brent, D. (2004). Traumatic grief among adolescents exposed to a peer's suicide. *American Journal of Psychiatry, 161,* 1411–1416.

Mitchell, A. M., Kim, Y., Prigerson, H. G., & Mortimer-Stephens, M. (2004). Complicated grief in survivors of suicide. *Crisis: The Journal of Crisis Intervention and Suicide Prevention, 25,* 12–18.

Miyabayashi, S., & Yasuda, J. (2007). Effects of loss from suicide, accidents, acute illness and chronic illness on bereaved spouses and parents in Japan: Their general health, depressive mood, and grief reaction. *Psychiatry and Clinical Neurosciences, 61,* 502–508.

Murphy, S. A., Das Gupta, A., Cain, K. C., Johnson, L. C., Lohan, J., Wu, L., & Mekwa, J. (1999). Changes in parents' mental distress after the violent death of an adolescent or young adult child: A longitudinal prospective analysis. *Death Studies, 23,* 129–159.

Murphy, S. A., Johnson, L. C., Chung, I.-J., & Beaton, R. D. (2003). The preva-lence of PTSD following the violent death of a child and predictors of change 5 years later. *Journal of Traumatic Stress, 16,* 17–25.

Murphy, S. A., Johnson, L. C., & Lohan, J. (2003). Challenging the myths about parents' adjustment after the sudden, violent death of a child. *Journal of Nursing Scholarship, 35,* 359–364.

Murphy, S. A., Johnson, L. C., Wu, L., Fan, J. J., & Lohan, J. (2003). Bereaved parents' outcomes 4 to 60 months after their children's death by accident, suicide, or homicide: A comparative study demonstrating differences. *Death Studies, 27,* 39–61.

Neimeyer, R. A. (2002). Traumatic loss and the reconstruction of meaning. *Journal of Palliative Medicine, 5,* 935–942.

Neimeyer, R. A. (2005). Tragedy and transformation: Meaning reconstruction in the wake of traumatic loss. In S. C. Heilman (Ed.), *Death, bereavement, and mourning* (pp. 121–134). New Brunswick, NJ: Transaction Publishers.

Neimeyer, R. A., Prigerson, H. G., & Davies, B. (2002). Mourning and meaning. *American Behavioral Scientist, 46,* 235–251.

Ness, D. E., & Pfeffer, C. R. (1990). Sequelae of bereavement resulting from suicide. *American Journal of Psychiatry, 147,* 279–285.

Ott, C. H., Lueger, R. J., Kelber, S. T., & Prigerson, H. G. (2007). Spousal bereavement in older adults: Common, resilient, and chronic grief with defining characteristics. *Journal of Nervous and Mental Disease, 195,* 332–341.

Prigerson, H. G., Horowitz, M. J., Jacobs, S. C., Parkes, C. M., Aslan, M., Goodkin, K., … Maciejewski, P. K. (2009). Prolonged grief disorder: Psychometric validation of criteria proposed for *DSM-V* and *ICD-11.* [Electronic version]. *PLoS Med 6(8),* e1000121. doi:10.1371/journal.pmed.1000121

Prigerson, H. G., & Maciejewski, P. K. (2005). A call for sound empirical testing and evaluation of criteria for complicated grief proposed for *DSM-V. Omega: Journal of Death and Dying, 52,* 9–19.

Prigerson, H. G., Vanderwerker, L. C., & Maciejewski, P. K. (2008). A case for inclusion of prolonged grief disorder in *DSM-V.* In M. S. Stroebe, R. O. Hansson, H. Schut, & W. Stroebe (Eds.), *Handbook of bereavement research and practice: Advances in theory and intervention* (pp. 165–186). Washington, DC: American Psychological Association.

Rando, T. A. (1993). *Treatment of complicated mourning.* Champaign, IL: Research Press.

Rando, T. A. (2000). *Clinical dimensions of anticipatory mourning: Theory and practice in working with the dying, their loved ones, and their caregivers.* Champaign, IL: Research Press.

Range, L. M. (1998). When a loss is due to suicide: Unique aspects of bereavement. In J. H. Harvey (Ed.), *Perspectives on loss: A sourcebook* (pp. 213–220). Philadelphia, PA: Brunner/Mazel.

Range, L. M., & Calhoun, L. G. (1990). Responses following suicide and other types of death: The perspective of the bereaved. *Omega: Journal of Death and Dying, 21,* 311–320.

Range, L. M., & Niss, N. M. (1990). Long-term bereavement from suicide, homicide, accidents, and natural deaths. *Death Studies, 14,* 423–433.

Reed, M. D. (1993). Sudden death and bereavement outcomes: The impact of resources on grief symptomatology and detachment. *Suicide and Life-Threatening Behavior, 23,* 204–220.

Reed, M. D. (1998). Predicting grief symptomatology among the suddenly bereaved. *Suicide and Life-Threatening Behavior, 28,* 285–301.

Ross, E. B. (1997). *Life after suicide: A ray of hope for those left behind.* New York, NY: Insight Books.

Rynearson, E. K. (2001). *Retelling violent death.* Philadelphia, PA: Brunner-Routledge.

Rynearson, E. K. (Ed.). (2006). *Violent death: Resilience and intervention beyond the crisis.* New York, NY: Routledge/Taylor & Francis Group.

Séguin, M., Lesage, A., & Kiely, M. C. (1995). Parental bereavement after suicide and accident: A comparative study. *Suicide and Life-Threatening Behavior, 25,* 489–498.

Stroebe, M. S., Folkman, S., Hansson, R. O., & Schut, H. (2006). The prediction of bereavement outcome: Development of an integrative risk factor framework. *Social Science & Medicine, 63,* 2440–2451.

Stroebe, M. S., Hansson, R. O., Schut, H., & Stroebe, W. (2008). *Handbook of bereavement research and practice: Advances in theory and intervention.* Washington, DC: American Psychological Association.

Sveen, C.-A., & Walby, F. A. (2008). Suicide survivors' mental health and grief reactions: A systematic review of controlled studies. *Suicide and Life-Threatening Behavior, 38,* 13–29.

Tall, K., Kõlves, K., Sisask, M., & Värnik, A. (2008). Do survivors respond differently when alcohol abuse complicates suicide? Findings from the psychological autopsy study in Estonia. *Drug and Alcohol Dependence, 95,* 129–133.

Thompson, K. E., & Range, L. M. (1992). Bereavement following suicide and other deaths: Why support attempts fail. *Omega: Journal of Death and Dying, 26,* 61–70.

Toynbee, A. (Ed.). (1968). *Man's concern about death.* London, United Kingdom: Hodder and Stoughton.

van der Wal, J. (1989). The aftermath of suicide: A review of empirical evidence. *Omega: Journal of Death and Dying, 20,* 149–171.

Wrobleski, A., & McIntosh, J. L. (1987). Problems of suicide survivors: A survey report. *Israel Journal of Psychiatry and Related Sciences, 24,* 137–142.

CHAPTER

The Impact of Suicide on Adults

John L. McIntosh and John R. Jordan

The goal of the present chapter is to provide existing information regarding common features, issues, and characterizations of bereavement among adults following death by suicide,[1] including its commonalities with other modes of death as well as its differences from death by other causes. In a general sense, the experience of adults who have lost a significant person in their lives to death by suicide involves the same information conveyed in Chapter 2's characterization of the nature of suicide bereavement. Therefore, the entire experience of suicide grief and bereavement is not repeated here. Rather, the issues that arise and the specific research findings in the developmental time period of adulthood associated with loss by suicide are discussed.

Some studies combine survivors from all kinship relations into a single group for comparisons, but the majority of these investigations have studied survivors of only one relationship category to the suicides they survive (i.e., parents only, widows only, etc.). Each specific relationship potentially involves its own aspects of grief and bereavement.

---

[1] Bereavement among children and families is addressed in Chapter 4.

Although much of the research has studied relationships, the need for many additional investigations—even among those few relationships previously studied—may reveal useful findings that enhance our knowledge and understanding as well as guide postvention efforts to assist survivors with their bereavement journey. Although all survivors will likely experience, to varying degrees, many of the reactions noted in Chapter 2, the individual's kinship relation—along with other variables—may affect the general and the specific reactions that are experienced. For example, the crucial role of kinship as an aspect of bereavement response (considerably larger than mode of death) was observed by Cleiren, Diekstra, Kerkhof, and van der Wal (1994) in their Netherlands investigation. As noted previously, few individual survivors will experience the full set of reactions or experience them in the same manner or at the same level as another survivor. The research on relationships has been reviewed in detail previously (e.g., McIntosh, 1987b, 1993, 1999) and will be brought up to date here.

Before proceeding to research on bereavement reactions for various kinship relations, the general research literature on public attitudes toward survivors has relevance here. Virtually all of this research has attempted to assess attitudes toward adult survivors, most often parents who survive the death of a child by suicide and spouses of individuals who died by suicide. The findings for this body of evidence (Calhoun & Allen, 1991; Calhoun & Selby, 1990; Rudestam, 1987) are largely consistent for both groups. Parents of child suicides and of suicide-bereaved spouses were more often blamed and held more responsible or accountable for the death than those of the same kinship relations who had lost someone by another mode of death. Attitudes suggested a belief that spouses had the opportunity to prevent their spouse's suicide and were more ashamed than survivors of other causes of death. Parents of children who died by suicide were not only more often blamed and held accountable, but they were also disliked more than other surviving parents. They were also seen as more emotionally disturbed. Somewhat surprisingly, these same attitudes were generally expressed even by those who already knew someone who had died by suicide or already knew a suicide survivor. These latter attitudinal studies found that coping with a suicide death was expected to be more difficult and that they were more uncomfortable talking to the surviving family members, expressing sympathy to them, or talking with them about the cause of death. Possibly helping to explain the existence of these attitudes, researchers also found that individuals expressed feeling great social discomfort and were uncertain about the "rules" associated with bereavement and offering support when the death was a suicide. Perhaps the results of Thompson and Range (1992–1993) are relevant here. The authors found greater variability in social support reported by suicide survivors compared with other survivors. The discomfort and uncertainty following a suicide death may well affect expressions and actions of support for the survivors (see also Séguin, Lesage, & Kiely, 1995, p. 495). It should be noted that there are several serious methodological issues with this dated body of research (see, e.g., Calhoun & Selby, 1990; McIntosh, 1987a; Rudestam, 1987), but the results may provide some insights into the social environment in which survivors of suicide find themselves following their loss and the personal as well as public problems that may arise as they seek to cope and adapt to it. Additionally, research has shown that feeling stigmatized was associated among survivors with greater grieving difficulties (Feigelman, Gorman, & Jordan, 2009; see Cvinar, 2005, and Sudak, Maxim, & Carpenter, 2008, for reviews of stigma and suicide).

☐ Comparison Group Studies: Kinship Relationships

With respect to adult loss, only the kinship relationships of parents who survive the suicide death of their child and suicide-bereaved spouses have been studied extensively in investigations that have included comparison or control groups.

Parent Survivors of Child Suicides

Of the 33,300 suicides in the United States in 2006, 940 were under the age of 18 (and 2,246 under the age of 21; Centers for Disease Control and Prevention [CDC], 2009). For each of these young deaths, there are most often two parents who survive the death (and even more, in the case of stepparents, for instance). In addition, for many of the suicides over the age of 18 (or 21), the death leaves behind a parent or parents as well. In other words, reaching "adult" ages does not produce the end of parenthood for the parents of these individuals. Most of the current research on parents as survivors has focused on the suicides that occur among children at young ages. Little is known about suicides of adult children and the effects on their parents, although there are many such deaths annually. We will consider deaths of adult children briefly later, but unless otherwise stated, the comments here are primarily related to parents who lost a child to suicide at a young age.

General Grief and Psychological Distress

Kovarsky (1989) administered grief and loneliness questionnaires to parents who either attended bereavement groups or participated in one of two bereavement conferences. Accident survivors indicated higher initial levels of grief than did parent survivors of child suicides, but the intensity for the parents of children who died in accidents diminished over time, whereas that of suicide-surviving parents either remained constant or even increased over time. Identical but nonsignificant trends were observed for loneliness between the two groups.

On the other hand, Séguin et al. (1995) found more symptomatology and psychological distress at an average of 6 months after the death for parents who had lost a son aged 18–35 years to suicide (i.e., young but not children or adolescents) than for parents whose son had died in an accident. However, the differences between the groups were not seen at an average of 9 months after the death for the two groups. At the same time, there were no differences in the overall grief measures for the two groups of surviving parents at either 6 or 9 months. The differences in results and patterns over time for parents found by Kovarsky (1989) and Séguin et al. may be attributable to any of several factors, including different recruitment methods (grief groups/conferences vs. contact through the coroner's office), the age of the children who died, or any number of other methodological differences. When the results of studies as diverse as these are combined based solely on kinship relation, mixed results (i.e., some support a particular reaction whereas others do not) are not surprising.

In a more recent study, Feigelman, Jordan, and Gorman (2008–2009) observed few differences between parents of suicide as compared with parents of traumatic death and natural causes (all parents were predominantly from support groups; 90% of the sample were below the age of 36 years) on most measures of general grief and distress. Emerging clearly, however, was that the most significant variable with respect to the reactions measured was the time since the death. Feigelman et al. found that between 3 and 5 years after the death, grief problems begin to lessen—a timeline for recovery longer than that generally observed for normative bereavement. Another difference that Feigelman et al. observed was that parents who had difficult relationships with the deceased child were more likely to experience greater difficulties in their grief. Similarly, Séguin et al. (1995) had observed that the parents of the children who had died by suicide more often reported "conflictual" relationships with their sons than did accident survivors.

Other investigators have failed to find overall differences between parents bereaved of suicide compared to other modes of death. Although

Dyregrov, Nordanger, and Dyregrov (2003) observed that more than a majority of all the parents who had lost children reported significant levels of traumatic grief reactions at 18 months after their loss, the suicide survivor (child's mean age at death = 22 years) and accident survivor (child's mean age at death = 11 years) parents were not different from one another (although both had significantly higher distress than parent survivors of sudden infant death syndrome [SIDS]). Similar to their other study (Feigelman et al., 2008–2009), Feigelman and colleagues' (2009) study of parents from support groups also found few differences in reactions or in the course of grief between parents of children who died by suicide compared to parents of children who died by other traumatic means. These findings of many similarities for suicide and traumatic grief are consistent with a larger body of evidence that has developed over time, are consistent with one of McIntosh's (1993) conclusions about the body of evidence, and fit with the model that we have set forth in Chapter 2 of this volume.

In a study focused specifically on mental health outcomes, Brent, Moritz, Bridge, Perper, and Canobbio (1996) followed up on a sample of parents (and siblings, but the focus here is on the parent data) who had lost an adolescent to suicide compared with a control group of parents who had not lost a child to suicide and had not been exposed to a suicide loss personally or in the last 2 years in their local community. At 6 months after the suicide, the researchers (Brent, Perper, Moritz, Liotus, et al., 1993) had observed that more mothers of adolescent suicides than mothers of controls displayed depressive symptoms and new-onset major depression. No differences were found for the fathers. At the 3-year follow-up time period, they observed that the mothers of suicides also exhibited more major depression and new-onset depression than did mothers of controls. Even 3 years after the death of their adolescent, mothers of suicides continued to have depressive problems.

Although Brent and colleagues concluded that depression was greater for mothers of young suicides, a series of published reports from a longitudinal prospective study of parents bereaved by the suicide, accident, or homicide of their children aged 12–28 years fails to support the general opinion that suicide grief is more difficult than that for other traumatic causes of death. The study followed the same bereaved parents over, ultimately, a 5-year period of time. These studies found at 2 years after the death that post-traumatic stress disorder (PTSD) was substantially more likely for parents of child homicides, with suicide and accident parents not being different (Murphy et al., 1999). Elsewhere, the researchers (Murphy, Tapper, Johnson, & Lohan, 2003) reported over the 5-year follow-up that parents whose child had died by suicide did not report the highest levels of suicide ideation of the three bereaved groups of parents. Rather, the suicide-bereaved parents showed the lowest percentage of the three groups. Finally, also reporting data from the entire 5-year period, Murphy and colleagues (Murphy, Johnson, Wu, Fan, & Lohan, 2003) looked at the parents' reports of acceptance of the death (at 4, 12, 24, and 60 months postdeath). They observed somewhat different patterns of acceptance for the three bereaved parent groups, but contrary to general expectations, parents of child suicides "had the *highest* acceptance scores at all data observation points compared with the other two groups" (emphasis added, p. 49). In reviewing the literature about some possible myths related to parents who are bereaved of sudden, violent child deaths, Murphy, Johnson, and Lohan (2003) concluded similarly that there was insufficient empirical evidence that child suicide death produced the worst bereavement outcomes for parents. These data support an interpretation that parents of children who died traumatic and violent deaths seem to have similar bereavement experiences.

Guilt, Shame, and Stigma

Both from a personal standpoint as parents as well as a societal view of parents, there are expectations and responsibilities associated with parenthood and parenting children that affect how parents and others react toward the parents whose child has died by suicide. As the attitudinal studies (briefly noted earlier) showed, parents are held accountable for their child's death by suicide more than when parents lose children by other modes of death. Personal feelings of responsibility for the death (i.e., guilt and its related dimensions such as shame and stigma) are perhaps the most prominent aspect of grief indicated among parents who have lost a child to suicide. Two mothers, both mental health professionals, who lost their young adult sons to suicide similarly describe some of the feelings of guilt they experienced. Bolton (1983) relays her feeling of being a total failure—as being "foul." "I thought I must indeed be foul for my son to prefer death to living with me and our family. Guilt hits hard and flits in and out of other moods" (p. 11). Regarding guilt and other parents' losses, Chance (1992) wrote in her diary after her son's death, "It's bad enough to lose a child ... but the guilt [that other parents who have lost a child to some other form of death] have over not getting them to a doctor 'soon enough,' the guilt over not being able to protect them from cancer or drunk drivers or whatever can't be as fundamental and soul-searing as knowing they couldn't endure the life you gave them" (p. 50).

Personal accounts often relate these and similar feelings, and although not all of the few studies of parents have found consistent results for guilt, shame, and stigma when compared to parent survivors of other modes of death, present findings often support this difference. At 9 months after the death, Séguin et al. (1995) found clear differences in shame among parents who had lost a son (aged 18--35 years) by suicide as compared with parents who had lost a son by accidental death. In a study of parents from support groups, Feigelman and colleagues (2009) found no differences in stigmatization between parents of children who died by suicide compared to parents of children who died by other traumatic deaths, but both were higher than for parents whose children had died of natural causes.

Kovarsky's (1989) parent survivors were also asked to respond to several specific questions related to their grief and blame. Significant differences were observed between suicide and accident parents for several aspects of blame—that is, parents of children who died by suicide blamed themselves, other family members, and doctors more than did parents of children who died by accidents. In the same way, the parents of children who died by suicide reported that their other family members blamed the child who died and the doctors more than did families of children who died by accidents.

These issues of blaming, as well as possibly discomfort and the uncertainty regarding how to interact with parents who are survivors of child suicides, are also relevant in the Australian findings of Maple, Edwards, Plummer, and Minichiello (2009). In this qualitative investigation, Maple and colleagues conducted in-depth interviews with 22 parents who had lost a young adult child to suicide. In their narratives, the parents reported that both they and others with whom they interacted "stayed silent" about their deceased child—that is, others either avoided or never mentioned the child who had died by suicide to the parents, and similarly, the parents stated that they had also felt compelled to do likewise. This "silencing" may well hinder the grieving process for the parents as well as decrease the social support available to them.

The exclusive emphasis of a study by Miles and Demi (1991–1992) was guilt among bereaved parents. Miles and Demi assessed various categories or types of guilt among parents who had lost a child to suicide, accident, or chronic disease. The authors found that 83% of these parents experienced guilt feelings, with suicide survivors most likely to report them (92%), although both accident survivors and chronic disease survivors reported high frequencies as well (78% and 71%, respectively). When asked to note the most distressing aspect of their grief, parents of children who had died by suicide most frequently listed guilt first, followed by feelings of loneliness. None of the parents of the other two groups listed guilt as the most distressing reaction (loneliness was first in both groups).

More important than the overall report of guilt, however, was that the researchers analyzed the parents' responses for content and categorized them into several sources of guilt that were based on a classification model of guilt that the authors themselves had previously developed (Miles & Demi, 1986). These sources are death causation, illness-related, childrearing, moral, survival, and grief guilt. About half of all parents reported one of the sources of guilt, and almost half of the suicide survivors reported two of the sources.

Overall, the three most common guilt sources that parents observed were death causation guilt (54% of all the parents), childrearing guilt (50%), and illness-related guilt (28%). *Death causation guilt* refers to various actions performed or not performed that the parents feel somehow contributed to their child's death. *Childrearing guilt* is indicated by parents' feelings about the kind of parenting style that they "should have" employed, that they perhaps should have been more loving, involved, and so forth, or perhaps "negative or ambivalent feelings toward the child" (Miles & Demi, 1991–1992, p. 210). *Illness-related guilt* centers on (a) feelings that parents did not provide or seek the needed or "best" care for their sick child or (b) guilt for not being present when the child died.

Great similarity was observed with respect to suicide and accidental death survivors (the two sudden-death groups). Death causation guilt was reported by more than half of both the suicide (63%) and accident survivors (64%) but only by 26% of the chronic illness survivors. Similarly, greater proportions of suicide- and accident-surviving parents expressed childrearing guilt than did the chronic disease–surviving parents (51%, 52%, and 44%, respectively). Not unexpectedly, the parents who survived a child's death by chronic disease most often felt illness-related guilt (41%), followed by suicide survivors (35%), whereas none of the accident survivors noted this type of guilt. In this case, it is likely that the suicide-bereaved parents were expressing their guilt related to the distress, depression, or related mental heath illness that they perceived on the part of their child and their own inadequacy to respond—or their unawareness of the degree of the problem.

As a final note on guilt-related issues, the vast majority of studies of the suicide bereaved used predominantly paper-and-pencil self-report questionnaires. Although these methodological issues are addressed later in Chapter 33, it is worth noting that other methods, such as qualitative analyses and techniques such as interviews, may provide different perspectives on the picture of suicide bereavement (see also Sveen & Walby, 2008). Although they did not include a comparison group, Owens, Lambert, Lloyd, and Donovan (2008) conducted semi-structured interviews with 14 parents of sons aged 18–30 years who had died by suicide. The narratives that the parents related were not found to focus on the medical/illness or psychological/psychiatric aspects of suicide. Instead, the narratives showed that the parents' pain and struggles focused on what the authors characterized as "moral" categories—that is, the parents grappled with issues of responsibility and who was to blame (or not) for the death (e.g., the dead son, themselves, others). These individual narratives support the personal accounts by survivors and clinical observations by support group leaders and mental health professionals with respect to blame and related themes.

Search to Understand "Why"

As noted in Chapters 2 and 11, one theme often occurring with respect to suicide survivors is trying to find an explanation for why their loved one died. In another qualitative study without a comparison group, Lindqvist, Johansson, and Karlsson (2008) interviewed the parents (as well as siblings, but again, the focus here is on parents) of 10 consecutive teenage suicides in a rural area of northern Sweden at 15 to 25 months after the suicide. The most striking theme that emerged from grounded-theory method with unstructured interviews was described by the authors as a "preoccupation" with a search for an answer to the question "Why?" These parents and their families were still struggling with the loss but had largely resumed their daily lives, albeit with continued pain and anxiety. However, they still grappled with finding "a rational answer that would make it possible for the bereaved to come to rest and [for them to] go on with their own lives" (open access, no pagination; see Chapter 11 for further discussion of issues of meaning making for survivors).

Family Functioning

Finally, as in all modalities of death, both positive and negative outcomes in family adaptation occur, with some studies finding that parents surviving a suicide may more often experience negative adaptation (e.g., Séguin et al., 1995). However, family dynamics difficulties have not always been observed when comparing suicide deaths to other modes. For instance, Nelson and Frantz (1996) studied the parents and siblings of children who had died by suicide (average age at death = 16 years) and the closeness of the relationships between parents and surviving siblings (that is, with either parent) as well as between the two parents. Four years (on average) after the death, no significant differences were observed among the suicide-, accident-, or illness-death families. In another investigation, Lohan and Murphy (2002) studied parents' perceptions of their family's functioning—in particular, its cohesiveness and adaptability. When comparing parents who had a child aged 12–18 years die by suicide and who still had other children in their homes, no significant differences were observed in the mother's perceptions of the family's functioning at 4, 12, and 24 months after the death of their child by suicide or accidents. Interestingly, at the first and last times of measure, fathers of children who had died by suicide perceived their family adaptability as higher than did fathers of children who had died by accidents; however, the reason for this perception is not clear.

Older Adults as Survivors of Offspring Suicide

One group of parent survivors that has been virtually absent from investigation are older adults who have lost their children to suicide. Instead, research has almost exclusively studied older adult survivors with respect to spouse suicides (see next subsection). An exception is a study by Clarke and Wrigley (2004) from Ireland. Among elderly psychiatric patients who had experienced the death of an adult child, deaths by suicide among those adult children were more common than for the elderly in the population as a whole. In fact, for half of these bereaved elderly psychiatric patients, the death that they had experienced by their adult child was a suicide. Another investigation, this one from Sweden (Waern, 2005), compared the suicide of older adults who had experienced the previous suicide of another family member with the suicide of those who had not. The information provided by the study's informants indicated that among the elders who had experienced a family suicide, the loss of a child to suicide had played an important role in the subsequent index suicide (whereas the loss of a sibling to suicide had not). These two studies suggest that the loss of a child by suicide, regardless of the child's or parent's age, can have a potentially important effect on the surviving parent, perhaps increasing their mental health risk as well as the risk of suicide by the parent. More research on this ignored subgroup of parent survivors is warranted.

Spouse Survivors

Suicides by married individuals account for the largest number of suicides by marital status (although the risk/rate is lowest because such large numbers of individuals are married). In 2006, of the American suicides by people 15 years of age and older, 37% were by married individuals (McIntosh, 2009). This means that in this single year, there were 12,280 surviving spouses of suicides. Of those individuals who had died by suicide, 9,669 were men and 2,611 were women. Not surprisingly, then, nearly all studies of spouse survivors are of widows—that is, wives whose husbands had died by suicide. This undoubtedly reflects the much higher levels of suicide by men (with rates and numbers 3 times higher than for women overall) and perhaps also the greater likelihood that women will more often agree to participate in research. Comparison and control group studies involving spouses of suicides represent a large proportion of the total studies of suicide bereavement conducted, and most of these investigations include exclusively or primarily widows. Details regarding some of the more common features of suicide grief in adulthood are noted here.

General Grief Features and Psychological Distress

It has long been suggested that the loss of a spouse (by any mode of death) is one of the most difficult and stressful losses or events that one can experience in a lifetime (e.g., Carr, 2008; Moss, Moss, & Hansson, 2001). Generally, the loss of a spouse by death usually occurs in mid or late life; however, it may happen at any age. Most of the research and writing here focuses, as would be expected, on later life losses among women— the group most likely to become (and remain) widowed. Reflecting this general information about spousal loss, Kitson's (2000) study observed that regardless of the mode of death, the bereaved spouses studied were distressed. From a larger longitudinal study of adjustment to widowhood, an investigation of 276 spouses at about 5 to 6 months after the death of their spouse found that mode of death (i.e., suicide, accident, homicide, and natural death [due to both short- and long-term illnesses]) had little effect on virtually any of the analyses of psychological adjustment (e.g., depression, overall psychological symptoms). The lack of cause-of-death results, however, may have been related to the relatively short time that has passed since the death. In most studies of suicide versus other modes of death, researchers have studied bereaved spouses at time periods after this early period. General bereavement studies have implied that widowed individuals will likely require longer periods after the death before they can be considered to have adapted to the loss. Generally, this period may well be 2 to 4 years (e.g., Weiss, 1998, p. 345).

Similar to Kitson's (2000) primary findings, one of the most common findings of the spouse survivor comparative research body has been that there are more similarities than differences for spouses of suicide and other modes of death—or fewer differences than had been expected. A study of a small sample of spouses of accidents and suicides (Pennebaker & O'Heeron, 1984) found no differences for any of the measures, including social support, coping, or health problems/illness. Rather, the results supported increased health problems among surviving spouses for both suicide and accidental deaths. Confiding in others following the death was a major factor in both coping and health in the two groups of surviving spouses. Demi (1984) also found more similarities than differences between the widows by suicides as compared to widows of natural deaths and accidents. During the second year of bereavement, no differences were found for overall social adjustment or social leisure role adjustment. Demi concluded that widowed suicide survivors "were not at greater risk than nonsuicide survivors for poor bereavement outcome" (p. 91).

Comparable conclusions were reached by McNeil, Hatcher, and Reubin (1988) with respect to widows they had interviewed and who had completed several standardized self-report instruments. No significant differences were found between those widowed by suicide and those widowed by accidental deaths on measures of family functioning, life stress, or psychiatric symptoms. However, clinically significant levels of psychiatric symptoms were observed in both survivor groups, reminiscent of Kitson's (2000) suggestion that the widowed individuals they studied were distressed.

A series of investigations have found more similarities than differences when looking at bereaved spouses across cultures as well as mode of death. Grad and Zavasnik (1996) studied spouses in Slovenia who survived either a death by suicide or traffic accident. In a subsequent report, Grad and Zavasnik (1999) added a comparison group of terminal illness–bereaved spouses to their groups of suicide and traffic accident–bereaved spouses from the 1996 study. The 1999 report included more complete results for all three groups. Combining the studies and their results, three measures—depression, general bereavement, and personality—were completed, and interviews were conducted at 2 and 14 months after the loss for all three groups. No differences on depression or the personality measures were observed between the three groups or at the two times. The general bereavement measure questions showed several differences for the groups. Particularly at the initial measure, suicide-bereaved spouses felt more shame, had more difficulty accepting the death, felt that it was unfair that the deceased had died, believed that the deceased had intentionally left them, and felt that the death had been a good solution for the deceased spouse. Measures at 14 months after the death for the suicide survivors showed more acceptance and lower feelings of unfairness and shame but a stronger belief that the deceased had intentionally left them. Feelings of abandonment by the deceased spouse did not change after 14 months for the suicide survivors. The accident survivors reported more sadness and more of a lack of perspective at the second measurement than did the suicide or terminal-illness survivors. In addition, feelings of shame and guilt were more prominent for accident survivors but not until the second time of measure (14 months). Thus, although there were many similarities, there were also some general issues of bereavement that differed, and the passage of time led to what can be seen as more adaptation behaviors on some feelings.

In addition, Cleiren, Grad, Zavasnik, and Diekstra (1996) studied spouses bereaved of suicide and traffic-accident deaths in Slovenia and the Netherlands, also using structured interviews and a standardized measure of depression, substance use, and social measures. The authors, as observed in Slovenia, concluded that more similarities than differences were observed in both countries and between the two groups of survivors. Depression, acceptance of the death, loss of friends, and self-blaming did not differ by cause of death. However, social measures such as feeling abandoned by society as well as being blamed and avoided by others were higher for the suicide survivors.

Not all studies have concluded or can be summarized as supporting few differences or more similarities than differences. Some specific study results have implicated differences between suicide-bereaved spouses compared with other modes of death, but often, there have been inconsistencies in the particular aspects of grief for which differences are observed—that is, some studies find differences that are not observed in other investigations, and studies frequently do not include the same aspects of grief in their investigations.

Among the studies that have observed differences is one by Barrett and Scott (1989, 1990). These researchers developed the Grief Experience Questionnaire (GEQ) not only to measure various aspects of grief, conducting their initial studies with spouse survivors, but also specifically to assess the general and specific grief experiences of suicide survivors. Barrett and Scott measured the grief reactions of spouses 2 to 4 years after the death, comparing the responses of groups of survivors of suicide, accidental death, natural-expected death, and natural-unexpected death.

No differences were observed for any of the subscales of the GEQ among the nonsuicide survivors; however, spouses of suicide survivors differed in several ways from the various nonsuicide survivors. Suicide survivors experienced a larger number of grief reactions than did either of the two natural-death survivor groups (although they did not differ significantly from accident survivors). With respect to specific grief reactions, suicide survivors experienced more rejection than did any of the other survivor groups—as well as several aspects of grief that Barrett and Scott present as relatively unique to suicide bereavement, including concealment of the cause of death from others and sensitivity to media coverage and portrayals of the death. Suicide survivors differed more from both natural-death spouse groups for stigmatization and shame. Alternatively, suicides were distinct from the natural-expected–death survivors only with regard to the search for an explanation and feelings of responsibility. No differences for any groups were observed for loss of social support, guilt, or self-destructive behavior. From these patterns, it should be emphasized—as has been observed in multiple studies—that there are many similarities in the grief experiences of traumatic-death survivors (suicide and accidental death).

Although they did not conduct a longitudinal study of these survivors, Barrett and Scott (1990) assessed the course and quality of grief recovery among these bereaved spouses. At the point in time of their study—that is, at 2 to 4 years after the death—no differences were found for any group in recovery. They particularly concluded that suicide survivors were not "stuck" in their bereavement process compared to the other bereaved spouses.

Though not without methodological difficulties, Farberow and colleagues (Farberow, Gallagher, Gilewski, & Thompson, 1987; Farberow, Gallagher-Thompson, Gilewski, & Thompson, 1992a, 1992b) reported the results of an exceptionally strong longitudinal investigation of more than 100 spouse-suicide survivors over a 2.5-year period. Well over a decade after its findings were reported, in addition to informing our knowledge about spouse survivors, it remains a model for future study designs and is reported here much as it was in McIntosh (1993). This investigation followed the grief experiences of surviving spouses of suicides as well as spouses of natural deaths and a nonbereaved control group, all of whom were aged 55 years and older at the beginning of the study. These survivors were interviewed at four time periods: within 2 months of the death of their spouse (in the case of the bereaved groups), and then again at 6 months, 12 months, and 30 months. In addition to interview responses, the participants provided self-report information regarding grief feelings, depression, and other symptoms of mental health problems.

In brief, this investigation showed that at 2 months, the suicide and natural-death survivors were not different from one another on any of the grief or mental health measures, but both bereaved groups showed more depression, psychological distress, and negative self-appraisal than did the nonbereaved control group. The same results were found at 6 months, with no differences between the bereaved groups but more psychological distress than for the controls. At 12 months, however, some differences between suicide and natural death groups appeared. Suicide survivors rated their mental health as poorer and reported higher levels of depression than did natural-death survivors. Grief and mental health symptoms generally decreased during the 12 months for both groups, but for the natural-death survivors, this improvement was predominantly seen during the first 6 months. Suicide survivors, on the other hand, improved only slightly during the entire first year.

At 2.5 years after the death, both bereaved groups showed significant improvement in their grief and mental health. However, suicide survivors continued to give poorer self-ratings of their mental health than did the controls, whereas the natural-death group did not. Once again, as at 2 and 6 months, the grief level for the two bereaved groups was similar. As might be expected, the levels of grief remained substantially higher than for the nonbereaved controls, even 30 months after the death. The findings suggest, therefore, that "the major mental health feelings experienced in bereavement by elderly survivors *do not differ so much in kind as in their course* during the first 2.5 years following a death and that these feelings will also vary in the survivor depending on the mode of death, [and] the time since the death" (Farberow et al., 1992b, p. P364; emphasis added).

The use of a longitudinal design and the information that it yielded regarding the course of change represents the major contribution of this investigation to understanding suicide survivorship. Only by longitudinal designs can true changes over time be assessed in survivors; this study remains one of only a small number of longitudinal control group studies that has been published to date. For suicide survivors, grief and mental health showed improvement in two stages. Grief levels remained high through all of the first year but dropped markedly by 30 months to levels similar to those of the natural-death survivors. The course for natural death, however, began with actually a slightly higher initial level of grief than that for suicide survivors, but grief feelings declined by 6 months and again by 30 months, with little change during the interim periods. Mental health improvements for suicide survivors occurred at the 6-month follow-up, did not change at 12 months, and improved further by 30 months. Natural-death survivors showed constant improvement in mental health measures over time periods through 30 months. The nonbereaved controls showed no changes over the study.

Depression also showed differential courses for the survivors. Suicide survivors and natural-death survivors showed higher levels of depression than did the controls at all time periods following the death. Suicide survivors' levels of depression did not lessen until the 30-month period. Natural-death survivors experienced great declines in depressive levels by the 6-month time period but showed only slight declines at 12 months and then a somewhat larger decline by 30 months.

Among the other findings of the study were that by 30 months, levels of emotional distress expressed by the survivors of suicide and natural death were virtually the same as those expressed by the nonbereaved controls. However, it was also observed that the suicide survivors were more anxious than either the natural-death survivors or nonbereaved controls even at 30 months after the death of their spouse.

Farberow and colleagues' (1987, 1992a, 1992b) results suggest that these bereaved groups of elderly spouses experience grief and mental health symptoms that decline over time but remain prominent even 2.5 years after their loss. It is also clear that the grief among suicide survivors follows a different course than that for natural-death survivors and that grief takes a longer period to subside among suicide survivors. The closing statements of Farberow and colleagues (1992b) suggest that suicide grief is more complicated than for natural causes, but "whereas the process seems a more difficult one for the SS [suicide survivors], especially during the first year, they seem after 2.5 years to be pretty much in the same place as the NDS [natural-death survivors], still feeling the loss, still carrying some grief, but generally functioning adequately" (p. P365). Similar studies and designs that include accidental-death control groups as well as other kinship relation categories are greatly needed.

Guilt, Shame, and Stigma

Results of spouse-survivor studies have produced mixed conclusions with respect to guilt and related experiences. Representative of this pattern, Demi (1984) found more similarities than differences in a comparison of widows of suicide and natural or accidental death during the second year of bereavement, although she observed more guilt and resentment among widows of suicides. Similarly, McNeil and colleagues (1988) identified more guilt and blaming reactions in suicide-survivor spouses than in accident-survivor spouses. As noted previously, however, Barrett and Scott (1989) did not find guilt differences among the four spouse-survivor groups that they studied (i.e., suicide death, accidental death, natural-expected death, and natural-unexpected death). At the same time, on several dimensions and issues related to guilt, the authors found differences for suicide survivors, including more stigmatization and shame, rejection, and a greater likelihood to report concealment of the cause of death from others. Suicide survivors were different only from the natural-expected–death survivors with regard to feelings of responsibility. The studies by Grad and Zavasnik (1996, 1999) of spouses in Slovenia found greater shame in suicide-bereaved spouses at 2 months, with these feelings lessened by 14 months, and found greater guilt and shame feelings by traffic-accident survivors at 14 months.

Another guilt- and stigma-related issue of bereavement is blaming. The stigma around suicide commonly involves blaming of the spouse, either overtly or covertly by the community, the neighbors, and, especially, the in-laws (e.g., Cain & Fast, 1966/1972; Saunders, 1981). The suicide widow in Silverman's (1972) study, in contrast to the accident and heart-attack survivors, was neither supported nor given sympathy by her neighbors. Rather, the neighbors were described as acting aloof and suspicious, spreading numerous stories and gossip about her role in the husband's death, and taunting and teasing the children. In some instances, gossip and ostracism may become severe enough to prompt a move to another community. Although this was not commonly observed in Shepherd and Barraclough's (1974) survivors, in one extreme case, a spouse "felt he could not go back to the town where he had lived with a suicide because of the gossip and blame he incurred" (p. 601). The suicide-bereaved widow described by Silverman (1972) moved within the year following her husband's death, and at least 5 of the 35 surviving spouses in Cain and Fast's (1966/1972) sample were "hounded out of [their] community by … sustained gossip, accusations, and ostracism" (p. 148).

Neighbors are not the only ones who blame, ostracize, or fail to provide support to suicide-bereaved spouses. Betsy Ross (1982) commented that after her husband had died by suicide, "[r]elatives from both families refused to attend the funeral. My family sent no flowers. My mother told neighbors not to bring food. Only 3 sympathy cards arrived" (pp. 99–100).

Search to Understand "Why"

Comparison-group spouse studies provide minimal evidence for the contention that suicide survivors experience a greater need to understand "why" with respect to their loved one's death. Among the few studies assessing this feature, Barrett and Scott (1989) found that suicide survivors were distinct from the natural-expected death survivors with regard to the search for an explanation but not from accidental- or natural-unexpected–death survivors. Activities such as searching for an explanation as well as looking for meaning by survivors are likely to be more prevalent among traumatic-death survivors than among natural-death survivors. These activities in response to loss may well mediate bereavement outcome and may have emerged as a common experience for traumatic-death survivors (e.g., Jordan, 2001).

Research Methods: Qualitative Research

As noted previously, results of bereavement studies often vary somewhat when comparing the findings of quantitative (often self-report instruments) and qualitative (often interview-based) investigations (Sveen & Walby, 2008). This variance may be seen in the findings of qualitative investigations of spouse survivors. For instance, a qualitative study of a small number of young widows aged 30–39 years (Saunders, 1981) suggested greater rejection from friends and the husband's family among suicide survivors than among survivors of other causes of death. However, suicide-surviving widows began dating sooner after the death than did the other widows.

Using a survey method, Stone (1972) studied the responses of 66 widowed individuals, a group that included 35 suicide survivors. Compared to the nonsuicide group, suicide survivors had been less healthy since the death of their spouse, had a poorer quality of their marriage at the time of the death, felt more compelled to move following the death (which Stone interpreted as stigma), felt more anger toward their deceased spouse, as well as more guilt and responsibility for the death. Similarly, Silverman (1972) analyzed the case histories of three widows following the sudden deaths of their husbands from a suicide, an accident, and a heart attack. The major difference observed in their grief experiences revolved around stigma and its ramifications.

These qualitative studies often present the same argument as that noted in Chapter 2 and by Ellenbogen and Gratton (2001): that the emphasis should be placed on differences among individual suicide survivors rather than on the differences between survivors of various modes of death. This was certainly the contention of Watford (2008), who provided a self-exploration of her grief following her husband's suicide. The literature contains many personal experience accounts of suicide survivorship for many kinship relations (see McIntosh, 1999, for a table of firsthand accounts by relationships). Consistent with these general arguments, Begley and Quayle (2007) conducted detailed interviews with eight suicide-bereaved spouses. The goal of the investigation was to discover common themes in the multiple interviews and individual experiences. The four themes that the researchers observed were (a) early attempts to gain some control over the death's impact, (b) a need to make sense of the loved one's death, (c) social discomfort, and (d) eventual accomplishment of a sense of purpose in their lives after the death.

Begley and Quayle noted the importance of "meaning making" or personal growth that has emerged as a focus in other investigations of suicide as well in recent years (e.g., Feigelman, Jordan, & Gorman, 2009; see also Chapter 11).

Risk Factors in Spouse-Suicide Survivors

Most spouse studies have been studies of widows—that is, women as survivors of their husband's death by suicide. Despite this, existing evidence (Agerbo, 2005) shows that suicide risk for the bereaved spouse was far more likely for men who had lost their wives or "cohabitee" by any mode of death; suicide risk was particularly elevated when the death had been by suicide (see also Hedström, Liu, & Nordvik, 2008). Virtually no studies specifically of men as survivors of their spouse's suicide have been conducted. In another study with implications about specific issues of risk with respect to bereavement features (Tall, Kõlves, Sisask, & Värnik, 2008), spouse survivors of suicide by an individual who was an alcohol abuser were more likely to report anger than were suicide-surviving spouses of individuals who were not alcohol abusers. The prevalence of alcohol abuse, in general, would suggest that this might be a factor in some proportion of suicide survivors and their adaptation to the loss.

☐ Other Relationships and Issues in Suicide Bereavement Among Adults

As noted earlier, there were 33,300 suicides in the United States in 2006. Of these deaths, 32,360 were aged 18 years and older, and 31,054 were aged 21 years and older (CDC, 2009). Although spouses represent a substantial number of these deaths among adults, there are many adults of various relationships to these adults who died by suicide, and many adults are involved in the lives of child and adolescent suicides, as well. Only a small number of specific relationships have received research attention. The paragraphs that follow detail some of those relationships proposed for systematic study, although many other relationships also could be investigated.

Adults as Survivors of Their Parent's Suicide

In Chapter 4, we discuss the case of those who lose a parent to suicide during childhood and adolescence. No research was identified regarding the impact of parental suicide loss during childhood and its impact during the individuals' remaining adulthood years. However, in another regard, with the large proportion of suicides that occur in midlife and late life, there are many adults who experience the suicide of a parent during their adulthood. Studies of adult children who survive the suicide of a parent are lacking, but the personal essays in Stimming and Stimming's (1999) book show possible common themes. Among the themes they noted were identification with the parent, feelings of abandonment, concerns about their own and their family members' risk of future suicide (including concerns about genetic factors in suicide), lack of an opportunity to know other adult child survivors with whom they can share their experience, and effects on their own family (spouse and children) and work relationships. Dane (1991) discussed the loss of a parent to suicide when an adult is middle aged, suggesting many of the same issues of grief that appear in Stimming and Stimming (1999) and adding other reactions often noted by suicide survivors, including guilt, anger, and the circumvention of usual mourning rituals to avoid dealing with the way in which the parent died. Much research is needed to investigate the impact of parent suicides on adult children.

Adults as Survivors of Their Sibling's Suicide

Similar to the situation of adults as survivors of their parent's suicide, adults who are siblings of suicides have not been studied. These suicides may well be those by a younger, adolescent sibling, such as the case of Edward Dunne and Karen Dunne-Maxim, two pioneers in the area of suicide survivorship who lost their 16-year-old younger brother by suicide (see Dunne, McIntosh, & Dunne-Maxim, 1987). Although Chapter 4 reviews the literature on sibling survivors, nearly all of the work has focused on siblings who are themselves also children or adolescents. Among the few studies of siblings that have appeared (e.g., Brent et al., 1996; Brent, Perper, Moritz, Liotus, et al., 1993), mixed results were observed regarding the vulnerability of sibling survivors to psychiatric illness and symptoms following the suicide when compared to controls. Studies of adult sibling survivors (for suicides by younger as well as adult siblings) are needed, as are investigations of the long-term impact of these sibling deaths.

Mixed-Relationship Studies of Adult Survivors

There have been several studies of adult survivors of suicide in which survivors have been combined into a single group for comparison to some other group or groups of survivors from other causes of death. As is discussed in some detail in Chapter 33, such designs have several undesirable methodological problems, and the wide diversity of the survivor relationships may well affect—and even negate—the reactions and features of the bereavement process. One recruitment or sampling method has been to study college students who identify as survivors of suicide and other causes of death (Bailley, Kral, & Dunham, 1999; McIntosh & Kelly, 1992; Range & Calhoun, 1990; Range & Niss, 1990). These studies, which use interviews or standardized instruments, have often observed differences for the bereaved groups, but differences have been observed for some grief experiences but not for others when comparing bereavement groups, and there has been no consistent pattern of findings between studies. However, Bailley et al. (1999) found clear differences among their bereaved groups (suicide, accident, and unanticipated and anticipated natural deaths), observing that suicide survivors had more frequent feelings regarding responsibility and rejection as well as more overall grief reactions and some unique reactions associated with suicide loss. It must be realized that these college student investigations consisted of predominantly close friends (and not immediate family members) of the suicide and other causes because of the population from which the samples were chosen.

Among the reasons to consider the findings from mixed-relationship studies is that such studies, although generally not the most desirable sampling methodology, may be both feasible and efficient with respect to time and resources as exploratory investigations. Although such studies of diverse samples might possibly wrongly identify issues for further study or fail to identify a potentially important variable (due to the variability introduced with the sample's diversity), such studies might identify variables of general interest to be studied in subsequent, better designed investigations (see Chapter 33 for more discussion). For instance, de Groot, de Keijser, and Neeleman's (2006) study of spouses and first-degree relatives of suicides and natural deaths looked at early bereavement measures. At 3 months after the death, they observed that on several domains of general health, the suicide bereaved showed worse health than did the natural-death bereaved. The suicide bereaved also showed more loneliness, depression, and complicated grief (CG). It should be cautioned, however, that the researchers believed that issues associated with recruiting via general practitioners may have affected their sample's representativeness. Although some of the studies noted previously have indicated that bereavement differences seem to disappear over time, coupled with the fact that many survivor studies are conducted many months—and, more often, many years—after a death, a study such as that of de Groot et al. might possibly indicate that differences in grief might be observed in the time period immediately after the death (see also Mitchell, Kim, Prigerson, & Mortimer-Stephens, 2004, and Mitchell, Sakraida, Kiim, Bullian, & Chiappetta, 2009; discussed later in this chapter). Another study (Miyabayashi & Yasuda, 2007) combining spouses and parents (no differences on any measures were noted between the two kinship groups) looked at survivor groups of suicide death, accident death, and acute-, short-, and longer-illness death. Several differences were observed between the suicide-bereaved group compared with one or more of the illness comparison groups, including poorer general health, greater social dysfunction, severe depression, and depression more generally among the suicide bereaved. Interestingly, no significant differences were observed for the suicide- and accident-bereaved groups, but the accident-bereaved group did not differ from the illness-bereaved groups as the suicide group did. Thus, similar to the contention regarding uniqueness of suicide grief, the authors concluded that "suicide was found to be the most distinctive bereavement" (Miyabayashi & Yasuda, 2007, p. 502).

In a somewhat unique approach to studying differential bereavement across mode of death, Houck (2007) compared grief responses among cancer-, HIV/AIDS-, and suicide-bereaved individuals who were involved in therapy or other forms of counseling and support. The participants represented those who had lost a parent, spouse, or life partner; sibling; child; close friend; or extended family member. The investigation used an instrument designed specifically for research on suicide bereavement (GEQ; Barrett & Scott, 1989; see Chapter 33 for a discussion of standardized measures as a methodological issue), and Houck argued that the three groups could be discriminated on the basis of their grief reactions; however, the most distinctive finding beyond unique features of suicide bereavement focused on the issue of stigmatization. Suicide is often characterized as a stigmatizing cause of death, but HIV/AIDS involves its own issues with respect to stigma. Houck found that the grief reactions that most differentiated the HIV/AIDS bereaved from the suicide and cancer bereaved was their experience of stigmatization. Houck concluded that "both the suicide and HIV/AIDS groups may be forced into a silence regarding grieving their losses openly" (p. 111), which can seriously affect the grieving process and has important implications for grief counseling.

Another potentially important issue with regard to suicide bereavement research in adults is apparent in multiple-relationship studies that focused on the quality of the relationship between survivors and the deceased. More specifically, a study of the effects of attachment and the kinship relation on grief (Reed & Greenwald, 1991) found, in general, that kinship relation was less important than attachment in affecting the intensity of grief. Higher levels of attachment significantly increased guilt and shame, shock, and mental preoccupation for suicide and accident survivors. The study also indicated that greater guilt and shame as well as rejection were experienced by suicide survivors than by accident survivors (the finding for rejection was observed also by Reed, 1998). However, suicide survivors showed less shock and emotional distress than did accident survivors. A desirable feature of survivor research would be the inclusion of measures of attachment and closeness of the survivor's relationship to the deceased. The emphasis on attachment has been a part of the larger bereavement perspective for some time (e.g., Mikulincer & Shaver, 2008; Shaver & Tancredy, 2001). This conclusion is also supported with respect to kinship relation closeness by two recent studies by Mitchell and colleagues (Mitchell et al., 2004, 2009).

In these studies, the closeness of the relationship (*close relations* were defined as spouses, parents, children, and siblings; *distant relations* were defined as in-laws, aunts or uncles, and nieces or nephews) was found to affect important aspects of bereavement. Measuring health, mental health, and grief within 1 month of the death by suicide of a relative in both studies, Mitchell et al. (2004) found higher levels of complicated grief (CG) among the close-relationship survivor group compared with the distant-relationship group, whereas Mitchell et al. (2009) found higher levels of depression and anxiety and lower levels of mental health quality of life among the close-relationship group. These studies support the inclusion of relationship and its attachment quality in investigations of suicide bereavement.

A final study of adult survivors that combined all relationship categories (spouses, first- and second-degree relatives, and friends) attempted to identify a group of suicide survivors who might be at differential risk for suicide bereavement responses. Parker and McNally (2008) observed that suicide-bereaved individuals who employ a "repressive coping" style may fare better in coping after a loss by suicide. This coping pattern, which was conceptualized as more "trait-like" than a trainable coping method, involves denying emotional disturbance and turning attention elsewhere when encountering threatening information. Compared with nonrepressors, repressors coped more effectively, had a milder course of grief, and coped better with the stress associated with their suicide bereavement.

Other Adult Relatives, Friends, and Nonkinship Survivors of Suicide

Although studies have been conducted of the impact on friends, peers, and acquaintances of youth who died by suicide (see Chapter 4; e.g., Brent, Perper, Moritz, Allman, et al., 1993), no such studies could be found of friends, peers, coworkers, neighbors, and so forth, regarding the variety of relationships in which adults are involved. Although at least one study of exposure to suicide (with *exposure* being defined as "knowing a suicide decedent from the previous year"; Crosby & Sacks, 2002) included more than 5,000 individuals aged 18 years and older, the categories of the telephone survey were immediate family, another relative, and friend or acquaintance. A total of 7% indicated that they did know someone who had died by suicide in the past year, with 80% of those being friends or acquaintances (and neighbors or coworkers), 3% being immediate family, and 14% being another relative. However, no indication of the closeness of the relationship was assessed, and the only reaction-related questions related to suicidal behavior on the part of the respondent. The researchers extrapolated these results to imply that for each suicide that occurs annually, more than 400 adults know of someone who died by suicide that same year. It seems clear that although this measure may be one aspect of suicide in society, it is far beyond the definition of "survivor" proposed in Chapter 1.

Rather than focusing on *exposure* as defined in the previous paragraph, we believe that more could be gained from studying those individuals who had relationships that ranged from noncasual to intimate; these were the people with whom those who died by suicide shared their lives. Campbell (1997) has reported that the bereavement support groups for suicide survivors at the Baton Rouge Crisis Intervention Center in Louisiana has had people from 28 different relationships attend the support meetings, seeking help with their grief. Clearly, the small set of relationships for which research findings are available does not represent the range of relationships or issues that affect suicide bereavement in adulthood. Research to determine the impact on other family relationships such as those of extended family should be investigated using both qualitative and quantitative methods, first-person accounts, and clinical experience. Such relationships might include widowers, grandparents, extended family members of various relationships (e.g., aunts, uncles, nieces, nephews, cousins, in-laws), fiancés, life partners and individuals in gay and lesbian relationships, same-sex marriage partners, coworkers, couples who are cohabitating but not legally married, closest friends and confidantes (as well as acquaintances and casual friends), and those who discovered the suicide or witnessed the death scene. Another relationship involves the therapist of a person who dies by suicide. This special relationship will be considered in Chapter 5. Such studies would extend and enhance the current knowledge base of suicide survivorship.

Survivors of Elderly Suicides

Just as a suicide death by an individual at a young age may have special implications regarding bereavement among survivors (see Chapter 4 and "Parent Survivors of Child Suicides" in this chapter), the life period of older adulthood may also be highlighted as potentially having special implications. The age group in adulthood traditionally at highest risk for death by suicide in the United States and many other nations is the older adult population (e.g., 65 years and older). With suicide rates approximately 50% higher than the rates of the nation as a whole (and young adulthood) in the United States, there are more than 5,000 elderly suicides annually, with most being men (in 2006, there were 5,299 total elderly suicides, 4,462 of which were men; CDC, 2009). Much of the evidence previously cited for spouses are studies of widows of elderly men's suicides. However, there are far more survivors of suicides in late life than their widows, and researchers have conducted few investigations to determine the impact of the late-life suicides on these other survivors. Some features that are more common in elderly suicides than in other age groups (e.g., more health problems; higher use of lethal, violent means; greater social isolation and living alone; multiple sources of loss, including people, social roles and networks, retirement, and economic independence) may affect survivors' reactions to the suicide of an elder loved one (see Balter, 1994; Cerel, Jordan, & Duberstein, 2008; McIntosh, Santos, Hubbard, & Overholser, 1994, pp. 45–53).

The methodologically strongest studies of elderly suicide survivors are those of Farberow and colleagues (Farberow et al., 1987, 1992a, 1992b), which are discussed at length earlier in this chapter (see the section on spouse survivors) and a more recent study by Harwood and colleagues (Harwood, Hawton, Hope, & Jacoby, 2002). As noted, Farberow and colleagues found much similarity between the spouses of elderly suicides and those who had lost a spouse to natural causes. Although the course of the grief patterns over time differed somewhat for the two groups, by 2.5 years after the death, the two groups of bereaved spouses had largely arrived at the same point: still somewhat anxious and troubled, but largely having adapted to the loss.

Whereas the Farberow studies (Farberow et al., 1987, 1992a, 1992b) included only spouses, Harwood and colleagues' (2002) study involved a mixed-relationship group of survivors of elderly suicide, including not only spouses but also children of the deceased (presumably adults, given that those who died by suicide were all older than the age of 60 years), friends, siblings, and "other relatives" (unspecified). The survivors of the elderly suicides were paired (on age and gender) with the bereaved members of a control group who had lost a loved one in late life by natural causes. Although age and gender were the same for the groups, the natural-cause bereaved group included more spouses and fewer friends than did the suicide group (i.e., the groups were not matched on relationship to the deceased). As observed in many studies reviewed here, the researchers found many similarities between the two groups of elder-bereaved individuals. For instance, no group differences were observed for overall grief, search for an explanation, guilt, or depressive symptoms. Differences were found, though, with suicide survivors displaying more stigmatization, shame, and rejection. The only kinship group large enough to permit statistically meaningful analyses in the two bereaved groups was children of the deceased elders. Although feelings of rejection were higher for the suicide bereaved among this group, the responses of stigma and shame did not differ. Thus, this study provided additional support for some aspects of social stigma but not others (e.g., guilt) and, once again, suggested a differential impact among those of various kinship and other relationships to those who die. However, many questions about, and factors in, elderly suicide bereavement remain to be addressed and answered.

Differential Bereavement, Sense Making, and Meaning Making

Before ending the consideration of adult bereavement after a loss by suicide, it is important to provide some focused attention on an emerging aspect of bereavement differences following loss. A common, though certainly not universal, finding in the literature reviewed previously has been that there is very mixed evidence for differences between suicide survivors and those with other losses. However, we would be leaving the reader with the wrong impression if the conclusion was drawn that there was simply no evidence for bereavement differences. In Chapter 2, we made the case for a more complex and nuanced perspective on the question of differences in bereavement based on mode of death. Also noted in some detail in Chapter 2 (and revisited in Chapter 33), the predominantly quantitative (e.g., as opposed to qualitative) methodologies used have revealed fewer differences than observed in qualitative investigations, which have often revealed more, considerable, and varied differences in not only symptomatology but also in the subjective experiences of survivors (e.g., what Jordan, 2001, called "themes"). More pointedly, Gillies and Neimeyer (2006, p. 31) expressed the opinion that "study methods and designs have constrained what can be concluded from" research on bereavement and the role of meaning making, for instance. In addition, as concluded in Chapter 2, the fewest differences in grief have most often been observed in investigations comparing those who have experienced loss due to traumatic deaths, of which suicide survivors are only one group (i.e., suicide, accidents, homicide). These losses are due to nonnormative, unexpected, and often violent causes. Researchers have found that survivors of traumatic and violent deaths have experienced more intense grief symptomatology than did survivors of nontraumatic deaths (e.g., Keesee, Currier, & Neimeyer, 2008).

In addition to the methodological limitations often observed in research on survivors, much evidence is emerging in the larger bereavement literature regarding the importance of sense making and meaning making after a loss; however, this issue has received little attention, thus far, in the research on suicide survivors. In Chapter 11, we present these issues in detail, but the themes associated with these important issues for the suicide bereaved will be briefly addressed here. For instance, Begley and Quayle (2007) conducted a qualitative study of eight mixed-relationship individuals, with four main themes emerging prominently in the interviews conducted. In addition to themes noted elsewhere in this chapter—that is, survivors' wish to "control the impact of the death" and experience considerable "social uneasiness"—Begley and Quayle (p. 26) found that suicide survivors expressed a tremendous desire to "make sense of the death" and indicated that they eventually felt a sense of "purposefulness" in their lives. As one indication of the importance of feelings of meaning, Keesee et al. (2008) observed that parents who had lost children to violent deaths made less sense of the loss experience than did parents who had lost children to other modes of death. Also, Keesee et al. noted that sense making was "the most salient predictor of grief severity" (p. 1145), with cause of death contributing considerably less to the prediction. Similarly, researchers found that adjustment to bereavement was predicted best by sense making (Holland, Currier, & Neimeyer, 2006), and sense making showed a strong relationship to CG symptomatology in the bereaved (Currier, Holland, & Neimeyer, 2006). As elaborated in Chapter 11, these aspects of grief hold great promise for revealing valuable information regarding our understanding and intervention with survivors following a death by suicide or other traumatic or violent causes.

☐ Special Postvention Issue: Impact of Suicide Attempts on Family and Friends of the Suicide Attempter

A final issue in the aftermath of suicide and suicidal behavior involves nonfatal suicide acts (i.e., suicide attempts). Although those who are bereaved by a suicide have generally embraced the idea of *postvention* as applying only to the aftermath of deaths by suicide, this term can also apply to the family and friends of someone who attempts suicide but who remains alive after the attempt. Postvention can also, of course, apply directly to the attempter and to the aftereffects of the attempt on the lives of all involved. This is not an issue exclusive to adulthood. The efforts surrounding this issue have, in some ways, mirrored some of the early efforts by suicide survivors: to bring attention to the issues; to organize, advocate, and come together to better understand and help the attempters and their loved ones in the time after their attempt; to lessen stigma surrounding suicide-attempt behavior; and to encourage the development of therapeutic approaches and support for the suicide attempt survivor and their significant others (see, e.g., Suicide Prevention Resource Center [SPRC], 2007).

Typically, the issues arising in the aftermath of nonfatal suicide acts have centered on the psychological well-being and treatment of the attempter; on the attempter's risk of depression, suicidality, and future suicidal behavior (e.g., Henriques, Wenzel, Brown, & Beck, 2005; Spirito, Boergers, Donaldson, Bishop, & Lewander, 2002; Stewart, Manion, & Davidson, 2002; van der Sande, Buskens, Allart, van der Graaf, & van Engeland, 1997); and even on the repercussions for clinicians, such as re-establishing therapy after serious suicide attempts by the client (Ramsay & Newman, 2005). Although more general mental health efforts with respect to the families of the mentally ill have existed for some time (e.g., Hatfield & Lefley, 1987; National Alliance on Mental Illness [NAMI] as an advocacy group), few efforts specific to survivors of suicide attempts could be found until some personal accounts of attempt survivors were published (e.g., Cook, 1993; Heckler, 1994). Later, the Organization for Attempters and Survivors of Suicide in Interfaith Services (OASSIS) was founded in 1997, and a book of personal accounts by attempt survivors was published (Clemons, 2001). In 2005, the first National Conference for Survivors of Suicide Attempts (SOSAs), Health Care Professionals, and Clergy and Laity was held (Litts, Beautrais, & Lezine, 2008). In Canada, the Suicide Information and Education Centre (SIEC), now the Centre for Suicide Prevention (CSP, 2001), published one of its *SIEC Alert* resource sheets in 2001 on suicide attempts and their impact, followed recently by another *SIEC Alert* from the perspective of attempters and yet another from that of the significant others (CSP, 2009a, 2009b). The U.S. Department of Health and Human Services (DHHS) developed a series of pamphlets in English and Spanish called "After an Attempt," with one intended for the attempter, one intended for family members, and another intended for medical providers (DHHS, 2006a, 2006b, 2006c), and NAMI has also developed a guide for the attempter and their relatives (NAMI, n.d.). The National Suicide Prevention Lifeline convened an Attempt Survivor Advisory Summit Meeting in New York City in 2007, at which eight survivors shared their experience and suggestions to advise future efforts (National Suicide Prevention Lifeline, 2007).

Research has begun to emerge that examines the feelings and experiences of significant others of suicide attempters, in particular. For example, Wagner, Aiken, Mullaley, and Tobin (2000) studied the verbal and emotional reactions of parents in the time period immediately following their adolescent's suicide attempt. Parents exhibited both positive and negative emotional reactions (e.g., caring, sadness, anxiety, hostility) but were more likely to express support and comfort for their adolescent than to express their angry feelings. Attempters experience a variety of feelings in the time after their attempt—including shame, depression, and the wish to keep the behavior secret to avoid stigma—and some felt a sense of relief that their attempt had not been fatal (CSP, 2009a; see, e.g., Chesley & Loring-McNulty, 2003). Similar in many ways to suicide survivors, significant others of the attempters exhibited reactions such as fear and concern for repeated behaviors and suicidal behavior on the part of other family members, feelings of responsibility for preventing future suicidal behaviors by the attempt survivor, anger, guilt, shame, and fear that others would find out about the attempt (CSP, 2009b). The goal of a qualitative study conducted in Ireland by Byrne and colleagues (2008) used a focus-group approach to identify the support needs of parents of attempt survivors. Among the themes derived from the analysis of the focus group, the parents stated their desire for a range of information as well as services in dealing with and understanding their child's attempt and to help them with approaches regarding further incidents. In addition, this Ireland-based group (Power et al., 2009) also conducted a pilot study to evaluate a support program for the parents of young people who had engaged in self-harming behavior. The 8-week program, meeting once weekly, provided support and educational services derived largely from the results of the earlier focus-group analysis. The program produced a number of improvements in measures of the parents' well-being, including psychological distress and parental satisfaction. Additionally, these improvements were maintained at a 6-month follow up. The parents also reported that their young people who had engaged in self-harming behaviors were experiencing lower levels of difficulties.

The research and clinical literature with respect to suicide-attempt survivors and their significant others is still relatively small, and many issues remain to be addressed. However, there are some commonalities with those who survive the suicide death of a loved one. Exploring these commonalities should assist in the development and availability of effective interventions for the attempters and their significant others in dealing with the aftermath of this suicidal behavior.

☐ References

Agerbo, E. (2005). Midlife suicide risk, partner's psychiatric illness, spouse and child bereavement by suicide or other modes of death: A gender specific study. *Journal of Epidemiology and Community Health, 59,* 407–412.

Bailley, S. E., Kral, M. J., & Dunham, K. (1999). Survivors of suicide do grieve differently: Empirical support for a common sense proposition. *Suicide and Life-Threatening Behavior, 29,* 256–271.

Balter, R. (1994). The elderly suicide: Those left behind. In D. Lester & M. Tallmer (Eds.), *Now I lay me down: Suicide in the elderly* (pp. 105–178). Philadelphia, PA: Charles Press.

Barrett, T. W., & Scott, T. B. (1989). Development of the Grief Experience Questionnaire. *Suicide and Life-Threatening Behavior, 19,* 201–215.

Barrett, T. W., & Scott, T. B. (1990). Suicide bereavement and recovery patterns compared with nonsuicide bereavement patterns. *Suicide and Life-Threatening Behavior, 20,* 1–15.

Begley, M., & Quayle, E. (2007). The lived experience of adults bereaved by suicide: A phenomenological study. *Crisis: International Journal of Crisis Intervention and Suicide Prevention, 28,* 26–34.

Bolton, I. (with Mitchell, C.). (1983). *My son … my son … : A guide to healing after a suicide in the family.* Atlanta, GA: Bolton Press.

Brent, D. A., Moritz, G., Bridge, J., Perper, J., & Canobbio, R. (1996). The impact of adolescent suicide on siblings and parents: A longitudinal follow-up. *Suicide and Life-Threatening Behavior, 26,* 253–259.

Brent, D. A., Perper, J., Moritz, G., Allman, C., Liotus, L., Schweers, J., … Canobbio, R. (1993). Bereavement or depression? The impact of the loss of a friend to suicide. *Journal of the American Academy of Child and Adolescent Psychiatry, 32,* 1189–1197.

Brent, D. A., Perper, J. A., Moritz, G., Liotus, L., Schweers, J., Roth, C., … Allman, C. (1993). Psychiatric impact of the loss of an adolescent sibling to suicide. *Journal of Affective Disorders, 28,* 249–256.

Byrne, S., Morgan, S., Fitzpatrick, C., Boylan, C., Crowley, S., Gahan, H., … Guerin, S. (2008). Deliberate self-harm in children and adolescents: A qualitative study exploring the needs of parents and carers. *Clinical Child Psychology and Psychiatry, 13,* 493–504.

Cain, A. C., & Fast, I. (1972). The legacy of suicide: Observations on the pathogenic impact of suicide upon marital partners. In A. C. Cain (Ed.), *Survivors of suicide* (pp. 145–154). Springfield, IL: Charles C Thomas. (Reprinted from *Psychiatry,* 1966, *29,* 406–411)

Calhoun, L. G., & Allen, B. G. (1991). Social reactions to the survivor of a suicide in the family: A review of the literature. *Omega: Journal of Death and Dying, 23,* 95–107.

Calhoun, L. G., & Selby, J. W. (1990). The social aftermath of a suicide in the family: Some empirical findings. In D. Lester (Ed.), *Current concepts of suicide* (pp. 214–224). Philadelphia, PA: Charles Press.

Campbell, F. R. (1997). Changing the legacy of suicide. *Suicide and Life-Threatening Behavior, 27,* 329–338.

Carr, D. (2008). Factors that influence late-life bereavement: Considering data from the Changing Lives of Older Couples Study. In M. S. Stroebe, R. O. Hansson, H. Schut, & W. Stroebe (Eds.), *Handbook of bereavement research and practice: Advances in theory and intervention* (pp. 417–440). Washington, DC: American Psychological Association.

Centers for Disease Control and Prevention. (2009). Web-Based Injury Statistics Query and Reporting System (WISQARS) [online; 2006 data]. WISQARS Fatal Injuries: Mortality Reports available from http://webappa.cdc.gov/sasweb/ncipc/mortrate.html

Centre for Suicide Prevention. (2001, July). *A suicide attempt is meaningful and significant* [SIEC Alert No. 45]. Calgary, Alberta, Canada: Author. Retrieved from http://www.suicideinfo.ca/csp/assets/alert45.pdf

Centre for Suicide Prevention. (2009a, January). *Attempted suicide: Part I. The perspective of attempters* [SIEC Alert No. 70]. Calgary, Alberta, Canada: Author. Retrieved from http://www.suicideinfo.ca

Centre for Suicide Prevention. (2009b, July). *Attempted suicide: Part II. The perspective of significant others* [SIEC Alert No. 71]. Calgary, Alberta, Canada: Author. Retrieved from http://www.suicideinfo.ca

Cerel, J., Jordan, J. R., & Duberstein, P. R. (2008). The impact of suicide on the family. *Crisis: International Journal of Crisis Intervention and Suicide Prevention, 29,* 38–44.

Chance, S. (1992). *Stronger than death: When suicide touches your life.* New York, NY: W. W. Norton.

Chesley, K., & Loring-McNulty, N. E. (2003). Process of suicide: Perspective of the suicide attempter. *Journal of the American Psychiatric Nurses Association, 9,* 41–45.

Clarke, C. S., & Wrigley, M. (2004). Suicide-related bereavement and psychiatric morbidity in the elderly. *Irish Journal of Psychological Medicine, 21,* 22–24.

Cleiren, M. P. H. D., Diekstra, R. F. W., Kerkhof, A. J. F. M., & van der Wal, J. (1994). Mode of death and kinship in bereavement: Focusing on "who" rather than "how." *Crisis: International Journal of Crisis Intervention and Suicide Prevention, 15,* 22–36.

Cleiren, M. P. H. D., Grad, O., Zavasnik, A., & Diekstra, R. F. W. (1996). Psychosocial impact of bereavement after suicide and fatal traffic accident: A comparative two-country study. *Acta Psychiatrica Scandinavica, 94,* 37–44.

Clemons, J. T. (Ed.). (2001). *Children of Jonah: Personal stories by survivors of suicide attempts.* Sterling, VA: Capital Books.

Cook, J. (1993). *How to help someone who is depressed or suicidal: Practical suggestions from a survivor.* Newington, CT: Rubicon Press.

Crosby, A. E., & Sacks, J. J. (2002). Exposure to suicide: Incidence and association with suicidal ideation and behavior: United States, 1994. *Suicide and Life-Threatening Behavior, 32,* 321–328.

Currier, J. M., Holland, J. M., & Neimeyer, R. A. (2006). Sense-making, grief, and the experience of violent loss: Toward a mediational model. *Death Studies, 30,* 403–428.

Cvinar, J. G. (2005). Do suicide survivors suffer social stigma? A review of the literature. *Perspectives in Psychiatric Care, 41,* 14–21.

Dane, B. O. (1991). Counselling bereaved middle aged children: Parental suicide survivors. *Clinical Social Work Journal, 19,* 35–48.

de Groot, M. H., de Keijser, J., & Neeleman, J. (2006). Grief shortly after suicide and natural death: A comparative study among spouses and first-degree relatives. *Suicide and Life-Threatening Behavior, 36,* 418–431.

Demi, A. S. (1984). Social adjustment of widows after a sudden death: Suicide and non-suicide survivors compared. *Death Education, 8*(Suppl.), 91–111.

Dunne, E. J., McIntosh, J. L., & Dunne-Maxim, K. (Eds.). (1987). *Suicide and its aftermath: Understanding and counseling the survivors.* New York, NY: W. W. Norton.

Dyregov, K., Nordanger, D., & Dyregrov, A. (2003). Predictors of psychosocial distress after suicide, SIDS, and accidents. *Death Studies, 27,* 143–165.

Ellenbogen, S., & Gratton, F. (2001). Do they suffer more? Reflections on research comparing suicide survivors to other survivors. *Suicide and Life-Threatening Behavior, 31,* 83–90.

Farberow, N. L., Gallagher, D. E., Gilewski, M. J., & Thompson, L. W. (1987). An examination of the early impact of bereavement on psychological distress in survivors of suicide. *Gerontologist, 27,* 592–598.

Farberow, N. L., Gallagher-Thompson, D., Gilewski, M., & Thompson, L. (1992a). The role of social supports in the bereavement process of surviving spouses of suicide and natural deaths. *Suicide and Life-Threatening Behavior, 22,* 107–124.

Farberow, N. L., Gallagher-Thompson, D., Gilewski, M., & Thompson, L. (1992b). Changes in grief and mental health of bereaved spouses of older suicides. *Journal of Gerontology: Psychological Sciences, 47,* P357–P366.

Feigelman, W., Gorman, B. S., & Jordan, J. R. (2009). Stigmatization and suicide bereavement. *Death Studies, 33,* 591–608.

Feigelman, W., Jordan, J. R., & Gorman, B. S. (2008–2009). How they died, time since loss, and bereavement outcomes. *Omega: Journal of Death and Dying, 58,* 251–273.

Feigelman, W., Jordan, J. R., & Gorman, B. S. (2009). Personal growth after a suicide loss: Cross-sectional findings suggest growth after loss may be associated with better mental health among survivors. *Omega: Journal of Death and Dying, 59,* 181–202.

Gillies, J., & Neimeyer, R. A. (2006). Loss, grief, and the search for significance: Toward a model of meaning reconstruction in bereavement. *Journal of Constructivist Psychology, 19,* 31–65.

Grad, O. T., & Zavasnik, A. (1996). Similarities and differences in the process of bereavement after suicide and after traffic fatalities in Slovenia. *Omega: Journal of Death and Dying, 33,* 243–251.

Grad, O. T., & Zavasnik, A. (1999). Phenomenology of bereavement process after suicide, traffic accident and terminal illness (in spouses). *Archives of Suicide Research, 5,* 157–172.

Harwood, D., Hawton, K., Hope, T., & Jacoby, R. (2002). The grief experiences and needs of bereaved relatives and friends of older people dying through suicide: A descriptive and case-control study. *Journal of Affective Disorders, 72,* 185–194.

Hatfield, A. B., & Lefley, H. P. (Eds.). (1987). *Families of the mentally ill: Coping and adaptation.* New York, NY: Guilford Press.

Heckler, R. A. (1994). *Waking up, alive: The descent, the suicide attempt, and the return to life.* New York, NY: Ballantine Books.

Hedström, P., Liu, K.-Y., & Nordvik, M. K. (2008). Interaction domains and suicide: A population-based panel study of suicides in Stockholm, 1991–1999. *Social Forces, 87,* 713–740.

Henriques, G., Wenzel, A., Brown, G. K., & Beck, A. T. (2005). Suicide attempters' reaction to survival as a risk factor for eventual suicide. *American Journal of Psychiatry, 162,* 2180–2182.

Holland, J. M., Currier, J. M., & Neimeyer, R. A. (2006). Meaning reconstruction in the first two years of bereavement: The role of sense-making and benefit-finding. *Omega: Journal of Death and Dying, 53,* 175–191.

Houck, J. A. (2007). A comparison of grief reactions in cancer, HIV/AIDS, and suicide bereavement. *Journal of HIV/AIDS and Social Sciences, 6*(3), 97–112.

Jordan, J. (2001). Is suicide bereavement different? A reassessment of the literature. *Suicide and Life-Threatening Behavior, 31,* 91–102.

Keesee, N. J., Currier, J. M., & Neimeyer, R. A. (2008). Predictors of grief following the death of one's child: The contribution of finding meaning. *Journal of Clinical Psychology, 64,* 1145–1163.

Kitson, G. C. (2000). Adjustment to violent and natural deaths in later and earlier life for Black and White widows. *Journal of Gerontology: Social Sciences, 55B,* S341–S351.

Kovarsky, R. S. (1989). Loneliness and disturbed grief: A comparison of parents who lost a child to suicide or accidental death. *Archives of Psychiatric Nursing, 3,* 86–96.

Lindqvist, P., Johansson, L., & Karlsson, U. (2008). In the aftermath of teenage suicide: A qualitative study of the psychosocial consequences for the surviving family members. *BMC Psychiatry, 8,* Paper 26 (open access). Retrieved from http://www.biomedcentral.com/1471-244X/8/26. doi:10.1186/1471-244X-8-26

Litts, D., Beautrais, A., & Lezine, Q. (2008, January). *First National Conference for Survivors of Suicide Attempts, Health Care Professionals, and Clergy and Laity: Summary of workgroup reports.* Retrieved from http://www.sprc.org/library/SOSAconf.pdf

Lohan, J. A., & Murphy, S. A. (2002). Family functioning and family typology after an adolescent or young adult's sudden violent death. *Journal of Family Nursing, 8,* 32–49.

Maple, M., Edwards, H., Plummer, D., & Minichiello, V. (2009). Silenced voices: Hearing the stories of parents bereaved through the suicide death of a young adult child. *Health and Social Care in the Community,* doi: 10.1111/j.1365-2524. 2009.00886.x. Retrieved from http://onlinelibrary.wiley.com/doi/10.1111/j.1365-2524.2009.00886.x/full

McIntosh, J. L. (1987a). Research, therapy, and educational needs. In E. J. Dunne, J. L., McIntosh, & K. Dunne-Maxim (Eds.), *Suicide and its aftermath: Understanding and counseling the survivors* (pp. 263–277). New York, NY: W. W. Norton.

McIntosh, J. L. (1987b). Survivor family relationships: Literature review. In E. J. Dunne, J. L. McIntosh, & K. L. Dunne-Maxim (Eds.), *Suicide and its aftermath: Understanding and counseling the survivors* (pp. 73–84). New York, NY: W. W. Norton.

McIntosh, J. L. (1993). Control group studies of suicide survivors: A review and critique. *Suicide and Life-Threatening Behavior, 23,* 146–161.

McIntosh, J. L. (1999). Research on survivors of suicide. In M. Stimming & M. Stimming (Eds.), *Before their time: Adult children's experiences of parental suicide* (pp. 157–180). Philadelphia, PA: Temple University Press.

McIntosh, J. L. (2009, May 4). Analysis of suicide data in the *Mortality Multiple Cause Files* for the year 2006 posted at the National Center for Health Statistics Web site http://www.cdc.gov/nchs/data_access/VitalStatsOnline.htm (data file: ftp://ftp.cdc.gov/pub/Health_Statistics/NCHS/Datasets/DVS/mortality/Mort2006us.zip).

McIntosh, J. L., & Kelly, L. D. (1992). Survivors' reactions: Suicide vs. other causes. *Crisis: International Journal of Crisis Intervention and Suicide Prevention, 13*, 82–93.

McIntosh, J. L., Santos, J. F., Hubbard, R. W., & Overholser, J. C. (1994). *Elder suicide: Research, theory and treatment.* Washington, DC: American Psychological Association.

McNeil, D. E., Hatcher, C., & Reubin, R. (1988). Family survivors of suicide and accidental death: Consequences for widows. *Suicide and Life-Threatening Behavior, 18*, 137–148.

Mikulincer, M., & Shaver, P. R. (2008). An attachment perspective on bereavement. In M. S. Stroebe, R. O. Hansson, H. Schut, & W. Stroebe (Eds.), *Handbook of bereavement research and practice: Advances in theory and intervention* (pp. 87–112). Washington, DC: American Psychological Association.

Miles, M. S., & Demi, A. S. (1986). Guilt in bereaved parents. In T. A. Rando (Ed.), *Parental loss of a child* (pp. 97–118). Champaign, IL: Research Press Company.

Miles, M. S., & Demi, A. S. (1991–1992). A comparison of guilt in bereaved parents whose children died by suicide, accident, or chronic disease. *Omega: Journal of Death and Dying, 24*, 203–215.

Mitchell, A. M., Kim, Y., Prigerson, H. G., & Mortimer-Stephens, M. (2004). Complicated grief in survivors of suicide. *Crisis: International Journal of Crisis Intervention and Suicide Prevention, 25*, 12–18.

Mitchell, A. M., Sakraida, T. J., Kim, Y., Bullian, L., & Chiappetta, L. (2009). Depression, anxiety and quality of life in suicide survivors: A comparison of close and distant relationships. *Archives of Psychiatric Nursing, 23*, 2–10.

Miyabayashi, S., & Yasuda, J. (2007). Effects of loss from suicide, accidents, acute illness and chronic illness on bereaved spouses and parents in Japan: Their general health, depressive mood, and grief reaction. *Psychiatry and Clinical Neurosciences, 61*, 502–508.

Moss, M. S., Moss, S. Z., & Hansson, R. O. (2001). Bereavement and old age. In M. S. Stroebe, R. O. Hansson, W. Stroebe, & H. Schut (Eds.), *Handbook of bereavement research: Consequences, coping, and care* (pp. 241–260). Washington, DC: American Psychological Association.

Murphy, S. A., Braun, T., Tillery, L., Cain, K. C., Johnson, L. C., & Beaton, R. D. (1999). PTSD among bereaved parents following the violent deaths of their 12- to 28-year-old children: A longitudinal prospective analysis. *Journal of Traumatic Stress, 12*, 273–291.

Murphy, S. A., Johnson, L. C., & Lohan, J. (2003). Challenging the myths about parents' adjustment after the sudden, violent death of a child. *Journal of Nursing Scholarship, 35*, 359–364.

Murphy, S. A., Johnson, L. C., Wu, L., Fan, J. J., & Lohan, J. (2003). Bereaved parents' outcomes 4 to 60 months after their children's deaths by accident, suicide, or homicide: A comparative study demonstrating differences. *Death Studies, 27*, 39–61.

Murphy, S. A., Tapper, V. J., Johnson, L. C., & Lohan, J. (2003). Suicide ideation among parents bereaved by the violent deaths of their children. *Issues in Mental Health Nursing, 24*, 5–25.

National Alliance on Mental Illness. (no date, downloaded 20 August 2009). *Suicide: Taking care of yourself and your family after an attempt.* Arlington, VA: Author. Retrieved from http://www.nami.org

National Suicide Prevention Lifeline. (2007, 30 July). *Lifeline service and outreach strategies suggested by suicide attempt survivors: Final report of the Attempt Survivor Advisory Summit Meeting and individual interviews.* Rockville, MD: Author. Retrieved from http://www.suicidology.org/c/document_library/get_file?folderId=229&name=DLFE-114.pdf

Nelson, B. J., & Frantz, T. T. (1996). Family interactions of suicide survivors and survivors of non-suicidal death. *Omega: Journal of Death and Dying, 33,* 131–146.

Owens, C., Lambert, H., Lloyd, K., & Donovan, J. (2008). Tales of biographical disintegration: How parents make sense of their sons' suicides. *Sociology of Health & Illness, 30,* 237–254.

Parker, H. A., & McNally, R. J. (2008). Repressive coping, emotional adjustment, and cognition in people who have lost loved ones to suicide. *Suicide and Life-Threatening Behavior, 38,* 676–687.

Pennebaker, J. W., & O'Heeron, R. C. (1984). Confiding in others and illness rate among spouses of suicide and accident-death victims. *Journal of Abnormal Psychology, 93,* 473–476.

Power, L., Morgan, S., Byrne, S., Boylan, C., Carthy, A., Crowley, S., Fitzpatrick, C., & Guerin, S. (2009). A pilot study evaluating a support programme for parents of young people with suicidal behaviour. *Child and Adolescent Psychiatry and Mental Health, 3,* 20. An open access journal. Electronic version of the article available at http://www.capmh.com/content/3/1/20; doi: 10.1186/1753-20000-3-20

Ramsay, J. R., & Newman, C. F. (2005). After the attempt: Maintaining the therapeutic alliance following a patient's suicide attempt. *Suicide and Life-Threatening Behavior, 35,* 413–424.

Range, L. M., & Calhoun, L. G. (1990). Responses following suicide and other types of death: The perspective of the bereaved. *Omega: Journal of Death and Dying, 21,* 311–320.

Range, L. M., & Niss, N. M. (1990). Long-term bereavement from suicide, homicide, accidents, and natural deaths. *Death Studies, 14,* 423–433.

Reed, M. D. (1998). Predicting grief symptomatology among the suddenly bereaved. *Suicide and Life-Threatening Behavior, 28,* 285–301.

Reed, M. D., & Greenwald, J. Y. (1991). Survivor-status, attachment, and sudden death bereavement. *Suicide and Life-Threatening Behavior, 21,* 385–401.

Ross, E. B. (1982, April). After suicide: A ray of hope [Abstract]. In C. R. Pfeffer & J. Richman (Eds.), *Proceedings of the 15th Annual Meeting of the American Association of Suicidology* (pp. 99–101). Denver, CO: American Association of Suicidology.

Rudestam, K. E. (1987). Public perceptions of suicide survivors. In E. J. Dunne, J. L. McIntosh, & K. L. Dunne-Maxim (Eds.), *Suicide and its aftermath: Understanding and counseling the survivors* (pp. 31–44). New York, NY: W. W. Norton.

Saunders, J. M. (1981). A process of bereavement resolution: Uncoupled identity. *Western Journal of Nursing Research, 3,* 319–335.

Séguin, M., Lesage, A., & Kiely, M. C. (1995). Parental bereavement after suicide and accident: A comparative study. *Suicide and Life-Threatening Behavior, 25,* 489–498.

Shaver, P. R., & Tancredy, C. M. (2001). Emotion, attachment, and bereavement: A conceptual commentary. In M. S. Stroebe, R. O. Hansson, W. Stroebe, & H. Schut (Eds.), *Handbook of bereavement research: Consequences, coping, and care* (pp. 63–88). Washington, DC: American Psychological Association.

Shepherd, D. M., & Barraclough, B. M. (1974, June 15). The aftermath of suicide. *BMJ: British Medical Journal, 2,* 600–603.

Silverman, P. R. (1972). Intervention with the widow of a suicide. In A. C. Cain (Ed.), *Survivors of suicide* (pp. 186–214). Springfield, IL: Thomas.

Spirito, A., Boergers, J., Donaldson, D., Bishop, D., & Lewander, W. (2002). An intervention trial to improve adherence to community treatment by adolescents after a suicide attempt. *Journal of the American Academy of Child and Adolescent Psychiatry, 41,* 435–442,

Stewart, S. E., Manion, I. G., & Davidson, S. (2002). Emergency management of the adolescent suicide attempter: A review of the literature. *Journal of Adolescent Health, 30,* 312–325.

Stimming, M., & Stimming, M. (Eds.). (1999). *Before their time: Adult children's experiences of parental suicide.* Philadelphia, PA: Temple University Press.

Stone, H. W. (1972). *Suicide and grief.* Philadelphia, PA: Fortress Press.

Sudak, H., Maxim, K., & Carpenter, M. (2008). Suicide and stigma: A review of the literature and personal reflections. *Academic Psychiatry, 32,* 136–142.

Suicide Prevention Resource Center. (2007, Winter). Survivors of suicide attempts. *Newslink* [a newsletter of the American Association of Suicidology], *34*(4), pp. 16–18.

Sveen, C.-A., & Walby, F. A. (2008). Suicide survivors' mental health and grief reactions: A systematic review of controlled studies. *Suicide and Life-Threatening Behavior, 38,* 13–29.

Tall, K., Kõlves, K., Sisask, M., & Värnik, A. (2008). Do survivors respond differently when alcohol abuse complicates suicide? Findings from the psychological autopsy study in Estonia. *Drug and Alcohol Dependence, 95,* 129–133. Retrieved from http://www.sciencedirect.com. doi:10.1016/j.drugalcdep.2007.12.015

Thompson, K. E., & Range, L. M. (1992–1993). Bereavement following suicide and other deaths: Why support attempts fail. *Omega: Journal of Death and Dying, 26,* 61–70.

U.S. Department of Health and Human Services. (2006a). *National Suicide Prevention Lifeline: After an Attempt. A Guide for Medical Providers in the Emergency Department Taking Care of Suicide Attempt Survivors* [CMHS-SVP-0161]. Rockville, MD: Author. Retrieved from http://mentalhealth.samhsa.gov/publications/allpubs/SVP-0161

U.S. Department of Health and Human Services. (2006b). *National Suicide Prevention Lifeline: After an Attempt. A Guide for Taking Care of Your Family Member After Treatment in the Emergency Department* [CMHS-SVP-0159]. Rockville, MD: Author. Retrieved from http://mentalhealth.samhsa.gov/publications/allpubs/SVP-0159

U.S. Department of Health and Human Services. (2006c). *National Suicide Prevention Lifeline: After an Attempt. A Guide for Taking Care of Yourself After Your Treatment in the Emergency Department* [CMHS-SVP-0157]. Rockville, MD: Author. Retrieved from http://mentalhealth.samhsa.gov/publications/allpubs/SVP-0157

van der Sande, R., Buskens, E., Allart, E., van der Graaf, Y., & van Engeland, H. (1997). Psychosocial intervention following suicide attempt: A systematic review of treatment interventions. *Acta Psychiatrica Scandinavica, 96,* 43–50.

Waern, M. (2005). Suicides among family members of elderly suicide victims: An exploratory study. *Suicide and Life-Threatening Behavior, 35,* 356–364.

Wagner, B. M., Aiken, C., Mullaley, P. M., & Tobin, J. J. (2000). Parents' reactions to adolescents' suicide attempts. *Journal of the American Academy of Child and Adolescent Psychiatry, 39,* 429–436.

Watford, M. L. (2008). Bereavement of spousal suicide: A reflective self-exploration. *Qualitative Inquiry, 14,* 335–359.

Weiss, R. S. (1998). Issues in the study of loss and grief. In J. H. Harvey (Ed.), *Perspectives on loss: A sourcebook* (pp. 343–352). Philadelphia, PA: Brunner/Mazel.

CHAPTER

The Impact of Suicide on Children and Adolescents

Julie Cerel and Rosalie S. Aldrich

For children and adolescents, bereavement following the suicide of some-one close to them may be traumatic and very different from bereavement following other types of death. However, studies that examine children's reactions to the suicide of a loved one compared with the nonsuicidal death of a loved one have yielded conflicting results. In this chapter, we examine what is known and unknown about the number of youth survivors as well as the recommended information that should be shared with children about suicides. Then, we examine the literature on specific populations of suicide-bereaved children—including parent-bereaved, sibling-bereaved, and peer-bereaved children. The chapter closes with recommendations for research that can help us better understand the experience and needs of suicide-bereaved children and their families. The term *child* is used interchangeably with the term *youth* to repre-sent individuals under the age of 18 years. *Adolescent* typically is used to describe individuals aged 13–18 years, but in some research, *adolescent* refers to individuals aged 13–24 years.

☐ Scope of the Problem

It is unknown how many children worldwide are affected by the suicide of a family member or other important person in their life. Estimates show that in the United States, approximately 60,000 youth under the age of 18 experience the suicide of a relative each year (Pfeffer et al., 1997). Cerel and Roberts' (2005) cross-sectional analysis of data from high school students collected in the National Longitudinal Study of Adolescent Health (Resnick et al., 1997) found that 3.9% of adolescents experienced a family member's suicide attempt in the year prior to the survey and 1.2% experienced a family member's death by suicide in the year prior to the survey. The numbers are undoubtedly substantially greater in larger countries with higher suicide rates, such as China or Japan. Furthermore, in the United States, approximately 2,300 children/teens under the age of 20 years die by suicide annually (Centers for Disease Control and Prevention [CDC], 2009), leaving sibling and peer survivors to cope with the loss. Up to 8,000 children experience sibling suicide in the United States annually from the loss of minor and adult siblings. This number is based on estimates that 80% of families in the United States and Europe contain more than one child (Dunn, 1985) and a smaller percentage contains three or more children.

For adults aged 25–44 years—the age group most likely to have children in the home—suicide is the fourth leading cause of death (CDC, 2009). Small and Small (1984) estimated that between 7,000 and 12,000 children in the United States experience the suicide of a parent each year. This is likely an underestimate, as it accounts for only one child per family. Pfeffer, Karus, Siegel, and Jiang (2000) estimated that the number of parent-bereaved child survivors in the United States each year was more likely somewhere between 10,000 and 20,000.

It is more likely that adolescents will have experiences with people outside their families (vs. inside their families) who have attempted or died by suicide. In an examination of a nationally representative sample of high school students, exposure to a peer's suicide attempt in the past year was reported by 15.5% of adolescents, and exposure to a peer's death by suicide in the past year was reported by 3.2% (Cerel, Roberts, & Nilsen, 2005). It is completely unknown how many college students experience the suicide of a peer such as a roommate or classmate during their college years.

☐ The Role of Genetics for Child Survivors

Genetics appears to play a role in the transmission of suicidal behavior, putting child survivors at special risk. The offspring of suicide decedents and attempters are at risk for psychopathology, future suicide attempts, and death by suicide (Brent et al., 2002; Pfeffer, Normandin, & Kakuma, 1998). Suicide rates have been shown to be twice as high in families of suicide decedents as in families in which a suicide has not occurred (Runeson & Asberg, 2003). Using twin designs, investigators have examined the genetic contribution to suicidal behavior and have determined that up to 45% of the variance in suicidal ideation and behavior may be attributable to genetic variables (Statham et al., 1998). Further, decreased responsiveness of the serotonergic system has been implicated in suicide and suicide attempts. These serotonergic abnormalities are thought to be "partially under genetic control" with as-yet-undetermined genetic factors then mediating "risk for suicidal behavior independently of the genetic factors responsible for the heritability of major psychiatric conditions associated with suicide" (Mann, Brent, & Arango, 2001, p. 467). It has been hypothesized that this hyporeactivity leads to impulsive and aggressive behavior that, in the context of psychiatric illness or other stressors, makes an individual more likely to act on thoughts of suicide (Kamali, Oquendo, & Mann, 2001). In a recent study of suicide attempters and their young adult offspring, children of suicide attempters with a mood disorder had 6 times the risk of a suicide attempt as the children of nonattempters who also suffered from a mood disorder (Brent et al., 2002). It has been shown that the suicide attempt of a mother is significantly more prevalent among adolescents with a lifetime history of a suicide attempt than among those adolescents who have not engaged in suicidal behavior (Pfeffer et al., 1998). In addition to considering the genetics associated with suicide, it seems just as important to consider how children are told about the suicide and the way in which they interpret the death.

☐ Telling Children

Families often struggle with whether to tell children that a death was a suicide. Once the choice is made to disclose that the death was a suicide, families face a difficult challenge—how to tell them. Early studies indicated that the majority of children were not told that the death was a suicide. Cain and Fast (1966) found that almost one quarter of the children in their study had directly witnessed the suicide or discovered the decedent but were told that the death was not a suicide but, rather, an accident or illness. More recent research (e.g., Cerel, Fristad, Weller, & Weller, 1999) has examined only those children who clearly knew that the cause of death was a suicide. Although research has not examined the effects of being lied to about the cause of death, it is likely that children often do not believe the lies they are told. Children often overhear the truth from another family member or peer; are directly told by someone else such as a peer; or simply do not believe that the death was not a suicide, on the basis of their own firsthand information. Some parents chose to tell the child certain information about the suicide, depending on the child's age or developmental level (Cain, 2002). Other variables that seem to influence whether a parent tells the child about the cause of death include whether the child witnessed the death, perceptions of the child's maturity and ability to cope, and the child's previous relationship with the decedent. These variables can sometimes lead various siblings within a family to be told or not told about the cause of death (Cain, 2002). Cain stresses that informing a child that their parent died by suicide is a process that needs to be revisited to determine how much they understand and retain over time. Mitchell and colleagues (2006) urge that children be told about a parent's suicide in language that is neither euphemistic nor metaphoric. The use of the word *suicide* with even a young child may be destigmatizing and may provide the basis for future discussions (Mitchell et al., 2006). Erica Goode, writing in the *New York Times,* described her experience of not being told about her father's suicide: "[F]or a very long time, nearly two decades, my mother told no one—not her children, not her brother and sister—that my father had killed himself, that she had found a note that morning and quickly destroyed it. Yet as I grew up, the mystery of my father's death defined my life in many ways" (Goode, 2003, paragraphs 6 and 7). This compelling firsthand account suggests that this area is clearly one that could benefit from additional research.

Although it has been declared that "imitation is not a major mechanism in familial transmission, given the results of adoption and twin studies and prospective studies of exposure to suicide" (Brent et al., 2002, p. 802), research has not specifically been conducted to examine the role that a child's knowledge and attributions about parental suicide plays in his or her future behavior. Joiner (2002) posits that an individual's past suicidal behavior may affect their future suicidal behavior through the mechanisms of cognitive sensitization and opponent process theory. *Cognitive sensitization* describes how previous suicidal behavior "sensitizes suicide-related thoughts and behaviors, such that they later become more accessible and active," whereas *opponent process theory* predicts that the impact of an emotion-laden stimulus is diminished through repetition (Joiner, 2002, p. 36). Carrying these ideas forward to the impact of parental suicide or suicide attempt on a child, it is possible that a parent's suicide can affect his or her children's future suicidal behavior through the very same mechanisms. The idea of suicide is primed—that is, it is more cognitively available and perhaps less taboo for the child, which then could be seen as a potential coping strategy when problems arise. The similarity of suicidal behavior over generations within a family would be evidence to support this model. Although data are not available on suicide method choice within families, anecdotal evidence indicates that successive generations do seem to use the same method of suicide (e.g., a family in which the same gun was used in multiple family suicides).

☐ Risk Behavior in Youth Survivors of Family Suicide

Adolescents who are bereaved following a suicide in the family or whose family member has attempted suicide are likely to engage in at-risk behaviors (Cerel & Roberts, 2005). In a secondary analysis of a large national dataset—Wave 1 of the National Longitudinal Study of Adolescent Health—Cerel and Roberts found that adolescents who had experienced the suicide attempt or death of a family member were more likely than those with no exposure to report cigarette, marijuana, and alcohol use; suicidal ideation and attempts; fighting and inflicting injuries; decreased life expectancy; emotional distress; and decreased adolescent reports of parent–child and family connectedness. Adolescents who had experienced a suicide death by a family member were 2.5 times more likely to report suicidal ideation, 6.5 times more likely to have a history of their own suicide attempt in the past year, and 3.1 times more likely to report inflicting serious injuries on others. Although exposure to suicide in the family, in itself, seems to be a risk factor for psychopathology, more in-depth research has examined psychopathology and grief reactions in child survivors of various relationships to the decedent.

☐ Psychopathology in Youth Survivors of Parental Suicide

A recent review of studies on the psychiatric and psychosocial outcomes for parent suicide–bereaved children indicated only nine unique studies of this population (Kuramoto, Brent, & Wilcox, 2009). Early studies of youth bereaved from parental suicide suffered from small sample sizes, varying lengths of time between the death and the assessment, and using parent report instead of directly interviewing the child. The earliest studies of parent suicide–bereaved children were of those children in treatment following the death (Cain & Fast, 1966; Pfeffer, 1981; Pfeffer, Conte, Plutchik, & Jerrett, 1980). Cain and Fast (1966) examined out-patient charts of 45 children whose parents had died by suicide, on aver-age, 4 years prior to the evaluation. Children's reactions tended to be either hostile, angry, and defiant, or sad, withdrawn, and guilt laden. Five children who were in inpatient psychiatric treatment were inter-viewed for Pfeffer's (1981) study. These children were found to be from families with chronic family turmoil, and children's reactions to the sui-cide appeared to mirror those of their surviving parents.

In a study of 36 children who had experienced the suicide of a parent, parent report indicated that one third of the children experi-enced anxiety, aggression, or withdrawal immediately after the death (Shepherd & Barraclough, 1976). More recent studies of community samples have compared parent suicide–bereaved children with children bereaved from other types of death.

Pfeffer and colleagues (2000) compared 11 families (including 16 children) in which a parent had died from suicide with 57 families (including 64 children) in which a parent had died of cancer. Suicide-bereaved children reported more depressive symptoms, especially those involving interpersonal problems, ineffectiveness, anhedonia, and nega-tive mood (Pfeffer et al., 2000). Interestingly, parental reports of chil-dren's behavior did not differ between the children bereaved by parental cancer or suicide and were within the normative range.

A study by Cerel and colleagues (1999) found that when psycho-pathology in 26 suicide-bereaved children was compared to psychopa-thology in 332 bereaved children from all other types of parental death, suicide-bereaved children showed an increased level of psychopathology. Psychopathology was especially evident in behavior problems prior to the death as well as increased behavioral and anxiety symptoms after the first few months following the death (Cerel et al., 1999). This study found no differences in post-traumatic stress disorder (PTSD) or in suicidal ideation or attempt between suicide-bereaved and nonsuicide-bereaved children.

Brown and colleagues (Brown, Sadler, Tein, Liu, & Haine, 2007) examined children (ages 8–16 years) who had been recruited into a bereavement program within 30 months of parental death; the authors compared 24 suicide-bereaved children with 302 nonsuicide-bereaved children participating in a family bereavement program. Prior to the intervention, children and surviving parents completed standard-ized measures. Results again showed no differences in internalizing or externalizing symptoms between the groups.

Most recently, Brent and colleagues have followed a cohort of youth who lost a parent to suicide, accident, or sudden natural death (Brent,

Melhem, Donohoe, & Walker, 2009; Melhem, Moritz, Walker, Shear, & Brent, 2007; Melhem, Walker, Moritz, & Brent, 2008). Biological offspring aged 7–25 years for whom one parent had died of suicide, accident, or sudden natural death (n = 176) were followed over time and were compared to controls who had two living parents (n = 168). Results indicated that children who had experienced parental suicide or accidental death had higher rates of depression than did control participants. Survivors of parental suicide had higher rates of alcohol or substance use than did control participants (Brent et al., 2009). Child survivors of parental suicide had higher rates of depression than did those bereaved from sudden death.

☐ Grief Emotions in Child Survivors of Parental Suicide

For children, the suicidal loss of a parent might lead to a variety of emotions. Cain and Fast (1966) identified two profiles of suicide-bereaved children with descriptions that mixed features of bereavement and psychopathology. Children in the study were categorized as showing a sad, guilt-laden, and withdrawn response or an angry, hostile, and defiant response. In their study of 26 children who had lost parents to suicide compared to children who experienced parental death from other causes, Cerel and colleagues (1999) explicitly measured grief emotions separately from symptoms of psychopathology and found that compared to nonsuicide-bereaved children, suicide-bereaved children were more likely to be anxious, angry, and ashamed but showed no differences in sadness and guilt over the first 2 years postdeath. Suicide-bereaved children also reported less acceptance and relief than did children bereaved from causes of parental death other than suicide (Cerel et al., 1999). To date, no research has established developmental patterns in grief emotions or whether some emotional responses might be associated with less psychopathology and more positive outcomes over time.

Melhem and colleagues (2007) examined complicated grief (CG) in 129 children and adolescents of parents who had died by suicide, accident, or sudden natural death. CG was found to be significantly related to functional impairment even after current depression, anxiety, and PTSD were controlled. In addition, CG also seemed to be associated with other measures of psychopathology, including suicidal ideation. The construct of CG has not been examined in other samples of suicide-bereaved adolescents and is an area that needs further research to determine its role for children and adolescents following a suicide.

☐ Effects on Family Systems

There is some evidence that families with minor children in which a suicide takes place seem to experience high levels of chronic turmoil and stressful events such as marital separation, trouble with the law, or domestic violence prior to the suicide (Cerel, Fristad, Weller, & Weller, 2000; Shepherd & Barraclough, 1976). Not all families experience this degree of disruption. Cerel and colleagues (2000) found three types of families in which the suicide of a parent had occurred. In *functional families,* characterized by no evidence of preexisting family conflict or psychopathology, usually the suicide had taken place in the context of chronic physical illness. In *encapsulated families*, psychopathology and conflict were observed only in the deceased and not in other family members. *Chaotic families* showed clear evidence of psychopathology in multiple family members and/or turmoil prior to suicide. The family system, prior psychopathology or conflict within the family, and the context of the suicide within the family need to be taken into account in future studies of child survivors.

☐ Responses to Sibling Suicide

Only a few studies have focused on child survivors of sibling suicide. Brent and colleagues (Brent, Perper, Moritz, Liotus, et al., 1993) examined 25 adolescent siblings of 20 suicide decedents and compared these individuals to nonbereaved, demographically matched controls in the 6 months following the suicide. New-onset depression was 7 times more common in siblings who had experienced a suicide than in the matched adolescents. The likelihood of depression was increased by a history of previous psychiatric disorder and family histories of depression and other psychiatric disorders. In a 5-year follow-up of this population, Brent, Moritz, Bridge, Perper, and Cannobbio (1996) found few differences between the bereaved and control adolescents in terms of depression. Siblings have also been examined in studies that combined survivors of multiple types of suicide loss (e.g., Pfeffer et al., 1997). The mixed nature of those studies makes it difficult to comment on the unique experience of sibling survivors. Pfeffer and colleagues (1997) examined 22 children aged 5–14 years from 16 families in which a parent or child had died by suicide. Children were recruited from schools and clinical referrals and were evaluated 1 month to 3 years after parental death. Suicide-bereaved children had internalizing symptoms and problems with school adjustment. Approximately 40%

of these children experienced symptoms of post-traumatic stress, and 25% of families contained children who experienced elevated Children's Depression Inventory scores (Kovacs, 1992). However, these studies relied primarily on clinically referred participants, and thus may not be representative of all children who experience parent or sibling suicide.

☐ Responses in Child Survivors of Peer Suicide

Few studies have examined children's reactions to the suicide of a peer. In a nationally representative sample of 5,852 youth in high school, Cerel et al. (2005) reported that youth exposed to peer suicidal behavior were significantly more likely to have their own suicidal ideation and attempts. These youth were also more likely than those who had not been exposed to any peer suicidal behavior to smoke cigarettes and marijuana, binge drink, be involved in a serious physical fight, and have inflicted injuries to others that required medical attention.

Brent and colleagues (Brent, Perper, Moritz, Allman, et al., 1993; Brent et al., 1995) interviewed 146 friends and acquaintances of 26 suicide decedents at four regular intervals in the 3 years following the suicide. Compared with matched controls who had not experienced the suicide of a friend, those youth who experienced the suicide of a friend showed elevated rates of major depression, PTSD, and suicidal ideation (Brent, Perper, Moritz, Allman, et al., 1993). Exposed youth were not more likely to engage in their own suicidal attempts. PTSD was predicted by a closer relationship to the suicide decedent, more severe exposure to the suicide itself, and a history of relationship problems (Brent et al., 1995). Traumatic grief was found in adolescents independent of depression and PTSD. Interestingly, traumatic grief at 6 months predicted the onset or course of depression and PTSD over time (Melhem et al., 2004). These findings suggest that the close friends of an adolescent who dies by suicide are not the only ones who are at risk of adverse outcomes. Youth in the social network of those who die by suicide should also be monitored for depression, PTSD, and future suicidal behavior.

☐ Conclusion

Many children and adolescents are exposed to the death of a loved one by suicide; however, the effects of such a death on children and adolescents are inconclusive. For example, some studies have found no overall differences in suicidal behavior and diagnosable depression in children bereaved from a suicide compared to children bereaved from other types of death. When compared to children who experienced other types of bereavement, child survivors appear to experience few differences in psychopathology. Suicide-bereaved children and adolescents do appear to experience more internalizing symptoms such as depression and anxiety as well as symptoms of PTSD. Studies of suicide-bereaved children suffer from small sample sizes, relatively short-term follow-ups, and differences in what children know about the cause of death (Kuramoto et al., 2009). It does not appear to be the suicide in itself that leads to problems for children but, rather, family functioning before and after the death, the child's perceptions of the suicide, and how the death was communicated to the child.

It is clear that there is a substantial need for research so that we can better understand child survivors of parent, sibling, other family, and peer death. Cerel and colleagues (Cerel et al., 2005; Cerel, Duberstein, & Jordan, 2008) suggest that research on child survivors should include longer follow-up, a determination of the relationship of survivor to risk behaviors, and an understanding of how treatment affects the course of bereavement and psychopathology. This longer follow-up needs to examine the effects of being a child survivor on an individual's experience as an adult and should include an examination of variables such as the child's age at the time of the suicide. The child's relationship to the decedent is another variable that has not been examined as a mediator or moderator of their reaction but that can definitely play a large role in the child's reaction following the death. Likewise, very little is known about the effect of suicide attempts of loved ones on children. Almost nothing is known about the effect of suicides on college students.

Children who experience the suicide of a loved one or someone close to them are at risk for adverse outcomes. It is important that adults tell children the truth about the cause of death in ways that are developmentally appropriate. Treatment for child survivors should focus on internalizing disorders, PTSD, and ways to help children deal with traumatic grief.

☐ References

Brent, D., Melhem, N., Donohoe, M. B., & Walker, M. (2009). The incidence and course of depression in bereaved youth 21 months after the loss of a parent to suicide, accident, or sudden natural death. *American Journal of Psychiatry, 166,* 786–794.

Brent, D. A., Moritz, G, Bridge, J., Perper, J., & Canobbio, R. (1996). The impact of adolescent suicide on siblings and parents: A longitudinal follow-up. *Suicide and Life Threatening Behavior, 26,* 253–259.

Brent, D. A., Oquendo, M., Birmaher, B., Greenhill, L., Kolko, D., Stanley, B., ... Mann, J. J. (2002). Familial pathways to early-onset suicide attempt: Risk for suicidal behavior in offspring of mood-disordered suicide attempters. *Archives of General Psychiatry, 59,* 801–807.

Brent, D. A., Perper, J. A., Moritz, G., Allman, C., Schweers, J., Roth, C., ... Liotus, L. (1993). Psychiatric sequelae to the loss of an adolescent peer to suicide. *Journal of the American Academy of Child & Adolescent Psychiatry, 32,* 509–517.

Brent, D. A., Perper, J. A., Moritz, G., Liotus, L., Schweers, Roth, C., ... Allman, C. (1993). Psychiatric impact of the loss of an adolescent sibling to suicide. *Journal of Affective Disorders, 28,* 249–256.

Brent, D. A., Perper, J. A., Moritz, G., Liotus, L., Richardson, D., Canobbio, R., ... Roth, C. (1995). Posttraumatic stress disorder in peers of adolescent suicide victims: Predisposing factors and phenomenology. *Journal of the American Academy of Child & Adolescent Psychiatry, 34,* 209–215.

Brown, A. C., Sandler, I. N., Tein, J. U., Liu, X., & Haine, R. A. (2007). Implications of parental suicide and violent death for promotion of resilience of parentally-bereaved children. *Death Studies, 31,* 301–335.

Cain, A. C. (2002). Children of suicide: The telling and the knowing. *Psychiatry–Interpersonal and Biological Processes, 65,* 124–136.

Cain, A. C., & Fast, I. (1966). Children's disturbed reactions to parental suicide. *American Journal of Orthopsychiatry, 47,* 196–206.

Centers for Disease Control and Prevention. (2009). Web-Based Injury Statistics Query and Reporting System (WISQARS). Retrieved from http://www.cdc .gov/ncipc/wisqars

Cerel, J., Duberstein, P. R., & Jordan, J. J. (2008). The impact of suicide on the family. *Crisis: The Journal of Crisis Intervention and Suicide Prevention, 29,* 38–44.

Cerel, J., Fristad, M. A., Weller, E. B., & Weller, R. A. (1999). Suicide-bereaved children and adolescents: A controlled longitudinal examination. *Journal of the American Academy of Child & Adolescent Psychiatry, 38,* 672–679.

Cerel, J., Fristad, M. A., Weller, E. B., & Weller, R. A. (2000). Suicide-bereaved children and adolescents: II. Parental and family functioning. *Journal of the American Academy of Child & Adolescent Psychiatry, 39,* 437–444.

Cerel, J., & Roberts, T. A. (2005). Suicidal behavior in the family and adolescent risk behavior. *Journal of Adolescent Health, 36,* 352.e8–352.e14. Available http://www.jahonline.org/article/S1054-139X(04)00436-7/abstract

Cerel, J., Roberts, T. A., & Nilsen, W. J. (2005). Peer suicidal behavior and adolescent risk behavior. *Journal of Nervous and Mental Disease, 193,* 237–243.

Dunn, J. (1985). *Sisters and brothers: The developing child.* Cambridge, MA: Harvard University Press.

Goode, E. (2003, October 28). And still, echoes of a death long past. *The New York Times.* Retrieved from http://www.nytimes.com/2003/10/28/science/and-still-echoes-of-a-death-long-past.html

Joiner, T. E. (2002). The trajectory of suicidal behavior over time. *Suicide & Life Threatening Behavior, 32,* 33–41.

Kamali, M., Oquendo, M. A., & Mann, J. J. (2001). Understanding the neurobiology of suicidal behavior. *Depression and Anxiety, 14,* 164–176.

Kovacs, M. (1992). *The Children's Depression Inventory (CDI) manual.* Toronto, Ontario, Canada: Multi-health Systems, Inc.

Kuramoto, S. J., Brent, D. A., & Wilcox, H. C. (2009). The impact of parental suicide on child and adolescent offspring. *Suicide and Life Threatening Behavior, 39,* 137–151.

Mann, J. J., Brent, D. A., & Arango, V. (2001). The neurobiology and genetics of suicide and attempted suicide: A focus on the serotonergic system. *Neuropsychopharmacology, 24,* 467–477.

Melhem, N. M., Day, N., Shear, M. K., Day, R., Reynolds, C. F., III, & Brent, D. (2004). Traumatic grief among adolescents exposed to a peer's suicide. *American Journal of Psychiatry, 161,* 1411–1416.

Melhem, N. M., Moritz, G., Walker, M., Shear, M. K., & Brent, D. (2007). Phenomenology and correlates of complicated grief in children and adolescents. *Journal of the American Academy of Child and Adolescent Psychiatry, 46,* 493–499.

Melhem, N. M., Walker, M., Moritz, G., & Brent, D. A. (2008). Antecedents and sequelae of sudden parental death in offspring and surviving caregivers. *Archives of Pediatrics & Adolescent Medicine, 162,* 403–410.

Mitchell, A. M., Wesner, S., Brownson, L., Gale, D. D., Garand, L., & Havill, A. (2006). Effective communication with bereaved child survivors of suicide. *Journal of Child and Adolescent Psychiatric Nursing, 19,* 130–136.

Pfeffer, C. R. (1981). Parental suicide: An organizing event in the development of latency age children. *Suicide and Life-Threatening Behavior, 11,* 43–50.

Pfeffer, C. R., Conte, H. R., Plutchik, R., & Jerrett, I. (1980). Suicidal behavior in latency-age children. An outpatient population. *Journal of the American Academy of Child & Adolescent Psychiatry, 19,* 703–710.

Pfeffer, C. R., Karus, D., Siegel, K., & Jiang, H. (2000). Child survivors of parental death from cancer or suicide: Depressive and behavioral outcomes. *Psycho-Oncology, 9,* 1–10.

Pfeffer, C. R., Normandin, L., & Kakuma, T. (1998). Suicidal children grow up: Relations between family psychopathology and adolescents' lifetime suicidal behavior. *Journal of Nervous & Mental Disease, 186,* 269–275.

Pfeffer, C. R., Martins, P., Mann, J., Sunkenberg, M., Ice, A., Damore, J. P., Jr., … Jiang, H. (1997). Child survivors of suicide: Psychosocial characteristics. *Journal of the American Academy of Child & Adolescent Psychiatry, 36,* 65–74.

Resnick, M. D., Bearman, P. S., Blum, R. W., Bauman, K. E., Harris, K. M., Jones, J., … Udry, J. R. (1997). Protecting adolescents from harm. Findings from the National Longitudinal Study on Adolescent Health. *JAMA, 278,* 823–832.

Runeson, B., & Asberg, M. (2003). Family history of suicide among suicide victims. *American Journal of Psychiatry, 160,* 1525–1526.

Shepherd, D. M., & Barraclough, B. M. (1976). The aftermath of parental suicide for children. *British Journal of Psychiatry, 129,* 267–276.

Small, A. M., & Small, A. D. (1984). Children's reactions to a suicide in the family. In N. Linzer (Ed.), *Suicide: The will to live vs. the will to die* (pp. 151–169). New York, NY: Human Sciences Press.

Statham, D. J., Heath, A. C., Madden, P. A., Bucholz, K. K., Bierut, L., Dinwiddie, S. H., … Martin, N. G. (1998). Suicidal behaviour: An epidemiological and genetic study. *Psychological Medicine, 28,* 839–855.

CHAPTER

The Impact of Suicide on Professional Caregivers

Nina Gutin, Vanessa L. McGann, and John R. Jordan

For psychotherapists and other mental health professionals, the loss of a patient or client to suicide is certainly not uncommon. Studies have found that one in five psychologists (Bersoff, 1999; Kleespies, 1993) and one in two psychiatrists (Chemtob, Hamada, Bauer, Kinney, & Torigoe, 1988; Ruskin, 2004) lose a patient to suicide in the course of their careers; this statistic suggests that such a loss constitutes a clear occupational hazard (Chemtob, Bauer, Hamada, Pelowski, & Muraoka, 1989; Rubin, 1990). Despite this fact, many mental health professionals continue to view suicide loss as an aberration. Consequently, there is often a lack of preparedness for such an event when it does occur.

Presently, there are many published articles on clinician suicide loss (see McIntosh, 2010, for a comprehensive bibliography), and several authors (Farberow, 2005; Jones, 1987; Plakun & Tillman, 2005; Schultz, 2005; Spiegelman & Werth, 2005; Quinnett, 1999) have developed suggestions, guidelines, and postvention protocols to help clinicians and mental health settings navigate the often-complicated sequelae to such a loss. In addition, a book edited by Weiner (2005) details the many issues pertaining to the therapeutic and legal issues involved in client suicide. However, these resources have not been integrated into clinical training and tend to be poorly disseminated. Thus, despite the existence of guidelines for optimal postvention and support, clinicians are often left to cope with the consequences of this difficult loss on their own and under less than optimal conditions.

In this chapter, we describe several factors that are likely to affect a clinician's response to a client's[1] suicide and highlight several aspects of the impact of such a loss on treating clinicians (as well as on others who may have worked in professional caregiving roles.) Such a loss typically affects clinicians on multiple levels, both personally and professionally. By highlighting the range of normative responses as well as the factors that may facilitate or inhibit subsequent healing and growth, we hope that (a) this knowledge may be used to help current and future generations of clinician–survivors[2] obtain optimal support and (b) institutions who treat potentially suicidal individuals will develop optimal postvention responses following a suicide loss (see Chapters 7 and 8 for more discussion and suggestions related to general postvention following suicide loss). Many aspects of the discussion are also applicable to clinicians who have experienced a suicide loss in their personal or family life, as this loss also tends to "spill over" into one's professional roles and identity.

☐ Grief After Suicide Loss

In many ways, the responses of clinicians after the suicide of a client are similar to the responses/reactions of other survivors after the loss of a loved one to suicide, which is generally considered a *traumatic loss*. Jordan and McIntosh (Chapters 1 and 2, this volume; Jordan, 2001) have detailed several elements and themes that differentiate suicide loss and its associated reactions from other types of loss and grief. In general, responses to suicide loss typically include initial shock, denial and numbness, intense sadness, anxiety, anger, and intense distress. Survivors are also likely

---

[1] From this point on, the term *client* refers to the individual who has completed suicide, and the term *clinician* refers to his or her professional caregivers.

[2] In general, the term *clinician–survivor* refers to clinicians who have lost either clients and/or family members to suicide; however, in this chapter, the term *clinician–survivor* refers to clinicians who have experienced only the suicide of a client. *Survivor* refers to relatives and loved ones who are bereaved after a suicide.

to experience post-traumatic stress disorder (PTSD) symptoms such as intrusive thoughts, experiences of detachment, and dissociation. In addition, suicide loss is often accompanied by intense confusion and existential questioning, reflecting a blow to one's core beliefs and assumptive world (see Chapter 11). Survivors of a loved one's suicide also commonly experience guilt and shame, and these feelings may be socially reinforced by the general stigma around suicide as well as the actual blaming and avoidance responses of others (Brown, 1987; Cvinar, 2005; Goffman, 1963, reissued 1986).

For clinicians, there are additional components of losing a client to suicide that may further complicate or exacerbate these reactions and extend their duration. First, such a loss affects clinicians on both personal and professional levels, a phenomenon that Plakun and Tillman (2005) termed a *twin bereavement*. Thus, in addition to the personal grief reaction entailed in losing a client with whom there was a therapeutically intense or intimate relationship, this loss is likely to affect clinicians' professional identities, their relationships with colleagues, and their clinical work.

Clinicians' professional identities are often predicated on generally shared assumptions and beliefs that, as trained professionals, they should have the power, aptitude, and competence to heal—or, at least, improve—the lives of clients, to lessen their pain, and to provide safety. In addition, specific assumptions about clinicians' responsibility and ability to prevent suicide are often reinforced in the clinical literature (Goldney, 2000; Litman, 1965). Often, this belief is accompanied by the assumption that clients, assuming the presence of a treatment alliance, will honestly disclose their level of distress and/or risk when clinicians inquire about this.

These assumptions are often challenged, if not shattered, when a client kills him- or herself. In her article on surviving client suicide, Rycroft (2005) describes a "professional void" following the loss of her client, in which "the world had changed, nothing was predictable any more, and it was no longer safe to assume anything" (p. 88). A clinician's sense of professional responsibility, the self-blame that may accompany this responsibility, the fear of and actual blame assigned by colleagues and family members, and the real or imagined threat of litigation may all greatly exacerbate a clinician's distress. Additional components of the grief reaction for clinicians may include "guilt, loss of self-esteem, self-doubts about one's skills and clinical competence, fear of being blamed for the suicide and fear of relatives' reactions" (Farberow, 2005, p. 14).

Hendin, Lipschitz, Maltsberger, Haas, and Wynecoop (2000) found that mental health therapists have described losing a client as "the most profoundly disturbing event of their professional careers" (p. 2022), noting that one third of these therapists experienced severe distress that lasted at least 1 year beyond the initial loss. Ruskin, in his 2004 study, similarly found that one quarter of psychiatrists and psychiatric trainees noted that losing a patient had a "profound and enduring effect on them" (p. 109). Many clinicians have noted that they considered leaving the field after such a loss, and it is hypothesized that many may have done so (Carter, 1971; Dewar, Eagles, Klein, Gray, & Alexander, 2000; Gitlin, 2007). Other clinicians have noted that, at least temporarily, they stopped treating clients who were potentially suicidal (Carter, 1971; Litman, 1965).

Several authors have proposed general models for describing the suicide grief trajectories of clinicians after a suicide. Tillman (2006) identified six distinct groups of responses to this event (traumatic, affective, those related to the treatment, those related to interactions with colleagues, liability concerns, and the impact on one's professional philosophy). She also found that Erikson's (1959) stages of identity provided an uncannily similar trajectory to the ways in which her research subjects—clinicians at a mental hospital—had attempted to cope with their clients' deaths, noting that the "suicide of a patient may provoke a revisiting of Erikson's psychosocial crises in a telescoped and accelerated fashion" (Tillman, 2004, p. 16). Maltsberger (1992) offered a detailed psychoanalytic analysis of the responses that clinicians may manifest in relation to suicide loss, including the initial narcissistic injury sustained in relation to their client's actions; the subsequent potential for melancholic, atonement, or avoidance reactions; and the eventual capacity for the resolution of these reactions. Bissell, in her 1981 study, found that psychiatric nurses who had experienced client suicides progressed through several developmental stages (naïveté, recognition, responsibility, individual choice), and she described these stages as enabling these nurses to come to terms with their personal reactions and place the ultimate responsibility for the suicide with the client.

☐ Professional Issues That May Affect the Grief Trajectory Following a Client Suicide

Many factors make the experience of client loss to suicide unique and variable for individual clinicians. Such factors include the amount of a clinician's professional training and experience, both in general and in working with potentially suicidal individuals. Several authors (Hendin et al., 2000; Kleespies, 1993; Ruskin, 2004) found that those who experienced the most distress were more likely to be trainees.

Chemtob et al. (1988) found that those with less training in suicide assessment and intervention were more likely to experience client suicide loss than more seasoned clinicians. Brown (1987) noted that many training programs were likely to assign the most "extraordinarily sick patients to inexperienced trainees" (p. 103). He noted that because the skill level of trainees has not yet tempered their personal aspirations, they are likely to experience a patient's suicide as a personal failure. However, Brown also suggested that the overall impact of client suicide may be greater for seasoned clinicians, when the "protective advantage" or "explanation" of being in training is no longer applicable (p. 104). This suggestion appears consistent with Munson's (2009) study, which found that greater number of years of clinical experience was negatively correlated with post-traumatic growth.

Other factors affecting a clinician's grief response include the context in which the treatment occurred (inpatient or outpatient, clinic or private practice, etc.), the presence and involvement of supportive mentors or supervisors, the length and intensity of the treatment, the quality and intensity of the clinical relationship and countertransference issues, and the time elapsed since the suicide occurred. In addition, the potential threat of liability issues can create tremendous anxiety and can easily delay or derail a clinician's ability to process grief in a "normative" way. Finally, each clinician's set of personal and life experiences can affect the way he or she moves through the grieving process. Any previous trauma or losses—particularly, prior exposure to suicide—will likely affect a clinician's reaction to his or her current loss, as will any susceptibility to anxiety or depression. Gorkin (1985) has suggested that the degree of omnipotence in the clinician's therapeutic strivings will affect his or her ability to accept the inherent ambiguity involved in suicide loss. Gender may also play a role: Grad, Zavasnik, and Groleger (1997) found that female clinicians felt more shame and guilt and professed more doubts about their professional competence than did male clinicians and were more than twice as likely as their male counterparts to identify talking with colleagues as an effective coping strategy. In addition to the clinician's individual circumstances, there are additional common factors that can affect the process and intensity of the grief response.

☐ Confidentiality Issues and Lack of Grief Rituals

Psychotherapists and their clients often have relationships that are deeply intimate, albeit in circumscribed ways. The development of trust and the sharing of pain are just two of the factors that can make the therapeutic encounter an intense emotional experience for both parties. Recent trends in the psychodynamic literature (particularly in the interpersonal, relational, and intersubjectivity-based approaches) acknowledge the profundity and depth of the personal impact that patients have on the clinician, an impact that is neither pathological nor an indication of poor boundaries in the therapy dyad but, instead, a recognition of how all aspects of the therapist's person—whether consciously or not—are used within the context of a therapeutic relationship. Vida (2003) has noted that this specific aspect of the often intimate therapeutic relationship is seldom acknowledged outside the treatment setting, with the possible exception of supervision or case consultation. Thus, when clinicians lose a client, it can feel as though the loss, although profound, has occurred in a void—an invisible space—that cannot be meaningfully shared with others due to the nature of psychotherapy and its accompanying restrictions on confidentiality. Furthermore, the usual grief rituals that facilitate the healing of loss and the processing of grief (gathering with others who know the deceased, sharing feelings and memories) are usually denied to the therapist and are often compounded by the reactions of the surviving family members and one's professional colleagues, who tend not to view the therapist's grief as "legitimate." Even the "psychological autopsies" that often follow such a loss are viewed more as fact-finding missions, in which the therapists' behaviors and notes are scrutinized but their interior experience is not recognized or validated. These responses are hardly conducive to facilitating the mourning process in the clinician. In addition, legal counsel may advise the clinician against speaking even to consultants or supervisors, for fear that any communication could be subpoenaed in legal proceedings. As one clinician in a clinician–survivor discussion group at a psychoanalytic conference stated, " I felt like I was grieving in a vacuum, that even if there had been a place to talk about my client, that I wasn't allowed to talk about how much she meant to me and how she had touched me" (Discussion group/personal communication, April 2004). The isolation of grieving alone is likely to be compounded by the lack of resources for supporting clinicians after such a loss. In contrast to the general suicide "survivor" network of support groups for family members who have experienced a suicide loss, there is an almost complete lack of supportive resources[3] for clinicians following such a loss, and most clinicians are not aware of those resources that are available. This often increases both personal and professional isolation in this unique form of disenfranchised grief (Doka, 2002).

---

[3] See the concluding section of this chapter for resources provided by the Clinician–Survivors Task Force of the American Association of Suicidology.

☐ Professional Relationships/ Reactions of Colleagues

Several authors have described potential responses within clinical communities that would optimally allow clinicians to both recover from and make good use of the experience of losing a patient to suicide. Farberow (2005) and others who have written on this issue have stressed that information about suicide, including both its statistical likelihood and its potential aftermath, should initially be presented as a general part of clinicians' education and training. These researchers have advised that clinical and training directors incorporate such information into their institutional policy and procedure manuals. Spiegelman and Werth (2005) have summarized the literature on the provision of optimal support for both clinical trainees and professional therapists, and several common suggestions emerged. These suggestions include ensuring that the clinician can obtain information about the circumstances of the suicide from a "neutral" source (e.g., a coroner); providing consultation from supervisors and/or colleagues that is supportive and reassuring rather than blaming; and providing opportunities for the clinician to talk about the experience of the loss, either individually or in group settings, without fear of judgment or censure. Quinnett (1999) noted that as director of his agency, he created a set of suicide postvention guidelines for all staff, and he enforces "a zero tolerance policy toward any staff person causing distress to another by reason of a client suicide" (Quinnett, 2008, personal communication).

Schultz (2005) detailed specific suggestions for supervisors of clinicians or trainees after a suicide. It should be noted that clinical supervisors are often quite invested in the outcome of these situations, particularly for unlicensed trainees, as they often bear at least some clinical and legal responsibility for the treatments that they supervise. Despite this, Schultz urges supervisors to allow extra time for the clinician to engage in the normative exploration of the "whys" that are unique to suicide survivors; to use education about suicide to help the clinician gain a more realistic perspective on their relative culpability; and to become aware of and provide education about normative grief reactions following a suicide. Because a suicide loss is likely to affect a clinician's subsequent clinical activity, she encourages supervisors to help clinicians monitor this impact on their work. Schultz also suggests that supervisors facilitate the clinician's contact with other clinicians who have experienced the suicide loss of a client. Throughout the document, she encourages supervisors to take an active stance in advocating for their supervisees, to encourage expressions of support from colleagues, and to discourage rumors and other stigmatizing reactions.

Unfortunately, many clinicians have experienced reactions from colleagues and supervisors that are antithetical to those suggested by these authors. According to Jobes and Maltsberger (1995, pp. 200–201), "the suicide death of a patient in active treatment is commonly taken as *prima facie* evidence that the therapist, somehow or another, has mismanaged the case," and thus the therapist often faces blame and censure from colleagues and supervisors. Hendin et al. (2000) noted that many trainees in his study found reactions by their institutions to be insensitive and unsupportive, one noting that the department's review of the case "felt more like a tribunal or inquest" (p. 2025). Quinnett (2008, personal communication) noted that many clinicians whom he interviewed following a suicide reported a pattern of isolation and interpersonal discomfort with their colleagues, who implicitly or explicitly expressed concerns about their competence. He described how a respected colleague received "no understanding, no support, only abuse" from her supervisor. Such responses—although perhaps surprising, considering they are coming from mental health professionals—probably reflect the longstanding cultural attitude of social condemnation of suicide and of those who are associated with it, particularly survivors.

Negative reactions from professional colleagues are most likely to occur immediately after the suicide loss and/or during the course of a subsequent investigation or psychological autopsy. Such reactions may lead to a well-founded ambivalence about disclosure to colleagues, and consequent resistance to seeking out optimal supervision/consultation or even personal therapy that could help clinicians gain clarity on the effects of these issues. Many professionals have described how, after the distressing experience of losing a client to suicide, they moved through this process in relative isolation and loneliness, feeling abandoned by their colleagues and by their own hopes and expectations for support.

☐ The Role of Professional Stigmatization

Another factor that may affect clinicians after a suicide loss is that of stigma. Stigma around the issue of suicide is well documented (Cvinar, 2005). David Satcher (former U.S. Surgeon General), in his *Call to Action to Prevent Suicide* (1999), specifically described stigma around suicide as one of the biggest barriers to prevention. In addition, researchers have found that the stigma associated with suicide "spills over" to the bereaved family members. Erving Goffman, in his seminal book, *Stigma: Notes on the*

Management of Spoiled Identity (1963, reissued 1986), refers to "disenfranchised grief," in which the bereaved person receives the message that his or her grief is not legitimate and, thus, is likely to internalize this view. Doka (2001) has expanded this idea more recently. Indeed, studies have shown that individuals bereaved by suicide are also stigmatized and are believed to be more psychologically disturbed, less likable, more blameworthy, more ashamed, and more in need of professional help than other bereaved individuals (Armour, 2006; Calhoun & Allen, 1991; Cvinar, 2005; Dunne, McIntosh, & Dunne-Maxim, 1987; Harwood, Hawton, Hope, & Jacoby, 2002; Jordan, 2001; McIntosh, 2003; Range, 1998; Sveen & Walby, 2008; Von Dongen, 1993). These judgments often mirror the survivor's self-punitive assessments, which then become exacerbated by and intertwined with both externally imposed and internalized stigma. Thus, it is not uncommon for suicide survivors to question their own right to grieve, to report low expectations of social support, and to feel compelled to deny or hide the mode of death. To the extent that they are actively grieving, survivors often feel that they must do so in isolation. Thus, the perception of stigma, whether real or imagined, can have a profound effect on decisions about disclosure, asking for support, and so forth—and, ultimately, on one's ability to integrate the loss. Indeed, Feigelman, Gorman, and Jordan (2009) found that stigmatization after suicide was specifically associated with ongoing grief difficulties, depression, and suicidal thinking.

As noted, when a client in treatment completes suicide, the treating clinician becomes an easy scapegoat for both family members and colleagues. To the extent that mental health professionals are not immune from the effects and imposition of stigma, this might also affect their previously mentioned tendency to place judgment, overtly or covertly, on the treating clinician and his or her degree of perceived competence.

In addition, there may also be stigma projected by colleagues in relation to a clinician's perceived emotional vulnerability. A traumatized clinician potentially challenges the notion of the implicit power imbalance between clients and the professionals who treat them: the former being needy, pathological, and looking to clinicians for care, and the professionals being the competent, healthy, and benevolent individuals who have the care to offer. This distinction may serve defensive functions if clinicians rely upon this type of "us/them" compartmentalization in order to reinforce their healthy, benevolent status to themselves. To the extent that these inherent assumptions underlying one's professional identity do serve to preserve or consolidate a clinician's professional esteem, then the apparent vulnerability in clinician–survivors may be threatening to their colleagues, evoking defensive condemnations of the survivor's professional handling of the case and/or of their "excessive" grief reactions after the suicide.

Thus, stigma that is associated both with suicide and with professional vulnerability can profoundly affect the ways in which colleagues relate to the clinician who has lost a client and may well be internalized by the clinician. When this occurs, it is likely to lead to even more isolation, shame, and self-blame. It is not surprising that many clinicians consider leaving the profession after this type of experience. To the extent that professional stigma continues to be an unexamined yet omnipresent aspect of suicide's aftermath, it even more clearly speaks to the need to address and disseminate information about optimal postvention.

☐ Effects on Clinical Work

In general, the literature on clinicians' loss of clients to suicide indicates that it commonly leads therapists to question their abilities as clinicians and to experience a sharp loss of confidence in their work with clients (Jobes & Maltsberger, 1995; Jones, 1987). Thus, in addition to the effects of personal grief and the issues that may affect a clinician's professional identity, a suicide loss is likely to affect a clinician's therapeutic work. As noted previously, the shattered beliefs and assumptions around the efficacy of the therapeutic process, a sense of guilt or self-blame, and any perceived or actual negative judgment from colleagues can dramatically compromise a clinician's sense of competence. Hendin et al. (2000) noted that even the most experienced therapists expressed difficulty in trusting their own clinical judgment or accurately assessing risk after the loss of a client to suicide. Such anxiety is likely to affect the clinical process, and it may be manifested in a multitude of ways.

In addition, the common responses to a suicide loss (including numbness, sadness, anxiety, and generalized distress) are likely to result in at least some temporary disruption of a clinician's optimal functioning. If PTSD symptoms are more pronounced, the effect and longevity of such impairment may be exacerbated. Quinnett (1999) notes that posttraumatic emotional states may" impair clinical response and therapeutic judgment" (p. 5). In addition, because such symptoms and states may be triggered by exposure to other potentially suicidal clients, they are more likely to affect clinical functioning when the clinician is working with suicidal individuals. Thus, the normative responses to a suicide loss are likely to affect a clinician's work, just as they may affect the personal and occupational functioning of any survivor of suicide loss.

In clinician–survivor discussion and support groups led by Gutin, many common areas of clinical impact were identified. Perhaps one of the most common early (anxiety-based) responses reported by clinician–survivors who continue to work with suicidal individuals was to become hypervigilant in relation to any perceived suicide risk, to interpret such risk in such a way as to warrant more conservative interventions than are necessary, and to consequently minimize the client's own capacities for self-care. Conversely, others reported tendencies to minimize or deny suicidal potential—for example, avoiding asking their clients directly about suicidal ideation, even when they retrospectively realized that it was indicated.

Suicide loss may also lead to more subtle countertransference reactions that have been observed primarily with suicidal clients, in addition to clients with loss or grief issues. Some clinicians have also noted that their reactions seemed to be more generic, affecting their entire caseloads. These include avoidant or even dissociative reactions in relation to their client's pain, which in turn affected the therapist's ability to "be fully present" or to be genuinely empathic in their clinical encounters (Gutin, 2004; Kolodny, Binder, Bronstein, & Friend, 1979). One therapist noted, "I felt as though I was seeing my patients through a glass wall, like an automaton going through the technical motions of being an adequate therapist, but I just didn't feel real or genuine" (Gutin, 2004). Others in discussion groups noted their tendency to "replace affect with intellect" as they engaged in a more didactic approach than they had in the past. One clinician, who identified herself as "primarily psychodynamic" in her orientation, noted that she became "a really good cognitive–behaviorist" subsequent to her loss of a client to suicide. Still others noted that they tended to project residual feelings of anger onto their current suicidal clients or envied clients who seemed to have mastered their grief. Consistent with Maltsberger's (1992) description of "atonement reactions," some clinicians found themselves doing more than should be expected for their clients, even losing their sense of professional boundaries in the process. Anderson (2005) noted that in pushing herself beyond what she knew were her optimal clinical boundaries, she was "punishing herself" for failing to prevent her client's suicide because, as she realized, "doing 'penance' was better than feeling helpless and powerless" (p. 28). Schultz (2005) described how therapists may have subsequent difficulty in trusting other patients, especially if clients who completed suicide did not disclose or denied their own suicidal intent.

☐ Effects of Potential Legal/Ethical Issues

As noted, several legal and ethical issues may also complicate and/or extend the grief process after a client's suicide. Confidentiality issues, as well as advice from attorneys to limit disclosure of information about the case, may preclude the clinician's ability to talk freely about the client, the therapeutic relationship, and their feelings about the loss—all of which are known to facilitate movement through the grief process. Furthermore, the clinician's concern about litigation, or an actual lawsuit, is likely to produce intense anxiety. This common fear is understandable, considering that according to Bongar (2002), malpractice related to suicide is the most common reason for the filing of a malpractice suit against a clinician.

In addition, an institution's concern about protecting itself from liability may compromise its ability to support the clinician or trainee who sustained the loss. As noted previously, the potential prohibitions around discussing the case can compromise the grief process. Additionally, the fear of (or actual) legal reprisals against supervisors and the larger institution may engender angry and blaming responses toward the treating clinician. Quinnett (personal communication, March 2008) described an incident in which a supervising psychologist stomped into the grieving therapist's office unannounced and shouted, "Now look what you've done! You're going to get me sued!" Other studies (Kolodny et al., 1979; Litman, 1965; Marshall, 1980) note that clinicians fear job loss and a reluctance on the part of colleagues and supervisors to assign new clients to them. Spiegleman and Werth (2005) also note that trainees grapple with additional concerns over negative evaluations, suspension or termination from clinical sites or training programs, and interruption of degree attainment. As noted previously, such supervisory and institutional reactions are likely to intensify a clinician's sense of shame and distress and are antithetical to postvention responses that promote optimal personal and professional growth. Such negative reactions are also likely to contribute (a) to a clinician's or trainee's subsequent reluctance to work with suicidal individuals or (b) to their decision to discontinue their clinical work altogether. Lastly, other ethical issues—such as contact with the client's family following the suicide, attending the funeral, and so forth—are explored more fully in Chapter 7, but the questions raised by these issues are likely to be a source of additional anxiety and distress, particularly if the clinician needs to address these problems in isolation.

☐ Positive Changes/Post-Traumatic Growth

Paradoxically, traumatic experiences can present a multitude of opportunities for new growth. Indeed, the relatively new literature on post-traumatic growth (Tedeschi & Calhoun, 2008) suggests that traumatic experiences often present opportunities for profound personal transformation. Interestingly, Fuentes and Cruz (2009) found that the occurrence of post-traumatic growth was significantly associated with "psychological-mindedness"—that is, the belief in the benefits of discussing one's problems, the willingness to discuss these problems with others, and openness to change. Perceived social support was also highly related to the degree of growth. These factors are consistent with the elements that have been previously identified as being most helpful to clinicians after the loss of a client to suicide.

Virtually all of the models of the clinician's suicide grief trajectory described earlier not only assume the eventual resolution of the distressing reactions accompanying the original loss but also suggest that mastery of these reactions can be a catalyst for both personal and professional growth. Clearly, not everyone who experiences such a loss will experience subsequent growth, for there are many anecdotal reports of clinicians leaving the field (Gitlin, 2007) or becoming "burned out" after this loss occurs. Although there is a lack of empirical studies (other than anecdotal case reports) that allow us to assess how common these negative reactions are, it does seem that the majority of clinicians who have described this loss in the literature and in discussion groups (e.g., ones conducted by the first author) have reported more positive eventual outcomes.[4]

The literature on the loss of a client to suicide as well as anecdotal reports confirm that clinicians are able to identify many retrospective benefits to their experience. These benefits include becoming better educated about suicide and the likelihood of its occurrence. Clinicians generally report that they are better able to identify potential risk and protective factors for suicide and are more knowledgeable about optimal interventions with suicidal individuals. They also describe an increased sensitivity toward suicidal clients and those bereaved by suicide. In addition, clinicians report a reduction in therapeutic grandiosity/omnipotence as well as more realistic appraisals and expectations in relation to their clinical competence. In their effort to understand the "whys" of their client's suicide, they are likely to retrospectively identify errors in treatment, "missed cues," or things that they might subsequently do differently (Hendin et al., 2000) and to learn from these mistakes. Optimally,

---

[4] It is difficult to establish whether this outcome is due to a cohort effect—namely, that those clinicians who are most likely to be interviewed for research studies and to seek out and participate in discussion/support groups may be more prone to find benefits in this experience, either by virtue of their nature or through the subsequent process of speaking about these experiences in a supportive atmosphere.

clinicians become more aware of their own therapeutic limitations, both in the short and long term, and they can use this knowledge to better determine how they will continue their clinical work. They also become much more aware of the issues involved in the aftermath of a client suicide, including perceived gaps in the clinical and institutional systems that could optimally offer support to both families and clinicians.

In addition to the positive changes related to knowledge and clinical skills, many clinicians also note deeper personal changes subsequent to their client's suicide. This is consistent with the literature on post-traumatic growth (Tedeschi & Calhoun, 2008). Joseph Munson (2009) explored internal changes in clinicians following the loss of a client to suicide and found that both post-traumatic growth and compassion fatigue coexisted within a clinician in the aftermath. Munson also found that the amount of time that elapsed since the client's suicide predicted post-traumatic growth in a positive direction as well as the seemingly counterintuitive result that the number of years of clinical experience prior to the suicide was negatively correlated with post-traumatic growth.

Huhra, Hunka, Rogers, Warbel, and Yamakoski (2004) have described some of the existential issues that a clinician is likely to confront following the loss of a client to suicide. A clinician's attempt to find a way to meaningfully understand the circumstances around this loss prompts reflection around mortality; freedom; choice and personal autonomy; and the scope and limits of one's responsibility toward others. To the extent that one's previous conceptions and expectations around these professional issues have been challenged by the suicide, the task remains to construct new paradigms that serve to integrate these new experiences and perspectives in a coherent way.

One of the most notable sequelae to this (and to other traumatic) experience is a subsequent desire to use the learning inherent in these experiences and to "give back." Many clinicians, once they feel that they are more resolved with their own grief process, have expressed the desire to support others with similar experiences. Indeed, it does seem notable that even when their experiences have been quite distressing, many clinicians have been able to view this as an opportunity to learn about ongoing limitations in the systems of support and to work toward changing these systems so that future clinician–survivors will have more supportive experiences. Many clinicians are able to view these new perspectives—and their consequent ability to be more helpful—as "unexpected gifts." They often express gratitude toward the people and resources that have allowed them to make these transformations. As Jones (1987) notes, "the tragedy of patient suicide can also be an opportunity for us as therapists to grow in our skills at assessing and intervening in a suicidal crisis, to broaden and deepen the support we give and receive, to grow in our appreciation of the precious gift that life is, and to help each other live it more fully" (p. 141).

☐ Recommendations for Future Research

Because clinicians' loss of a client to suicide is a relatively new area of research, there are many ways to enhance the understanding of how, why, and when the experience of client suicide affects professionals. Clinician variables such as gender, cultural background, the extent and type of training and supervision, and one's history of personal loss or trauma may all play a role in determining how such a loss may affect an individual. There may also be variable experiences for different types of clinicians, such as medically trained psychiatrists and other mental health clinicians, but also for others who take on a caregiving role in relation to suicidal individuals, such as clergy, teachers, and school personnel, as well as those in less "formalized" support positions. Client variables such as the known degree of suicide risk, the method of suicide, diagnostic history, and age may also affect the impact on clinicians. Finally, situational variables such as the setting in which the suicide took place (in the hospital, after hospital discharge, etc.) as well as the degree of publicity rendered after the suicide are likely to have an effect. Additional research on these and related topics can shed more light on the impact of this loss and on the ways in which it might best be addressed for surviving individuals.

☐ Conclusion and Recommendations

In general, losing a client to suicide is a complicated, potentially traumatic process, and its impact may be mediated by many of the contextual factors discussed previously. As noted, there have been many efforts to identify those aspects of the aftermath of a client suicide that are most likely to facilitate healing and subsequent growth in clinicians. It is clear that the task remains to use this existing information by consistently integrating it into more formal training and education around suicide assessment and intervention. This information, which would include realistic appraisals of the actual likelihood of patient suicide and information about optimal organizational postvention and clinician self-care, should be presented early on in the training careers of mental health professionals and should be reinforced and updated at regular intervals.

In addition, information about additional resources for clinician–survivors should be disseminated and used. Jones (1987) noted that clinicians who have lost clients to suicide need "a place to acknowledge and carry forward their personal loss; that although therapists may be good at facilitating others' emotional work, they are not so adept at dealing with their own emotional needs … [thus they could] benefit both personally and professionally from the opportunity to talk with other therapists who have survived the loss of a patient through suicide" (p. 136). As a result of these realizations, Jones went on to found the first support group for therapist–survivors in 1982.

Subsequently, the Clinician–Survivors Task Force[5] (CSTF) of the American Association of Suicidology (AAS) was formed to support the needs of clinicians after the loss of a client to suicide. In its present form, the CSTF supports clinicians who have lost clients and/or family members, with the recognition that both types of losses carry implications within clinical and professional domains. The CSTF provides an electronic mail list and a Web site, on which there are opportunities to read and post narratives about one's experience with suicide loss as well as possibilities to access telephone and e-mail contact with other clinicians who have experienced such a loss. In addition, the chairs of this task force conduct clinician–survivor support activities at annual AAS conferences and in their respective geographic areas. Future goals for the CSTF include (a) empowering current clinician–survivors (and others who support suicidal individuals, such as teachers, clergy, etc.) to advocate for future clinician–survivors and for the changes described in this chapter, (b) to disseminate the information that is currently available on the sequelae of clinicians' loss of a client to suicide, and (c) to increase the research that is conducted on this topic.

☐ References

Anderson, G. O. (2005). Who, what, when, where, how, and mostly why? A therapist's grief over the suicide of a client. In K. M. Weiner (Ed.), *Therapeutic and legal issues for therapists who have survived a client suicide: Breaking the silence* (pp. 25–34). New York, NY: Haworth Press.

---

[5] To access the CSTF Web site, visit the AAS Web site (http://www.suicidology.org) and scroll down to the "I am" section of the home page or go to the "Survivor" page and click on the "Clinician–Survivor" link. To request to join the electronic mail list, please contact Vanessa L. McGann at vlmcgann@aol.com.

Armour, M. (2006). Violent death: Understanding the context of traumatic and stigmatized grief. *Journal of Human Behavior in the Social Environment, 14*(4), 53–90.

Bersoff, D. N. (1999). *Ethical conflicts in psychology* (2nd ed.). Washington, DC: American Psychological Association.

Bissell, B. P. H. (1981). The experience of the nurse therapist working with suicidal cases: A developmental study. *Dissertation Abstracts International, 42*(06), 2307B. (UMI No. AAT 8126678)

Bongar, B. (2002). *The suicidal patient: Clinical and legal standards of care* (2nd ed.). Washington, DC: American Psychological Association.

Brown, H. B. (1987). The impact of suicide on therapists in training. *Comprehensive Psychiatry, 28,* 101–112.

Calhoun, L. G., & Allen, B. G. (1991). Social reactions to the survivor of a suicide in the family: A review of the literature. *Omega: Journal of Death and Dying, 23,* 95–107.

Carter, R. E. (1971). Some effects of client suicide on the therapist. *Psychotherapy: Theory, Research, and Practice, 8,* 287–289.

Chemtob, C. M., Bauer, G. B., Hamada, R. S., Pelowski, S. R., & Muraoka, M. Y. (1989). Patient suicide: Occupational hazard for psychologists and psychiatrists. *Professional Psychology: Research and Practice, 20,* 294–300.

Chemtob, C. M., Hamada, R. S., Bauer, G., Kinney, B., & Torigoe, R. Y. (1988). Patients' suicides: Frequency and impact on psychiatrists. *American Journal of Psychiatry, 145,* 224–228.

Cvinar, J. G. (2005). Do suicide survivors suffer social stigma? A review of the literature. *Perspectives in Psychiatric Care, 41,* 14–21.

Dewar, I., Eagles J., Klein S., Gray, N., & Alexander, D. A. (2000). Psychiatric trainees' experiences of, and reactions to, patient suicide. *Psychiatric Bulletin, 24,* 20–23.

Doka, K. J. (Ed.). (2002). *Disenfranchised grief: New directions, challenges, and strategies for practice* (2nd ed.). Champaign, IL: Research Press.

Dunne, E. J., McIntosh, J. L., & Dunne-Maxim, K. (Eds.). (1987). *Suicide and its aftermath: Understanding and counseling the survivors.* New York, NY: W. W. Norton.

Erikson, E. H. (1959). *Identity and the life cycle.* New York, NY: International Universities Press.

Farberow, N. L. (2005). The mental health professional as suicide survivor. *Clinical Neuropsychiatry: Journal of Treatment Evaluation, 2,* 13–20.

Feigelman, W., Gorman, B. S., & Jordan, J. R. (2009). Stigmatization and suicide bereavement. *Death Studies, 33,* 598–601.

Fuentes, M. A., & Cruz, D. (2009, Winter). Posttraumatic growth: Positive psychological changes after trauma. *Mental Health News, 11*(1), pp. 31, 37. Retrieved from http://www.mhnews.org

Gitlin, M. (2007). Aftermath of a tragedy: Reaction of psychiatrists to patient suicides. *Psychiatric Annals, 37,* 684–687.

Goffman, E. (1963, reissued 1986). *Stigma: Notes on the management of spoiled identity.* Englewood Cliffs, NJ: Prentice Hall.

Goldney, R. D. (2000). The privilege and responsibility of suicide prevention. *Crisis: Journal of Crisis Intervention and Suicide Prevention, 21,* 8–15.

Gorkin, M. (1985). On the suicide of one's patient. *Bulletin of the Menninger Clinic, 49,* 1–9.

Grad, O. T., Zavasnik, A., & Groleger, U. (1997). Suicide of a patient: Gender differences in bereavement reactions of therapists. *Suicide and Life-Threatening Behavior, 27,* 379–386.

Gutin, N. J. (2004, March). *Clinician survivors of family suicide: Implications for practice and professional identity.* Unpublished paper presented at the American Psychological Association Division of Psychoanalysis (39) Conference, Miami, FL.

Harwood, D., Hawton, K., Hope, J., & Jacoby, R. (2002). The grief experiences and needs of descriptive and case-control study. *Journal of Affective Disorders, 72,* 185–194.

Hendin, H., Lipschitz, A., Maltsberger, J. T., Haas, A. P., & Wynecoop, S. (2000). Therapist's reactions to patients' suicides. *American Journal of Psychiatry, 157,* 2022–2027.

Huhra, R., Hunka, N., Rogers, J., Warbel, A., & Yamakoski, C. (2004, April). *Finding meaning: Theoretical perspectives on patient suicide.* Paper presented at the 2004 annual conference of the American Association of Suicidology, Miami, FL.

Jobes, D. A., & Maltsberger, J. T. (1995). The hazards of treating suicidal patients In M. B. Sussman (Ed.), *A perilous calling: The hazards of psychotherapy practice* (pp. 200–214). New York, NY: Wiley & Sons.

Jones, F. A., Jr. (1987). Therapists as survivors of client suicide. In E. J. Dunne, J. L. McIntosh, & K. L. Dunne-Maxim (Eds.), *Suicide and its aftermath: Understanding and counseling the survivors* (pp. 126–141). New York, NY: W. W. Norton.

Jordan, J. (2001). Is suicide bereavement different? A reassessment of the literature. *Suicide and Life-Threatening Behavior, 31,* 91–102.

Kleespies, P. M. (1993). The stress of patient suicidal behavior: Implications for interns and training programs in psychology. *Professional Psychology: Research and Practice, 24,* 477–482.

Kolodny, S., Binder, R. L., Bronstein, A. A., & Friend, R. L. (1979). The working through of patients' suicides by four therapists. *Suicide and Life-Threatening Behavior, 9,* 33–46. (Reprinted in A. S. Cook & K. A. Oltjenbruns (1989), *Dying and grieving: Lifespan and family perspectives* (pp. 457–471). New York, NY: Holt, Rinehart and Winston.)

Litman, R. E. (1965). When patients commit suicide. *American Journal of Psychotherapy, 19,* 570–576.

Maltsberger, J. T. (1992). The implications of patient suicide for the surviving psychotherapist. In D. Jacobs (Ed.), *Suicide and clinical practice* (pp. 169–182). Washington, DC: American Psychiatric Press, Clinical Practice No. 21.

Marshall, K. (1980). When a patient commits suicide. *Suicide and Life-Threatening Behavior, 10,* 29–40.

McIntosh, J. L. (2003). Control group studies of suicide survivors: A review and critique. *Suicide and Life-Threatening Behavior, 23,* 146–161.

Munson, J. S. (2009). *Impact of client suicide on practitioner posttraumatic growth.* Unpublished doctoral dissertation, University of Florida.

Plakun, E. M., & Tillman, J. G. (2005). Responding to clinicians after loss of a patient to suicide. *Directions in Psychiatry, 25,* 301–310.

Quinnett, P. (1999). *Postvention guidelines for agency suicides: QPR Institute administrative directory.* Spokane, WA: QPR Institute.

Range, L. M. (1998). When a loss is due to suicide: Unique aspects of bereavement. In J. H. Harvey (Ed.), *Perspectives on loss: A sourcebook* (pp. 213–220). Philadelphia, PA: Brunner/Mazel.

Rubin, H. L. (1990). Surviving a suicide in your practice. In S. J. Blumenthal & D. J. Kupfer (Eds.), *Suicide over the lifecycle: Risk factors, assessment and treatment of suicidal patients* (pp. 619–636). Washington, DC: American Psychiatric Press.

Ruskin, R. (2004). Impact of patient suicide on psychiatrists and psychiatric trainees. *Academic Psychiatry, 28,* 104–110.

Rycroft, P. (2005). Touching the heart and soul of therapy: Surviving client suicide. In K. M. Weiner (Ed.), *Therapeutic and legal issues for therapists who have survived a client suicide: Breaking the silence* (pp. 83–94). New York, NY: Haworth Press.

Satcher, D. (1999). *The Surgeon General's call to action to prevent suicide.* Washington, DC: Department of Health and Human Services. Retrieved from http://www.sprc.org/library/surgeoncall.pdf

Schultz, D. (2005). Suggestions for supervisors when a therapist experiences a client's suicide. In K. M. Weiner (Ed.), *Therapeutic and legal issues for therapists who have survived a client suicide: Breaking the silence* (pp. 59–69). New York, NY: Haworth Press.

Spiegelman, J. S., & Werth, J. L., Jr. (2005). Don't forget about me: The experiences of therapists-in-training after a client has attempted or died by suicide. In K. M. Weiner (Ed.), *Therapeutic and legal issues for therapists who have survived a client suicide: Breaking the silence* (pp. 35–57). New York, NY: Haworth Press.

Sveen, C. A., & Walby, F. A. (2008). Suicide survivors' mental health and grief reactions: A systematic review of controlled studies. *Suicide and Life-Threatening Behavior, 38,* 13–29.

Tedeschi, R. G., & Calhoun, L. G. (2008). Beyond the concept of recovery: Growth and the experience of loss. *Death Studies, 32,* 27–39.

Tillman, J. G. (2004, March). *Exploring the responses of therapists to the suicide of a patient.* Paper presented at the American Psychological Association Division of Psychoanalysis (39) Conference, Miami, FL.

Tillman, J. G. (2006). When a patient commits suicide: An empirical study of psychoanalytic clinicians. *The International Journal of Psycho-Analysis, 87,* 159–177.

Van Dongen, C. J. (1993). Social context of postsuicide bereavement. *Death Studies, 17,* 125–141.

Vida, J. (2003). A dialogue of unconsciouses: A contribution to the panel "Jung and Ferenczi—'The emergent conversation.'" *Journal of Analytical Psychology, 48,* 491–497.

Weiner, K. M. (Ed.). (2005). *Therapeutic and legal issues for therapists who have survived a client suicide: Breaking the silence.* New York, NY: Haworth Press. [Published with the same pagination in the journal *Women & Therapy, 28*(1), 2005.]

SECTION

2

Helping Survivors

CHAPTER

Research on the Needs of Survivors

John R. Jordan, William Feigelman,
Jannette McMenamy, and Ann M. Mitchell

It has long been recognized that the loss of a loved one to suicide can be a devastating and sometimes life-altering experience. Many studies have found that suicide survivors are an at-risk population, comprising individuals who are likely to suffer from elevated rates of suicidality, psychiatric disorders, and psychosocial difficulties as a result of the loss (Jordan, 2001; see also Chapters 1 through 5 of this book for full reviews of this literature). It is both surprising and distressing, then, that so little has been done to provide organized help for survivors and to scientifically study interventions meant to assist them (Campbell, Cataldie, McIntosh, & Millet, 2004). In their recent review of the literature, Jordan and McMenamy (2004) noted that

> [w]e also know very little about the coping strategies that survivors develop on their own, and only slightly more about what types of formal and informal assistance survivors receive from professional caregivers, family, friends, and others in their social network. Careful longitudinal

research with a diverse, community-based sample of survivors would greatly increase our understanding of the challenges involved and the coping skills required after a suicide. (p. 345)

In this chapter, our goal is to review the small number of studies that have analyzed survivors' efforts to cope with their loss and what types of resources they have found helpful or unhelpful in their healing process. We appraise the small but growing literature on studies that ask survivors directly about their perceived needs and coping mechanisms, including reports on recent research conducted by the authors of this chapter on this important topic.

☐ What Do Survivors Need?

Most treatment approaches in the mental health field have emerged in a "top-down" fashion. Typically, professionals—whether clinicians or researchers—have created the services that they believe will be helpful for those coping with a problem, even though they may not have experienced the problem themselves. Although this approach may have its advantages, a strong case can be made that a "bottom-up" approach, particularly when dealing with bereavement, is likely to be more beneficial and more relevant to those seeking assistance (Myers & Fine, 2007). We believe that there is hard-won wisdom acquired by those who are living with the loss of a loved one to suicide—wisdom to which clinicians, program administrators, and researchers should pay careful attention. Therefore, we begin this chapter with a review of the few studies that have looked at the resources and reported needs of suicide survivors, including recent research by each author of this chapter.

Research on Survivor Needs

Provini, Everett, and Pfeffer (2000) conducted research that included an archival review of staff notes of telephone conversations with 144 adult next-of-kin suicide survivors. The domains of interest included concerns or problems after the suicide, needs for both formal and informal assistance, actual assistance received, and barriers to obtaining help after the death. Of the participants who expressed concerns, family difficulties (e.g., difficulty maintaining family routines) were the most frequently mentioned problem (65% of sample), followed by stressors (e.g., financial problems: 62%), psychiatric symptoms (e.g., depression: 54%), and bereavement-related problems (e.g., trouble expressing grief: 38%). In terms of assistance needed and received, 72% of the respondents who disclosed their needs indicated that they wanted formal, professional help (e.g., psychotherapy with a mental health professional), whereas 47% indicated that they had, in fact, received such help. Similarly, 16% said they wanted informal assistance (e.g., help from family or friends), and 41% said they had received such help. Twelve percent of the sample said they were in need of—and had received—a combination of both types of assistance. Also of note, families with children or adolescents expressed significantly more problems or concerns than did families without children. Barriers to receiving assistance included family disputes about the need for help, language barriers (i.e., non-English-speaking family members), and practical problems such as lack of financial resources to obtain help. The authors concluded with a discussion of the need to raise public awareness about the resources available to the bereaved and destigmatizing help seeking on the part of survivors, while also increasing the availability of culturally competent services.

Dyregrov and colleagues (K. Dyregrov, 2002, 2003; K. Dyregrov & A. Dyregrov, 2008) conducted a comprehensive quantitative and qualitative study with parents in Norway who had lost a child to suicide, sudden infant death syndrome (SIDS), or accident. One hundred twenty-eight of the participants had lost a child to suicide. The study looked at—among other variables—the self-perceived needs of bereaved parents as well as the ideal forms of assistance desired. Also studied was the match between the help received and the reports of community caregivers about the help that they believed was offered to traumatically bereaved parents. Eighty-eight percent of the parents indicated that they felt a need for professional assistance in terms of helping affected children in the family, dealing with problems in their social networks, and managing personal grief reactions (particularly post-traumatic stress disorder [PTSD] symptoms). Many of the parents stressed that they were often deeply traumatized and depressed after the death and were unable to mobilize themselves to seek professional help. Instead, they recommended that services should be routinely offered to all traumatically bereaved persons and that the providers of such services should be proactively reaching out to new survivors. These parents also felt that support services should provide both professional assistance and written information about suicide bereavement and available local resources and should be of longer duration than the typical 6 months or less (at least 1 year, and many suggested 2 or more years). In addition, local authorities (physicians, community nurses, clergy, etc.) often overestimated the amount of help that had been offered to survivors when compared with the survivors' perceptions of the help that they actually received. Both survivors and community caregivers, however, recognized that the amount and kinds of help offered were often inadequate for the needs of traumatically bereaved parents.

De Groot, de Keijser, and Neeleman (2006) conducted a well-designed comparison study of people bereaved by suicide and by natural causes. Participants were recruited through their general practitioner medical doctors and included 153 suicide-bereaved and 70 naturally bereaved individuals. The self-report measures included loneliness, neuroticism, depression, complicated grief, suicidality, general health functioning, and sense of self-esteem and mastery. On virtually every measure, the suicide survivors reported worse functioning and greater distress than the naturally bereaved participants. Of particular note for this chapter is the finding that the suicide-bereaved individuals indicated a significantly greater need for professional help/intervention with their grief difficulties than did naturally bereaved survivors.

Feigelman Survivors Child Loss Survey

The next section of this chapter reports on a recent series of survey studies by Feigelman, Gorman, and Jordan (Feigelman, Gorman, Beal, & Jordan, 2008; Feigelman, Gorman, & Jordan, 2009; Feigelman, Jordan, & Gorman, 2009a, 2009b). Specifically, we describe three studies that have been published, and then we present original and unpublished data on the use of resources by survivors over a longer duration (Feigelman, Gorman, & Jordan, 2007). To the best of our knowledge, the participants were the largest sample of suicide survivors ever studied. This sample included 540 bereaved parents who had used some type of bereavement support group, 86% of whom were survivors of the suicide of a child. There were also 45 cases of accidental-death survivors, 24 natural-death survivors, 4 homicide-death survivors, and 5 survivors of deaths that occurred under ambiguous circumstances. The sample included bereaved parents who were using face-to-face support groups, Internet-based support groups, or both. Nine percent had experienced the loss of their child within the last 12 months, and 40% had experienced the loss between 1 and 4 years earlier (for further details on the samples, see the studies mentioned earlier in this section).

The first study contrasted survivors who used Internet support groups with those who participated in face-to-face groups (Feigelman et al., 2008). Contradicting the expectation that Internet participants would be concentrated in underserved rural areas, results showed similar levels of urban, suburban small city, and rural participation in both Internet and face-to-face groups. Several elements of Internet groups were described as important, including their 24/7 availability and the increased opportunities for participation they afforded. Internet participants reported higher levels of depression and grief difficulties than did those who attended face-to-face groups—as well as more stigmatization from their families and other associates.

A second study compared stigmatization responses of the 462 parents who lost a child to suicide with 54 other traumatic-death-surviving parents and 24 natural-death survivors (Feigelman, Gorman, & Jordan, 2009). Results showed that parents encountering hurtful responses and strained relations with family members and friends also experienced heightened grief difficulties. After controlling for the type of death and the time since the loss, stigmatization continued to be associated with grief difficulties, depression, and suicidal thinking. Findings also showed few differences between the amount of reported stigmatization experienced by suicide survivors and that experienced by survivors of other traumatic deaths.

A third study (Feigelman, Jordan, et al., 2009a) examined the differences in grief difficulties and general mental health problems for suicide survivors when compared with survivors of other types of traumatic- and natural-death survivors. Results were mixed, with suicide survivors showing greater grief difficulties on a suicide-specific measure of grief but not on most of the other measures—a finding that conforms to the results of a recent review by Sveen and Walby (2008). The study also investigated differences in grief difficulties among suicide survivors as a function of elapsed time since the death, exposure to the body at the time of death, the relationship with the decedent, and reported feelings of surprise at the child's suicide. Results indicated that a history of repeated suicide attempts and a negative relationship with the decedent prior to the death were associated with greater grief difficulties during the early years of bereavement, although not when subjects were 5 or more years past the date of death. This data analysis also suggested that between 3 and 5 years usually marked a turning point—a time when acute grief difficulties accompanying a suicide loss began to subside.

Lastly, the previously unpublished data studied by Feigelman and colleagues (2007) refer to how the sample of 462 parent suicide survivors evaluated common helping resources. The study asked respondents about their use of six resources commonly sought by suicide survivors as well as a rating of the helpfulness of the resource, if it was used. The most helpful resource was suicide-specific support groups, followed closely by general bereavement support groups. (Note that these findings quite likely reflect the fact that the convenience sample in this study was primarily drawn from people participating in bereavement support groups.) In contrast, clergy, mental health professionals, and bereavement counselors received lower ratings of helpfulness, with psychics or spiritualists receiving intermediate ratings—although this last group was the least frequently consulted by participants.

Interesting findings also emerged from the data regarding frequency of and changes in the use of various services by the parents who were suicide survivors (see Table 6.1).

General and suicide-specific bereavement support groups were the most frequently used resources (again, this is quite likely characteristic of this particular sample, which was drawn mostly from support groups), and psychics were the least frequently used service. The use of all resources declined as time since the death increased. However, Table 6.1 also reveals that participation in bereavement support groups dropped after 5 years but tended to plateau after that, with approximately 40% still going to general bereavement groups or SOS groups 10 or more years after their loss. Use of other resources (e.g., mental health professionals, bereavement counselors, psychics) continued to decline over time or else was relatively flat throughout the entire time period (e.g., clergy). Examination of the data that inquired about the reasons for support-group participation revealed that there was a subset of "long-term" support group members (more than 5 years since the death) who rated friendship and personal growth as more salient reasons for participation than did the more recently bereaved. These preliminary data suggest that there may be some people for whom the community of other survivors becomes not just a temporary support resource but an ongoing and important part of their social network. It should be understood that the participation rates presented in Table 6.1 were not mutually exclusive categories. For example, participants could be seeing bereavement counselors and psychics and attending support groups at the same time.

Mitchell Qualitative Study

Mitchell and colleagues (Mitchell, Sakraida, Grabiak, & Barton, 2005) conducted an unpublished study using a focus group methodology employing semistructured interviews combined with qualitative analysis of the transcribed discussion data. The convenience sample consisted of 21 adult survivors of suicide who discussed their perceptions of currently available bereavement support services. The results identified 12 themes during the discussions, and highlighted in the paragraphs that follow are several of the themes that relate most directly to the issue of providing support for survivors.

TABLE 6.1 Differences in Treatment Seeking Among Parents Losing
Children to Suicide With Differing Lengths of Time Since Loss

In the past year, sought help from…	Length of time since loss (N = 462) (% per sample/number responding)		
	≤ 4.9 years (n = 258)	5.00–9.99 years (n = 126)	10 or more years (n = 71)
General bereavement group			
Never	47.5/122	60.0/75	57.8/41
1–5 times	28.0/72	23.2/29	19.7/14
6 or more times	24.5/63	16.8/21	22.5/16
Suicide-survivor support group			
Never	44.2/111	59.0/72	55.9/38
1–5 times	23.9/60	16.4/20	22.1/15
6 or more times	31.9/80	24.6/30	21.1/15
Professional bereavement counselor			
Never	69.1/177	78.7/96	89.9/62
1–5 times	14.1/36	12.3/15	5.8/4
6 or more times	16.8/43	9.0/11	4.4/3
Psychiatrist/psychologist/ social worker			
Never	54.3/139	73.8/93	85.5/59
1–5 times	19.1/49	14.3/18	5.8/4
6 or more times	26.6/68	11.9/15	8.7/6

(*continued*)

TABLE 6.1 Differences in Treatment Seeking Among Parents Losing Children to Suicide With Differing Lengths of Time Since Loss (continued)

In the past year, sought help from…	Length of time since loss (N = 462) (% per sample)		
	≤ 4.9 years (n = 258)	5.00–9.99 years (n = 126)	10 or more years (n = 71)
Member of the clergy			
Never	70.6/180	78.1/96	80.3/57
1–5 times	22.8/58	18.7/23	16.9/12
6 or more times	6.7/17	3.3/4	2.8/2
Psychic or spiritualist			
Never	72.8/185	87.1/108	92.5/62
1–5 times	23.2/59	11.3/14	4.5/3
6 or more times	3.9/10	1.6/2	3.0/2

Source: From Feigelman, W., Gorman, B. S., & Jordan, J. R., Survivors Child Loss Survey, unpublished data, 2007.

First, a key concept that was heard frequently was the idea of family, friends, professionals, and other survivors being available in order to provide needed support to the survivor. This theme of "Being There For Us" reflected the knowledge that there were people within the survivors' networks to whom these survivors could turn. This knowledge decreased feelings of being alone and also became a valuable and necessary source of information.

Another common theme had to do with the notion of commonality and bonding among survivors, especially as it related to the role of other family members and friends. As seen in the following quote, having family and friends was a source of support but often was not enough. The theme of "Not Meaningful Until Personal" is exemplified in the following quotation:

Your friends and all are helpful, but if they've never experienced anything like that they're…. They just can't do it.

The participant's comment suggested that although it was important for survivors to have family and friends around, participants also were aware of the limitations of nonsurvivors in their social networks. This was especially true when people have not lived through the experience themselves, which highlights the importance of contact with other survivors.

Third, one of the most personal and emotional aspects of survivorship had to do with the importance of having people available who have lived the common experience. The theme of "Commonality and Bonding" is exemplified in the following quote:

> So it actually gave you a sense of normalcy while you were with the group because they were all going through it. And you could say ... one word or I could just describe a situation I had been through and know that other people would just ... go "yeah, I know."

The individuals who had found a support group always spoke positively about the support and information that they received from the other group members. There was a bonding that took place that sometimes extended past the time-limited group format.

Fourth, participants in the focus groups expressed tremendous frustration when they were unable to locate services and/or knowledge related to the specific issue of suicide survivorship, as demonstrated in the following quotes related to the theme of "Service Issues and Knowledge Seeking" about the uniqueness of suicide bereavement:

> Compassionate Friends which we never did actually go to ....And suicide is different from any other losses. And there are similarities and differences and we just felt that this was what we needed so we came here [to Survivors of Suicide]. And it's been very helpful for us—a lifeline.

> So that was my first thing. I felt like I just needed something, whether I'm talking to somebody or reading something and I read ... cover to cover and highlighted, did that kind of thing. And then Sue started meeting with us separately, like you said, and to me that was like a god-sent [sic]. And we met together which was wonderful because we were dealing with it together and so that really helped.

Hearing from others who had managed to live through the experience already was a source of great comfort for the survivors who participated in the focus groups. They were often amazed that so many others experienced a death by suicide, too.

McMenamy Survivor Needs Assessment Survey

McMenamy, Jordan, and Mitchell (2008) developed a comprehensive self-report needs assessment survey that asked survivors about four domains: (a) practical, psychological, and social difficulties; (b) formal and informal sources of support; (c) resources for support (e.g., support group or self-help books); and (d) barriers to obtaining assistance. A pilot investigation of the Survivor Needs Assessment Survey (McMenamy et al., 2008) was conducted with a convenience sample of 63 adult survivors of suicide. Mean time since the suicide for the sample was 47.9 months, with 52% of the sample having experienced the suicide within 2 years or less. Consistent with past research (Jordan, 2001; McIntosh, 2003), the findings suggested that the trajectory of suicide bereavement is long and difficult, characterized by many difficulties in the practical, psychological, and social domains. For example, more than 61% of participants reported moderate to high levels of functional impairment in daily activities at work or home. The majority of participants also indicated that they had suffered moderate to high levels of depression, guilt, intense sadness and yearning, anxiety, and trauma symptoms. Almost one quarter of the sample met the diagnostic criteria for complicated grief (Gray & Prigerson, 2004; Lichtenthal, Cruess, & Prigerson, 2004; Prigerson & Maciejewski, 2005). Furthermore, more than 60% of participants reported moderate to high levels of difficulty with social relationships such as sharing grief and talking about the suicide within the family. Problems relating to withdrawal from friends and family and social isolation were also prevalent.

The pilot study also revealed important information about the support resources used by suicide survivors. Table 6.2 shows the number of respondents (out of a total sample of 63) who used various support resources, along with their mean rating of helpfulness and the percentage of respondents who rated the resource as moderately to highly helpful.

More than three-quarters of the sample used mental health professionals, and the majority of participants rated the support received from mental health professionals as at least moderately helpful or better. At the same time, the sample relied upon a broad range of other support resources, including friends, neighbors, colleagues, funeral directors, and clergy. Although many participants reported that expressing grief within the family was difficult, the majority viewed family members as important sources of support.

This study's sample relied on many different types of resources for healing—ranging from suicide bereavement support groups to individual therapy to talking one on one with another survivor to books and Internet sites. Table 6.3 shows the number of respondents who used

TABLE 6.2 Participants' Use of Support Resources and Ratings of Helpfulness for Each Resource

Support resources	Number using each resource[a] (n)	Mean helpfulness	% rating the item moderately to highly helpful (i.e., 3 or higher)
Formal resources			
Police	39	2.64	49
Emergency room	22	2.18	36
Funeral director	43	3.33	70
Clergy	41	3.20	63
Mental health professional	49	3.80	80
Primary care provider	38	2.68	47
Teacher	15	1.73	20
Informal resources			
Parents	36	3.14	67
Spouse/partner	45	4.00	82
Children	47	3.91	85
Siblings	51	3.55	70
Grandparents	8	2.25	38
Extended family	35	2.91	60
Friends	54	4.04	87
Neighbors/work colleagues	39	3.54	74

Note: [a]$N = 63$. Means are based on a scale of 1–5 (1 = *not helpful;* 5 = *extremely helpful*).

TABLE 6.3 Participants' Use of Resources for Healing and Ratings of
Helpfulness for Each Resource

Resources for healing	Number using each resource[a] (n)	Mean helpfulness	% rating the item moderately to highly helpful (i.e., 3 or higher)
General grief support groups	33	3.09	27
Suicide support groups	53	4.72	94
Individual therapy	46	4.07	80
Elder services	7	1.57	14
Information/referral services (e.g., United Way resource hotline)	12	1.75	17
Pastoral counseling	34	3.47	65
School-based services	12	2.25	50
Books on grief and suicide	53	3.92	85
Hotlines	9	1.44	11
Church/religious organization	29	3.10	66
Psychotropic medications	32	3.37	69
Help from primary care provider	28	2.64	46
Internet resources	32	3.25	72
Substance abuse treatment	6	1.67	33
Advocacy organizations (e.g., AFSP, SPAN)	32	3.59	78
Couples therapy	16	3.10	69
One-to-one interaction with another suicide survivor	52	4.62	100

Note: [a]N = 63. Means are based on a scale of 1–5 (1 = not helpful; 5 = extremely helpful).

various resources for healing, along with their mean rating of helpfulness and the percentage of respondents who rated the resource as moderately to highly helpful.

Importantly, talking one on one with another survivor was viewed as at least moderately to highly helpful by all (52/52) survivors who used that resource. Similarly, participation in a suicide-specific bereavement support group was viewed as moderately to highly helpful by virtually all (50/53) survivors who used that resource.

Perhaps the most important findings from the study are those that demonstrated relationships between functional impairment and help-seeking behaviors. More than half the sample indicated that depression was a moderately severe or greater barrier to receiving support, and more than one third of the sample reported at least moderately severe difficulties with finding resources or having resources available to them. Furthermore, the participants who reported the highest levels of functional impairment were those who met diagnostic criteria for complicated grief, reported the highest levels of psychological distress (e.g., depression, guilt, anxiety, anger), and reported very high levels of social isolation and withdrawal from family and friends. These individuals were also the participants who viewed books and Internet sites as particularly effective while simultaneously reporting considerable barriers to finding other resources.

☐ Implications for Intervention Programs

In this review of studies on perceived survivor needs, there are several convergences that are worth noting. As noted in "Risk Associated With Exposure to Suicide" (Chapter 1), the data suggest that as a group, suicide survivors are a significantly distressed population, one that reports a high and persistent degree of psychological symptoms after the suicide. Of note are trauma-related symptoms that many survivors describe as particularly disturbing and for which they would like professional assistance. This symptomatology suggests that all suicide survivors should be screened for PTSD as well as other anxiety and depressive disorders that appear to be common sequelae of the experience. Likewise, survivors will often need skilled professional help to deal with and find some relief from these trauma-based symptoms (see Chapter 9).

Moreover, the data make clear that the experience of losing a loved one to suicide can be seriously disruptive of social connections, both within the family unit and with the larger social network. It appears that survivors seek help from their closest associates but also encounter strain in these relationships as a result of the suicide. These social disruptions may be the consequence of many factors, including the "grief overload" that happens when all members of a family are grieving the loss simultaneously and are unable to be available in usual ways to provide support. Another likely factor is the stigmatization that has surrounded psychiatric disorders and suicide for centuries. This process of stigmatization may include the withdrawal of some persons in the network who blame the survivors for the suicide or see them as somehow "tainted" by the death. However, it is equally important to note that survivors may self-stigmatize (Dunn & Morrish-Vidners, 1987) and withdraw from potentially supportive interactions with others out of a belief that they will be judged negatively as a result of the suicide. Lastly, there is great social ambiguity around the "rules" of social interaction with survivors. Because suicide is a stigmatized and relatively low-frequency death, many people are likely to be uncertain about how to behave "appropriately" with survivors. They may, therefore, withdraw from the bereaved due to the social awkwardness created by the death and resulting bereavement (K. Dyregrov & A. Dyregrov, 2008). For example, friends and family may be unsure whether it is acceptable to use the word *suicide* when speaking about the death, whether to inquire about the reasons for the suicide, and simply whether the survivor wishes to discuss the subject at all. This ambiguity may lead to misunderstanding and avoidance on the part of both survivor and support person, thereby contributing to the increase in social strain and isolation that seems to occur for many survivors after a suicide.

Underlying all of these problems of social disruption is the experience of what Neimeyer and Jordan (2001) have termed the *empathic failure* inherent in disenfranchised grief. Empathic failure in the context of disenfranchised grief is the inability of one person or group to understand and empathize with the internal experience of another person who is grieving. The research reviewed here suggests that—whether accurate or not—survivors often feel that others who have not lived through the suicide of a loved one cannot fully understand what the survivor is experiencing. By extension, then, most of these studies confirm the perceived helpfulness of interaction with other survivors in the recovery process. The most popular form of this contact is through participation in face-to-face survivor support groups (Cerel, Padgett, Conwell, & Reed, 2009), but this is not the only type of survivor-to-survivor contact that might be helpful. Other forms could include one-on-one individual interaction (whether through telephone, online, or face-to-face contact), participation in online support groups and electronic mailing lists, and even *bibliotherapy* (involving the personal narratives of other survivors). As popular as survivor support groups are, it is important to note a caveat about this apparently salutatory impact of contact with other survivors. Most of these studies on survivor needs have drawn their convenience samples from survivors who are already attending support groups, and hence they may represent people for whom survivor-to-survivor contact is particularly helpful. We simply do not know enough about the needs of survivors who do not choose to participate in these types of contact with other survivors or who try them only briefly and find them unsatisfactory (Cerel et al., 2009). As we discuss in Chapter 33 of this book, there is a great need for community-based longitudinal research with all survivors after a suicide, not simply with convenience samples of people who are currently participating in survivor support groups.

Finally, these studies suggest that support services for survivors may be inadequate in meeting the survivors' needs. The data make clear that survivors often find that there are no services available to them, or when they do exist, they are difficult to locate in a timely fashion. Moreover, survivors are often severely depressed and traumatized in the initial stages of their grief, and thus a health care delivery model that requires survivors to mobilize themselves to locate and access services at this exceedingly difficult time may be an unrealistic expectation. Rather, Campbell and colleagues have argued forcefully for an *active postvention model*—one that provides proactive outreach to new survivors and facilitates their ability to access the services they need when they need them (Campbell, 1997; Campbell et al., 2004; Cerel & Campbell, 2008). We strongly agree with this recommendation. In addition, the data suggest that people bereaved by suicide may need different types of services at different points in their bereavement trajectories and that "one size does not fit all" in terms of services (see Chapter 34 and Cerel et al., 2009). Thus, interventions will likely need to be available for longer than just the short-term and crisis-oriented response that is typically offered in communities after a suicide, at least for people who are deeply affected by the death. Instead, these data imply to us that the ideal program of support services would allow for "multiple points of access to multiple types of services." All of these observations about the development of "infrastructure" for survivors are covered in more depth in Chapter 34, which focuses on recommendations for national programs for suicide survivors.

☐ References

Campbell, F. R. (1997). Changing the legacy of suicide. *Suicide and Life-Threatening Behavior, 27*, 329–338.

Campbell, F. R., Cataldie, L., McIntosh, J., & Millet, K. (2004). An active postvention program. *Crisis: The Journal of Crisis Intervention and Suicide Prevention, 25,* 30–32.

Cerel, J., & Campbell, F. R. (2008). Suicide survivors seeking mental health services: A preliminary examination of the role of an active postvention model. *Suicide and Life-Threatening Behavior, 38,* 30–34.

Cerel, J., Padgett, J. H., Conwell, Y., & Reed, G. A., Jr. (2009). A call for research: The need to better understand the impact of support groups for suicide survivors. *Suicide and Life-Threatening Behavior, 39,* 269–281.

de Groot, M. H., de Keijser, J., & Neeleman, J. (2006). Grief shortly after suicide and natural death: A comparative study among spouses and first-degree relatives. *Suicide and Life-Threatening Behavior, 36,* 418–431.

Dunn, R. G., & Morrish-Vidners, D. (1987). The psychological and social experience of suicide survivors. *Omega: Journal of Death and Dying, 18,* 175–215.

Dyregrov, K. (2002). Assistance from local authorities versus survivors' needs for support after suicide. *Death Studies, 26,* 647–668.

Dyregrov, K. (2003). *The loss of a child by suicide, SIDS, and accidents: Consequences, needs, and provisions of help.* Bergen, Norway: University of Bergen.

Dyregrov, K., & Dyregrov, A. (2008). *Effective grief and bereavement support: The role of family, friends, colleagues, schools, and support professionals.* Philadelphia, PA: Jessica Kingsley Publishers.

Feigelman, W., Gorman, B. S., Beal, K. C., & Jordan, J. R. (2008). Internet support groups for suicide survivors: A new mode for gaining bereavement assistance. *Omega: Journal of Death and Dying, 57,* 217–243.

Feigelman, W., Gorman, B. S., & Jordan, J. R. (2009). Stigmatization and suicide bereavement. *Death Studies, 33,* 591–608.

Feigelman, W., Gorman, B. S., & Jordan, J. R. (2007). [Survivors Child Loss Survey]. Unpublished data.

Feigelman, W., Jordan, J. R., & Gorman, B. S. (2009a). How they died, time since loss, and bereavement outcomes. *Omega: Journal of Death and Dying, 58,* 251–273.

Feigelman, W., Jordan, J. R., & Gorman, B. S. (2009b). Personal growth after suicide loss: Cross-sectional findings suggest growth after loss may be associated with better mental health among survivors. *Omega: Journal of Death and Dying, 59,* 181–202.

Gray, M. J., & Prigerson, H. G. (2004). Conceptual and definitional issues in complicated grief. In B. T. Litz (Ed.), *Early intervention for trauma and traumatic loss* (pp. 65–84). New York, NY: Guilford Press.

Jordan, J. (2001). Is suicide bereavement different? A reassessment of the literature. *Suicide and Life-Threatening Behavior, 31,* 91–102.

Jordan, J., & McMenamy, J. (2004). Interventions for suicide survivors: A review of the literature. *Suicide and Life-Threatening Behavior, 34,* 337–349.

Lichtenthal, W. G., Cruess, D. G., & Prigerson, H. G. (2004). A case for establishing complicated grief as a distinct mental disorder in *DSM-V. Clinical Psychology Review, 24,* 637–662.

McIntosh, J. L. (2003). Suicide survivors: The aftermath of suicide and suicidal behavior. In C. D. Bryant (Ed.), *Handbook of death & dying, Vol. 1* (pp. 339–350). Thousand Oaks, CA: Sage Publications.

McMenamy, J. M., Jordan, J. R., & Mitchell, A. M. (2008). What do suicide survivors tell us they need? Results of a pilot study. *Suicide and Life-Threatening Behavior, 38,* 375–389.

Mitchell, A. M., Sakraida, T., Grabiak, B., & Barton, K. (2005, April). An investigation of suicide survivors' perceptions of bereavement services. *Proceedings of the 38th Annual American Association of Suicidology Conference: Partnerships for Change: Advancing Suicide Prevention Services and Practices,* American Association of Suicidology (AAS), Broomfield, CO.

Myers, M. F., & Fine, C. (2007). Touched by suicide: Bridging the perspectives of survivors and clinicians. *Suicide and Life-Threatening Behavior, 37,* 119–126.

Neimeyer, R. A., & Jordan, J. R. (2001). Disenfranchisement as empathic failure: Grief therapy and the co-construction of meaning. In K. J. Doka (Ed.), *Disenfranchised grief: New directions, challenges, and strategies for practice* (pp. 95–118). Champaign, IL: Research Press.

Prigerson, H. G., & Maciejewski, P. K. (2005). A call for sound empirical testing and evaluation of criteria for complicated grief proposed for *DSM-V. Omega: Journal of Death and Dying, 52,* 9–19.

Provini, C., Everett, J. R., & Pfeffer, C. R. (2000). Adults mourning suicide: Self-reported concerns about bereavement, needs for assistance, and help-seeking behavior. *Death Studies, 24,* 1–19.

Sveen, C.-A., & Walby, F. A. (2008). Suicide survivors' mental health and grief reactions: A systematic review of controlled studies. *Suicide and Life-Threatening Behavior, 38,* 13–29.

CHAPTER

Guidelines for Postvention Care With Survivor Families After the Suicide of a Client[1]

Vanessa L. McGann, Nina Gutin, and John R. Jordan

Hopefully, our ability to identify and to empathically connect with other survivors helps us to simultaneously heal ourselves as we endeavor to help others.

C. Fine & M. Myers
Suicide Survivors: Tips for Health Professionals, 2003

It is estimated that at least one third of the roughly 30,000 annual suicide victims in the United States have had contact with mental health providers within a year of the suicide, many of them being in active treatment

[1] The authors gratefully acknowledge the following people for their careful reviews and helpful suggestions for this manuscript: David Browning, LICSW; Carla Fine; Eric Harris, EdD, JD; Michael Myers, MD; Robert Simon, MD; and Skip Simpson, JD.

(Luoma, Martin, & Pearson, 2002). Thus, approximately 10,000 U.S. clinicians per year face the loss of someone with whom they have worked, often intimately and intensively. Given these staggering numbers, there has been surprisingly little written for clinicians, not only on the psychological aftereffects of suicide in general but also on their roles and responsibilities toward the surviving family after such a devastating event. There has been almost no systematic research regarding the costs and benefits, either legally or emotionally, of clinicians and families communicating with one another after a death to suicide.

After a suicide, it is very common for family members to wish to discuss questions and concerns about their loved one with the treating clinician. As noted in previous chapters, it is also very common for survivors to have multiple questions about the whys and hows around the suicide, and many hope that their loved one's clinician can provide answers to these questions. However, families are often unsure as to whether contact is "allowed," or they wait for contact to be initiated by the treating clinician. Clinicians, in turn, are often concerned about how the family will react to them, the constraints of confidentiality, and the prospect of a lawsuit. Clinicians can also feel unprepared for contact with survivors, confused about their responsibility to provide follow-up care to the surviving family, and overwhelmed with their own complex feelings about the suicide (see Chapter 5). Often, for both surviving families and clinicians, communication after a suicide is limited and stilted, if indeed communication occurs at all.

Is contact with the surviving family legal? Ethical? Can it be therapeutic? We believe that the answers are yes, yes, and yes—given certain guidelines, clinical acumen, and care. However, the issues implicit in these questions are complex, and the recommendations coming from agencies and/or legal consultants may seem confusing if not contradictory or overly simplistic. In addition, a clinician's mental clarity and judgment around postvention issues may be affected by his or her own grief around the loss of the client, as noted in Chapter 5. Thus, the more aware and educated clinicians can become in relation to these issues, the more likely they are to play a positive role in an optimal outcome, both for families and for themselves.

After the suicide of a client, the clinician must walk a fine line. The goals of communication with the family should be to honor the deceased, to help surviving family members with their loss, to minimize legal risk, and to meet the clinician's own emotional needs to pay respects to his or her client. Keeping each of these goals in mind without allowing any of them to eclipse the others can be difficult, especially when the clinician is often coping with his or her own shock and grief. There may be times or circumstances in which some of these goals appear to be in conflict.

Often, there may be no clear choice or course of action. In this chapter, our goal is to highlight relevant aspects of this complex situation so that a clinician placed in this position can find a way to orient him- or herself when making the necessary but difficult decisions.

In this chapter, we explore the legal, ethical, and therapeutic issues involved in contact with family members after a suicide; highlight pertinent literature and research in this area; and offer general principles to keep in mind when planning outreach to and interventions with family members (although some suggestions and topics are specific to postvention, many points may also pertain to contact with families after a serious suicide attempt; see Chapter 3). To the extent that clinicians are knowledgeable about their legal and ethical responsibilities, trained in the repercussions of a suicide, and supported (both professionally and emotionally) by their institutions and colleagues, they can have a much easier time negotiating decisions in the days, weeks, and months following such a loss. In addition, they can potentially help themselves as well as the family survivors by offering timely and appropriate postvention care. Conversely, as C. Campbell and Fahy (2002) state, "[T]he reluctance of the profession as a whole to address systematically the issues that arise in the aftermath of patient suicide has far-reaching implications for mental health professionals, the families of patients who have committed suicide, and, of course, the patients themselves" (p. 44).

In this chapter, we also present a series of postvention guidelines that parallel a contemporary trend in medicine regarding the handling of poor outcomes and medical error, where greater transparency and more active involvement with a family on the part of the doctor is considered the most beneficial stance to take for family and doctor alike (Garbutt et al., 2007; Waterman et al., 2007).

☐ Considerations in Postvention

Legal Issues

In considering legal issues, hospitals and agencies seem to vary widely in their approach to postvention guidelines, if indeed they have guidelines at all.[2] Knowing and adhering to these guidelines can have positive legal ramifications. In contrast, consider a suicide that occurs in private

---

[2] This section on legal issues pertains to U.S. law; other countries may differ in their approach. Readers should investigate the laws of their individual countries regarding rules of confidentiality.

practice: Although there are no set guidelines to which the clinician must adhere, consultation with a lawyer can help guide one's actions in regard to the family and especially may help if litigation does occur. In general, it is wise to be familiar with all state and agency regulations that may contain restrictions that affect the specific circumstances with which the clinician is dealing. However, there is often much ambiguity around the issues of suicide postvention in the legal arena, and any actions should also be informed by consideration of how the family may react to one's interventions.

Before reviewing salient legal issues regarding postvention, it is important to state that the best protection against litigation after a suicide takes place is what the clinician does before it occurs. When working with clients at risk of suicide, it is often wise to actively include families in the treatment (with the client's permission), discussing with the families the potential risk of suicide (S. Simpson, personal communication, October 2009). In addition, regular peer or supervisory consultations as well as careful assessments of suicidality, a clinically sound rationale for and implementation of all interventions, and diligent documentation of these actions will go a long way toward demonstrating that the clinician has met the prevailing standards of care for professionals in their discipline (Bongar, 2002). The decision of a plaintiff's attorney to take on and potentially win a case of negligence or malpractice will be greatly influenced by the facts about what the clinician has done in the treatment before the suicide (S. Simpson, personal communication, October 2009). Whether consultations have been sought and assessments have been well documented before a suicide, a common first reaction upon hearing of a client's self-inflicted death is to worry about litigation. There is often much confusion about the scope of confidentiality regarding the content of the client's sessions and treatment history, the therapist's own verbal reactions to the suicide, and the hospital's or agency's policies in the aftermath of a suicide. What follows is a brief and general overview of the legal issues that generally arise for clinicians in relation to a client's family. Again, because some of the legal issues vary from agency to agency, state to state, and nation to nation, the clinician should speak with any institution involved in the client's care; contact their malpractice carrier; and seek legal counsel, as necessary, as soon as possible after hearing about the suicide. Indeed, as Simpson (S. Simpson, personal communication, October 2009) notes, some malpractice insurance companies have a clause in their contract giving them the legal right to deny coverage if they feel that the clinician has acted in ways to hinder his or her defense.

Clinicians often have questions or misunderstandings about the confidentiality of a client's treatment. In the United States, a client's confidentiality extends beyond his or her death, and when that client dies, decisions regarding any and all disclosures can be made only by the legal representative of the client's estate. In most states, medical records can be released only to the decedent's legal representative, and permission to share records with third parties can be given only upon written request by that representative. This permission includes granting requests for information by the police.[3] In addition, it is not appropriate to disclose the content and theme of therapy sessions to family members or other individuals without the specific consent of the person who holds the legal power to authorize that disclosure.

Although legal mandates regarding a client's confidentiality might be straightforward, it is sometimes difficult to balance the family's need for answers with the clinician's need to protect the client's confidentiality, thereby potentially alienating family members. However, this problem is not qualitatively different from keeping confidentiality at other times in the therapy process. Usually, the clinician can help satisfy the family's need to understand the outcome without having to disclose potentially confidential information by (a) providing an explanation at the outset as to the legal and ethical reasons why confidentiality exists, (b) taking an empathic stance toward the family's need for answers, and (c) responding to their questions with understanding and nondefensive openness; these approaches can ameliorate antagonism or prevent an adversarial relationship. In addition, clinicians can help families become better educated about factors relevant to suicide in general, perhaps tailoring this information to the specific context of the client (e.g., factors involved in adolescent suicide when the deceased was an adolescent). Also, there may be times when following the letter of the law may actually antagonize or cause more harm to a family member than disclosing certain impressions and information, so clinical judgment must still be used. For instance, telling an upset and agitated mother that she has to wait until she comes to the clinician's office to sign a consent form before the therapist can talk to another family member with whom she urgently wants the clinician to talk may be the wrong course of action from both a clinical and risk-management standpoint. We believe that the guiding ethical principle in all interactions with surviving family members after a suicide should be a wise and flexible combination of compassion, support, and adherence to the standard of "first do no harm" rather than a rigid adherence to a legalistic view of the situation. Genuine, honestly communicated concern for the well-being of the surviving family serves

---

[3] Many states do make an exception for coroners or state medical examiners. If someone asserts a right to access, it may make sense to consult an attorney or at least request that the person provide citations to the relevant statutes (E. Harris, personal communication, March 2009).

as the best deterrent to legal action against the clinician and facilitates the healing process of both the family and the clinician (see Chapter 5).

In addition to issues regarding the client's confidentiality, clinicians are often unsure about the confidentiality of what they say to others regarding their own reactions to the suicide. Often, after hearing of a client's suicide, a clinician will grapple with feelings of guilt and want to share their thoughts and feelings with friends and colleagues. However, many legal advisors (Bongar, 2002; Simon & Hales, 2006) point out that the only truly confidential space in which to discuss feelings of self-blame, guilt, and responsibility is a legally protected therapeutic, husband–wife, or attorney–client relationship. Thus, a clinician grappling with these feelings may do better to enter therapy than to discuss these feelings openly with friends, colleagues, and supervisors. Indeed, the American Psychological Association (APA) Insurance Trust, in its book *Assessing and Managing Risk in Psychological Practice: An Individualized Approach* (Bennett et al., 2006) cautions against engaging in self-recrimination in nonconfidential relationships after a suicide.

Unfortunately, the litigious era in which we live puts the clinician in a difficult place. On the one hand, he or she may need to share the experience of client loss with others in order to feel less isolated, process thoughts, and grapple with strong feelings. As noted in Chapter 5, these are precisely the recommendations for survivors, including clinicians, who are coping with suicide grief. However, clinicians must also consider the need to protect themselves from potential legal ramifications. Spiegelman and Werth (2005) elaborate on this paradox and note that the fear of being subpoenaed if a lawsuit is filed needs to be weighed against the emotional and training needs of the clinician in order to ensure that optimal judgments and decisions are made at all times. In addition, Harris (E. Harris, personal communication, March 2009) points out that although the provider's pre-suicide behavior may figure heavily from a legal risk perspective, this is rarely true of the provider's postsuicide behavior unless it is very problematic.

A related issue involves the legal consequences of certain statements of condolence to the family. There is some confusion in the literature as to whether and what statements might be used against a clinician in a court of law. Strasburger (1990, as cited in Kaye & Soreff, 1991) suggests that a statement such as "I'm sorry this happened" is not an admission of responsibility and can often help to soothe and calm a family member. Certainly, statements expressing sorrow for another's loss are considered normal and appropriate in most contexts. However, Bongar (2002) cautions that any statement a clinician makes can be subjected to judicial scrutiny and, as such, suggests that statements such as "I am so sorry" or "I feel awful about this" should be carefully avoided. The law on these matters is changing; there is evidence that in the larger arena of adverse events and medical error, clinicians are being encouraged to be "fully compassionate" toward the family (D. Browning, personal communication, June 2009), but again, laws vary from state to state (F. R. Campbell, 2006). Thus, it is wise to consult with agencies and/or a legal advisor prior to speaking with the family. Notwithstanding any specific limitations on statements that could imply culpability—and, again, depending on the circumstances—heartfelt condolences and open acknowledgement of shared grief often decrease rather than increase a family's animosity (see literature cited in the paragraphs that follow).

A similar issue arises in relation to unpaid services and whether to bill the estate for sessions. Although some clinicians may feel uncomfortable contacting the family for the collection of fees for fear of inciting anger, not asking for payment for services rendered may imply guilt. Again, although there is no law stating that fees must be collected, actions should be considered from a risk-management standpoint. It has been noted that billing is more likely to cause animosity than not collecting is to cause risk (E. Harris, personal communication, March 2009) and that rigorous attempts to collect fees after a suicide are often viewed poorly by a jury (S. Simpson, personal communication, October 2009). Thus, it is wise to consider the level of animosity, the family's style, and their previous relationship to money and billing when deciding how formal or lax to be in the collection of fees. In addition, tact—such as including a compassionate note stating, "I am sorry to bother you with such mundane matters at this time, but I have enclosed my last invoice for you to take care of at your convenience"—may be received more warmly than a standard, impersonal bill.

Ethical Issues

Beyond legal mandates and cautions, confusion often arises as to the therapist's ethical responsibilities after a suicide. Before the death, the clinician's ethical responsibility is clearly to their client. As part of this responsibility and in forming a therapeutic relationship, the clinician attempts to be empathic to the client's needs and respectful of his or her decisions. For instance, the client may have expressed anger at his or her family or even a wish to have distance from them. In the aftermath of a client's suicide, when this same family approaches the clinician, the clinician may feel protective of the client or indeed angry at the family for their role in their loved one's struggles. Even when a family has had a positive relationship with the person who died by suicide, the clinician may feel conflicted about contact with the family, and ethical questions may arise such as "Who am I here to help?", "Who is the client now?", and "Beyond legalities, what do I owe to my client after their death versus what do I owe to their family?".

Sometimes, the client's feelings and intentions are clear, as in the following example:

> A week or so after his death, I got a call from the mother, asking me if I would consider speaking at her son's funeral. I wasn't really sure how to handle this. A few days later, I received a letter from my deceased patient. It read "Forgive me, I couldn't go on. And please, look after my mom." Thus, my decision as to whether or not to speak at the funeral was made. The mother chose to make our relationship known, and beyond that, I didn't break confidentiality. I just spoke generally about his courage and struggles, and commented on what a special man he was to me. I believe, in this case at least, my decision benefited all involved. (M. Myers, personal communication, June 2009)

However, often the feelings of the deceased are not so clear, and the clinician needs to think through how to weigh the needs of the client, the family, and him- or herself. This issue is explored further in a later subsection, "Treating the Family."

Therapeutic Issues

In addition to legal and ethical decisions involved in one's postvention response, there are myriad therapeutic issues that arise when considering the extent of contact with the surviving family. Notifying the family of a death, attending a funeral, speaking at a funeral, writing a condolence card, meeting with the family, and educating the family—as well as working with the family, making referrals, and checking on their progress—all have the potential to be either therapeutically harmful or helpful.

Consider these two contrasting composite vignettes.

> After my daughter died, I felt like I wanted to understand everything about her last days, hours, and moments. I was like a detective on a mission to understand where she was and what she was thinking; anything to get close to her. When I met with her therapist, I was taken aback by how withholding and frightened

he was. He kept acting like I was looking for someone to blame. It never occurred to me to blame anyone, not even my daughter. But his stance made me angry at him and made me more guilty as well, wondering what he was hiding.

My husband's therapist contacted me right away, and told me to come see her. The next day, we spent over an hour together and met again after the hospital review and the autopsy. She summarized the findings and helped me with all the jargon. It was clear to me that she was deeply affected by this. We talked about many things—about me, my children, about my husband's struggles and all of the many emotions I had. She made it clear that I could call her again if I needed to, but she also suggested support groups as well as a trustworthy and talented colleague of hers that I might want to see in the future to help with my own mourning. I will never forget how much her presence helped in those first weeks.

As the literature cited in the following paragraphs shows, the way in which communication with the family is approached and handled can make an enormous difference in the grief journeys of both family and clinician alike.

☐ Review of the Literature on Postvention

Broadly stated, the types of postvention strategies suggested in the literature reflect two seemingly opposing schools of thought regarding contact with family after a suicide. With regard to the need to protect oneself legally, ethically, or emotionally, these two schools of thought reflect two ends of a spectrum. Anecdotal evidence suggests that after a suicide, clinicians are often encouraged to be conservative and to err on the side of caution with regard to family contact, believing that this is the best strategy to protect the agency or clinician from legal actions. For example, Weiner (2005), in the introduction to her book, *Therapeutic and Legal Issues for Therapists Who Have Survived a Client Suicide: Breaking the Silence,* mentions hearing of an agency policy—allegedly based on guidance from the agency's insurance carrier—that forbade therapists from attending funeral services or having any contact with surviving family members. Eric Harris, a lawyer/psychologist who is the risk management consultant to the APA Insurance Trust, believes that this or similar policies are quite common and that, unfortunately, legal and risk-management advice often suggest that the clinician remain at a distance from the family survivors, regardless of the particulars of the case (E. Harris, personal communication, March 2009).

A contrasting viewpoint, and one that is reflected much more often in the literature, is that distance from family members only increases the likelihood of mistrust and animosity, thus increasing the likelihood of litigation. In this vein, writing for the APA Insurance Trust, Bennett and colleagues (2006) state that

> it may be clinically indicated to respond to an outreach from the family of the patient...when permitted by state law, you may discuss some of the general therapeutic issues with the patient's family, share your condolences, and try to give the family a sense of closure. Not only is this the humane thing to do, [but] it also reduces your risk of being sued if you are open, caring, and forthright with the family. (p. 170)

The literature suggests that there are many actions a clinician can take in the aftermath of a suicide to reduce the likelihood of animosity leading to litigation. For example, some authors urge quick initial contact because it has been shown that early help and support reduce the displacement of anger onto the psychiatrist (Bongar, 2002; Ruben, 1990). It has also been noted that depending on facts and circumstances, and with the permission of the family, attending a funeral is often very much appreciated and in no way implies guilt (Kaye & Soreff, 1991). In contrast, when clinicians do not initiate contact, many commentators believe that families can feel disappointed, angry, rejected, and blamed (C. Campbell & Fahy, 2002; Davis & Hinger, 2005; Van Dongen, 1993), thus increasing the risk of litigation (Bongar, 2002; Peterson, Luoma, & Dunne, 2002). In addition, many authors suggest that speaking candidly to a family is the best policy (Bongar, 2002; F. R. Campbell, 2006). Indeed, although there may be legal restrictions on disclosure, Harris (E. Harris, personal communication, March 2009) points out that when walking a line between confidentiality and disclosure, he would rather defend a licensing complaint about a breach of confidentiality of a deceased individual that occurred when a psychologist was trying to help the family with its healing than enter into a malpractice suit precipitated by a detached or rejecting attitude on the part of the clinician. In summary, although a clinician may fear that contact with family members may expose one to blame, almost all of the literature emphasizes that compassion over caution is the best way to reduce the risk of litigation.

Beyond litigation concerns, contact with the family—when handled well—can also be therapeutically beneficial for both parties. For the family, appropriate information given by the clinician can help answer questions and increase the family's sense of connection to their loved one (Weiner, 2005). Sometimes, simply meeting the clinician helps the family broaden the picture of their loved one's personality, problems, and experiences. This additional insight into their loved one may help survivors to more realistically understand the factors that have contributed to the suicide while facilitating the necessary work of putting the suicide into a larger perspective (see Jordan, 2008, and Chapter 9 of this book). In particular, many families may not understand the role of psychiatric disorder as the foundation for most suicides. Thus, sensitively provided psychoeducational work with surviving family members around the multiple factors that contribute to suicide can be tremendously helpful in facilitating understanding of the death and reducing the sense of personal failure felt by family members (F. R. Campbell, 2006). Dunne (1987) also suggests that when a therapist acknowledges his or her own grief, the family feels relieved. In addition, families who receive information about the special nature of grieving after a suicide can be prepared for some of the likely relational strains that may emerge after the death (Cerel, Jordan, & Duberstein, 2008; Jordan, 2001, 2008). For instance, providing knowledge that the grieving process may be more complex and painful than other losses and that family members are likely to use different coping methods and do their grief work at different paces can mitigate later struggles. Indeed, this information may be vital to the survivors' recovery (F. R. Campbell, 2006; Kaye & Soreff, 1990; Scott, 1989). In addition, the clinician can be of help to the family by assessing each individual's abilities and making appropriate and timely therapeutic interventions, if indicated. Given the distress created by a suicide—and the small but increased risk of suicide in people who are survivors (see Chapter 2)—it is also appropriate to realistically discuss this risk with family members. An open discussion of the issue can address family members' fears about the possibility of another suicide occurring and can provide guidance and support for appropriate help-seeking for any family member who is feeling suicidal him/herself.

In contrast to the suggestions just discussed, if communication with family members is handled poorly and without adequate preparation, families can feel increased guilt, isolation, and confusion after contact with a clinician, in addition to increased anger and blame. They may leave a meeting with more questions and intensified bad feelings about their loved one's suicide and the quality of treatment of the deceased. The resulting anger, confusion, and disappointment can increase the chances of litigation and interfere with the surviving family's ability to mourn their loss.

Another poor outcome of meeting with a family can occur when the family feels compelled to help the clinician. This behavior is especially likely if the clinician has difficulty modulating his or her own sadness or guilt during a phone call or meeting. However, Ruben (1990) stresses that if a circumstance arises in which the psychiatrist feels unable to offer support, he or she should still make contact in order to refer family members to a colleague. Making the family feel obligated to extend an invitation to a funeral, to keep in contact, or to take care of the clinician in other ways is not appropriate and should be avoided. This is the reason why a clinician must make their emotions available but keep them sufficiently under their control before meeting with a family (Kalsow & Aronson, 2001). The clinician has to be in touch with his or her own feelings in order to be truly helpful to the family. The empathic connection that happens when the clinician allows him- or herself to feel, while also being able to modulate those feelings, is extremely helpful. However, either excessive constriction or excessive emotionality on the part of the clinician is likely to be unhelpful.

A meeting with the family that results in a poor outcome can interfere with the clinician's ability to mourn his or her own loss, as well. In their study, Hendin, Haas, Maltsberger, Szanto, and Rabinowcz (2004) found that even if the therapist did nothing negligent or wrong in the treatment, anger from the patient's family produced guilt and shame. Ruben (1990) also found that feelings of guilt in the clinician can increase when the family and/or legal representatives communicate anger or blame toward the clinician.

Finally, the literature also indicates that contact with the family may help the clinician (Kaslow & Aronson, 2001). It can help with his or her own sense of closure by giving the clinician a place in which to process the loss and share their sorrow with people who knew the patient in a different but intimate way (Grad & Michel, 2005). If he or she is invited, attending a funeral may be one of the few public rituals in which a clinician can take part to help with saying good-bye. When done well, meeting with the family can increase a clinician's sense of safety regarding future litigation and can thus offer tremendous emotional relief. It may also help to provide missing details about the client's life and give the clinician a new perspective on that client's struggles and suicide. In fact, contact with families has often been cited as being more helpful to the clinician's grief process than is contact with colleagues or involvement in psychological autopsies (Kaslow & Aronson, 2001; Rycroft, 2005). In summary, although anecdotal, the literature suggests that when clinicians are prepared and initiate contact with families, positive outcomes are often achieved for all involved.

☐ Recommendations and Guidelines

We have several recommendations for approaching a family following a suicide.[4] These recommendations are based on three overarching principles:

1. Knowledge and preparation are essential, and nothing should be done in haste.

2. Each case or situation is different and should be approached with individual, historical, and cultural differences in mind.

3. When in doubt, err on the side of empathically based compassionate outreach when deciding on what level of involvement to have with a family.

Knowledge and Preparation: Don't Do This Alone

As previously stated, it is essential that clinicians contact their malpractice carriers, speak with any institution involved in their client's care, and seek legal consultation (as indicated) as soon as possible after hearing about the suicide. In addition to providing vital information, these consultations can provide additional support, as many clinicians feel relief at knowing what may lie ahead for them and less alone in their journey after they hear that others have gone through it before.

It is also helpful—if not essential—to seek out a trusted colleague in order to conduct a thorough case review. This can be done in addition to an agency-led psychological autopsy, especially if the autopsy was brief,

---

[4] We would like to acknowledge the four major postvention guidelines that have been published to date, all of which we have heavily incorporated into our thinking. We refer interested readers to review them in detail: (1) Question, Persuade, Refer (QPR) Institute's *Postvention Guidelines for Agency Suicides* (Quinnett, 1999); (2) The Calgary Health Region of Canada's Suicide Response Initiative (SRI) pamphlet (Trew, Maloff, & Pryce, 2006); (3) "Aftermath of Suicide: The Clinician's Role" (F. R. Campbell, 2006); and (4) "The Psychiatrist's Role, Responses, and Responsibilities When a Patient Commits Suicide" (Kaye & Soreff, 1991).

was unhelpful, or left questions of any kind. In addition to going over the treatment to gain insights into the reasons for the suicide, the review can help contain anxieties and be an additional means of gaining support.[5] As part of this review, the clinician should thoroughly discuss issues pertinent to contacting the family. The clinician should prepare for the outreach by thinking carefully and critically about the circumstances of the suicide, the family's relationship to the deceased, their cultural values, and their familiarity with the clinician. This examination of the cultural, historical, and emotional issues—as well as the clinician's previous contact with the family—should help in developing a detailed plan for outreach.

We strongly recommend that clinicians seek out other well-informed supervisors, mentors, and colleagues for personal support, as well. If communication with others must be limited because of legal concerns, personal therapy can be vital.[6] It is difficult to overemphasize the isolation that many, if not most, therapists feel after a client suicide (see Chapter 5). Having a knowledgeable and compassionate person who can listen without judgment or bias can be an essential component of the clinician's psychological recovery process. Therapists and colleagues who have themselves lost a client to suicide can be particularly helpful. Although the circumstances surrounding the suicides may be quite different, knowing that a colleague has also dealt with the shock, questions, fears, and need to cope can go a long way in containing anxieties and helping in the challenges ahead. Indeed, support is crucial in these circumstances; suicide is an occupational hazard, and clinicians need a way to feel the normal range of feelings but to also appreciate the normalcy of what they are going through (D. Browning, personal communication, June 2009). Also, these colleagues can help with broader questions that may arise about general clinical competence, professional identity, and professional or life choices. Exploring these and other issues can help clinicians feel more grounded and assured in their decisions.

Another person to consider involving is a cofacilitator to accompany the clinician when he or she meets with the family. Although some have suggested that a cofacilitator might be helpful if the clinician is not in sufficient control of his or her emotions (Ruben, 1990), others (E. Harris, personal communication, March 2009) caution that the presence of an outside person might be misconstrued by the family. We believe

---

[5] Psychological autopsies are not always protected under state peer review laws (E. Harris, personal communication, October 2009).

[6] Simpson (S. Simpson, personal communication, October 2009) also suggests that if, due to litigious reasons, confidentiality with colleagues is an issue, the lawyer can hire a nontestifying consultant as part of the legal team—and, as such, that consultant can hold privileged information.

that even when a clinician feels prepared to handle the situation alone, an extra person who has specific training in suicide prevention and postvention, as well as experience in responding to grieving families, has the potential to facilitate the meeting in ways that are beneficial to all. Of course, the choice to introduce an outsider should ultimately be decided based on the comfort level of the therapist as well as that of the family. Having a stranger present at a meeting has some potential to make those who are gathering feel more awkward, self-censoring, or, on the part of the clinician, infantilized or judged. However, if done well, a skilled and compassionate yet objective third party can facilitate communication, take care that the goals of both parties are met, offer information and perspective on factors related to suicide, and suggest resources and strategies for survivors about which the clinician may be unaware.

Compassionate Outreach—Initial Contact

Families should be contacted as soon as possible after the death, preferably by the treating clinician. However, if the clinician is too overwhelmed by grief, or concerned about his or her own guilt and defensiveness, a senior clinician familiar with the case as well as with suicide grief should make the call. Heartfelt condolences should be given, and an offer should be extended to meet with the family in person at some point in the near future and at their convenience. Given cultural considerations, one might also offer to attend funeral services, but if the clinician makes such an offer, he or she should underscore that this is being done primarily to comfort the family, not oneself (e.g., "If it would help you at all, I would be more than willing to attend the funeral—however, if that does not feel right, that would be fine as well."). If directly asked to attend services, the therapist should make every effort to do so. At the end of the call, the therapist should also be sure to leave his or her name and telephone number and an explicit offer to give any further assistance that is within his or her power to provide to the family.

Setting Up a Meeting

If the family wishes to have a meeting, the therapist should decide ahead of time whether he or she, another agency representative or colleague, or both should attend. This decision should be based on the wishes of the family, the therapist's comfort level, and the likelihood of animosity from the family (in some circumstances, having a third party present may be helpful; see previous paragraph). Usually, the meeting should take place in the therapist's office. If a larger or more comfortable place is needed, the therapist should ascertain this need ahead of time. If the family seems too overwrought or prefers that the therapist come to their home, then the therapist should honor their wishes. If there are divisions within a family that might be awkward or problematic, such as ex-spouses, the therapist should offer to meet with people separately if the family feels that doing so would avoid unnecessary tensions. We recommend not charging for this initial meeting and planning to allow as much time as possible—a minimum of 2 hours. If subsequent meetings are to be held, the therapist should think this through and be clear with the family about any charges that they will incur for additional time spent with the therapist.

In the first few days after a suicide, the family may be in shock and may be unable to handle attending a meeting. In addition, they may be busy with funeral arrangements, religious practices, or condolence visits. Although early telephone contact with the family soon after the suicide is advisable, waiting 1 to 3 weeks to have a face-to-face meeting may be wise in that it will give the family time to organize their thoughts, feelings, and questions as well as to think about whom they might want to invite. This time can also be valuable to the therapist, as it can allow him or her to seek proper consultation and allow his or her own thoughts and feelings to settle. Of course, if a family wishes to meet right away, the therapist should make every effort to accommodate them. Also, if a psychological autopsy or review is planned, it might make sense to postpone the meeting until afterward (although the specific information in that review is likely to be privileged).

Conducting the Family Meeting

There may be many goals for a family meeting after the suicide of a client, some of which will take precedence over others, depending on the situation. These goals include hearing the stories of each family member, answering questions about the loved one (keeping in mind the fine line between discussing details of the client's treatment and protecting his or her postmortem right to confidentiality, as discussed previously—the therapist should think about what might be most helpful to the family's psychological well-being), processing the loss together, talking about and assessing how the family is coping, educating the family about unique aspects of survivor grief, and planning for ongoing therapy, including the provision of information about additional resources and referrals.

Knowledge about the family is helpful when planning a meeting. The therapist should spend time thinking about the family's possible questions and concerns regarding their loved one, the treatment, and their own futures. The therapist should try to anticipate questions about the patient's unique treatment history and diagnosis. If there is a hospital or clinic review and the information is not privileged, the therapist should plan to summarize the findings in a direct and straightforward manner, using as much detail as the family needs. The therapist can offer to discuss the findings with them again if they have any other questions in the future. Also, the therapist should plan for questions about the nature of suicide and impulsivity as well as suicide in specific populations (e.g., teenagers, the elderly, etc.).

It is advised to not necessarily expect expressions of anger but to still be prepared for them and to allow psychological room for them. In fact, the therapist should remember that anger is a reasonable, appropriate, and understandable reaction to the suicide of a loved one. The therapist should try not to become overly defensive or upset by expressions of anger or blame from the family. He or she should not try to overly rationalize or contextualize it. As a general rule, working to understand the emotional pain that underlies the expression of anger can help the therapist to reframe for his or herself—and, when appropriate, for the family—the source of the anger. Also, if survivors express guilt, it is important to realize that this reaction is reasonable, appropriate, and understandable as well. The therapist should not attempt to talk them out of this quickly, but rather, should listen respectfully and validate the normality of this response in survivors.

Suicide survivors can also feel quite ashamed, stigmatized, and alone. The therapist can help them by normalizing their reactions, letting them know that their grief may be more intense, prolonged, and complex than reactions to other losses that they have experienced, and that guilt and ongoing questions about "why" are very common. It is recommended that they be encouraged to get help or call the therapist in the future if they feel that their lives are becoming unmanageable. The therapist can tell them of resources available such as local suicide-survivor support groups, Web-based support groups, and literature (see the Web sites of the American Foundation for Suicide Prevention [http://www.afsp.org] or the American Association for Suicidology [http://www.suicidology .org] for suggested resources).

The reviews of the literature in Chapters 1 through 5 in this book make it clear that negative social and psychological sequelae after a suicide are distinct possibilities for survivors. Thus, it can be argued that making sure that the surviving family gets adequate attention and support is an ethical responsibility of the treating clinician. There are ethical and clinical advantages that accrue to assisting the family. These advantages include providing some information about their loved one, offering psychoeducation about suicide and suicide grief, making an assessment of family survivors' specific needs, and suggesting resources and/or referrals based on these needs. This assistance can also include referrals to other clinicians who are familiar with suicide grief, suicide grief support groups, and Web sites and books that aim to support survivors. The complicated question of whether the therapist should engage in ongoing treatment of the family is discussed next.

Treating the Family

Beyond the initial meeting with the family in the immediate aftermath of a client suicide, issues may arise when therapists are considering whether to provide longer-term grief counseling for surviving family members. This decision may be based, in part, on one's training and theoretical orientation, as those trained in a disease or individual model of treatment may take a hands-off approach in the aftermath of suicide (Hendin et al., 2004), whereas therapists trained in a systems model of treatment may feel more of an obligation to continue working with the family (Kaslow & Aronson, 2001, 2004). Reasons for these differing approaches may also be culturally driven, considering that in some countries, it is indeed common for the treating clinician to work with the family after a suicide (F. R. Campbell, 2006).

The relevant literature suggests that it may be tempting for clinicians to treat a member or members of the family following a suicide, and in some circumstances, this might be of value to the family (Weiner, 2005). However, as the therapist makes a decision about whether to work in an ongoing way with an individual survivor or family, he or she must be certain that this is the best choice for the family's grief work and not simply the best choice to meet his or her own psychological needs. More specifically, there may be many motivations at work that contribute to the desire to work with a surviving family member(s). For example, a therapist might wish to work with a family in order to learn details or gain insight into his or her client's decision. In addition, the therapist might feel that productive and successful work with the family could relieve his or her feelings of guilt or helplessness, particularly if the therapist feels that he or she was unable to help the deceased. It may also feel curative for the therapist to see the family come to respect and rely on him or her. All of these and other reasons for treatment may have more to do with the therapist's needs than the needs of the family.

Additional issues that may potentially compromise the ability to provide optimal family treatment in the face of a client's suicide include the therapist's considerations about his or her own grief reactions. As noted in Chapter 5, the loss of a client to suicide may disrupt the therapist's ability to access his or her best clinical judgment, particularly early on after the suicide. In addition, any unresolved countertransference issues, either in relation to the client or to family members, can potentially compromise the therapist's capacity for empathy and appropriate judgment.

Although there are many anecdotal accounts of successful treatments of family members following a suicide (Weiner, 2005), there may be as many or more unhelpful treatment experiences that have not been so openly reported in the literature. Some have suggested that if the family was not already part of the treatment, working with them in an ongoing way is a multiple relationship and might leave the therapist vulnerable to charges of unethical and unlawful practice (E. Harris, personal communication, March 2009). Thus, if the therapist chooses to do ongoing treatment with the family, we believe that he or she should do so only after consultation with an experienced colleague, with careful consideration of one's own grief and countertransference issues, cultural factors, family needs, and other possible referrals and resources for the surviving family. If, after this assessment, treating the family seems counterindicated, the therapist should explain the rationale for this decision and offer referrals to other clinicians who have expertise in suicide grief. The therapist can tell them that he or she thinks they might be better served by someone else in a way that minimizes any feeling of rejection. Even if therapists believe that they are capable of treating the survivors, it is wise to always offer the option to the family of seeing someone else, as some families may believe that they are obligated to work with the therapist.

Follow-Up and Assessment

If the contact and meetings have gone well, goals have been met, and no other intervention is deemed necessary, it is also advisable to check in with the family after some time has gone by. If it feels awkward to do this without prior agreement, we suggest checking in on an important date such as a birthday or the anniversary of the suicide. Because survivors often feel discomfort in discussing the loss with so many people around them, hearing from their deceased loved one's therapist can be a deeply moving and much-appreciated gesture (F. R. Campbell, 2006). However, if the family seems to have ambivalent or angry feelings toward the therapist or a desire to forget the part of their loved one's life associated with treatment and suicide, it is appropriate and helpful for the therapist to conclude contact with the family after the first meeting.

If ongoing treatment with the family has been agreed upon and is going well, that is ideal. If, on the other hand, it has begun to feel difficult or has reached a stalemate, the therapist might consider additional consultation or referring out. We believe that this can be done without a sense of failure or blame. With statements such as, "I believe the two of us together have really done a good job of looking at Matt's suicide. At this point, I am wondering if you would be best served by exploring some of these other issues with someone else," the time together can be seen as productive and honoring the life of their loved one while minimizing feelings of rejection or abandonment.

Of course, it is often difficult to judge the long-term positive or negative impact of one's actions. If a family says they are thankful for the clinician's outreach, they may be saying so out of politeness rather than real gratitude. However, without more research, we base our recommendations on our anecdotal experience of talking with many hundreds of survivors in support groups, individual therapy, and casual encounters. From them, we have heard the repeated desire for clinicians to err on the side of offering survivors compassionate and proactive attention rather than avoiding survivors out of a misguided "respect for privacy" or discomfort on the part of the clinician.

☐ Summary and Conclusion

In summary, we cannot emphasize strongly enough the idea that before a suicide ever takes place, training institutions and agencies should teach and disseminate information on the legal, ethical, and therapeutic responsibilities toward survivors as well as educate their students about the grief processes of clinicians and families alike (Schwartz, Kaslow, & McDonald, 2007). It is not a given that families will be angry with clinicians after a suicide. If training and education in this area were universal, we believe that many painful experiences in regard to clinician contact with families could be avoided, and significant assistance in the grieving process for family and clinician alike could routinely be provided. In addition, we suggest that therapists use an overarching principle of compassion over caution—as well as a careful consideration of the unique circumstances of each clinician/family dyad—when making decisions about the types and extent of family contact. If this is done, the grief process for both parties can be facilitated and oriented toward healing for all concerned.

Research in this area is so sparse that it has left a multitude of questions that need to be examined. Some questions that can be addressed in future research are as follows:

- Is there a relationship between the amount of clinician contact and the likelihood of a lawsuit?

- Are there characteristics of clinician response that are associated with fewer lawsuits?

- Is there a quality of family contact associated with better coping in the clinician?

- Are there cultures or family types that are more comfortable with involvement on the part of the treating clinician?

- Are there clinical populations, circumstances of a suicide, or treatment modalities of the deceased that would indicate that a family is more likely to benefit from more involvement on the part of the treating clinician (e.g., young vs. old, sudden vs. chronic, intensive psychotherapy vs. medication only)?

We recognize that it is very difficult to weigh the legal, ethical, and therapeutic issues in the aftermath of a client suicide; to strike the correct balance in content and tone; to feel confident in oneself; and, ultimately, to have a beneficial exchange with a family. However, we have worked in this chapter to delineate all of the pertinent issues so that a full appreciation of the factors involved in this important moment in time can be taken into account. We feel that the lack of guidelines and confusion about the law, ethics, and good clinical practice often lead to isolation, defensiveness, hostilities, and poor outcomes for both families and clinicians. In contrast, clear guidelines for responding, proper support for both the clinician and family, and a proactive outreach effort by a caring and compassionate clinician can do much to ease the suffering of survivors and facilitate the healing process for all who are affected by the loss of a client and family member to suicide.

☐ References

Bennett, B. E., Bricklin, P. M., Harris, E. H., Knapp, S., VandeCreek, L., & Younggren, J. N. (2006). *Assessing and managing risk in psychological practice: An individualized approach.* Rockville, MD: The Trust.

Bongar, B. (2002). *The suicidal patient: Clinical and legal standards of care.* Washington, DC: American Psychological Association.

Campbell, C., & Fahy, T. (2002). The role of the doctor when a patient commits suicide. *Psychiatric Bulletin, 26,* 44–49.

Campbell, F. R. (2006). Aftermath of suicide: The clinician's role. In R. I. Simon & R. E. Hales (Eds.), *The textbook of suicide assessment and management* (pp. 459–476). Washington, DC: American Psychiatric Publishing.

Cerel, J., Jordan, J. R., & Duberstein, P. R. (2008). The impact of suicide on the family. *Crisis: Journal of Crisis Intervention and Suicide Prevention, 29,* 38–44.

Davis, C., & Hinger, B. (2005). *Assessing the needs of survivors of suicide: A needs assessment in the Calgary Health Region (Region 3).* Calgary, Alberta, Canada: Calgary Health Region.

Dunne, E. J. (1987). A response to suicide in the mental health setting. In E. J. Dunne, J. L. McIntosh, & K. Dunne-Maxim (Eds.), *Suicide and its aftermath: Understanding and counseling the survivors* (pp. 182–190). New York, NY: W. W. Norton.

Fine, C., & Myers, M. (2003, September 17). Suicide survivors: Tips for health professionals. *Medscape General Medicine, 5*(3) [Online journal]. Retrieved from http://cme.medscape.com/viewarticle/460958

Garbutt, J., Brownstein, D., Klein, E., Waterman, A., Krauss, M., Marcuse, E., … Gallagher, T. (2007). Reporting and disclosing medical errors: Pediatricians' attitudes and behaviors. *Archives of Pediatric and Adolescent Medicine, 161,* 179–185.

Grad, O., & Michel, K. (2005). Therapists as client suicide survivors. In K. M. Weiner (Ed.), *Therapeutic and legal issues for therapists who have survived a client suicide: Breaking the silence* (pp. 71–81). New York, NY: Haworth Press.

Hendin, H., Haas, A. P., Maltsberger, J. T., Szanto, K., & Rabinowcz, H. (2004). Factors contributing to therapists' distress after the suicide of a patient. *American Journal of Psychiatry, 161,* 1442–1446.

Jordan, J. (2001). Is suicide bereavement different? A reassessment of the literature. *Suicide and Life-Threatening Behavior, 31,* 91–102.

Jordan, J. R. (2008). Bereavement after suicide. *Psychiatric Annals, 38,* 679–685.

Kaslow, N. J., & Aronson, S. G. (2001). The consequences of caring: Mutual healing of family and therapists following a suicide. In S. H. McDaniel, D.-D. Lusterman, & C. L. Philpot (Eds.), *Casebook for integrating family therapy: An ecosystemic approach* (pp. 373–383). Washington, DC: American Psychological Association.

Kaslow, N. J., & Aronson, S. G. (2004). Recommendations for family interventions following a suicide. *Professional Psychology: Research and Practice, 35,* 240–247.

Kaye, N. S., & Soreff, S. M. (1991). The psychiatrist's role, responses, and responsibilities when a patient commits suicide. *American Journal of Psychiatry, 148,* 739–743.

Luoma, J. B., Martin, C. E., & Pearson, J. L. (2002). Contact with mental health and primary care providers before suicide: A review of the evidence. *American Journal of Psychiatry, 159,* 909–916.

Peterson, E. M., Luoma, J. B., & Dunne, E. (2002). Suicide survivors' perceptions of the treating clinician. *Suicide and Life-Threatening Behavior, 32,* 158–166.

Quinnett, P. (1999). *Postvention guidelines for agency suicides: QPR Institute administrative directory.* Spokane, WA: QPR Institute.

Ruben, H. L. (1990). Surviving a suicide in your practice. In S. J. Blumenthal & D. J. Kupfer (Eds.), *Suicide over the lifecycle: Risk factors, assessment and treatment of suicidal patients* (pp. 619–636). Washington, DC: American Psychiatric Press.

Rycroft, P. (2005). Touching the heart and soul of therapy: Surviving client suicide. In K. M. Weiner (Ed.), *Therapeutic and legal issues for therapists who have survived a client suicide: Breaking the silence* (pp. 83–94). New York, NY: Haworth Press.

Schwartz, A. C., Kaslow, N. J., & McDonald, W. M. (2007). Encountering patient suicide: A requirement of the residency program curriculum. *Academic Psychiatry, 31,* 338–339.

Scott, D. (1989). *Coping with suicide.* London, United Kingdom: Sheldon Press.

Simon, R. I., & Hales, R. E. (Eds.). (2006). *Textbook of suicide assessment and management.* Washington, DC: American Psychiatric Publishing.

Spiegelman, J. S., & Werth, J. L., Jr. (2005). Don't forget about me: The experiences of therapists-in-training after a client has attempted or died by suicide. In K. M. Weiner (Ed.), *Therapeutic and legal issues for therapists who have survived a client suicide: Breaking the silence* (pp. 35–57). New York, NY: Haworth Press.

Trew, M., Maloff, B., & Pryce, C. (2006). *Calgary Health Region's caregiver response after suicide: Supporting families, clinicians, staff, co-patients and communities.* Calgary, Alberta, Canada: Calgary Health Region.

Van Dongen, C. J. (1993). Social context of postsuicide bereavement. *Death Studies, 17,* 125–141.

Waterman, A. D., Garbutt, J., Hazel, E., Dunagan, W. C., Levinson, W., Fraser, V. J., & Gallagher, T. H. (2007). The emotional impact of medical errors on practicing physicians in the United States and Canada. *Joint Commission Journal on Quality and Patient Safety, 33,* 467–476.

Weiner, K. M. (2005). Introduction: The professional is personal. In K. M. Weiner (Ed.), *Therapeutic and legal issues for therapists who have survived a client suicide: Breaking the silence* (pp. 1–7). New York, NY: Haworth Press.

CHAPTER 8

Organizational Postvention After Suicide Death

Lawrence Berkowitz, James McCauley,
Donna L. Schuurman, and John R. Jordan

The term *postvention* was coined by Edwin Shneidman (1972), the founder of contemporary suicidology, to describe planned interventions with those affected by a suicide death that would facilitate the grieving process. Over the last several decades, others have expanded the goals of postvention to include stabilizing the environment and reducing the risk of negative behaviors, most notably the risk of contagion (Brock, 2002, 2003; Centers for Disease Control and Prevention [CDC], 1988; Kerr, Brent, McKain, & McCommons, 2003; Poland, 2003; Underwood & Dunne-Maxim, 1997).

Many organizations, schools, and communities fail to develop prevention or postvention plans in advance of a crisis, leaving them with time, resource, and personnel constraints rather than the ability to compassionately and methodically implement a well-researched and documented plan. This may be explained, in part, by our society's reluctance to talk openly about death in general complicated after a suicide by numerous factors. Cultural and religious attitudes may contribute to stigmatization of the deceased, the mode of death, and/or family and friends left behind. The fear of suicide contagion or "copycat" behavior, particularly among youth, may constrain reasoned approaches. Concerns about the legal liability of the organization may also paralyze leaders into nonaction. Additionally, how we conceptualize the cause(s) of suicide informs how we respond to the bereaved and to those who may be at risk for suicidal behaviors. Although we may ask the question "Why?" about any death, there is a magnified and charged quality to the question following a suicide death. How we explain the act of suicide informs how we conduct postvention activities after a suicide. For example, some refer to the deceased as "one who chose to end his/her own life" (Underwood & Dunne-Maxim, 1997, p. 31) or one who made a poor choice (Poland, 2003). What is often not emphasized is that psychiatric disorders interfere with the functioning of the brain, thereby impairing the individual's ability to make clear choices. With these issues in mind, this chapter will examine a variety of factors that present challenges to providing comprehensive postvention in organizational, school, and community settings; describe several controversies relating to efforts to articulate plans for postvention; and propose universal tasks to guide postvention in these varied settings.

Given the challenges already identified, along with a dearth of reliable research and conflicting conclusions among professionals, it is not difficult to see why some conclude that a "safe response" to suicide may be "no response." This, however, is a mistake with potentially serious consequences. Those grieving a suicide death often receive less social support for their loss, leading to more isolation (Cvinar, 2005; Farberow, Gallagher-Thompson, Gilewski, & Thompson, 1992; Sveen & Walby, 2008). Not dealing openly with suicide death also perpetuates the stigmatization of mental illness. To paraphrase Shneidman (1972), we strongly agree with the idea that good postvention *is* prevention of future suicides.

☐ Literature Review

Research tells us that exposure to the suicide death of a peer may have deleterious consequences. Brent and colleagues found that adolescents exposed to the suicide death of a peer have elevated levels of depression, post-traumatic stress disorder (PTSD), complicated grief (CG), and traumatic grief when followed up 3 to 6 years beyond the death (Brent, Moritz, Bridge, Perper, & Canobbio, 1996; Melhem et al., 2004a, 2004b; see also

Chapter 4 of this book). Similarly, a large, national longitudinal survey of adolescents has shown that even exposure to suicide attempts increased suicidal ideation and attempts among friends (Bearman & Moody, 2004). Moreover, a recent Swedish study provided further evidence of the negative impact of a suicide death on others in the workplace. This population-based study of 1.2 million people from 1991 to 1999 in Stockholm found that men working in small companies (fewer than 100 employees) who were exposed to the suicide death of a coworker were 3.5 times more likely to die of suicide than were nonexposed men, whereas those exposed to a suicide within the family were 8.3 times as likely to die of suicide (Hedström, Ka-Yuet, & Nordvik, 2008). Further evidence of the potential risks of being exposed to a suicide attempt or suicide death was recently presented by de Leo and Heller (2008). Summarizing several large-scale, international studies, they related one finding that 54% of all subjects who had attempted suicide reported knowing at least one person who had previously attempted or died of suicide.

What might be the mechanism underlying this apparent influence of one suicide death on others? Some posit a social learning model (henceforth known as *modeling*) to explain why some who are exposed to suicide are more likely to die of the same cause. Madelyn Gould and colleagues have used strong epidemiological models to look at this phenomenon, known as *contagion* or *clustering*, and they found that 1%–5% of suicide deaths of adolescents and young adults may be attributable to such contagion—another potential risk of exposure to suicide (Gould & Kramer, 2001; Insel & Gould, 2008). Likewise, de Leo and Heller (2008), using data from studies in Australia and several European countries, provide robust statistical reports of correlations between nonlethal suicidal behaviors and exposure to peer and family suicide attempts or suicide deaths as evidence for modeling. Citing a related concept, Rubinstein (1983), in his studies of the high suicide rates among young Micronesians, proposed that "familiarity" with suicide leads to an acceptance by peers of the act. Although all the contributing factors of contagion are not well established, the risk factors—emotional illness, substance abuse, previous suicide attempts, loss, and family instability or dysfunction—for youth suicide during a cluster appear to be common to suicide in general.

Several excellent articles and manuals recommend postvention strategies for educational systems after a suicide death. These resources include, for example, guidelines for managing sudden loss such as suicide in schools (DiCara, O'Halloran, Williams, & Brooks, 2009; Kerr et al., 2003; Underwood & Dunne-Maxim, 1997) and comprehensive tasks delineated for people in varied roles (police, clergy, medical examiner, etc.) who respond to schools and communities following the suicide death of a young person (National Alliance for Mental Illness, New Hampshire [NAMI-NH], 2010). Although there is seemingly broad consensus that something should be done to support others following a suicide death, we know of no systematic evaluation of the benefits of postvention response to one or more suicide deaths in school, organizational, or community settings. What does exist consists of expert and practitioner consensus. This broad consensus points to several goals and challenges for postvention.

Goals of Organizational Postvention

What is it that we hope to accomplish by providing postvention? On the basis of the little that has been written on the subject, and upon our own growing experience in responding to organizations and communities, several goals guide our work. At the organizational level, a primary goal is to help restore equilibrium and functioning within the organization. Schools need to return to the business of educating and nurturing students. Businesses need to return to a functioning status in which employees feel productive and meaningfully engaged. In addition, at the individual and group level, postvention aims to promote healthy grieving and to commemorate the deceased for all who are affected members of the community. We want to provide comfort to those who are distressed; minimize adverse personal outcomes (depression, PTSD, CG); and reduce the risk of suicide imitation or contagion. To engage in such efforts, we must try to identify individuals who are most likely to need support. These individuals are likely to include—but are not limited to—people who were psychologically close to the deceased (e.g., friends and family members), people who were already depressed and possibly suicidal themselves before the death, and those who might psychologically identify with the deceased as being similar in lifestyle, values, or life circumstances. Particularly after suicide, it is also important to identify members of the community who may have felt responsible for the well-being of the deceased—and, by extension, for preventing the suicide. For example, teachers, coaches, and counselors in a school setting who were closely involved with an adolescent who has died of suicide are at risk. Likewise, in a workplace setting, supervisors and colleagues of a person who takes his or her life may feel particularly guilty and/or ashamed for not preventing the death.

Another goal of postvention is to use the experience as a "teachable moment"—that is, taking the opportunity to educate the organization and community about psychiatric disorders, contributing factors in suicide, and the availability of resources for getting help. Additional broad goals include increasing the organization's or community's sense of empowerment and mutual support for members of the community as well as ensuring the development of plans to prevent and/or respond to future deaths.

☐ Issues and Challenges in Postvention Planning

The challenges in implementing healthy postvention are significant. How do we appropriately remember and honor the life of the deceased—as we would if he or she had died from cancer or in a car accident—without (a) glorifying the act of suicide, thereby encouraging others toward imitation or (b) demonizing the deceased, while (c) simultaneously honoring the wishes of the family and (d) the needs of the bereaved community?

How do we balance promoting healthy commemoration while simultaneously reducing the risk of contagion? Concerns about imitation or contagion are valid (de Leo & Heller, 2008; Gould & Kramer, 2001; Hedström et al., 2008; Insel & Gould, 2008). Imitative suicide deaths may be carried out by an individual or may be part of a *contagion* (defined earlier) of suicides, which assumes either direct or indirect awareness of the prior suicide. *Clusters* are groups of suicide attempts or deaths that occur closer together in time and space than would normally be expected just by chance in a given community. Although the magnitude of this contagion or clustering effect tends to be relatively small (estimates are 1%–5% among teens and young adults; Gould, n.d.), it is widely believed that this class of suicide deaths is highly susceptible to the glamorizing or sensationalizing of the death. Some people also assume that many efforts to memorialize those who have died may inadvertently glamorize—or, at least, highlight—suicide as a method of dealing with significant life challenges. We agree that no postvention efforts should glamorize or sensationalize a suicide death. Unfortunately, it has been our experience that some efforts to avoid glamorizing or sensationalizing leave peers and families feeling that they are being stigmatized or even overtly punished as a result of the type of death.

The CDC (1988) states that the role of imitation or contagion is less well established than other risk factors such as depressive illness and a history of past suicide attempts. In summary, there is evidence to support the existence of a contagion effect primarily in adolescents and young adults, for whom the underlying mechanism is, most likely, modeling (Insel & Gould, 2008).

So, given these concerns about imitation by those who may be vulnerable, how do we handle the natural desire to commemorate a suicide death and memorialize the person who is suddenly gone? Although we provide a more specific discussion concerning the tasks of postvention in the section that follows, we believe that the principles that should guide the issue of memorials are (a) fairness in policy about handling all types of death in the organization and (b) a concerted effort to avoid an inordinate emphasis on the cause of death. Policies or guidelines should be created that not only guide the response to all deaths in a generally equivalent manner but also attend to the risks inherent to memorializing a suicide death.

Another tension sometimes experienced in providing postvention results from applying different frames of reference to the activity. Is the goal of the postvention to facilitate grief or to reduce trauma and prevent future suicide deaths? We contend that schools and organizations need to embrace both these frames of reference. It may be argued that following a single death, the balance might be tipped more toward facilitating grieving, but if a second death or additional suicide deaths occur, we believe that the balance must reorient toward reacting to trauma, facilitating prevention, and identifying those who might be at elevated risk.

When offering assistance to organizations, we often find a tension between the role of outside "experts" and the use of the organization's internal resources. Part of our role as consultants is to build and support the resources internal to the organization—after all, they know their constituents best. Fortunately, suicide remains a relatively low-incidence event. The school counselor or workplace human resources (HR) professional may come across this situation only a limited number of times, if at all. As external resources, we have more depth of experience but little or no relationship with those most affected by the loss. Many organizations wrestle with the question of whether to invite outside experts in to help with a postvention. As a guest in their space, we must tread gently as we support and enable the organization to follow the proposed guidelines and tasks (which will be articulated in the sections that follow) in a way that best fits the culture of its individual setting.

☐ General Guiding Principles for Organizational Postvention

For the purposes of brevity and clarity, the term *organization* as used here includes institutions such as schools, businesses, places of worship, military units, medical institutions, fraternal groups, and other settings in which a group of people have regular interaction with one another and a shared history of relationship with the deceased.

What follows is a list of some generally accepted guidelines for postvention plans, which should be considered within the context of the challenges and tensions identified above.

- Avoid oversimplifying the causes of suicide, murder–suicides, or suicide pacts. Emphasize that suicide is not the result of a single factor or event in the life of the deceased (e.g., the breakup of a relationship); rather, it is a complex and complicated interplay of events. Also avoid presenting the causes as inexplicable or unavoidable. Emphasize that there are alternatives to suicide when one is feeling distressed or hopeless, and make clear what resources are available for getting help. It can be useful to characterize the act of suicide as a serious mistake in judgment on the part of the deceased, in which their recognition of alternatives and resources for help was impaired by the psychological pain from which they suffered.

- Emphasize the correlation among depression, mental illness, and suicide, and stress that help or treatment is available. Reducing the stigma of mental illness and help-seeking behavior will enhance the likelihood that people will seek help, particularly if they learn the pathways through which help can be accessed.

- Avoid romanticizing or glamorizing someone who has died by suicide—that is, do not portray the deceased as a hero or having died a noble or romantic death (as in Romeo and Juliet). Conversely, do not portray the deceased as a villain or worthy of contempt. Emphasize that almost all suicide is associated with psychiatric disorder and the impairment in judgment that accompanies this disorder.

- Provide a structure that facilitates ongoing suicide prevention efforts (Gould & Kramer, 2001; Graham et al., 2000; Suicide Prevention Resource Center [SPRC], 2008). (More information about prevention efforts following a suicide death is included in the "Postvention Tasks" section that follows.)

- Discourage a focus on the method of the suicide, which is often the subject of gossip and sensationalization. Report the method factually (e.g., he hung himself), but emphasize that the important information is that the person mistakenly felt that he or she could not get help for his or her problems—when, in fact, help was possible.

Although there is significant agreement about these guidelines, there are also considerable differences of opinion about how to put these guidelines into practice. Previously mentioned articles detail postvention strategies for educational systems (DiCara et al., 2009; Kerr et al., 2003; NAMI-NH, 2010; Underwood & Dunne-Maxim, 1997), but very few articles address postvention strategies in other organizations: workplace, civic, athletic, religious organizations, and communities. Although the potential for contagion and a destabilized environment appears to be higher in the group aged 15–24 years (Gould, n.d.), a strong need for a postvention response occurs in many settings other than schools. A death or several suicide deaths can be devastating to a community and can undermine a sense of cohesion.

Postvention Tasks

Several universal tasks that are found in most effective postvention strategies can be used in school settings as well as many other organizations or communities. We recommend that these tasks be sequenced in the order in which they are presented in the subsections that follow.

Verification of Death and Cause

All responsible postvention efforts begin with verification of the death: who died, when, the circumstances, location, and whether or not the death was a suicide—that is, self-inflicted and apparently self-intended. Most officials—school superintendents, chief executive officers (CEOs), and community leaders—initially are swamped with information and rumors from students, parents, and colleagues, and are hounded by the press asking if they have heard that a given person has died. In an age of cell phones, social networking sites, and Twitter, responsible leaders should assume that much of the information will be inaccurate and that rumors will prevail. No official release of information should be distributed until the circumstances of the death have been confirmed by the appropriate authority: police chief, medical examiner, immediate family member. Even if a family member requests secrecy about the cause of death, it may not be possible to keep the circumstances a secret. In many municipalities around the world, the cause of death is public information, although in the United States, federal laws (i.e., Family Educational Rights and Privacy Act [FERPA] and Health Insurance Portability and Accountability Act [HIPAA]) take precedence. We suggest gently helping the family to think through the pros and cons of trying to keep the cause of death a secret—and the difficulty in doing so. If the family still does not want to disclose this information, then the institution must uphold their wishes. However, as Hollingsworth (2007, p. 53) notes, "[N]ot disclosing the cause of death as a suicide leads to confusion, rumors, speculation, decreases trust among staff and students, puts school supportive staff in the position of not discussing this openly with students, puts other students' parents in a position of not knowing how to support their sons and daughters, and increases the likelihood of contagion."

Coordination of External and Internal Resources

In the case of a school system, the superintendent or principal will immediately notify his or her crisis response team and plan for an initial meeting within hours or early the next day. Most crisis teams have written protocols delegating actions and responsibilities in the case of sudden traumatic death. Schools that have working relationships with local mental health agencies, neighboring school districts, and other local resources will often invite these partners to the crisis response meeting. Ideally, this will not be the first time that school personnel and community programs have met. Although some school systems are inclined to handle a crisis on their own with staff familiar to the students, these local resources can provide valuable consultation for school administrators and teachers, who may be unfamiliar with how to handle this devastating loss and who may, themselves, be grieving the death of a student. Nearby school systems can send additional counselors to cover students who are in acute grief, and the nearby school may also be able to provide backup to teachers and school staff who might want to attend the wake or funeral. Perhaps the most important reason for using outside resources is to ensure that school personnel who are on the front lines of postvention efforts are themselves being supported throughout the entire postvention effort.

When a death occurs in a business or other organization, it might be more difficult to identify and mobilize resources. A small business might have little experience with the death of a colleague, and death from suicide might complicate any response due to lack of knowledge about suicide and the stigma associated with it. The CEO—or his or her designee—may contact the HR director to obtain guidance and to strategize on how best to support staff. Mid- to large-sized companies typically have contracts with employee assistance programs (EAPs) whose staff members are usually well trained in managing sudden death or other personnel emergencies. EAPs often are on call as a valuable resource in the aftermath of a suicide death. Local mental health agencies also can provide this assistance to a business or civic association.

Another possible resource for an effective postvention plan may be a member of the clergy. Few professionals know more about grief and grief rituals than the clergy, and those who have been trained in suicide postvention and trauma are a potential resource to support schools and organizations. Unfortunately, many school systems and communities may be wary of crossing the line between church and state and do not use this potential resource. However, we (LB and JM, the authors) have had good experience working with clergy when they have been trained in crisis response, post-traumatic stress management, or suicide postvention (Macy et al., 2004; NAMI-NH, 2010). Local funeral homes may also be excellent resources for information and are usually willing to answer questions. The funeral director can provide specific information about what will happen during the wake and funeral. For many adolescents, this may be their first funeral, so knowledge about specific details can be extremely helpful: Will the casket be open or closed? Has the family decided on cremation or burial? Who will preside over the funeral? Are there religious rituals that can be explained ahead of time?

Dissemination of Information

The most effective strategy for providing known details of the death is a written statement that can be distributed to everyone in the school or organization and community. It should include factual information about the death and an acknowledgment that the cause of death was suicide; condolences to family and friends; plans to provide support for those affected; information about funeral plans, if known (or acknowledgment that the information will be provided once known); and any changes in school or work schedule during the upcoming days. It is also strongly advised that an announcement not be read over a public address system. Conducting this conversation in smaller groups (e.g., homerooms, work groups, team meetings) gives responders a chance to gauge individual and group reactions. When everyone in the community gets exactly the same information—teachers reading the statement in the classroom; e-mails to parents; a press release to the local media—then rumors will begin to subside.

Provide Support for Those Most Affected by the Death

Close friends, fellow team or club members, colleagues on the same work team, and neighbors in the community may have a particularly hard time and may need extra support for a period of time. Those individuals who need support might also include, for example, a colleague who recently argued with the deceased or a romantic partner who initiated a breakup. In schools, counselors will frequently follow the schedule of the deceased student; EAP personnel may want to spend the day being available to the deceased's shift or work group. A neighbor may host a gathering for families who live on the deceased's block. The emphasis in these activities is on mourning the loss. Although postvention counselors traditionally try to minimize discussions about the details and means of the death, trying to divert grieving friends and colleagues away from such discussion may be counterproductive. People struggle to make sense of the question, "Why did my friend/classmate/colleague/neighbor die by suicide?" and they will wrestle with that question for a very long time. Indeed, this question may be the lead-in to a "teachable moment," in which key points can be emphasized in discussions: Suicide is never the result of one thing but, rather, the "perfect storm" of multiple factors converging; one of those factors is almost always a psychiatric disorder. Important information to share includes evidence that 90% of those who die from suicide have an underlying depression, substance abuse problem, anxiety disorder, or other psychiatric issue that contributed to their deaths (Moscicki, 2001).

Identification of Those at Risk and Prevention of Contagion

After a suicide death, some attention must be devoted to identifying whether close friends or others in the school or organization might be at risk for suicide attempts or other risky behaviors. Those at risk could include individuals having a history of suicidal behavior or depression; a history of tragic loss or suicide in their family; peers who start to identify with the deceased even though the connection was quite remote; and students, coworkers, or staff who likely felt responsible for somehow contributing to or preventing the suicide. Generally, in a school, someone on the crisis team should keep a master list of the students and staff who are at risk. These individuals may need someone who knows them well enough to check in with them or their family. Most of those individuals identified will not need an immediate referral or evaluation but may be encouraged to ask for support and may be asked to identify who can be of most help to them if they are feeling scared, overwhelmed, or depressed.

Identification of those at risk is not a task for schools or colleges only. Some workplaces may have a high percentage of young employees or employees with traumatic histories. There has been little research on the potential for contagion following the suicide death of a coworker. However, as you will recall, the unique study from Stockholm (Hedström et al., 2008)—noted near the beginning of this chapter—demonstrated that there was a significant increase in the number of suicide deaths in smaller work settings following the suicide death of a coworker. Coupled with the finding by Crosby and Sacks (2002) suggesting that about 80% of suicide exposure occurs with the death of an acquaintance, rather than a family member, these studies (a) imply that exposure to suicide is statistically much more likely in the workplace or school setting than through the death of a family member and (b) support the need to attend to those who may be at risk in work settings as well as educational settings (de Leo & Heller, 2008).

Provide Opportunities for Commemoration

Although the original purpose of postvention activity was to facilitate grief (Shneidman, 1972), over the years, the focus of postvention activities has shifted to reducing the possibility of contagion. This goal has sometimes led to misguided efforts to maintain secrecy after a suicide death, including blaming or stigmatizing the deceased. Little effort has focused on facilitating healthy grieving as a necessary form of prevention. School, business, and community officials can take the lead in offering public condolences to family and friends, encouraging appropriate commemorative activities, and allowing flexibility in work or class schedules so that members of the community can attend memorial services. Generally, our experience has been that large, all-school events during the school day (requiring the participation of students) are not ideal. When commemoration activities and funerals are held after school hours, participation is voluntary, and it is more likely that parents may accompany their children or teenagers to the funeral or wake, a practice that should be encouraged. Supportive postvention activities in the workplace or community do not have to be highly formal events but might include activities as simple as providing meals, transportation, and other concrete ways of supporting the grieving families and peers.

There is considerable controversy about memorializing a student who dies of suicide for fear that glorification will lead to contagion. As mentioned previously, we believe that commemoration activities should be the same for any death of a student or colleague, regardless of the cause. The CDC (1988) discourages permanent memorials such as planting of trees and placement of benches in a student's memory. Our experience has been that memorializing students by encouraging and supporting suicide prevention activities of local or national organizations, raising scholarship money through activities, becoming involved in helping other suicide survivors, and so forth, are preferable to concrete, permanent memorials (Kerr et al., 2003; Poland, 2003). Encouraging such "mobilizing" activities is also consistent with approaches to helping survivors deal with the potentially traumatic experience of a suicide loss by supporting a sense of agency rather than helplessness (Brymer et al., 2006). When developing policies, it is important to ensure consistency of the response, regardless of the type of death. Similar questions arise about how to handle memorials in a yearbook or related publication. Again, the recommendation is to make it consistent with how any other death would be recognized and to make mention of those attributes and activities about the person that will be remembered rather than focus on the cause of death.

Provide Psychoeducation on Grieving, Depression, PTSD, and Suicide

The goals of this task are to provide individuals with an understanding of the grieving process as well as to provide education about signs and symptoms of depression, PTSD, and suicidality. For younger people who may not have experienced a prior loss, understanding that their reactions are normative may be comforting. Regarding education on the signs and symptoms of depression and suicidality, the underlying assumption is that we might prevent further suicide deaths by detecting depressive symptoms or suicidal tendencies in others or by helping individuals recognize such symptoms in themselves. Appropriate psychoeducation may counter such risks by reinforcing important social messages such as "suicide is a permanent solution to a temporary problem" and by encouraging adaptive coping and problem-solving strategies such as help-seeking. If, as postulated, familiarity with suicidal behavior as a coping strategy increases the risk of others modeling this behavior (de Leo & Heller, 2008; Insel & Gould, 2008; Rubinstein, 1983), then it is appropriate, in schools, to educate students and staff about other options for coping with difficulties. We recommend using a curriculum that has been determined to have best practice or evidence-based status (see the SPRC Web site: http://www.sprc.org) such as the Signs of Suicide Curriculum ([SOS]; Aseltine & DeMartino, 2004).

Although few interventions have been developed and tested for providing psychoeducation in a work setting, programs such as the United States Air Force Suicide Prevention program (Knox, Litts, Talcott, Feig, & Caine, 2003) may provide guidance. Similarly, a program such as Question, Persuade, Refer ([QPR]; Wyman et al., 2008) serves as an example of psychoeducation that may be provided in an occupational setting.

At the community level, psychoeducation about suicide and prevention can take place in a wide range of settings, with a goal of educating *gatekeepers*—those in the social network of at-risk persons—who are likely to recognize the warning signs of distress and refer the person for help. The Connect project (formerly called Frameworks) is an evidence-based approach to prevention of youth suicide that targets a wide range of gatekeepers (Baber & Bean, 2009; NAMI-NH, 2010). In our work in Massachusetts (JM and LB, the authors), we have provided trainings for community and civic organizations (garden clubs, senior centers, chambers of commerce, etc.), for interfaith clergy groups, and for parent groups. The range of gatekeepers for whom training can potentially be provided is limited only by the creativity of the trainers. For example, in one community, the suicide prevention coordinator attempted to gather the town's bartenders for training. Although we thought it was a clever idea, unfortunately, only one bartender came to the meeting, but it nonetheless demonstrates that nonconventional and "embedded" caregivers may be good targets for psychoeducation about suicide prevention.

Case Finding/Screening

Because we know that there is a possibility of copycat deaths or contagion, especially following a suicide death among adolescents or young adults, we believe that we have a responsibility to screen others for depression or suicidal risk. This imperative is bolstered by the 2007 National Youth Risk Behavior Survey (CDC, 2008) findings indicating that 28% of students met screening indicators for depression and 14.5% seriously considered suicide. Additionally, case finding is consistent with a public health approach to preventing an illness. In the case of schools, we use the Brief Screen for Adolescent Depression (Lucas, 2001), which includes two suicide-specific items. This tool is incorporated into the SOS curriculum (Aseltine & DeMartino, 2004), in which students are instructed to self-score and encouraged to self-refer for assistance if they reach criteria for possible depression or suicidality. In our work with schools, we include a few additional questions and ask students to identify themselves on—and then return—the screening tool. Any student whose screening meets criteria for possible depression and/or suicidality is seen for an onsite screening by a school adjustment counselor or mental health professional at the school that day. Parents are notified of in-person screenings, and recommendations are communicated to the parent/guardian. Our experience in schools following these education and screening programs is that approximately 5%–7% of students participating in screening are seen for an in-person screening, with a smaller percentage referred for further evaluation or counseling. Equally important as the direct reports of students about their personal status, we have experienced multiple instances in which students have used the screening as an opportunity to discuss concerns about a peer or other personal troublesome issues, such as domestic violence. Anecdotally, many students have commented that they find the discussion groups helpful and have asked why we didn't "do something like this sooner." Recently, we have begun characterizing comments written on the response cards as generally positive (found the groups helpful, felt that they had learned new material); generally negative (found it unhelpful, upsetting, or, as one student bluntly stated, "it was boring"); or neutral ("I already knew everything we talked about today"). In one mostly rural setting, 147 of 300 students who participated wrote comments. In that sample, 60% wrote mostly positive comments, 10% wrote negative comments about the program, and the remaining 30% were neutral. We will continue to use student feedback to help shape our programs in schools.

Screening for those at risk at a workplace is a more challenging undertaking. With the exception of the military or, possibly, a public safety employment setting, we assume that employers would agree that screenings for mental health conditions or suicidality must be voluntary. An online tool, such as that developed by Screening for Mental Health (2010) (SOS; see Aseltine, James, Schilling, & Glanovsky, 2007), is an example of an instrument that workers may be encouraged to complete, with recommendations to seek assistance depending on the screening results. When used, screenings in the workplace are often conducted by EAPs. Another consideration following a suicide death in the workplace is to ensure that managers are trained to recognize warning signs of depression and suicidality. Such action may lead supervisors to refer for help those employees who appear to be struggling with depression or other mental health challenges. The company's HR department should be involved in any organized training or referral efforts. Unfortunately, our experience coincides with that of others in the field in finding that managers are often reluctant to address depression or suicide prevention in the workplace. Perhaps those of us advocating for postvention in the workplace need to do a better job of (a) highlighting the potential lost productivity that may be associated with workers reacting to the suicide death of a coworker and (b) sharing the new evidence of potential for increased deaths when members of an organization are exposed to the suicide death of a coworker (Hedström et al., 2008). We understand that this reluctance is another manifestation of the larger cultural taboo about dealing directly with psychiatric disorder and suicidality.

Second or Subsequent Suicide

Depending upon the size of the setting or community, a second suicide death in a short period of time or within the same peer group may increase the risk that a cluster is developing within the community. Although it is our experience that many communities may wait until a third or fourth suicide to take action, we recommend beginning to form a *community coordinating committee* (CDC, 1988) following a second death. The role of a coordinating committee is to elevate suicide prevention to a community level and to include a wide range of school, community, and regional or state leaders in the prevention plan. Such a committee should include school officials, public safety officials, community leaders, local mental health agencies, local media, and clergy, and it should be linked to the state or regional coalition for suicide prevention as well as the state's strategic plan for suicide prevention (see, e.g., Massachusetts Coalition for Suicide Prevention, 2009).

The committee's responsibility is to develop plans for a response to any future deaths and to begin a plan for prevention in the community. Post-traumatic stress management (PTSM; Macy et al., 2004) is the model that has been used in several communities recently in Massachusetts to assist individuals and groups reacting to subsequent suicide deaths. In these communities, a wide range of community members are trained to respond to students, family members, and others. Additionally, coordinated plans and protocols are established for responding to suicidal ideation and threats noted in schools, organizations, young people taken into police custody, mental health centers, and so forth. In-depth training is provided for local mental health clinicians to improve skills for assessing and managing suicide risk using the best-practices curriculum developed by the American Association of Suicidology (AAS) and the SPRC (SPRC, 2008). State agencies or grants have provided additional clinical resources to the schools to assist with implementing prevention services as well as identifying, triaging, and consulting regarding students considered to be at elevated risk.

Linking to Resources

An important part of responding to any potentially traumatic event is linking individuals and groups to other resources for continued, local support as needed. Ideally, we will leave individuals, family members, and the school or workplace with a list of local mental health resources, including contact information for emergency mental health assessment. As noted previously, when multiple suicide deaths occur in a given locale, a crucial part of the response includes ensuring that the many local community professionals are collaborating according to a single vision and plan. Community coalitions should also be linked to state-wide and federal organizations that focus on suicide prevention and postvention.

Evaluate and Review Lessons Learned

Ongoing feedback should be sought from all involved in the postvention process: students, workers, those involved with implementing the plan, and management and local officials, if appropriate. Even if the postvention is a one-time event, plans should include follow-up support and the development of ongoing organizational and community structures to respond in the event of future suicide deaths. Plans should address potentially sensitive milestones such as graduation and anniversaries, and those occasions may again be used as opportunities to evaluate and review the process. If the postvention is a larger, ongoing project that involves a planning or organizing committee, the committee should build in periods for review and soliciting feedback from all constituents, and the results of the feedback should be built into the ongoing plan.

Develop a Systemwide Prevention Plan

Many school districts or communities who have a suicide death will respond to the tragedy determined to do anything they can to prevent further deaths from suicide. They may form a task force or a community coalition and begin looking at strategies for suicide prevention. Excellent resources exist to guide such efforts (see the SPRC Web site: http://www.sprc.org). A few strategies are common to most of these prevention efforts. First, identify and promote protective factors. In the case of a community-wide effort, part of the work of a school, workplace, or coalition is to identify and promote factors that are likely to mitigate further suicide deaths. The following list identifies protective factors that are associated with "lessened risk for suicide or suicidal behaviors across the lifespan," as identified by the Assessing and Managing Suicide Risk workshop developed jointly by the SPRC and AAS (SPRC, 2008, *Resource Sheet No. 5*, p. 2):

- Clinical care: Effective care for mental and physical health and for substance abuse disorders, positive therapeutic relationships for those having a mental health challenge, ready access to care, and support for help-seeking

- Family and community support: For example, strong connections to family and community, responsibility to children and pets, and support from medical or mental health relationships

- Resilience

- Coping skills

- Frustration tolerance and emotional regulation

- Cultural and religious beliefs that affirm life and discourage suicide

Some of these protective factors are easier to build and support than others. Workplaces, schools, and communities can all develop policies and practices that promote strong connections with family, workgroup, and community. Schools can include curricula that teach effective coping and problem-solving strategies, and sports and civic organizations can teach or encourage frustration tolerance. The demographics of suicide tell us much about which cultural groups have lower rates of suicide than others (see, e.g., http://www.sprc.org). Conducting future research into these differences and learning from these groups might help inform our interventions in organizational and community settings.

A second strategy for prevention efforts is means reduction. Reducing access to the methods by which suicide may occur is an essential component of postvention. The Harvard Injury Control Research Center has reviewed dozens of research studies demonstrating that under certain circumstances, decreasing access to lethal means of suicide actually decreases the suicide deaths in a given area (Harvard School of Public Health, n.d.). This is particularly true for reducing access to higher lethality means such as firearms (Marzuk et al., 1992). For example, information provided to parents of at-risk peers and students following the suicide death of a peer should include suggestions that families secure or remove weapons from the home. Similarly, families should be encouraged to purge their medicine cabinets (in an environmentally safe manner) of unused medications. Medication prescribed for individuals considered to be at risk should be provided in safe—that is, small—quantities. Similar precautions should be considered for other means—for example, with architectural and physical barriers on bridges and buildings. Balancing this recommendation, however, is the importance of exercising care to not draw excessive attention to a specific method following a suicide death.

☐ Conclusions

Although formalized postvention in schools and other organizations is recommended by many, few formal and comprehensive guidelines have been written to assist those who conduct the work. Moreover, as we have identified, the work is complicated by a variety of complex factors concerning beliefs about death and suicide that include the stigma associated with suicide; philosophical beliefs about why individuals die of suicide; and the unique "cultural" factors of a given school, workplace, or community. Thus, to be delivered effectively in a fashion that meets the needs of a particular organization, postvention must be seen as an active, evolving process that attends to the guidelines and principles outlined in this chapter. Yet, it must be done with the flexibility to acknowledge and respond to the variety of challenges raised by a suicide death.

How will we know if we have delivered postvention effectively? That question must be answered by those whom we seek to support: the survivors. Do they feel that they have been helped in the process of grieving? Have they been provided opportunities to commemorate the life of their friend/classmate/colleague in ways that feel meaningful and that the clinical community would consider to be safe? Have those who experienced trauma as part of the loss been helped to respond to the traumatic aspects of the loss? Has the organization found a way to be compassionate yet continue to advance their organizational goals? Have people in the community learned about suicide and the warning signs to help others who might be potentially at risk? Have we helped reduce suicide rates in a community? This last question is particularly challenging, as we know of no research that has investigated how long the effects of "familiarity" with suicide or modeling as a perceived means for dealing with psychic anguish might persist.

The questions raised are not only part of assessing a particular postvention but should be considered questions to guide research on postvention as a form of intervention. Longitudinal and comparative studies are needed to follow groups that have experienced the suicide loss of a community member. Qualitative analyses of what people in schools, work settings, and other organizations have found helpful in the aftermath of a suicide loss could help guide future postventions. Continued dialogue about best practices among those in the field is essential for the refinement of effective postvention.

☐ References

Aseltine, R. H., Jr., & DeMartino, R. (2004). An outcome evaluation of the SOS Suicide Prevention Program. *American Journal of Public Health, 94,* 446–451.
Aseltine, R., James, A., Schilling, E., & Glanovsky, J. (2007). Evaluating the SOS suicide prevention program: A replication and extension. *BMC Public Health* 7(161).

Baber, K., & Bean, G. (2009). Frameworks: A community-based approach to preventing youth suicide. *Journal of Community Psychology, 37,* 684–696.

Bearman, P. S., & Moody, J. (2004). Suicide and friendships among American adolescents. *American Journal of Public Health, 94,* 89–95.

Brent, D. A, Moritz, G., Bridge, J., Perper, J., & Canobbio, R. (1996). Long-term impact of exposure to suicide: A three-year controlled follow-up. *Journal of the American Academy of Child and Adolescent Psychiatry, 35,* 646–653.

Brock, S. E. (2002). School suicide postvention. In S. E. Brock, P. J. Lazarus, & S. R. Jimerson (Eds.), *Best practices in school crisis prevention and intervention* (pp. 553–575). Bethesda, MD: National Association of School Psychologists.

Brock, S. E. (2003, May). *Suicide postvention.* Paper presented at the Department of Defense Education Activity (DoDEA) Safe Schools Seminar, Honolulu, HI (online seminar).

Brymer, M., Jacobs A., Layne C., Pynoos, R., Ruzek J., Steinberg, A.,...Watson, P. (2006). *Psychological first aid field operations guide* (2nd ed.). Rockville, MD: National Child Traumatic Stress Network and National Center for PTSD. Retrieved from http://ncptsd.va.gov/ncmain/ncdocs/manuals/PFA_2ndEditionwithappendices.pdf

Centers for Disease Control. (1988, August 19). CDC recommendations for a community plan for the prevention and containment of suicide clusters. *Morbidity and Mortality Weekly Report, 37*(Suppl. S-6). Retrieved from http://www.cdc.gov/mmwr/preview/mmwrhtml/00001755.htm

Centers for Disease Control and Prevention. (2008). Youth Risk Behavior Surveillance—United States, 2007. Surveillance Summaries. *Morbidity and Mortality Weekly Report, 57* (Whole No. SS-4):1–131.

Crosby, A. E., & Sacks, J. J. (2002). Exposure to suicide: Incidence and association with suicidal ideation and behavior: United States, 1994. *Suicide and Life-Threatening Behavior 32,* 321–328.

Cvinar, J. G. (2005). Do suicide survivors suffer social stigma? A review of the literature. *Perspectives in Psychiatric Care, 41,* 14–21.

de Leo, D., & Heller, T. (2008). Social modeling in the transmission of suicidality. *Crisis: International Journal of Crisis Intervention and Suicide Prevention, 29,* 11–19.

DiCara, C., O'Halloran, S., Williams, L., & Brooks, C. C. (2009). *Youth suicide prevention, intervention and postvention guidelines: A resource for school personnel (4th ed.).* Augusta, GA: The Maine Youth Suicide Prevention Program. Retrieved from http://www.maine.gov/suicide/docs/Guidelines%2010-2009—w%20discl.pdf

Farberow, N. L., Gallagher-Thompson, D., Gilewski, M., & Thompson, L. (1992). The role of social supports in the bereavement process of surviving spouses of suicide and natural deaths. *Suicide and Life-Threatening Behavior, 22,* 107–124.

Gould, M. S. (n.d.). *Suicide contagion (clusters).* Retrieved from Suicide and Mental Health Association International (SMHAI) Web site at http://suicideandmentalhealthassociationinternational.org/suiconclust.html

Gould, M. S., & Kramer, R. A. (2001). Youth suicide prevention. *Suicide and Life-Threatening Behavior, 31*(Suppl.), 6–31.

Graham, A., Reser, J., Scuderi, C., Zubrick, S., Smith, M., & Turley, B. (2000). Suicide: An Australian Psychological Society discussion paper. *Australian Psychologist, 35,* 1–28.

Harvard School of Public Health (n.d.). *Means matter: Suicide, guns, and public health.* Retrieved from Harvard School of Public Health Web site at http://www.hsph.harvard.edu/means-matter

Hedström, P., Ka-Yuet, L., & Nordvik, M. K. (2008). Interaction domains and suicide: A population-based panel study of suicides in Stockholm, 1991–1999. *Social Forces, 87,* 713–740.

Hollingsworth, J. (2007). *Oregon youth suicide prevention. Youth suicide prevention, intervention, & postvention guidelines: A resource for school personnel (2nd revision)* [A modification for Oregon of the May 2002 edition of *Youth suicide prevention, intervention and postvention guidelines: A resource for school personnel.* Augusta, GA: The Maine Youth Suicide Prevention Program.]. Eugene, OR: Looking Glass Youth and Family Services. Retrieved from http://www.oregon.gov/DHS/ph/ipe/ysp/docs/yspipg.pdf

Insel, B. J., & Gould, M. S. (2008). Impact of modeling on adolescent suicidal behavior. *Psychiatric Clinics of North America, 31,* 293–316.

Kerr, M. M., Brent, D. A., McKain, B., & McCommons, P. S. (2003). *Postvention standards manual: A guide for a school's response in the aftermath of sudden death (4th ed.).* Pittsburgh, PA: University of Pittsburgh Medical Center. Retrieved from http://www.starcenter.pitt.edu/files/document/Postvention.pdf

Knox, K. L., Litts, D. A., Talcott, G. W., Feig, J. C., & Caine, E. D. (2003). Risk of suicide and related adverse outcomes after exposure to a suicide prevention programme in the U.S. Air Force: Cohort study. *BMJ: British Medical Journal, 327,* 1376–1378.

Lucas, C. (2001). *Brief Screen for Adolescent Depression.* New York, NY: Columbia DISC Development Group.

Macy, R. D., Behar, L., Paulson, R., Delman, J., Schmid, M., & Smith, S. F. (2004). Community-based acute posttraumatic stress management: A description and evaluation of a psychosocial-intervention continuum. *Harvard Review of Psychiatry, 12,* 217–228.

Marzuk, P. M., Leon, A. C., Tardiff, K., Morgan, E. B., Stajic, M., & Mann, J. J. (1992). The effect of access to lethal methods of injury on suicide rates. *Archives of General Psychiatry, 49,* 451–458.

Massachusetts Coalition for Suicide Prevention. (2009). *Massachusetts strategic plan for suicide prevention.* Boston, MA: Massachusetts Coalition for Suicide Prevention, Massachusetts Department for Public Health, Massachusetts Department of Mental Health. Retrieved from http://www.sprc.org/stateinformation/PDF/stateplans/plan_ma.pdf

Melhem, N. M., Day, N., Shear, M. K, Day, R., Reynolds, C. F., III, & Brent, D. (2004a). Predictors of complicated grief among adolescents exposed to a peer's suicide. *Journal of Loss and Grief, 9,* 21–34.

Melhem, N. M., Day, N., Shear, M. K, Day, R., Reynolds, C. F., III, & Brent, D. (2004b). Traumatic grief among adolescents exposed to a peer's suicide. *American Journal of Psychiatry, 16,* 1411–1416.

Moscicki, E. K. (2001). Epidemiology of completed and attempted suicide: Toward a framework for prevention. *Clinical Neuroscience Research, 1,* 310–323.

National Alliance for Mental Illness, New Hampshire. (2010). *Connect Suicide Prevention Program* (Web site home). Retrieved from http://www.naminh .org/frameworks.php

Poland, S. (2003). *After a suicide: Answering questions from students.* National Association of School Psychologists Resources Web site. Retrieved from http://www .nasponline.org/resources/principals/aftersuicide.aspx

Rubinstein, D. H. (1983). Epidemic suicide among Micronesian adolescents. *Social Science and Medicine, 17,* 657–665.

Screening for Mental Health, Inc. (2010). SOS Signs of Suicide® Prevention Program. Wellesley Hills, MA: Screening for Mental Health, Inc.

Shneidman, E. S. (1972). Foreword. In A. C. Cain (Ed.), *Survivors of suicide* (pp. ix–xi). Springfield, IL: Charles C Thomas.

Suicide Prevention Resource Center. (2008). *Assessing and managing suicide risk: Core competencies for mental health professionals* [A workshop and program developed by the Suicide Prevention Resource Center and the American Association of Suicidology]. Web page description available at http://www .sprc.org/traininginstitute/amsr/clincomp.asp

Sveen, C. A., & Walby, F. A. (2008). Suicide survivors' mental health and grief reactions: A systematic review of controlled studies. *Suicide and Life-Threatening Behavior, 38,* 13–29.

Underwood, M., & Dunne-Maxim, K. (1997). *Managing sudden traumatic loss in the school: New Jersey adolescent suicide prevention project.* Piscataway, NJ: University Behavioral Health Care.

Wyman, P. A., Brown, C. H., Inman, J., Cross, W., Schmeelk-Cone, K., Guo, J., & Pena, J. B. (2008). Randomized trial of a gatekeeper program for suicide prevention: 1-year impact on secondary school staff. *Journal of Consulting and Clinical Psychology, 76,* 104–115.

Principles of Grief Counseling With Adult Survivors

John R. Jordan

In Chapter 1, we defined a *suicide survivor* as "someone who experiences a high level of self-perceived psychological, physical, and/or social distress for a considerable length of time after exposure to the suicide of another person" (see Chapter 1, "A General Definition of Survivorship"). A great deal has been written about the impact of losing a loved one to suicide. Chapters 1 through 5 of this book summarize the extensive empirical literature on this topic. The general conclusion is that for those who meet this definition of a suicide survivor, the impact can be severe and life altering, with an attendant risk of psychiatric morbidity and even mortality. Given this consensus, it is surprising that so little effort has been made to study how bereavement caregivers can be of help to suicide survivors. Indeed, the effectiveness of bereavement-related interventions for the all mourners has been subject to question, as most people seem to recover from the loss of a loved one without the aid of formal, professional intervention (M. S. Stroebe, Hansson, Schut, & W. Stroebe, 2008a), and interventions designed to facilitate recovery or ameliorate the negative effects of bereavement have demonstrated a surprising lack of robustness (Currier, Holland, & Neimeyer, 2007; Currier, Neimeyer, & Berman, 2008; Jordan & Neimeyer, 2003). With regard to interventions specific to suicide survivors, Jordan and McMenamy (2004) and McDaid, Trowman, Golder, Hawton, and Sowden (2008) have completed recent reviews of evidence-based interventions for this group. Both reviews noted that the small number of relevant studies do show some positive effects for participants. However, both reviews also came to similar conclusions about the paucity of such studies, the methodological weakness of the research that has been done, and the need for more and better designed investigations into interventions to help suicide survivors (see also Chapter 33 of this book). While noting that there are many descriptions of clinical work with survivors, Jordan and McMenamy stated that

> we must conclude that the efficacy of formal interventions for survivors has yet to be scientifically established. The state of our knowledge about how, when, and with whom to intervene after a suicide is still quite primitive, suggesting a pressing need for further research that addresses several key issues. (p. 345).

Accordingly, this chapter will draw from the limited body of studies of interventions for survivors, from the general clinical literature on bereavement-related interventions, and from the clinical experience of the author and others who have worked extensively with suicide survivors.

☐ Guidelines for Working With Survivors

Common Issues and Problems for Survivors

There has been some controversy as to whether and in what ways bereavement after a suicide is different from bereavement after other types of losses. In Chapter 2, we review the ways and evidence that suicide bereavement may be different while also sharing common aspects of the grief response after traumatic deaths—particularly, deaths that are sudden, unexpected, and traumatic, such as homicide. In Chapter 2, we also present a model for understanding how the experience of suicide loss may be simultaneously the same and different from other loss trajectories. Jordan (2001) has previously referred to these suicide-specific aspects of bereavement as the thematic differences in the subjective experience of suicide survivors. Next, we briefly review these heightened themes as a guide for clinicians about the kinds of intense and complicated problems with which suicide survivors are likely to present. For more details, please see Jordan (2001, 2008, 2009).

Questions of "Why" and Responsibility

The loss of someone important to suicide assaults the assumptive world of the mourner (Currier, Holland, Coleman, & Neimeyer, 2008; Currier, Holland, & Neimeyer, 2006; Kauffman, 2002; Owens, Lambert, Lloyd, & Donovan, 2008; Sands, 2009). The suicide brings into question all of the things that the bereaved individual took for granted about the identity of the deceased, the nature of their relationship with that individual, and the mourner's own identity. Suicide is an inexplicable death for most people, one that may come as a complete shock to the mourner and that sometimes appears to have no obvious cause. Of course, not all suicide deaths fit this profile, and some may actually be expected and feared by loved ones, particularly when the deceased had a long psychiatric history that included previous attempts. Still, suicide inherently challenges the belief that all human beings fear death and want to live, as well as many other guiding assumptions by which the survivor may have operated. Suicide thus remains a cause of death that cries out for explanation.

A 21-year-old student makes a serious suicide attempt during her senior year at college. The girl had no history of previous suicide attempts and went through a seemingly "normal" period of mourning after the death of her adoptive mother 2 years ago. Her father is stunned to hear of her attempt, finding it hard to comprehend that the child to whom he felt closest in the family could have done this. The girl spends a week in a psychiatric unit close to her college and then is discharged to her father's care; she is advised to seek a day treatment program. After returning to her home, and while awaiting admission to the program, she overdoses on medication and drives her car off an embankment, ending her life. In subsequent grief counseling sessions, her father condemns himself for his failure to believe that his daughter could really have wanted to die—her death was simply a brutal violation of everything that he thought he knew about his daughter.

These profound challenges to the assumptive world of the survivor usually set in motion the need for a personal psychological autopsy of the suicide that includes an attempt to "reconstruct" the state of mind of the deceased prior to the suicide and an investigation into the events leading up to the death that might help explain the reasons for the suicide.

Closely related is the need on the part of most survivors to establish accountability for the suicide. Because it is often ambiguous as to whether suicide was a freely made choice of the deceased or, conversely, was an action to which they were driven by external stressors and/or psychiatric disorder, most survivors struggle with the question of whom to hold accountable for the death. Many begin the process of seeking answers by blaming themselves. This "inquest" into the death typically includes a review of the self-perceived failings of the mourner in his or her dealings with the deceased, a process that frequently manifests itself as intense and ruminative guilt. But the inquiry into responsibility may also be extended to others in the social network of the deceased (i.e., their spouse, parents, therapist, etc.)—and sometimes to the deceased him- or herself. The construction of a coherent narrative that helps the mourner make at least partial sense of the suicide is a central healing task for most survivors, and must be both respected and actively facilitated by the clinician if the survivor is to successfully come to terms with the trauma of the suicide. (Jordan, 2008, 2009; see also Chapter 11 for a more thorough discussion of this perspective)

Horror/Trauma

The loss of a loved one to suicide often produces some degree of clinical trauma symptoms in the survivors, even if they do not reach full syndromal level post-traumatic stress disorder (PTSD; Armour, 2006; Melhem et al., 2004b; Melham et al., 2001; Murphy et al., 1999; Neria & Litz, 2004; Raphael, Martinek, & Wooding, 2004; Simon et al., 2007). These symptoms can include an intrusive reliving of the dying process and the death scene, along with rumination about the amount of mental and physical suffering experienced by the deceased just before the suicide. Likewise, avoidance symptoms are common. For example, survivors may be very reluctant to enter into physical proximity with the location at which the suicide occurred. Avoidance can also extend to social connections, as some survivors seek to avoid contact with other people who are likely to trigger reminders of the deceased. Of course, this social withdrawal can also be the result of the stigma associated with suicide (see next subsection on social disruption). Hyperarousal symptoms that include insomnia, difficulty concentrating, irritability, and various other physiological and psychological symptoms of traumatization are also common in survivors. Although these responses seem to be exacerbated by actually witnessing the suicide or finding the body (Callahan, 2000), it is very important for caregivers to understand that survivors can experience traumatic reliving and avoidance symptoms even if they did not directly witness the suicide or view the death scene.

Perceived Abandonment, Rejection, and Social Disruption

The suicide of a loved one can have profound effects on the relational life of survivors—including their symbolic connection with the deceased—and their actual relationship with their family and their larger social network. To the extent that survivors construe the suicide as a willful choice on the part of the deceased, it may engender profound feelings of rejection and abandonment in the mourner, and intense anger at the deceased (Bailley, Kral, & Dunham, 1999; Jordan, 2001; Sveen & Walby, 2008). The "intentionality" of the suicide and the perceived betrayal by the deceased is a central problem for many survivors (Sands, 2008). Clinical work to repair this relational rupture is often a focus of the ensuing therapeutic work.

Likewise, a considerable body of research supports the proposition that suicide survivors experience more stigma, social disruption, and isolation than survivors of most other types of deaths (Allen, Calhoun, Cann, & Tedeschi, 1993; Bailley et al., 1999; Cleiren, Grad, Zavasnik, & Diekstra, 1996; Cvinar, 2005; Range, 1998; Saarinen, Hintikka, Lehtonen, Lönnqvist, & Viinamäki, 2002; Sveen & Walby, 2008). Survivors often confront the general cultural stigmatization of suicide and psychiatric disorders, along with what K. Dyregrov (2003b; K. Dyregrov & A. Dyregrov, 2008) has termed the *social ineptitude* of their social networks, meaning the lack of cultural norms and interpersonal skill sets within the network for making helpful social responses after a suicide. The encounter with the failure of their social network to appropriately respond to their distress often leaves survivors feeling isolated and abandoned by family members and their larger communities. Similarly, these same problems can develop within the immediate family of the survivor. Families can experience scapegoating, secrecy about the cause of death (e.g., withholding the actual cause of death from children or extended family), and a general disruption of family rituals after the suicide of a member. Please see Cerel, Jordan, and Duberstein (2008) for a recent review of the impact of suicide on families, plus several additional resources (Jordan, 2001; Jordan, Kraus, & Ware, 1993; Kaslow & Aronson, 2004; McMenamy, Jordan, & Mitchell, 2008). Chapter 13 also offers an overview of interventions with families after a suicide.

Complicated Grief and Suicidality

Chapters 1 through 5 have reviewed the evidence for the elevated rates of psychiatric morbidity and mortality after the death by suicide of a loved one, close intimate, or client. There is convincing evidence that exposure to suicide and suicidal behavior, particularly of an immediate family member (or a close friend, in the case of adolescents) is associated with elevated suicidal ideation, behavior, and completions in survivors (Agerbo, 2003, 2005; Agerbo, Nordentoft, & Mortensen, 2002; Brent & Mann, 2006; Brent et al., 1993, 2002; Crosby & Sacks, 2002; Hedstrom, Liu, & Nordvik, 2008; Mann et al., 2005; Qin, Agerbo, & Mortensen, 2002, 2005; Roy & Janal, 2005). As Shneidman (1972) noted long ago, this research means that postvention with suicide survivors is a crucial form of prevention of future suicides.

Beyond the risk for mortality, there also appears to be a risk for elevated rates of psychiatric morbidity after suicide. Chapters 1 through 5 have reviewed this evidence in detail. Of particular relevance for this chapter is the growing evidence that suicide survivors may be at elevated risk for the newly defined syndrome called *complicated grief* (CG) or *prolonged grief disorder* (PGD; de Groot, de Keijser, & Neeleman, 2006; Knieper, 1999; Melhem et al., 2004a; Mitchell, Kim, Prigerson, & Mortimer-Stephens, 2004). Research has shown that the presence of this disorder is associated with a number of negative social, medical, and psychiatric sequelae that add morbidity over and above any comorbid depression or PTSD (Latham & Prigerson, 2004; Lichtenthal, Cruess, & Prigerson, 2004; Ott, 2003; Prigerson & Maciejewski, 2005).

Revision of the Clinician's Assumptive World About Working With Suicide Bereavement

Most mental health and related counseling professionals (e.g., clergy who do pastoral counseling) have at least some experience working with bereavement as a presenting problem. Typically, most of this work has been with clients presenting with the loss of an older spouse or parents to natural causes. These more normative losses have been written about extensively (Balk, Wogrin, Thornton, & Meagher, 2007; Hansson, Hayslip, & Stroebe, 2007). The majority of empirical studies of bereavement have also been done with these developmentally "on-cycle" losses, and they have begun to yield valuable data about what might be considered the "typical" trajectory of bereavement (Bonanno & Boerner, 2008; Ott & Lueger, 2002). From this, norms have also emerged for defining pathological deviations from the typical trajectory of bereavement. For example, the criteria for the new diagnostic category of CG or PGD currently specifies a 6-month symptom duration as the cutoff point for distinguishing normal from complicated or prolonged bereavement (Prigerson et al., 2009; Prigerson, Vanderwerker, & Maciejewski, 2008).

The difficulty for clinicians arises, however, when norms about these much more common losses are applied to bereavement after non-normative deaths such as suicide and other forms of traumatic death. To work with clients who have experienced a suicide, particularly those who meet the criteria outlined in Chapter 1 for survivorship, clinicians may need to revise their expectations about what constitutes a "normal" bereavement response. For example, there is evidence that a significant number of parents who have lost a child to a traumatic cause (suicide, homicide, and accident) continue to show elevated levels of mental distress for 5 and up to 10 years after the death—a much longer period of time than the proposed 6-month criteria for the PGD diagnosis (Murphy, Johnson, & Lohan, 2002, 2003; Murphy, Johnson, Wu, Fan, & Lohan, 2003; Saarinen et al., 2002; Saarinen, Hintikka, Viinamäki, Lehtonen, & Lönnqvist, 2000). Both Murphy (Murphy, Johnson, Wu, et al., 2003) and Feigelman, Jordan, and Gorman (2009) also found that suicidally bereaved parents reported that it was not until the third to fifth year that their grief symptoms began to subside and they were able to regain a sense of perspective and a "new normal" in their lives.

These findings suggest that clinicians must readjust their own and their clients' expectations about the mourning process when working with traumatic loss (Jordan, 2008). Three areas of expectation should be considered for revision by the clinician. First, practitioners must be aware of their own general beliefs and attitudes about suicide. Across cultures and throughout history, suicide has been viewed from many perspectives. It has been interpreted as immoral and selfish behavior; as an act of cowardice; as possession by an external and evil force; as the result of a medical or psychological disorder; and, in certain circumstances, as an understandable, acceptable, and even honorable action by the deceased (Colt, 2006). Clinicians are, of course, also influenced by these cultural perceptions and are unlikely to be simply neutral about the act of suicide. Thus, their own values and beliefs about what leads to suicide and how it should be "judged" are likely to be evoked in working with survivors. This is particularly true if the clinician has directly experienced the suicide of someone close to them, whether a family member, friend, or client. As with all such countertransferential responses, the goal should not be to rid oneself of the response but, rather, to be aware of it so that it does not interfere with the therapy. Ideally, such reactions on the part of the caregiver can then be used as a source of empathy and insight into the experience of the client.

Second, many therapists are likely to find that the duration and intensity of their client's distress will often exceed the levels found after most other types of losses. For example, the intensity of the feelings of guilt and failure in survivors are often manifested as a rigidly perceived failure on the part of the survivor to recognize the "warning signs" and to intervene to stop the suicide. The reality of the circumstances of the suicide may strike the clinician as being at odds with this apparently unreasonable and retroactive demand on themselves made by clients. Consequently, clinicians may find themselves wanting to quickly challenge this irrational self-condemnation. However, when viewed from the perspective of trauma mastery, this rumination may serve important functions in coming to terms with the universal trauma questions about what happened, why it happened, whose fault it was, and how can it be prevented from happening again (Taku, Calhoun, Cann, & Tedeschi, 2008). As a clinician who has worked with many suicide survivors, the author of this chapter often tries to prepare clients for this internal need to have a "trial" to see if they deserve to be "convicted." The proposal to the client is that the clinician and survivor work together to make sure that there is a "fair trial" and that all of the "evidence" is considered before reaching a "verdict." This validation of the intense need to review one's actions usually proves much more empathic with the survivor's internal experience than a premature attempt to pathologize or invalidate their sense of culpability.

Again, clinicians should also monitor their own responses when confronted with this type of anguished rumination in their survivor clients. Countertransferential responses can include a premature need to push their "stuck" clients to "get over it" (often mirroring the messages that survivors receive from others in their social network), frustration and helplessness at the inability to fix the client's suffering, and clear empathic failures in which the therapist minimizes and emotionally distances him- or herself from the extent of the client's distress (Neimeyer & Jordan, 2001). The caregiver may also find themselves feeling a need that is similar to the client's to blame someone for the havoc created by the suicide. This "someone" can be the client him- or herself, the deceased, another clinician, or a family member. All of these understandable reactions emerge from the shared need of both the client and the clinician to affix accountability for the death and restore a sense of an orderly and "just" world. These reactions can also reflect a lack of familiarity with the profound and life-changing nature of traumatic loss on the part of the clinician and client alike. The heart of therapeutic skill with suicide survivors involves the ability to remain emotionally present in the face of deep emotional pain—without needing to quickly resolve it, minimize it, or move on from it.

The third expectation that may need revision when working with survivors involves the general goals of therapy. Contemporary psychotherapy has come to be dominated by a medically based psychiatric model that is built around the analogy that therapy is essentially the same as other medical treatment (Neimeyer & Raskin, 2000; Wampold, 2001). From this perspective, therapists are presumed to "diagnose" their clients' discreet disorders based on the presence of specific symptoms, which are then remediated by the application of treatments that are linked to those specific diagnoses. Such factors as the person who has the disorder, their history (except for previous episodes of the "disorder"), the social context in which their problems occur, the meaning that the symptoms hold for the client, their understanding of the existential reasons for their loss and suffering, and the personal and professional history of the person who is providing the therapy are all considered to be mostly extraneous to the treatment process, just as they would be presumed to be irrelevant to the treatment of a sore throat with antibiotics by a medical doctor (Neimeyer, 2005a, 2009; Neimeyer & Raskin, 2000). From this medical analogy perspective, healing is essentially a homeostatic process that involves amelioration of symptoms and a return to the preloss status quo of functioning. Although acknowledging that there are benefits to this orientation, the author's opinion is that the medical model also has profound limitations as a foundational framework for assisting suicide survivors (and probably for most grief counseling). In contrast, emerging orientations in thanatology that concentrate on the subjective meaning of the loss for clients seem to hold a much greater promise for understanding the true nature of the healing process as well as the role of clinicians in facilitating that process. For example, constructivist or narrative models focus on the disruption of the internal and social narratives of the traumatized survivor (Currier, Holland, et al., 2008; Currier, Holland, Coleman, & Neimeyer, 2006; Currier & Neimeyer, 2006; Neimeyer, 2005b), as do adaptational models of mourning that conceptualize healing as a process of complex adjustment to a dramatically changed world and the integration of loss into the client's larger identity (Attig, 1996, 2001). Likewise, the understanding that the clinician is a fellow sojourner and "expert companion" (Tedeschi & Calhoun, 2003) who facilitates this process of reintegration and meaning reconstruction as it reverberates throughout the psychological life-space of the client also opens the door to a very different understanding of the therapy process—one that has more in common with a traditional spiritual guide than a neutral and detached technician. This more holistic view also incorporates the pos-sibility of post-traumatic growth in the bereaved person rather than a simple "return to baseline," emphasizing recovery as a collaborative process of change rather than homeostatic repair (Tedeschi & Calhoun, 2003, 2006, 2008; see also Chapter 11). From this perspective, the jour-ney of survivors is facilitated not by the "expert knowledge" of the clini-cian but, rather, by his or her relational skills and invitational posture of collaboratively exploring the newfound territory in which survivors must live the remainder of their lives.

In summary, in this author's opinion, grief counseling is best viewed from a "binocular" perspective that, while incorporating this dominant medical model of treatment, also holds that the heart of grief counseling is a concentrated form of empathically attuned and skillfully applied social support, not medical treatment. Grief counseling from this point of view is primarily person focused, rather than symptom focused, and intervention is primarily relationally focused rather than technique focused. Although this dialectic about the nature of change is evident in the larger discussion about what constitutes the "heart and soul" of all psychotherapeutic change (Duncan, Miller, Wampold, & Hubble, 2010), it has particular resonance when the presenting issue is the loss of a meaningful relationship, as in all grief counseling. Neither viewpoint is exclusive of the other, and both can be useful to the practitioner who seeks to be of maximal assistance to their clients and who is open to drawing from all relevant metaphors when seeking to help with the suf-fering of their traumatically bereaved clients.

☐ Assessment

There are a number of issues to consider in beginning counseling with suicide survivors; some of these issues are specific to suicide loss, whereas others are more generic to counseling after any type of loss. The first and most obvious is a mapping of the problems that the individual is having as a result of the loss. These problems can include familiar intrapsychic "symptoms" of grief; disruption of physical, cognitive, and social functioning; and bereavement-related damage to the assumptive world of the client. These common intrapsychic symptoms of grief are well known and well documented (Balk et al., 2007; Hensley & Clayton, 2008) and may include shock and disbelief at the fact of the death; pre-occupation with the deceased and an intense yearning to have them return; a need to "search" for the deceased, fearfulness about coping in the world without the loved one; and anger at the unavailability of the deceased. All of these are congruent with the human response to the loss of a psychologically important attachment figure (Shear & Shair, 2005).

Beyond these more universal aspects of the grief response, suicide survivors should be monitored for signs and symptoms of psychiatric disorders that are common specifically after traumatic, sudden, and violent losses. As noted previously, there is evidence that survivors of such losses are more likely to experience trauma symptoms of intrusive reliving of the death, coupled with attempts to avoid these disturbing memories and the accompanying arousal symptoms of hypervigilance, sleep disturbance, irritability, difficulty with concentration, and other markers of heightened autonomic arousal (Shear et al., 2007).

A second symptom that may be found in suicide survivors is *suicidal ideation*. As established in Chapter 1, exposure to the suicide of a loved one elevates the risk of suicidality in those exposed, including the risk of suicide completion. Moreover, the new tripartite model of suicide bereavement (Sands, 2009; see also Chapter 11) notes that a form of identification with the suffering and suicidality of the deceased may be a common part of the grieving process for many suicide survivors, a clinical phenomenon that the author has also observed in many clients. Thus, assessing the risk level of a suicide attempt in the suicidally bereaved is no simple task for clinicians.

Usually, the suicidality takes the form of a passive wish to be freed from the pain of grief and/or a wish for reunion with the deceased. And, as Sands (2009) has noted for some survivors, there is an intense need to understand the mindset of the deceased—part of the need for a personal psychological autopsy mentioned previously in this chapter. Less frequently, the survivor may experience active suicidality that includes planning a method to end his or her life, taking steps toward implementing that plan (e.g., saving up pills or purchasing a firearm), and engaging in rehearsal behaviors of the suicidal act. In this author's experience, this is most commonly (although not exclusively) found in individuals who had a history of suicidal ideation and behaviors prior to the loss of their loved one, and the death has re-activated and/or intensified these preexisting problems. Regardless, the discovery of all thoughts of suicide, no matter how understandable in light of the loss, must be followed up with a careful risk assessment and development of a plan for safety for the client, depending on the assessed level of suicide risk. Clients who have a previous history of suicidal ideation or attempts are particularly vulnerable and should be monitored more carefully. Moreover, risk must be reassessed going forward throughout the course of therapy, not simply during assessment, because the risk for suicide can fluctuate and is likely to rise at certain predictable times for the survivor. These can include anniversaries of the death, holidays, or the period when the initial numbing response to the death begins to "wear off" (for more on conducting a thorough suicide risk assessment, see Joiner, Van Orden, Witte, & Rudd, 2009; Joiner, Walker, Rudd, & Jobes, 1999; Shea, 2002).

Lastly, the presence of other comorbid psychiatric symptoms and syndromes should be assessed, particularly mood and anxiety disorders. It is beyond the scope of this chapter to address the complex questions involved in differentiating the grief response from a major depressive disorder. The reader is referred to recent articles by Zisook and colleagues for an informed and updated discussion of these issues (Auster, Moutier, Lanouette, & Zisook, 2008; Kendler, Myers, & Zisook, 2008; Zisook & Kendler, 2007; Zisook & Shuchter, 2001). Of importance here is a recognition that depressive symptoms, although common early in bereavement, usually subside in a way that allows them to be differentiated from the longer-lasting grief response. The persistence of depressive symptoms (anhedonia, sleep and appetite dysregulation, unremitting and intensifying guilt, suicidality, etc.)—and, particularly, their intensification over time—should be considered a red flag that a syndromal level of depression is developing and must be addressed in addition to the grief. Moreover, clients who have a history of mood-related disorders seem to be particularly susceptible to developing a major depressive episode after a traumatic loss and should be considered earlier as possible candidates for pharmacological treatment of the depressive symptoms (Hensley, 2006a, 2006b; Hensley & Clayton, 2008). Likewise, the development of CG or PGD may require the use of specialized treatment protocols that are under development (see the section later in this chapter on techniques, as well as articles by Shear et al. [2005]; Shear, Gorscak, & Simon [2006], and Shear et al. [2001]). In general, the author has found it more useful to consider the trend or direction of the client's grief-related distress rather than the duration of its presence—that is, as long as the client's physical, psychological, and social problems are gradually improving, he or she can be considered "on track." When the symptoms are not improving at all—or, more ominously, are growing worse with time—then additional intervention may be necessary, ranging from pharmacological treatment to referral to additional specialists (e.g., to a sleep clinic for persistent sleep disorder). The only caveat to this guideline is that some evidence shows that for clients who are traumatized, the initial period of emotional numbness may give way to an intensification of grief distress, particularly as the "emotional anesthesia" of shock and disbelief begins to wear off and the social support around the survivor begins to withdraw (generally between 6 months and 1 year after the loss).

Problems With Social Connection

Beyond the presence of these psychiatric-type symptoms, clinicians should assess—and, when needed, assist—clients with disruptions in their functioning in the larger world. Central to this is the impact of the suicide on the mourner's social connections. As has been documented in Chapter 2 and previously in this chapter, there is considerable evidence that suicide survivors experience more stigmatization and social ostracism than do survivors of most other modes of death (Armour, 2006; Cvinar, 2005; Sveen & Walby, 2008; Thompson & Range, 1992). Survivors may also have their ability to elicit social support from others severely compromised, either from the general traumatization and grief that they are experiencing or from a kind of "self-stigmatization" and self-imposed isolation from others (K. Dyregrov & A. Dyregrov, 2008; K. Dyregrov, Nordanger, & A. Dyregrov, 2003; Van Dongen, 1993). Even in the absence of overt stigmatization, the "competence" of social networks to provide effective social support to survivors can be quite variable (K. Dyregrov, 2003b; K. Dyregrov & A. Dyregrov, 2008). Clients who have a history of social isolation, relatively impoverished social connections, or involvement with hostile or disenfranchising social networks are at elevated risk for prolonged grief distress. The research literature on the role of social support in buffering the impact of traumatic loss is complicated and sometimes contradictory (W. Stroebe, Schut, & M. S. Stroebe, 2005; W. Stroebe, Zech, M. S. Stroebe, & Abakoumkin, 2005). However, in this author's opinion, there is sufficient empirical and clinical evidence that good social support, as perceived by the survivor, is associated with a reduced overall level of bereavement distress and depressive symptoms to make this a major focus of assessment and possible intervention with survivors (K. Dyregrov, 2003a; K. Dyregrov & A. Dyregrov, 2008; K. Dyregrov et al., 2003; Farberow, Gallagher-Thompson, Gilewski, & Thompson, 1992; Feigelman, Gorman, & Jordan, 2009; Murphy, Chung, & Johnson, 2002; Reed, 1998).

In addition, a suicide may also significantly affect the quality of connectedness within the smaller network of the family system (Cerel et al., 2008; Jordan, 2001, 2008, 2009; Jordan et al., 1993; Kaslow & Aronson, 2001, 2004; McMenamy et al., 2008). Traumatic losses such as a suicide may destabilize family rituals, produce shut-downs in communication, and reduce family members' practical and emotional availability to one another in ways that can profoundly affect the cohesiveness of the family system. Of particular note for clinicians doing suicide postvention is the potential emergence of blaming or scapegoating among family members. The anger generated by a suicide can literally destroy previously stable and functional family relationships and is particularly problematic in relationships that were already strained with hostility and resentment. It is imperative that clinicians assess at the beginning of therapy, as well as in an ongoing fashion, the impact of the suicide on all family members and on the functioning of the family as a unit.

The assessment should include the impact of the suicide on the family's ability to restore the many role functions of its members (Jordan et al., 1993). This restoration includes re-establishment of daily rituals such as a shared meal, provision of support and structure for children such as helping with homework and chores, and resuming pleasurable activities of the marital pair bond, such as sexual and companionate interaction. Losses often produce "coping asynchrony" between family members, as each person attempts to contain their pain and gather their personal resources to begin the healing process. Profound losses may produce profound pain in family members, and each person's method of coping with that pain is a unique combination of personality, personal history with loss, and cultural socialization (e.g., gender roles). For example, a husband may cope with the grief of a child's suicide by intensifying his involvement with work and withdrawing into himself at home, whereas his wife seeks affiliation with her husband and repeated opportunities to discuss the child's death with him. Moreover, family members may experience transformational change as a result of this type of loss, and the new, "postloss" person may be significantly different from the "preloss" individual, producing an additional sense of loss and abandonment among family members. These changes in identity and personality may be a significant source of relational strain and, in some cases, family dissolution.

After the shocking suicide of their adolescent daughter, a married couple finds themselves experiencing radically different priorities and needs in their attempts to cope with the tragedy. The father, who had suffered for many years from depression, told the therapist that his goal for therapy was to prevent a reoccurrence of his own depression, to keep his previously troubled marriage from falling apart completely, and to minimize the emotional consequences of the suicide for his remaining children. He wanted the family to return to "normal" as quickly as possible. His wife, however, was consumed with the need to allow herself time and space to fully grieve her daughter's death. This included a more or less complete "shutdown" of her functioning, along with withdrawal from almost all contact with friends, extended family, and, at times, even her husband and other children. She wanted mainly to be left alone to grieve in her room and to have contact with her husband only around their shared sorrow over their daughter's death. Their diverging ways of coping with their grief soon led to increasing tension between the spouses as each became more resentful of the other's unavailability and inability to find a common way of mourning. Each was also frightened by the changes happening in the relationship that seemed beyond anyone's control.

It is crucial that clinicians monitor the evolving family system for these sequelae of the loss and, when possible, offer psychoeducational and other interventions to reduce the negative consequences of the suicide for the family's cohesive balance.

☐ Intervention

The range of intervention options for survivors encompasses the usual alternatives available for psychological distress, including individual, group, and family counseling as well as more nontraditional choices such as bereavement support groups, visits from survivor outreach teams, bibliotherapy, and use of online resources. Individual grief counseling is a crucial component of healing for many survivors (de Groot et al., 2006; McMenamy et al., 2008; see also Chapter 6). It affords the clinician time for a more extensive evaluation of the problems and resources that the survivor brings to the experience as well as more careful monitoring of serious psychiatric complications of the loss, such as suicidality, PTSD, clinical depression, and alcohol/drug involvement. Individual therapy also allows the survivor to experience an interpersonal "safe harbor," where all aspects of the relationship with the deceased, the events of the suicide, and the psychological and social difficulties after the loss can be explored. Frequently, there is no other such protected setting in the life-space of the survivor. Individual therapy is also the optimal arrangement for exploring the damage to the mourner's assumptive world and for implementing specific techniques to help repair that damage (see sections that follow, as well as Chapter 11).

Conjoint therapy with an affected family can also be very useful. Many of the communication difficulties that are common after a suicide can be successfully addressed with the help of a skilled clinician who can play an impartial facilitating role in promoting empathy and mutual support among family members (Cerel et al., 2008; Kaslow & Aronson, 2004). Psychoeducational guidance on the normative responses to profound grief, including their impact on family relationships, can be tremendously helpful for families whose lives have been disrupted by the suicide of a member. Parents, in particular, often seek professional guidance about how to protect their children from the negative effects of a suicide (K. Dyregrov, 2002; K. Dyregrov & A. Dyregrov, 2005; Provini, Everett, & Pfeffer, 2000). The effects of differences in coping styles and the resulting relational strains can also be normalized and addressed in conjoint family or marital meetings. All of this can help with the debilitating effect that traumatic losses may have on the functioning and cohesiveness of a family. Anything that the clinician can do to promote a sense of mutual support and respect for individual differences will be helpful in the family's attempt to recover from the trauma of a suicide.

Despite these salutatory effects, clinicians should be cautious about starting immediate conjoint meetings with bereaved family members after a suicide. Rather, clinicians should do some assessment to understand the relationship history of family members (particularly conflictual ones), the degree of blaming or scapegoating that is occurring around the suicide, and the distress that members may feel in being asked to disclose their grief experience in a family where such intimate sharing is not the norm. Although the clinician should always have an awareness of family issues and functioning, for some families, conjoint meetings may do more harm than good. Sound clinical judgment must be used about when to bring people together and when to see them individually or in smaller subsystems of the family. Also, please see the work of Kaslow, Cerel, and Boyd-Weber and their colleagues—as well as Chapters 4, 10, and 13 of this book—for additional guidance on child- and family-oriented suicide postvention work (Cerel, Fristad, Weller, & Weller, 1999, 2000; Cerel et al., 2008; Kaslow & Aronson, 2001, 2004; Kaslow, Ivey, Berry-Mitchell, Franklin, & Bethea, 2009; Schuurman & DeCristofaro, 2007; Webb, 1993, 2002, 2003).

Contact With Other Survivors

In addition to formal psychotherapeutic interventions, there is growing evidence that contact with other suicide survivors is an important part of the healing process for many after a suicide loss (Cerel, Padgett, Conwell, & Reed, 2009; Jordan & McMenamy, 2004; McMenamy et al., 2008). The most common form of contact is participation in a bereavement support group. Participation can reduce the sense of isolation and stigmatization felt by many survivors while also instilling hope for recovery from the intense psychic pain of the loss. Survivors also have an opportunity to learn new strategies from the coping efforts shared by other participants. Chapter 12 offers a fuller exploration of the role of bereavement support in groups in helping survivors heal.

Beyond support groups, there are many other forms of survivor-to-survivor contact that may be beneficial. These forms of contact include receiving visits from outreach teams that do home visits with new survivors (for examples, see the Promising Programs section of this book [Chapters 14 through 32] and research by Campbell [Campbell, 2006; Campbell, Cataldie, McIntosh, & Millet, 2004]); participation in online support activities (Feigelman, Gorman, Beal, & Jordan, 2008); involvement in educational or fundraising gatherings of survivors (such as the National Survivors of Suicide Day activities of the American Foundation for Suicide Prevention; see Chapter 26); and becoming an "activist" in organized community efforts to prevent suicide and help other survivors. All such participatory activities with other survivors can have valuable healing effects for many survivors. They should be encouraged for, but not forced upon, clients who seek help from a mental health clinician.

Tasks of Healing and Therapeutic Goals

Worden (2009), Rando (1993), and others have found it useful to conceptualize the recovery process after loss as a series of tasks that must be addressed in order for psychological healing to proceed. Likewise, it is useful to consider the tasks that are faced by suicide survivors as they seek to integrate the loss into their ongoing life narrative. The magnitude and form that these challenges take, and the manner in which they are mastered, will of course vary from one survivor to another. Nonetheless, almost all survivors will, at some point, need to wrestle with variations of these tasks, as they form the heart of the survivor's journey. The overarching goal of clinical intervention then becomes one of facilitating the mastery of these tasks. The specific tasks are discussed in the subsections that follow.

Containment of the Trauma

Common to all trauma is the intrusive nature of the experience and its power to capture the psychological resources of the survivor. Rynearson (2001) has aptly termed this the "possession" of the bereaved by the "three Vs" of violent dying: the *violence* inherent in the manner of the death, the *violation* of the psychological and physical life-space of the mourner, and the human *volition* involved in the death. In the case of a suicide, volition involves the perceived choice of the person who died by suicide to end his or her own life, what Sands (2008) has referred to as the "intentionality" of the death. Modulation of the trauma response produced by these three Vs becomes a central task for the survivor to accomplish. This includes containment of the shock and horror at the circumstances of the death (e.g., rumination over mental images of the death scene, the look of the body, etc.) and attenuation of the instinctive identification with the suffering of the deceased as they were dying (e.g., ruminating about "What was it like for my loved one as they tried to breathe while hanging from the rope?"). At a minimum, the survivor must learn to compartmentalize these reactions so that they are not invasive of his or her day-to-day functioning. Recent research on repressive coping in bereavement, in which the mourner is able to avoid dwelling on painful bereavement-related thoughts and emotions, shows the potential utility of this style of coping (Bonanno, Keltner, Holen, & Horowitz, 1995; Bonanno, Papa, Lalande, Zhang, & Noll, 2005; Coifman, Bonanno, Ray, & Gross, 2007), including after suicide bereavement (Parker & McNally, 2008). In addition to avoidance strategies, some survivors may intuitively learn to desensitize themselves to triggers that elicit the trauma response (e.g., by deliberately returning to the scene of the death rather than avoiding it). New treatment approaches to dealing with CG may assist with this desensitization process (see the later section "Specialized Treatment Techniques" as well as research by Shear [Shear et al., 2005, 2006; Shear & Frank, 2006]).

Learning Skills for Dosing Grief, Finding Sanctuary, and Cultivating Psychic Analgesia

For many survivors, the separation distress experienced after the suicide of their loved one is the most intense psychological pain they have ever endured.

A father whose son died by suicide on a Sunday afternoon calls his therapist on the Sunday 2 weeks later in a terrified panic. At the same hour of day that his son died, he finds himself now sitting on the floor with his heart racing, his mind conjuring the scene of his son dying at this moment 2 weeks earlier, and his tears for the loss of his son flowing uncontrollably. He tells the therapist of his fear that he is losing his mind, that he will never be able to bear the death of his beloved son, and that "I've never felt anything like this in my life." The therapist offers measured and compassionate reassurance about his ability to survive, checks for any suicidal ideation, and helps the father develop some immediate coping activities to manage the wave of anxiety and grief that he is experiencing.

Similar to intense physical pain, early in mourning these "grief spasms" are typically relentless and all consuming, and can be functionally very debilitating. An important goal for treatment, then, is to help the individual cultivate sources of comfort and control over the pain, a kind of psychic analgesia. Learning what will bring relief is often a collaborative trial-and-error process for the therapist and client. The solutions are often idiosyncratic for each person and may range from going "toward" the pain to allow it to run its course (e.g., visiting the grave and talking with the deceased; reminiscing with others about the deceased) to engaging in active efforts to distract oneself from the pain and self-soothe (e.g., engaging in intense physical exercise, watching engaging movies or television, etc.). As with other intrusive trauma symptoms, over time, the goal is for the survivor to be able to "dose" their exposure to the pain and to more voluntarily experience it at moments of their own choosing while also regulating its intensity.

A relatively new description of the grieving process, the *dual process model* (DPM; Hansson & M. S. Stroebe, 2007; M. Stroebe & Schut, 1999; M. S. Stroebe, Hansson, Schut, & W. Stroebe, 2008b), offers a valuable format for understanding the recovery efforts of suicide survivors in learning to dose their separation distress. Essentially, the DPM posits that adaptive mourning involves an oscillation between two broad orientations. The first is the *loss orientation,* which includes confronting and working through the loss with the goal of integrating it and restoring psychological equilibrium. The other orientation is the *restoration orientation,* in which the mourner directs his or her energy toward adapting to the changed world created by the loss. This adaptation can include learning new skills and developing new relationships that facilitate adaptation after the loss. This model is innovative because it emphasizes the value of acquiring the psychological skills necessary to both (a) approach the loss and (b) compartmentalize and avoid it. From the perspective of the DPM, the mourning process can, therefore, be understood as a process of skill acquisition—in this case, the skill to regulate exposure to internal bereavement-related thoughts and emotions. Suicide and other traumatic losses can be profoundly dysregulating for the bereaved—physiologically, emotionally, and cognitively. The development of the skills to dose one's exposure to the loss is central to the slow process of re-regulating oneself after the trauma of suicide. The increasing ability to control one's reactivity also helps provide hope for the mourner that the intense pain and anhedonia that accompany a traumatic loss can indeed be controlled and that the ability to experience pleasure and happiness can be restored.

Creation of a Complex, Realistic, and Compassionate Narrative of the Suicide Through a Personal Psychological Autopsy

As described previously, suicide is often incomprehensible to the survivor and, thus, profoundly challenges his or her assumptive world (see Chapter 11 of this book). This collapse of the ability to experience one's personal world as orderly, understandable, and benevolent is a devastating sequelae of many suicides and may produce tremendous anxiety in the survivor. As Chapter 11 illustrates, the survivor's understanding of the deceased and the relationship that he or she had with that person, the survivor's connections with other people in his or her social network, and the survivor's sense of his or her own identity may all be shaken by the suicide. In an effort to rebuild this profound breach of their assumptive world, the majority of survivors engage in an intense review of what happened, why it occurred, and of the accountability of various people in the process. In this author's experience, most survivors begin this urgent inquiry with an examination of their own role in the suicide. This includes their perceived failure to provide sufficient support to the deceased, along with a perceived failure to recognize the level of risk and take action to prevent the suicide. Survivors usually overestimate their own power to influence or control the events that led to the suicide and are unaware of, or underestimate, all the other elements that contributed to the death. They also frequently make the cognitive error of evaluating their actions before the suicide in light of what they have come to know after the suicide. A client of the author's once aptly labeled this compulsive second-guessing of the self as the "tyranny of hindsight." It can become a tormenting demon for many survivors.

Gradually over time, most survivors come to recognize the many and complex factors that contributed to the suicide but that were not knowable or in their control before the death. They also begin to understand that they are unlikely to arrive at a completely satisfactory understanding of the suicide, so that learning to tolerate "not knowing" and living with an incomplete understanding of the death becomes a more realistic goal (Sands, 2009). Indeed, although searching for more information about the suicide is an important component of the development of a healing narrative, the objective is not necessarily the discovery of the absolute "truth" about the suicide but, rather, the construction of an account that is bearable for the survivor. This entails a "believable enough" story of the death that the survivor is relieved from the need to compulsively search for an answer to the question "Why?" and can instead reinvest psychological energy into rebuilding their life without the deceased.

This section can be summarized by noting that a crucial goal of the treatment process for many survivors is the development of a narrative of the death and of their own accountability in it that is complex ("the suicide was the result of many factors, not just one thing"), realistic ("my role in contributing to the death was limited or even nonexistent, and I recognize the limitations of what I could have done"), and compassionate ("I, others around me, and my loved one did the best that was possible, given who we were and what we had to deal with").

Learning Skills to Manage Changed Social Connections

As noted, becoming a suicide survivor often changes or even disrupts the interpersonal connections of the survivor, both within and outside the family. Survivors and those around them are thrust into a social world in which the norms of interaction are ambiguous and often strained. Survivors may be unsure about when and to what extent others want to hear about the details of the death or the truth about their level of distress (e.g., when someone asks "How are you doing?" it is often unclear to survivors how much the questioner really wants to know the truth). Indeed, more than after other types of loss, survivors hide the nature of the death from others (Range, 1998; Range & Calhoun, 1990). In similar fashion, supporters of the survivor are often uncertain about how to be of help and specifically about whether talking about the details of the death is appropriate. Most suicide survivors thus face the complicated task of discerning what their own needs are for self-disclosure to others, who in their social network can be empathic with their situation, and how to effectively communicate their needs to others.

Repair and Transformation of the Bond With the Deceased

The field of thanatology has moved beyond the belief that grief is resolved by "decathecting" the relationship with the deceased and toward an understanding that the psychological work after loss is better understood as a transformation of the attachment to the deceased (Field, 2006b; Klass, Silverman, & Nickman, 1996; Neimeyer, Baldwin, & Gillies, 2006; Schut, M. S. Stroebe, Boelen, & Zijerveld, 2006). More nuanced understandings of this process are emerging as research begins to discriminate adaptive from maladaptive ways of "holding on" to the deceased (Boelen, M. S. Stroebe, Schut, & Zijerveld, 2006; Field, Gao, & Paderna, 2005; Schut et al., 2006; M. Stroebe & Schut, 2005; M. Stroebe, Schut, & W. Stroebe, 2005). If a transformation of the attachment to the deceased is a necessary part of grief work (Field, 2006a, 2008), and if suicide commonly produces a serious rupturing of that attachment, then the task of repairing the relationship after a suicide can be daunting. The perception that the deceased voluntarily chose to leave the mourner can produce tremendous feelings of abandonment, anger, and unworthiness in the survivor. As with other types of relational rupture (e.g., a marital affair or divorce), the emergence of such strong emotions usually requires considerable psychological work to repair the damage, yet the effort is obviously made more complicated by the death of the other person. Hence, an important goal of grief counseling with suicide survivors is the review of the relationship with the deceased, coupled with an exploration of how the life of the deceased and their relationship with the mourner can be disentangled from the manner of their death and the perceived abandonment of the mourner by the deceased. This work is intimately tied with the work described previously in constructing a narrative of the death—one that is complex, realistic, and compassionate.

Memorialization of the Deceased

After most deaths, it is common for mourners to seek ways to remember and honor the life of a loved one, both privately and publicly. Walter (1996) describes this process as the cocreation between the mourner and his or her social network of a "durable biography" of the deceased. Moreover, human beings usually have a strong wish to see their dead in a positive light, and most social networks support the attempts by the bereaved to accomplish this goal through eulogizing the deceased, sharing memories about his or her positive actions and traits, and so forth.

However, this process can become problematic after stigmatized and disenfranchised deaths such as a suicide (Doka, 2001). Social condemnation of suicide as a selfish or sinful act may converge with the survivor's own anger and sense of betrayal, leading to a great deal of ambivalence about whether and how to honor the deceased. The response of the community may also actively discourage attempts to publicly honor the deceased, as when school administrators refuse to allow any memorialization of a student who has died by suicide (see Chapter 8 for more discussion about the tension between prevention of contagion after suicide and honoring the life of the deceased). The central task for most survivors lies in being able to find a less negative and more neutral interpretation of the act of suicide (e.g., "It was the result of an illness, not of selfishness") and then to separate their feelings about the suicide from their feelings about the rest of the life of the deceased (e.g., "Even though he died by suicide, he was a good person"). In the beginning, the manner of death may seem to be the only important fact in the biography of the deceased. Revisiting and expanding that life story to include the positive characteristics and achievements of the deceased is a significant healing task after suicide, one that is closely tied to the transformation of the attachment to the deceased. For some survivors, it may involve a need to better understand and empathize with the distress that led to the suicide, and for others, it may also include a need to forgive the deceased for their actions.

Restoration of Functioning and Reinvestment in Life

The last task for suicide survivors is to psychologically reinvest in their own living. For some, this involves a need to "dis-identify" with the suicidal part of the deceased and to reaffirm the survivor's own reasons for continuing to choose life over death (Sands, 2008). For others, it can include rebuilding sources of meaning and pleasure in the survivor's own life that are not "tainted" by the suicide. And for still others, this task manifests itself in the form of post-traumatic growth (Calhoun & Tedeschi, 2001; Tedeschi & Calhoun, 2008). Post-traumatic growth involves the finding of benefit and psychological or spiritual growth after loss. This, too, can take many forms that include becoming a more compassionate person, changing one's spiritual orientation toward life and death, and developing a reordered set of priorities (usually involving service to others). These changes can be the culmination of all of the tasks outlined previously, as the survivor comes to a deeper understanding of his or her own life and that of the deceased, finds ways to bear the trauma of the suicide, and reorients him- or herself toward finding meaning in the death of a loved one to suicide. See Chapter 11 for additional comments on post-traumatic growth in suicide survivors.

Roles of the Grief Counselor

The skills of providing grief counseling to suicide survivors are both the same and different from those needed to provide assistance after any loss and will be reviewed in this section. These skills can also be conceptualized as key roles that a clinician plays during the course of the client's journey from the emotional injury to integration of the loss and reinvestment in living. The roles to be described here include bearing witness, expert guide, and psychotherapist.

Bearing witness. In the comparison made previously to a medical versus expert companioning model of psychological treatment, an explicit assumption that guides this author's understanding of grief counseling was articulated: "[G]rief counseling is a concentrated form of empathically attuned and skillfully applied social support" (see earlier in this chapter). The heart of that social support is bearing witness to the suffering of the mourner and to their attempt to integrate that suffering into their ongoing life trajectory. The central skill required of the therapist to perform this role has been termed "the gift of presence" (Rando, 1993). This conceptualization of the clinician as the provider of a safe and available "safe harbor" for the bereaved individual is congruent with the emerging literature on the role of attachment figures in recovery from trauma. The critical role of an empathically attuned attachment figure in the healing of childhood relational trauma has been widely discussed in the recent literature on child development (Herman, 1992; Hughes, 2006; Kagan, 2004; A. N. Schore, 2002a, 2003a, 2003b; J. R. Schore & A. N. Schore, 2008). Likewise, the importance of empathic resonance between therapist and patient has become a major focus of modern psychoanalytic and "self-psychology" approaches to psychotherapy (McCluskey, 2005; Spiegel, Severino, & Morrison, 2000). This also fits with the growing empirical support for the crucial role of the therapist–client alliance in producing favorable outcomes across all forms of psychotherapy (Norcross, 2002).

From this perspective, therapists serve as attachment figures who provide a "secure base" from which a bereaved individual is able to martial their own resilience to absorb a life trauma. At a basic level, consider the universal response of social networks in very acute grief reactions. Members of the family and community provide what human beings need for soothing and re-regulation of their biological systems (most particularly, the central nervous system)—physical touch and holding, calming vocalizations, and most importantly, their reassuring availability that signals to the individual that he or she is safe and will be protected by the group during this time of heightened vulnerability. In short, members of the mourner's social network engage in attachment-based caregiving behaviors. All of this is what happens (or should happen) in the beginning hours and days of acute grief, with the funeral as a culminating symbolic gathering of the community to literally and symbolically "hold" the wounded member of the group.

Over a much longer period of time, a similar process happens on a less physical and less public—but no less important—transactional level. That is, grieving individuals need the presence of stable, available, and empathically attuned figures in their social network who provide longer term "psychological holding" while the self-soothing and self-healing capacity of the individual is allowed to work. Crucial to this process are attachment figures whose presence allows the integration of the fragmented and dissociated experience of the trauma into a more coherent verbal narrative that helps the individual to make sense of, learn to carry, and ultimately move on from the wounding traumatic event(s) (Currier & Neimeyer, 2006; Neimeyer, 2001b, 2002). This understanding of the central role of attachment figures in facilitating "self-repair" after trauma provides an extremely useful foundational perspective for understanding the role of the therapeutic relationship in grief counseling with survivors of suicide and other traumatic losses.

Expert Guidance and Psychoeducation

The function of bearing witness to the story of the client requires a stance of humility and "beginner's mind" (a reference to Buddhist thinking that entails approaching an experience without preconception about what it means or what will happen—in this case, about what the loss means to the client or what they will need therapeutically from the clinician (see Suzuki, 1973). Put differently, bearing witness requires that the clinicians understand that they themselves are the "student" and the client is the "teacher" about the client's own experience. However, this alone is often not sufficient to help with the healing of most clients and must be counterbalanced with its exact opposite—a clinician who knows more about the experience of traumatic loss and what the client needs than does the client him- or herself.

Consultative psychoeducation with survivors plays a tremendously important role because bereavement after suicide is a truly alien experience for most people, something for which they have no reference point by which to judge their responses. For example, survivors often have no idea whether the intensity, form, and duration of their distress is normal. Typically, they underestimate how long the process of recovery will take, sometimes using guidelines from their own or other people's experience with much more normative losses ("You'll feel better in a few weeks" or "You'll be done with your grief in a year"). The perceived failure to grieve "correctly and on schedule" may add to the already intense level of the client's feelings of defectiveness and unworthiness. More rarely, clients may overestimate the amount of distress that they should be experiencing and think that they are not in sufficient pain for a long enough time to have "successfully" grieved. This sometimes engenders worries that they will be stricken later with symptoms of unresolved grief if they "fail" to grieve correctly now. This can also apply to family members' expectations of one another. For example, a mother may seek counseling for her adolescent son after the death of his father to suicide because he "won't talk about it" and "doesn't seem to be expressing his feelings enough" or "hasn't cried yet." The clinician's knowledge of grief after traumatic loss such as suicide, as well as his or her understanding of the heterogeneity of individual grief responses (in this case, the difference between adolescent males and adult females) is crucial in helping clients benchmark their own or others' responses.

However, psychoeducation for the survivor can go beyond simply offering normative guidelines about recovery. Another important expert role is the active anticipation of potential problems and the teaching of new skills to the client for coping with those problems. For example, survivors may be unaware of and unprepared for the intensity of their grief around the death anniversary or holidays. Devising a plan for coping with these predictably difficult periods can be helpful in allowing the client to feel more in control of their reactions as the dates approach. Likewise, many survivors have never thought about and are unprepared for the changes in their social connections that may occur after a suicide. They may encounter a plethora of insensitive comments from others ("They're in a better place now."; "How could they have done such a selfish thing to you?"; "Didn't you see it coming?") that are quite disturbing. Others may find that key people who were expected to stand by them are now instead pulling away. Experienced bereavement therapists can play an essential role in helping survivors to anticipate and learn skills for managing these difficult social encounters. Likewise, contact with other survivors can also serve much of the same psychoeducational role as did contact with the clinician in the transmission of coping skills for surviving after a suicide.

Lastly, the clinician's role as "grief expert" may reach its zenith with regard to specialized techniques that can be of tremendous value to clients and which they are unable to obtain anywhere else in their social network. Several examples of these techniques are described in the *Specialized Treatment Techniques* section later in this chapter. In addition to application of the techniques that are of direct help in ameliorating the client's experience of grief- and trauma-related symptoms, use of such procedures also serves to reinforce the client's expectation that the "grief expert" holds specialized knowledge that will assist the client in his or her journey, thus invoking the relational placebo effect that is a universal but underappreciated curative aspect of the medical model of treatment. It also fits well with the understanding of the role of affiliation with an attachment (i.e., a symbolic parental) figure whose presence can bring reassurance and comfort in the face of devastating psychological pain and loss.

Traditional Psychotherapist

Caregivers who primarily do grief counseling sometimes view all the client's difficulties through the lens of the presenting loss. Yet not every problem presented will be a result of the loss, even if the loss is due to suicide. Bereavement never happens in a vacuum—instead, it happens to individuals who have an ongoing life trajectory, a history, and a personality structure. In other words, people come to the experience of losing someone to suicide with a number of factors that are likely to influence the course of their bereavement and entail problems that predate the suicide (M. S. Stroebe, Folkman, Hansson, & Schut, 2006).

The first of these factors is the survivor's history with loss, separation, and trauma. It is beyond the scope of this chapter to review all of the research indicating that developmental processes, particularly with important attachment figures, influence how people deal with subsequent losses in their life. However, suffice it to say that there is considerable evidence that a history of previous trauma experiences in childhood creates a vulnerability to the development of PTSD after adult exposure to trauma (A. N. Schore, 2002a, 2002b). Likewise, one of the risk factors emerging from the research on CG or PGD is a history of insecure attachment relationships in the mourner, particularly in spousal loss (Gray, Prigerson, & Litz, 2004; Lichtenthal et al., 2004; Shear et al., 2007; Shear & Shair, 2005; Vanderwerker, Jacobs, Parkes, & Prigerson, 2006). In general, the survivor's history with other traumatic separations will influence the meaning that the loss has for them as well as how they attempt to cope with the psychic pain of the loss.

There is also convincing evidence that a history of previous psychiatric disorder is associated with an elevated risk for the redevelopment of these disorders after a loss (Hensley & Clayton, 2008). This seems to be particularly true for affective disorders (depression and bipolar disorder) but may also hold true for PTSD, other anxiety disorders, sleep disturbance, and difficulties with substance abuse. Likewise, preexisting relationship problems in a client's marriage or family are often intensified by the relational strain created by a suicide (Cerel et al., 2008; Jordan et al., 1993; Kaslow & Aronson, 2004).

Of course, not all of these issues will necessarily become a focus of clinical work with survivors. Rather, the decision about whether to address related problems is a complex and evolving one that must be decided collaboratively between the client and the therapist over the course of therapy. In some cases, such comorbid problems and disorders will directly interfere with the survivor's recovery (e.g., an alcohol abuse problem that grows worse after a traumatic loss). In other instances, treatment of these comorbid problems may need to be postponed for another time—or, perhaps, for another therapist who is more qualified to work with the difficulty in question (e.g., longstanding marital problems that might be exacerbated by a treatment focus on marital conflict and run the risk of further dissolution of family cohesion; or a client history of sexual abuse that has never been addressed).

A couple requests help in coping with the recent suicide of their only son. The son had shown some signs of depression, but both parents were unaware of his suicidal ideation. They were consequently stunned when his body was discovered by the police after shooting himself with a firearm that belonged to the father. The mother believed the father when he had previously promised to remove the firearm. The presence of weapons in the house was but one of many longstanding conflicts in the marital history, which had included a conflictual and, at times, abusive relationship between the father and his wife and children, as well as a prior marital separation. Despite the problems, both individuals indicated that they needed and wanted to stay together. Although both parents were deeply grieved by the death of their son, it quickly became apparent that the couple's coping styles were radically different. The mother needed to mourn openly and intensely for her son and was furious with the father for his deceit about the removal of the firearm. The father, in contrast, desperately needed to psychologically "wall off" his feelings of guilt and remorse about the death and responded to anger from his wife with defensiveness and denial. In light of the longstanding marital problems, and the current need for grief support by each partner, the therapist and couple agreed early in the treatment to do separate individual therapy sessions with the therapist rather than the more typical conjoint meetings. The initial focus on working on their grief in a private context, where the marital problems could also be discussed without threatening the already-fragile marriage, seemed to help keep the couple together while allowing each person to work on the grief in his or her own fashion and to gain a better appreciation of the partner's coping needs.

In general, clinicians are advised to follow the principle that "comorbid" problems should be named by the therapist as possible issues to be addressed early on in therapy but that clients should take the lead in deciding what problems are to be addressed and the sequencing of when those issues are to be confronted. The only exception to this would be problems that are potentially life threatening (e.g., suicidality in the client) or that so markedly interfere with the therapy that a failure to address them would lead to a failure of the treatment itself. Of course, therapists must also consider their own expertise and experience in dealing with other issues that may arise during the course of evaluation and treatment and, when appropriate, refer the survivor to other clinicians with the appropriate skills for additional therapy.

Specialized Treatment Techniques

Although it has been argued here that the core of grief counseling lies in the relational aspects of the therapy, this does not exclude the important role for specialized techniques that may be of significant value to survivors. Three broad goals of such specialized techniques, along with examples of each type of technique, are described in the subsections that follow. These broad goals include trauma reduction, meaning reconstruction, and relational repair. Many of these techniques can be helpful with more than one of these goals. Readers are also encouraged to learn about a new treatment protocol for CG (Shear et al., 2005; described briefly in the text that follows) that incorporates elements of all three of these types of techniques.

Trauma Reduction

From the field of traumatology a number of theoretically grounded and empirically supported techniques have evolved that may be helpful for suicide survivors who experience PTSD-type symptoms. These symptoms include evidence of reliving the traumatic experience (e.g., intrusive visual images of the death scene, nightmares); behaviors that serve to avoid any triggering of these distressing reliving experiences (e.g., avoidance of going into the room where the suicide happened); and hyperarousal of the autonomic nervous system (e.g., difficulty sleeping, irritability, startle reaction, etc.). Most of these procedures involve some combination of imaginal and/or in vivo exposure procedures to deal with the avoidance behaviors (e.g., imagining being in or actually spending time in the room where the suicide occurred) coupled with cognitive–behavioral techniques that help the individual attenuate distorted and dysfunctional cognitions that have developed as a result of the trauma (e.g., "I should have foreseen the suicide, and I didn't do enough to prevent it from occurring"). One technique with considerable empirical support is eye movement desensitization and reprocessing (EMDR; Shapiro, 2002; Shapiro & Forrest, 2004; Shapiro & Maxfield, 2002). EMDR involves having the client receive bilateral stimulation of the right and left hemispheres of the brain (through left/right eye movement or other alternating sensory input) while engaging in imaginal exposure to disturbing images or memories. It also includes psychoeducation about trauma, relaxation training, and cognitive restructuring of negative beliefs about the self that have developed from the traumatic experience.

Another relevant technique is prolonged exposure therapy (PE; Foa, Hembree, & Rothbaum, 2007; Yadin, & Foa, 2007). Similar to EMDR, PE involves education about trauma, training for diaphragmatic breathing, and in vivo and imaginal exposure. A hallmark of PE is the use of homework. The homework involves practicing the breathing exercises, carrying out in vivo exposure to traumatic stimuli, and listening to taped recordings of treatment sessions. The imaginal exposure includes a first-person, present-time, and detailed description of the traumatic event (e.g., "I'm walking into the room. There is blood everywhere. I see his body lying on the bed. ...").

Although neither EMDR nor PE were specifically developed for the treatment of traumatic grief, bereavement-oriented techniques that borrow heavily from EMDR and PE are beginning to appear in the literature (Boelen, 2006; Boelen, de Keijser, van den Hout, & van den Bout, 2007; Boelen, van den Hout, & van den Bout, 2006; Shear, 2006; Shear & Frank, 2006). Trauma reduction techniques such as these offer tremendous potential to help suicide survivors with the specific aspects of their experience that are anxiety producing and intrusive. These techniques are likely to be of particular help to survivors who witnessed the suicide or found the body but can also be very useful for survivors who have developed traumatic images of their loved one's death, despite the lack of direct eyewitness exposure to the event.

A father whose son ended his life by hanging is subsequently plagued by images of the last moments of his son's life, despite not being an eyewitness to the death or the death scene. He wonders how much his son struggled for breath, whether he attempted to place his feet on the ground, and how long it took him to lose consciousness and die. When these images begin to enter his thoughts, he actively tries to suppress them through distraction and avoidance, with only partial success. After preparation, the father engages in a session of EMDR where he is asked to call up these deeply disturbing images while receiving bilateral stimulation of pulses to the left and right palms of his hands. He almost immediately has an extraordinarily intense bodily and emotional reaction, beginning to weep, calling out his son's name, pleading with him not to hang himself, and visibly shaking. The session lasts for approximately 25 minutes. Both the therapist and the father are in awe of the power of the experience, and at the end of it and in subsequent sessions, the father reports a dramatic change in his experience of his grief. He states that he feels that, while still deeply saddened by the loss, he can now somehow confront and accept what his son has done. He also reports significant changes in the physicality of his grief, including a newfound sense of lightness in his body and an ability to sleep restfully that has been absent since his son's death.

Meaning Reconstruction

In this chapter, we have emphasized the impact that suicide can have on the assumptive world of the survivor. In a series of seminal articles and books, Neimeyer and colleagues have argued for the central role of meaning reconstruction in the trajectory of recovery from loss (Neimeyer, 2001a; Neimeyer, Prigerson, & Davies, 2002; Neimeyer & Wogrin, 2008). They also have provided empirical support for the central role of meaning making in the healing process (Currier, Holland, et al., 2008; Currier & Neimeyer, 2006; Gillies & Neimeyer, 2006; Holland, Currier, & Neimeyer, 2006; Keesee, Currier, & Neimeyer, 2008; Neimeyer, Baldwin, & Gillies, 2006) and have offered a variety of clinical case examples and techniques that are informed by this perspective (Neimeyer, 1999, 2006b, 2006c; Neimeyer, Herrero, & Botella, 2006; Neimeyer, Keesee, & Fortner, 2000; Stewart & Neimeyer, 2007).

This group has suggested that meaning making after traumatic loss can be understood along at least three different dimensions. *Sense making* is the attempt to "emplot" the traumatic events into a narrative that has coherence for the mourner, including an accounting of the events of the death, the key actors in the story (including the mourner), and their motivations for acting as they did. The second dimension is *benefit finding* in the loss, which entails discovering positive benefits for self and/or others that emerge from the loss experience. Third is finding a new identity that incorporates the death and reworked identity as a survivor of suicide loss. Chapter 11 of this book offers an in-depth exploration of these issues as well as clinical applications of this approach.

A number of meaning-making techniques that have relevance to work with suicide survivors have been developed in recent years. For example, although primarily developed for use with homicide survivors, a protocol has been developed by Rynearson (2001, 2006) for "restorative retelling" of the narrative of a violent death that has potential for healing after a suicide. The novel aspect of the protocol involves asking the client to first draw the death scene as they either witnessed it or imagined it to be and then to repeatedly re-draw (and, hence, retell) the scene in a way that is more bearable to the survivor. For example, a parent might re-draw the scene of his or her child being enveloped by a protective angel who lifts the child's spirit from his or her body up to heaven after the suicide. This more comforting image of the dying experience seems to provide a soothing alternative "memory image" to which the survivor may turn when they are plagued by intrusive and disturbing memories of the actual death scene. Similar constructivist approaches to trauma emphasize the need to "re-story" the death as a way to develop a coherent narrative of the death and its impact on the life of the mourner (Neimeyer, 2006c; Neimeyer, Herrero, & Botella, 2006; Shear & Frank, 2006; Stewart & Neimeyer, 2007). Cognitive–behavioral approaches also call attention to the value of engaging in a careful review of the mourner's accounting of a death and his or her perceived role in the event, helping the bereaved to re-examine their assumptions about the death and the cognitive "errors" that are often contained in those assumptions (Boelen, 2006; Stubenbort et al., 2006). These approaches seem to converge with constructivist approaches to meaning making after a loss (Neimeyer, 2006a) and also are beginning to generate empirical evidence for their efficacy (Boelen et al., 2007; de Groot et al., 2007).

Lastly, the therapeutic benefits of expressive writing or journaling about traumatic experiences of all types have received considerable empirical support and have been conceptualized as a way of facilitating meaning making and development of a coherent narrative of the loss and its impact (Neimeyer, van Dyke, & Pennebaker, 2008; Pennebaker, 2003, 2004; Pennebaker & Chung, 2007; Smyth & Pennebaker, 2008). Letter writing to the deceased may also have benefits for the third category of specialized techniques to facilitate relational repair of the connection with the deceased (see the next subsection).

Relational Repair

Intimate relationships are usually grounded in a mutual sense of affection, loyalty, psychological trust, and reciprocal availability as attachment figures (or, in the case of parents and offspring, as caregiver and attachment figures). As described previously, suicide is often experienced by the survivor as a profound betrayal of the "contract" of the intimate relationship with the deceased, such that the trust has been violated and the availability of the deceased taken away. This rupturing of the relationship can, in turn, contribute to the intense emotions of anger, abandonment, and unworthiness felt by many survivors. Thus, the relationship with the deceased often needs—and can benefit from— repair, but this is often seen as impossible by the survivor, considering the individual is gone.

However, the use of enactment techniques that encourage conversation with the deceased can be tremendously helpful in producing a psychological repair of the connection. These techniques can include having the mourner write letters to (and then back from) the deceased, guided imagery exercises that allow the mourner to have imaginal conversations with the deceased, and discussions with the deceased at the graveside or in classic "empty chair" conversations in the counselor's office setting. All of these interventions may be useful for survivors who are particularly troubled by the perceived relational betrayal embedded in the suicide. These interventions can help foster forgiveness of the deceased and of oneself as well as allow the development of a transformed but continuing psychological bond with the deceased that has been thwarted by the perceived intentionality of their suicide.

☐ Summary and Conclusion

Focused grief counseling with a knowledgeable, experienced, and compassionate grief counselor can be of enormous help to many suicide survivors. According to survey studies, aside from contact with other survivors, formal psychotherapy is perhaps the most useful form of formal postvention sought by suicide survivors (de Groot et al.,

2006; K. Dyregrov, 2002, 2003a; McMenamy et al., 2008; Saarinen, Viinamäki, Hintikka, Lehtonen, & Lönnqvist, 1999). This chapter has outlined many of the common grief reactions and problems faced by survivors and has described detailed goals for clinical intervention that facilitate the healing tasks that are common for most survivors. It has also outlined the foundational roles played by a therapist working with survivors as well as specific and targeted techniques that may be helpful in the recovery process. When combined with general clinical skills, a respectful validation of the remarkable resilience shown by most suicide survivors, and no small measure of wisdom about the complicated journey by which human beings heal from deep emotional trauma, the role of grief counseling in the healing process for suicide survivors can be invaluable.

☐ References

Agerbo, E. (2003). Risk of suicide and spouse's psychiatric illness or suicide: Nested case-control study. *BMJ: British Medical Journal, 327,* 1025–1026.

Agerbo, E. (2005). Midlife suicide risk, partner's psychiatric illness, spouse and child bereavement by suicide or other modes of death: A gender specific study. *Journal of Epidemiology & Community Health, 59,* 407–412.

Agerbo, E., Nordentoft, M., & Mortensen, P. B. (2002). Familial, psychiatric, and socioeconomic risk factors for suicide in young people: Nested case-control study. *BMJ: British Medical Journal, 325,* 74–77.

Allen, B. G., Calhoun, L. G., Cann, A., & Tedeschi, R. G. (1993). The effect of cause of death on responses to the bereaved: Suicide compared to accident and natural causes. *Omega: Journal of Death and Dying, 28,* 39–48.

Armour, M. (2006). Violent death: Understanding the context of traumatic and stigmatized grief. *Journal of Human Behavior in the Social Environment, 14*(4), 53–90.

Attig, T. (1996). *How we grieve: Relearning the world.* New York, NY: Oxford University Press.

Attig, T. (2001). Relearning the world: Making and finding meanings. In R. A. Neimeyer (Ed.), *Meaning reconstruction and the experience of loss* (pp. 33–53). Washington, DC: American Psychological Association.

Auster, T., Moutier, C., Lanouette, N., & Zisook, S. (2008). Bereavement and depression: Implications for diagnosis and treatment. *Psychiatric Annals, 38,* 655–661.

Bailley, S. E., Kral, M. J., & Dunham, K. (1999). Survivors of suicide do grieve differently: Empirical support for a common sense proposition. *Suicide and Life-Threatening Behavior, 29,* 256–271.

Balk, D., Wogrin, C., Thornton, G., & Meagher, D. (Eds.). (2007). *Handbook of thanatology: The essential body of knowledge for the study of death, dying, and bereavement*: New York, NY: Routledge/Taylor & Francis Group.

Boelen, P. A. (2006). Cognitive-behavioral therapy for complicated grief: Theoretical underpinnings and case descriptions. *Journal of Loss & Trauma, 11*, 1–30.

Boelen, P. A., de Keijser, J., van den Hout, M. A., & van den Bout, J. (2007). Treatment of complicated grief: A comparison between cognitive-behavioral therapy and supportive counseling. *Journal of Consulting and Clinical Psychology, 75*, 277–284.

Boelen, P. A., Stroebe, M. S., Schut, H. A. W., & Zijerveld, A. M. (2006). Continuing bonds and grief: A prospective analysis. *Death Studies, 30*, 767–776.

Boelen, P. A., van den Hout, M. A., & van den Bout, J. (2006). A cognitive-behavioral conceptualization of complicated grief. *Clinical Psychology: Science and Practice, 13*, 109–128.

Bonanno, G. A., & Boerner, K. (2008). Trajectories of grieving. In C. B. Wortman, M. S. Stroebe, R. O. Hansson, H. Schut, & W. Stroebe (Eds.), *Handbook of bereavement research and practice: Advances in theory and intervention* (pp. 287–307). Washington, DC: American Psychological Association.

Bonanno, G. A., Keltner, D., Holen, A., & Horowitz, M. J. (1995). When avoiding unpleasant emotions might not be such a bad thing: Verbal-autonomic response dissociation and midlife conjugal bereavement. *Journal of Personality and Social Psychology, 69*, 975–989.

Bonanno, G. A., Papa, A., Lalande, K., Zhang, N., & Noll, J. G. (2005). Grief processing and deliberate grief avoidance: A prospective comparison of bereaved spouses and parents in the United States and the People's Republic of China. *Journal of Consulting and Clinical Psychology, 73*, 86–98.

Brent, D. A., & Mann, J. J. (2006). Familial pathways to suicidal behavior: Understanding and preventing suicide among adolescents. *New England Journal of Medicine, 355*, 2719–2721.

Brent, D. A., Oquendo, M., Birmaher, B., Greenhill, L., Kolko, D., Stanley, B., … Mann, J. J. (2002). Familial pathways to early-onset suicide attempt: Risk for suicidal behavior in offspring of mood-disordered suicide attempters. *Archives of General Psychiatry, 59*, 801–807.

Brent, D. A., Perper, J. A., Moritz, G., Allman, C., et al. (1993). Bereavement or depression? The impact of the loss of a friend to suicide. *Journal of the American Academy of Child & Adolescent Psychiatry, 32*, 1189–1197.

Calhoun, L. G., & Tedeschi, R. G. (2001). Posttraumatic growth: The positive lessons of loss. In R. A. Neimeyer (Ed.), *Meaning reconstruction and the experience of loss* (pp. 157–172). Washington, DC: American Psychological Association.

Callahan, J. (2000). Predictors and correlates of bereavement in suicide support group participants. *Suicide and Life-Threatening Behavior, 30*, 104–124.

Campbell, F. R. (2006). Aftermath of suicide: The clinician's role. In R. I. Simon & R. E. Hales (Eds.), *The textbook of suicide assessment and management* (pp. 459–476). Washington, DC: American Psychiatric Publishing.

Campbell, F. R., Cataldie, L., McIntosh, J., & Millet, K. (2004). An active postvention program. *Crisis: The Journal of Crisis Intervention and Suicide Prevention, 25*, 30–32.

Cerel, J., Fristad, M. A., Weller, E. B., & Weller, R. A. (1999). Suicide-bereaved children and adolescents: A controlled longitudinal examination. *Journal of the American Academy of Child & Adolescent Psychiatry, 38*, 672–679.

Cerel, J., Fristad, M. A., Weller, E. B., & Weller, R. A. (2000). Suicide-bereaved children and adolescents: II. Parental and family functioning. *Journal of the American Academy of Child & Adolescent Psychiatry, 39,* 437–444.

Cerel, J., Jordan, J. R., & Duberstein, P. R. (2008). The impact of suicide on the family. *Crisis: The Journal of Crisis Intervention and Suicide Prevention, 29,* 38–44.

Cerel, J., Padgett, J. H., Conwell, Y., & Reed, G. A., Jr. (2009). A call for research: The need to better understand the impact of support groups for suicide survivors. *Suicide and Life-Threatening Behavior, 39,* 269–281.

Cleiren, M. P. H. D., Grad, O., Zavasnik, A., & Diekstra, R. F. W. (1996). Psychosocial impact of bereavement after suicide and fatal traffic accident: A comparative two-country study. *Acta Psychiatrica Scandinavica, 94,* 37–44.

Coifman, K. G., Bonanno, G. A., Ray, R. D., & Gross, J. J. (2007). Does repressive coping promote resilience? Affective-autonomic response discrepancy during bereavement. *Journal of Personality and Social Psychology, 92,* 745–758.

Colt, G. H. (2006). *November of the soul: The enigma of suicide.* New York, NY: Scribner.

Crosby, A. E., & Sacks, J. J. (2002). Exposure to suicide: Incidence and association with suicidal ideation and behavior: United States, 1994. *Suicide and Life-Threatening Behavior, 32,* 321–328.

Currier, J. M., Holland, J. M., Coleman, R. A., & Neimeyer, R. A. (Eds.). (2006). *Bereavement following violent death: An assault on life and meaning.* Amityville, NY: Baywood.

Currier, J. M., Holland, J. M., Coleman, R. A., & Neimeyer, R. A. (2008). Bereavement following violent death: An assault on life and meaning. In R. G. Stevenson & G. R. Cox (Eds.), *Perspectives on violence and violent death* (pp. 177–202): Amityville, NY: Baywood.

Currier, J. M., Holland, J. M., & Neimeyer, R. A. (2006). Sense-making, grief, and the experience of violent loss: Toward a mediational model. *Death Studies, 30,* 403–428.

Currier, J. M., Holland, J. M., & Neimeyer, R. A. (2007). The effectiveness of bereavement interventions with children: A meta-analytic review of controlled outcome research. *Journal of Clinical Child and Adolescent Psychology, 36,* 253–259.

Currier, J. M., & Neimeyer, R. A. (2006). Fragmented stories: The narrative integration of violent loss. In E. K. Rynearson (Ed.), *Violent death: Resilience and intervention beyond the crisis* (pp. 85–100). New York, NY: Routledge/Taylor & Francis Group.

Currier, J. M., Neimeyer, R. A., & Berman, J. S. (2008). The effectiveness of psychotherapeutic interventions for bereaved persons: A comprehensive quantitative review. *Psychological Bulletin, 134,* 648–661.

Cvinar, J. G. (2005). Do suicide survivors suffer social stigma? A review of the literature. *Perspectives in Psychiatric Care, 41,* 14–21.

de Groot, M., de Keijser, J., Neeleman, J., Kerkhof, A., Nolen, W., & Burger, H. (2007). Cognitive behaviour therapy to prevent complicated grief among relatives and spouses bereaved by suicide: Cluster randomised controlled trial. *BMJ: British Medical Journal, 334,* 994.

de Groot, M. H., de Keijser, J., & Neeleman, J. (2006). Grief shortly after suicide and natural death: A comparative study among spouses and first-degree relatives. *Suicide and Life-Threatening Behavior, 36,* 418–431.

Doka, K. J. (Ed.). (2001). *Disenfranchised grief: New directions, challenges, and strategies for practice* (2nd ed.). Champaign, IL: Research Press.

Duncan, B. L., Miller, S. D., Wampold, B. E., & Hubble, M. A. (2010). *The heart and soul of change: Delivering what works in therapy* (2nd ed.). Washington, DC: American Psychological Association.

Dyregrov, K. (2002). Assistance from local authorities versus survivors' needs for support after suicide. *Death Studies, 26,* 647–668.

Dyregrov, K. (2003a). *The loss of a child by suicide, SIDS, and accidents: Consequences, needs, and provisions of help.* Bergen, Norway: University of Bergen.

Dyregrov, K. (2003b). Micro-sociological analysis of social support following traumatic bereavement: Unhelpful and avoidant responses from the community. *Omega: Journal of Death and Dying, 48,* 23–44.

Dyregrov, K., & Dyregrov, A. (2005). Siblings after suicide—"The forgotten bereaved." *Suicide and Life-Threatening Behavior, 35,* 714–724.

Dyregrov, K., & Dyregrov, A. (2008). *Effective grief and bereavement support: The role of family, friends, colleagues, schools, and support professionals.* Philadelphia, PA: Jessica Kingsley Publishers.

Dyregrov, K., Nordanger, D., & Dyregrov, A. (2003). Predictors of psychosocial distress after suicide, SIDS and accidents. *Death Studies, 27,* 143–165.

Farberow, N. L., Gallagher-Thompson, D., Gilewski, M., & Thompson, L. (1992). The role of social supports in the bereavement process of surviving spouses of suicide and natural deaths. *Suicide and Life-Threatening Behavior, 22,* 107–124.

Feigelman, W., Gorman, B. S., Beal, K. C., & Jordan, J. R. (2008). Internet support groups for suicide survivors: A new mode for gaining bereavement assistance. *Omega: Journal of Death and Dying, 57,* 217–243.

Feigelman, W., Gorman, B. S., & Jordan, J. R. (2009). Stigmatization and suicide bereavement. *Death Studies, 33,* 591–608.

Feigelman, W., Jordan, J., & Gorman, B. S. (2009). How they died, time since loss, and bereavement outcomes *Omega: Journal of Death and Dying, 58,* 251–273.

Field, N. P. (2006a). Continuing bonds in adaptation to bereavement: Introduction. *Death Studies, 30,* 709–714.

Field, N. P. (2006b). Unresolved grief and continuing bonds: An attachment perspective. *Death Studies, 30,* 739–756.

Field, N. P. (2008). Whether to relinquish or maintain a bond with the deceased. In M. S. Stroebe, R. O. Hansson, H. Schut, & W. Stroebe (Eds.), *Handbook of bereavement research and practice: Advances in theory and intervention* (pp. 113–132). Washington, DC: American Psychological Association.

Field, N. P., Gao, B., & Paderna, L. (2005). Continuing bonds in bereavement: An attachment theory based perspective. *Death Studies, 29,* 277–299.

Foa, E. B., Hembree, E. A., & Rothbaum, B. O. (2007). *Prolonged exposure therapy for PTSD: Emotional processing of traumatic experiences: Therapist guide.* New York, NY: Oxford University Press.

Gillies, J., & Neimeyer, R. A. (2006). Loss, grief, and the search for significance: Toward a model of meaning reconstruction in bereavement. *Journal of Constructivist Psychology, 19,* 31–65.

Gray, M. J., Prigerson, H. G., & Litz, B. T. (2004). Conceptual and definitional issues in complicated grief. In B. T. Litz (Ed.), *Early intervention for trauma and traumatic loss* (pp. 65–84). New York, NY: Guilford Press.

Hansson, R. O., Hayslip, B., Jr., & Stroebe, M. S. (2007). Grief and bereavement. In J. A. Blackburn & C. N. Dulmus (Eds.), *Handbook of gerontology: Evidence-based approaches to theory, practice, and policy* (pp. 367–394). Hoboken, NJ: John Wiley & Sons.

Hansson, R. O., & Stroebe, M. S. (2007). The dual process model of coping with bereavement and development of an integrative risk factor framework. In R. O. Hansson & M. S. Stroebe (Eds.), *Bereavement in late life: Coping, adaptation, and developmental influences* (pp. 41–60). Washington, DC: American Psychological Association.

Hedstrom, P., Liu, K.-Y., & Nordvik, M. K. (2008). Interaction domains and suicide: A population-based panel study of suicides in Stockholm, 1991–1999. *Social Forces, 87,* 713–740.

Hensley, P. L. (2006a). A review of bereavement-related depression and complicated grief. *Psychiatric Annals, 36,* 619–626.

Hensley, P. L. (2006b). Treatment of bereavement-related depression and traumatic grief. *Journal of Affective Disorders, 92,* 117–124.

Hensley, P. L., & Clayton, P. J. (2008). Bereavement: Signs, symptoms, and course. *Psychiatric Annals, 38,* 649–654.

Herman, J. (1992). *Trauma and recovery.* New York, NY: Basic Books.

Holland, J. M., Currier, J. M., & Neimeyer, R. A. (2006). Meaning reconstruction in the first two years of bereavement: The role of sense-making and benefit-finding. *Omega: Journal of Death and Dying, 53,* 175–191.

Hughes, D. A. (2006). *Building the bonds of attachment: Awakening love in deeply troubled children* (2nd ed.). Lanham, MD: Jason Aronson.

Joiner, T. E., Van Orden, K. A., Witte, T. K., & Rudd, M. D. (2009). *The interpersonal theory of suicide: Guidance for working with suicidal clients.* Washington, DC: American Psychological Association.

Joiner, T. E., Walker, R. L., Rudd, M. D., & Jobes, D. A. (1999). Scientizing and routinizing the assessment of suicidality in outpatient practice. *Professional Psychology: Research and Practice, 30,* 447–453.

Jordan, J. (2001). Is suicide bereavement different? A reassessment of the literature. *Suicide and Life-Threatening Behavior, 31,* 91–102.

Jordan, J. (2009). After suicide: Clinical work with survivors. *Grief matters: The Australian Journal of Grief and Bereavement, 12*(1), 4–9.

Jordan, J., & McMenamy, J. (2004). Interventions for suicide survivors: A review of the literature. *Suicide and Life-Threatening Behavior, 34,* 337–349.

Jordan, J., & Neimeyer, R. A. (2003). Does grief counseling work? *Death Studies, 27,* 765–786.

Jordan, J. (2008). Bereavement after suicide. *Psychiatric Annals, 38,* 679–685.

Jordan, J., Kraus, D. R., & Ware, E. S. (1993). Observations on loss and family development. *Family Process, 32,* 425–440.

Kagan, R. (2004). *Rebuilding attachments with traumatized children: Healing from losses, violence, abuse, and neglect.* Binghamton, NY: Haworth Maltreatment and Trauma Press/The Haworth Press.

Kaslow, N. J., & Aronson, S. G. (2001). The consequences of caring: Mutual healing of family and therapists following a suicide. In S. H. McDaniel, D.-D. Lusterman, & C. L. Philpot (Eds.), *Casebook for integrating family therapy: An ecosystemic approach* (pp. 373–383). Washington, DC: American Psychological Association.

Kaslow, N. J., & Aronson, S. G. (2004). Recommendations for family interventions following a suicide. *Professional Psychology: Research and Practice, 35,* 240–247.

Kaslow, N. J., Ivey, A. Z., Berry-Mitchell, F., Franklin, K., & Bethea, K. (2009). Postvention for African American families following a loved one's suicide. *Professional Psychology: Research and Practice, 40,* 165–171.

Kauffman, J. (2002). *Loss of the assumptive world: A theory of traumatic loss.* New York, NY: Brunner-Routledge.

Keesee, N. J., Currier, J. M., & Neimeyer, R. A. (2008). Predictors of grief following the death of one's child: The contribution of finding meaning. *Journal of Clinical Psychology, 64,* 1145–1163.

Kendler, K. S., Myers, J., & Zisook, S. (2008). Does bereavement-related major depression differ from major depression associated with other stressful life events? *American Journal of Psychiatry, 165,* 1449–1455.

Klass, D., Silverman, P. R., & Nickman, S. L. (1996). *Continuing bonds: New understandings of grief.* Washington, DC: Taylor & Francis.

Knieper, A. J. (1999). The suicide survivor's grief and recovery. *Suicide and Life-Threatening Behavior, 29,* 353–364.

Latham, A. E., & Prigerson, H. G. (2004). Suicidality and bereavement: Complicated grief as psychiatric disorder presenting greatest risk for suicidality. *Suicide and Life-Threatening Behavior, 34,* 350–362.

Lichtenthal, W. G., Cruess, D. G., & Prigerson, H. G. (2004). A case for establishing complicated grief as a distinct mental disorder in *DSM-V. Clinical Psychology Review, 24,* 637–662.

Mann, J. J., Bortinger, J., Oquendo, M. A., Currier, D., Li, S., & Brent, D. A. (2005). Family history of suicidal behavior and mood disorders in probands with mood disorders. *American Journal of Psychiatry, 162,* 1672–1679.

McCluskey, U. (2005). *To be met as a person: The dynamics of attachment in professional encounters.* London, United Kingdom: Karnac Books.

McDaid, C., Trowman, R., Golder, S., Hawton, K., & Sowden, A. (2008). Interventions for people bereaved through suicide: Systematic review. *British Journal of Psychiatry, 193,* 438–443.

McMenamy, J. M., Jordan, J. R., & Mitchell, A. M. (2008). What do suicide survivors tell us they need? Results of a pilot study. *Suicide and Life-Threatening Behavior, 38,* 375–389.

Melhem, N. M., Day, N., Shear, K., Day, R., Reynolds, C. F., III, & Brent, D. (2004a). Predictors of complicated grief among adolescents exposed to a peer's suicide. *Journal of Loss & Trauma, 9,* 21–34.

Melhem, N. M., Day, N., Shear, K., Day, R., Reynolds, C. F., III, & Brent, D. (2004b). Traumatic grief among adolescents exposed to a peer's suicide. *American Journal of Psychiatry, 161,* 1411–1416.

Melham, N. M., Rosales, C., Karageorge, J., Reynolds, C. F., III, Frank, E., & Shear, K. (2001). Comorbidity of Axis I disorders in patients with traumatic grief. *Journal of Clinical Psychiatry, 62,* 884–887.

Mitchell, A. M., Kim, Y., Prigerson, H. G., & Mortimer-Stephens, M. (2004). Complicated grief in survivors of suicide. *Crisis: The Journal of Crisis Intervention and Suicide Prevention, 25,* 12–18.

Murphy, S. A., Braun, T., Tillery, L., Cain, K. C., Johnson, L. C., & Beaton, R. D. (1999). PTSD among bereaved parents following the violent deaths of their 12- to 28-year-old children: A longitudinal prospective analysis. *Journal of Traumatic Stress, 12,* 273–291.

Murphy, S. A., Chung, I.-J., & Johnson, L. C. (2002). Patterns of mental distress following the violent death of a child and predictors of change over time. *Research in Nursing & Health, 25,* 425–437.

Murphy, S. A., Johnson, L. C., & Lohan, J. (2002). The aftermath of the violent death of a child: An integration of the assessments of parents' mental distress and PTSD during the first 5 years of bereavement. *Journal of Loss & Trauma, 7,* 203–222.

Murphy, S. A., Johnson, L. C., & Lohan, J. (2003). Finding meaning in a child's violent death: A five-year prospective analysis of parents' personal narratives and empirical data. *Death Studies, 27,* 381–404.

Murphy, S. A., Johnson, L. C., Wu, L., Fan, J. J., & Lohan, J. (2003). Bereaved parents' outcomes 4 to 60 months after their children's death by accident, suicide, or homicide: A comparative study demonstrating differences. *Death Studies, 27,* 39–61.

Neimeyer, R. A. (1999). Narrative strategies in grief therapy. *Journal of Constructivist Psychology, 12,* 65–85.

Neimeyer, R. A. (Ed.). (2001a). *Meaning reconstruction & the experience of loss.* Washington, DC: American Psychological Association.

Neimeyer, R. A. (2001b). Reauthoring life narratives: Grief therapy as meaning reconstruction. *Israel Journal of Psychiatry and Related Sciences, 38,* 171–183.

Neimeyer, R. A. (2002). Traumatic loss and the reconstruction of meaning. *Journal of Palliative Medicine, 5,* 935–942.

Neimeyer, R. A. (2005a). The construction of change: Personal reflections on the therapeutic process. *Constructivism in the Human Sciences, 10,* 77–98.

Neimeyer, R. A. (2005b). Tragedy and transformation: Meaning reconstruction in the wake of traumatic loss. In S. Heilman (Ed.), *Death, bereavement, and mourning* (pp. 121–134). New Brunswick, NJ: Transaction Publishers.

Neimeyer, R. A. (2006a). Complicated grief and the reconstruction of meaning: Conceptual and empirical contributions to a cognitive-constructivist model. *Clinical Psychology: Science and Practice, 13,* 141–145.

Neimeyer, R. A. (2006b). Narrating the dialogical self: Toward an expanded toolbox for the counselling psychologist. *Counselling Psychology Quarterly, 19,* 105–120.

Neimeyer, R. A. (2006c). Re-storying loss: Fostering growth in the posttraumatic narrative. In L. G. Calhoun & R. G. Tedeschi (Eds.), *Handbook of posttraumatic growth: Research & practice* (pp. 68–80). Mawah, NJ: Erlbaum.

Neimeyer, R. A. (2009). *Constructivist psychotherapy: Distinctive features.* New York, NY: Routledge/Taylor & Francis Group.

Neimeyer, R. A., Baldwin, S. A., & Gillies, J. (2006). Continuing bonds and reconstructing meaning: Mitigating complications in bereavement. *Death Studies, 30,* 715–738.

Neimeyer, R. A., Herrero, O., & Botella, L. (2006). Chaos to coherence: Psychotherapeutic integration of traumatic loss. *Journal of Constructivist Psychology, 19,* 127–145.

Neimeyer, R. A., & Jordan, J. R. (2001). Disenfranchisement as empathic failure: Grief therapy and the co-construction of meaning. In K. J. Doka (Ed.), *Disenfranchised grief: New directions, challenges, and strategies for practice* (pp. 95–117). Champaign, IL: Research Press.

Neimeyer, R. A., Keesee, N. J., & Fortner, B. V. (2000). Loss and meaning reconstruction: Propositions and procedures. In R. Malkinson, S. S. Rubin, & E. Witztum (Eds.), *Traumatic and nontraumatic loss and bereavement: Clinical theory and practice* (pp. 197–230). Madison, WI: Psychosocial Press.

Neimeyer, R. A., Prigerson, H. G., & Davies, B. (2002). Mourning and meaning. *American Behavioral Scientist, 46,* 235–251.

Neimeyer, R. A., & Raskin, J. D. (2000). *Constructions of disorder: Meaning-making frameworks for psychotherapy.* Washington, DC: American Psychological Association.

Neimeyer, R. A., van Dyke, J. G., & Pennebaker, J. W. (2008). Narrative medicine: Writing through bereavement. In H. C. W. Breitbart (Ed.), *Handbook of psychiatry in palliative medicine* (pp. 454–469). New York, NY: Oxford University Press.

Neimeyer, R. A., & Wogrin, C. (2008). Psychotherapy for complicated bereavement: A meaning-oriented approach. *Illness, Crisis, & Loss, 16,* 1–20.

Neria, Y., & Litz, B. T. (2004). Bereavement by traumatic means: The complex synergy of trauma and grief. *Journal of Loss & Trauma, 9,* 73–87.

Norcross, J. C. (2002). *Psychotherapy relationships that work: Therapist contributions and responsiveness to patients.* New York, NY: Oxford University Press.

Ott, C. H. (2003). The impact of complicated grief on mental and physical health at various points in the bereavement process. *Death Studies, 27,* 249–272.

Ott, C. H., & Lueger, R. J. (2002). Patterns of change in mental health status during the first two years of spousal bereavement. *Death Studies, 26,* 387–411.

Owens, C., Lambert, H., Lloyd, K., & Donovan, J. (2008). Tales of biographical disintegration: How parents make sense of their sons' suicides. *Sociology of Health & Illness, 30,* 237–254.

Parker, H. A., & McNally, R. J. (2008). Repressive coping, emotional adjustment, and cognition in people who have lost loved ones to suicide. *Suicide and Life-Threatening Behavior, 36,* 676–687.

Pennebaker, J. W. (2003). Writing about emotional experiences as a therapeutic process. In P. Salovey & A. J. Rothman (Eds.), *Social psychology of health: Key readings* (pp. 362–368). New York, NY: Psychology Press.

Pennebaker, J. W. (2004). Theories, therapies, and taxpayers: On the complexities of the expressive writing paradigm. *Clinical Psychology: Science and Practice, 11,* 138–142.

Pennebaker, J. W., & Chung, C. K. (2007). Expressive writing, emotional upheavals, and health. In H. S. Friedman & R. C. Silver (Eds.), *Foundations of health psychology* (pp. 263–284). New York, NY: Oxford University Press.

Prigerson, H. G., Horowitz, M. J., Jacobs, S. C., Parkes, C. M., Aslan, M., Goodkin, K., … Maciejewski, P. K. (2009). Prolonged grief disorder: Psychometric validation of criteria proposed for *DSM-V* and *ICD-11.* [Electronic version]. *PLoS Med 6(8),* e1000121. doi:10.1371/journal.pmed.1000121

Prigerson, H. G., & Maciejewski, P. K. (2005). A call for sound empirical testing and evaluation of criteria for complicated grief proposed for *DSM-V. Omega: Journal of Death and Dying, 52,* 9–19.

Prigerson, H. G., Vanderwerker, L. C., & Maciejewski, P. K. (2008). A case for inclusion of prolonged grief disorder in *DSM-V.* In M. S. Stroebe, R. O. Hansson, H. Schut, & W. Stroebe (Eds.), *Handbook of bereavement research and practice: Advances in theory and intervention* (pp. 165–186). Washington, DC: American Psychological Association.

Provini, C., Everett, J. R., & Pfeffer, C. R. (2000). Adults mourning suicide: Self-reported concerns about bereavement, needs for assistance, and help-seeking behavior. *Death Studies, 24,* 1–19.

Qin, P., Agerbo, E., & Mortensen, P. B. (2002). Suicide risk in relation to family history of completed suicide and psychiatric disorders: A nested case-control study based on longitudinal registers. *Lancet, 360,* 1126–1130.

Qin, P., Agerbo, E., & Mortensen, P. B. (2005). Factors contributing to suicide: The epidemiological evidence from large-scale registers. In K. Hawton (Ed.), *Prevention and treatment of suicidal behavior* (pp. 11–28). Oxford, United Kingdom: Oxford University Press.

Rando, T. A. (1993). *Treatment of complicated mourning.* Champaign, IL: Research Press.

Range, L. M. (1998). When a loss is due to suicide: Unique aspects of bereavement. In J. H. Harvey (Ed.), *Perspectives on loss: A sourcebook* (pp. 213–220). Philadelphia, PA: Brunner/Mazel.

Range, L. M., & Calhoun, L. G. (1990). Responses following suicide and other types of death: The perspective of the bereaved. *Omega: Journal of Death and Dying, 21,* 311–320.

Raphael, B., Martinek, N., & Wooding, S., (2004). Assessing traumatic bereavement. In J. P. Wilson & T. M. Keane (Eds.), *Assessing psychological trauma and PTSD* (2nd ed.; pp. 492–510). New York, NY: Guilford Press.

Reed, M. D. (1998). Predicting grief symptomatology among the suddenly bereaved. *Suicide and Life-Threatening Behavior, 28,* 285–301.

Roy, A., & Janal, M. (2005). Family history of suicide, female sex, and childhood trauma: Separate or interacting risk factors for attempts at suicide? *Acta Psychiatrica Scandinavica, 112,* 367–371.

Rynearson, E. K. (2001). *Retelling violent death.* Philadelphia, PA: Brunner-Routledge.

Rynearson, E. K. (Ed.). (2006). *Violent death: Resilience and intervention beyond the crisis.* New York, NY: Routledge/Taylor & Francis Group.

Saarinen, P. I., Hintikka, J., Lehtonen, J., Lönnqvist, J. K., & Viinamäki, H. (2002). Mental health and social isolation among survivors ten years after a suicide in the family: A case-control study. *Archives of Suicide Research, 6,* 221–226.

Saarinen, P. I., Hintikka, J., Viinamäki, H., Lehtonen, J., & Lönnqvist, J. (2000). Is it possible to adapt to the suicide of a close individual? Results of a 10-year prospective follow-up study. *International Journal of Social Psychiatry, 46,* 182–190.

Saarinen, P. I., Viinamäki, H., Hintikka, J., Lehtonen, J., & Lönnqvist, J. (1999). Psychological symptoms of close relatives of suicide victims. *European Journal of Psychiatry, 13,* 33–39.

Sands, D. (2008). *Suicide grief: Meaning making and the griever's relational world.* Sydney, Australia: University of Technology.

Sands, D. (2009). A tripartite model of suicide grief: Meaning-making and the relationship with the deceased. *Grief Matters: The Australian Journal of Grief and Bereavement, 12*(1), 10–17.

Schore, A. N. (2002a). Dysregulation of the right brain: A fundamental mechanism of traumatic attachment and the psychopathogenesis of posttraumatic stress disorder. *Australian and New Zealand Journal of Psychiatry, 36*, 9–30.

Schore, A. N. (2002b). The neurobiology of attachment and early personality organization. *Journal of Prenatal & Perinatal Psychology & Health, 16*, 249–263.

Schore, A. N. (2003a). *Affect dysregulation and disorders of the self*. New York, NY: W. W. Norton & Co.

Schore, A. N. (2003b). *Affect regulation and the repair of the self*. New York, NY: W. W. Norton & Co.

Schore, J. R., & Schore, A. N. (2008). Modern attachment theory: The central role of affect regulation in development and treatment. *Clinical Social Work Journal, 36*, 9–20.

Schut, H. A. W., Stroebe, M. S., Boelen, P. A., & Zijerveld, A. M. (2006). Continuing relationships with the deceased: Disentangling bonds and grief. *Death Studies, 30*, 757–766.

Schuurman, D. L., & DeCristofaro, J. (2007). After a parent's death: Group, family, and individual therapy to help children. In N. B. Webb (Ed.), *Play therapy with children in crisis: Individual, group, and family treatment* (3rd ed.; pp. 173–196). New York, NY: Guilford Press.

Shapiro, F. (2002). EMDR 12 years after its introduction: Past and future research. *Journal of Clinical Psychology, 58*, 1–22.

Shapiro, F., & Forrest, M. S. (2004). *EMDR: The breakthrough therapy for overcoming anxiety, stress, and trauma*. New York, NY: Basic Books.

Shapiro, F., & Maxfield, L. (2002). Eye movement desensitization and reprocessing (EMDR): Information processing in the treatment of trauma. *Journal of Clinical Psychology, 58*, 933–946.

Shea, S. C. (2002). *The practical art of suicide assessment: A guide for mental health professionals and substance abuse counselors*. Hoboken, NJ: John Wiley & Sons.

Shear, K. (2006). Adapting imaginal exposure to the treatment of complicated grief. In B. O. Rothbaum (Ed.), *Pathological anxiety: Emotional processing in etiology and treatment* (pp. 215–226). New York, NY: Guilford Press.

Shear, K., & Frank, E. (2006). Treatment of complicated grief: Integrating cognitive-behavioral methods with other treatment approaches. In V. M. Follette & J. I. Ruzek (Eds.), *Cognitive-behavioral therapies for trauma* (2nd ed.; pp. 290–320). New York, NY: Guilford Press.

Shear, K., Frank, E., Houck, P. R., & Reynolds, C. F., III. (2005). Treatment of complicated grief: A randomized controlled trial. *JAMA: Journal of the American Medical Association, 293*, 2601–2608.

Shear, K., Gorscak, B., & Simon, N. (2006). Treatment of complicated grief following violent death. In E. K. Rynearson (Ed.), *Violent death: Resilience and intervention beyond the crisis* (pp. 157–174). New York, NY: Routledge/Taylor & Francis Group.

Shear, K., Monk, T., Houck, P., Melhem, N., Frank, E., Reynolds, C., … Silowash, R. (2007). An attachment-based model of complicated grief including the role of avoidance. *European Archives of Psychiatry and Clinical Neuroscience, 257*, 453–461.

Shear, K., & Shair, H. (2005). Attachment, loss, and complicated grief. *Developmental Psychobiology, 47,* 253–267.

Shear, K., Frank, E., Foa, E., Cherry, C., Reynold, C. F., III, Vander Bilt, J., … Masters, S. (2001). Traumatic grief treatment: A pilot study. *American Journal of Psychiatry, 158,* 1506–1508.

Shear, K., Zuckoff, A., Melhem, N., Gorscak, B. J., Schein, L. A., Spitz, H. I., … Vargo, S. (2006). The syndrome of traumatic grief and its treatment. In S. Vargo (Ed.), *Psychological effects of catastrophic disasters: Group approaches to treatment* (pp. 287–333). New York, NY: Haworth Press.

Shneidman, E. S. (1972). Foreword. In A. C. Cain (Ed.), *Survivors of suicide* (pp. ix–xi). Springfield, IL: Charles C Thomas.

Simon, N. M., Shear, K. M., Thompson, E. H., Zalta, A. K., Perlman, C., Reynolds, C. F., … Silowash, R. (2007). The prevalence and correlates of psychiatric comorbidity in individuals with complicated grief. *Comprehensive Psychiatry, 48,* 395–399.

Smyth, J. M., & Pennebaker, J. W. (2008). Exploring the boundary conditions of expressive writing: In search of the right recipe. *British Journal of Health Psychology, 13,* 1–7.

Spiegel, J., Severino, S. K., & Morrison, N. K. (2000). The role of attachment functions in psychotherapy. *Journal of Psychotherapy Practice & Research, 9,* 25–32.

Stewart, A. E., & Neimeyer, R. A. (2007). Emplotting the traumatic self: Narrative revision and the construction of coherence. In S. Krippner, M. Bova, & L. Gray (Eds.), *Healing stories: The use of narrative in counseling and psychotherapy* (pp. 41–62). San Juan, Puerto Rico: Puente Publications.

Stroebe, M., & Schut, H. (1999). The dual process model of coping with bereavement: Rationale and description. *Death Studies, 23,* 197–224.

Stroebe, M., & Schut, H. (2005). To continue or relinquish bonds: A review of consequences for the bereaved. *Death Studies, 29,* 477–494.

Stroebe, M., Schut, H., & Stroebe, W. (2005). Attachment in coping with bereavement: A theoretical integration. *Review of General Psychology, 9,* 48–66.

Stroebe, M. S., Folkman, S., Hansson, R. O., & Schut, H. (2006). The prediction of bereavement outcome: Development of an integrative risk factor framework. *Social Science & Medicine, 63,* 2440–2451.

Stroebe, M. S., Hansson, R. O., Schut, H., & Stroebe, W. (2008a). Bereavement research: Contemporary perspectives. In M. S. Stroebe, R. O. Hansson, H. Schut & W. Stroebe (Eds.), *Handbook of bereavement research and practice: Advances in theory and intervention* (pp. 3–25). Washington, DC: American Psychological Association.

Stroebe, M. S., Hansson, R. O., Schut, H., & Stroebe, W. (Eds.). (2008b). *Handbook of bereavement research and practice: Advances in theory and intervention.* Washington, DC: American Psychological Association.

Stroebe, W., Schut, H., & Stroebe, M. S. (2005). Grief work, disclosure and counseling: Do they help the bereaved? *Clinical Psychology Review, 25,* 395–414.

Stroebe, W., Zech, E., Stroebe, M. S., & Abakoumkin, G. (2005). Does social support help in bereavement? *Journal of Social & Clinical Psychology, 24,* 1030–1050.

Stubenbort, K., Cohen, J. A., Schein, L. A., Spitz, H. I., Burlingame, G. M., & Muskin, P. R. (2006). Cognitive-behavioral groups for traumatically bereaved children and their parents. In S. Vargo (Ed.), *Psychological effects of catastrophic disasters: Group approaches to treatment* (pp. 581–628). New York, NY: Haworth Press.

Suzuki, S. (1973). *Zen mind, beginner's mind*. New York, NY: Weatherhill.

Sveen, C.-A., & Walby, F. A. (2008). Suicide survivors' mental health and grief reactions: A systematic review of controlled studies. *Suicide and Life-Threatening Behavior, 38*, 13–29.

Taku, K., Calhoun, L. G., Cann, A., & Tedeschi, R. G. (2008). The role of rumination in the coexistence of distress and posttraumatic growth among bereaved Japanese university students. *Death Studies, 32*, 428–444.

Tedeschi, R. G., & Calhoun, L. G. (2003). *Helping bereaved parents: A clinician's guide*. New York, NY: Brunner-Routledge.

Tedeschi, R. G., & Calhoun, L. G. (2006). Time of change? The spiritual challenges of bereavement and loss. *Omega: Journal of Death and Dying, 53*, 105–116.

Tedeschi, R. G., & Calhoun, L. G. (2008). Beyond the concept of recovery: Growth and the experience of loss. *Death Studies, 32*, 27–39.

Thompson, K. E., & Range, L. M. (1992). Bereavement following suicide and other deaths: Why support attempts fail. *Omega: Journal of Death and Dying, 26*, 61–70.

Van Dongen, C. J. (1993). Social context of postsuicide bereavement. *Death Studies, 17*, 125–141.

Vanderwerker, L. C., Jacobs, S. C., Parkes, C. M., & Prigerson, H. G. (2006). An exploration of associations between separation anxiety in childhood and complicated grief in later life. *Journal of Nervous and Mental Disease, 194*, 121–123.

Walter, T. (1996). A new model of grief: Bereavement and biography. *Mortality, 1*, 7–25.

Wampold, B. E. (2001). *The great psychotherapy debate: Model, methods, & findings*. Mawah, NJ: Erlbaum.

Webb, N. B. (1993). Suicidal death of mother: Cases of silence and stigma. In N. B. Webb (Ed.), *Helping bereaved children: A handbook for practitioners* (pp. 137–155). New York, NY: Guilford Press.

Webb, N. B. (2002). Assessment of the bereaved child. In N. B. Webb (Ed.), *Helping bereaved children: A handbook for practitioners* (2nd ed.; pp. 19–42). New York, NY: Guilford Press:.

Webb, N. B. (2003). Play and expressive therapies to help bereaved children: Individual, family, and group treatment. *Smith College Studies in Social Work, 73*, 405–422.

Worden, J. W. (2009). *Grief counseling and grief therapy* (4th ed.). New York, NY: Springer.

Yadin, E., & Foa, E. B. (2007). Cognitive behavioral treatments for posttraumatic stress disorder. In L. J. Kirmayer, R. Lemelson, & M. Barad (Eds.), *Understanding trauma: Integrating biological, clinical, and cultural perspectives* (pp. 178–193). New York, NY: Cambridge University Press.

Zisook, S., & Kendler, K. S. (2007). Is bereavement-related depression different than non-bereavement-related depression? *Psychological Medicine, 37*, 779–794.

Zisook, S., & Shuchter, S. R. (2001). Treatment of the depressions of bereavement. *American Behavioral Scientist, 44*, 782–792.

10
CHAPTER

Grief Counseling With Child and Adolescent Survivors of Parental Suicidal Deaths

Nancy Boyd Webb

Death is difficult for survivors of any age. However, when an individual's intentional actions result in suicide death, the loss qualifies as traumatic for all surviving family members. Child and youth survivors of parental suicide are multiply and profoundly bereft because of their dependency and need for a parenting role model and caregiver, in addition to their need for a parent's unconditional love. Furthermore, young children have difficulty understanding the concept of death itself; when they find out their parent's death was self-inflicted, they may be overcome with troubling feelings of confusion and anger. Timely bereavement counseling in the form of crisis/trauma therapy can help young people process their experiences of complicated traumatic bereavement so that their development can proceed despite their terrible loss.

This chapter applies the principles of crisis intervention, grief counseling, and trauma treatment in therapy with suicide-bereaved children and youth of three different developmental stages: preschool, elementary-school age, and adolescence. Children's typical responses to trauma will be presented to highlight some of the differences between the grief reactions of young people and adults. Brief case vignettes illustrate the specific methods and principles of crisis intervention play therapy, cognitive therapy, and psychodynamically oriented treatment with children and youth of different ages. Although several literature reviews have cast doubts about the necessity and efficacy of grief counseling for all bereaved persons, empirical evidence as well as considerable clinical wisdom suggest that for people exposed to traumatic losses such as suicide, formal professional interventions may be of significant value (Currier, Neimeyer, & Berman, 2008; Fortner, 1999; Jordan & Neimeyer, 2003; Larson & Hoyt, 2007). The only review to consider bereavement interventions specifically for children (Currier, Holland, & Neimeyer, 2007) found similar results, but acknowledged that most of the studies did not screen for or select children based on membership in a high-risk category, such as suicide exposure. Although no control cases were available to compare the children and youth discussed in this chapter with those who did not receive treatment, improvement after therapy was evident in several of the individual cases as well as in the cases treated in the cognitive-behavioral treatment model described by Cohen, Mannarino, and Deblinger (2006). Sometimes, many intervening variables can complicate and negate individual therapy when the family insists on denying the suicidal death, or when unstable families cannot provide the necessary support to the bereaved young person. Hopefully, future research will document the helpfulness of different counseling methods so that children and adolescents who suffer the complicated and traumatic grief associated with suicide deaths will be able to receive and benefit from the supportive help they so desperately need.

☐ Traumatic Grief in Children and Adolescents

Childhood traumatic grief (CTG) has been described as "a condition in which both unresolved grief and post-traumatic stress disorder (PTSD) symptoms are present, often accompanied by depressive symptoms" (Cohen et al., 2006). Without treatment, PTSD symptoms can increase the risk of other serious psychiatric conditions, such as depression, substance abuse, and borderline personality disorder (Cohen et al., 2006). Survivors' bereavement responses differ depending on the nature of the death, the individual's personal qualities and past experiences, and the interaction of these factors with the surrounding support system, including the larger culture. In a previous publication, I conceptualized these three groups of factors as *The Tripartite Assessment of the Bereaved Child* (Webb, 2002).

The Nature of the Death

The death of an elderly grandmother can be quite sad for her family, but the sudden suicidal death of a family member in adolescence or midlife brings about many other emotions in addition to sadness. The recognition of this difference has led to the development of the concept of traumatic grief (TG) as applicable to survivors' emotional responses following traumatic deaths, such as suicide. Researchers studying these reactions agree that TG, unlike ordinary bereavement, exists when the experience of a traumatic death significantly interferes with normal grief processes (Cohen, Mannarino, & Greenberg, 2002; Pynoos, 1992). Since suicide involves intentional acts that result in a deliberately instigated death, survivors become preoccupied with the traumatic details of *how* the person died, and this preoccupation interferes with their ability to grieve their loss. The persistent and frightening mental images about the nature of the death dominate and interfere with the typical reminiscences about the dead person that constitute a natural part of mourning. Thus, suicide clearly constitutes a *traumatic* experience for survivors. Therefore, a practice principle in providing therapy for people after a traumatic death advises clinicians to begin by dealing with the trauma before moving the focus to bereavement issues (Cohen et al., 2002; Nader, 2002). This will be discussed in the section "Trauma-Focused Cognitive Behavioral Therapy Model."

Individual Factors

As discussed in Chapter 4, the age of the child/adolescent will significantly affect his or her ability to comprehend the reality of death. Since young children typically think that they have the power to prevent events or cause them to happen, they may believe that something that they did or did not do precipitated the death. This belief will need to be addressed in therapy to reduce the child's inappropriate sense of guilt about the suicide. Preschoolers also do not understand the finality of death, and believe that the dead person can return. They may become angry when that does not happen, and part of the therapy should focus on clearing their confusion. School-age children have a more mature understanding about death, but they associate it primarily with older people and do not realize that it can happen to anyone of any age, and that a person can actually cause his

or her own death. Older children may want to know *"Why?"* their parent made the decision to end his or her life. The older the children are,
the more they may struggle with feelings of abandonment and confusion about how their parent could have made the decision to leave them.
Adolescents, who have a cognitively more mature understanding about
death, may become preoccupied with the meaning behind this deliberate and fatal act, and these worries can lead to serious changes in their
assumptions about the world, about good and evil, sickness and health,
and about the role of relationships and spirituality in supporting or negat-
ing one's will to live. These serious concerns may be addressed in either
individual or group therapy, as discussed later in this chapter.

The *nature of the relationship* with the person who died also affects
the survivor's feelings about the suicide. For example, the death of a
father who has been detached or abusive to the youth will have different
ramifications than that of a father who had a loving and supportive relationship with his children. When survivors have an abundance of negative feelings toward the deceased, their guilt may be magnified because
of unrealistic feelings that somehow their negativity had a role in causing
the death, which will be an issue in therapy.

Family, Social, Religious, and Cultural Factors

Suicide does not occur in a vacuum, and the responses of the family
and social network can have a profound impact on the child or youth
survivor. Many families feel a sense of shame about the nature of the
death, as suicide may be viewed with strong disapproval in some religions and cultures. Because of the perceived stigma surrounding suicide,
young persons may not be told the truth about the death, or they may be
instructed not to talk about it. This veil of secrecy can seriously interfere
with a therapist's attempts to form a trusting therapeutic relationship
with the young person.

☐ Bereavement Programs and Other Counseling Interventions for Children and Youth Suicide Survivors

Therapy with suicide survivors is extremely challenging. Talking about
and remembering traumatic details of the death stir up anxiety, and

this discomfort leads to avoidance in dealing with memories of the person. This is true both for adults and young persons. Thinking about the deceased leads to recollections about the circumstances in which the death occurred, and this is very painful. In addition, if the family has imposed a shroud of silence about the nature of the death, survivors feel guilty if they talk about their feelings. Typically, bereaved children feel "different" from their nonbereaved peers, regardless of the circumstances of the death. This perception adds to the reluctance of bereaved youth to talk about their loss and contributes to their sense of isolation. However, when children and youth are referred to groups in which *all* the members have experienced the death of a loved one, they may feel tremendous relief because they are no longer alone. This section describes two specific programs that offer bereavement support in the form of group, individual, and family counseling. Often, the groups utilize various expressive arts methods as aids to stimulate the expression of feelings about the deceased person.

The Dougy Center

The Dougy Center is a pioneering program in Portland, Oregon, dedicated to providing group peer support to bereaved children and families. Founded in 1982, it has become a model for replication by hospices and other programs across the country. The program consists of groups that are set up according to the ages of the participants and the type of death, such as sibling death, parent death, healing from a homicide or violent death, and healing from a suicide death. The age groups include the "Littles" (ages 3–5), the "Middlers" (ages 6–12), and teens (ages 13–18), plus young adult, adult, and caretaker groups. Whenever possible, participants are given choices as to which group they prefer, such as a sibling death group, a parent death group, or a healing from a suicide death group. Most *suicide survivors* choose the suicide-specific group because they do not like to be the "only one" grieving a suicide death in a group where others may be dealing with deaths caused by accidents, illnesses, or disease (D. L. Shuurman, personal communication, June 2008). Of course, the numbers of suicide-bereaved persons varies from time to time, and it is not always possible to offer an age-specific group for this specialized population. In that case, it is the responsibility of the group facilitator to open a discussion about suicide that will help remove the stigma associated with it so that the suicide survivor experiences support, not criticism, related to his/her relative's manner of death.

Children and youth usually experience a range of emotions and feelings that facilitators help them explore in the groups. These include the following typical bereavement reactions: fear and anxiety, guilt and regret, anger and frustration, and sorrow and sadness. Although these would be applicable to *all* types of bereavement, specifically the suicide bereaved often experience extreme levels of guilt and anger. The goals of the trained group facilitator include helping the children and youth to experience social support in the group and realize that their responses are "normal," giving them an outlet for their feelings, and helping them to keep a connection with the deceased. Examples of actual group sessions can be found in Shuurman and DeCristofaro (2007).

The Trauma-Focused Cognitive-Behavioral Therapy Model

The Trauma-Focused Cognitive-Behavioral Therapy Model for treatment of traumatic grief in children and adolescents, developed by Judith Cohen, Anthony Mannarino, and Esther Deblinger (2006) is an evidence-based approach that focuses on both the individual grieving child and the parent. The model employs a variety of directive methods, including psychoeducation about typical grief reactions, discussion of ambivalent feelings toward the deceased, and preserving positive memories. This approach recommends working on trauma content first, before addressing the grief. This is accomplished using educational materials, teaching relaxation and meditation methods, encouraging the development of a narrative of the trauma, and processing the traumatic experience alone and in conjoint parent-child sessions. The model, originally developed to deal with domestic violence and child sexual abuse exposure, would also seem to be appropriate to help survivors of suicidal deaths.

Other Interventions

Two other exemplary bereavement programs will be discussed below in the sections specific to their respective modalities of treatment. These are Irwin Sandler's Family Bereavement Program (Sandler et al., 2003) and Cynthia Pfeffer's group intervention for suicide survivors (Pfeffer, Jiang, Kakuma, Hwang, & Metsch, 2002).

☐ Different Forms of Bereavement Groups

A recent review of the effectiveness of bereavement interventions with children (Currier et al., 2007) found that the 13 studies that met the criteria of the review did not support the assumption that bereavement interventions with children had a significant influence on their adjustment. However, there are a number of weaknesses in this overview, and the finding must be considered in view of the small numbers of studies represented and other factors, including a substantial amount of time between the child's loss and the beginning of treatment. In the absence of definitive research findings related to the effectiveness of bereavement therapy, we must continue to rely on clinical practice reports.

As mentioned earlier, anecdotal clinical experience maintains that groups for suicide survivors often help a young person realize that he or she is not the only one who has suffered this type of bereavement, and this helps lessen the stigma associated with suicide. An example of such a support group for children bereaved by parental suicide (Mitchell, Wesner, Garand, Gale, Havill, & Brownson, 2007) found that an outpatient group meeting every other week over an 8-week period helped children aged 7–13 years understand the facts about suicide even as they received support from others who had gone through a similar experience.

Group therapy is often the treatment of choice for traumatized *adolescents* because they usually are more comfortable with peers than with individual treatment with an adult therapist. Group participation allows adolescents to express their feelings therapeutically through a variety of methods, such as music, dance, poetry, and journal writing, in addition to verbal discussion (Malekoff, 2004). When there are insufficient numbers of suicide survivors within a particular age cohort to form a group focused on that form of death, the group facilitator should attempt to have at least two children who are bereaved by suicide in a group so they will not feel isolated and misunderstood. Another option is to offer treatment by pairing two students together, as described in the case example of Rosa later in this chapter. Whatever the treatment approach, the methods must be age appropriate, and must respect developmental abilities and preferences regarding activities intended to foster communication and promote healing.

The Bereavement Group Intervention (BGI)

Cynthia Pfeffer's program specifically targeted children bereaved by the suicide of a parent or a sibling (Pfeffer et al., 2002). Using a manualized group intervention, this approach documented reductions in anxiety and depressive symptoms among children who received the group intervention compared to those who did not. The 10 weekly group sessions, each 90 minutes long, used psychoeducational and support components to focus on strengthening coping skills, as well as responses to death and suicide. Separate but concurrent sessions were held for children and their parents. Parents' symptoms of depression also were found to have decreased from the initial to outcome assessments. For more information, see Pfeffer et al. (2002).

Family Bereavement Program

It also is highly recommended to offer the family support in the form of family therapy or referral to a family group consisting of suicide survivors (Sandler et al., 2003). However, this may be difficult or even contraindicated in some situations where a surviving parent is inconsolable or raging against the deceased. Children and youth may be reluctant to express their true feelings because of concerns that they might upset other family members. These matters may best be addressed in separate sessions initially, with family therapy postponed until a later time, when individuals have had the opportunity to deal with their personal feelings.

One model of a family bereavement program that has been successful was created by Irwin Sandler and his colleagues at the University of Arizona (Sandler et al., 2003). This theoretically derived intervention program for children who have experienced parental death attempts to promote resiliency in 12 group sessions and two individual sessions, with six sessions including conjoint activities for caregivers and youth. Personal goals were identified at the beginning of the program, and each session contained discussion of home practice of skills and progress toward achieving these personal goals. Cognitive reframing was used with both the children and the caregivers, with attention focused on avoiding "gloom and doom thoughts."

The 156 families with children and adolescents between the ages of 8 and 14 were randomly assigned to the behavioral program or a comparison group. Evaluation findings demonstrated improved mental health outcomes and self-esteem for the behavioral intervention group, both at program termination and 6 years later. The research focused on resiliency and the important role of parenting in helping children/youth recover from the stresses of bereavement.

☐ Individual Counseling and Therapy With Children and Youth

Therapy for child/adolescent suicide survivors can take the form of individual psychoanalytically oriented or cognitive-behavioral play therapy, bereavement counseling (in either individual or group format), family therapy, or a combination of these. Play therapy has been recognized for more than 6 decades as the oldest and most popular form of child therapy, and empirical studies of treatment outcomes using this method are beginning to emerge (Reddy, Files-Hall, & Schaefer, 2005). The literature demonstrating successful treatment outcomes using different forms of play therapy include examples of art therapy (Malchiodi, 1997; Roje, 1995), music therapy (Loewy & Stewart, 2004), sandbox (Carey, 1999, 2006), puppets/dolls (Webb, 1999, 2002), and storytelling (O'Toole, 2002). Many of these expressive arts methods have been incorporated into the bereavement programs already discussed, and will be illustrated in the case vignettes to follow.

The examples below focus on the various procedures that crisis-intervention bereavement counselors and play therapists have developed in their work with traumatized child and youth survivors of suicide. Practice principles intrinsic to this work are as follows:

1. Establish a safe, comfortable relationship with the child/youth before attempting to deal with the topic of suicide.

2. Provide toys and activities that will assist the child/youth in recreating the traumatic event.

3. Acknowledge that remembering and talking about the person who died may be hard because of the way that person died.

4. Formulate a statement about *why* the person took his or her life, and explore the child's and youth's reactions to this.

5. Teach relaxation methods and techniques of positive imagery to control and contain anxiety.

6. Once the child/youth has mastered some relaxation and worry-reduction techniques, the therapist can encourage a gradual reenactment or recall of the traumatic death. This must be done slowly and after telling the child/youth that he/she will be "in charge" of how much of the upsetting content he/she wants to deal with in any one session.

7. Encourage both positive and negative (scary) memories.

8. Acknowledge that it is acceptable for the child or youth to have fun despite the death.

Establish a Safe, Comfortable Relationship With the Child or Youth Before Attempting to Deal With the Topic of Suicide

It is essential that the child or youth knows that the therapist is a person trained to help young people and their families, and that the purpose of the meeting is to help them with their feelings. This should be explained in age-appropriate language simply and directly. For example, with younger children, one might say, "I am a special kind of doctor who helps kids and families after scary things happen in their lives. I know about your father's death, and your mom has given you permission to talk with me about any of your worries. I have lots of toys and art materials here. Sometimes we talk, and sometimes we play or draw or make up stories. It's up to you. You can ask me any questions you want, or you can choose something now to draw or play."

When an adolescent is bereaved by suicide, the school counselor might approach the youth and mention that the youth is invited to attend the next session of a bereavement group that is composed of kids of the same age, all of whom have experienced the deaths of family members from different causes, including suicide (parental permission should be obtained prior to approaching the youth). The counselor can offer to introduce the youth to one of the members prior to the next meeting. The counselor may ask the teen to agree to attend the group at least two times before deciding if he or she wants to continue to discourage premature termination.

Provide Toys and Activities That Will Assist the Child or Youth in Recreating the Traumatic Event

For Young Children

Some disagreement exists among play therapists as to whether guns, swords, and other "aggressive" equipment should be included among the toys available in the play therapy room because of the belief that these toys may stimulate the child's aggression. However, the introduction of such equipment may be of benefit in cases of suicide bereavement. For example, when the therapist knows that a father shot himself, the therapy with the child or youth survivor could be facilitated if a toy gun is present on the toy shelf. Of course, most child suicide survivors would probably not approach this toy in early sessions because it would elicit too much anxiety. Once the child felt safe in a comfortable relationship with the therapist, the presence of the gun could encourage discussion with children about what they think about having guns in the house, and then about what they think happened to their parent and why.

For Adolescents

Most teenagers will not play with toys, although some may be interested in working with clay, tossing a Koosh ball, or doodling with markers and colored paper during a discussion with the therapist. Having some books about death and suicide or some pamphlets describing Web sites for teens who are suicide survivors can help break the ice. One such book for preteens and adolescents is *What on Earth Do You Do When Someone Dies?* (Romain, 1999). A useful journal designed to help teens work through the grieving process is *Fire in My Heart, Ice in My Veins* (Traisman, 1992). Many hotlines exist; two that will put the caller into contact with the closest certified crisis intervention center are 1-800-273-TALK (8255) and 1-800-784-2433.

Acknowledge That Remembering and Talking About the Person Who Died May Be Hard Because of the Way That Person Died

With Younger Children

Some children and youth express their feelings through play or art work. Play therapists look for symbolic themes in the child's play activities and make comments that refer to the underlying message in the drawing or in the play scene created by the child. For example, a 6-year-old boy whose father shot himself because he had been terminated from his employment began the therapy session by throwing all the toys in the center of the room and then saying repeatedly "It's a mess." The play therapist, who assumed that the child was talking about his own life, responded without being specific, "It *is* a mess, and it's hard to know what will make it better." In a separate session, this child's 9-year-old brother, who had been getting into fights in school since the father's death, drew a picture of a volcano. The play therapist said to this boy, "This volcano has been quiet for a long time, but now it can't hold its lava in any more and it is going to erupt." The boy then made the connection to his father's death and responded, "That's the way I feel now." This comment enabled the therapist to state that the boy "had gone through a lot since his father's death, and that those feelings must be hard for him to hold inside." The boy then mentioned that people have been telling him that now he is the "man of the house" and that he "should be strong." This made him very uncomfortable. The therapist responded that because he was only 9 years old, and not a man yet, it was not fair to expect that he could become an adult overnight!

With Adolescents

The boys' 14-year-old sister did not want to participate in individual therapy, but she did agree to attend a bereavement group at her school. In a brief meeting with this girl following the family meeting, the therapist said to the girl that she realized that it must be very painful to think about *how* her father died. Acknowledging that "this would be hard for *anyone* to have to deal with," the therapist then added that often it takes a while before anyone can share this terribly frightening information with other people. The therapist then reassured the girl that she would not be pushed to talk before she was ready.

Formulate a Statement About *Why* the Person Took His or Her Life, and Explore the Child's and Youth's Reactions to This

This is a very sensitive issue and must be discussed first with the adult family members to ensure that the youth will be given a message that is accurate, age-appropriate, and consistent. Usually it helps to make some kind of statement about the fact that the person who died was "so sick and sad in their feelings and thoughts that they could not make the right decision; they just wanted to stop their hurting feelings and they didn't know how, and they didn't know or believe that there were other ways to help." The Dougy Center (2001) has published a child-friendly activity book, *After a Suicide Death*, which includes chapters about answering questions, talking about the suicide with friends, going back to school, and advice about feeling better. This is an excellent resource for children, families, and therapists to review together. Other helpful books include Goldman's (1996) *Breaking the Silence,* Cammarata's (2001) *Someone I Love Died by Suicide,* and Requarth's (2006) *After a Parent's Suicide: Helping Children Heal.* Adolescents will appreciate Grollman's (1993) *Straight Talk About Death for Teens.* Of course, an experienced child therapist will understand how much information to share at a given time with children of different ages. Similar to giving facts about sex, the caveat is not to overwhelm the child or youth by telling too much at any one time. It also is very important to know what the family is saying about the suicide death since the young person will have heard this and drawn some conclusions (correct or incorrect) about what may have been overheard. An example I use in teaching refers to a 7-year-old boy who refused to go with his family to attend his grandfather's wake. After much prodding, the boy's mother managed to find out that the boy had overheard a telephone call in which he heard her say, "We lost the head of the family." The boy took this literally and thought that he would see his grandfather in the casket without his head!

Teach Relaxation Methods and Techniques of Positive Imagery to Control and Contain Anxiety

Sometimes children and youth have trouble sleeping, or they develop stomachaches or headaches, without realizing that these symptoms appear after they have been thinking about the person who died. It often helps when the therapist asks if the young person would like to learn some methods to control these upset or uncomfortable feelings by changing them to happy feelings. Most kids are curious and want very much to be able to control their own bodies. The idea of control is especially appealing to adolescents. The therapist can use a rag doll (such as Raggedy Ann/Andy or Dora the Explorer) to encourage the youth to pretend to hang loose like the dolls with no worries. Kids love to imitate the floppy dolls and often end up laughing and relaxed. This is a good time to tell the young person that it is possible to learn how to control his or her thoughts, and to make "bad thoughts go away by crowding them out with good thoughts in their heads." I ask the children or youth to imagine and then draw a stop sign, telling them that they can imagine the stop sign in their heads every time they have some thoughts that they do not like.

The next step is to have them draw their "own special safe place, where no one can hurt them, and where they can feel very safe and happy." After they draw their safe place picture, the therapist tells them that they are in control of the pictures that go through their heads. If they don't like some pictures, they can put up a stop sign and then "change the channel" by substituting their own safe place picture. This cognitive-behavioral method helps the young person feel more in control of his/her feelings.

Encourage a Gradual Reenactment or Recall of the Traumatic Death

Encouraging reenactment or recall must be done slowly and after telling the child or youth that he or she will be "in charge" of how much of the upsetting content is dealt with in any one session. Usually this recall or reenactment occurs after several weeks during which the young person has developed a trusting relationship with the therapist.

With Younger Children

For example, during his fourth session, the 6-year-old boy whose father shot himself reenacted the death scene spontaneously by setting up a house with blocks and then had a male doll scream, "I can't take it any-more!", then held a gun to his head and made a loud shooting noise. He then said matter-of-factly, "He's dead." The therapist kept saying that this was "so very sad" and that "his family was going to miss him very, very much!" The boy then said we had to bury the body and have a funeral, which was then reenacted, with great concentration on the child's part. This child heaved a big sigh of relief at the end of this session, and the therapist noticed from his intense concentration that the reenactment of his father's death scene and burial had been very meaningful to him. In the event that a child does not spontaneously play out his or her version of the suicide scene, the therapist may invite the child to show with the toys what happened with the loved one who died by suicide.

With Adolescents

The process of reenactment with older children might begin by looking at some photos of the deceased person and then asking the youth what he or she thinks led the person to decide to kill him/herself. This may result in a very painful account in which the therapist should listen quietly and respectfully. However, sometimes the young person is "stuck" and unable to verbalize mixed emotions. The therapist must be patient and understanding, acknowledging that this is very difficult to discuss. Clinical judgment will guide the therapist in how to proceed. Sometimes it is helpful for the clinician to say, "Other kids who have gone through similar experiences have told me that they felt a mixture of sadness, anger, and disgust. Do you have any of these feelings when you think about your Dad's death?" When the youth expresses personal regrets or guilt, the therapist makes note of this for future discussion. At the end of the youth's narrative about the death, the therapist may acknowledge that the facts about the death are very sad and unfortunate, but that this does not wipe out some of the happy memories that also were a part of the person's life and relationships. Ideally, in future therapy sessions the youth will be able to recall all kinds of memories about the dead person. The therapist may comment that this recall may be both exhausting and a relief. The goal is to try to deal with the ambivalent feelings that are inevitable in situations like this.

Encourage Both Positive and Negative (Scary) Memories

Everyone has both positive and negative feelings toward other family members. When this is acknowledged in a matter-of-fact way, the young person can begin the healing process of reminiscence. I use the form "A Letter to the Person Who Died" (Webb, 2002), which is a sheet of lined paper with simple instructions for the young person to write a letter to the person who died and tell what is missed and not missed about the person. This enables the young person to deal with "unfinished business" due to the suddenness of the death. If the young person cannot write, he or she can dictate the letter. It is important to plan with the young person about what to do with the letter once it is written. Some choose to read the letter out loud in front of a picture of the dead person, others may take it to the cemetery and read it there, while others may want to put it inside a balloon and release it into the sky. Some may wish to share the letter with a parent, and others may prefer to keep it private. Even very young children try to avoid upsetting their parents and may deliberately refrain from bringing up memories that they think might cause a parent to cry.

The balloon release, an activity promoted by some hospice programs, is often conducted as a group activity. There is some danger, however, that children younger than 6 or 7 years of age may consider this as true communication with the dead person and may expect to receive some kind of response from on high. Therefore, adults who engage young children in this activity need to prepare them for the fact that they will not receive a reply from heaven. Children in mid-elementary grades usually have the ability to appreciate the symbolism of this activity.

Adolescents may be interested in keeping a journal of memories about the person who died. This might include, for example, some funny activities in which the deceased person participated with other family members. It also might involve recollections of special activities shared with the deceased, such as going to baseball games or baking cookies. Adolescents should be instructed to write about memories that are important to them.

Acknowledge That It Is Acceptable for the Child or Youth to Have Fun Despite the Death

The author has commented elsewhere that children have "short sadness spans" (just like some have short attention spans). They cannot endure long periods of feeling sad and regretful. Often, family members misinterpret a child's or youth's desire to participate after a death in the same fun activities they have enjoyed in the past. They may not want to cancel previously scheduled events. The younger the child, the more allowances should be made for the child to continue with the usual routine of school and other activities as far as possible. However, even older youth will become tired and overwhelmed in the course of the bereavement process, and may need a "break" from grieving family members. This should be permitted and even encouraged.

☐ Reenactment of the Traumatic Event: Pros and Cons

As outlined by Nader (2001), most trauma treatments include the following procedural components:

- Review of the traumatic event(s)

- Reprocessing or redefinition of the traumatic memories

- Restoration of a sense of safety and self-confidence

- Promotion of an increased sense of control

The literature recommends that trauma therapists help the traumatized person tell what happened, or draw or play out the scene, when verbalization is too frightening (Cohen et al., 2006; Gil, 1991; Malchiodi, 1998; Pynoos & Nader, 1988). The goal in this review process is to increase the individual's understanding about the traumatic situation, with appropriate attribution of blame, to be able to put the experience in the past and thereby restore and promote a sense of confidence, self-control, and safety. However, there is a lack of unanimity about the benefits of encouraging a trauma review, with more than one report (Litz, 2004) cautioning that this is *not* helpful, and in some instances may even be harmful. The case examples of therapy with child and youth survivors of parental suicide provided below illustrate the use of various play and cognitive methods to help young suicide survivors process and recover from their painful memories.

Case Example: A Preschooler Tries to Understand Her Father's Suicidal Death[1]

Presenting Problem

Cathy, a 4½-year-old girl, was referred for therapy 1 month after her father's suicide by gunshot that was related to a psychotic depressive episode. Cathy's behavior following her father's death consisted of frequent crying and clinging, sulking, and insisting on sleeping with her mother.

Issues in Play Therapy With Cathy

The play materials most frequently chosen by this child were dolls and plasticine (Play-Doh). She washed the dolls carefully and arranged them properly in their beds before leaving the session. This type of play is age appropriate and seemed to give her a sense of comfort, control, and safety that she could take care of the dolls in a competent manner. The play therapist commented to Cathy that she liked to have the dolls safe in their beds.

In contrast, Cathy's play with the Play-Doh revealed some spontaneous trauma reenactment. She created five "cookie faces," with the

---

[1] Adapted from Hurley (1991). Two of the three cases presented here were previously published in books edited by the chapter author. They are summarized here with permission of the original authors/child therapists.

last one having only one eye and no mouth. She then became fearful as the therapist-in-training tried to make connections to the people in her family (not recommended, since it aroused too much anxiety and caused her to leave this activity). Later, in supervision, the therapist-in-training was encouraged to consider a more helpful response that would not have frightened Cathy. A possible alternative would have been for the therapist to empathize with the cookie that was disfigured and to say something to the child like, "That poor cookie, what happened to his face?" By keeping the dialog in the realm of fantasy, the child might have been able to explain her view of what happened to her father; that is, "the cookie got hurt; a gun shot his eye," or some such explanation. Ideally, this would allow the therapist to express empathy ("Oh, that's too bad!") and to refer to the other cookies' grief ("They must be very sad about this."). The important point in using play therapy with young children is that it allows the child to express fears/anxieties/beliefs in a *displaced* manner, so that confusions and emotions can be expressed through the play object, using the child's imagination and ability to project.

Another play episode with Cathy occurred when she found a male toy figure in the sandbox. This stimulated her to talk about people ("like my Dad") who are buried. Since the child herself made the connection to her father's death, it was appropriate for the therapist to engage Cathy in a discussion about her father's body in the ground, and her wish to be able to see her father again. She wondered whether her father could come back or not, and how he died. She knew her father had shot himself, but she was not clear about the permanence of death. The therapist said to the child, "When a person is dead, they cannot come back, even if they want to."

This short description presents only a brief snapshot of how play therapy can assist a young suicide survivor to deal with some of her worries and grief about her father's death. One year later, the therapist reported that Cathy was more independent of her mother, was crying less, and preparing to enter kindergarten.

Summary of Play Themes

Some of this child's traumatic grief responses were evident during the first three sessions. When she created the five "cookie faces," it seemed evident that they represented her family, one of whom had been severely injured. Children use play in therapy to express and displace their own fears and anxieties onto the toys and play materials, without conscious awareness that they are playing out aspects of their own lives. This child did later refer to death and coffins while she was playing in the sandbox, thereby demonstrating how the medium of sand can lead naturally to burying and uncovering activities and associations. The next case example reworks this same theme with older school-age children.

Case Example: A Fourth-Grader Tries to Understand Her Mother's Suicidal Death[2]

Presenting Problem

Rosa was 9½ years old. Her mother, who had been previously psychiatrically hospitalized and expressed suicidal thoughts daily, shot herself at the beginning of the school year. After about a month of weekly individual therapy with the school social worker, Rosa expressed interest in talking to other children who had a parent die, and the social worker decided to offer a peer therapy experience to Rosa and to another girl whose father had died suddenly of a heart attack. The two girls, Rosa and Cindy, were seen together because both had similar fears about the death or disappearance of their single surviving parent, and they both also were having difficulties with peer relationships and with their school work.

Issues in Therapy

As weekly sessions progressed, the girls spoke openly about missing their deceased parents, and about how these feelings intensified when they were in bed and sometimes caused them to cry. The girls both spoke longingly of their dead parent, but resisted the therapist's attempt to have them elaborate further on their feelings. Instead, they spontaneously decided to put on a puppet show because, "We don't want to talk anymore."

The theme of the puppet show involved puppet characters who sold drugs that eventually killed all the various puppet characters. The show thereby symbolically continued to deal with the topic of death in the girls' chosen play scenario.

The next week, the play therapist suggested that some of the characters who died in the previous show could come back to life. The girls immediately verbalized their wish that they could see their dead parents again and acted out a scene in which (in the role of puppets) they

---

[2] Adapted from Bluestone (1999).

went to heaven and visited their dead parents. This was a very emotional and meaningful enactment of the children's natural wishes to be reunited with their parents, *even for one day* (as the script had specified). They continued the same play the following week in which there was more expression of open grief and the desire to remain in heaven to stay with their dead parent. In this scene, the therapist took the role of Rosa's mother and expressed her ongoing love, but also her wish to have her daughter return to her "home on Earth and be happy with her friends." After a very powerful farewell scene, the puppets sang a goodbye song and hugged each other.

Summary of Play Therapy Themes

Although these girls were in the fourth grade, it was too difficult for them to speak at length about their feelings of longing for their deceased parents. However, they needed to work on these feelings, and they used play effectively to help them deal with their emotional issues. After they had developed a degree of comfort with the therapist and with each other, they spontaneously created a puppet play that expressed the themes of death and an imagined visit to heaven so they could have contact with their parent who died. They were able to convey their questions and their wishes more effectively through the play enactment than either girl could have done by verbal means alone.

Case Example: Typical Responses of a Teen to the Suicidal Death of a Parent[3]

Presenting Problem

Michael, aged 17, lived with his mother following his parents' divorce 5 years earlier. He saw his father, who had remarried and lived in a neighboring town, every other weekend. Michael's mother was a nurse who worked full-time in the local hospital. Michael had a part-time job after school, and was looking forward to going away to college in the coming fall. Michael's relationship with his mother was not close; he did not know that she had recently been diagnosed with inoperable cancer. One day, when he returned home from his after-school job, his

---

[3] This is a fictional case, based on a composite of several cases.

father was there and told him that his mother had taken an overdose of medication and then sat in her car in the garage with the motor running until she died.

Michael was distraught and blamed himself for not realizing that his mother was depressed. His father, a physician, made arrangements for Michael to move in with him and attend a bereavement group at the local hospice.

Issues in Therapy

In the group, Michael kept repeating how he could not believe that his mother was dead and that she had actually killed herself. He kept wondering why she had not told him about her diagnosis. He also kept asking why he had not noticed that she was worried or depressed. Since both of his parents were in the medical field, he had grown up with the idea that illnesses were curable. He could not understand how this had happened to his mother without any warning.

The group members were sympathetic to Michael's questions. One commented that even though Michael was almost 18, his mother still considered him her child and she probably didn't want to cause him worry. Michael's mother had left a note addressed to her son in which she said that when she found out that her condition was not treatable, she had begun to make plans to die. She had arranged for Michael to inherit her pension so that he would have money for his school books and other needs. In her note, she expressed her love for Michael and her wish to spare him the grief of watching her die gradually. She said that she had seen patients waste away, and that she didn't want to inflict that on herself or on Michael.

When Michael read the note, he felt weak and looked for some alcohol to give him strength. He told the group that he thought he needed the alcohol to keep him strong. One of the group members whose parents were alcoholics mentioned that his view was that alcohol can be a trap, and once a person starts drinking it, they can't stop. This kid warned and even begged Michael not to fall into the trap.

Summary of Therapeutic Themes

Membership in the bereavement group soon after his mother's death proved to be extremely supportive for Michael. Although he was not particularly close to his mother, he knew he could count on her if he needed something, and now he felt alone. The group members spoke about their relationships with other family members, and Michael realized that he wanted to get to know his father better. Due to the bitterness of the divorce, he had not wanted to take sides, and tried to distance himself from both parents. Now he realized that he could share some activities and develop a relationship with his father. Additionally, he gradually made friends with some of the group members who understood the pain of his loss and who wanted to support him. He began to interact with the boy whose father had died from the consequences of alcoholism. When the group concluded after the school year ended, Michael remained in contact with him and with several other members who had become his friends.

☐ Conclusion

If death is difficult for children to comprehend, how much more complicated is the knowledge that one's parent deliberately caused an end to his/her own life? Whereas young children experience a parent's departure as abandonment, as they get older, they begin to ponder why the parent chose to leave their family. Although numerous explanations may be given to them, many young people continue to feel the suicide was an act that failed to take account of their own future without the presence of this parent. The difficult emotions of anger, guilt, and shame may continue to surge in waves for years to come.

Different types of therapy can attempt to help the child and adolescent suicide survivor. Anecdotal case reports as described here suggest that play therapy and peer and group counseling can help these young people feel supported and understood. Although at this time no one method has been empirically shown to provide long-term helping effects, clearly the relationship with a bereavement counselor who offers encouragement and support seems to help in the short term. Also, cognitive methods that help clarify confusions about the death can help diminish various symptoms.

Because the grief over a parent's suicide is never completely resolved, it may be appropriate to consider and recommend a model of sequential therapy that will address the stresses of the *ongoing* bereavement process. For example, the loss of the parent may be felt acutely at certain milestones of the youth's life, such as at graduation. When the young person knows that the recurrence of painful grief can be expected, he or she may accept the idea of returning to therapy periodically for short-term counseling focused on the loss experience. Hopefully, future research will become available to direct counselors and therapists about empirically validated helping methods for traumatically bereaved children and youth.

☐ References

Bluestone, J. (1999). School-based peer therapy to facilitate mourning in latency-age children following sudden parental death: Cases of Joan, age 10½, and Roberta, age 9½, with follow-up 8 years later. In N. B. Webb (Ed.), *Play therapy with children in crisis: Individual, group, and family treatment* (2nd ed.), 225–251. New York, NY: Guilford Press.

Cammarata, D. (2001). *Someone I love died by suicide: A story for child survivors and those who care for them.* Palm Beach Gardens, FL: Grief Guidance, Inc.

Carey, L. (1999). *Sandplay: Therapy with children and families.* Northvale, NJ: Jason Aronson.

Carey, L. (2006). (Ed.). *Expressive and creative arts methods for trauma survivors.* London, England: Jessica Kingsley.

Cohen, J. A., Mannarino, A. P., & Deblinger, E. (2006). *Treating trauma and traumatic grief in children and adolescents.* New York, NY: Guilford Press.

Cohen, J. A., Mannarino, A. P., & Greenberg, T. (2002). Childhood traumatic grief. Concepts and controversies. *Trauma, Violence, & Abuse, 3*, 307–327.

Currier, J. M., Holland, J. M., & Neimeyer, R. A. (2007). The effectiveness of grief interventions with children: A meta-analytic review of controlled outcome research. *Journal of Clinical Child and Adolescent Psychology, 36*, 253–259.

Currier, J. M., Neimeyer, R. A., & Berman, J. S. (2008). The effectiveness of psychotherapeutic interventions for bereaved persons: A comprehensive quantitative review. *Psychological Bulletin, 134*, 648–661.

Dougy Center. (2001). *After a suicide death: An activity book for grieving kids.* Portland, OR: Author.

Fortner, B. V. (1999). *The effectiveness of grief counseling and therapy: A quantitative review.* Memphis, TN: University of Memphis.

Gil, E. (1991). *The healing power of play.* New York, NY: Guilford Press.

Goldman, L. (1996). *Breaking the silence.* Washington, DC: Accelerated Development.

Grollman, E. (1993). *Straight talk about death for teens.* Boston, MA: Beacon Press.

Hurley, D. J. (1991). The crisis of paternal suicide: Case of Cathy, age 4½. In N. B. Webb (Ed.), *Play therapy with children in crisis: Individual, group, and family treatment* (pp. 237–253). New York, NY: Guilford Press.

Jordan, J., & Neimeyer, R. A. (2003). Does grief counseling work? *Death Studies, 27*, 765–786.

Larson, D., & Hoyt, W. (2007). What has become of grief counseling? An evaluation of the empirical foundation of the new pessimism. *Professional Psychology, 38*, 347–355.

Litz, B. (2004). *Early interventions for trauma and traumatic loss.* New York, NY: Guilford Press.

Loewy, J. V., & Stewart, K. (2004). Music therapy to help traumatized children and caregivers. In N. B. Webb (Ed.), *Mass trauma and violence: Helping families and children cope* (pp. 191–215). New York, NY: Guilford Press.

Malchiodi, C. (1997). *Breaking the silence: Art therapy with children from violent homes* (2nd ed.). Bristol, PA: Brunner/Mazel.

Malchiodi, C. (1998). *Understanding children's drawings.* New York, NY: Guilford Press.

Malekoff, A. (2004) *Group work with adolescents: Principles and practice* (2nd ed.). New York, NY: Guilford Press.

Mitchell, A. M., Wesner, S., Garand, L., Gale, D. D., Havill, A., & Brownson, L. (2007). A support group intervention for children bereaved by parental suicide. *Journal of Child and Adolescent Psychiatric Nursing, 20,* 3–13.

Nader, K. (2001). Treatment methods for childhood trauma. In J. P. Wilson, M. J. Friedman, & J. D. Lindy (Eds.), *Treating psychological trauma and PTSD* (pp. 159–192). New York, NY: Guilford Press.

Nader, K. (2002). Treating children after violence in schools and communities. In N. B. Webb (Ed.), *Helping bereaved children. A handbook for practitioners* (pp. 214–244). New York, NY: Guilford Press.

O'Toole, D. (2002). Storytelling with bereaved children. In N. B. Webb (Ed.), *Helping bereaved children: A handbook for practitioners* (pp. 323–345). New York, NY: Guilford Press.

Pfeffer, C. R., Jiang, H., Kakuma, T., Hwang, J., & Metsch, M. (2002). Group intervention for children bereaved by the suicide of a relative. *Journal of the American Academy of Child & Adolescent Psychiatry, 41,* 505–513.

Pynoos, R. S. (1992). Grief and trauma in children & adolescents. *Bereavement Care,* 11, 2–10.

Pynoos, R. S., & Nader, K. (1988). Psychological first aid treatment approach for children exposed to community violence: Research implications. *Journal of Traumatic Stress, 1,* 445–473.

Reddy, L. A., Files-Hall, T. M., & Schaefer, C. E. (2005). *Empirically based play interventions for children.* Washington, DC: American Psychological Association.

Requarth, M. (2006). *After a parent's suicide: Helping children heal.* Sebastopol, CA: Healing Hearts Press.

Roje, J. (1995). LA 94 earthquake in the eyes of children: Art therapy with elementary school children who were victims of disaster. *Art Therapy, 12,* 237–243.

Romain, T. (1999). *What on earth do you do when someone dies?* Minneapolis, MN: Free Spirit.

Sandler, I. N., Ayers, T. S., Wolchik, S. A.,Tein, J.-Y., Kwok, O.-M., Haine, R. A., … Griffin, W. A. (2003). The Family Bereavement Program: Efficacy evaluation of a theory-based prevention program for parentally bereaved children and adolescents. *Journal of Consulting and Clinical Psychology, 71,* 587–600.

Schuurman, D. L., & DeCristofaro, J. (2007). After a parent's death: Group, family, and individual therapy to help children. In N. B. Webb (Ed.). *Play therapy with children in crisis: Individual, group, and family treatment* (3rd ed.) (pp. 173–196). New York, NY: Guilford Press.

Traisman, E. S. (1992). *Fire in my heart, ice in my veins.* Omaha, NE: Centering Corporation.

Webb, N. B. (1999). (Ed.). *Play therapy with children in crisis: Individual, group, and family treatment* (2nd ed.). New York, NY: Guilford Press.

Webb, N. B. (2002). (Ed.). *Helping bereaved children: A handbook for practitioners* (2nd ed.). New York, NY: Guilford Press.

11

The Meanings of Suicide
A Narrative Approach to Healing

Diana C. Sands, John R. Jordan, and Robert A. Neimeyer

There are many things that we take for granted about our world, perhaps most importantly our relationships with those to whom we are closest. Our assumptions about the world include its safety and predictability, and the continued availability of our loved ones. A sudden death, such as suicide, may violate much of what we believe to be true about our lives. Perhaps more than any other death, a suicide leaves those left behind searching for an answer to the question "Why?" The quest to make sense of that which makes no sense often becomes a central healing task for suicide survivors (see Chapter 9). As Chapter 1 noted, one of the characteristics that all unexpected deaths seem to share is this "shock effect" on the assumptive world of the mourner (Currier, Holland, Coleman, & Neimeyer, 2008; Currier, Holland, & Neimeyer, 2006).

Suicide appears to be particularly potent in its ability to shatter the most fundamental of assumptions in life. For a period of time, many survivors are truly unable to make sense of why the suicide has happened, what role they played in the death, and its implications for their identity and their understanding of the world. Although clinical experience suggests that these effects are most prominent when the mourner was "blindsided" by the suicide and had no awareness that their loved one was considering ending his or her life, this shock effect appears to be a central issue to some extent after almost all suicide bereavements (see Chapter 9).

In this chapter, we seek to explore a central question: How does the suicide of a loved one affect the assumptive world of a survivor? Our intention is to respond to this question from a constructivist approach to mental health, one predicated on the construction and reconstruction of meaning to accommodate the vicissitudes of living (Neimeyer, 2009; Neimeyer & Mahoney, 1995). We begin with a brief overview of the constructivist, or narrative, approach to bereavement. Next, we describe a number of domains of a survivor's assumptive world that can be affected by a suicide. We then present a new meaning-oriented model of bereavement after suicide called the Tripartite Model of Suicide Bereavement (TMSB) (Sands, 2008, 2009). We also discuss ways that the work of rebuilding one's assumptive world may contribute to the emergence of post-traumatic growth after the suicide of a loved one. Finally, we conclude the chapter with a case study that uses the story of one family's journey through the loss of a daughter to offer an example of therapeutic interventions that facilitate the healing process of meaning reconstruction after a suicide.

☐ Grief and the Quest for Meaning: A Constructivist Contribution

A constructivist theory of bereavement posits that grieving entails an active effort to reaffirm or reconstruct a world of meaning that has been challenged by loss (Neimeyer, 2001, 2006b). In this perspective, people are viewed as meaning-makers, drawing on personal, social, and cultural resources to construct a system of beliefs that permit them to anticipate and respond to the essential themes and events of their lives (Kelly, 1955/1991). Across time, this "effort after meaning" confers a sense of identity and intelligibility, giving rise to a *self-narrative* that integrates the "micro-narratives" of daily life into a "macro-narrative" regarding life's purpose and direction (Neimeyer, 2006a). The death of a loved one, however, can challenge this framework, sometimes calling into question the most basic premises that anchor one's "assumptive world" (Janoff-Bulman & Berger, 2000), necessitating efforts to integrate the discrepant experience of loss into one's autobiographical memory (Boelen, van den Hout, & van den Bout, 2006).

According to this conceptualization, *resilient survivors*, who take the loss in stride without profound distress, would likely be those who are able to assimilate the loss into a stable and positive meaning system, perhaps drawing on secular or spiritual beliefs that help them make sense of the loss and the life transition they are forced to undergo. *Adaptive grievers*, by comparison, may wrestle profoundly for a time with practical or existential questions concerning the death of their loved one and its implications for their sense of self, but ultimately accommodate their self-narrative to the changed reality in a way that engenders renewed stability and perhaps even personal growth. In contrast to these resourceful responses, a minority of *foreclosed survivors* may assimilate the loss into a stable, but predominantly negative or pessimistic meaning system, finding in their loss yet another life experience that validates their sense of life's cruelty and meaninglessness or their own failings. Finally, *chronic grievers* may contend with an anguishing invalidation of their central assumptions about God, the universe, their loved one, and other people, often experiencing an ongoing struggle to reconstruct a life narrative that accounts for their past loss, their present circumstances, and their changed future (cf. Neimeyer, 2006b).

This basic theoretical perspective accords well with a growing body of research that associates resilient and adaptive trajectories through loss with an absence of searching for meaning in the first instance and a successful quest for meaning in the second (Bonanno, Wortman, & Nesse, 2004; Calhoun & Tedeschi, 2006; Coleman & Neimeyer, in press; Davis, Wohl, & Verberg, 2007). Conversely, an ongoing attempt to search for meaning in the loss and a chronic inability to make sense of it is associated with profound and protracted grieving among such groups as bereaved young adults (Holland, Currier, & Neimeyer, 2006), parents who have lost children (Keesee, Currier, & Neimeyer, 2008), and older widows and widowers (Bonanno et al., 2004; Coleman & Neimeyer, in press). In fact, "sense making" is such a critical predictor of adjustment to loss that one study found it to be a near-perfect mediator of the impact of bereavement by violent death. That is, although loss through suicide and other forms of violent death was indeed associated with higher levels of complicated grief symptoms than loss through natural death, nearly all of the difference could be attributed to a failure to find meaning in the loss in the former instance (Currier et al., 2006). More suggestively, recent evidence also accords with the conceptualization of a group of *foreclosed survivors*, whose world assumptions are pessimistic, fragile, and self-critical, and whose distress is exacerbated by the loss of a loved one (Currier, Holland, & Neimeyer, 2009).

In sum, a constructivist approach that views the challenge of bereavement through the lens of a meaning-making model seems to hold considerable promise in understanding a survivor's attempt—whether successful or unsuccessful—to rebuild a workable model of the self and world in the wake of loss. Such a perspective seems to hold particular promise when applied to the seismic event of suicide, which can rock the foundations of a survivor's personal world of meaning and launch a protracted search for sense in a seemingly inexplicable death. To further mine this promise, we turn to an exploration of the many ways that suicide may devastate the assumptive world of its survivors. After that, we present one specific conceptualization—the Tripartite Model of Suicide Bereavement (TMSB)—of particular relevance to this tragic form of loss, before considering its implications for post-traumatic growth and anchoring these in a brief case study.

☐ Suicide and the Challenge to the Assumptive World

The experience of each mourner is unique to that mourner. Attempts to describe a universal set of responses after any type of death must always be seen as incomplete and imperfect. Nonetheless, clinical experience and the small amount of research on this subject suggest that certain domains of an individual's assumptive world may be particularly challenged after a suicide, what Jordan (2001) has called the "thematic issues" of suicide bereavement. This damage to the assumptive world becomes apparent as survivors seek to repair the psychological havoc created by the death (Jordan, 2008; Neimeyer et al., 2002). Sands has set forth in the TMSB a tripartite organization for understanding these domains, including the survivors' relationship with the deceased, with themselves, and with others in their social networks (see below and Sands, 2008, 2009). The impact of a suicide on these three foundational elements of a survivor's assumptive world will be discussed below.

Relationship of the Self With the Deceased

With a long-term relationship with another individual comes a feeling that "I understand the thinking, feelings, and motivations of this person—I know this person." Through this understanding, people also come to believe that they can predict the behavior of their loved one and organize their relationship accordingly. In reality, however, people can really only know the observable behavior of another person. Internal thoughts and feelings can be understood only if an individual is honest about his or her internal experience, or shows it in a way it can be correctly deciphered from verbal and nonverbal behavior. The inherent ambiguity in this interpretive process of the behavior of others (including their words) is made more difficult by the fact that human beings are capable of masking their inner thoughts and feelings, while outwardly acting in ways that can be quite incongruent with their internal state. They can also engage in behaviors that are kept hidden from their close associates (e.g., sexual activities, use of drugs, etc.). This existential "separateness" of the inner consciousness of each one of us from others is the foundation for the psychological boundary between self and others. In a very real sense, it is also the condition that allows suicide to happen in a way that people who "know" the deceased may be utterly stunned by the act.

> A woman seeks therapy after the suicide of her husband. He had been charged with embezzling from his employer and was scheduled for a court appearance. He had managed to keep all of this information hidden from his wife. On the day of his court appearance, his attorney informed him that he was probably going to be convicted and would have to serve time in prison. Shortly after receiving this news, he shot himself in the family car near his home. His wife had absolutely no idea that her husband was in legal trouble or facing a probable prison sentence, let alone that he had been considering suicide for the last several months. She was utterly dumbfounded that her husband could have kept this hidden from her.

It is not unheard of that survivors report that their loved one seemed untroubled, goal directed, and enjoying life just prior to the suicide. It is also not unusual for survivors to be deeply surprised not only by the suicide of their loved one, but also by some of the behaviors that may have preceded the act. For this reason, suicide can be a profoundly disorienting experience for the survivor because the observable behavior of the loved one masks the inner experience of the deceased, including the intent to die.

Of course, in many instances, the trajectory leading to suicide was more obvious, and the suicide may have been feared but not really unexpected. The deceased may have communicated (sometimes for years) his or her wish to die, leaving survivors on "suicide watch" for a considerable period of time before the death. This pathway seems most common when a suicide occurs at the endpoint of a long struggle with depression, substance abuse, or chronic suicidality, making the suicide "fit" with the person known to the survivor. Still, even when the life trajectory of the deceased seemed to clearly point toward an eventual suicide, it is remarkable how many survivors find it difficult to believe that their loved ones could actually die by their own actions.

A mother who came to a survivor support group reported that her son had battled bipolar disorder for many years prior to his death. He had been hospitalized on several occasions, had made a number of previous suicide attempts, and had told his mother directly on many occasions that he expected to kill himself some day. In the past, when he had become suicidal, she had been able to talk him out of carrying out the action, convincing him to seek emergency psychiatric treatment. On the day of his death, however, he called his mother and told her that he was standing outdoors with a firearm, and that he had made an irrevocable decision to die. He said goodbye, hung up the phone, and shot himself. Despite her son's longstanding suicidality, his mother expressed disbelief that this time she had been unable to stop her son from carrying out the suicide. She had been sustained through previous crises by believing that somehow, she would always be able to rescue him from his death. His suicide destroyed the hope that had sustained her through the long ordeal of dealing with his psychiatric illness and chronic suicidality.

A suicide may also reveal to the survivor that the deceased had aspects of his or her life that were unknown to the mourner, thereby challenging assumptions survivors may hold about the nature of the deceased's life and of his or her relationship with the survivor. Established relationships evolve relatively stable patterns of interaction within confines of the relationship. Human beings then draw conclusions about the "nature" of the relationship from these habitual patterns. After suicide, survivors may be stunned to find out that these conclusions were mere assumptions, not unchanging truths. For example, the survivor may believe that the relationship with the deceased was very close psychologically, that the deceased trusted the survivor and was in turn trustworthy, and that the deceased would naturally turn to the survivor for help if really desperate. These and many other assumptions about the nature of the relationship can be violated by the suicide of a loved one.

> A middle-aged man who had been a stable provider and loving husband and father had recently been diagnosed with some potentially life-threatening heart problems. He was also facing a possible, though not certain, lay-off from the company at which he had worked for many years. He had been somewhat agitated and physiologically dysregulated for the previous two weeks, sleeping and eating poorly. Although he confided some of his worries to his wife and family doctor, he gave no hint that he might be considering ending his life. Both of these people, in turn, had no idea that he might have been suicidal, seeing the man as only mildly and understandably worried about his work and health. Returning home from school, his daughter found his body in the family garage, where he had asphyxiated himself with fumes from the family car. The couple had lived a very close and confiding relationship over the course of their long marriage, and the man's doctor had been his primary care physician for most of his adult life. Both survivors were incredulous and deeply upset that their partner/patient had not confided the level of his distress to them, nor asked for their help in finding alternative solutions.

Relationship of the Self With the Self

The suicide of someone to whom we are intimately attached changes how we think and feel about ourselves. From a constructivist perspective, the "self" experienced by most people can be viewed as a psychological "fiction" that appears to have solidity and continuity, but is actually better thought of as a flowing process (like a flowing river that is simultaneously constant yet always changing). A central component of the construction of this self is the manner in which others relate to and treat our own self (Guidano, 1991; Neimeyer, 2000). Consider then, what "relational messages" about the self a survivor might perceive in the suicide of a loved one, and what those messages might mean for the survivor's own identity.

Many survivors experience the suicide of their loved one as a deep rejection or abandonment by the deceased. The suicide is interpreted as a profound statement about the unworthiness of the survivor as a person. This is perhaps most obvious when the suicide is of a spouse or partner, where the feelings evoked may resemble those of someone whose life partner leaves the relationship for another person—a profound combination of abandonment, anger, and failure.

Another possible interpretation of the suicide might be as an act of hostility, abuse, or aggression by the deceased that is meant to punish the survivor. Early psychoanalytic formulations suggested that the motivation for suicide might include just such murderous feelings toward the survivor that are acted out by murdering oneself (Menninger, 1933).

> A man divorces his wife after a long and highly conflicted marriage. She is enraged with this perceived abandonment by her husband. That rage is intensified when he remarries two years later. On the first Thanksgiving morning after his remarriage, his former wife telephones her former husband and angrily tells him "This is because of you!" She then shoots herself while on the phone with him.

Understandably, being the recipient of such enmity can permanently "scar" a survivor, producing feelings of both deep shame and unworthiness, or of intense counter-rage at the assault on the survivor's self acted out in such an "other-directed" suicide. Other survivors seem to experience the suicide as a statement about their general competence in the world. For example, parents who lose a child to suicide almost always feel that the death reflects on their capabilities as a parent. They may believe that a "good" parent would surely know that their child was suicidal and would naturally take the "proper" steps to save them. Unfortunately, this perception is sometimes held by people in the larger community, who also attribute problematic behavior in children exclusively to their upbringing (Range, 1998; Range & Goggin, 1990). Most survivors experience what a client of the second author once called "the tyranny of hindsight." That is, after a suicide, survivors can often see warning signs of the deceased's suicidality that were not apparent before the death. Nonetheless, survivors feel that this evidence would have been obvious had they been more knowledgeable or more vigilant. To other people not so closely involved with the deceased (including therapists), these deductive conclusions about the self are cognitive distortions. Nonetheless, they are extraordinarily powerful and emotionally compelling beliefs for survivors, ones that are not easily reasoned away.

To summarize, from a constructivist perspective, the attitudes that we have toward ourselves, most importantly our worthiness to be loved and our competence to navigate in the world, are to a great degree a compilation of the relational judgments about these traits that others have communicated to us through their behavior toward us. Suicide is frequently understood by the survivor as a relational communication from the deceased about the worthiness and competence of the survivor. Both the ambiguity of the intended message in the suicide ("What was he trying to say to me?"), and the obvious negative connotations that are easily constructed about a suicide ("She did this at home because she wanted to punish me—she must have hated me," or "I couldn't have been very important to him if he could do such a selfish thing," etc.) can add greatly to the bereavement burden of suicide survivors.

Relationship of Self With Others

Suicide also changes how we relate to, and are related to by other people in our family, work, and community networks (Calhoun, Selby, & Walton, 1985; Range, 1998). In other historical settings, the stigmatization of survivor families by the community was overt and usually brutal. The body of the deceased might be dismembered and placed in a public setting as a warning to others. Moreover, the family would be prohibited from inheriting the assets of the deceased, and members were frequently shunned by the community for many years to come (Colt, 2006; Cvinar, 2005).

At least in most developed nations, such overt prejudice appears to be giving way to a more subtle form of unhelpful interaction with survivors. Suicide can create an ambiguity about the "rules" of social interaction between the survivor and their social networks (Calhoun, Abernathy, & Selby, 1986; Jordan, 2001; van Dongen, 1993). That is, friends, colleagues, and even family members are often uncertain about what kind of response is appropriate or needed after a suicide death. Although this can occur after any type of bereavement, it is often particularly problematic after a suicide. As in most social situations where the "correct" behavior is unclear, people tend to stay away from emotionally charged and socially ambiguous issues altogether, attempting to avoid interpersonal situations that might result in awkwardness and misunderstanding.

From this perspective, social avoidance by family and friends that actually springs from simple discomfort may be misinterpreted by survivors as condemnation of their "failure" to be a good enough spouse, parent, sibling, and so forth. It is also probable that some survivors "self-stigmatize," that is, they assume that others are thinking negatively of them because of the suicide (Dunn & Morish-Vidners, 1987; Jordan, 2001). Survivors may isolate themselves to avoid what they expect to be emotionally painful interactions with others (Neimeyer & Jordan, 2002). Paradoxically, although this social withdrawal of the bereaved may serve some positive functions for a mourner (energy conservation, attending to family members first, etc.), it can sometimes be viewed by members of the social network as an abandonment of them by the mourner. Thus, reciprocal avoidance between members of the community and the mourner may set up a self-reinforcing feedback loop of misunderstanding and hurt feelings that make future interaction more difficult (Séguin, Lesage, & Kiely, 1995). This process may account for much longer term social disruption that can follow a suicide. Many survivors report that after the loss of their loved one to suicide, they "found out who my real friends were," referring to those who did not avoid or abandon them, but instead stayed engaged and available.

Note that these same processes can occur within family systems, and the loss of relational availability of family members to one another can lead to strain and estrangement between intimates (Cerel, Jordan, & Duberstein, 2008; Kaslow & Aronson, 2004). The suicide of a family member may alter the relational dynamics between marital partners and between parents and children. Established relationship systems such as families typically evolve toward stable patterns of interaction, with shared constructions about the personalities of the family members and the meaning of certain behaviors. Catastrophic losses such as a suicide can drastically destabilize these patterns of interaction and their related meaning systems (Nadeau, 1998).

After an intense argument with her parents, an adolescent daughter storms up to her bedroom and hangs herself. Her parents cope with this catastrophic event very differently. The father responds by focusing on restoring orderly functioning within the family, seeking to shield his other children from the negative psychological effects of the suicide and protect his already strained marriage from dissolving. He expects that everyone in the family, including himself, will return within a few weeks to their "jobs" as breadwinner, housekeeper, parent, and child/ student. His wife, in contrast, spends enormous amounts of time in her bedroom crying, sleeping, and ruminating about where her daughter's spirit is after the death. She is barely able to function as a parent with her other children, let alone relate to her husband as a marital partner. She feels misunderstood and abandoned by her husband for his failure to literally and metaphorically "be with me in the bedroom." The relational strain between the couple escalates rapidly as resentment about their radically different ways of coping grows.

To a great extent, such tensions within the family as these can reflect different—and often gendered—styles of coping with bereavement, in which "instrumental" grievers may adopt a more controlled, "cognitive" and practical style, while "intuitive" grievers naturally adopt a more "emotional," expressive stance (Doka & Martin, 2010). Marital partners may find their mate "becoming a different person" as each individual seeks to heal their own internal psychic wounds, thereby changing the familiar emotional availability of partners to one another. Thus, a suicide may change the perceptions that family members have of one another and of the typical patterns of interaction that have guided family life prior to the death. Direct scapegoating of the survivor may also emerge within families; with one or more members developing a narrative about responsibility for the suicide that directly places blame for the death upon another family member. This disruption of emotional and role availability of family members to one another may have long-term consequences for family developmental processes, reverberating on into the dynamics of the next generation in the family (Bradach & Jordan, 1995; Jordan, Kraus, & Ware, 1993).

Similar to the dynamics within families, a suicide may change the perceptions and interactional patterns between survivors and members of their larger social network of friends, colleagues, professional caregivers, and others with whom they interact. Many survivors report the feeling that others interact with them differently after a suicide (Range & Calhoun, 1990). Friends may sometimes become intrusive, asking for an explanation of an event that the survivors themselves cannot understand. More commonly, friends may avoid interaction with the survivors around the specific subject of the suicide, or may withdraw from social contact completely. In a fashion quite similar to scapegoating within a family, survivors may also encounter outright stigmatization and blaming from members of their community. Recent empirical evidence on bereavement following traumatic death links the occurrence of such negative interactions with more complicated grief symptomatology in survivors (Burke, Neimeyer, & McDevitt-Murphy, 2010; Feigelman, Gorman, & Jordan, 2009).

> A father in a family takes his life after struggling with alcoholism and depression and eventually losing his job. A neighbor, whose children have played with the deceased's children for many years, forbids her children from interacting with them anymore. She tells her children that the man has committed a sin, and is now in hell. The children of the deceased are no longer invited to birthday or holiday parties at the neighbor's house, and the woman also withdraws from socializing with the man's wife.

Lastly, for survivors whose loved one was involved with the mental health or other institutional caregiving systems, the comforting assumption that professionals are experts who always have the knowledge and skill to "save" someone who is suicidal may be shattered by personal and institutional realities. For example, evidence exists to suggest that at least for beginning counselors, suicide threat in a client can engender more anxiety (and possibly avoidance) than a range of other serious presenting problems, such as substance abuse or incest (Kirchberg & Neimeyer, 1991). Moreover, even when competent clinicians are involved, the limitations of the system to prevent all suicide may become all too evident, as the frequency of suicide in psychiatric hospitals suggests (Ajdacic-Gross, Lauber, Baumgartner, Malti, & Rossler, 2009). This loss of faith in trusted institutions can add to the distress burden of survivors.

> A devoutly religious woman who loses her young adult daughter to suicide turns to her church and pastor of many years for solace and answers about how this could have happened, and what it means for her daughter's soul. Her pastor, however, is clearly made uncomfortable by her distress, and seems at a loss

for words when she pleads for guidance about the reassurance of her daughter's acceptance into heaven. After an initial and perfunctory condolence call on the family, he avoids contact with the mother in the weeks following the girl's death, and avoids bringing up the subject when he unexpectedly finds himself alone with her. He also declines to let the mother engage in certain memorialization activities that are commonly allowed after other deaths in the church. Moreover, the woman finds that many members of her congregation avoid talking with her about her daughter's death after the initial few weeks. She attributes this behavior to her pastor's failure to help the community deal with the suicide in a forthright and open manner. The woman is left feeling bitter and abandoned by the response of the clergy and church community, whom she assumed would be the obvious source of support to help her through her grief. She ends up changing churches, feeling that she no longer can find a home in her previous faith community.

In all of these examples, the suicide results in profound changes in the relational meanings and associated interactional patterns that occur between survivors and their social networks. Both the survivors themselves, and often those around them, now view the survivor through the newly acquired identity of suicide survivor, an identity that can be saturated with misinformed and often negative connotations for all concerned. How the survivor negotiates this status and attempts to reconstruct meaning in the wake of devastating loss is the subject of the next section.

☐ Meaning Reconstruction and the Tripartite Model of Suicide Bereavement

The TMSB (Sands, 2008, 2009) is a meaning-making model that focuses on key themes that the bereaved struggle with as they re-story their loss in the aftermath of a suicide death. The model is a relational model that considers meaning-making themes within the context of the bereaved person's relationship with self, the deceased, and significant others. The search for meaning-making proceeds through discourse, dialogue, and re-storying, but the model stresses that it is emotional engagement with relationships that is at the heart of adaptive and transformative grief processes (Sands & Tennant, 2010). The TMSB identifies how relationships are changed, modified, and reframed as the bereaved construct flexible and more emotionally tolerable narratives about their loss. The model sets out a nonlinear, three-by-three matrix, providing a framework to identify meaning reconstruction in suicide bereavement (Figure 11.1).

Drawing on narrative and relational theories, the model conceptualizes suicide bereavement as a nonlinear process of adaptation in which the bereaved engage, with fluctuating degrees of intensity, in recursive meaning-making processes concerned with the intentional nature of suicide, reconstruction of the death story, and repositioning of the suicide and pain of the deceased's life. The metaphors of "trying on the shoes," "walking in the shoes," and "taking off the shoes" of the deceased are used to illustrate the different dimensions of the grief process (Sands, 2008, 2009). Range (1998) described the search for meaning by those bereaved by suicide as, "emotionally draining ... because they are struggling with existential questions for which there are not ultimate answers" (p. 215). However, as previously described, research confirms that the ability to make meaning that is tolerable is linked with improved grief outcomes and self-growth (Currier et al., 2006; Murphy, Johnson, & Lohan, 2003), and indeed, that in the wake of violent death, such sense-making is a far stronger predictor of overcoming adverse grief symptomatology than is the passage of time (Holland & Neimeyer, in press). The grief literature provides many lists of indicators or symptoms describing suicide grief, including guilt, blame, abandonment, and broken trust; the TMSB groups these issues within an integrated relational meaning-oriented framework to illustrate a transformative process of adaptation in suicide loss.

The core of the TMSB is concerned with the development of the ongoing relationship with the deceased. The postloss attachment of the bereaved to the deceased has been termed the "continuing bond" by Klass, Silverman, and Nickman (1996). It is important to note that the relationship between the bereaved and the deceased can be adaptive or maladaptive (Klass, 2006). Research suggests that the formation of the continuing bond and imaginal communications between the bereaved and the deceased are part of a complex process in which the bereaved readjust from the living person to a constructed imaginal presence of the deceased that attains an ongoing place in the bereaved person's life (Klass et al., 1996; Walter, 1996). The continuing relationship with the deceased undergoes a process of adaptation, as the bereaved disengages from the living person and transfers the attachment to a transformed reconstructed mental representation of the deceased (Boerner &

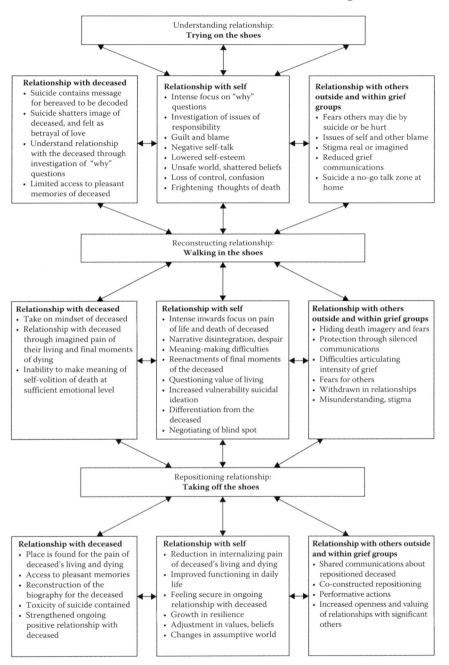

FIGURE 11.1 The Tripartite Model of Suicide Bereavement.

Heckhausen, 2003). In this process, meaning-making about the life of the deceased and the manner of his or her death is pivotal in the formation of the ongoing relationship (Walter, 1996). For example, factors such as whether the deceased suffered, whether the death was expected and in keeping with the natural order of life and death, and whether it was considered by the bereaved to be a "good death" are significant markers in the bereavement process (Nadeau, 1998). A death by suicide can therefore create a number of complex meaning-making challenges for the bereaved that can complicate bereavement and the development of the ongoing relationship (see "Suicide and the Challenge to the Assumptive World" earlier in this chapter). Rynearson (2001) discussed these challenges and noted a disjuncture between the violent actions of the deceased and the caring behavior of the bereaved that complicated construction and narration of the death story, creating a structural "dead end" (p. 21). Of particular importance is research that confirms that when there is an intense attachment or bond to the deceased coupled with an inability to make meaning, the bereaved are at risk of grief complications developing (Neimeyer, Baldwin, & Gillies, 2006). The model draws attention to meaning-making difficulties in a death due to suicide that may influence the maladaptive or adaptive nature of the ongoing relationship with the deceased.

The TMSB also highlights how the ability to make meanings that assist the construction of an adaptive relationship with the deceased has consequences for the bereaved person's sense of self. Rappaport (2009) stated, "Suicide demands to be explained by the living as a way to absolve or condemn the survivors" (p. 7). For the bereaved, the suicide of a loved one is a devastatingly personal and intimate act that can fundamentally question the relationship with the self (Barrett, 1989; Bolton, 1986; Jamison, 1999; Lukas & Seiden, 1990; Neimeyer, Prigerson, & Davies, 2002). The intimate nature of suicide is captured in the words of a suicide-bereaved child asking, "Why did he do that to me?" (Sands, 2003). It is acknowledged that grieving is a uniquely personal process, and it is understood that this process involves profound changes to an individual's sense of self and assumptions about his or her world (Hedtke & Winslade, 2004; Janoff-Bulman & Berg, 1998; Neimeyer, Botella, Herrero, Pacheco, Figueras, & Werner-Wilder, 2002).

The TMSB identifies how the assault on meaning-making also has implications for the bereaved person's relationships with significant others. Nadeau (1998) demonstrated that meaning-making conversations are a major factor in storying the death of a family member, friend, or work colleague. However, issues of confusion, contagion, stigma, blame, and responsibility all tend to reduce meaning-making opportunities and compromise communication following a suicide death. As Jamison

(1999) pointed out, suicide causes fear and confusion in others and disrupts grief conversations. A bereaved child speaks of her confusion in trying to make sense of her father's suicide: "I would rather him die of a heart attack because it's more understandable than killing yourself ... [and] you wouldn't have to think why and stuff" (Sands, 2003). In her autobiographical account following her sister's suicide, Linn-Gust (2004) explained that the death of her sister left her family vulnerable to community censure, as the suicide "exposed to society what we thought was wrong with our family. After all, society says something must be amiss with the family if one of its members decided not to live anymore" (p. 119). The suicide of a family member can irrevocably change family interactions and the way the family experiences itself. This experience within the family can be understood as a microcosm of the "empathic failure," isolation, and stigma in the wider relational web and community that tends to disenfranchise and silence grief following a suicide death, thus severely impeding survivors' capacity to narrate and construct meaning in their loss (Neimeyer & Jordan, 2002).

Trying on the Shoes

To capture the overwhelming nature of the grief process following a suicide death, the TMSB uses the metaphor of "trying on the shoes." Carl Rogers (1951) argued that to understand and empathize with another person we need to stand in their shoes. For the bereaved, trying on the shoes of the deceased is prompted by their need to understand and make meaning of the intentional nature of a suicide death. Rynearson (2001) noted his compulsion to return repeatedly to the suicide death of his wife in an effort to find a way to live with the intentional actions that ended her life. The bereaved often believe there is an implied message in a suicide death, a message that is confusing and difficult to decode. The following quote illustrating the model is taken from conversations and writings of a study participant in Sands' (2008) research.

> A wife talks of her profound bewilderment: "There was absolutely no prelude to anything, he was the most wonderful father, husband, my soul mate, [and] I have to try and comprehend something that happened so out of the blue."

Rappaport (2009) shares her sense of bafflement over her mother's suicide note written at the same time as a grocery list in preparation for the arrival of her children that day. Confusion and concerns with regard to the intentional nature of suicide present in a range of relational themes that saturate the thinking and conversations of those bereaved, frequently explored through various forms of "why" questions. As another of Sands' participants acknowledged, "I ask all these questions. Why didn't I know? Why didn't I see anything?" These questions can be understood as part of an ongoing dialogue that is both internal and external. The intentionality of suicide tends to subsume other aspects of the deceased's life and challenges the grievers' understanding of the fundamental basis of their relationship with the deceased.

Walking in the Shoes

Chapter 9 of this book describes one of the healing tasks for survivors as the need to conduct a personal "psychological autopsy" of the state of mind of the deceased. In similar fashion, the TMSB conceptualizes the focus on meaning reconstruction of the death story with reference to the Native American adage that to understand the experience of someone else, we must "walk in his or her moccasins." The metaphor "walking in the shoes" focuses on the prevalence of themes concentrating on details and material related to the pain of the life and death of the deceased. The model draws attention to themes in which the bereaved either physically or mentally repeatedly revisit the death scene, as well as the sequence of events prior to the death, and the difficult issues in the deceased's life, in an effort to make sense of the actions of the deceased. A bereaved person in Sands' (2008) study captures the visceral, embodied sense of this quest for meaning, writing "[I] can now feel your pain ... your emptiness ... your loneliness." Sands (2008, 2009) observed that often the bereaved feel an intense need to understand the frame of mind of the deceased. It is suggested that the process of reconstructing the imagined, or known pain in the deceased's life, and the events preceding the death, assist the bereaved in meaning reconstruction efforts that facilitate integration of the loss (Rynearson, 2001; Walter, 1999). A bereaved daughter in Sands' (2008) research explains how thoughts of the deceased led inescapably to the shock and distress of the death: "It's there every day, I think it colors—it's in every pore of my skin ... I can't get that vision out of my head." A bereaved mother says, "I obsess about what she went through when she was dying." In a similar vein, another bereaved mother, 2 years after the death of her son, reflects, "I often go there, in my mind ... [I] think about the actual suicide: How? And how long did it take?" Sands found that for a pro-portion of those bereaved, in the initial stages, the ongoing relationship with the deceased was primarily formed through the pain of the death event. Quotes such as the following capture the exhausting nature of these reconstruction efforts: "I think about the day [he] was found a lot, any time of day ... [I] still can't come to terms with it ... the suicide issue is just huge."

Significantly, the TMSB identifies the function of reconstruction efforts in assisting with psychological differentiation processes. The fol-lowing reflections by a young woman in Sands' (2008) study as she walks in her father's shoes illustrate this process.

> Like a forensic investigator, the young woman reconstructs the death event, stating, "I re-enacted my dad's hanging ... I put the chair in the exact place dad kicked it from. Everything was the same." The daughter tells us, "I put the rope on, and I now know if Dad wanted to get out of it, he could have, the chair was close enough." The meaning she makes is significant, "My dad did not want to stop or pull out." This knowledge becomes a point of differentiation and adaptation in her relationship with her father as she reflects, "I get much more peace knowing he didn't want to get out and could—so this has helped me."

A similar process is mapped in the following quote, in which a sis-ter describes the impact of her sister's suicide.

> "The violence of her jumping haunts me." The sister walks in her sister's shoes, wanting "to know what she was feeling," and reports her experi-ence that it is "[as if] I am walking on tha cliff, and to fall off would be the natural progression." She imagines her sister's death: "The violence, the image of her being airborne, the image of her smashed up body." However, as she openly makes meaning she articulates her ambivalence, "I want to run either to the edge, or as far away as possible," and affirms her dif-ference, "The effort is to pull back ... I can't bear to be near the edge of a cliff."

It is clear that those walking in the shoes of a person who died by suicide can experience a similar challenge to their assumptive world to that experienced by the person who died by suicide. Survivors undertak-ing this are vulnerable to experiencing comparable feelings of hopeless-ness and suicidal ideation. Some of the bereaved may stay interminably ruminating within the mindset of the deceased. It is difficult and some-times frightening to listen to death story reconstruction attempts that contain suicidal ideation and traumatic detail, but without a listener, the bereaved are silenced and left to navigate this process in isolation. The deceased's death leaves a potent message for the bereaved about the futility of dealing with the pain of living, a message that can cause the bereaved to doubt their meaning-making efforts and ability to resolve the pain of their grieving. It is important that the bereaved are supported with appropriate interventions that assist reconstruction of static, fixed narratives to increase narrative flexibility, affirm the focus on the bereaved person's own experience, and assist with the differentiation processes that are central to reconstruction of the death story and navigation of what Sands (2008) refers to as the *blind spot* at the core of suicide.

The blind spot refers to the inherent inability of the survivor to ever fully comprehend the mind and motivation of the deceased, and therefore the reasons for the suicide. Finding a way through the blind spot is not about making meanings that are profoundly comprehensive so much as getting to a place of meaning that allows the bereaved to reinvest energy in themselves and re-engage in daily life (Sands, 2008, 2009). Rappaport (2009), commenting on her own exhaustive meaning-making efforts to reconstruct and understand her mother's suicide, noted "knowledge helps ... The accumulation of details may never add up completely, but they do provide scaffolding for understanding and work-lights for the darkness" (p. 278).

Taking off the Shoes

With the metaphor "taking off the shoes," the model identifies the differentiation of the bereaved from the deceased. Repositioning themes tend to become more prevalent once the bereaved have differentiated from the deceased and negotiated the incomprehensibility of the blind spot (Sands, 2008, 2009). As ruminations on intentionality and the death story lessen, a transformative space is created for positive remembering, repositioning, and development of and adjustment to an adaptive valued relationship with the deceased. Repositioning themes illustrate how reconstruction processes integrate difficult and complicated material with more positive memories of the deceased. For example, a mother in Sands' study stresses she is no longer focused on walking in the shoes reconstruction efforts: "I choose to remember him when he was well and when we shared so much of our lives together." A bereaved sister explains that she is bringing her deceased sister back into the family: "She might have given up on herself and removed herself, but that's not the place that I ... want her in our lives. I want her in there as much as my other [family members]." Transformative shifts in the relationship with the deceased from maladaptive to adaptive can be identified in repositioning themes that separate painful death story ruminations from more positive and hopeful memories of the deceased's life. A mother is able to smile as she recalls, "At work today, I felt like a butterfly kiss on my cheek. And this to me is like a sign from her." Repositioning themes reconstruct the death story in ways that bear witness to the suffering of the deceased, but do not sanction the manner of their death. Repositioning themes also function to increase a sense of worthiness and personal autonomy, and importantly, assist in healing broken trust and recreating a sense of order and safety in the world.

> A bereaved brother explains, "I have learned to focus on the rest of his life ... and see the whole picture, not just the bad part ... Good and bad washed in together." He affirms, "There is no point focusing on the worst point in his life."

Although grieving continues, the pain of the deceased's life and death are separated from more nurturing memories that support growth through grief. For clinicians, the implications of "taking off the shoes" suggest the benefit of "punctuating" micro shifts in the way the bereaved are talking about their grief. It is important to notice and affirm small differences while creating opportunities that support meaning reconstruction through rituals that honor, celebrate, and value the best memories, qualities, and legacy of the deceased.

The TMSB maps pathways in suicide bereavement in the context of meaning-making and the griever's relational world, but we would stress that many people bereaved by suicide will manage their grieving without experiencing the themes and features identified in this model. The way in which individuals negotiate suicide bereavement is inevitably intertwined with the manner in which the loss challenges their assumptive world, sometimes even changing it in ways that deepen the survivors' sense of purpose in living. It is this prospect of positive reconstruction in the aftermath of suicide bereavement that we will now consider, drawing further on the metaphors inherent in the TMSB model.

☐ Post-traumatic Growth After Suicide

When do the bereaved accept the knowledge that the unfamiliar landscape in which they find themselves is the place where they now live?

Attig (2004) described the process of picking up the pieces and beginning again as *relearning the world*, explaining that when a significant other dies, a person's life patterns are disrupted and the shape of that person's life is forever changed, requiring the griever to relearn the world. It is generally accepted that there is no "recovery" of the griever's preloss state of being; bereaved people do not "get over" losses, but rather they "adapt and adjust to the changed situation" (Stroebe, Hansson, Stroebe, & Schut, 2001, p. 9). The process of adaptation to the changed reality provoked by grief is uniquely individual, involving options that may continue to be revisited and reworked over a lifetime. And for some grievers, given the circumstances of the loss and their own personal factors, only limited adaptation and adjustment is possible. Many researchers, however, have commented that paradoxically there are possibilities for growth through the suffering and struggle that grief provokes (Calhoun & Tedeschi, 2001, 2006; Neimeyer et al., 2002). As the wheel turns and returns, every ending carries within it the space of a new beginning. It is important to note that growth through grief does not suggest an absence of suffering. Given this understanding, the optimal conditions for growth through grief would allow "room for a relationship with grief that is livable, acceptable, creative," and that supports the changes and personal development that accompany grieving (Moules, Simonson, Prins, Angus, & Bell, 2004, p. 100). Tedeschi and Calhoun (2006) studied growth through grief and noted, "Post-traumatic growth might be considered the highest form of change associated with grief" (p. 31). In their research, Calhoun and Tedeschi (2006) identified five domains of positive post-traumatic growth: the development of personal strength, new possibilities, including an increased ability to relate and connect with others, a greater appreciation of life, and spiritual and existential change.

Suicide bereavement studies are consistent with Calhoun and Tedeschi's (2006) findings in their descriptions of the trauma, degree of disruption, and patterns of post-traumatic growth through grief following a suicide death (Begley & Quayle, 2007; Jordan, 2009; Neimeyer et al., 2002; Rynearson, 2001). There are, however, thematic differences in suicide bereavement post-traumatic growth narratives. Sands' (2008, 2009) research described rumination and reconstruction themes in suicide bereavement that preceded post-traumatic growth, and identified a number of post-traumatic narrative themes. Taku, Calhoun, Cann, and Tedeschi (2008) also noted the significant role of rumination and cognitive reconstruction processes in post-traumatic growth. Like alchemy, in suicide bereavement, reconstruction narratives transmute and integrate complex grief elements into a valuable resource in the bereaved person's life to assist growth through grief. Sands (2008) noted *redemptive narratives* that transformed the death separating the deceased from the trauma of the death in ways that validated the suffering of the deceased but not the action of suicide. The following quotes illustrating post-traumatic growth through grief in suicide bereavement are taken from conversations and writings of study participants in Sands' (2008) research, and are referred to within the TMSB as repositioning relationship themes; that is, taking off the shoes.

A suicide-bereaved parent's *redemptive narrative* illustrates this distinction between the deceased and the manner of their death: "I am not angry with him [for killing himself]. I feel great compassion and sadness ... for somebody who was so brave with the mental illness that he suffered."

A bereaved sister reflecting on the transformed role of the deceased as a supportive guide also makes this distinction, "I feel so guided by him [the deceased]—and I didn't feel that before ... And the way he died [suicide] ... well that just happened then, and now we are over here and he is helping."

Narratives of containment functioned to control and contain a range of fearful and toxic elements associated with the death to assist reconstruction of order and safety, and reduced suicidality.

A bereaved person talks of how she has recovered her sister from the black hole of suicide and in doing so restored her own sense of safety, "[I feel] safer ... I'm not scared anymore that I [also] have a mental illness. I have been able to bring my [deceased] sister back from the black hole I felt she had disappeared into."

In a similar manner, a mother's narrative suggests reduced suicidality and increased resilience and stability. "I am starting to learn that ... I can survive, now, but ... I would have been really high on that suicide list. I was not stable."

Narratives of forgiveness are another distinctive theme in post-traumatic growth in suicide bereavement. Having struggled with complex meaning-making issues, the bereaved may reach a place in their growth where they are able to talk of forgiving both themselves and the deceased for leaving them in that way. The bereaved in Sands' (2008) research reported increased resilience and feeling "calmer and more at peace" and less hard on themselves about the way the death happened.

A mother reflected, "I no longer feel that my daughter's death was my fault. It's like a great weight has been lifted ... I have the strength to go on with life ... I am finding a place in my life for her suicide."

A sibling's narrative also illustrates growth through forgiveness: "To survive this loss has required every strength and every ounce of knowledge and experience gained throughout my life ... I never thought I could forgive myself for what happened ... it has found a place within me."

Sands (2008) also found *narratives of reconnection* that mapped relational efforts to reconnect in ways that integrated the suicide. Significantly, many narratives talked of reconstructing an ongoing connection with the deceased, for example when the relationship had been severed due to the overwhelming nature of the pain saturating the deceased's life and death.

A mother's comments illustrate the quality of this kind of reconnection, "I just kind of draw her essence back into my life ... you don't stop your relationships with the people that you care about when they are alive so ... you [don't] stop developing a relationship with someone that's died ... some bits are good and lots aren't good ... but you try and ... move on with it."

Notably, *narratives of reconnection* are also about repairing relational connections damaged by issues of blame, guilt, and stigma within the bereaved family and the community of grievers. The following quote illustrates family and friends working together to integrate and move past the manner of death. "The family ... [and] close friends ... all of us moving on ... and trying to hold him [the deceased]—to get past the way that he died ... [and] celebrate the good things ... the good times."

In accord with findings by Calhoun and Tedeschi (2006), suicide bereavement narratives demonstrated *narratives of increased appreciation of life*. These narratives also frequently contained spiritual and existential themes, as evident in this man's words, "I will live out my days with a better appreciation of life and people and relationships ... then when I eventually pass, there will be plenty of forever to spend time with him [the deceased]." Community service is another aspect of growth through grief found in suicide bereavement narratives. Armour (2003) noted that narratives of performative actions such as community service or volunteer work promoted a sense of agency and continuity. In this quote, a bereavement group member asks others to join her in such an endeavor: "This group has such a wealth of diversity and people that we could help, maybe another group." Those who have suffered a loss through suicide may become involved in increasing public awareness of suicide postvention and prevention through the media, educational talks, arranging remembrance days, setting up foundations, raising funds for services, participating in research, writing, and numerous other activities to benefit the community.

Distinctive themes in post-traumatic growth in suicide bereavement can be traced in *redemptive narratives* that reconstruct the death story in ways that reclaim the deceased and validate their suffering but not the manner of their death. *Containment narratives* confine and hold toxic, traumatic, and fearful elements concerned with the death to rebuild trust, order, and safety and reduce suicidality. *Narratives of forgiveness* function to release the bereaved and deceased from blame, anger, and guilt and illustrate the development of resilience. Post-traumatic growth *narratives of reconnection* illustrate relational reconnection themes that integrate the suicide in relationship with the deceased, the self, the family, and extended relational web. Finally, and consistent with other forms of grief, *narratives of increased appreciation of life* illustrate a valuing of life and service to community within a redefined sense of self and reconstructed existential beliefs, as the bereaved engage in the process of living in a world forever changed.

☐ A Case Observed

The day that Tricia and Scott received the fateful notification of the suicide of their 19-year-old daughter, Christine, was, in their words, "a Monday after work, an ordinary day like any other." Although their daughter's increasingly volatile life over the past few years had placed her on the brink of self-destruction on at least one other occasion, the news ruptured any sense of normality in their world, and, as Tricia said, "left a lot of questions unanswered, and the *guilt*. And so by the time we reached for help, I was having trouble sleeping and concentrating, I couldn't stop thinking about her. I thought about her 24-hours a day and I felt like I wasn't a good mom if I didn't think about her. I wasn't doing her memory justice if I didn't think about her all the time, and I couldn't get on with life because I was just mourning her all the time." As a result, she and her husband sought therapy with one of the authors (RAN) some 6 weeks after this traumatic loss and began a 6-month journey through an alien terrain, which can be aptly described in terms of the components of the TMSB.

Trying on the Shoes

When Tricia and Scott arrived for their first session, their encapsulation in the harrowing experience of the suicide was palpable, as was Tricia's preoccupation with the death and its significance. As she noted, "How could I go on with life and not think about her every minute because she has gone? And it just didn't seem right that life went on without her, that the birds would keep singing, that people would get in their cars and go to work. How could that be when my daughter had died?" To which Scott added, "That was the cruel injustice of it all ... that Christine passed away and the rest of the world just continued to go forward without her. Our world stopped, but nobody else's did." The surreal landscape of loss was made still more threatening by the collapse of foundational assumptions in their own ability to protect their children from adversity, and by the erosion of their belief in a beneficent universe. Wrestling with the perturbing question of the cause of their daughter's fatal decision, Scott acknowledged, "You find you're blaming yourself for what happened. What could I have done differently? What did I do to make her do this?"

If anything, this corrosive quest to decode the meaning of their daughter's death cut still deeper for his wife, who shared that, "It made me question God and the whole thing about, 'How can God create this beautiful girl with this fatal flaw?' You know, 'Why did God do this to her? Why would he allow this?' Your whole belief system is changed. It's like, 'Why did I have this child with this defect, and how could she be so perfect in so many other ways and just so wrong in this part of her being?'" The result was a ruminative engagement with an elusive explanation for the death, accompanied by a "24/7" form of grieving from which Tricia, in particular, found no respite.

As their immersion in the quicksand of anguished questioning deepened, the couple began to grow disengaged from each other and increasingly concerned for the safety of their younger daughter, Chelsea, who seemed to be sinking into her own suicidal morass in the wake of her sister's death. At the same time, Tricia feared that she was "going crazy," as all that she could recall about Christine was the "bookends" of her birth and death, with all the years of pleasant memories between rendered inaccessible by the trauma.

Therapy in this early period attempted to stabilize the family system, to reach out to Chelsea, to provide a safe context for articulating and pursuing answers to the seemingly impossible questions that Christine's death posed, and to help Tricia and Scott as individuals and as a couple to "dose" their grief work by also finding ways to re-engage their changed world without guilt for "leaving Christine behind." For example, faced with Tricia's apparently obligatory grief, the therapist asked her whether she "had ever put her daughter down, perhaps in her bed or bassinet, when she was a baby." Surprised, Tricia acknowledged that she had, of course, many times during the course of a given day. The therapist then asked, "And did that make you a poor mother?" To this Tricia shook her head, as she replied, "Of course not, I was a good mother to her," a claim fully supported by her husband. "What then prevents you from putting her down now from time to time," the therapist continued, "without failing her as a mother?" Tricia registered a slight look of shock, and for the first time in the week that followed, found herself able to "take breaks from the grief without guilt," in order to reconnect with her husband and the world. Returning for the next session, Scott remarked, his arm around his smiling partner, "I feel I have my wife back." Though much work remained to be done, each was learning to modulate the intense affect engendered by the suicide, without losing themselves or one another.

Walking in the Shoes

A second phase of therapy began with a more experiential engagement with the "blind spot" at the center of their daughter's elective death. Informed by a constructivist view of suicide as an act that, however bizarre and tragic when viewed from the perspective of others, appears to represent a "logical" or ineluctable choice from the perspective of the suicidal person herself (Neimeyer & Winter, 2006), the therapist prompted the couple to pursue the quest for meaning differently. "How," he asked, might they "look at her suicide from the *inside out*, instead of looking from the *outside in*, and wondering, 'How do we explain this inexplicable event?,' [but instead] to try and step into *her* view and look at it and ask, 'What did her death mean to *her*?'" Reflecting on this question in a follow-up session 3 months after the termination of their formal therapy, Scott noted, "That was a big change for me. I look back on that now and I saw something that I didn't see until we started talking to you, that maybe this is something that she really *wanted*, and for whatever reason, being here on this earth with us just was too much for her." What followed was a reconstruction, led entirely by the couple, of their understanding of the existential pain and anguish implied by their daughter's tragic choice, in which they came to understand her death as the result of her escalating "mental illness." However, the perturbing questions about "How God could make a person with this fatal flaw, when she had always been so perfect as a child?" continued to haunt them, giving rise to a "crisis of faith," with which they contended for months to come.

Particularly trenchant were Tricia's self-accusations for having "failed" her daughter, despite nearly 3 years of devoted mothering that repeatedly pulled her daughter back from the dark abyss into which she ultimately tumbled. As this self-blame was coupled to Tricia's agonizing attempt to understand why her daughter, now living a thousand miles away, had not called her at the moment of her final crisis, the therapist suggested that they "reopen the dialogue with Christine that was interrupted by her death, and pose the question to her directly." Perplexed but intrigued, Tricia accepted the suggestion to place her daughter symbolically in an empty chair in the office, and address to her in an emotionally resonant way the burning questions that were yearning for answers. With courage and tears, Tricia plaintively gave them voice, and then, with the therapist's gesture, switched chairs and assumed the position of her daughter. Instantly her voice changed to a more teenage timbre, as she voiced Christine's response: "Mom, this is *so* not about you." She went on to explain that when she was little she had "orbited around" her mom as the center of her universe, but that as she moved toward adulthood, Tricia was "no longer her *sun*, but more like her *moon*," as Christine herself was drawn into the thrall of a darker star. Completing the 10-minute dialogue, as Scott witnessed the scene with intense concentration, Tricia expressed nearly immediate relief from the self-accusation that had dogged her for months. Looking back on this "pivot point" in therapy in the follow-up session, Tricia recalled,

When we did our counseling together, there was the one thing where you said that I didn't have to end the relationship with Christine, that I could still have conversations with her, talk to her, or have moments with her. And it's been helpful when I find myself having a question, I do the role-playing: "Christine, *why?*" And then I let her answer. I can hear her, you know.... And that role-playing really helped me as I could talk to her. And I found that I couldn't do that before, like I had lost that and I couldn't. I would be like paralyzed and I couldn't answer the questions until I really spoke directly to her, and then that really helped to answer those questions. And it continued at home. I took that home, and like talked to her in the shower, or in the kitchen. I told Christine, "Why did you do this, why didn't you call me? *Why? Why? Why?*" It was as if I could hear her telling me, "Mom, don't be ridiculous. It wasn't about that. You are *so* off the mark here." I could hear what she would've said and that really, really helped me.

Gradually, her "conversations" with Christine melded into "special moments" of privacy in her car, as she would play music reminiscent of her daughter, and began to access and share with the family the loving story of Christine as a young girl that had previously been obscured by the "dominant narrative" of her traumatic death.

Taking off the Shoes

As Scott and Christine began to reconnect more fully to one another, to Chelsea, and to pleasant memories of Christine, they also began to harvest the bittersweet fruit of their loss in the form of post-traumatic growth. In part, this growth was seeded by some remarkable "coincidences." One such was finding a business card containing on one side an image of Vincent van Gogh's *Starry Night* in the darkness under the bed of their hotel room as they prepared to return home from the funeral. For the grieving parents, the image invoked the turbulence in Christine's soul, as in the painter's before he took his own life, and also conjured Don McLean's song *Vincent*, which recounts the beauty and tragedy of van Gogh's life. In an uncanny conjunction, Tricia had been learning that very song on the guitar the week of her daughter's death, and it replayed endlessly in her head as she flew to bury her. The plastic card—which also functioned as a compact flashlight—struck her profoundly as a "message from God" that her child was in a place of light, and that the family would ultimately find their own way through the darkness.

With courage and determination, both Scott and Tricia began to sift through the pieces of their lives following this seismic loss, and reassemble a framework for living that, in its own way, took on still greater meaning for all their family had suffered. As Tricia noted in the follow-up session of therapy, "I think it has brought us closer as a family. I think we value our relationships more. We know that any moment could be your last moment. So you value those moments. And the one thing we have really learned as a family is that there is a lot of stuff that just doesn't matter. There are so many things that we stress over until you lose somebody, and then all of a sudden everything has a new perspective, life has a new perspective. You think, 'That doesn't really matter, that's not important, no one died.' Your *perspective* changes and in that way, I can say that it has been a *positive* thing, I guess.'" Echoing this, Scott noted, "I try to live for the moment now. I try to appreciate what I have, at this moment, and I try not to look too far in the future now, because I can really drive myself crazy if I do that. In my profession it is a lot about planning for what could happen and I always find myself looking at the future and thinking probably more negatively of, 'Oh, what if this happens, or what if that happens?' And I really just try not to go there anymore. I try to live my life for today, appreciate what I have today, and what tomorrow brings.'"

For both, life ultimately took on a deeper value, though they continued to seek a workable psychological and spiritual framework that acknowledged that life had no "sure bets," and that God gave no guarantees that the lives we cherish today will continue tomorrow.

☐ Coda

Viewed through a constructivist lens, suicide bereavement typically poses distinctive challenges to survivors' worlds of meaning, as they engage in an anguishing attempt to reconstruct their relationships with the deceased, with themselves, with significant others, and with a broader community. In keeping with recent research on bereavement that links an inability to "make sense" of this seemingly senseless loss with a profound and protracted course of grieving, we have sketched a tripartite model of the psychological, relational, and existential tasks faced by survivors as they attempt to grasp, step into, and ultimately differentiate from the mindset that led their loved one toward a tragic relinquishment of life. In our own clinical practice, we have found this to offer a useful heuristic for creative engagement with our clients' efforts, and hope that the TMSB will offer something of value to other readers who provide professional companionship to those who strive to move from mourning to meaning, and from grief to growth, in the wake of this devastating loss.

☐ References

Ajdacic-Gross, V., Lauber, C., Baumgartner, M., Malti, T., & Rossler, W. (2009). In-patient suicide: A 13-year assessment. *Acta Psychiatrica Scandinavica, 120,* 71–75.

Armour, M. (2003). Meaning making in the aftermath of homicide. *Death Studies, 27,* 519–540.

Attig, T. (2004). Meanings of death seen through the lens of grieving. *Death Studies, 28,* 341–360.

Barrett, T. (1989). *Life after suicide: The survivor's grief experience.* Fargo, ND: Aftermath Research.

Begley, M., & Quayle, E. (2007). The lived experience of adults bereaved by suicide: A phenomenological study. *Crisis: The Journal of Crisis Intervention and Suicide Prevention, 28,* 26–34.

Boelen, P., van den Hout, M., & van den Bout, J. (2006). A cognitive-behavioral conceptualization of complicated grief. *Clinical Psychology: Science and Practice, 13,* 109–128.

Boerner, K., & Heckhausen, J. (2003). To have and have not: Adaptive bereavement by transforming mental ties to the deceased. *Death Studies, 27,* 199–226.

Bolton, I. (with C. Mitchell), (1986). *My son, my son: A guide to healing after death, loss or suicide.* Atlanta, GA: The Bolton Press.

Bonanno, G. A., Wortman, C. B., & Nesse, R. M. (2004). Prospective patterns of resilience and maladjustment during widowhood. *Psychology and Ageing, 19,* 260–271.

Bradach, K. M., & Jordan, J. R. (1995). Long-term effects of a family history of traumatic death on adolescent individuation. *Death Studies, 19,* 315–336.

Burke, L. A., Neimeyer, R. A., & McDevitt-Murphy, M. E. (2010). African American homicide bereavement: Aspects of social support that predict complicated grief, PTSD and depression. *Omega: Journal of Death and Dying, 61,* 1–24.

Calhoun, L. G., Abernathy, C. B., & Selby, J. W. (1986). The rules of bereavement: Are suicidal deaths different? *Journal of Community Psychology, 14,* 213–218.

Calhoun, L. G., Selby, J. W., & Walton, P. B. (1985). Suicidal death of a spouse: The social perception of the survivor. *Omega: Journal of Death and Dying, 16,* 283–288.

Calhoun, L. G., & Tedeschi, R. G. (2001). Posttraumatic growth: The positive lessons of loss. In R. A. Neimeyer (Ed.), *Meaning reconstruction and the experience of loss* (pp. 157–172). Washington, DC: American Psychological Association.

Calhoun, L. G., & Tedeschi, R. G. (2006). *Handbook of posttraumatic growth: Research and practice* (pp. 3–23). Mahwah, NJ: Lawrence Erlbaum Associates.

Cerel, J., Jordan, J. R., & Duberstein, P. R. (2008). The impact of suicide on the family. *Crisis: The Journal of Crisis Intervention and Suicide Prevention, 29,* 38–44.

Coleman, R. A., & Neimeyer, R. A. (in press). Measuring meaning: Searching for and making sense of spousal loss in later life. *Death Studies.*

Colt, G. H. (2006). *November of the soul: The enigma of suicide.* New York, NY: Scribner.

Currier, J. M., Holland, J. M., Coleman, R. A., & Neimeyer, R. A. (2008). Bereavement following violent death: An assault on life and meaning. In R. G. Stevenson & G. R. Cox (Eds.), *Perspectives on violence and violent death* (pp. 177–202). Amityville, NY: Baywood.

Currier, J. M., Holland, J. M., & Neimeyer, R. A. (2006). Sense-making, grief, and the experience of violent loss: Toward a mediational model. *Death Studies, 30,* 403–428.

Currier, J. M., Holland, J., & Neimeyer, R. A. (2009). Assumptive worldviews and problematic reactions to bereavement. *Journal of Loss and Trauma, 14,* 181–195.

Cvinar, J. G. (2005). Do suicide survivors suffer social stigma: A review of the literature. *Perspectives in Psychiatric Care, 41,* 14–21.

Davis, C. G., Wohl, M. J. A., & Verberg, N. (2007). Profiles of posttraumatic growth following an unjust loss. *Death Studies, 31,* 693–712.

Doka, K., & Martin, T. (2010). *Grieving beyond gender.* New York, NY: Routledge/Taylor & Francis.

Dunn, R. G., & Morrish-Vidners, D. (1987). The psychological and social experience of suicide survivors. *Omega: Journal of Death and Dying, 18,* 175–215.

Feigelman, W., Gorman, B. S., & Jordan, J. R. (2009). Stigmatization and suicide bereavement. *Death Studies, 33,* 591–608.

Guidano, V. F. (1991). *The self in process.* New York, NY: Guilford.

Hedtke, L., & Winslade, J. (2004). *Re-membering lives: Conversations with the dying and the bereaved.* Amityville, NY: Baywood.

Holland, J., Currier, J., & Neimeyer, R. A. (2006). Meaning reconstruction in the first two years of bereavement: The role of sense-making and benefit-finding. *Omega: Journal of Death and Dying, 53,* 173–191.

Holland, J., & Neimeyer, R. A. (in press). An examination of stage theory of grief among individuals bereaved by natural and violent causes: A meaning-oriented contribution. *Omega: Journal of Death and Dying.*

Jamison, J. R. (1999). *Night falls fast: Understanding suicide.* London, England: Picador.

Janoff-Bulman, R., & Berg, M. (1998). Disillusionment and the creation of value: From traumatic losses to existential gains. In J. H. Harvey (Ed.), *Perspectives on loss: A sourcebook* (pp. 33–47). Philadelphia, PA: Brunner/Mazel.

Janoff-Bulman, R., & Berger, A. R. (2000). The other side of trauma: Towards a psychology of appreciation. In J. H. Harvey & E. D. Miller (Eds.), *Loss and trauma: General and close relationship perspectives* (pp. 29–44). New York, NY: Routledge.

Jordan, J. (2001). Is suicide bereavement different? A reassessment of the literature. *Suicide and Life-Threatening Behavior, 31,* 91–102.

Jordan, J. (2008). Bereavement after suicide. *Psychiatric Annals, 38,* 679–685.

Jordan, J. (2009). After suicide: Clinical work with survivors. *Grief Matters: The Australian Journal of Grief and Bereavement, 12,* 4–9.

Jordan, J., Kraus, D. R., & Ware, E. S. (1993). Observations on loss and family development. *Family Process, 32,* 425–440.

Kaslow, N. J., & Aronson, S. G. (2004). Recommendations for family interventions following a suicide. *Professional Psychology: Research and Practice, 35,* 240–247.

Keesee, N. J., Currier, J. M., & Neimeyer, R. A. (2008). Predictors of grief following the death of one's child: The contribution of finding meaning. *Journal of Clinical Psychology, 64,* 1145–1163.

Kelly, G. A. (1991). *The psychology of personal constructs.* New York, NY: Routledge. (Original work published 1955).

Kirchberg, T. M., & Neimeyer, R. A. (1991). Reactions of beginning counselors to situations involving death and dying. *Death Studies, 15,* 603–610.

Klass, D. (2006). Continuing conversation about continuing bonds. *Death Studies, 30,* 843–858.

Klass, D., Silverman, P. R., & Nickman, S. L. (1996). Concluding thoughts. In D. Klass, P. R. Silverman, & S. L. Nickman (Eds.), *Continuing bonds: New understandings of grief* (pp. 349–355). Washington, DC: Taylor & Francis.

Linn-Gust, M. (2004). *Do they have bad days in heaven? Surviving the suicide loss of a sibling.* Albuquerque, NM: Chellehead Works.

Lukas, C., & Seiden, H. M. (1990). *Silent grief: Living in the wake of suicide.* London, England: Papermac division of Macmillan.

Menninger, K. A. (1933). Psychoanalytic aspects of suicide. *International Journal of Psychoanalysis, 14,* 376–390.

Moules, N. J., Simonson, K., Prins, M., Angus, P., & Bell, J. M. (2004). Making room for grief: Walking backwards and living forward. *Nursing Inquiry, 11,* 99–107.

Murphy, S. A., Johnson L. C., & Lohan, J. (2003). Finding meaning in a child's violent death: A five-year prospective analysis of parents' personal narratives and empirical data. *Death Studies, 27*, 381–404.

Nadeau, J. W. (1998). *Families making sense of death.* Thousand Oaks, CA: Sage.

Neimeyer, R. A. (2000). Narrative disruptions in the construction of self. In R. A. Neimeyer & J. D. Raskin (Eds.), *Constructions of disorder: Meaning making frameworks for psychotherapy* (pp. 207–241). Washington, DC: American Psychological Association.

Neimeyer, R. A. (Ed.). (2001). *Meaning reconstruction and the experience of loss.* Washington, DC: American Psychological Association.

Neimeyer, R. A. (2006a). Re-storying loss: Fostering growth in the posttraumatic narrative. In L. G. Calhoun & R. G. Tedeschi (Eds.), *Handbook of posttraumatic growth: Research and practice* (pp. 68–80). Mahwah, NJ: Lawrence Erlbaum Associates.

Neimeyer, R. A. (2006b). Widowhood, grief and the quest for meaning: A narrative perspective on resilience. In D. Carr, R. M. Nesse, & C. B. Wortman (Eds.), *Spousal bereavement in late life* (pp. 227–252). New York, NY: Springer.

Neimeyer, R. A. (2009). *Constructivist psychotherapy.* New York, NY: Routledge.

Neimeyer, R. A., Baldwin, S. A., & Gillies, J. (2006). Continuing bonds and reconstructing meaning: Mitigating complications in bereavement. *Death Studies, 30*, 715–738.

Neimeyer, R. A., Botella, L., Herrero, O., Pacheco, M., Figueras, S., & Werner-Wilder, L. A. (2002). The meaning of your absence: Traumatic loss and narrative reconstruction. In J. Kauffman (Ed.), *Loss of the assumptive world: A theory of traumatic loss* (pp. 31–47). New York, NY: Brunner Routledge.

Neimeyer, R. A., & Jordan, J. R. (2002). Disenfranchisement as empathic failure. In K. Doka (Ed.), *Disenfranchised grief* (pp. 97–117). Champaign, IL: Research Press.

Neimeyer, R. A., & Mahoney, M. J. (Eds.). (1995). *Constructivism in psychotherapy.* Washington, DC: American Psychological Association.

Neimeyer, R. A., Prigerson, H. G., & Davies, B. (2002). Mourning and meaning. *American Behavioral Scientist, 46*, 235–251.

Neimeyer, R. A., & Winter, D. (2006). To be or not to be: Personal constructions of the suicidal choice. In T. E. Ellis (Ed.), *Cognition and suicide: Theory, research, and therapy* (pp. 149–169). Washington, DC: American Psychological Association.

Range, L. (1998). When a loss is due to suicide: Unique aspects of bereavement. In J. H. Harvey (Ed.), *Perspectives of loss: A sourcebook* (pp. 213–220). Philadelphia, PA: Brunner/Mazel.

Range, L. M., & Calhoun, L. G. (1990). Responses following suicide and other types of death: The perspective of the bereaved. *Omega: Journal of Death and Dying, 21*, 311–320.

Range, L. M., & Goggin, W. C. (1990). Reactions to suicide: Does age of the victim make a difference? *Death Studies, 14*, 269–275.

Rappaport, N. (2009). *In her wake: A child psychiatrist explores the mystery of her mother's suicide.* New York, NY: Perseus Books Group.

Rogers, C. (1951). *Client-centered therapy: Its current practice, implications and theory.* London, England: Constable.

Rynearson, E. K. (2001). *Retelling violent death.* Philadelphia, PA: Brunner-Routledge.

Sands, D. (Producer and director). (2003). *The red chocolate elephants: Children bereaved by suicide* (DVD film). Sydney, Australia: Karridale.

Sands, D. (2009). A tripartite model of suicide grief: Meaning-making and the relationship with the deceased. *Grief Matters: The Australian Journal of Grief and Bereavement, 12,* 10–17.

Sands, D., & Tennant, M. (2010). Transformative learning in the context of suicide bereavement. *Adult Education Quarterly, 60,* 99–121.

Sands, D. C. (2008). *A study of suicide grief: Meaning making and the griever's relational world.* Unpublished doctoral thesis, University of Technology, Sydney, Australia. http://utsescholarship.lib.uts.edu.au/iresearch/scholarly-works/handle/2100/777

Séguin, M., Lesage, A., & Kiely, M. C. (1995). Parental bereavement after suicide and accident: A comparative study. *Suicide and Life-Threatening Behavior, 25,* 489–498.

Stroebe, M. S., Hansson, R. O., Stroebe, W., & Schut, H. (2001). Introduction: Concepts and issues in contemporary research on bereavement. In M. S. Stroebe, R. O. Hansson, W. Stroebe, & H. Schut (Eds.), *Handbook of bereavement research: Consequences, coping, and care* (pp. 3–22). Washington, DC: American Psychological Association.

Taku, K., Calhoun, L.G., Cann, A., & Tedeschi, R. G. (2008). The role of rumination in the coexistence of distress and posttraumatic growth among bereaved Japanese university students. *Death Studies, 32,* 428–444.

Tedeschi, R. G., & Calhoun, L. G. (2008). Beyond the concept of recovery: Growth and the experience of loss. *Death Studies, 32,* 27–39.

van Dongen, C. J. (1993). Social context of postsuicide bereavement. *Death Studies, 17,* 125–141.

Walter, T. (1996). A new model of grief: Bereavement and biography. *Mortality, 1,* 7–25.

Walter, T. (1999). *On bereavement: The culture of grief.* Berkshire, MA: Open University Press.

Group Work With Suicide Survivors

John R. Jordan

Suicide bereavement support groups have been described and recommended for many years in the literature on suicide survivors (Appel & Wrobleski, 1987; Clark et al., 1993; Gaffney, Jones, & Dunne-Maxim, 1992; Rogers, Sheldon, Barwick, Letofsky, & Lancee, 1982), and they continue to be suggested as a helpful experience for many survivors of suicide loss (Cerel, Padgett, Conwell, & Reed, 2009; Cerel, Padgett, & Reed, 2009; Feigelman, Gorman, Beal, & Jordan, 2008; Jordan & Harpel, 2007; Lifeline Australia, 2009; McMenamy, Jordan, & Mitchell, 2008; Mitchell et al., 2007; World Health Organization [WHO}, 2008). This chapter begins with a brief review of the empirical literature on bereavement support groups in general, as well as suicide bereavement-specific groups in particular. This is followed by a discussion of the various functions that support groups might serve for survivors, and the various types of support group formats that can be adopted. It concludes with some general guidelines for facilitators of survivor support groups, as well as some observations about the future direction of support groups as a form of postvention after suicide.

☐ Literature Review

General Bereavement Support Groups

Mutual support groups have been widely suggested as a helpful form of intervention for adults after a variety of losses (Hughes, 1995; Jordan & Ware, 1997; Lehmann, Jimerson, & Gaasch, 2001; Ryan & Crawford, 2002; Schneider, 2006; Schwab, 1995; Vernon, 2002; Zulli, 2001), as well as for other life stressors (Pistrang, Barker, & Humphreys, 2008). They have also been recommended for children and adolescents (Haasl & Marnocha, 2000; Lehmann et al., 2001; Stubenbort et al., 2006; Tedeschi, 1996). Despite their apparent widespread usage, there has been relatively little controlled research on the effectiveness or efficacy of bereavement support groups. Perhaps the best example of a well-conceptualized, designed, and executed family group intervention for parentally bereaved children is the Family Bereavement Program (FBP), developed by Sandler and his associates (Sandler et al., 2003; Sandler, Wolchik, & Ayers, 2008; Sandler, Wolchik, Ayers, Tein, et al., 2008; Tein, Sandler, Ayers, & Wolchik, 2006). The FBP has been shown to have positive effects at both the systemic level (e.g., improvement in parenting skills) and the intrapsychic level (e.g., reduction in both internalizing and externalizing behaviors in girls participating in the intervention). The FBP has also demonstrated positive effects that appear to increase over time as much as 6 years after delivery of the intervention (Sandler, Wolchik, Ayers, Tein, et al., 2008).

Goodkin, in a series of reports, has shown the partial efficacy of bereavement support groups for men affected by the loss of a partner to HIV (Goodkin et al., 2001; Goodkin et al., 1999; Goodkin et al., 1997). His theory-based intervention was designed to address the domains of stressor appraisal, social support, and coping style, and was found to produce reductions on a measure of global dysphoria in participants. Likewise, Cohen and her associates have empirically demonstrated the efficacy of a cognitive behaviorally based and family-oriented program for treating traumatic grief in children (Cohen & Mannarino, 2006; Cohen, Mannarino, & Deblinger, 2006; Cohen, Mannarino, & Knudsen, 2004). The program, which involves both children and parents, is divided into components that focus on dealing with post-traumatic stress reactions and grief reactions separately, and then culminates in conjoint work with children and parents together (Cohen et al., 2006). Piper, McCallum, and their associates have presented a well-articulated, psycho-dynamically oriented, short-term group therapy for people suffering from loss and complicated grief (though not just loss through death) (Piper, McCallum, & Azim, 1992). In an extensive series of reports, they have studied many of the predictors of successful outcome for their intervention, including expression of affect, aspects of the relationship with the deceased, and personality characteristics of the patient (McCallum, Piper, & Morin, 1993; McCallum, Piper, Ogrodniczuk, & Joyce, 2003; Ogrodniczuk, Piper, Joyce, McCallum, & Rosie, 2003; Ogrodniczuk, Piper, Joyce, Rosie, & McCallum, 2002; Ogrodniczuk, Piper, McCallum, Joyce, & Rosie, 2002; Piper, McCallum, Joyce, Ogrodniczuk, & Rosie, 2001; Piper et al., 2001). They have also begun examining differential responses to different types of group therapy for patients with different types of grief responses (Ogrodniczuk, Piper, Joyce, McCallum, Rosie, et al., 2003) and differing levels of object relations quality and psychological mindedness (McCallum et al., 2003; Ogrodniczuk, Piper, McCallum, et al., 2002). This pioneering work is among the first to attempt to match patients with loss as a presenting problem to differing types of bereavement interventions. Finally, Murphy and her colleagues have reported on a group intervention for parents who have lost a young adult child to traumatic causes (suicide, homicide, and accident) (Murphy, 2000; Murphy et al., 1998). The intervention showed partial efficacy for mothers who were the most distressed at the beginning of the intervention, but failed to show any effects for fathers participating in the program, or any long-term effects on follow-up.

Suicide-Specific Support Groups

The literature regarding support groups specifically for the bereaved after suicide consists primarily of clinical descriptions and models of existing support group programs for survivors (Clark et al., 1993; Farberow, 2001; Mitchell et al., 2007; Renaud, 1995; Wrobleski, 1984). Likewise, Sections 3 and 4 of this volume on promising programs contain excellent descriptions of many survivor support programs that are built primarily around bereavement support groups. Mirroring the larger domain of general bereavement support groups, however, has been a dearth of empirical investigation of the efficacy of these support groups (or any other type of intervention) for survivors (Jordan & McMenamy, 2004; McDaid, Trowman, Golder, Hawton, & Sowden, 2008). In a controlled study that lacked random assignment, Farberow found that participants in his group intervention showed a greater reduction in several distress responses than nonparticipants, although they also showed increases in depression and puzzlement about the suicide (Farberow, 1992). Participants also indicated high satisfaction with the service. Likewise, in uncontrolled pre- and posttest studies of survivor interventions, Constantino et al. (Constantino & Bricker, 1996; Constantino, Sekula, & Rubinstein, 2001), Rogers et al. (1982), and Renaud (1995) found that their structured support group interventions showed some reduction in symptoms on most measures and high satisfaction with the program. Mitchell and Kim (2003) found that participants in a single-session debriefing intervention after a suicide did better on some measures than participants in a treatment-as-usual control group. In a randomized, controlled design, Pfeffer and colleagues (Pfeffer, Jiang, Kakuma, Hwang, & Metsch, 2002) studied the efficacy of a manual-based intervention for suicide-bereaved children. She found that the intervention produced a significant reduction in anxiety and depressive symptoms for participants when compared to the no-treatment control group. Lastly, Feigelman reports in Chapter 6 of this book on the largest study of suicide-survivor support group participants ever conducted (see also Feigelman et al., 2008; Feigelman, Gorman, & Jordan, 2009; Feigelman, Jordan, & Gorman, 2009a, 2009b, for more reports from the study). Although not specifically an intervention study, the authors did find that support group members rated their participation as a highly valuable part of their recovery, more helpful than contact with clergy, bereavement counselors, or mental health professionals. This replicates the findings by McMenamy and associates (2008) regarding the perceived value for many survivors of support group participation.

To summarize these empirical findings, there is tentative evidence that bereavement support groups are an important part of the recovery process for many suicide survivors. Unfortunately, much of this evidence is anecdotal or from methodologically weak studies, rather than the result of well-designed randomized and controlled trials of support group interventions. Given these methodological limitations, as well as the generally small number of studies of survivor interventions of any type (Jordan & McMenamy, 2004; McDaid et al., 2008), it is not yet possible to state that support group interventions have been scientifically established as an effective intervention for suicide survivors. Moreover, as with the general bereavement intervention outcome research (Currier, Holland, & Neimeyer, 2007; Currier, Neimeyer, & Berman, 2008), there are probably moderator variables that determine which types of groups are likely to benefit which types of survivors and at which point in their recovery process.

In a recent thorough review of the subject, Cerel and her colleagues present the persuasive case for doing more research on the impact of support groups on the healing process of many survivors (Cerel, Padgett, Conwell, et al., 2009). Until that research has been conducted, the field will need to rely on clinical judgment and the few empirical studies that have been done to determine who is most likely to benefit from participation in a suicide-survivor support group. Drawing primarily on my clinical experience and study of the literature, the next section describes some of the functions that such participation may serve in helping survivors in their healing journey.

☐ Functions of Survivor Support Groups

The experience of sharing one's grief in the context of a well-facilitated and compassionate group of survivors seems to serve many functions for the bereaved. Above all, the experience helps to reduce the sense of isolation that is commonly reported after suicide (Dyregrov, 2003a; Saarinen, Hintikka, Lehtonen, Lönnqvist, & Viinamäki, 2002; Wrobleski & McIntosh, 1987). Although support groups may help meet this need after any type of loss (Schwab, 1995; Tedeschi & Calhoun, 1993), this may be a particularly important aspect of the group experience after a stigmatized loss such as suicide. A suicide may create ambiguity about the appropriate rules for social interaction with the bereaved individual (Dyregrov, 2003b). Given the nonnormative nature of the death, members of the survivor's social network may be unclear about how to support the mourner. Participation in a support group can have a counterbalancing effect on this damaging experience of social avoidance or even outright stigmatization that survivors sometimes encounter (Armour, 2006; Cvinar, 2005; Feigelman, Gorman, et al., 2009). Typically, support groups operate on a norm of nonjudgmental acceptance of the members and their unique experience of grief, providing a psychologically safe environment in which members can explore and express the intense thoughts and feelings associated with suicide bereavement without fear of burdening others, being judged as responsible for the suicide, or viewed as overreacting or inappropriately "dwelling" on the loss.

The experience of participation in a support group also affords survivors valuable opportunities for social learning. For example, in ongoing groups with "veteran" members who have participated for many months or years, new participants often use these veterans as role models for the survivability of the loss. This inspiration of hope for recovery can be a significant factor that helps new survivors endure the suffering of early bereavement. Other role modeling effects can be seen as survivors learn from one another about coping strategies that have worked for other people. Examples include learning how other participants prepare for the death anniversary or the seasonal holidays. Discussion with other members also permits participants to benchmark their own grief reactions, allowing them to gauge and normalize their own strong responses. This process of comparison also allows survivors to recognize the ways that their grief is different from the grief of others. The appreciation of differences in grieving styles may enhance the survivor's clarity about their own unique needs, while simultaneously increasing empathy with other members of their family who cope differently. There also appear to be benefits accrued from acting in the "helper" role with other bereaved individuals. Helping another survivor is likely to feel empowering for survivors who may feel tremendously disempowered by their own loss (Appel & Wrobleski, 1987). Lastly, through group participation, survivors may obtain valuable knowledge from the leader or other members about the nature of psychiatric disorder and suicide, while also learning about additional coping resources within the community such as local "survivor-friendly" therapists, Internet resources, and self-help books.

☐ Types of Survivor Support Groups

Support groups for suicide survivors can take many forms (Cerel, Padgett, & Reed, 2009), each with strengths and weaknesses. Two broad types of group format can be identified. Closed-format groups typically have a fixed number of sessions for each cycle of the group (usually 8 to 12 sessions that meet monthly, bimonthly, or weekly). The same group members start and finish together as a unit. Participants usually have some form of screening contact with the facilitator before beginning the group, and are typically asked to commit to attending all of the scheduled meetings on a regular basis. The closed format seems to enhance the development of cohesion and a "group identity" as members share the experience of starting as a group, increasing self-disclosure and mutual understanding over time, and then saying good-bye together. Closed groups are also sometimes psychoeducational in nature, with specific topics or themes for each meeting and a structure for shared discussion of the topic. Closed groups are typically, although not always, run by a non-bereaved facilitator, often a mental health professional. Closed groups have the advantage of allowing members to know each other as "equals" (as opposed to more "veteran" members having a kind of higher status in open format groups—see next paragraph). Their greater structure may also be more suitable for survivors who value clear organization and focus within a group meeting. On the other hand, a closed format offers less flexibility in meeting the differing needs of survivors. For example, since a sufficient number of committed members are needed to begin a closed group, potential members may have to wait longer to start.

Likewise, some survivors may be unwilling or unable to commit to the required number of meetings involved in a closed format.

Open-format groups (also referred to as drop-in groups) have a different structure. They typically meet at a regular time and place, but new members may join the group at any meeting. Open-format groups are usually less structured than closed groups, allowing more open discussion of any topic that the members wish to address, although the leader may sometimes suggest topics for the group to consider. In open-format groups, members may attend as frequently (or infrequently) as they wish, allowing them to use the group on an "as needed" and drop-in basis. Open groups that have been in existence for some time typically have veteran members who serve as role models for new members, although this can sometimes create a feeling among new entrants of being "outsiders."

Hybrid group structures incorporate a mixture of open- and closed-group formats. For example, open groups may limit the frequency with which new members can join, only admitting new members periodically at fixed times, rather than at any meeting. Some closed groups may allow members to repeat a cycle as often as needed, thus providing a more or less continuous group involvement. Other variations of groups may reflect differences in leadership or focus for the groups. Survivor support groups may be led by professional leaders, such as mental health professionals or clergy, or by peer survivors who are not professionally trained but are motivated by a wish to help other survivors in their grief. Survivor groups can also be co-led by a combination of a professional and a peer survivor. Sections 3 and 4 of this volume offer illustrations of many different types of open, closed, and hybrid format groups.

A study by Rubey and McIntosh (1996) found that the majority of survivor support groups in the United States and Canada used an open format and were run by trained peer survivors or sometimes by professional and peer teams. A recent update of that survey, with much useful information about current survivor groups in the United States, found that most groups in the United States were still run as open-format groups, but were now much more likely to be run by peer survivors rather than mental health professionals, perhaps reflecting the development of an active "survivor movement" within the United States that views survivor issues as outside the province of mental health treatment (Cerel, Padgett, & Reed, 2009).

Other Variations in Support Groups

Survivor support groups may vary along other dimensions. For example, groups differ with regard to the type of kinship relationship with the deceased. Although most survivor groups are "mixed," allowing parents, spouses, siblings, children, and even friends of the deceased to attend, some restrict the membership to a particular kinship relationship (most frequently, parents who have lost a child to suicide). Groups may also vary by kinship and gender (e.g., a group for mothers who have lost a child to suicide), by time since death (e.g., a group for people who are several years out from the loss), or even by mode of death (e.g., suicide survivors may participate in a general bereavement group that includes people with mixed causes of death). It has been my experience that groups that are more homogeneous with regard to the kinship to the deceased and mode of death are often better at serving the needs of suicide survivors. Perceived similarity to other group members is a crucial factor in producing cohesion and a feeling of empathic belonging among members; the more diverse the group, the longer and more difficult it may be before these essential group characteristics are achieved. Most group participants want to know that there is someone else in the group who is "like" them and dealing with a comparable situation. Thus, similarity along these dimensions seems to facilitate the process of mutual identification. Other demographic variables, such as social class, ethnicity, religion, and so forth, may make group members more comfortable in the beginning, but appear to be less important in developing cohesion within the group.

Lastly, survivor support groups are also developing in formats other than face-to-face meetings. For example, the use of the Internet as a way for bereaved individuals, including suicide survivors, to connect with one another appears to be growing rapidly (Feigelman et al., 2008; Stroebe, Van Der Houwen, & Schut, 2008; see also Chapter 21, this volume). These forms of contact can range from message boards where individuals read and respond to messages left by other bereaved individuals to facilitated, "real-time" meetings of survivors online that, like a face-to-face group, have a designated date, time, and cyberspace "location" for the meeting. Likewise, telephone conference calling technology is being utilized to bring survivors together to share experiences and offer support (Lifeline Australia, 2009).

☐ General Guidelines for Group Facilitation

A number of comprehensive training manuals for the facilitation of suicide survivor support groups have been written (Archibald, 2003; Flatt, 2007; Jordan & Harpel, 2007; Lifeline Australia, 2009; WHO, 2008). What follows is drawn from these resources, and the reader is encouraged to consult them directly for more detailed suggestions.

The facilitator of a suicide survivor support group endeavors to create a psychological "space" that is emotionally safe, where processing of the members' grief can proceed. It is crucial to keep in mind that suicide survivors have been psychologically wounded and are in a vulnerable emotional condition in which they can easily be reinjured in their social interactions with others. Thus, the overarching job of the facilitator is to ensure that the group is as emotionally safe as possible for all participants. Conversely, a group culture that is not psychologically secure will produce guardedness, conflict, and ultimately, withdrawal of the members from the group. To promote group interaction that manifests this group attribute of psychological safety, the facilitator must monitor and protect the process of the group to make sure that it stays within the guidelines designed to promote emotional security for the members.

A distinction can be made between process and content in group member interactions. The content of interactions refers to the "topic" of the discussions between people. Although there is some specific content that may be psychologically distressing or harmful to some members (e.g., hearing the specific details of a death scene described by another member or hearing the belief stated that people who die by suicide go to hell), the primary concern of the facilitator must be with the process, not the content of the group's discussions. This means attending to the *way* in which people interact with each other around the content. For example, a group member who is interrupting and giving unsolicited advice to others or who is judging the "correctness" of another's grief responses, no matter how well-meaning he or she may be or how "truthful" the content of the feedback seems to be, is likely to be doing more harm than good. In such situations, the facilitator generally needs to intervene in a way that redirects the problematic member to interact in more helpful ways. Assuming this responsibility for protecting the process of the group is the primary distinction between the facilitator's role and that of other members, and it is crucial to a well-functioning group.

Facilitators protect the process of the group by following through on three related activities. First, they must establish and introduce the members to the norms or guidelines of the group that serve to make it psychologically secure. This is usually done by the recitation of explicit "ground rules" for interaction at the beginning of each meeting (see Jordan & Harpel, 2007, for written examples of such guidelines). These guidelines can include providing positive support rather than critical judgments, not interrupting, refraining from judging the grief of others, sharing the discussion time with other members, and other such rules that promote helpful interactions among the members. Second, the facilitator must make sure that the group members are, in fact, staying within these guidelines in their interactions with one another over the course of the group meeting. That is, it is not sufficient to introduce the guidelines at the beginning of the group and then to expect that people will simply and automatically follow them throughout the rest of the time together. Third, the facilitator must intervene, sometimes in a proactive way, when a member acts in a way that violates these guidelines and jeopardizes the psychological safety of other members (e.g., a member criticizes another member's choice of a holiday ritual to honor a loved one), or less seriously, makes the meeting less helpful than it might otherwise be (e.g., a member repeatedly brings the content of discussions back to themselves, without responding to the comments and needs of other members).[1] Learning to monitor and, when necessary, proactively protect the process of the group, is perhaps the single most important function of a support group facilitator.

Other Facilitator Functions

In addition to the overarching role of protecting the process of the group, and by extension, the psychological safety of its participants, the facilitator usually serves several other functions in a survivor support group. First, the facilitator takes an active leadership role at certain points in the meeting, acting as a convener of the meeting and sometimes performing an opening ritual to formally begin the event. The ritual can include welcoming members, reading the behavioral guidelines or "rules" of the meeting, and initiating a "go-around" where participants introduce themselves and their loss. The opening ritual can also include performing more expressive activities such as reading poetry, playing music, etc., that serve as a kind of "invocation" for the meeting. Likewise, the facilitator is usually responsible for the performance of a closing ritual at the end of the meeting that may also contain similar emotionally symbolic expressions of the grief felt by members and the solidarity among group members (see Jordan & Harpel, 2007, for examples of opening and closing group rituals).

Second, during the course of the meeting, the facilitator often enhances the group process by engaging in activities that encourage sharing and participation among the members. These activities can include asking open-ended questions (e.g., "What was that like for you?" or "Has anyone else felt the same way?"), empathically reflecting the experience of members in their grief, and reflecting upon and summarizing

---

[1] The reader is referred to the manual by Jordan and Harpel (2007) for a more detailed discussion of this topic of protecting the process of the group.

common themes that emerge in group discussions. Facilitators may also provide specific information that is sought by the membership and that they are qualified to answer (e.g., a mental health professional might describe some of the symptoms of depression or bipolar disorder), and may suggest specific topics or activities for the group (e.g., suggesting that members discuss their plans for dealing with their grief over the upcoming holidays). All of these active leadership functions are valuable, but facilitators should use them sparingly. In a very real sense, in a well-functioning support group, the leader remains largely in the background, allowing the members to provide support and lead the discussion for each other rather than through the leader.

The facilitator may also serve organizational functions that include screening potential members, finding a location for and publicizing the meeting, raising funds, etc. If the group is being run under the auspices of a larger organization or agency, these functions may be performed by other individuals in the agency. The screening function requires some elaboration since it is an important but sometimes controversial one. Some survivor group facilitators have an admirable "everyone is welcome" philosophy. However, not all suicide survivors are able to be contributing members of a support group, nor will a group necessarily be helpful for them. This could be true for several reasons, including that they are so new in their grief that participation in the group will be overwhelming, that they have a particular "agenda" that they need to "proselytize" to other members (e.g., that suicide is a sin and prayer is the only way to cope), or that they have acute psychiatric or personality problems beyond the group's capacity to ameliorate that get in the way of their appropriate participation in the group. In my opinion, the facilitator's first priority must always be the welfare of the group as a whole, and at times, that priority may clash with the needs of a given individual. Although members cannot always be screened before attending the group, whenever possible, prior contact with potential members (such as a telephone conversation) is recommended. This benefits both the group and potential members, as helping them find appropriate services and support outside the group may also be in their best interest.

Lastly, on rare occasions the facilitator must be prepared to deal with an acute emergency. Suicide survivors show higher levels of suicide risk themselves (see Chapters 1 and 2 of this book), and occasionally group participants will disclose their own suicidal thinking or behavior during the course of a meeting. Although it is not the job of a group facilitator to perform a full suicide risk assessment (although they may have legal liability if they are a mental health professional leading the group and do not do so), it behooves all facilitators to understand the warning signs of a member who may be at risk for suicide, and to have a plan for handling such a situation. This can include talking with the member one-on-one after the meeting, following up with a family member or therapist of the at-risk member, or knowing the phone numbers and locations of the local crisis intervention center or hospital emergency department.[2]

Cofacilitation

Although it is not always possible, in this author's experience, having two facilitators to lead a meeting is usually the preferable arrangement. A well-functioning cofacilitator team permits a fluid division of labor about facilitation tasks. For example, one facilitator may become engaged with helping a member who is having a very difficult time, while the other facilitator continues to monitor the other members in the group. Different facilitators can also bring complementary skills that are additive in helping the group to function. For example, one person may be better at dealing with members who are overbearing or monopolizing, while another may be more skilled at helping a particularly quiet member to participate. Together, this facilitator dyad has a range of skills to assist the group. Likewise, two facilitators can provide a "binocular" view of the group's process and individual members that enriches the perspective of each facilitator. In addition, a shared sense of responsibility for the group is preferable to the sometimes lonely or overwhelming feeling of running a group by oneself. This can be particularly helpful if there are problems in the group functioning or with a particular member. The only typical drawback of a cofacilitator arrangement occurs when the dynamics of their relationship creates problems in their functioning in the group. Cofacilitators must develop a consensus about the sharing of the leadership of the group, have a genuine respect for each other's skills, and have sufficient openness and trust in their dyadic process to work out conflicts satisfactorily. The inability to establish this kind of adaptive working relationship can create problems for the functioning of the group and stand in the way of members receiving the group support they seek.

---

[2] See the Web sites of the American Association of Suicidology (http://www.suicidology .org) and the American Foundation for Suicide Prevention (http://www.afsp.org) for more information about suicide risk assessment. In the United States, facilitators can also call the National Suicide Prevention Lifeline (1-800-273-TALK [8255]) for assistance in finding emergency resources.

☐ Conclusion: Future Directions for Support Groups

Although their efficacy has not yet been established through rigorous scientific testing, there is considerable anecdotal and some empirical support for the conclusion that bereavement support groups are an important and valuable form of postvention for many suicide survivors. However, not all survivors participate in support groups, and support groups may not be helpful for all participants. Research has suggested that survivors often have difficulty finding a group in their area (McMenamy et al., 2008). Even for mourners who are able to locate a group, there may be barriers that prevent the group from becoming a useful resource, ranging from groups that are poorly facilitated to ones that are not affordable or are "full" (as in a professionally led, closed group) to groups that seem to be a compositional mismatch (e.g., being the only person with spousal or sibling loss in a group with mostly bereaved parents). And of course, there may simply be people who will never feel comfortable in a setting in which they are expected to discuss their grief with strangers. We have no data about survivors who choose never to attend a support group or who come only once or twice and then stop. Vitally important research is needed to help understand who does or does not choose to attend support groups, what influences those decisions, and what would help improve the functionality of support groups for a greater percentage of survivors. Given the prevalence of support groups as one of the most popular interventions after a suicide, this type of research should be a priority for the field (Cerel, Padgett, Conwell, et al., 2009; Jordan & McMenamy, 2004) (see also Chapter 33 in this book).

There appear to be several trends in survivor support groups that are likely to increase over the next decade. First, the sheer number of support groups (as well as other support services for survivors such as home-visiting teams) seems to be on the rise in the United States and around the world (Cerel, Padgett, Conwell, et al., 2009; Harpel, 2009). This is a much needed development since anecdotal evidence suggests that many survivors continue to experience difficulties in finding such groups.

Second, the quality of facilitation of such groups, whether peer or professionally led, is also continuing to increase as more facilitators receive some type of training (Cerel, Padgett, & Reed, 2009). Promising and innovative training programs to help lay and professional people who wish to lead a support group have been developed and are being implemented (Jordan & Harpel, 2007; Lifeline Australia, 2009; see also

Chapters 15, 17, and 26 for examples of training programs). These programs will hopefully increase the skill of facilitators at enhancing group interaction and protecting the psychological safety of the group.

Third, new formats that bring survivors together are emerging, most prominently on the Internet (Feigelman et al., 2008; Stroebe et al., 2008; see Chapter 21 in this book and visit http://www.parentsofsuicide.com/parents.html for examples). These new forms of connection hold great promise for making the support group experience more accessible and comfortable for survivors who otherwise might not choose to participate in face-to-face meetings or who need more intensive involvement than the monthly or bimonthly meetings that are typical of in-person gatherings. These innovative group formats, combined with the continued development of more traditional support group formats and improved research on the efficacy and effectiveness of such groups, suggest that the future of this important form of healing support for survivors is likely to grow in coming years.

☐ References

Appel, Y. H., & Wrobleski, A. (1987). Self-help and support groups: Mutual aid for survivors. In E. J. Dunne, J. L. McIntosh, & K. Dunne-Maxim (Eds.), *Suicide and its aftermath: Understanding and counseling the survivors* (pp. 215–233). New York, NY: W. W. Norton & Co.

Archibald, L. (2003). *HEARTBEAT survivors after suicide, groups of mutual support, leaders guide.* Retrieved from http://heartbeatsurvivorsaftersuicide.org/docs/guidelines.doc

Armour, M. (2006). Violent death: Understanding the context of traumatic and stigmatized grief. *Journal of Human Behavior in the Social Environment, 14,* 53–90.

Cerel, J., Padgett, J. H., Conwell, Y., & Reed, G. A., Jr. (2009). A call for research: The need to better understand the impact of support groups for suicide survivors. *Suicide and Life-Threatening Behavior, 39,* 269–281.

Cerel, J., Padgett, J. H., & Reed, G. A., Jr. (2009). Support groups for suicide survivors: Results of a survey of group leaders. *Suicide and Life-Threatening Behavior, 39,* 588–598.

Clark, S. E., Jones, H. E., Quinn, K., Goldney, R. D., et al. (1993). A support group for people bereaved through suicide. *Crisis: The Journal of Crisis Intervention and Suicide Prevention, 14,* 161–167.

Cohen, J. A., & Mannarino, A. P. (2006). Treating childhood traumatic grief. In E. K. Rynearson (Ed.), *Violent death: Resilience and intervention beyond the crisis* (pp. 255–273). New York, NY: Routledge/Taylor & Francis Group.

Cohen, J. A., Mannarino, A. P., & Deblinger, E. (2006). *Treating trauma and traumatic grief in children and adolescents.* New York, NY: Guilford Press.

Cohen, J. A., Mannarino, A. P., & Knudsen, K. (2004). Treating childhood traumatic grief: A pilot study. *Journal of the American Academy of Child & Adolescent Psychiatry, 43,* 1225–1233.

Constantino, R. E., & Bricker, P. L. (1996). Nursing postvention for spousal survivors of suicide. *Issues in Mental Health Nursing, 17,* 131–152.

Constantino, R. E., Sekula, L. K., & Rubinstein, E. N. (2001). Group intervention for widowed survivors of suicide. *Suicide and Life-Threatening Behavior, 31,* 428–441.

Currier, J. M., Holland, J. M., & Neimeyer, R. A. (2007). The effectiveness of bereavement interventions with children: A meta-analytic review of controlled outcome research. *Journal of Clinical Child and Adolescent Psychology, 36,* 253–259.

Currier, J. M., Neimeyer, R. A., & Berman, J. S. (2008). The effectiveness of psychotherapeutic interventions for bereaved persons: A comprehensive quantitative review. *Psychological Bulletin, 134,* 648–661.

Cvinar, J. G. (2005). Do suicide survivors suffer social stigma: A review of the literature. *Perspectives in Psychiatric Care, 41,* 14–21.

Dyregrov, K. (2003a). *The loss of a child by suicide, SIDS, and accidents: Consequences, needs, and provisions of help.* Bergen, Norway: University of Bergen.

Dyregrov, K. (2003b). Micro-sociological analysis of social support following traumatic bereavement: Unhelpful and avoidant responses from the community. *Omega: Journal of Death and Dying, 48,* 23–44.

Farberow, N. L. (1992). The Los Angeles Survivors-After-Suicide Program: An evaluation. *Crisis: The Journal of Crisis Intervention and Suicide Prevention, 13,* 23–34.

Farberow, N. L. (2001). Helping suicide survivors. In D. Lester (Ed.), *Suicide prevention: Resources for the millennium.* (pp. 189–212). New York, NY: Brunner-Routledge.

Feigelman, W., Gorman, B. S., Beal, K. C., & Jordan, J. R. (2008). Internet support groups for suicide survivors: A new mode for gaining bereavement assistance. *Omega: Journal of Death and Dying, 57,* 217–243.

Feigelman, W., Gorman, B. S., & Jordan, J. R. (2009). Stigmatization and suicide bereavement. *Death Studies, 33,* 591–608.

Feigelman, W., Jordan, J. R., & Gorman, B. S. (2009a). How they died, time since loss, and bereavement outcomes. *Omega: Journal of Death and Dying, 58,* 251–273.

Feigelman, W., Jordan, J. R., & Gorman, B. S. (2009b). Personal growth after suicide loss: Cross-sectional findings suggest growth after loss may be associated with better mental health among survivors. *Omega: Journal of Death and Dying, 59,* 181–202.

Flatt, L. (2007). *The Basics: Facilitating a Suicide Survivors Support Group.* Retrieved from http://www.spanusa.org/files/General_Documents/The_Basics_Facilitator_Guide.pdf

Gaffney, D. A., Jones, E. T., & Dunne-Maxim, K. (1992). Support groups for sibling suicide survivors. *Crisis: The Journal of Crisis Intervention and Suicide Prevention, 13,* 76–81.

Goodkin, K., Baldewicz, T. T., Blaney, N. T., Asthana, D., Kumar, M., Shapshak, P., … Zheng, W. L. (2001). Physiological effects of bereavement and bereavement support group interventions. In M. S. Stroebe, R. O. Hansson, W. Stroebe, & H. Schut (Eds.), *Handbook of bereavement research: Consequences, coping, and care* (pp. 671–703). Washington, DC: American Psychological Association.

Goodkin, K., Blaney, N. T., Feaster, D. J., Baldewicz, T., Burkhalter, J. E., & Leeds, B. (1999). A randomized controlled clinical trial of a bereavement support group intervention in human immunodeficiency virus type 1-seropositive and -seronegative homosexual men. *Archives of General Psychiatry, 56,* 52–59.

Goodkin, K., Burkhalter, J. E., Blaney, N. T., Leeds, B., Tuttle, R. S., & Feaster, D. J. (1997). A research derived bereavement support group technique for the HIV-1 infected. *Omega: Journal of Death and Dying, 34,* 279–300.

Haasl, B., & Marnocha, J. (2000). *Bereavement support group program for children: Participant workbook* (2nd ed.). Philadelphia, PA: Accelerated Development.

Harpel, J. (2009). *AFSP support group facilitator training program—Follow-up survey of attendees 2002–2006 Executive Summary.* Unpublished document prepared for the American Foundation for Suicide Prevention.

Hughes, M. (1995). *Bereavement and support: Healing in a group environment.* Philadelphia, PA: Taylor & Francis.

Jordan, J., & Harpel, J. (2007). *Facilitating suicide bereavement support groups: A self-study manual.* New York, NY: American Foundation for Suicide Prevention.

Jordan, J., & McMenamy, J. (2004). Interventions for suicide survivors: A review of the literature. *Suicide and Life-Threatening Behavior, 34,* 337–349.

Jordan, J., & Ware, E. S. (1997). Feeling like a motherless child: A support group model for adults grieving the death of a parent. *Omega: Journal of Death and Dying, 35,* 361–376.

Lehmann, L., Jimerson, S. R., & Gaasch, A. (2001). *Grief support group curriculum: Facilitator's handbook.* New York, NY: Brunner-Routledge.

Lifeline Australia. (2009). *Practice handbook: Suicide bereavement support group facilitation.* Retrieved from http://www.lifeline.org.au/__data/assets/pdf_file/0016/40075/38786_LIFELINE_SBSG_Handbook_.pdf

McCallum, M., Piper, W. E., & Morin, H. (1993). Affect and outcome in short-term therapy for loss. *International Journal of Group Psychotherapy, 43,* 303–319.

McCallum, M., Piper, W. E., Ogrodniczuk, J. S., & Joyce, A. S. (2003). Relationships among psychological mindedness, alexithymia and outcome in four forms of short-term psychotherapy. *Psychology and Psychotherapy: Theory, Research and Practice, 76,* 133–144.

McDaid, C., Trowman, R., Golder, S., Hawton, K., & Sowden, A. (2008). Interventions for people bereaved through suicide: Systematic review. *British Journal of Psychiatry, 193,* 438–443.

McMenamy, J. M., Jordan, J. R., & Mitchell, A. M. (2008). What do suicide survivors tell us they need? Results of a pilot study. *Suicide and Life-Threatening Behavior, 38,* 375–389.

Mitchell, A., & Kim, Y. (2003, May). *Debriefing approach with suicide survivors.* Paper presented at the Survivors of Suicide Research Workshop, sponsored by NIMH/NIH Office of Rare Diseases and the American Foundation for Suicide Prevention. Washington, DC.

Mitchell, A. M., Wesner, S., Garand, L., Gale, D. D., Havill, A., & Brownson, L. (2007). A support group intervention for children bereaved by parental suicide. *Journal of Child and Adolescent Psychiatric Nursing, 20,* 3–13.

Murphy, S. A. (2000). The use of research findings in bereavement programs: A case study. *Death Studies, 24,* 585–602.

Murphy, S. A., Johnson, C., Cain, K. C., Gupta, A. D., Dimond, M., Lohan, J., ... Baugher, R. (1998). Broad-spectrum group treatment for parents bereaved by the violent deaths of their 12- to 28-yr-old children: A randomized controlled trial. *Death Studies, 22*, 209–235.

Ogrodniczuk, J. S., Piper, W. E., Joyce, A. S., McCallum, M., & Rosie, J. S. (2003). NEO-Five Factor personality traits as predictors of response to two forms of group psychotherapy. *International Journal of Group Psychotherapy, 53*, 417–442.

Ogrodniczuk, J. S., Piper, W. E., Joyce, A. S., McCallum, M., Rosie, J. S., Azim, H. F., ... Rosie, J. S. (2003). Differentiating symptoms of complicated grief and depression among psychiatric outpatients. *The Canadian Journal of Psychiatry/ La Revue canadienne de psychiatrie, 48*, 87–93.

Ogrodniczuk, J. S., Piper, W. E., Joyce, A. S., Rosie, J. S., & McCallum, M. (2002). Social support as a predictor of response to group therapy for complicated grief. *Psychiatry: Interpersonal and Biological Processes, 65*, 346–357.

Ogrodniczuk, J. S., Piper, W. E., McCallum, M., Joyce, A. S., & Rosie, J. S. (2002). Interpersonal predictors of group therapy outcome for complicated grief. *International Journal of Group Psychotherapy, 52*, 511–535.

Pfeffer, C. R., Jiang, H., Kakuma, T., Hwang, J., & Metsch, M. (2002). Group intervention for children bereaved by the suicide of a relative. *Journal of the American Academy of Child & Adolescent Psychiatry, 41*, 505–513.

Piper, W. E., McCallum, M., & Azim, H. F. A. (1992). *Adaptation to loss through short-term group psychotherapy.* New York, NY: Guilford Press.

Piper, W. E., McCallum, M., Joyce, A. S., Ogrodniczuk, J. S., & Rosie, J. S. (2001). Patient personality and time-limited group psychotherapy for complicated grief. *International Journal of Group Psychotherapy, 51*, 525–552.

Piper, W. E., Ogrodniczuk, J. S., Joyce, A. S., Weideman, R., Azim, H. F., & McCallum, M. (2001). Ambivalence and other relationship predictors of grief in psychiatric outpatients. *Journal of Nervous and Mental Disease, 189*, 781–787.

Pistrang, N., Barker, C., & Humphreys, K. (2008). Mutual help groups for mental health problems: A review of effectiveness studies. *American Journal of Community Psychology, 42*, 110–121.

Renaud, C. (1995). Bereavement after a suicide: A model for support groups. In B. L. Mishara (Ed.), *The impact of suicide* (pp. 52–63). New York, NY: Springer Publishing Co.

Rogers, J., Sheldon, A., Barwick, C., Letofsky, K., & Lancee, W. (1982). Help for families of suicide: Survivors support program. *Canadian Journal of Psychiatry, 27*, 444–449.

Rubey, C. T., & McIntosh, J. L. (1996). Suicide survivors groups: Results of a survey. *Suicide and Life-Threatening Behavior, 26*, 351–358.

Ryan, B. S., & Crawford, P. (2002). Creating loss support groups for the elderly. In S. Henry, J. F. East, & C. L. Schmitz (Eds.), *Social work with groups: Mining the gold* (pp. 151–162). New York, NY: Haworth Press.

Saarinen, P. I., Hintikka, J., Lehtonen, J., Lönnqvist, J. K., & Viinamäki, H. (2002). Mental health and social isolation among survivors ten years after a suicide in the family: A case-control study. *Archives of Suicide Research, 6*, 221–226.

Sandler, I. N., Ayers, T. S., Wolchik, S. A., Tein, J.-Y., Kwok, O.-M., Haine, R. A., … Griffin, W. A. (2003). The Family Bereavement Program: Efficacy evaluation of a theory-based prevention program for parentally bereaved children and adolescents. *Journal of Consulting and Clinical Psychology, 71*, 587–600.

Sandler, I. N., Wolchik, S. A., & Ayers, T. S. (2008). Resilience rather than recovery: A contextual framework on adaptation following bereavement. *Death Studies, 32*, 59–73.

Sandler, I. N., Wolchik, S. A., Ayers, T. S., Tein, J.-Y., Coxe, S., & Chow, W. (2008). Linking theory and intervention to promote resilience in parentally bereaved children. In M. S. Stroebe, R. O. Hansson, H. Schut, & W. Stroebe (Eds.), *Handbook of bereavement research and practice: Advances in theory and intervention* (pp. 531–550). Washington, DC: American Psychological Association.

Schneider, R. M. (2006). Group bereavement support for spouses who are grieving the loss of a partner to cancer. *Social Work with Groups, 29*, 259–278.

Schwab, R. (1995). Bereaved parents and support group participation. *Omega: Journal of Death and Dying, 32*, 49–61.

Stroebe, M. S., Van Der Houwen, K., & Schut, H. (2008). Bereavement support, intervention, and research on the Internet: A critical review. In M. S. Stroebe, R. O. Hansson, H. Schut, & W. Stroebe (Eds.), *Handbook of bereavement research and practice: Advances in theory and intervention* (pp. 551–574). Washington, DC: American Psychological Association.

Stubenbort, K., Cohen, J. A., Schein, L. A., Spitz, H. I., Burlingame, G. M., & Muskin, P. R. (2006). Cognitive-behavioral groups for traumatically bereaved children and their parents. In S. Vargo (Ed.), *Psychological effects of catastrophic disasters: Group approaches to treatment* (pp. 581–628). New York, NY: Haworth Press.

Tedeschi, R. G. (1996). Support groups for bereaved adolescents. In C. A. Corr & D. E. Balk (Eds.), *Handbook of adolescent death and bereavement* (pp. 293–311). New York, NY: Springer Publishing Co.

Tedeschi, R. G., & Calhoun, L. G. (1993). Using the support group to respond to the isolation of bereavement. *Journal of Mental Health Counseling, 15*, 47–54.

Tein, J.-Y., Sandler, I. N., Ayers, T. S., & Wolchik, S. A. (2006). Mediation of the effects of the Family Bereavement Program on mental health problems of bereaved children and adolescents. *Prevention Science, 7*, 179–195.

Vernon, A. (2002). Group counseling: Loss. In D. Capuzzi & D. R. Gross (Eds.), *Introduction to group counseling* (3rd ed.) (pp. 321–349). Denver, CO: Love Publishing Company.

World Health Organization (WHO). (2008). *Preventing suicide: How to start a survivors' group*. Retrieved from http://www.who.int/mental_health/prevention/suicide/resource_survivors.pdf

Wrobleski, A. (1984). The Suicide Survivors Grief Group. *Omega: Journal of Death and Dying, 15*, 173–184.

Wrobleski, A., & McIntosh, J. L. (1987). Problems of suicide survivors: A survey report. *Israel Journal of Psychiatry and Related Sciences, 24*, 137–142.

Zulli, A. P. (2001). The aftercare worker and support group facilitation. In O. D. Weeks & C. Johnson (Eds.), *When all the friends have gone: A guide for aftercare providers* (pp. 199–213). Amityville, NY: Baywood Publishing Co.

A Family-Oriented and Culturally Sensitive Postvention Approach With Suicide Survivors[1]

Nadine J. Kaslow, Tara C. Samples,
Miesha Rhodes, and Stephanie Gantt

☐ Epidemiology

Every time a person dies by suicide, 6 to 10 loved ones are bereaved (Jordan & McMenamy, 2004). Each year, there are 180,000 to 300,000 newly bereaved suicide survivors (Mitchell, Kim, Prigerson, & Mortimer, 2005) and 1.1% of the population loses an immediate or extended family member to suicide (Crosby & Sacks, 2002). Further, each year, 1.2% of

[1] This work was supported in part by a grant from the American Foundation for Suicide Prevention, "Culturally Competent Family-Based Intervention Versus Enhanced Usual Care in the Community for Reducing Psychological Distress and Enhancing Functioning in Suicidally Bereaved African Americans," awarded to the first author.

adolescents have a suicide death in their family (Cerel & Roberts, 2005), and 7,000 to 12,000 children in the United States lose a parent to suicide (Cerel, Jordan, & Duberstein, 2008). Suicide often is a devastating experience for family members who are left behind. Unfortunately, only about 10,000 survivors in the United States receive postvention efforts each year (Andriessen, 2009).

☐ Suicide Grief

There has been considerable debate and discussion about whether or not bereaved groups of suicide survivors experience more significant mental health problems (depression, anxiety, post-traumatic stress disorder [PTSD], suicidal behavior) and more complicated and prolonged grief reactions than other bereaved groups (Cerel et al., 2008; McMenamy, Jordan, & Mitchell, 2008; Sveen & Walby, 2007). Some have argued that suicide survivors are similar to other bereaved groups (McIntosh, 1993). Other researchers have highlighted differences between groups and have suggested that suicide survivors have more severe responses, including more psychological distress (sadness, fear, guilt, anxiety, anger, shame), higher levels of loneliness, and lower levels of positive social functioning (de Groot, de Keijser, & Neeleman, 2006; Ellenbogen & Gratton, 2001; Jordan, 2001; Jordan & McMenamy, 2004; Kaslow & Aronson, 2004; Sveen & Walby, 2007). These differences have been attributed to the fact that suicide survivors, in addition to dealing with the loss of a loved one, need to contend with profound feelings of shame and guilt, fear, rejection, anger, and blame. The researchers who highlight the differences in the groups have found that suicide bereavement differs from other forms of bereavement in terms of the complexity of the grief reaction, the thematic content of the grief, the social processes surrounding the survivor, and the impact suicide has on the family system. Even when families return to their normal daily routines, many still are plagued by their loss and often isolate themselves because they do not want to burden others with talk about the death. Further, survivors report the need for professional help at rates nine times higher than that of the naturally bereaved (de Groot et al., 2006; Lindqvist, Johanson, & Karlsson, 2008).

Grief Reactions

Compared with persons who have lost loved ones to other causes, individuals and families who lose members to suicide experience a more complex grieving pattern. This complicated grief reaction is associated with a much greater vulnerability to suicidal ideation (Mitchell et al., 2005). Common aspects of complicated grief reactions include shock, disbelief, and denial, and these emotions are particularly likely to be intense and of long duration. Anger and rage toward the deceased are not uncommon, and sometimes the anger is projected toward other systems involved with the loved one and the death, such as mental health providers, insurance companies, friends, community members, and other family members (Kaslow & Aronson, 2004). Family members may feel guilt or shame for having the aforementioned feelings (Lindqvist et al., 2008; Parrish & Tunkle, 2005). Furthermore, in families where there was interpersonal conflict between members and the deceased loved one, guilt and blame may predominate and can sometimes be reinforced by other family members. Another hallmark of these complex grief reactions includes problems accepting the suicide, particularly if the cause of death is questionable or if suicide is not acceptable in the survivors' culture (Kaslow & Aronson, 2004). Further, grief may negatively affect people's identity and sense of self, making it challenging for them to feel good about themselves and function effectively in society.

Thematic Content

Compared with other mourner groups, suicide survivors struggle more with questions regarding the meaning of the death; feelings of guilt, blame, and responsibility for the death; experience a greater sense of rejection or abandonment and shame; and acknowledge a more significant need to conceal the cause of the death. The nature of the kinship relationship (e.g., closeness, quality) with the deceased also influences the grief process (Andriessen, 2009; Jordan, 2008; Mitchell, Kim, Prigerson, & Mortimer-Stephens, 2004).

Social Processes

Attention has been paid to feelings of stigmatization and isolation that surround the bereaved. More stigmatization appears to be attached to people who have lost a loved one to suicide. Concern about being judged or perceived negatively by others may result in the suicide bereaved hiding the real cause of the death. Feeling stigmatized can heighten people's feelings of shame and lower their self-esteem (Demi & Howell, 1991). Further, families occasionally experience self-stigmatization because of feelings of guilt and shame (Dunne, McIntosh, & Dunne-Maxim, 1987). In addition to issues of stigmatization, communication distortions may occur between bereaved families and their social networks in the following ways: Family members (a) may isolate and feel the need to keep the suicide a secret because they believe they are to blame; (b) may experience a breakdown of family bonds because of angry blaming among family members; and (c) may have difficulty talking with others about the suicide due to the secrecy surrounding the death, which often causes issues with intimacy and individual and family life cycle development (Cerel et al., 2008; McMenamy et al., 2008).

Suicide affects families differently, and death by suicide may be more challenging for family systems than death from other causes (Jordan, 2001). There is evidence of increased levels of psychopathology in family members; greater distance in family relationships; and more dysfunctional family patterns, including communication difficulties, disruption of role functioning, conflicts regarding coping, and destabilization of family coalitions and intergenerational boundaries (Cerel et al., 2008). Additionally, lack of adequate family coping skills and the increase in stressors related to the suicide are associated with greater levels of family disintegration. It should be noted, however, that some families grow closer and communicate more openly following a suicide (Provini & Everett, 2000).

Access to Services

Given the profound impact on family members who lose a loved one to suicide, it is imperative that families have appropriate mental health services available to them. Hence, survivors of suicide have been targeted by the field of postvention as it has emerged over the past 40 years (Shneidman, 1969). Much of this postvention work has been in the form of support groups, which offer invaluable services (Jordan & McMenamy, 2004; Mitchell et al., 2007). However, many families also seek more traditional family intervention services. It is important that such family interventions be made easily accessible, as many families who are bereaved by suicide report significant barriers to seeking help, despite the fact that when they do receive care, they find professional help to be beneficial (McMenamy et al., 2008).

☐ Recommendations for Working With Suicide-Bereaved Families

The recommendations for clinicians working with suicide-bereaved families that are described below are based on the relevant literature, our review of proposed family intervention models, and the existing evidence base. Our suggestions also reflect our own clinical experience through the Healing and Understanding Grieving Suicide Survivors (HUGSS) project. More information on this project is presented later in this chapter in the section "Relevant Evidence Base."

Role of the Therapist

Before beginning family therapy, ethical therapists should examine their own beliefs and attitudes about suicide to ensure their personal biases and fears do not affect the therapeutic atmosphere (Kaslow & Aronson, 2004). Providing therapeutic support for families who have lost a member to suicide can be emotionally and professionally challenging for even the most skilled therapists. Suicide is a culturally and emotionally laden topic, and exposure to the pain and loss of multiple family members can provoke feelings of fear and dread for therapists. It is recommended that therapists seek regular supervision and consultation during family therapy, as the content of such therapy is likely to be an emotional experience for therapists. Self-exploration will ensure that personal fears and beliefs do not interfere with the therapeutic role of supporter for the families with whom therapists work. Successful postvention efforts require that therapists believe in the healing potential and strengths of families and communicate that belief to them. The ability to remain present, without the compulsion to avoid painful affective expressions or to rush the members to fix their grief, is the fundamental responsibility of treating professionals (Jordan, 2008).

The responsibilities of therapists in postvention family therapy entail conducting careful assessments of risk and protective factors; building trust with and among family members; helping families develop an understanding of and respect for one another's grief process; and carefully offering support, providing psychoeducation, and utilizing theory-driven, empirically based interventions.

Support

Providing support is key to conducting a meaningful assessment with suicide-bereaved families, as well as throughout all aspects of the intervention process. The provision of support requires the creation of a "holding environment" (Winnicott, 1965), in which family members feel empowered to express their feelings and needs in a safe and nonaggressive setting (Rudd, Joiner, & Rajab, 2001).

Much of family therapy after a suicide is focused on facilitating the grieving process for the survivors of the devastating loss. This facilitation can be guided by a variety of theoretical approaches, but should be empirically driven and take into account the common themes experienced by families after a member's suicide. Some of these themes may be more prominent in certain family members than in others, and their order and intensity may also vary. Interventions that target these themes can help families heal from their psychological distress, boost resiliency, and decrease morbidity and mortality. In addition, strategies used to support families may depend on the nature and quality of the family relationships. Therapists should prepare families for potential tension and conflict between members, as each member's unique grieving process will likely conflict with the unique pattern of other members (Jordan, 2008).

Effective therapists recognize the challenges that families experience as they cope with this devastating loss, and are careful not to place blame for the death on the deceased, family members, or other caregivers. Therapists must strive to prevent disengagement within the family and redress emotional cutoffs by underscoring that the family can serve as a potent source of comfort in the healing process; therapists must also communicate that withdrawal of support or blaming prolongs the grief process. Survivors should be encouraged to seek solace from each other and their individual social networks. It is essential to highlight that despite intense pain, grief, and fears of personal and family disintegration, the family as a unit, along with individual members, will be able to continue to function and eventually thrive (Kaslow & Aronson, 2004).

One key component of providing support to suicide-bereaved families is sensitivity to the protective functions of denial, as well as a focus on helping family members move past this stage. For example, people may deny that the death was a suicide, deny some or all of their own negative reactions to the death, or deny the impact of the death on the family unit. It behooves therapists to meet the family unit and/or individual members at the point they are at in the grief cycle (e.g., shock/denial, anger, bargaining, depression/sadness, acceptance) and patiently help them move successfully through the various stages to acceptance (Kübler-Ross & Kessler, 2005). Working through the grief process is the pathway to healing. Family members and other supportive adults should help children to work through their denial by answering their questions honestly, which will entail talking openly about the suicide (Dunne et al., 1987; Kaslow & Aronson, 2004). When caregivers are unable to help children with their emotional needs, it exacerbates their own feelings of denial, guilt, and powerlessness. This further complicates their grief (Kaslow & Aronson, 2004). Therefore, family therapists should help adult family members learn effective ways to communicate with children about such a difficult family event.

Assessment

The assessment of each family member involved in the intervention should address the following variables to determine their role in the family's grief experience: family structure, role of the deceased, quality of interpersonal relationships within the family, family reorganization following the death, perceived stigma, social support, family's experience with loss and grief, and family's view of itself (Kaslow & Aronson, 2004; Scocco, Frasson, Costacurta, & Pavan, 2006). Additionally, therapists should assess individual and family life cycle stages, openness of the system, levels of respect and acceptance, modes of emotional expression, communication and problem-solving patterns, cultural and religious beliefs about death and suicide, views of seeking and utilizing mental health services, and preexisting psychological disorders.

Therapists should be flexible with the types of interventions offered based upon the data gleaned from the assessment. Families may benefit from family therapy with the whole unit or various subsystems, as well as from referrals to family-oriented support groups. Individual members may find relief through the addition of individual therapy sessions, support group participation, and medications. Further, recommendations may be made for home or graveside visits, attendance at the burial, and possible phone consultations (Dunne et al., 1987; Kaslow & Aronson, 2001, 2004).

Assessment and Culturally Diverse Families

Attention to assessing culturally diverse families who have lost a loved to suicide is scarce. Therefore, therapists must be attuned to cultural factors that may affect a family's bereavement processes and help-seeking when conducting postvention assessments. When assessing individuals from racial or ethnic minority groups, several factors should be considered (Westefeld, Range, Greenfeld, & Kettman, 2008). First, family members from racial or ethnic minority groups may be less likely to disclose personal information regarding their suicidality and be less open to share their thoughts and feelings about a loved one's suicide when compared to persons from the majority group (Westefeld et al., 2008). For example, although asking direct questions about thoughts of self-harm or completing suicide are important, research suggests that African Americans are less likely to admit suicidality when asked directly (Morrison & Downey, 2000; Westefeld et al., 2008). In this case, therapists conducting assessments should have insight into other suicide risk factors, particularly experiencing the loss of a loved one to suicide, depression, attitudes toward suicide, and attitudes toward seeking help from mental health professionals.

Second, mental health professionals conducting assessments with families from racial or ethnic minority groups who have lost a loved one to suicide should possess general knowledge about different minority groups (Westefeld et al., 2008). Such awareness can facilitate the process of rapport building with families, lay the groundwork for the development of a safe and comfortable therapeutic environment, reduce resistance with families who feel ambivalent about seeking and utilizing mental health treatment, and help address issues with stigma related to suicide in the general population as well as within minority groups.

Third, cultural sensitivity while undertaking such evaluations should involve careful attention to cultural issues. This may include, but is not limited to, such issues as racial discrimination, religious and spiritual beliefs, perceptions of the acceptability of suicide, and levels of social support, as these variables have been found to be key risk and protective factors for suicide and for coping with stress (Anglin, Gabriel, & Kaslow, 2005; Boyd-Franklin, 2003; Brown, 2008; Kaslow, Ivey, Berry-Mitchell, Franklin, & Bethea, 2009; Kaslow et al., 2005; Kaslow, Thompson, Brooks, & Twomey, 2000; Westefeld et al., 2008). Assessing the three aforementioned facets not only gives therapists a broad perspective of the risk factors that need to be addressed in the treatment process, but also highlights protective factors that are useful to the family's treatment progress.

Another consideration for assessing culturally diverse suicide survivors is the use of culturally appropriate instruments. Such tools should definitely address the three facets discussed earlier and have included ethnic minorities in the samples used for their development and/or standardization. Examples of measures that fit this criterion, that tap risk and protective factors, and that thus may be appropriate include, but are not limited to, the Suicide Behaviors Questionnaire (Linehan & Nielsen, 1981), the Reasons for Living Inventory (Linehan, Goodstein, Nielsen, & Chiles, 1983), and the Suicide Resilience Inventory–25 (Osman et al., 2004). Along with these measures, the Survivor Needs Assessment Survey may be invaluable to incorporate in assessment batteries as it addresses four categories:

1. Practical, psychological, and social difficulties that occurred since the suicide

2. Formal and informal sources of support to aid with coping

3. Resources utilized in healing

4. Barriers to finding support (McMenamy et al., 2008)

Instruments like this help guide therapists in focusing on attaining as much accurate information about the family history as possible, particularly as it relates to the suicide of their loved one.

Psychoeducation

In addition to supporting families, a significant responsibility of therapists is the dissemination of information about suicide and recovery from complex grieving. Due to the stigma attached to suicide, many family members will be unaware of basic information about suicide and the grieving process (Jordan, 2001). Therapists may provide psychoeducation about risk factors for suicide, gently address the presence of commonly held myths about suicide, and teach effective coping strategies and communication patterns (Kaslow & Aronson, 2004). In response to the complexity of the family's grief, therapists must inform families about the grief process and normative responses to suicide, and communicate to them the acceptability of open expression of all aspects of the grieving experience (Bolton, 1984; Kaslow & Aronson, 2001). Therapists should encourage families to read literature about coping with suicide, participate in a survivors support group, access relevant Internet sites, and contact suicide survivor hotlines if needed (Kaslow & Aronson, 2004).

Therapists must work quickly to teach positive coping skills and effective communication skills to maintain family connectedness. They also should help the family identify roles and responsibilities of family members that existed prior to their loved one's death, and assist in the transition to developing new roles and responsibilities if necessary. It is helpful if therapists highlight the importance of the difficult, yet necessary reengagement process. Caregivers for children should receive assistance with addressing the children's questions or misconceptions as they relate to their social systems. School officials should be informed and included in the intervention. The family members' concerns about judgment should be acknowledged and discussed (Kaslow & Aronson, 2004).

Creation of a Suicide Story

One key way to build trust and respect within family systems is through encouraging family members to create a suicide story and providing an opportunity in family sessions for these stories to be shared (Kaslow et al., 2009; Van Dongen, 1993). Creating a suicide story helps families work through the psychological distress and painful emotions that they experience following the death. Additionally, it enables them to gradually accept that certain questions will not be answered. Through the process of creating and sharing their suicide stories, family members feel more connected to one another, satisfy their longing for meaning and understanding, create a new theoretical framework about the event, and feel less stigmatized (Kaslow & Aronson, 2004; Van Dongen, 1991). When looking at unbearable medical or psychological illness that led to the suicide of a loved one, constructing the story assists family members with acceptance of their loved one's challenges prior to the death (Kaslow & Aronson, 2001). Therapists can facilitate this process by providing education about the illness. Throughout this process, therapists should be mindful of cultural and religious beliefs that may complicate the construction of a suicide story. Information should be gathered from families and their support systems about suicide acceptability and used to help guide the process in a culturally appropriate way.

It is essential that therapists support family members in crafting their own stories, while at the same time constructing a shared narrative among the family (Kaslow et al., 2009). In inviting families to create suicide stories, it is recommended that therapists offer sample stories, convey that it is acceptable for family members to share only as much detail as they are comfortable with, and underscore the fact that each family member will have a different story to tell and all experiences of the deceased person and grief process are normal and acceptable. It is helpful if therapists provide guidance regarding the elements of a suicide story. This may be done through the use of probe questions related to family members' relationship with the loved one, how they found out about and reacted to the suicide, their personal experience since the loss, their understanding about why their loved one killed him or herself and the events leading up to the death, what their experience was of the funeral/memorial service and other rituals, what they miss most about their loved one, and what one last thing they would like to say to their loved one. Therapists must be willing to encourage individuals further in sharing their thoughts and feelings related to their suicide stories, help them explore painful emotions, and dispel myths that may have been apparent in the storytelling.

Clinical judgment must be used to explore what is challenging about the exercise, particularly if individuals are reluctant to participate. In addition, therapists need to ascertain families' levels of comfort in having children present as they share the details of the suicide. Children should be allowed to share their own stories through drawings or written or oral communications. The development of the story is a vital component of the treatment and may take place throughout the course of the intervention. However, it is imperative to assist families in moving beyond this point and engaging more fully in their lives (Kaslow & Aronson, 2004).

Healing Rituals

Creating healing rituals also is beneficial (Imber-Black, Roberts, & Whiting, 2004). Rituals underscore the fact that everyone needs to reflect about people they have lost. Each family member should be encouraged to participate in the decision making and ceremony. Rituals should be designed to honor the loved one and the relationship that family members had with that person. These rituals may be sacred, secular, traditional, or something that is created by the family. They may incorporate creative expression through music, dance, art, and writing. During rituals, families can share their common grief and offer support to one another. In addition, rituals reconfirm social support systems and make families aware that they are not alone during their time of mourning and celebrating the life of their loved ones (Castle & Phillips, 2003).

The observation of anniversaries, holidays, and other marker events are also important because they help to cultivate healing (Kaslow & Aronson, 2004). Thus, it behooves therapists to help families be flexible about how they approach holidays and family occasions (Myers & Fine, 2006). Further, the emotional reactions that emerge at significant anniversaries change as the context of the loss shifts. Therefore, therapists need to work with families to alter their rituals to accommodate their emotions associated with loss and create new ways of acknowledging and celebrating events that are key in the family's life (Alexander, 1991).

Although the work with families related to rituals typically occurs in the months and years following a suicide, therapists who work with a family prior to or immediately after the death may help the family make decisions regarding death rituals. These rituals can aid families in mourning, healing, and commemoration (Walsh & McGoldrick, 2004). Assisting families in this process may be a particularly challenging process for therapists who are also grieving the loss of the person who died by suicide.

Authentic healing rituals, whether they occur immediately following the death or at a later point in time, are likely to elicit intense emotions in family members. Therefore, it is beneficial to have a time boundary around the experience, which offers a safe context for emotional expression (Imber-Black et al., 2004). These boundaries also foster active engagement for multiple family members. Further, a well-defined ritual can afford family units with the opportunity to experiment with new behaviors and ways of interacting. In addition, by providing specific times and ways of doing so, rituals enable people to feel free to reflect on things other than the deceased person and the death at other times (Smolin & Guinan, 1993). Rituals may occur out of or in session. The creation of a suicide story, as described above, is one example of an in-session ritual.

Relevant Evidence Base

The conduct of postvention work should be informed by the relevant evidence base. Evidence-based practice incorporates pertinent research findings, clinical expertise, and patient characteristics (American Psychological Association, 2006). There have been some empirical efforts to ascertain if intervention can prevent complicated grief reactions. The following is a brief, nonexhaustive review of relevant randomized controlled trials (RCT) that focus on family-based interventions. Although there are a few intervention trials for family members who are suicide bereaved (Jordan & McMenamy, 2004; McDaid, Trowman, Golder, Hawton, & Sowden, 2008), there is a paucity of studies that examine family treatments (Rogers, Sheldon, Barwick, Letofsky, & Lancee, 1982); even fewer of these use an RCT methodology.

One RCT of a brief family-based cognitive behavioral grief counseling program revealed that participation in this four-session intervention was not associated with greater reductions in the risk for complicated grief, suicidal ideation, or depressive symptoms as compared to usual care. However, there was some suggestion that the intervention might be beneficial with regard to ameliorating maladaptive grief responses and perceptions of blame (de Groot et al., 2007).

Another investigation primarily for bereaved children also included a psychoeducational intervention for parents (Pfeffer, Jiang, Kakuma, Hwang, & Metsch, 2002). When compared with those randomized to the no-treatment condition, youth in the intervention showed marked reductions in symptoms of depression and anxiety, although no between-group differences were noted in terms of trauma or social adjustment. However, there were no between-group differences in terms of parental levels of depressive symptoms, a finding likely attributable to the fact those parents received education about their children's bereavement, rather than treatment that directly targeted their own grief reactions.

In addition to data from RCTs, some family postvention models have been proposed in the literature. The family debriefing model, an adaptation of critical incident stress debriefing, has been proposed for parents and older sibling suicide survivors (Juhnke & Shoffner, 1999). This model is theoretically based in critical incident stress debriefing and is a five-session brief therapy approach to suicide postvention. Published evaluation of this method is limited to one study of anecdotal reporting. Eleven families, 10 of them Caucasian, were reported to have completed the five-session model with anecdotal indications of improved family communication, grief sharing, and parent-child interaction. No empirical investigation of this model has been published to date.

Another model based on family support theory was designed as part of a community collaboration (Forde & Devaney, 2006). This strengths-based approach underscores the relevance of the family's informal social networks and seeks to consolidate these, ensures that support is offered as a result of genuine concern, recognizes the interdependency and interconnectedness of the family system, and emphasizes that respect for the family's wishes is paramount.

A third example is the Active Postvention Model, known as the Local Outreach to Suicide Survivors (LOSS) Program (Campbell, Cataldie, McIntosh, & Millet, 2004). This model includes a first-response team that delivers immediate services to survivors following the death (see Chapter 33). Receiving such outreach reduces the lag time to when survivors receive services.

A fourth example is the Helping and Understanding Grieving Suicide Survivors (HUGSS) model for African American families developed by our team (Kaslow et al., 2009). Families in the HUGSS study attend a 10-session, manualized, and culturally relevant psychoeducational intervention. The protocol builds on research data and is grounded on the theory of symbolic interactionism, a theory that has been applied in multiple studies to African American families. The key themes associated with this perspective that are integrated into the HUGSS project are the meaning of suicide in the African American community; the influence of the kinship network; the recognition of the impact of cultural history as well as current realities of racism, prejudice, and differential treatment; and the impact of these factors on the family and the larger community, in addition to a mindful incorporation of common cultural communication patterns such as the reliance on nonverbal cues, gestures, tone, and respect for privacy. Each 2-hour session, which is cofacilitated by an African American therapist and a cotherapist of another race, includes a supportive discussion, problem-focused psychoeducation, skill building, and an activity. The sessions cover the grief process, myths and facts about suicide, safety planning, the sharing of the suicide story, effective communication, problem solving, self-talk, coping skill development, mobilizing social support, and identifying community resources (Kaslow et al., 2009).

Special Considerations in Postvention Family Therapy

Although common themes are present in most suicide postventions, some groups and individuals merit special consideration when designing specific postvention treatment plans. Therapists must be attuned to gender differences in response to therapy, the impact of religious belief on grieving, the developmental needs of children and adolescents in the therapeutic environment, and cultural differences among various ethnic or racial minorities. Each group introduces important additional factors that must be honored and addressed for successful postvention.

Gender

Male and female suicide survivors may not respond to interventions in the same way (Jordan & McMenamy, 2004; Murphy, 2000). For example, one study found that mothers who attended a group intervention and who initially presented with elevated distress demonstrated a decrease in symptoms when the intervention was complete (Murphy, 2000). In contrast, in the same study, fathers indicated an increase in PTSD symptoms after the intervention. Socialized gender norms of grief expression may affect the response of individuals to the therapeutic process. Males may not respond as well as females to support groups due to the emphasis in such groups on expressing feelings and disclosure (Jordan & McMenamy, 2004). The literature reflects a need to examine gender differences in the design, implementation, and outcomes of grief interventions (Jordan & McMenamy, 2004; Murphy, 2000). When providing postvention family therapy, it is important that therapists monitor the effectiveness of their intervention strategies on each member and that they remain aware of potential gender differences.

Age

Another relevant subpopulation for special consideration in treatment design is minors. In families with children, therapists should include other family members (blood and fictive kin) and members of the community whom the children know and are comfortable with because the adult survivors may have difficulty engaging and helping the children through their grief due to their own psychological distress. The supportive adults should be educated about the unique processes of grief for children and connected to resources to assist them and the children.

Children and adolescents may experience the suicide of a family member differently than adults due to their increased feelings of powerlessness, as well as developmental limitations in comprehending the death (Cerel et al., 2008). Child suicide survivors may experience grief reactions involving stronger feelings of shame, guilt, self-blame, rejection, family dysfunction, and social stigmatization (Hawton & Simkin, 2003). The role of the individual who died by suicide (parent, sibling, etc.) further impacts the child's grief and loss (Cerel, Fristad, Weller, & Weller, 2000). For example, with parental suicide, the child will not only experience grief, but also may experience compounding stressors such as economic distress, disruption of housing, change in school, and separation from peer support (Cerel et al., 2008).

When implementing therapeutic techniques with children and adolescents, therapists must remain cognizant of the differences among children in verbal ability, cognitive development, and conceptualizations of death (Mitchell et al., 2006). Therapists must create a therapeutic atmosphere that is child friendly when providing psychoeducation regarding death, suicide, and grief in a developmental framework. Furthermore, it is helpful to assist children with identifying and expressing thoughts and emotions regarding the loss; to foster the development of coping skills; and to encourage family support and assist caregivers in helping children navigate the stigmatization, shame, and guilt associated with survivorship (Barnes, 2006; Kaslow et al., 2009).

Race and Ethnicity

Racial and ethnic identity is also a relevant factor to consider when choosing an intervention style. Despite the increased focus on the creation of culturally informed family interventions, no research examines evidence-based, culturally competent postventions for specific ethnic/racial groups of survivors (Kaslow et al., 2009). The lack of such interventions is significant, as empirically validated interventions are not always generalizable to every racial/ethnic group. This lack of generalizability is in part related to differential cultural grief practices, as well as the presence of additional stressors such as discrimination and racism that are salient to the grieving process for family members from historically oppressed groups. Investigation is needed to determine the applicability of theory-driven interventions, the usefulness of specific techniques, and the potential for integrating cultural grief practices into therapy with families from historically oppressed groups.

The HUGSS project, designed specifically for African Americans, provides one example of the ways in which intervention programs need to be tailored. Although quantitative data collection is still in progress for the HUGSS project, the endeavor has produced meaningful feedback from participants. A significant challenge of the project has been the recruitment of families, rather than single individuals, as many potential participants are suspicious of the therapeutic process. Participants who have completed the program expressed that direct discussion about the impact of racism and the examination of culturally held suicide myths, such as the tendency for African American family members to attribute the death to other causes, are extremely helpful (Poussaint & Alexander, 2000).

Religion

Religious beliefs are another variable that influences the grieving process. Therapists must be mindful of ethical and treatment concerns when integrating religious views in the therapeutic context. While religious beliefs often are considered a positive structure for the grieving process, religious convictions about suicide may complicate the grieving process. Therapists providing family postvention must remain educated about the suicide beliefs of major religious movements.

The act of suicide has been traditionally condemned in most major religious traditions (Gearing & Lizardi, 2009). In Christianity, although there are no specific biblical statements about the eternal destiny of those who died by suicide, the church historically has taught that suicide condemned an individual to eternal damnation (Vandecreek & Mottram, 2008) and individuals often are denied religious burial rites (Gearing & Lizardi, 2009). Historically, Jewish traditions have also forbidden suicide, as people are forbidden by Jewish law from intentionally causing harm to their bodies, in particular taking their own lives. Some conservative Jewish traditions have also denied individuals burial rites (Gearing &

Lizardi, 2009). Likewise, the Koran forbids people from killing themselves, and Islamic tradition maintains that suicide always excludes an individual from heaven and can never be forgiven (Kamal & Lowenthal, 2002). Adherents to Hinduism or Buddhism, while not fearful of eternal damnation, may fear that the deceased loved one will have difficulty in their reincarnation due to the suicide (Kamal & Lowenthal, 2002; Vandecreek & Mottram, 2008). Due to the myriad competing interpretations and cultural expressions of spiritual beliefs within the dominant religious traditions, individual family members may have individually distinctive views about suicide based on their religious predilections. Therefore, as in other forms of multicultural therapy, therapists must be educated about the common beliefs of specific religions without assuming that their clients' beliefs are reflective of the group norms.

Therapists must become comfortable with assessing religion and spirituality, and discussing such matters in the context of family postvention (Hathaway, Scott, & Garver, 2004). It is suggested that therapists assess for the significance of religious beliefs in previous crisis experiences and in daily life, and the impact of such views on postvention efforts must be considered (Gearing & Lizardi, 2009). For families who are very religious, or when therapists lack knowledge regarding the suicide beliefs and healing rituals of a family's religious heritage, the inclusion of a clergy member such as a pastor, rabbi, or imam in the therapeutic context or as a supplemental support may be helpful. Therapists may choose to utilize religious rituals and other spiritual practices as therapeutic tools for healing. Religious rituals may enhance therapeutic effectiveness with spiritually inclined families if administered with appropriate ethical care. Therapists may use bibliotherapy or incorporate sacred text readings if they are relevant to treatment. There is evidence from several studies in Christian and Muslim societies where the incorporation of sacred readings enhanced treatment (Worthington & Sandridge, 2001), a finding that may prove true with families who have lost a loved one to suicide. Therapists may encourage endogenous values, such as forgiveness, faith, family prayer, and the incorporation of prayer into healing rituals (Abernathy, Houston, Mimms, & Boyd-Franklin, 2006; Worthington & Sandridge, 2001; Yarhouse & VanOrman, 1999). Whenever religious beliefs or rituals are incorporated into therapy, even when therapists share the family's spiritual heritage, it is imperative appropriate roles be maintained and therapists not usurp the role of spiritual advisor. When appropriate ethical boundaries are maintained, spiritually meaningful interventions can be powerful tools for healing. However, therapists must be mindful to maintain respect for the tradition and to avoid trivializing the sacred meaning of the ritual or belief.

☐ Conclusion

Suicide is one of the most catastrophic of losses that families can experience (Jordan, 2008). Given the complex nature of bereavement due to suicide, an integrative approach to family assessment and intervention can provide the stability and support that families need to acknowledge the role of the deceased and accept the suicide, enhance family structures and improve family dynamics, increase family members' capacities to cope with psychological distress, ensure the family members maintain helpful social connections, and support family members in leading healthy and productive lives. Family postvention requires a sophisticated therapeutic balance of attending to family units as wholes, as well as to the individual members within the system. Careful attention should be given to the impact of age, gender, ethnicity and cultural identification, and religious belief of the individuals' suicide beliefs and the family healing process.

When intervening with families who have lost a loved one to suicide, it is essential that therapists provide a safe context for family members to explore their myriad responses to the death, create and share their suicide stories, modify and optimize family interaction patterns, engage with extended family and family members' social support networks, and access appropriate treatment for psychiatric and social problems.

Engagement in effective postvention efforts is empowering to family members. They become more active in their healing and recovery process. They experience more hope about their individual futures and the future of their family. Participation in postvention efforts helps family members to find more meaning in their lives and creates a different legacy for the deceased.

☐ References

Abernathy, A. D., Houston, T. R., Mimms, T., & Boyd-Franklin, N. (2006). Using prayer in psychotherapy: Applying Sue's differential to enhance culturally competent care. *Cultural Diversity and Ethnic Minority Psychology, 12*, 101–114. doi: 10.1037/1099-9809.12.1.101

Alexander, V. (1991). *In the wake of suicide: Stories of the people left behind*. San Francisco, CA: Jossey-Bass Publishers.

American Psychological Association. (2006). Evidence-based practice in psychology: APA Presidential Task Force on Evidence-Based Practice in Psychology. *American Psychologist, 61*, 271–285. doi: 10.1037/0003-066X.61.4.271

Andriessen, K. (2009). Can postvention be prevention? *Crisis, 30*, 43–47. doi: 10.1027/0227-5910.30.1.43

Anglin, D., Gabriel, K. O. S., & Kaslow, N. J. (2005). Suicide acceptability and religious well-being: A comparative analysis in African American suicide attempters and nonattempters. *Journal of Psychology and Theology, 33*, 140–150. Retrieved from https://wisdom.biola.edu/jpt/index.cfm

Barnes, D. H. (2006). The aftermath of suicide among African Americans. *Journal of Black Psychology, 32*, 335–348. doi: 10.1177/0095798406290470

Bolton, I. (1984). Families coping with suicide. In T. T. Frantz (Ed.), *Death and grief in the family* (Vol. 8, pp. 35–47). Rockville, MD: Aspen Systems Corporation.

Boyd-Franklin, N. (2003). *Black families in therapy: Understanding the African American experience* (2nd ed.). New York, NY: Guilford.

Brown, D. L. (2008). African American resiliency: Examining racial socialization and social support as protective factors. *Journal of Black Psychology, 34*, 32–48. doi: 10.1177/0095798407310538

Campbell, F. R., Cataldie, L., McIntosh, J. L., & Millet, K. (2004). An active post-vention program. *Crisis, 25*, 30–32. doi: 10.1027/0227-5910.25.1.30

Castle, J., & Phillips, W. L. (2003). Grief rituals: Aspects that facilitate adjustment to bereavement. *Journal of Loss and Trauma, 8*, 41–71. doi: 10.1080/15325020390168681

Cerel, J., Fristad, M. A., Weller, E., & Weller, R. (2000). Suicide-bereaved children and adolescents: II. Parental and family functioning. *Journal of the American Academy of Child and Adolescent Psychiatry, 39*, 437–444.

Cerel, J., Jordan, J. R., & Duberstein, P. R. (2008). The impact of suicide on the family. *Crisis, 29*, 38–44. doi: 10.1027/0227-5910.29.1.38

Cerel, J., & Roberts, T. A. (2005). Suicidal behavior in the family and adolescent risk behavior. *Journal of Adolescent Health, 36*, 352.e8-352.e14. doi:10.1016/j.jadohealth.2004.08.010

Crosby, A. E., & Sacks, J. J. (2002). Exposure to suicide: Incidence and association with suicidal ideation and behavior: United States, 1994. *Suicide and Life-Threatening Behavior, 32*, 321–328. Retrieved from http://www.guilford.com/cgi-bin/cartscript.cgi?page=pr/jnsl.htm&dir=periodicals/per_psych&cart_id=

de Groot, M., de Keijser, J., & Neeleman, J. (2006). Grief shortly after suicide and natural death: A comparative study among spouses and first-degree relatives. *Suicide and Life-Threatening Behavior, 36*, 418–431. Retrieved from http://www.guilford.com/cgi-bin/cartscript.cgi?page=pr/jnsl.htm&dir=periodicals/per_psych&cart_id=

de Groot, M., de Keijser, J., Neeleman, J., Kerkhof, A., Nolen, W., & Burger, H. (2007). Cognitive behaviour therapy to prevent complicated grief among relatives and spouses bereaved by suicide: Cluster randomised controlled trial. *BMJ: British Medical Journal*, doi:10.1136/bmj.39161.457431.457455.

Demi, A. S., & Howell, C. (1991). Hiding and healing: Resolving the suicide of a parent or sibling. *Archives of Psychiatric Nursing, 5*, 350–356. doi: 10.1016/0883-9417(91)90036-5

Dunne, E. J., McIntosh, J. L., & Dunne-Maxim, K. (Eds.). (1987). *Suicide and its aftermath: Understanding and counseling the survivors*. New York, NY: W. W. Norton and Company.

Ellenbogen, S., & Gratton, F. (2001). Do they suffer more? Reflections on research comparing suicide survivors to other survivors. *Suicide and Life-Threatening Behavior, 31,* 83–90. Retrieved from http://www.guilford.com/cgi-bin/cartscript.cgi?page=pr/jnsl.htm&dir=periodicals/per_psych&cart_id=

Forde, S., & Devaney, C. (2006). Postvention: A community-based family support initiative and model of responding to tragic events, including suicide. *Child Care in Practice, 12,* 53–61. doi: 10.1080/13575270500526303

Gearing, R. E., & Lizardi, D. (2009). Religion and suicide. *Journal of Religious Health, 48,* 332–341. doi: 10.1007/s10943-008-9181-2

Hathaway, W., Scott, S. Y., & Garver, S. A. (2004). Assessing religious/spiritual functioning: A neglected domain in practice? *Professional Psychology: Research and Practice, 35,* 97–104. doi: 10.1037/0735-7028.35.1.97

Hawton, K., & Simkin, S. (2003). Helping people bereaved by suicide. *BMJ: British Medical Journal, 327,* 177–178. doi: 10.1136/bmj.327.7408.177

Imber-Black, E., Roberts, J., & Whiting, R. (Eds.). (2004). *Rituals in families and family therapy* (Rev. ed.) (pp. 57–66). New York, NY: W. W. Norton and Company.

Jordan, J. (2001). Is suicide bereavement different? A reassessment of the literature. *Suicide and Life-Threatening Behavior, 31,* 91–102. Retrieved from http://www.guilford.com/cgi-bin/cartscript.cgi?page=pr/jnsl.htm&dir=periodicals/per_psych&cart_id=

Jordan, J. (2008). Bereavement after suicide. *Psychiatric Annals, 38,* 1–5. Retrieved from http://www.psychiatricannalsonline.com

Jordan, J., & McMenamy, J. (2004). Interventions for suicide survivors: A review of the literature. *Suicide and Life-Threatening Behavior, 34,* 337–349. Retrieved from http://www.guilford.com/cgi-bin/cartscript.cgi?page=pr/jnsl.htm&dir=periodicals/per_psych&cart_id=

Juhnke, G. A., & Shoffner, M. F. (1999). The Family Debriefing Model: An adapted critical incident stress debriefing for parents and older sibling suicide survivors. *Family Journal: Counseling & Therapy for Couples and Families, 7,* 342–348. Retrieved from http://tfj.sagepub.com/

Kamal, Z., & Lowenthal, K. M. (2002). Suicide beliefs and behavior among young Muslims and Hindus in the UK. *Mental Health, Religion, and Culture, 5,* 111–118. doi: 10.1080/13675670210141052

Kaslow, N. J., & Aronson, S. G. (2001). The consequences of caring: Mutual healing of family and therapists following a suicide. In S. H. McDaniel, D.-D. Lusterman, & C. L. Philpot (Eds.), *Casebook for integrating family therapy: An ecosystemic approach* (pp. 373–383). Washington, DC: American Psychological Association.

Kaslow, N. J., & Aronson, S. G. (2004). Recommendations for family interventions following a suicide. *Professional Psychology: Research and Practice, 35,* 240–247. doi: 10.1037/0735-7028.35.3.240

Kaslow, N. J., Ivey, A. Z., Berry-Mitchell, F., Franklin, K., & Bethea, K. (2009). Postvention for African American families following a loved one's suicide. *Professional Psychology: Research and Practice, 40,* 165–171. doi: 10.1037/a001402.3

Kaslow, N. J., Sherry, A., Bethea, K., Wyckoff, S., Compton, M., Bender, M.,... Parker, R. (2005). Social risk and protective factors for suicide attempts in low income African American men and women. *Suicide and Life-Threatening*

Behavior, 35, 400–412. Retrieved from http://www.guilford.com/cgi-bin/cartscript.cgi?page=periodicals/jnsl.htm&cart_id=

Kaslow, N. J., Thompson, M., Brooks, A., & Twomey, H. (2000). Ratings of family functioning of suicidal and nonsuicidal African American women. *Journal of Family Psychology, 14,* 585–599. Retrieved from http://www.apa.org/journals/fam/index.aspx

Kübler-Ross, E., & Kessler, J. D. (2005). *On grief and grieving: Finding the meaning of grief through the five stages of loss.* New York, NY: Scrivner.

Lindqvist, P., Johanson, L., & Karlsson, U. (2008). In the aftermath of teenage suicide: A qualitative study of the psychosocial consequences of the surviving family members. *BioMed Central Psychiatry, 8,* 1–7. doi: 10.1186/1471-244X-8-26

Linehan, M. M., Goodstein, J. L., Nielsen, S. L., & Chiles, J. A. (1983). Reasons for staying alive when you're thinking of killing yourself: The Reasons for Living Inventory. *Journal of Consulting and Clinical Psychology, 51,* 276–286. Retrieved from http://www.apa.org/pubs/journals/ccp/index.aspx

Linehan, M. M., & Nielsen, S. L. (1981). Assessment of suicide ideation and parasuicide: Hopelessness and social desirability. *Journal of Consulting and Clinical Psychology, 49,* 773–775. Retrieved from http://www.apa.org/pubs/journals/ccp/index.aspx

McDaid, C., Trowman, R., Golder, S., Hawton, K., & Sowden, A. (2008). Interventions for people bereaved through suicide: A systemic review. *British Journal of Psychiatry, 193,* 438–443. doi: 10.1192/bjp.bp.107.040824

McIntosh, J. L. (1993). Control group studies of suicide survivors: A review and critique. *Suicide and Life-Threatening Behavior, 23,* 141–161. Retrieved from http://www.guilford.com/cgi-bin/cartscript.cgi?page=pr/jnsl.htm&dir=periodicals/per_psych&cart_id=

McMenamy, J. M., Jordan, J. R., & Mitchell, A. M. (2008). What do suicide survivors tell us they need? Results of a pilot study. *Suicide and Life-Threatening Behavior, 38,* 375–389. Retrieved from http://www.guilford.com/cgi-bin/cartscript.cgi?page=pr/jnsl.htm&dir=periodicals/per_psych&cart_id=

Mitchell, A. M., Kim, Y., Prigerson, H. G., & Mortimer-Stephens, M. (2004). Complicated grief in survivors of suicide. *Crisis, 25,* 12–18. doi: 10.1027/0227-5910.25.1.12

Mitchell, A. M., Kim, Y., Prigerson, H. G., & Mortimer, M. K. (2005). Complicated grief and suicidal ideation in adult survivors of suicide. *Suicide and Life-Threatening Behavior, 35,* 498–506. Retrieved from Retrieved from http://www.guilford.com/cgi-bin/cartscript.cgi?page=pr/jnsl.htm&dir=periodicals/per_psych&cart_id=

Mitchell, A. M., Wesner, S., Brownson, L., Dysart-Gale, D., Garand, L., & Havill, A. (2006). Effective communication with bereaved child survivors of suicide. *Journal of Child and Adolescent Psychiatric Nursing, 19,* 130–136. doi: 10.1111/j.1744-6171.2006.00060.x

Mitchell, A. M., Wesner, S., Garand, L., Dysart-Gale, D., Havill, A., & Brownson, L. (2007). A support group intervention for children bereaved by parental suicide. *Journal of Child and Adolescent Psychiatric Nursing, 20,* 3–13.

Morrison, L. L., & Downey, D. L. (2000). Racial differences in self-disclosure of suicidal ideation and reasons for living: Implications for training. *Cultural Diversity and Ethnic Minority Psychology, 6,* 372–386. doi: 10.1037//1099-9809.6.4.374

Murphy, S. A. (2000). The use of research findings in bereavement programs: A case study. *Death Studies, 24*, 585–602. doi: 10.1080/07481180050132794

Myers, M. F., & Fine, C. (2006). *Touched by suicide: Hope and healing after loss*. New York, NY: Gotham Books.

Osman, A., Gutierrez, P. M., Muehlenkamp, J. J., Dix-Richardson, F., Barrios, F. X., & Kopper, B. A. (2004). Suicide Resilience Inventory–25: Development and preliminary psychometric properties. *Psychological Reports, 94*, 1349–1360. doi: 10.2466/PRO94.3.1349-1360

Parrish, M., & Tunkle, J. (2005). Clinical challenges following an adolescent's death by suicide: Bereavement issues faced by family, friends, schools, and clinicians. *Clinical Social Work Journal, 33*, 81–102. doi: 10.1007/s10615-005-2621-5

Pfeffer, C., Jiang, H., Kakuma, T., Hwang, J., & Metsch, M. (2002). Group intervention for children bereaved by the suicide of a relative. *Journal of the American Academy of Child and Adolescent Psychiatry, 41*, 505–513. doi: 0890-8567/02/4105-0505C

Poussaint, A. F., & Alexander, A. (2000). *Lay my burden down: Unraveling suicide and the mental health crisis among African Americans*. Boston, MA: Beacon Press.

Provini, C., & Everett, J. R. (2000). Adults mourning suicide: Self-reported concerns about bereavement, needs for assistance, and help-seeking. *Death Studies, 24*, 1–19. doi: 0748-1187/00

Rogers, J., Sheldon, A., Barwick, C., Letofsky, K., & Lancee, W. (1982). Help for families of suicide: Survivors support program. *Canadian Journal of Psychiatry, 27*, 444–449. Retrieved from http://publications.cpa-apc.org/browse/sections/0

Rudd, M. D., Joiner, T., & Rajab, M. H. (2001). *Treating suicidal behavior: An effective, time-limited approach*. New York, NY: Guilford Press.

Shneidman, E. (1969). *On the nature of suicide*. San Francisco, CA: Jossey-Bass.

Scocco, P., Frasson, A., Costacurta, A., & Pavan, L. (2006). SOPRoxi: A research-intervention project for suicide survivors. *Crisis, 27*, 39–41. doi: 10.1027/0227-5910.27.1.39

Smolin, A., & Guinan, J. (1993). *Healing after the suicide of a loved one*. New York, NY: Simon and Schuster.

Sveen, C.-A., & Walby, F. A. (2007). Suicide survivors' mental health and grief reactions: A systematic review of controlled studies. *Suicide and Life-Threatening Behavior, 38*, 13–29. Retrieved from http://www.guilford.com/cgi-bin/cartscript.cgi?page=pr/jnsl.htm&dir=periodicals/per_psych&cart_id=

Van Dongen, C. J. (1991). Survivors of a family member's suicide: Implications for practice. *The Nurse Practitioner, 16*, 31–35.

Van Dongen, C. J. (1993). Social context of postsuicide bereavement. *Death Studies, 17*, 125–141. Retrieved from http://www.tandf.co.uk/journals/titles/07481187.html

Vandecreek, L., & Mottram, K. (2008). The religious life during suicide bereavement: A description. *Death Studies, 33*, 741–761. doi: 10.1080/07481180903070467

Walsh, F., & McGoldrick, M. (Eds.). (2004). *Living beyond loss: Death in the family* (2nd ed.). New York, NY: W. W. Norton & Company.

Westefeld, J. S., Range, L., Greenfeld, J. M., & Kettman, J. J. (2008). Testing and assessment. In F. T. L. Leong & M. M. Leach (Eds.), *Suicide among racial and ethnic minority groups: Theory, research, and practice* (pp. 229–253). New York, NY: Routledge Taylor and Francis Group.

Winnicott, D. W. (1965). *The maturational process and the facilitating environment.* New York, NY: International Universities Press.

Worthington, E. L., & Sandridge, S. J. (2001). Religion and spirituality. *Psychotherapy: Theory, Research, and Practice, 38,* 473–478. Retrieved from http://www.apa.org/pubs/journals/pst/index.aspx

Yarhouse, M. A., & VanOrman, B. T. (1999). When psychologists work with religious clients: Applications of the general principles of ethical conduct. *Profesional Psychology: Research and Practice, 30,* 557–562. Retrieved from http://www.apa.org/pubs/journals/pro/index.aspx

SECTION 3

Promising Programs of Support for Survivors

U.S. Programs

CHAPTER

Baton Rouge Crisis Intervention Center's LOSS Team Active Postvention Model Approach

Frank R. Campbell

In 1998, when the LOSS (Local Outreach to Suicide Survivors) team was founded, Louisiana had a suicide rate of 11.0 per 100,000 (480 suicides) people and ranked 35th in rate of suicide in the United States. Its rate was close to that of the national average of 11.3 (McIntosh, 2000). In 1997, the state had a suicide rate of 12.1 per 100,000 (528 suicides) people and ranked 26th in the nation. Its rate in 1997 was above the national average of 11.4 for that same year. Until 1998, Louisiana's suicide had remained consistently above the national average and has remained eighth in the United States in the ranking of suicides by firearms.[1] In 1997, resources for suicide survivors in Louisiana were limited to metropolitan areas with populations over 400,000. The resources were limited to two communities,

---

[1] Data for the most recent year available, 2006, show Louisiana with 492 suicides and a rate slightly above the national average, at 11.5 per 100,000 compared to 11.1, respectively (McIntosh, 2009).

with only one of the two having a formal organizational approach providing 24-hour availability of services to survivors of suicide.

Rather than challenge a system that had consistently underutilized the opportunity to make referrals for survivor services, it was my intent (at that time I was Executive Director of the Baton Rouge Crisis Intervention Center [BRCIC; http://www.brcic.org] and the agency's director of survivor services) to institute a more structured, research-based, and achievable method for providing survivor services and referrals at the time of death. The method included aspects of "postvention," a term coined by Shneidman to describe "appropriate and helpful acts that come after a dire event" (1973, p. 33). The term postvention has been used primarily within the field of suicidology and is currently seen as those efforts intended to reduce the aftermath of a death by suicide for those impacted by that death. It was Shneidman's contention that "the largest public health problem is neither the prevention of suicide … nor the management of suicide attempts …, but the alleviation of the effects of stress in the survivor-victims of suicidal deaths, whose lives are forever changed" (1973, p. 33). By providing services in an Active Postvention Model (APM; i.e., in the LOSS team approach, services are delivered to the survivors at the time of death, typically at the death scene), our ability to identify all potential survivors was greatly increased, and our ability to make referrals enhanced. This approach was able to significantly reduce the time between referral and treatment (see Table 14.1) when comparing APM to more traditional (e.g., Rubey & McIntosh, 1996) passive approaches to survivor referrals in which the survivors typically must seek the support.

Baton Rouge, Louisiana, located in East Baton Rouge Parish,[2] has an established survivors program that began in 1981, with ongoing support from a 24-hour crisis intervention center. The center had a positive relationship with the local coroner and received survivor referrals from around the state as well as the surrounding communities. Because of the wealth of existing resources for survivors, the relationship with the coroner, the access to survivors, and the 24-hour access for services, the site was well suited to study how services for survivors might be enhanced. Perhaps most important to the goal was that the crisis intervention center in this parish was able to provide an APM, beginning in 1998. The APM was designed to be implemented by a team dedicated to the Local Outreach to Survivors of Suicide, better known as the LOSS team. The LOSS team includes staff members of the Crisis Center and survivors who have had additional training to help them respond to survivors at the scenes of suicide deaths.

---

[2] A parish is the state's equivalent of a county.

TABLE 14.1. Suicides and Postvention Service Intakes Involving and Not Involving LOSS Team Contacts in Baton Rouge Parish, 1999–2006, After 8 Years of Providing an Active Postvention Model (APM)

Year	Number of suicides*/number of LOSS team visits (%)	Number of intakes–passive model	Mean elapsed time in days since the death–passive model	Number of intakes—Active Postvention Model (APM)	Mean elapsed time in days since the death–APM
1999	46/27 (59%)	40	1,210	28	32
2000	28/22 (79%)	26	944	25	68
2001	33/19 (57%)	36	832	20	49
2002	43/25 (58%)	48	839	19	30
2003	38/21 (55%)	33	358	22	42
2004	40/24 (60%)	37	2,427	30	40
2005	29/21 (52%)	40	568	10	93
2006	33/17 (52%)	28	430	8	41
8-year mean	37/23 (62%)	36	951 Days	20	49 Days

*Number of suicides as reported by the East Baton Rouge Parish Coroner (L. Cataldie, personal communication).

During the program's first 3 years, the team members and a large comparison group of survivors who were attending survivor groups at the BRCIC but not going to the scenes each completed three measures— Beck Depression Inventory (BDI-II), Beck Anxiety Inventory (BAI), Hayes-Jackson Bereavement survey—every 60 days. Results of that study have been widely circulated through publications and presentations since 2001 (e.g., Campbell, Cataldie, McIntosh, & Millet, 2004), and can be succinctly summarized as showing that being a LOSS team member had no negative impact when compared with a group of survivors. The LOSS team was a unique concept in 1998 and different in several significant ways when compared with other outreach services for suicide survivors:

1. The LOSS team goes to the scenes of suicides and begins helping the survivors as close to the time of death or notification as possible.

2. The LOSS team depends heavily on survivors to be the primary resource at the scene.

3. The APM of the LOSS team provides referrals to all those identified as potential survivors of suicide for additional support services while at the scene of the suicide. This award-winning response team has been viewed by the other first responders as a welcome addition to the scene of such tragic events in the community.

4. Most importantly, the survivors have served as an installation of hope to the newly bereaved that they will survive. Survivors can be a resource for change and recovery (Cutcliffe, Stevenson, & Campbell, 2007).

The program has now been adopted in communities around the world and has been modified to meet the specific needs and the resources of each of those adopting communities. Many of those who wish to bring an APM to their communities will benefit by making a capacity building preinvestment to ensure the successful launch of an APM. This capacity building can be accomplished by bringing all the stakeholders (law enforcement, mental health professionals, first responders, medical personnel, hospital and health care agency representatives, elected officials, and volunteer survivors of suicide) together to explore how active postvention and support for an APM similar to the LOSS team could be helpful to the entire community. This preinvestment by building capacity for an APM recognizes the importance of stakeholders being on board with the concept while respecting all of the first responders who are at the scenes of suicides. These stakeholders are vital to the success of an APM and by involving them in the decision process, the opportunity for their support is increased. It is also vital to grow support from the broader community by including service delivery leaders that ha `e been helping suicide survivors prior to bringing an APM to the comm inity. This collaborative approach will promote a more successful launch by reducing conflict that could arise from stakeholders feeling excluded. This community collaboration approach has been facilitated through workshops that are focused on building the capacity to provide an APM; the workshops have begun to be requested and provided to communities as interest in an APM has grown.

In addition to first responders and the broad community, it is wise to also include leaders from the clinical community to see if they are open to learning about the impact of sudden and traumatic death scenes, as well as how they might be impacted by the suicide of a client. Some therapists and mental health providers could be threatened by such a model, and they will need to be reassured this is not a model that replaces them in the community since in communities where an APM exists, they can remain a resource to the survivors of their clients who die by suicide (Campbell, 2006).

Resistance can come from many areas and patience is important in setting out to develop an APM in your community. It took 10 years and a new coroner for our team to become a reality. We have now provided the service since December 1998, and many of those who are on the team today were recipients of a LOSS team call themselves. Some said that from that tragic day, they knew they wanted to do whatever it takes to heal so they could be someone who could come out to a scene and give to others what was given to them. This altruistic need is often reported in survivors, but the thing that most survivors miss is the need to first heal themselves before helping others. This might mean attending the weekly support group for an undetermined amount of time, and then being trained as a LOSS team observer until they reach a place where they sign up as a responder and not an observer. The ability to be reflective and accept "knowing when you are ready" as a process, not a time factor, is key to success.

Other than the previously mentioned study of LOSS team members to demonstrate that they are not harmed by providing this service to other survivors at the death scenes, no formal assessments have yet been conducted of the LOSS team and the APM. Evaluation research to demonstrate the effectiveness of the program for the survivors who receive assistance at the death scene of their loved ones are needed to complement the work with team members. In addition, the assessment should focus on measuring the community effects of the program's existence.

This concept of going to the scene of a suicide began as a result of my desire to let survivors know where to get help so they did not have to discover resources on their own. Knowing help is available could mean survivors getting help sooner rather than later. Most survivors I met in the weekly SOS group had stumbled on to the help that was available following their loss. As a result of having to find help on their own, the elapsed time between death and getting assistance was long and the process difficult. Too many had suffered longer than necessary because they did not know where to go for help when the suicide occurred. What I did not know was how this APM would transform our community into one that would value the effort of a few so much.

The LOSS team is still coordinated by a survivor, and the team is mostly composed of survivors who have received help at the scene from the LOSS team members in the past. To date, there are LOSS teams in communities from Singapore to Northern Ireland, and they operate on the local community level based on the APM that began in Baton Rouge, Louisiana (lossteam.com). I believe any community can and should investigate the benefits of offering the APM because the result will be a more caring and healed community.

☐ References

Campbell, F. R. (2006). Aftermath of suicide: The clinician's role. In R. I. Simon & R. E. Hales (Eds.), *The textbook of suicide assessment and management* (pp. 459–476). Washington, DC: American Psychiatric Publishing.

Campbell, F. R., Cataldie, L., McIntosh, J., & Millet, K. (2004). An active postvention program. *Crisis, 25,* 30–32.

Cutcliffe, J., Stevenson, C., & Campbell, F. (2007). Suicide "survivors," reciprocity and recovery: Issues around survivors as therapeutic agents in the care of other suicidal people. In J. R. Cutcliffe & C. Stevenson, *Care of the suicidal person* (pp. 180–195). Edinburgh, Scotland: Churchill Livingstone/Elsevier.

McIntosh, J. L. (2000, August 3). *U.S.A. suicide: 1998 official final data.* Washington, DC: American Association of Suicidology. Retrieved from http://mypage.iusb.edu/~jmcintos/datayrarchives.htm

McIntosh, J. L. (2009, April 25). *U.S.A. suicide: 2006 official final data.* Washington, DC: American Association of Suicidology .Retrieved from http://www.suicidology.org

Rubey, C. T., & McIntosh, J. L. (1996). Suicide survivors groups: Results of a survey. *Suicide and Life-Threatening Behavior, 26,* 351–358.

Shneidman, E. S. (1973). *Deaths of man.* New York, NY: Quadrangle.

15
CHAPTER

The Link Counseling Center and The Link's National Resource Center for Suicide Prevention and Aftercare

Doreen S. Marshall and Iris M. Bolton

The Link Counseling Center (LCC) is a nonprofit community counseling center established in 1971 in Atlanta, Georgia. It thrives today with four basic programs: Counseling and Psychotherapy (for individuals, couples, families, and groups), Children and Adolescents in Crisis and Grief, The Link's National Resource Center (NRC) for Suicide Prevention and Aftercare, and The Marriage and Family Therapy (MFT) Training Institute (for graduate students who are pursuing MFT licensure in the state of Georgia).

With support from The Link, Iris Bolton officially founded The Link's NRC for Suicide Prevention and Aftercare in 1996 after providing informal services to survivors since 1978. Iris Bolton was The Link's Executive Director for 36 years and is internationally known for her work with survivors. She is also the coauthor of *My Son ... My Son ...: A Guide to Healing After Death, Loss, or Suicide*, a book written with her father, Curtis

Mitchell (Bolton & Mitchell, 1983), following the suicide death of her son, Curtis Mitchell Bolton, in 1977. Jack Bolton, her husband and the father of "Mitch," continues to publish this resource for survivors from Bolton Press Atlanta (http://www.boltonpress.com). Services provided since the program's inception include the following:

- Grief counseling for individual and families by licensed clinical professionals

- Telephone counseling, information, and national referral

- Survivors of Suicide (SOS) support groups for adults and children

- Support group facilitator training and survivors of suicide support team training

- SOS support team providing home visits

- Suicide survivor services for businesses, schools, clergy, and law enforcement

- Resource materials, including a Suicide Grief Support Packet and an online national newsletter, *The Journey* (http://www.thelink.org)

- A resource library

- Speeches and seminars on prevention, intervention, and postvention

The Link provides approximately 14,000 hours of counseling services, most of them on a sliding-fee scale. In addition, The Link provides $600,000 in pro bono and reduced-fee services to the community annually. The Link's clinical staff also trains and supervises 25 volunteers who provide administrative support to the counseling center.

☐ History of The Link's National Resource Center for Suicide Prevention and Aftercare

Iris Bolton, now Director Emeritus of The Link Counseling Center, began one of the first support groups for bereaved parents in the United States in 1977. She started the first group following a request from a local minister who knew about the death of Iris' son by suicide. That group later became one of the first Compassionate Friends support groups in 1978. By the end of 1978, there was a need for a group specifically for those devastated by suicide. In conjunction with The Link, Iris Bolton then established one of the first known suicide-specific support groups for anyone who had lost a loved one to suicide.

Iris would later learn that others around the country recognized the same need for survivor support. For example, in California, Norman Farberow, and later Charlotte Ross, initiated support groups. It was as though a collective unconscious was finally responding to the specific needs of those impacted by the tragedy of suicide and the movement spread across the country. These support groups have different names, such as HEARTBEAT (LaRita Archibald), Friends for Survival (Marilyn Koenig), Ray of Hope (Betsy Ross), LOSS (Charlie Ruby), and SOS (Stephanie Weber) (see Sections 3 and 4 of this volume on promising programs for descriptions of most of these models). Currently, hundreds of survivor support groups can be found across the country that have been started by survivors.

☐ Survivors Giving Back: Joan and Bill Glover

On November 18, 1985, Joan and Bill Glover came to Iris Bolton's office at The Link 3 days after their son ended his life with his father's revolver. Bill stated, "The gun I kept in my nightstand to protect my family is the gun my son used to destroy my family. How do you live with that?" The couple shared their story of how their son was bullied at school, how he became depressed, and how he had died by suicide 3 days earlier. They shared their disbelief, pain, confusion, and hopelessness. After a 3-hour visit, they agreed to attend The Link's support group at least three times before deciding if it was right for them. They received a home visit from Bolton a few days later, attended three support group meetings, and stayed with The Link for several years, eventually helping others by becoming facilitators of survivor support groups.

Bill and Joan Glover also became members of the Survivors of Suicide (SOS) Support Team, speakers for United Way, and other civic organizations, and speakers for suicide prevention and aftercare at local churches and synagogues. Their lives were enhanced by giving back to the Atlanta community with loving support from The Link's programs of healing and hope.

The Glovers are a typical example of those who have participated in The Link's support groups, SOS Support Team, and Facilitator and Team

Training. Bill and Joan's story is just one of many about individuals that has contributed to the survivor movement, both at The Link and around the United States. (Note: Joan died in June 2007 of cancer and Bill continues to live a life of service through his volunteer work.)

☐ Outreach to Survivors: The Development of the SOS Support Team Program

In the mid-1980s, The Link was receiving too many requests for home visits for Iris to handle alone. To address this need, she asked her husband Jack, the Glovers, and two other couples, the Weyrauchs (Elsie and Jerry) and the Klosterbors (Joyce and Milt), both of whom had lost a child to suicide, to travel with her to learn the process of conducting a home visit. This informal arrangement led to the development of a local 8-week course, a manual, and The Link's NRC's outreach program, the SOS Support Team. The SOS Support Team and its training were developed in cooperation with several different agencies and therapists in Atlanta. The program is believed to be the first of its kind in the United States.

The SOS Support Team officially began in 1996 with the formalization of The Link's NRC program. Since the program's inception, clinical support has been provided by five part-time clinicians: Kathleen Gildea, MEd, LMFT, (clinician-survivor) 1985–1987, Tracy T. Dean, MS, LPC (clinician-survivor) 1996–2000, Doreen S. Marshall, PhD, LPC (clinician-survivor) 2000–2005, Donna Johnson, MS (clinician) 2005–2006, and Stuart Smith, Clinical Coordinator, MA, LPC (clinician) 2008–present. The program was also staffed by part-time Program Managers Karen Marshall, Ginny Sparrow, Maureen Roe, and currently Karen Opp, MS. These staff members serve to coordinate the support team visits. The NRC is administered by Gene Bridges, Clinical Director of The Link, and Janet Mainor, Director.

Approximately 25–30 survivor (nonprofessional) volunteers have conducted visits in the Atlanta area and across the state of Georgia over the duration of the program. The program also has had approximately five to six professional (nonsurvivor) volunteers participate since its inception. Each volunteer who has conducted a visit with the Atlanta team has completed a 2-day training at The Link's NRC; many of the volunteers are also involved in facilitating support groups or advocacy efforts for survivors.

Because the annual trainings often have individuals from outside the Atlanta area in attendance, several individuals have developed teams in their own areas and adapted the training to fit their local needs. The

Local Outreach to Survivors of Suicide (LOSS) teams in Baton Rouge, Louisiana (see Chapter 14), and Sioux Falls, South Dakota, are two examples of such teams. These teams have adapted the model of the NRC's program and have survivors assist emergency personnel in responding to deaths by suicide. Over the years, hundreds of people have received The Link's Support Team Training.

The SOS Support Team provides unique survivor-to-survivor contact following the death of a loved one by suicide. These contacts are not clinical visits, and volunteers with clinical backgrounds conduct these visits in a nonprofessional capacity after suicide-specific sensitivity training. A primary goal of the support team visits is to connect newly bereaved survivors with survivors who have been engaged in support groups, advocacy, or other volunteer work that has helped to bring them healing. This connection provides hope and reassurance to the newly bereaved survivor that surviving a loved one's death by suicide is possible and helps the newly bereaved survivor connect to a larger community of survivors coping with a suicide loss.

Visits are initiated by the newly bereaved survivor, who requests a home visit by calling the central number of The Link's NRC. Visits generally either occur in the home of the newly bereaved, at The Link Counseling Center, or at a neutral location decided by the survivor and the volunteers. The team visits typically occur within 1 week of the initial call to The Link's NRC, though the time since the death may vary up to several weeks. These calls are received by the program manager, who explains the program to the requesting survivor and gathers pertinent information, such as the date and relationship of the loss, family members and/or friends who are likely to be present for the visit, and possible times and dates for the visit. The program manager then contacts volunteers to determine their availability for the visit and works to coordinate a mutual time between the two parties.

The visits typically last between 1 and 3 hours, depending on the circumstances, the volunteer's availability, and the family members' request. In most cases, two volunteers are sent on each visit, though more may be sent given a particular circumstance. For example, a visit was conducted that involved a group of neighborhood families and their children following the death of a high school student by suicide. Several members of the team were sent to the deceased's home at the request of the family since approximately 30 to 40 survivors had planned to attend. Typically, the program manager tries to match volunteers with the family based on loss (i.e., sending a volunteer who lost a child to a family where parents who lost a child would be present).

During the visit, the volunteers' main role is to listen, to be a sign of hope, to provide support, and to encourage the survivor to seek out resources to support his or her grieving process. Newly bereaved survivors are encouraged to discuss aspects of the loss, how they are coping, and to ask questions of the volunteers related to coping with the suicide death and the resources available to them. Volunteers bring a packet of resources to the home, including a Suicide Grief support packet and bibliography, a copy of *The Journey* newsletter, and a listing of support groups in the state.

Following the visit, team members have the opportunity to debrief with each other and the program clinician. They complete a form following the visit to keep a record of the visit. They also update the program manager as to what transpired during the visit in the event that a follow-up phone call is requested by the newly bereaved survivor. Survivors who have received a visit often contact the NRC for information about the other services available through The Link Counseling Center and The Link's NRC.

The NRC's Support Team program is publicized locally through the efforts of The Link's staff and through affiliation with other suicide prevention and survivor groups, at public speaking engagements, and through the efforts of the survivor volunteers. Volunteers who decide to complete the Support Team training are required to be at least 18 months away from the death of their loved one by suicide, allowing time for their own essential grief process. In addition, new volunteers are usually paired for the first visit with a volunteer who has already completed several visits.

The Support Team program was expanded to provide postvention to local schools, businesses, and congregations in the Atlanta area. The Link's support to organizations varies according to the needs of the institution served. The Link may spend several hours or an entire day in response to a crisis in the community. Following a loss that significantly affected an entire study body and faculty, The Link's clinical staff spent an entire week on campus in support of those grieving and to provide education about the grieving process. This is an example of a typical postvention that is provided by The Link many times a year at no charge.

☐ Lessons Learned

Since 1996, more than 150 support visits have been conducted with requesting families. Although there has not been a systematic evaluation of the services provided, there is convincing evidence that these visits have created a bridge helping survivors to engage in other support services, particularly in light of the continuing large enrollment in survivor support groups hosted by The Link's NRC. The NRC has been hosting three support groups per month in the Atlanta area since 1999, and there are many anecdotal accounts of survivors attending the groups because of the support team connection. Given the large numbers of survivors that request support team visits and subsequently attend support groups, formal evaluation of the role of the support team visits in assisting survivors to engage additional support is needed. This type of research and program evaluation would help demonstrate the efficacy of this program, and may help to identify factors that support survivors in their grief process.

Some unique aspects of The Link's NRC's program have helped to sustain this endeavor. First, the program is housed in a community-based counseling center, providing the NRC with its own facility from which to run the program. This provides a visible community marker, as well as a place for visits that cannot occur in the home. Second, the history of The Link in the Atlanta community and the work of Iris Bolton are well known, assisting efforts in publicizing the program. Finally, all of the programs at the NRC are funded through private donations, income from fee-based services such as counseling, and private grants. This allows paid staff to coordinate and provide oversight to the NRC's programs, including the Support Team.

Although the program has been very well received by the community, there have been some challenges in sustaining a program of this type despite its many successes. As trainings for new volunteers occur annually, some time may transpire between a volunteer receiving the training and receiving a call for an actual visit. It has been important to find ways to keep volunteers engaged given that it could be several months after completing the training before they are called to conduct a visit.

Another challenge has been addressing requests for visits outside the metro Atlanta area, as most of the trained volunteers reside in Atlanta and cannot always travel to more remote parts of the state. This poses a problem when visits are requested far from the metro Atlanta area where there are not trained volunteers. In some of these instances, phone contact has occurred in lieu of an in-person visit. Providing adequate, survivor-specific referrals to individuals out of the metro area can be difficult, particularly when the closest survivor of suicide support group may be hours away.

Yet another obstacle is ensuring that volunteers are managing their own grieving process while being involved in volunteer activities. Ensuring that volunteers have opportunities to debrief following visits, encouraging volunteer self-care, and monitoring the number of visits any one volunteer completes to avoid burnout are important considerations in sustaining the program and its volunteers.

Finally, follow-up with those who have received a visit has posed an additional hurdle. Although many of those who have received visits later engaged in a support group, counseling, or another resource to support them in their grief, little is known about what impact the visits had on the decision to pursue support. A systematic evaluation of these efforts would help determine whether additional follow-up is needed and provide information as to the type of follow-up services that would be helpful to those not likely to engage a support group.

The services of The Link and The Link's NRC have assisted hundreds of people bereaved by suicide, helping them to share their stories with others, to make meaning out of their loss, to advocate and educate about suicide prevention and aftercare, to honor the memories of their loved ones, and to recover productive lives after a loss by suicide.

☐ Reference

Bolton, I., & Mitchell, C. (1983). *My son… my son…: A guide to healing after death, loss, or suicide* Atlanta, GA: Bolton Press.

16
CHAPTER

Samaritans Grief Support Services

Roberta Hurtig, Emily Bullitt, and Kim Kates

Samaritans is an international crisis intervention/suicide prevention organization that began in England in 1953 (http://www.metanoia.org/suicide/samaritans.htm) and was established in Boston in 1974 (http://www.samaritansofboston.org). Its mission has remained strong over the years. Its purpose is to alleviate despair, isolation, distress, and suicidal feelings among individuals in our community, 24 hours a day; to educate the public about suicide prevention; and to reduce the stigma associated with suicide. Samaritans also wants to be the place survivors turn when they are in need of support, resources, or just a place to grieve. All of our programs are based on the practices and principles of befriending, which is unconditional and nonjudgmental listening.

From the beginning, Samaritans has offered important resources to individuals who are lonely, depressed, or in crisis. The first service available in Boston was the 24-hour Helpline, which continues to this day. Staffed by trained volunteers, this phone number is available to anyone who wishes to pick up the phone and talk about their struggles, pain, or challenges. People do not need to be suicidal to call the Helpline;

our befriending service is there for individuals who are feeling alone or hopeless, and for those who might be grieving.

As the years have gone by, Samaritans' services have increased and been augmented to better serve the community. We frame our programs around three basic elements: prevention, intervention, and postvention.

☐ Prevention and Intervention

Prevention work is done on the Helpline before a caller has reached a state of crisis. We are here to listen and help individuals gain back some sense of control and to give people the support they need in the moment. Most of our callers are not actively suicidal when they pick up the phone, they just need a caring person to hear their story and validate their feelings. We are there before a person feels like suicide is the only option.

Our prevention work also takes place in our Community Education and Outreach Program. Samaritans reaches out to high-risk popula- tions and provides free workshops on suicide prevention and self-care. We also educate the community and survivors on the unique grief experienced after the loss to suicide. We feel this is very important in our efforts to support the survivor community, both to help survivors understand what they themselves are going through, and to help the people around them appreciate their anguish and be better equipped to support them.

We speak with members of community organizations all over the greater Boston, Metrowest, and Worcester areas. We facilitate workshops in schools, churches, senior centers, prisons, and hospices. We talk to police officers, home health aides, school nurses, addiction specialists, correction officers, clergy, and mental health clinicians. Suicide knows no boundaries. Samaritans' goal is to create awareness so that communi- ties have the education to end the stigma of suicide and the tools to be there for members at risk.

Samaritans is also actively involved in suicide intervention. Primarily through the befriending services offered on the 24-hour Helpline, volunteers and staff provide an outlet for callers to talk through the feelings and circumstances behind their suicidal ideation. Although Samaritan volunteers sometimes offer to provide references or to call an ambulance, they never do so without the consent of the caller, and they never trace a call. Therefore, intervention is focused on supporting people through difficult periods, rather than on physically intervening.

☐ Postvention

Samaritans' postvention work happens in our Grief Support Services. We have always been committed to the needs of survivors, wanting to be there to offer support and space that is safe and free of stigma. Yet it has only been in the last few years that our agency has fully understood how big the need of the survivor community truly is and how important it is for Samaritans to develop innovative programs and ways to meet that need.

Samaritans believes that for survivors to be able to grieve, they need (a) time; (b) a safe and gentle environment; (c) permission to tell their stories; (d) the ability to integrate the loss into their own lives; (e) the chance to talk about all their feelings and have those feelings heard and acknowledged; and (f) to be around other survivors who allow them to talk about the person they lost without having to defend that person, their relationship, or themselves. Our programs allow them to see that they are not alone in their confusion or guilt in their constant rehashing of events and investigating all the circumstances and details of what happened before their loved one died.

Samaritans also believes that survivors need information to help put together the pieces of their ordeal. We help them to have a better comprehension of suicide, mental illness, and the unique nature of survivor grief. We offer collective knowledge through other survivors' experiences and stories, literature and materials, and our own work in suicide awareness that helps the survivors gain perspective and some clarity. Our hope is that through this education and perspective, survivors can remember their loved one as a whole person, and can define him or her by the fashion they lived their life, not by the way they died.

SafePlace

Our Grief Support Services are evolving. We have six separate survivor support groups in the greater Boston, Metrowest, and Worcester areas, called SafePlace. These meetings provide open, caring, and nonjudgmental support for people who have lost a loved one to suicide. The groups are facilitated by survivors who have had time to heal and rebuild their lives. SafePlace offers the opportunity to be quiet, to explore feelings, to grieve, and to share. It is a space for people to feel accepted and understood. Every SafePlace meeting has a life of its own, depending on what the group needs at the time. The group discussion frames the evening and allows the facilitators to steer the conversation around what people want to talk about and the areas where they need support and validation. There is an opening statement to welcome everyone. Following that the facilitators and participants go around and introduce themselves, and if they wish, say who they lost. After this introduction, there is no formal program or presentation. The facilitators help guide the conversation to ensure the meeting is supportive for all its members.

In the mid-1980s, Samaritans took over the first SafePlace group in Somerville, MA, from Catholic Charities. This group was later moved to Medford, where it continues to meet. In the 1990s, another group location was added in Boston. Parallel to these groups, the Framingham SafePlace group ran independently until the Boston and Framingham Samaritans merged in 2005. That summer, Samaritans began the Quincy SafePlace location, filling a much-needed service gap on the South Shore. In January 2007, a Worcester-based location started, opening the door to providing services in Central Massachusetts. The sixth group was established in August 2008 in South Boston. In every case, Samaritans was responding to a need for people to have a support group in their community, giving survivors a place to be safe and heard.

Helpline

The Samaritans' 24-hour Helpline is also a wonderful service for survivors. Survivors can always reach a caring, compassionate person who will provide unconditional support. Helpline volunteers understand the pain and complicated emotions that survivors face. They provide a listening ear and no judgments or demands. These volunteers are empathetic and are aware of resources available to the survivor community. Individuals can call as often and as many times as they need. It is not unusual for survivors to rely upon emotional support over an extended period. Samaritans is here to listen to whatever a person is experiencing.

Memorial Events

Every January, Samaritans hosts a memorial event that honors those who have died by suicide. All survivors are welcome. This beautiful non-denominational service is an opportunity to not only remember loved ones, but also for survivors to reconnect with each other, offer comfort and support, and share memories.

Every autumn, Samaritans holds a 5K-Run/Walk and Family Fun Festival. On this day, hundreds of people come together to remember those lost to suicide, and help raise awareness for suicide prevention. It is a wonderful day. Many survivors run or walk in honor of a friend or family member. Teams and individuals create a page on the Samaritans' Web site (http://www.samaritanshope.org/index.php/5k.html) to recognize a loved one and allow others to get a sense of who this person was and how valued their life was. In the fall of 2010, we celebrated our 12th 5K-Run/Walk.

Survivor to Survivor Network

In the summer of 2006, Samaritans started a new service for survivors called the Survivor to Survivor Network. This unique initiative is an outreach program that sends a pair of trained volunteers to meet with newly bereaved survivors in their home or in another comfortable setting. Every team has at least one person who is a survivor. People are welcome to invite any family members or friends who could benefit from the meeting. This visit is a time for survivors to talk about their loved one, their loss, and their grief. They can ask questions, cry, be quiet, or share worries and concerns. Survivor to Survivor Network team members are there to listen, befriend, and offer information. They are there to support and help survivors, and to alleviate some of the isolation and confusion often felt by survivors. They provide information about Samaritans' programs and community resources and share educational literature about bereavement after a suicide. Samaritans staff coordinates these visits, then follows up with participants. Families have the option of up to five more contacts with this team after the initial visit. They can invite others to join these future meetings.

The path toward creating the Survivor to Survivor Network began in 2002 when Roberta Hurtig, Samaritans' executive director, and Jack Jordan met at the American Foundation for Suicide Prevention Day of Healing. Soon after, the two were called in by the Massachusetts Department of Public Health at the request of Massachusetts State Senator Robert Antonioni. During this meeting, it became clear that while Samaritans' SafePlace and Helpline were good and important services, additional, different services were needed so that more people could be served.

Samaritans realized support groups were not for everyone—sometimes, the nights the groups met were not convenient, and often a group's meeting could be too soon for recent survivors to hear the stories and sadness of other recent survivors. It was hard enough for survivors to get out of bed some days, never mind showing up at a group twice a month.

Our goal was to make the whole experience safe, simple, and as minimally stressful as possible.

All Samaritans programs are free, and to qualify for Grief Support Services, all a survivor needs to do is let Samaritans know they need the services. They can come to a SafePlace meeting years after they have lost a loved one, have a Survivor to Survivor Network visit even if they were not a direct relative of the person who died, and call the Helpline anytime for any reason. For survivors, this is very important because often a suicide causes much paperwork and bureaucracy on top of the heartache and sadness. Thus, to be able to attend a support group without worrying about insurance, or have a Survivor to Survivor visit without having to fill out any paperwork or call for a referral, is monumental.

Volunteers are at the heart of the organization. They participate at all levels of service that we provide and truly steer the organization. Our SafePlace meetings are facilitated by trained volunteers who are also survivors. This is what has made the meetings so welcoming and successful. Therefore, we realized we had to staff the Survivor to Survivor Network using the same model.

All our SafePlace facilitators and Survivor to Survivor Network team members go through a rigorous screening process that includes a written application and interviews with the director of Grief Support Services and our clinical consultant, Dr. Jack Jordan. We do reference and criminal offender record information checks. This whole process helps ensure that Samaritans finds extremely caring and compassionate people who are committed to our mission and ready to take on such a big challenge. Our Grief Support Services volunteers need to be in a place in their own healing that allows them to be present for the people attending SafePlace meetings and Survivor to Survivor visits. As survivors themselves, they are able to understand the pain and hopelessness that a suicide can bring.

☐ Lessons Learned

As our Grief Support Services program grows, we continue to learn. We have realized the importance of having survivors be there for other survivors and that those connections are priceless. We have learned that sending a card or thoughtful e-mail can make a world of difference. Volunteers and staff work hard to reach out to survivors in ways that are supportive and not invasive. We follow up with participants in our programs in gentle ways, always letting people know we are here but not making them feel like they are obligated to take part in our services.

We have learned that we need to provide more resources for bereaved children and teens. We were able to quickly create a wonderful relationship with a local organization, the Children's Room. We have shared trainings and conducted in-services for each other. The Children's Room staff has talked to our Grief Support Services team on the unique needs of grieving children and teens; Samaritans has offered workshops on issues of suicide loss for the Children's Room staff and volunteers. We refer families to each other's programs. The Children's Room staff and Samaritans have collaborated on different projects, and have developed a good set of resources for families who have lost a loved one to suicide and need to support children and teens through the loss.

We have learned how important it is to provide many different options for families and loved ones, and to be as flexible as possible. Originally, we thought that the Survivor to Survivor Network would be the gateway to SafePlace meetings. Yet, we are finding many families are attending SafePlace meetings and requesting Survivor to Survivor Networks simultaneously. We are also discovering that many of our Survivor to Survivor Network visits are with only one person, not entire families as we first anticipated. Many individuals have included other people in the second visit. We have also seen that often one or two Survivor to Survivor visits are enough, and it is rare for a person or a family to use all six of the allotted meetings.

We are learning how important it is for families and friends to "do something" after a suicide; they want to feel that they are helping others and keeping the memory of their loved one alive. They want to take something tragic and find some good. Hence, we have started to create ways people can become involved with Samaritans other than becoming SafePlace facilitators or Survivor to Survivor Network team members. Survivors have accompanied staff on outreach presentations, have formed 5K-teams in memory of their loved ones, and have joined Samaritan committees. They have supported our work in the office doing clerical tasks, or working on specific projects such as our fundraising events and community outreach. Volunteering seems to offer them some hope and a feeling of connectedness and community.

Samaritans has always known how important it is to take care of its volunteers. Yet, we are learning with our Grief Support Services how critical and essential ongoing support, training, and supervision are. Over the years, we have fine-tuned our training and added to its curriculum. After listening to what our volunteers need and want, we have adjusted the way we facilitate our quarterly supervision meetings. We continue to offer resources and training opportunities to our volunteers, creating new ways to be supportive and to show how much we value all they do. This work demands a great deal emotionally and physically from our volunteers. The more we ask of them, the more vital it is that the Samaritans staff is there to help sustain their energy, organize the logistics of the programming, and offer guidance and caring.

The biggest challenge of our work has been getting the word out to the community that Grief Support Services exist. It has been slow going, but with each year, more and more people are using our services. We have reached out to first responders, faith-based communities, clergy, funeral home directors, and mental health providers. We have developed a workshop on grieving after suicide that we can share with members of the wider community. Our Grief Support Services volunteers have undertaken grassroots networking, letting people in their circles know about our services. The Internet has been a wonderful way for people to find Samaritans, and we continue to investigate other methods to reach people online.

The Grief Support Services staff attempt to solicit feedback from participants. Each new person who comes to a SafePlace meeting receives an evaluation form and a stamped envelope. We also give an evaluation form to Survivor to Survivor participants. Facilitators encourage members of the group to take evaluations out with our survivor literature and return them. Most of the feedback we gather comes from anecdotes and word of mouth. Our hope as we move forward is to reach out more directly to new survivors with caring and supportive phone calls from Grief Support team members, asking them directly how they experienced our services. Samaritans wants to meet the needs of survivors, so we need to listen to their reactions and requests.

Our advice to anyone beginning a program like our Grief Support Services is simple: Listen to survivors, get them involved, and take what they say to heart. It is also important to reach out to other organizations, schools, and agencies in your community. Let them know what you are doing and educate them about the needs of survivors. Initially, this can be time-consuming and slow, but with time, the momentum builds and people become aware of what you are doing and of its importance.

Samaritans is committed to suicide survivors. We want to be there for them. Samaritans wants to give survivors the tools and resources they need to weather this hard and unfair storm, offering them glimpses of hope and community. We want to help survivors remember their loved ones as a whole person, defined by the way they lived, not by the way they died.

HEARTBEAT Survivors After Suicide, Inc.

LaRita Archibald

"Healing by helping others heal" epitomizes the benefit of mutual support grief groups. That is, grief groups are gatherings of individuals with like experience who reinforce and encourage one another toward resolution of, and adaptation to, the consequence of the like experience. HEARTBEAT Survivors After Suicide, Inc. is such an organization.

The objective of HEARTBEAT is to relieve isolation created by suicide for those left behind, to offer permission to grieve freely by normalizing emotional response to an abnormal death, to model healthy coping, and to extend hope for a positive and productive future.

The name HEARTBEAT acknowledges the almost physical effort of making one heartbeat follow another in the immediate aftermath of a loved one's suicide. The letters in HEARTBEAT define the healing philosophy of the organization. The name symbolizes:

Healthy coping through
Empathy and understanding reinforced by

Acceptance without judgment and **A**ffirmation of self-worth,
Resolution of conflict and **R**einvestment in life supported by the
Truth ... responsibility for the death rests with the one who ended
their life.

The philosophy further encourages "seasoned" survivors to:

Be a source of reinforcement to newly bereaved,
Effect public prevention education, and
Acknowledgement of suicide as a preventable health problem, thus
Transforming one's personal tragedy into positive action that lends meaning and purpose to the loss.

With the support of my husband, I founded HEARTBEAT in 1980, 2 years after the suicide of our 24-year-old son in 1978. Forming HEARTBEAT was a direct result of meeting and sharing with another surviving mother during an American Association of Suicidology conference I attended in Denver in May 1979, 6 months after my son's death. Finally, there was someone who understood my anguish, fear, sense of responsibility, frustration, and impotence. Interaction with this single mother, alienated from her only surviving child, made me acutely aware of the blessing of a loving, supportive family and the healing benefit of shared grief. This encounter also made me determined that no one bereaved by suicide in my community would ever again be without empathetic consolation.

I became a volunteer telephone respondent to suicide survivor callers through a hotline sponsored by a local community health association. Callers often asked to meet with me to talk about suicide loss. Meeting with callers was against hotline policy, but the number of requests convinced me that group meetings could be beneficial.

Serendipity played a role in the formation of HEARTBEAT. A *Family Circle* magazine article I read while waiting in my dentist's office provided my first information about support groups and their purpose. My personal loss experience and the grief needs described by suicide-bereaved callers dictated a philosophy of healing that offered validation, encouragement, and hope. The name HEARTBEAT defined the philosophy and acknowledged the physical effort of survival. When I approached the director of the community health association for advice, she confided that her father had ended his life when she was a young girl and, without hesitation, supported my vision of a suicide-survivor support group. She offered sponsorship under the association's umbrella, meeting space, telephone screening, photocopy privileges, publicity, minimal funding, invaluable suggestions, and encouragement when my resolve wavered. Efforts to gain endorsement, advisors, or referrals from the faith and mental health communities were another matter. None was willing to risk involvement in such a controversial endeavor.

I drafted a meeting agenda based on my grief research, personal experience, and a great amount of divine guidance. The Meeting Welcome stated the group's purpose and the need for courteous sharing. Participant introductions, group sharing, and the Serenity Prayer to close the meeting completed the agenda. Eventually, time was allocated for sharing in separate relationship groups.

Anyone losing a friend or family member to suicide could attend meetings at any time for as long as they benefited from receiving or giving support. With help from the sponsoring agency, a brochure was developed and distributed. The agency's network publicized the new group, and with support from my family, I gathered the courage to promote HEARTBEAT support group meetings for survivors after suicide through a local newspaper interview. I relied upon experience in leading discussion groups to guide me in facilitating the meeting.

On November 15, 1980, in Colorado Springs, four survivors attended the first HEARTBEAT meeting—my husband and I, a gentleman who survived his younger brother, and a woman who had lost a cousin. By late summer 1981, as word of HEARTBEAT spread through the sponsoring agency's network, suicide survivors from other communities and even other states were calling to speak of their tragedies. Many traveled hundreds of miles to spend 2 hours at monthly HEARTBEAT meetings, sharing the pain of a loved one's suicide and the comfort of being in the presence of others who understood the meaning of suicide loss. By 1982, when meeting attendance grew too large for productive sharing (between 40 and 50 attendees each meeting), the Denver Catholic Diocese volunteered to sponsor a HEARTBEAT chapter in that city. After two other Colorado cities requested a HEARTBEAT group, I authored a manual to assist in starting groups. The original photocopied manual, *HEARTBEAT Leadership Guide*, was many times revised, updated, and widely circulated throughout the country. The advent of the Internet now allows the *HEARTBEAT Leadership Guide* to be downloaded free from http://www.heartbeatsurvivorsaftersuicide.org. Although forming chapters was never the initial intent, 42 chapters in nine states and two foreign countries presently offer comfort and encouragement to suicide-bereaved individuals.

HEARTBEAT Survivors After Suicide was incorporated as a non-profit organization in June 1993. The founding chapter received IRS nonprofit determination in 2001, and now operates autonomous of any agency. The organization's operating expense is minimal with an all-volunteer staff and donated space. Funding for support materials is through donations, memorials, and small grants.

To open a chapter, prospective chapter leaders contact LaRita Archibald, founder/director, usually after visiting the HEARTBEAT Web site and downloading the HEARTBEAT guidelines or after participating in another chapter. They are informed that there are no charges assessed to form a HEARTBEAT chapter, that all leadership is by volunteers, and that most chapter meeting spaces are donated. New leaders are encouraged to seek funding support from local mortuaries, faith-based organizations, or mental health agencies rather than depending upon personal finances for initial funding. This serves two purposes: a vested interest from the agencies that support the group through referrals, and funds to print quality brochures and create a library.

Where distance permits, I meet with prospective leaders. Most new groups are formed after numerous e-mails and telephone exchanges assure me of the suitability and commitment of the individual as a HEARTBEAT chapter founder/leader. We discuss their motivation for starting a chapter. "Seasoned" survivors are usually excellent suicide-bereavement support group leaders because of the seemingly inexhaustible passion they are willing to invest in providing support to other survivors. However, many successful support groups are formed and led by compassionate, knowledgeable individuals other than survivors, who are willing to commit the time and energy necessary to lead a suicide grief support group. When prospective chapter founders are employed by mental health, faith-based, or government agencies, and have been designated by their employer to form a chapter, we discuss their grief experience and leadership knowledge, educational background, and agency oversight.

Leadership selection is a nondiscriminatory process, although many leaders are women. When the prospective chapter leader is a suicide survivor, I inquire about his or her loss, time since the death, and the healing achieved. There is no set time frame following a suicide required for starting and leading a HEARTBEAT chapter. Nearly 30 years of working with survivors has taught me that there are survivors stable and strong enough to lead a group after a year, and others who would not be satisfactory leaders after 5 or 10 years. We discuss the prospective leader's support system, the need for a suicide grief group in the locale, and community support of a chapter. I inquire about the individual's involvement in grief support beyond his or her personal experience, whether he or she has attended a bereavement support group, and past facilitating experience or willingness to pursue training. We discuss the time and energy involved in working with suicide bereaved outside group meetings, whether a coleader is being considered, the potential sponsoring agency, how the new chapter will be funded, and the vision for the chapter. I do not understate the needed time, energy, commitment, or the difficulties and demands, nor do I understate the reward and satisfaction.

As a grassroots support group founder, without guidelines or an experienced advisor, I learned that being the sole group leader is very confining and exhausting. I emphasize the practicality of a coleader to share the responsibility in providing a productive, ongoing group. As well, I strongly recommend forming a steering committee to help shoulder the administrative responsibilities.

Further, we speak of values and spiritual beliefs. We discuss chapter administration, the purpose and benefit of a steering committee or board of directors to provide checks and balances, fiscal responsibility, administrative support, oversight assurance that the support group is operating within the HEARTBEAT guideline parameters to the best of its ability, and some assurance of group perpetuity. When interviews determine an individual is not appropriate or ready to assume the responsibility of a chapter, I kindly suggest that he or she invest more time in personal healing, or become involved in other pursuits.

Prospective leaders are strongly encouraged to solicit coleaders among the survivor, faith-based, and mental health communities, to avoid leader burnout, ensure meeting constancy, and provide balanced facilitation. All new leaders are provided with the opportunity to receive facilitator training from the founding chapter training team. When distance makes this impractical, new leaders are encouraged to seek facilitator training through a resource in their own communities. A leadership prerequisite is knowledge of symptoms of suicidal ideation to help identify and refer any meeting participant demonstrating a need for mental health help.

Marks of leadership inappropriateness are bias, bigotry, poor verbal skills, lack of sensitivity or empathy, being uninformed about suicide risk, or a reluctance to refer an at-risk participant for mental health help. Politicizing and proselytizing are unacceptable, as is disregard for HEARTBEAT standards and philosophy.

Each chapter operates autonomously, both fiscally and administratively. Most chapters are funded by donation, fundraising events, or small grants. The HEARTBEAT director provides ongoing assistance to new leaders, brochure design, and copies of the HEARTBEAT incorporation certificate, and bylaws to assist leaders in developing strong chapters consistent in operation with other HEARTBEAT chapters.

Chapter leaders sign a Memorandum of Understanding (MOU) with the HEARTBEAT director for the purpose of quality control and to ensure group perpetuity. The MOU is the only agreement between the HEARTBEAT director and chapter leaders. New chapter leaders are allowed flexibility to adapt procedure to meet the needs of the survivor population in their respective community. By facilitating various chapters, I have noted considerable differences in community personalities, usually determined by culture or socioeconomics, although the pain of suicide loss is a common trait. What works well for a chapter in a high-tech community may not work in a blue-collar community, or in a large metropolitan area versus an agricultural community.

Any leader abusing his or her role as a HEARTBEAT leader by creating conflict with sponsors, harm to a survivor, or damage to the credibility of the organization is asked to resign. Only once has the HEARTBEAT director needed to act as arbitrator between coleaders. The director provides each chapter with both a support group directory and Web site directory to encourage communication and referrals between chapters and to link them to state and national suicide-related organizations and resources.

When a community no longer has survivors needing support, a chapter may be discontinued, as occurred in a sparsely populated Kansas farming community where no suicides occurred in a 2-year period following the five that were the impetus for the chapter. Such chapters are listed as "At Rest" in the HEARTBEAT directory. On the other hand, if leaders are willing to serve as a support contact should a need arise, their information is instead listed as "On Call."

HEARTBEAT support groups are encouraged to be involved with suicide prevention organizations and activities in their communities. For example, the founding chapter, one of the partners of the Suicide Prevention Partnership/Pikes Peak Region, appoints a "seasoned" survivor to represent HEARTBEAT as postvention committee chair and to serve as a director on the Partnership Board. Beginning in 1989, the HEARTBEAT Founding Chapter presented a well-attended, biennial, 2-day "Healing After Suicide" conference in Colorado Springs. Recently, this conference has been discontinued due to the advent of an annual state-sponsored suicide prevention conference that also addresses survivor issues.

HEARTBEAT has developed other resources for survivors beyond mutual support grief groups. Compassion Teams were formed in 1998 to respond in the near-immediate aftermath of a suicide death upon request of the bereaved. These teams are most often activated following a suggestion to newly bereaved individuals by fire or police chaplains at the scene. New survivors report tremendous benefit from having a "seasoned" survivor offer understanding and consolation, listen as they struggle with the reality of suicide, offer the comfort that they are not alone and the assurance that they will survive this tragedy, and offer to be available for ongoing support. "Seasoned" survivors volunteer to serve as Compassion Team members. An interview with the HEARTBEAT director determines their readiness to serve as a responder. Following 4 hours of training, the new team member accompanies an experienced team member on calls.

A 6-week Teen HEARTBEAT is activated when at least six teens are enrolled. During the 6 weeks, the teen group leader, a young clergy-woman survivor with a gift for "teen speak," engages the teen survivors in suicide grief-specific curriculum and activities. A HEARTBEAT leader simultaneously meets with the parents/guardians of the teens.

The first Tuesday evening of every December, HEARTBEAT hosts a candlelight memorial at a local church. This event is preceded by the ceremonial lighting of an enormous blue spruce decorated with hundreds of tiny lights (courtesy of a local landscaping company). Hung on the tree are several hundred memorial ornaments requested by surviving families; these 3-inch round, gold, shatterproof ornaments have the names and dates of persons who have ended their lives calligraphied on them by the HEARTBEAT staff. In addition to memorializing loved ones at a difficult time of year, this event makes the public aware of the scope of the local suicide problem. There is no charge for the ornaments, but donations are accepted and result in substantial funds to help support the organization's work.

Although there is no systematic evaluation of the HEARTBEAT program's efficacy, the fact that none of the hundreds of HEARTBEAT participants are known to have ended their own life and the increasing referrals to HEARTBEAT chapters from therapists lends credibility to the program. Perhaps individual survivor accounts are the best measure of the program's benefits.

John, an 86-year-old man, attended only one HEARTBEAT meeting. He was accompanied by his wife and daughter, who were concerned about John's recent obsession with his father's suicide. John's father, an early 20th-century North Dakota homesteader, disillusioned by dust, wind, and drought, had hung himself from a windmill on the family farm when John was 9 years old. John, his mother, and neighbors buried his father, and no one spoke of his father again. John's memory of his father was distorted by shame. During the meeting, John tearfully spoke of his love for his father in conflict with his shame of how his father had died and the terrible sin he had committed. HEARTBEAT participants shared their own learning with John—that suicide was often the result of depression, an illness, and not a shameful act to be hidden. They offered him the reassurance of their own beliefs—God had known and understood his father's state of mind and forgiven his choice. They encouraged John to speak of the love he shared with his father and to refuse to carry shame for the manner of his father's death. At the end of the meeting, John stood in the center of the grief circle, tears running down his cheeks, and said, "You have given me back my father. I'm no longer ashamed of how he died. For the first time in more than 70 years, I can breathe without the weight of shame sitting on my chest."

John's story of lifelong shame and sorrow is one of many that have been assuaged through HEARTBEAT. Participants share the pain of parents whose adult child killed his wife and children before ending his own life; wives with small children left destitute by their husband's suicide; bereaved individuals who have lost several family members to suicide and fear for their surviving family; military dependents whose loved one survived battle to end his or her life upon returning home; gay survivors who lost their partners to suicide and had their right to grieve denied; as well as the unique grief of every group attendee.

HEARTBEAT was built from God-given direction following indescribable loss and soul-searing emotional agony. Its grassroots beginning was awkward and unsure, but it has grown into a widespread ministry that exemplifies what can happen when wounded people reach out of their own anguish to extend the hand of empathy and encouragement to other like-wounded individuals.

18

CHAPTER

Friends for Survival

Marilyn Koenig

In 1982, Marilyn Koenig and Chris Moon shared their experience of the death by suicide of their teenage sons at a Compassionate Friends meeting for grieving parents. That shared experience gave birth to a support group for all survivors of a suicide death. In the early 1980s, no other such resource was available in the Sacramento, CA, area, and very few organizations existed nationally. The founding families of Friends for Survival (FFS) envisioned an organization that would provide emotional support, education, and insight into the problems faced by those who have been affected by a suicide loss, and in so doing, help break the cycle of death by suicide. A mission statement was developed and adopted by the FFS Board of Directors in 1996. It states

> Friends for Survival, Inc. is an organization of people who have been affected by a death caused by suicide. We are dedicated to providing a variety of peer support services that comfort those in grief, encourage healing and growth, foster the development of skills to cope with a loss, and educate the entire community regarding the impact of suicide.

357

The first FFS meeting on February 3, 1983, was attended by eight grieving survivors. By the end of 2009, we had responded to more than 7,300 grieving families nationwide, mailed 652,470 monthly newsletters, facilitated 1,410 monthly education/support meetings, and presented 24 all-day conferences and retreats. Our 2010 budget was $75,000. All of this would not have been possible without the backbone and brains of the 568 dedicated volunteers who have donated more than 80,000 hours of their time. For the first 26 years, we had been an all-volunteer organization. In July 2009, we hired part-time staff to support our programs and help with the phones.

This amazing growth has been accomplished by the visionary efforts and planning of a board of directors who have been affected by a suicide death. The first planning meeting started with two critical goals: developing a brochure and becoming a nonprofit agency. Those founding families each donated $25, for a total of $100, to print our brochure. What they donated in time and skills created this successful program that has reached thousands of families and saved many lives.

FFS is more than a support group. It is a diverse program that offers a variety of services to meet the complicated needs of families and friends following a suicide death, as well as the needs of the community at large. We have found that approximately 10% of the families that call us actually come to meetings. However, we are contacted by 55% of the families that experience a suicide death in our extended area. It is our goal to provide services to everyone who contacts us, whether they attend meetings or not. Our services are outlined here.

☐ Monthly Newsletter

Our monthly newsletter offers a small dose of healing on a consistent basis; it could be called a support group in printed form. It includes articles on coping with our particular grief, poems, education on suicide, reviews of new books, national events of interest, meeting times, and topics. It reminds people of the how, what, and where of meetings at a time when they cannot remember where to go, when to be there, or where they have been. Although no formal evaluation has been conducted, the feedback we get confirms this truly is the best and most important resource that we offer. Comments such as "This newsletter is a great part of healing, understanding, forgiving, and carrying on," or "Your newsletter helps me to cope," indicate the importance of our monthly newsletter. It is free, but we encourage donations and the recipients respond with grateful notes and compensation. At the end of

2009, we were mailing our monthly newsletter to 3,500 families in all 50 states.

☐ Monthly Meetings

Our meetings are open-ended, with several options available every month. We set up our meetings around tables laden with treats, drinks, and colorful napkins. Our goal is to establish an atmosphere of hospitality, like sitting with a friend around the kitchen table. The table is not a crutch, but rather, a support; a place to put your cup of coffee, tea, or lemonade; write notes; review handouts; and reach for tissues if needed. We collaborate with our local professional health care community, the members of which offer their skills and time to our support/education meetings. Those professionals who speak are requested to present an interactive talk. Each month, there is a topic relevant to suicide, such as anger, guilt, depression and medication, journaling, getting through the holidays, trauma, remembering the good memories, different grief styles in families, children and grief, preservation of photos, and so forth. We do not go around the room asking people to share their entire experience, as we have found that this can retraumatize attendees. We each have our own horror story, and having to listen to several people relate their tragedy can be very depressing. Therefore, each meeting has a topic for discussion. We have found only a small percentage of people will attend meetings due to impediments such as work schedules, distance, lack of transportation, and a belief that perhaps they would not be comfortable in a group. However, average attendance at our education support meetings is 35 people. We also offer sharing meetings at several outlying locations. Each of our meetings has a minimum leadership team of three. Leadership team members are survivors who meet our qualifications, attend our trainings, and sign a leadership agreement for a minimum of 1 year.

☐ Day-Long Conferences and Retreats

Our speakers and workshop leaders are well-known professionals who have a special expertise in suicide grief. Typically, our keynote speakers have national-level reputations. Our conferences and retreats are planned to provide those attending with specific information for coping and a sense of hope so that they may leave our events with a smile on their face. We plan ways to pamper them with special treats, surprises, and always a memento to take with them. We have also sponsored professional conferences for first responders, school personnel, and health care professionals.

☐ Suicide Loss Helpline

Our helpline telephone service (1-800-646-7322 or 1-800-6-HOPE CA; also, locally, at 916-392-0664) is answered by survivors. Training is provided, and over the many years in service, we have never changed our phone number. The phone is almost always the first contact with and by survivors. This is a very subtle way to screen persons to ensure they are contacting us because they have had a suicide death. With the initial call, we spend as much time listening and talking to them as they need. This helps to develop a bond with them and gives them a level of comfort and confidence that gives them hope. We offer them information and resources, and always follow up with a packet of information and a recent monthly newsletter. We continue to send them our newsletter until they notify us that they no longer need it. In more than 25 years, we have had only two people decline to receive a packet.

☐ Other Services and Resources

In addition to the services above, we have three memorial quilts, composed of squares created by families; a free lending library at our meetings; information about and referral to local resources; a pen-pal program (for survivor-to-survivor contact); a speakers bureau; and our Web site (http://www.friendsforsurvival.org). We have about 100 volunteers, and all these programs are coordinated and closely monitored by a board of directors to maintain integrity and stability.

We have a diverse base of funding, including donations from the families we serve, United Way designations, an annual raffle, the sale of restaurant and entertainment discount books, board fundraising, community donations, garage sales, and grants. Our brochures are distributed by funeral homes and law enforcement chaplains. We are listed in numerous local and national directories. We receive referrals from faith-based organizations, health care professionals, employee assistance programs, crisis lines, mental health associations, families already receiving our services, and so forth.

☐ **Lessons Learned**

In 1983, when we started this organization, we thought it would be a small, community resource. We have been amazed at the growth and the willingness of people to reach out to us after such a tragic event. Offering a variety of services has allowed us to help more survivors and meet the diversity of their needs and the needs of the community at large. Our collaboration with the professional health community has not only enhanced our services, but we have received its endorsement of our services as well. Our challenge at this time is to build long-term sustainability and broaden our administrative structure to include some paid staff. Funding is, of course, a challenge that we are confidently and constantly overcoming.

Since 1983, we have had disappointments. For example, we have found that our grieving families will not attend social events, such as baseball games, picnics, and so forth. We have found sponsoring a fireworks booth as a fundraiser is too labor-intensive for the profit derived from it. We have also found that meetings that involve only sharing (no topic) are not as well attended as our educational support meetings, but they do serve a purpose for those few attendees. We have found that our attendees are negligent in returning library books, but the library is still important to maintain.

We know there are specific aspects of our organization that have contributed to our success. First, each of us has experienced a suicide death, and that experience has given us personal insight into the struggles with which our callers are grappling. That initial phone call offers us the opportunity to comfort, offer hope, and acquaint survivors with our program. We firmly believe the minimum leadership team of three survivors is necessary to have a successful community resource. The leadership team of three, with broad leadership and skills, ensures the program will not falter due to the illness, vacations, or perhaps burnout of one solitary leader. From our experience, a comprehensive brochure is one of the best ways to advertise our services. A dedicated phone number with an appropriate message is very important. Proper phone etiquette allows the caller to know immediately that they have reached the appropriate resource. Disconnected phone numbers and calls not being returned are discouraging to grieving persons who may only have the energy to make that one call.

Thus far, we have relied on the comments and suggestions from survivors, internal surveys, and so forth, to guide us in the development of our programs. We recognize, however, the need to pursue a professional evaluation of our program. Approximately 25 new families contact us each month, and without paid staff, responding to them has become overwhelming. Presently, our most important task is to raise the funds for full-time staff and add more volunteers for the necessary clerical tasks.

We believe the millions of survivors in this country and abroad deserve quality support and specific information that can aid in their coping and healing. When survivors call, they are really asking, "Tell me how I am going to get through this!" We have the ability and experience to offer hope and services to these very grateful, loving people who are looking for answers. We can use our own experience with suicide to make a difference in their grief journey and save lives.

19
CHAPTER

Didi Hirsch Mental Health Services Survivors After Suicide Program (SAS)

Lyn Morris and Norman L. Farberow

Didi Hirsch's Suicide Prevention Center's (SPC) Survivors After Suicide Program (SAS; formerly known as the Los Angeles Survivors After Suicide Program) is a multitasked program specifically designed to provide emotional support and counseling to persons who have lost a loved one to suicide (as opposed to the "survivor" of a nonfatal suicide attempt). The program was initiated in 1981 and grew out of the experiences of the SPC staff in conducting psychological autopsies on suicide and equivocal deaths for the coroner of Los Angeles County. Interviews with the families and other witnesses in investigations of the deaths disclosed a frequently severe emotional impact of the death on the survivors. The SAS program was developed to help survivors resolve their reported feelings of guilt, confusion, and grief.

Referrals to the service have come from announcements to the professional mental health community, self-referrals, previous clients of the service, articles in mental health journals, the Internet, reports in newspapers and magazines, and public presentations by survivor volunteers. The process most often starts with a telephone call to the SAS program coordinator from the prospective client. Details are gathered about the suicide, and information about the program and its group format is offered. The groups, with five to ten members, meet once a week for 90 minutes for 8 weeks. Survivors are identified as anyone who experiences significant emotional distress in the bereavement of a loss by suicide. The loss is usually recent, ranging mostly from 1 week to 6 months, and averaging 3.5 months. Not infrequently, however, the loss may have occurred many years ago, sometimes in the childhood of the adult caller. Group members are usually adults, 18 years of age and older, most often members of the immediate family, such as parents, older children, siblings, extended family members, lovers and/or sweethearts, and, less frequently, close friends, colleagues, or fellow workers. Callers are told when the next group in their area will be starting, and a package is sent consisting of pamphlets describing the service, helpful resources, and a pregroup questionnaire requesting information about the suicide.

Group membership is mixed in terms of age, sex, race, and kinship or relationship. Clinical experience has found the mixture generally to be advantageous in furthering understanding of suicide from the varied points of view that emerge in the meetings. For example, an angry sibling who blamed his parents for the loss of his sister learned from the discussion by the parents in his group of how much pain and effort had gone into their trying to prevent the death; or a gap was bridged as the lover and the suicide's estranged family members revealed the pain of their mutual loss.

The groups are led by a mental health professional and a survivor-facilitator, a survivor who has gone through the group experience and has received training in the group process. The professional directs the group, ensuring each person the opportunity to participate and to share feelings, normalizing feelings and reactions (such as grief, guilt, shame, anger, depression, denial, shock, etc.), offering professional information about suicide and suicide behavior when needed, and monitoring the discussions for indications of unattended medical or physical problems (such as sleep and appetite disruptions) or serious psychological disturbance possibly requiring individual attention or therapy (such as complicated grief, post-traumatic stress disorder, suicidal depression, etc.). The professional also arranges for hospitalization if necessary.

The survivor-facilitator most often is one of the members of a group who has expressed a strong interest in helping other survivors to overcome their grief. In some instances, the survivor may be invited by the professional group leader to serve as a facilitator because he or she has shown empathy and nonjudgmental support for other survivors. The facilitator shares his or her own experiences and suggests through questions or comments the problem areas most frequently encountered. The facilitator also serves as an onsite model for the new group members, providing living "proof" that it is possible to survive the overwhelming feelings of grief, and that a future still exists in which it will be possible to function in society again.

Although topics are scheduled for each of the meetings, the discussion generally emerges spontaneously from the feelings or problems the members want to discuss, or they may emerge from the handouts of publications about suicide and related areas that have been provided to members. The process includes sharing, often as frequently by members as by the leaders, of information, advice, counsel, and guidance for new, unfamiliar experiences, such as social stigma, contacts with the police and the medical examiner/coroner, the need for toxicology and autopsy reports, death certificates, insurance claims, funeral and burial problems, legal and bureaucratic complications, and (sometimes) contacts with the media.

Data for evaluation purposes are collected from each member before entering the group and after the eight sessions. Donations are requested before each session, but no one is excluded because of an inability to pay. In addition to donations from the group sessions, other funding and support are provided by individual donations in memory or in honor of a loved one, grants from United Way of Greater Los Angeles, United Hostess' Charities, and fundraising. At the end of the eight sessions, participants are invited to return to a monthly drop-in group (no fee) led by an experienced facilitator, where the client can discuss new experiences examined in the light of insights gathered from the group. The monthly group also provides evidence of continuing availability and support from the program if needed.

A guiding principle in conducting the group program is the recognition that the participants, for the most part, are regarded as clients, not as patients. Generally, they are functioning, capable people who have been in adequate control of their lives. The suicide of a loved one is frequently a disruptive, catastrophic experience. The individual is faced with what feels like a monumental, overwhelming task of reconstruction. Most participants are not in need of an intensive search for hidden conflicts and obscure dynamics. The group experience allows them to say the word "suicide" without the feeling of stigma often encountered in social exchange, to share with like-minded others experiencing grief, guilt, and shame in a nonjudgmental atmosphere, and to learn a variety of coping attitudes that will reinforce positive changes.

An evaluation of the program was conducted in 1992 (Farberow, 1992). The subjects were 60 participants who had completed the program; 22 survivors who had applied for admission to the program but either did not attend or dropped out after only one session served as a control group. Questionnaires, administered before and after the 8-week program, asked participants to estimate the level of intensity of nine emotions: depression, grief, anxiety, shame, guilt, anger at the deceased, anger at self or others, puzzlement, and own suicidal feelings—at three points in time: retrospectively within the first 4 weeks after the suicide, before the group intervention started, and after the program ended. The results showed no significant differences between the groups in their retrospective ratings of their feelings in the period immediately after the death—all nine feelings were rated high. The ratings as the groups started, 4 to 5 months after the death, significantly decreased in intensity of all feelings for both groups; however, the experimental group reported significantly higher levels of feelings of grief, guilt, and shame than the controls. Postintervention assessment at the end of the program indicated a significant decline on eight of the nine feelings for the experimental group; the controls declined significantly on only one of the feelings (anxiety).

The study indicated that the program had reduced significantly high feelings of guilt, grief, and shame to approximately the same level as the controls. However, slight increases in the levels of depression and confusion for participants significantly differentiated them from the controls. It was possible that the group experience, while helping to diminish the self-blaming feelings of shame and guilt, had also made participants' sadness over the loss feel more current. Also, the repeated discussions of their losses with others in their group had forced participants to recognize that it was unlikely that a satisfactory answer to the question of "why" would ever be reached. A significant question remains as to how long the beneficial impact of the group experience lasts. Needed are follow-up studies at selected intervals, such as 6, 12, and 24 months, to determine levels of feeling, community resources accessed, and the process of adjustment.

☐ Other Services

Telephone Support Counseling (TSC)

Although the SAS support groups are offered on a quarterly basis in five locations in the Los Angeles area, there can be up to a 2-month wait before the next group is started. Understandably, the wait can be distressing and can feel like an eternity to a survivor reaching out for resources and support. The SAS program coordinator offers telephone support counseling to those survivors who have to wait until the next SAS support group begins. If the survivor accepts, the coordinator partners him or her with a telephone support counselor with whom the survivor can consult during the waiting period. The counselor is a survivor who has completed the SAS 8-week support program and has received "facilitator" training in providing emotional support for new survivors. The counselor is provided with all the contact information obtained during the survivor's first call, including the type of loss experienced. The counselor will contact the survivor within 24 to 48 hours and begin a dialogue with the survivor that continues until the group begins. It is common that the new survivor will request a TSC counselor with the same type of loss he or she has experienced. Efforts are made to accommodate such requests, based on the availability among the counselors.

During the first call, the counselor will arrange the frequency, time, and length of the calls based on individual situations. Generally, the counseling is offered once a week for an hour, but it can be more or less frequent or longer or shorter depending on the need. For some survivors, the relationship may continue as a friendship, and for others, it fulfills the purpose of getting them through the difficult waiting period. TSC is an integral component to SAS, ensuring every survivor who calls for support has access to services immediately.

Suicide Response Team

The Suicide Response Team (SRT) works in collaboration with the Mayor's Crisis Response Team (CRT) of the City of Los Angeles. The CRT assists police officers faced with crises or emergencies in which emotional aspects are a major feature. A member of the SRT is called to assist the CRT when the situation is one in which a suicide has occurred. The aim of the partnership is to provide comfort, resources, information, and referrals to survivors, assuring them they are not alone with their fresh burden of grief and that help is available.

The process begins with either the police department or the fire department calling the CRT for help in addressing a situation in which there is considerable emotional distress or mental illness. When the problem is suicide, the CRT will activate the SRT by calling the 24-hour crisis line to request an SRT responder. The crisis line shift supervisor will contact the SRT responder who is geographically closest to the scene. The SRT responder goes immediately to the scene and contacts the CRT responder to learn the facts of the situation and determine the best response. All SRT responders have prepackaged envelopes with resources and information to give to the primary survivor or a family member at the close of the callout. Before leaving, the SRT responder asks if the primary survivor would mind a follow-up call within the next 2 weeks to see how they are doing, provide further support, and to assist them in accessing resources.

The SRT responder most often is a volunteer in our Suicide Prevention Center who has expressed a strong interest in helping the survivors of a suicide when the suicide is first discovered or reported. In some instances, a volunteer may be invited by the professional staff to become an SRT responder because he or she has been judged to have the ability to recognize and respond to the heightened emotional impact of a suicide that leaves survivors with feelings that are painful, raw, overwhelming, and shocking. SRT responders need to be easy to talk with, open-minded, and empathic, and must have the emotional stability to handle crises so they can provide support and resources to new survivors.

All SRT responders attend a 1-day training in which they learn coroner and police procedures in handling a situation in which a suicide death has occurred; how to assess family and/or friends for suicidal thoughts; how to deal with the wide variety of grief reactions, which may range from wild, uncontrolled behavior to withdrawn, uncommunicative silence; how to deal with normal grief reactions; and how to manage their own reactions. Debriefing of the SRT responders is provided at the end of each callout, at regular intervals, and when needed.

Suicide Survivor Prevention Outreach

As with the Suicide Prevention Center, the Survivor After Suicide Program receives many requests for education, information, and training. These requests may come in from teachers and or students in community high schools, school psychologists, school nurses, parent-teacher associations, professional and community mental health associations, community crisis agencies, 911 operators, and others. Survivors who have committed themselves to educating the public about suicide provide lectures not only about suicide and its statistics, myths, warning signs, and risk factors, but also about its impact on family, friends, and community. The survivor is able to relate from personal experience the devastating impact of the sudden loss of a spouse, sibling, or child; the ensuing grief and depression; the loss of social support; or the awkwardness of friends who do not know what to say. The aim is to erase the stigma, allowing the cry for help to be made and the capability to respond increased.

Newsletter

Didi Hirsch's SAS program publishes its own quarterly newsletter, which is sent to every survivor, past and present, who has attended the SAS support group. It keeps the survivors connected to each other and the survivor community. The newsletter lists current and coming events of interest to survivors, reports of newsworthy events, helpful resources, and Web sites. Occasionally it will print abstracts of publications about survivorship and/or suicide prevention and reports of pertinent research. Many survivors submit articles sharing memories of their loved one, or sharing coping skills they feel might be helpful to other survivors. Some survivors write beautiful poems honoring their loved ones and expressing their feelings about their loss. The newsletter is not only educational, informative, and interesting, but also heartfelt and touching due to the survivors' personalized contributions.

Survivor Potlucks

Survivors, their families, and friends attend two potlucks held each year, one in the summer and the other in the winter. Each potluck has a theme, such as coping through the holidays, honoring traditions, and sharing words that either were the favorites of their loved ones or were written by them. The survivors share their stories or memories of their loved ones as it relates to the theme.

The potlucks end with a closing ceremony. It may be lighting a candle, attaching a note to a balloon and releasing it into the sky, or giving each survivor a flower to attach to a message, written to his or her loved one, that the survivor reads aloud. Survivors have built relationships and made lifelong connections with other survivors through the potlucks. Survivors who attend the potlucks say they learn from them and that they are inspired by the strength and courage of other survivors.

Alive and Running for Suicide Prevention 5K/10K

The Alive and Running for Suicide Prevention 5K/10K is an annual event that brings together people from all walks of life, young children, expert runners, entire families, and volunteers to call attention to the devastating impact of suicide in the community. The event honors and memorializes the loved ones lost to suicide. Close to 4,000 participants show up on race day to participate in running, walking, or volunteering to bring awareness to the community that suicide is preventable.

☐ Reference

Farberow, N. L. (1992). The Los Angeles Survivors After Suicide Program: An evaluation. *Crisis: Journal of Crisis Intervention and Suicide Prevention, 13*, 23–34.

The Retrospective Profile and the Facilitated Family Retreat

Madelyn Schwartz

The Retrospective Profile (RP) and the Facilitated Family Retreat (FFR) grew out of my work as a coroner's death investigator and my subsequent interactions with survivors of suicide. The RP is an expanded psychological autopsy (a contemporary adaptation of the psychological autopsy work of Edwin Shneidman and colleagues, e.g., Shneidman & Farberow, 1961), which has evolved over time from being an interview between the investigator and one to two individuals at a time, to the broader context of the extended family and those whom they would invite to join the conversation. It has been used effectively for more than 15 years as both an investigative tool in the examination of known suicides as well as equivocal deaths, and as a means to help families understand what was likely to have been happening in the life of a loved one to cause that person to opt for suicide. The FFR is an original concept I developed after years of working with survivors of suicide. It combines a contemporary version of the model of the psychological autopsy with group process and grief counseling theory to create a safe haven for survivors to explore their emotions, history, and knowledge of and interconnectedness with the deceased individual and each other. FFR arose as a response to the request of a survivor for a family intervention after the suicide death of her brother. The RP is used as the means of accumulating information in the larger context of a gathering of numerous individuals who knew the decedent, and the information is processed with everyone present.

Although the psychological autopsy has been used primarily as either a research or a risk assessment tool, when conducted with understanding and empathy, it also functions extremely well as a step in the healing process for survivors of suicide. If a person's life is viewed as a three-dimensional jigsaw puzzle, family members often are familiar with the pieces around or near the center, but do not necessarily know how they fit together, or what the larger puzzle looks like. They may not realize how or why the colors and patterns change from one side of the picture to the other. Further, they may not even know how big the puzzle really is, what the overall picture represents, or whether they have the most vital pieces. Where a forensic autopsy is a deconstruction of the body to draw conclusions about how a death occurred, the psychological autopsy is a reconstruction of all known historical data, current events, relationships, physical and emotional health status, psychopathology, substance use, and lifestyle values of the deceased person. When this information is laid out by a knowledgeable facilitator, the triggers and underlying issues preceding the suicidal event frequently become apparent, similar to the way the picture of the puzzle emerges when enough pieces are fit together.

Over time, the original assessment tool has grown from 12 to more than 400 questions, to accommodate my growing understanding of the myriad puzzle pieces that could be operational for any given individual. These questions are intended to tweeze out information about individuals' relationships with themselves and with the world around them. A forensic pathologist criticized the term "psychological autopsy," and in deference to that objection, the tool was renamed the Retrospective Profile. After seeing the value of interpreting the information as it is received, and in the context of the relationship of the person being interviewed, the format of the FFR was developed to offer the same explorative and healing opportunity to family systems. The RP is used as the means to draw out information from those attending the FFR.

The FFR provides a comprehensive system within which we can begin to understand the impact of suicide on individuals and families, and on kinship systems as a whole. Participants gain insights into their own worldview and the shared and differing perceptions of the family unit(s), and develop tools for recognizing and taking action regarding the potential suicidality of other family members or friends. Using the RP, workshop participants are assisted in an exploration of their unique relationships with the deceased person. Their observations and knowledge of the deceased person's psychological well-being, cognitive functioning, physical health, and social and spiritual connectedness to others and to self at the time of and prior to death are examined. When the answers to the questions of the RP are laid out, the triggers and underlying issues preceding the suicide frequently become apparent.

The FFR can be offered as either a 1-day or 2-day seminar for families and/or extended kinship networks healing from the tragedy of suicide. It is conducted in modules and can be customized to work for the needs of the group. Participants gather in a safe and neutral environment of their own choosing to learn, share, hold, and understand the energy of what they have experienced in the context of their relationships with the decedent, each other, and themselves. They are encouraged to bring their own stories, feelings and perceptions, memories, and mementos to share. They explore what is reasonable to expect of each other, learn skills to assist and support each other through any future difficult times, and obtain information about additional resources that may exist within the family and community.

During the first module, participants check in and are welcomed to the event. The reasons for gathering are discussed, as well as the priorities of the workshop, and the agenda is set for the rest of the time together. Ground rules for group process and issues of confidentiality are discussed at the beginning of the retreat. The specific agenda is developed through consensus of participants with input from the facilitators. Residual questions about the process are addressed. The deceased individual is acknowledged as the reason for the gathering, and any tangible items brought by participants are gathered and set out in a collage of the deceased person's life.

The next module involves doing "the work." Using the psychological autopsy as the rubric through which information is gathered, the facilitators engage various psychological models (theoretical models include attachment theory, behavioral, cognitive and humanistic approaches, gestalt, lifespan and family systems theories, psychoanalysis, and others) for individual and group dynamics to guide the participants, provide interventions as needed, and create a context for honest expression of feelings and perceptions. Handout materials, books, and bibliographies about grief after suicide and its aftermath are made available. Psychodynamic educational information, guided meditation, art, and creation of ritual by and for the family are included, as appropriate and desired by the group.

Many of us wear slightly different hats in the diverse roles we play: at home as a partner or a parent; as an employee or employer; or as a friend, student, acquaintance, parishioner, client, and so forth. Sometimes, information about one aspect of a person's life—how they handled the news of an imminent layoff, a friend's death, a lawsuit, a medical diagnosis—is known only by those in a specific area of one's life. Young people in particular often have lives with their friends that may differ considerably from the lives they maintain with their families. Confidences are not always shared with those with whom we live closest—out of fear; to protect others; or due to confusion, lack of communication skills, substance abuse, or a myriad of other reasons. The facilitator is a trained neutral and objective observer of the facts of the deceased person's life.

The RP consists of a series of questions about a person who has died by possible suicidal means. The questions serve as an outline to assess the physical health, psychological well-being, cognitive functioning, and social and spiritual connectedness of an individual. Many other ideas and directions will arise from the answers, and the facilitators must be astute enough to follow leads provided by a statement, an off-hand remark, a tangential topic, or the body language of participants. Family members, friends, coworkers, physicians, teachers, therapists, mentors, and clergy are all appropriate resources to ask to be members of a retreat.

The RP can be used regardless of the deceased person's age. Clearly, some of the questions might not be appropriate for all individuals, and younger persons might not have had enough life experience for some of the questions to be applicable to their life and death. A version of the RP was developed with the intention of using it with the peers of younger people (under the age of 16). Although the breadth of the questionnaire is limited, the questions are straightforward and more simply worded. Teenagers are often not given credit for the depth of their emotions, the commitments they feel in their friendships, or their need for interconnectedness. The abridged profile seeks to address these feelings and concerns without appearing to talk down to or override the very real and potent passions and emotions inherent in younger people.

The inclusion of minors in the retreat *must* be at the discretion of their parents. Although some young people are mature enough to understand the implications of suicide, others might be further traumatized by a frank discussion of what went on prior to the death. An alternative to the retreat being done strictly for family and adult friends would be to do an abridged version for only the young friends of a minor deceased individual. In this case, parental permission *must* be obtained for each attendee. The best retreat would be one where the young people felt safe enough to be open and expressive. This often means the absence of adults, with the exception of the retreat facilitators and perhaps a school counselor or other adult accepted by the majority of the young attendees. As in the adult retreat, attention would have to be paid to the responses of individuals to questions and discussions. If a particular individual exhibits behaviors of concern, follow-up with the appropriate resources would be highly recommended.

The facilitators help the family and friends fill in the missing pieces of the puzzle. This is not simply a "memory" event, but rather an active verbalization and collection process. During the FFR, the RP ultimately assists participants in uncovering evidence for how a decision was arrived at by sharing what they know about the decedent. Personality traits or patterns of behavior not obvious to family members or close friends might be revealed. Historical information that set behaviors into motion may surface. The information inherent in this discussion is not always positive, and there may be adverse reactions to details previously unknown by some present at the event. Parents, spouses, and siblings often do not know or see their loved one away from the orbit of the family. Information about an individual from several sources gives family members a more global perspective of what factors motivated the decision to stop living.

The RP does not assign blame or responsibility, although in the course of a retreat, a family member or friend, coworker, physician, or other individual may see something they construe as such. The skills of the facilitators become critical if someone begins to take on responsibility for the suicidal event. A thorough working knowledge of suicidology by facilitators can safeguard a sense of appropriate grief and connection, and potentially intercept a spiral into a more serious depression. Facilitators work in tandem with each other, such that one of them is always observing the group and noting any signs of distress in the group members.

Group facilitators provide mirroring, deepening of meanings and understandings, gentle confrontation, and clarity to group members within the context of the RP as the basis for all discussion with the retreat attendees. Answers to the questions in the profile are tracked and collated, to be fed back to the group as the puzzle comes together. Family dynamics and individual values and priorities are acknowledged and addressed in terms of the family system. Myths and fallacies about suicide are focused upon as they arise. If time allows, private individual or family sessions can be made available by appointment and are strictly confidential. When participants' addresses are provided in advance, the names of therapists in their area who specialize in supporting survivors in their healing after a suicide may be made available.

A closing ritual created by the facilitators at the end of the retreat draws on all the information that has come forth. If the group is so inclined, guided or reflective meditations may be included, as well as art projects and ceremonies about letting go and achieving closure. Examples of rituals used have been the use of a talking stick, passed to all attendees to allow them to address the group and the facilitators; a bowl has also been passed around to be filled metaphorically by those who choose to. Family members and friends have been encouraged to write letters, draw their heartfelt feelings, or otherwise express their emotions to the decedent, each other, and themselves. The goal is to assist participants to feel they have come to the end of a journey of exploration within themselves and the larger community.

Currently, there is no organizational structure to the program, nor is it administered by any definitive entity. When a death by suicidal means is investigated by the county coroner's office, I am available to the family for a more in-depth look at the decedent's life and choices. This can be done informally as part of the investigation, or formally as a retreat, as the family wishes. The most significant obstacle to getting the program up and running has been the apparent reluctance of many families to take an in-depth look at the decedent, the individual relationships he or she had with family members and friends, and the functionality, or lack thereof, of the family system. At times, several members of a family will want to do the workshop, but when other members object or make excuses, they back down. The taboos about suicide are still in play: For many people, the idea of speaking about the private matters of the decedent or the family system, and the fear of exposure are not overcome, even within the context of a "safe" and confidential retreat environment.

The retreat is staffed by facilitators who must have a familiarity and comfort level with the medical examiner's or coroner's investigative report, as well as with the content and use of the RP. It is imperative that anyone who leads this kind of seminar be able to easily understand and interpret, for lay individuals, the potentially graphic language of a forensic investigation, while simultaneously reading and responding to the needs of those gathered for the program. A background in forensics, group process, suicidology and grief counseling, systems, and developmental psychology is extremely helpful. Having at least two facilitators (depending on the size of the group)—one to be speaking, eliciting information, interpreting and teaching, while the other watches, supports, and responds to those at the event—is imperative. Facilitators trade roles throughout the program, always playing off each other, explaining information as they progress through the facts, and coaching when necessary, as they support participants working through their emotions.

Other hurdles that must be overcome are the time and cost of producing such a workshop, and the training necessary to be able to run one. No family has ever been charged for the proceedings. The facilitators have donated their time, knowledge, and energy to the program. Grants have been considered; however, because the program is not affiliated with a university or mental health agency, it has been difficult to identify funding sources. Costs affiliated with the program can be kept minimal, depending on who is organizing the event and how resourceful they are willing to be. The author has found restaurants willing to donate private rooms and light snacks, as well as families willing to host a 1-day event in their home.

The time involved in developing the concept and curricula for both the RP and the FFR has been donated by the author, and all of the training has been on the job. One other facilitator has been trained to date. The retreats are always labor intensive. Thus far, more than 80 RPs and 5 FFRs have been conducted. There has been no systematic evaluation of the efficacy of either of the programs, but the feedback from 85%–90% of the participants has been that, although often extremely difficult, the program was worth doing. The author acknowledges a formal evaluation would be of great value. Since these programs have always been evolving, ideas, suggestions, and feedback are welcome.

☐ Examples of the Program

One of the first, informal retreats was held in a private area of a local restaurant, where seven friends of a decedent gathered with the author to talk about their thoughts, feelings, and perceptions of their friend. The answers to questions about her family history, academic, psychosocial and spiritual connectedness, and medical and psychological health issues gelled into a palpable image of her as an extremely depressed individual. As the discussion ranged over the depth and breadth of each participant's relationships, and as participants individually and collectively expressed regrets about not having recognized the extent of their friend's suicidality, I was able to paint the multiple emotional and cognitive dimensions of the decedent in a way that made sense and answered many of their "why" questions. Participants left the meeting feeling more informed and perhaps less guilty and angry than they had been earlier. Several years later, I was introduced to a version of the psychological autopsy, which was presented as a risk assessment instrument in a counseling center where a client had died by suicide. It was clearly the beginning of an exploratory tool for the investigation of deaths from potentially suicidal means.

In a second example, the death of a 32-year-old male at his parents' home left the extended family upset and shaken. He was the second-youngest child of five, and was living with his parents after release from a drug and alcohol treatment center. His eldest sister discovered him deceased in his childhood bedroom, with a bottle of hard liquor and several empty pill containers nearby. No note was found. The parents, who were in their seventies, refused to believe his death was a suicide, and insisted it was an accidental overdose. The sister, with the support of two of her three surviving siblings, requested the profile and family retreat to uncover more information and thus assist with an accurate determination of the cause and manner of death. The profile and retreat were conducted at the family's home within 5 days of the death, with the parents, two sisters, and two brothers in attendance.

As we went through the questions in the RP, the family dynamics became very clear. The mother was the undisputed head-of-household. The father preferred to defer to her rather than risk her substantial anger. The eldest sister was an almost histrionic advocate for understanding her deceased brother's motivations for dying. The youngest, a brother only 1 or 2 years younger than the decedent, staunchly supported his mother's contempt for the proceedings. The other brother and sister, along with the eldest, were 12 to 15 years older and quiet, but nonetheless supported their sister in wanting to understand what had happened.

Several hours into the discussion, and with much stonewalling by the mother, it was clear to the author there were family secrets that were not being addressed. The eldest sister was becoming increasingly emotional as her father withdrew and her mother insisted they were a normal, loving family, and that her son's death was an accident. He simply succumbed to his unwillingness to step up to the proverbial plate and take responsibility for his life. Whenever one of the other older siblings attempted to support the eldest sister, he or she was increasingly and rudely shot down by the mother and youngest son. Gentle prodding to go deeper was clearly not working. In an effort to break through some of the denial, the eldest sister was asked what was behind her questions and assumptions. She started screaming at her mother, lost what remained of her frazzled emotional control, and ran from the room sobbing. The mother interrupted her other daughter as she started to speak, and turned on the facilitators as the perceived enemy. We were given 5 minutes to pack up and leave the premises or there would be unnamed "consequences." We left.

The older brother and sister followed us out to our vehicle and apologized for the way things had fallen apart. We were starting to say that sometimes happens, when the sister interrupted. She then disclosed the family secret: Her eldest sister was in fact the mother of the decedent. Her pregnancy was due to incest by another family member, and the pregnancy was hidden from the rest of the family and community. The baby was adopted at birth and raised by the parents as one of their own, with the youngest brother conceived potentially to justify late-in-life childbearing. As an adult, the eldest sister eventually sought counseling and, in an effort to come to terms with her past, had disclosed to her "brother" that he was in fact her son. Already an alcoholic with other substance abuse issues, she feared this may have pushed him over an emotional edge, hence her own histrionic affect. The mother, who had long ago assumed the mantle of maternal responsibility, was furious when her daughter divulged she had sought healing for an act that had long ago supposedly been put to rest by the adoption. When she found out her daughter had disclosed the true relationship to her brother/son, the mother disowned her daughter and held her responsible for her "son's" death, which she insisted was an accidental overdose. Although this family information was not included in the official investigative report, the death certificate as signed indicated the cause of death as an acute intoxication of alcohol and prescription drugs. Manner of death was determined to be suicide. No further contact was initiated with the family. A one-line thank-you note was received about a month later from the eldest sister.

☐ Reference

Shneidman, E. S., & Farberow, N. L. (1961). Sample investigations of equivocal suicidal deaths. In N. L. Farberow & E. S. Shneidman (Eds.), *The cry for help* (pp. 118–128). New York, NY: McGraw-Hill.

CHAPTER 21

Parents of Suicides–Friends & Families of Suicides Internet Community

Karyl Chastain Beal

What would you do if your son or daughter had taken his or her life, and you somehow knew that a key to your survival was connecting with others whose losses were just like yours? In 1998, a small group of parents whose lives had been devastated by the suicide death of their children found each other on the Internet and banded together. They formed a small e-mail support "group" on October 9, 1998. Their mission was day-to-day survival, nothing more. They voted on the name for the group; Parents of Suicides (POS) won. The mission of POS is to offer understanding, support, information, connections, and hope to parents bereaved by suicide.

Word spread, and other bereaved parents found the group and joined. The members were not just from the United States; they came from Australia, Brazil, Canada, the United Kingdom, Ireland, Jamaica, Luxembourg, New Zealand, France, Germany, Israel, the Philippines, Poland, Spain, South Africa, and Zimbabwe. In June 2010, the membership of POS was about 750.

One main challenge in the early years of POS was turning people away. Friends, siblings, spouses, cousins, in-laws, grandparents, and other family members applied to join the group. Many were upset when they were not accepted as members, so on September 30, 2000, a second e-mail group was started. It was named Friends & Families of Suicides (FFOS), and its mission was to serve anyone whose life had been affected by the suicide of someone for whom they cared. In June 2010, the membership of FFOS was about 425.

Many people are unfamiliar with e-mail support groups and how they compare to face-to-face support groups. Basically, both groups have the same general purpose. There are leaders or facilitators, and there are members who are at various places along the way in their grief, sharing, discussing, listening, and encouraging each other. Face-to-face groups allow people to look each other in the eye, to actually hug each other, and to sit and cry together. E-mail groups allow people to read or write to the group when it is convenient for them. Also, e-mail group members may connect with others at 2 a.m., dressed in their pajamas and slippers, if they wish.

In addition to mode of connection, several differences affect the interaction of the members. First, face-to-face groups generally have a small number of attendees, with 5 to 20 being average. In online groups, hundreds of people may be connecting. Next, in a face-to-face group, most attendees have similar backgrounds. They may attend the same churches, work together, or share similar social and cultural views. The online community, however, connects its members with people whose lives may be very different culturally, religiously, and socially. Finally, some people may prefer an online connection because they get a fresh start with people who may not already have negative views about them or the person who died.

☐ Membership in an E-mail Group

Most people learn about e-mail groups through search engines, Web site links, or referrals from counselors or friends. Membership in both POS and FFOS is restricted to adults; no minors are allowed. In POS, the person must be a birth or adoptive parent. Although stepparents are not allowed in POS, they are welcome in FFOS, along with anyone else who has lost someone to suicide.

Anyone who wants to join either of the groups must complete an application through the group Web site or by e-mail and return it to the administrator. A prospective member must use his/her real name, and must list the state (or country) in which he or she lives. If there is any doubt about validity, the administrator may ask for more information before giving approval to join the group.

After an application is approved, the person is sent an invitation through the group service (Yahoo! Groups). She or he must follow the directions on the invitation to sign up. The administrator will then send a message out introducing the new person to the group. As new members join, they are sent several messages to help them become oriented to the group. The volume of messages is typically about 3,400 messages through POS each month and approximately 1,250 through FFOS. Members are given options for the manner in which they want their messages delivered. Most people choose regular e-mail. However, for those who do not want a large amount of e-mail, there is a "digest" option. Choosing digest means that group messages are collected by Yahoo! Groups and sent periodically in single, combined e-mails that hold about 25 messages each. A third option people sometimes use if they want to take a break or want a lighter connection is called Special Notices. People who opt for Special Notices do not receive regular messages from the group. They receive *only* group announcements and the e-newsletters.

The messages sent through the group are the key to the connection. The members write about the person they lost to suicide and their experiences and feelings. They discuss issues unique to suicide; issues they cannot discuss with other people. They rant and rave. Inspirational and educational materials are also sent through the group regularly, and each day, a thought-provoking question is sent for discussion. Most important, the group members read and listen, then write replies to offer help and support to each other.

☐ POS–FFOS Internet Community

POS and FFOS have grown to be much more than two separate e-mail groups. They have become thriving communities of people who connect in a variety of ways, who take on meaningful projects together, and who sometimes express a sense of belonging to an extended family. Among these are the following projects and activities.

Memorial Web Site

A memorial Web site was created for POS in November 1999 and another for FFOS in 2001 by one of the members. The two Web sites were later merged into a new Web site, http://www.pos-ffos.com. The Web site now serves as a clearinghouse with a variety of memorials and resources.

E-newsletter and Private Chat Room

Another distinctive service volunteers create for each of the groups is an e-newsletter. *The Butterfly Net* is published biweekly for POS, and *Journey of Peace* is published monthly for FFOS members. The members of the groups can meet in a private chat room to socialize with others or to participate in special programs, such as the Holiday Remembrance Chat each December.

Retreats

Retreats are held for members of the groups each spring and fall in Columbia, Tennessee. These informal gatherings provide an opportunity for members to meet each other in person and to participate in face-to-face sharing circles and other significant activities.

Memorial Projects

The members of the groups have also joined together to create several special memorial projects. For example, in 2004, 2007, and 2009, hard-back memorial cookbooks were published. In 2005, members published a professional-quality memorial book, and volunteers from the groups have created eight memorial quilts.

Another memorial project of the groups was the establishment of the International Suicide Memorial Wall, located in Columbia, Tennessee. The Wall currently holds almost 500 memorial tiles with names, dates, locations, and photos. The memorial is on private property and is open to viewing by appointment only. A photo and list of names of those on the International Suicide Memorial Wall can be seen at http://www.posffos .com/memorials/names.htm

Other Web Sites and Groups

The group members have also created and maintain several other Web sites to further the mission of suicide awareness, grief support, and education. *The Suicide Memorial Wall* (http://www.suicidememorialwall.com) was created in 2001, *The Suicide Grief Support Forum* (http://www.suicidegrief.com) began in 2002, and the *Faces of Suicide* site (http://www.facesofsuicide.com) started in 2007.

Some of the members also lead small partner groups, which were created to meet a specific focus of other members, in several cases not specific to suicide loss. The partner groups are:

- AUNZ–POS and AUNZ–FFOS are for people who are bereaved by suicide and live in Australia and New Zealand.

- POS–Christian Sharing (POS–CS) is for members who wish to discuss the specifics of their Christian faith as they grieve.

- Parents Forever (PF) is for members who are at least 3 years away from the death of their children and who are ready to focus on living again. The group is not specific to suicide.

- Still Our Children (SOC) serves members whose sons or daughters suffered from symptoms of schizophrenia.

- Mourning Our Brothers & Sisters (MOBS) is a group for adults whose siblings have died. MOBS is not specific to suicide.

- Distant Drums (DD) is for Native Americans or Canadian Aboriginals who have lost someone to suicide.

☐ Leadership

One reason for the effectiveness of the groups is the fact that many of the "older" members stay connected to the group. More specifically, 30 members who joined POS during its first year still belong. The charter members help keep the group stabilized and focused. They also offer the priceless gift of experience.

Another reason the groups are so effective can be attributed to a solid core of extraordinary volunteers and moderators who tend to everything. They are the people who take care of the extra Web sites and groups. They are the people who do the work behind the scenes to help meet the needs of all of the other members. They help monitor all group activities, including the chat room. They serve as mentors to newer members, reaching out gently with understanding and compassion. About 40 dedicated volunteers and moderators are the heart of both POS and FFOS.

☐ Special Issues

After almost 12 years of existence, the POS–FFOS Internet Community has grown in size and complexity. Some of the special issues that affect the group are listed below.

- Activism. Some of the group members become inspired to help others and make a difference in memory of the person who died. Through the group, they find out about local, state, and national suicide prevention organizations and join them. Some of them promote suicide prevention in their own communities.

- Participation. About 10% of the members participate by writing to the group regularly. Newer members tend to read every message that comes through the group. After a while, however, most members become a little more selective; they identify the messages that interest them the most or meet their needs, and they delete the other messages. Many members say that even if they do not read or write to the group, just having the connection available in case they feel the need to communicate is important.

- Conflicts. Considering the size, diversity, and activity of the groups, it is amazing there are very few significant problems within the membership. From time to time, minor conflicts may develop, mostly due to communication problems rather than malicious intent. Moderators work privately with the members involved to resolve these issues.

- Boundaries. Some members of the group may suffer from mental illness, addiction, or other problems that are beyond the scope of the group or with which the group cannot deal. Moderators and designated volunteers understand that they are not professionals, and they may not give advice. They also encourage people to seek professional help when needed.

- Private information. Members are not required to provide their home phone numbers and addresses to join the group, but many do submit contact information voluntarily. This information is kept in a confidential file that is available only to moderators.

- Crises. From time to time, members admit to having suicidal thoughts that may be beyond their control. Moderators are prepared to call emergency services to help, and they sometimes do.

- Leaving the group. Some members stay a few months, while others may stay involved a few years and then decide they do not need the group any longer, so they leave. It is not uncommon for members to leave the group and then rejoin later.

- Cost. The POS–FFOS community is completely volunteer driven, so no fees are charged, and no money is solicited. No one within the groups is paid for services. The money needed to maintain the Web site domain names and hosting costs comes from small private donations.

☐ Research and Evaluation

Members of the groups have participated in several informal surveys designed to evaluate the group during the years. The most comprehensive research has been conducted by William Feigelman, PhD, of Nassau Community College, New York, during 2007. Summaries of the research were shared with the group, and research findings were published in a professional journal and national organization newsletter (Feigelman, 2007; Feigelman, Gorman, Beal, & Jordan, 2008). Informal survey results were also shared with the group, and some of the recommendations were implemented.

The POS–FFOS Internet Community is continuously evolving. Frequent and regular evaluation of the group's effectiveness is needed for continued growth. The rising popularity of Internet social networks is having a subtle impact on the group. This is an issue that may be of particular interest for research because some of the members now use these other sites to communicate with each other.

☐ Suggestions

Advice to someone else who wants to start an Internet group or community follows.

- Identify the group mission clearly and focus on it.

- Make sure you are willing and able to commit time and effort to establishing and building the group, and that you are committed to it for a long time before you begin.

- Some people instinctively understand the dynamics of support group facilitation, but for most people, formal training and similar experience are the keys to good leadership. The same guidelines for face-to-face group facilitation will generally work with online groups as well.

- Do not argue with group members, and never reply to them with sarcasm or disrespect.

- Give other members of the group opportunities to be involved, and mentor and communicate regularly with those who are willing to help.

- Resolve most of your own issues before you try to lead others. The group should not be about you.

☐ References

Feigelman, W. (2007). Research update: Internet support groups for survivors of suicide. *Surviving Suicide* (quarterly newsletter of the American Association of Suicidology), *19*(4), 1, 8–9.

Feigelman, W., Gorman, B. S., Beal, K. C., & Jordan, J. R. (2008). Internet support groups for suicide survivors: A new mode for gaining bereavement assistance. *Omega: Journal of Death and Dying, 57,* 217–243.

Loving Outreach to Survivors of Suicide (LOSS) Program
A Postvention Service for Survivors of Suicide

Charles T. Rubey

☐ How LOSS Began

Toward the end of 1978, three couples met at a group called Compassionate Friends, an international support group for parents grieving the loss of a child from an accident, terminal illness, SIDS, or any other means (http://www.compassionatefriends.org). These three couples—Carol and Ernie Fluder, Elsie and Joe Settanni, and Marie and Bill Churchill—all had lost a child from suicide. They formed a natural bond and developed their own informal support group. One of the couples had a sister who worked at the Catholic Charities of the Archdiocese of Chicago (http://www.catholiccharities.net). They approached her and mentioned that the Catholic Charities should do something special for people grieving the death of a loved one from suicide. Although these three couples felt that they had a lot in common with the other parents of Compassionate Friends, they felt there was something different about their loss, as suicide presents a set of issues that other grieving parents do not have to grapple with, such as guilt, shame, or embarrassment.

The couples approached the Catholic Charities with the issue, and Father Charles T. Rubey, Director of Mental Services of the Catholic Charities at the time, was given the assignment. He began meeting with these three couples and challenged them as to why a separate group should be formed. The issues that they presented convinced him that a special organization should be formed because suicide was different from death by other means. Thus, LOSS was born and began meeting in the homes of the various participants. The meetings were run by Father Rubey with the active participation of the three founding couples and other survivors of a death by suicide. The meetings were held on Sunday evenings beginning at 7:00 P.M. and lasted about 2 hours. A short break in the middle of the meetings allowed people to talk informally and take a break from the emotional heaviness of the meeting. After a time, the meetings were moved to a local Catholic parish to give the group a more public identification. At about the same time, another meeting on the southwest side of Chicago was initiated because of the proliferation of the phenomenon of suicide that was beginning to grip our society. This meeting was held at a Catholic parish on the southwest side of Chicago. Some members wanted to give the organization a name. A few names were suggested, and Elaine Fluder came up with "Loving Outreach to Survivors of Suicide." The group now had a name: LOSS.

☐ Purpose of the Group

One of the main purposes of this group is to create a safe environment for people to engage in the journey of grief. This is particularly important because grief from suicide is different from grief associated with other forms of death. People who come to the LOSS group have a very safe environment in which they can express their feelings. They are not told what to feel or how to feel. Rather, they are allowed to express any feelings without being judged or told that the feeling is not appropriate. Feelings are neither right nor wrong. They are just feelings, and people have a right to their personal feelings without worrying that they might be judged negatively. The environment is nonjudgmental and nurturing. It is up to the facilitator and the clinician to maintain that type of an environment.

☐ Evolution of LOSS

In addition to the group experience, some members expressed a need to receive individual counseling. There were issues that they wanted to address, but they felt uncomfortable discussing these issues with the group. Some issues might be too personal, and the need for privacy was paramount. Other issues might be limited to a particular family, and to avoid wasting the time of the other group members, the family sought individual counseling. These individual sessions proved to be productive. In addition, some people are frightened by the concept of group interaction. They are private people by nature, and the thought of addressing such a personal experience as a suicide in front of a group of strangers can be overwhelming. Such individuals often suffer alone, in the privacy of their homes, and in the company of their families. Realizing the needs of the range of suicide survivors, LOSS began offering individual counseling as part of the overall program.

To keep track of the various people calling for inquiries about the program, a mailing list was compiled and a monthly reminder provided about the meetings in terms of location and time. Originally, the reminder was in the form of a postcard. However, some members would submit articles that they felt were helpful for the group. As there was not much written at that time, any article was of great interest to group members. The postcard evolved into a letter as well as an enclosed article for the members to read and use as a point of discussion at the meeting. As LOSS grew, more people were calling in for information, and the mailing list expanded. The monthly newsletter became part of the structure of the program.

The name of the monthly newsletter is *Obelisk*. The name was chosen as a symbol for the LOSS Program to describe the grief process. This symbol came from the definition of an obelisk: a solid, upright, four-sided pillar gradually tapering as it rises. Obelisks are rare structures that can be seen rising above the landscape. The most famous obelisk in the United States is the Washington Monument in Washington, DC.

The original obelisks were erected in Egypt. The monuments were constructed by many people working together to pull a single block of granite into place. Writings were carved into the stone on the sides of the obelisk, recording battles and victories of great kings as a permanent testimony to the rulers of ancient Egypt. The LOSS *Obelisk* contains the writings of survivors and survivor-related issues. This is a record of the struggles, and the battle to survive. It represents the support that is gained from meeting with other survivors so that survivors are not alone on their journey of grief. As strength is gained, the grief tapers off, spirits rise, and survivors are able to look up again and to have hope for the future.

By the time the newsletter was developed, one person could no longer handle all of the requests for individual counseling and another counselor was added to the program on a part-time basis. As time went on, the two counselors talked and discovered a common theme woven into many of the individual sessions. A discussion followed about how the individual sessions could be folded into group discussions, not as a substitute for the individual counseling, but in addition to the individual sessions. These groups would meet on a weekly basis and be more structured than the regular monthly meetings. Further, these groups would be an interim resource between the monthly meetings and the individual sessions. The weekly sessions would be chaired by the clinicians.

From the beginning, it was always the dream of Father Rubey to have a survivor on the staff who would be the first person to speak to those seeking help from LOSS. The thinking behind this was that no one knows the visceral reaction to a death from suicide better than another survivor. That is a very special but unwanted "gift" that goes with losing a loved one to suicide. Therefore, a position was created for a survivor whose responsibility would be to listen and care for those who called to inquire about LOSS services. The person hired for this position also had the creative skills to further develop the monthly reminder about the meetings into a newsletter specifically geared to survivors of a suicide. The articles and information would be suicide-related to better acquaint readers about mental illness, suicide, and issues surrounding grief.

Simultaneous to the hiring of a survivor was the idea that the meetings should be led/facilitated by survivors. The program began selecting some survivors who might be good leaders and had skills that could be used in the groups. They would have to be 2 years removed from their own experience with a suicide. It was believed that sooner than that would be too much for them to handle emotionally. They would be exposed to some very basic information and training regarding running a meeting and other information germane to the group. In addition, they would facilitate the meetings and make sure they began on time and had structure. They would work hand-in-hand with the clinician who would be present at all of the meetings. The facilitator training sessions would take place on a weekly basis, with five or six sessions in all. At the completion of the training, each facilitator would be given a certificate of completion. The facilitators have been as integral to the program as the clinicians. Facilitators and clinicians work well together and have a mutual respect for one another.

☐ **Purpose of LOSS**

Many segments of society expect survivors to "get over" the loss of a loved one from suicide. The expected time for this process to be completed might range from a few months to a year. It is our opinion that grief goes on throughout the lifetime of survivors. In other words, survivors are never finished with grief work. That does not mean that survivors feel the intense feelings of grief for the rest of their lives. From the experiences of Father Rubey, there seem to be steps in the grief process, and the first step is typically a period of very intense and extremely raw pain. This is the most critical period of the journey. After much work and time, the tasks of this stage of grief are accomplished.

The second critical step is the accepting of the death and absorbing the loss and calling it what it is—a suicide. As a third step, survivors must learn to express the myriad feelings that accompany their loss. Among those feelings are guilt, anger, and shame or embarrassment, as well as a feeling of abandonment. The next step is the acceptance of the fact that this loss is permanent and determining how the survivor is going to go on with life.

The last step in the initial stage of the grief journey is the incorporation of this loss into one's psychic system and moving on with one's life. The survivor moves on to the other stages of grief. The pain becomes less intense, and over time, ordinary, in that it is not so piercing, and just an aching pain. The main message to survivors is that while the pain is never completely over, it does diminish, and a survivor is able to resume living and feel pleasure and happiness. The loss is always going to be there, and it is important for survivors to know that. They do not "get over" the experience. Instead, they learn to live with it. Survivors have a choice in addressing their grief. They can look upon this experience as either their enemy or their companion. If it is going to be their enemy, then they will fight it and try to flee from it. LOSS tries to assist survivors on the journey of grief to look upon the pain as their companion. Pain will be there, and the best way to survive is to develop a comfort level with this companion. Survivors do not have to like it, but they must realize that it will be present.

☐ **Role of Rituals**

One of survivors' greatest fears is that their loved ones will fade from memory and their very existence forgotten as if they never existed.

Most major religions have rituals that make God present during a ceremony or event. Such ritualistic activities may include attending Catholic Masses, Jewish Shabbat services, or Islamic Friday prayers; reading from the Bible; or being cleansed at a sacred river. The purpose of the ritual is to make participants aware of God in their lives. It could be God, Yahweh, Allah, or some other deity, but the rituals address the fact that the deity is important and sovereign to the worshippers. The deity is remembered in a special sacred way, and the worshippers commune with this deity in a deep prayerful way and remember the importance of this deity in their lives. Similarly, to make certain that loved ones will not be forgotten, rituals can be employed to ensure that the loved ones will be a part of a family's gathering for special occasions. Initially, the rituals can be uncomfortable and painful, but as time goes on, they become part of a family getting together. A ritual can be simple, such as a favorite song of the one who has died or reading a poem. It might be a toast made before dinner or serving the favorite dessert of the deceased. It can be religious or secular, depending on the practices of those participating. The ritual makes present the one who has died by suicide. A tragedy worse than a loved one's suicide death (if a survivor can imagine something worse) would be for that loved one to be forgotten. As long as loved ones are remembered through the performing of a ritual, they will never be forgotten at family gatherings. They are still part of the family, and they should be treated as such.

☐ The LOSS Model

The reason that the LOSS program has been so successful is that there has been a dynamic working relationship between the clinician and the facilitator. No meeting takes place without both positions being present. In fact, usually there are two survivor facilitators and one clinician. The leaders work out their respective roles, and there is a mutual respect between the roles. The facilitators lead the meetings, and the clinician answers any technical questions that might arise and ensures the group dynamics are followed and respected. The clinician and facilitators are active participants, working together to keep the meeting flowing and getting as much group participation as possible. Consistent with the LOSS model, they make sure that the environment is conducive to helping the members feel safe and nurtured. This principle is one of the main reasons that LOSS has been successful and endured for 30 years.

☐ Addenda

As noted above, LOSS is a program of the Catholic Charities of the Archdiocese of Chicago. There is great value in a survivor group being connected with a larger organization, particularly at the beginning of the program. For LOSS, the Catholic Charities absorbed start-up costs such as mailing, coffee and cookies, and the director's salary. As part-time staff came to work for LOSS, their salaries also were paid for by the Catholic Charities. Other hidden costs involved in the provision of services for survivors were absorbed by the larger agency as well. Stand alone groups have nowhere to turn for money except writing grants or receiving donations. Father Rubey doubts that the LOSS program would have been able to thrive as it has without the help, connection, and support of the Catholic Charities of Chicago.

In addition to financial support, another benefit of being a part of the larger agency is that the larger agency can provide ancillary services that the survivor group may not have as part of its services. One such ancillary service provided for LOSS was the provision of other professionals to assist in the work the survivors of suicide needed to successfully traverse the journey of grief.

Below is an example of results achieved by a client who engaged with the group counseling services provided by the LOSS Program. The names have been changed for confidentiality purposes.

☐ LOSS Program Success Story

Mary is a 54-year-old married female who lost her only daughter 6 years ago. Her daughter, Jan, was 17 years old, a senior in high school, and the youngest of Mary's three children. Jan was artistic, thoughtful, creative, and a beloved little sister to her older brothers. She had struggled with a history of mental illness, and Mary and her husband, Jim, had worked hard to get her to doctors and counselors, on medication, and in a safe place emotionally. They were aware of her struggles with dark thoughts and depression. They were supportive and loving. One night, after Mary had spent the entire evening watching television with Jan, Mary kissed her good night and went to bed. During the night, Jan took her life by hanging herself from a tree in the backyard. Jim found her in the morning and cut her down.

Mary's life spiraled out of control. The wake, the funeral, and subsequent weeks were a blur for her. She came to an 8-week group a few months later and sobbed uncontrollably through the entire meetings. One night near the end of the group's run, she gathered the courage to ask the facilitators, a couple who had lost a son to suicide 17 years before, if this pain that she was feeling would ever end. She said she did not think she could make it through another day. She said she could not get out of bed many days, cried all through work when she could get there, and felt that she had been paralyzed by her grief and loss. The facilitators honored every word she said and told her that she would not always feel this way. They gave her hope and helped her to see that even then she had made some strides by being there and sharing her pain with others.

Mary now serves LOSS as a facilitator and extends hope to newly bereaved members.

CHAPTER

A Bereavement Crisis Debriefing Intervention for Survivors After a Suicide

Ann M. Mitchell and Susan Wesner

The suicide of a family member or significant other is one of the most stressful life events with which a person may have to cope. For survivors who must cope with this type of loss, the death may be a critical incident that affects their functional ability, making suicide a significant public health problem. After working for a number of years with suicide survivors and observing the length of time it takes many survivors to come to terms with a death by suicide, we saw a pressing need to determine effective ways to help meet the needs of survivors early on in their bereavement process. As a result, we implemented a Bereavement Crisis Debriefing Intervention for Survivors after a Suicide within 1 month of the death of a significant other.

Empirical research has shown that sudden bereavement is often associated with numerous psychological problems and, at times, even physical illnesses. Critical incidents happen suddenly and without warning, and severely disrupt a person's feeling of control and faith in their surroundings (Slaikeu, 1994). For survivors after a suicide, the death may be a critical incident that affects their functional abilities through associated affective, behavioral, cognitive, and even physiological consequences. Persons in crisis commonly feel vulnerable, but are often open to suggestions as to how to proceed, making this an opportune time to intervene. However, few programs are available to help during a survivor's bereavement, especially in the acute phase, and the effectiveness of existent programs has not been carefully evaluated and is largely undetermined.

Crisis intervention, including psychological debriefings after critical incidents, has been widely accepted clinically, but has not previously been used with survivors of suicide. Critical incident stress debriefing is an intervention designed to mitigate the impact of a critical incident and accelerate the return of routine functioning after such an incident (J. T. Mitchell & Everly, 1993). Although debriefings have been successful in initially lowering some stress symptoms in emergency medical services personnel and police officers, two meta-analyses (Rose, Bisson, & Wessely, 2002; Van Emmerick, Kamphuis, Hulsbosch, & Emmelkamp, 2002) found no evidence that single-session, individual debriefings reduced post-traumatic stress disorder or improved recovery from psychological trauma. In some situations, the analyses found, such interventions may increase symptoms. However, a study by Richards (2001) evaluating the effectiveness of critical incident stress debriefing (CISD) within the context of a total critical incident stress management (CISM) framework found that the CISM group had less post-trauma morbidity compared to the CISD intervention alone.

Because the suicide of a family member or significant other may be a critical incident in the life of the survivor, a modified bereavement crisis debriefing intervention program within an integrated mental health system was implemented during the acute phase of bereavement (within 1 month of a death by suicide). The program provided suicide survivors with a one-time, family-focused crisis intervention, which was modified from the original Mitchell model (J. T. Mitchell & Everly, 1993; 1996). The program was staffed by two advance practice psychiatric-mental health nurses and one peer-survivor of suicide, all of whom had been specifically trained for the program. We made numerous agencies aware of the program, advertised, then received referrals by word-of-mouth and from local community agencies, funeral homes, social service agencies, and other mental health agencies, including a local survivor of suicide bereavement support group.

After a referral, the organizational structure of the program included making an appointment with the contacting individual, informing him or her about the program and obtaining consent to participate. The individual then invited family and members of his or her social support network to attend the Bereavement Crisis Debriefing Intervention session. The sessions generally lasted between 1.5 and 3 hours, depending on the size of the network and the needs of each particular family network and its individual members.

The transactional theory of stress by Lazarus and Folkman (1984) suggests that stress is related to a particular type of person-environment transaction or relationship in which demands are appraised as taxing or exceeding one's coping resources and endangering one's sense of well-being. A crisis is a temporary state of upset and disorganization, characterized chiefly by an individual's inability to cope with a particular situation using customary methods of problem-solving and by the potential for a radically positive or negative outcome (Slaikeu, 1994). Crisis theory is embedded in the concept of loss, although loss may encompass much more than death. For example, for survivors after a suicide, loss may also include the loss of belief in the "rightness" of the world. Cognitive appraisal and coping are viewed as important mediators of the relationship between stressful situational demands and emotional stress responses. Couched within this stress and coping framework, the Bereavement Crisis Debriefing Intervention for Survivors after a Suicide is based in both crisis theory, adapted from the critical incident stress management framework, and in cognitive behavioral therapy (CBT) principles. A major premise of the intervention is that problems do and will exist, and that procedures involved in the process of coping with life's challenges constitute skills to be acquired. Family and social support network member strengths and competencies are emphasized. This intervention utilizes approaches designed to decrease the stress and tension that often accompany suicide bereavement and increase the individual's adaptive coping and problem-solving skills, which will lead to more positive affective, behavioral, and cognitive responses.

The National Institute of Mental Health (NIMH) Mass Violence and Early Intervention Consensus Conference (NIMH, 2002) outlined tasks that need to be accomplished within a framework for early and later interventions. Once a violent or traumatic event occurs, the sequence of reactions begins with the impact (incident to 72 hours postincident, generally) and involves basic survival and protection activities. In the aftermath of a suicide death is when the rituals associated with funeral arrangements, burial, and estate issues must also be a priority. Next, rescue (within the first 7 days after the incidence) involves adjusting to, orienting oneself to, and providing for basic and immediate needs. The recovery phase (from 1 to 4 weeks after the incident) is when appraisal, reappraisal, planning, narrative formation, and adjustment begin as one continues to "return to life" (from 2 weeks to 2 years). The Bereavement Crisis Debriefing Intervention program shares features of both the early intervention guidelines and CBT principles. For example, it includes a psychoeducational component designed both to educate survivors about common stress reactions and sequelae, and to teach individuals adaptive coping skills for managing stress. Using the short-term CBT approaches of Foa, Hearst-Ikeda, and Perry (1995) and Bryant, Harvey, Dang, Sackville, and Basten (1998), it also involves cognitive restructuring techniques. These features are high-lighted in the intervention, which also incorporates those unique aspects of suicide bereavement outlined by Jordan (2001).

Specifically, the intervention was designed for use by families and their social support network members, and includes specific information related to suicide, bereavement, and suicide bereavement, specifically. In general, it is a process that encourages family members and significant others to discuss the suicide, the events surrounding it, and bereavement-related symptomatology. The process promotes the family's ability to share affective, behavioral, and cognitive markers that suggest healthy family and individual responses to coping with a death by suicide. Information provision and health promotion activities are important components of the intervention. The session is designed to increase the family's under-standing of suicide and suicide bereavement, and to educate members about symptoms of anxiety, depression, and post-traumatic stress. All participants are also provided with information about known available local community resources, emergency phone numbers, and any other survivor of suicide-specific bereavement support group information that may be available within their own communities.

When we examined depression, complicated grief, perceived stress, and quality of life measures taken together postintervention, a positive effect was seen on these mental health outcomes from pre- to postint-ervention. Otherwise, when these outcomes were examined separately, we found a positive effect on perceived stress and on mental health quality of life. Anecdotally, participants stated that not only did they receive support, but they also had a greater understanding of suicide and suicide bereavement, and were made aware of local resources that were also available to them. One of the biggest strengths of the program was having the peer-survivor of suicide participate in the Bereavement Crisis Debriefing Intervention. This supports McMenamy, Jordan, and Mitchell's (2008) finding that 100% of 52 participants' use of resources for healing found one-to-one interaction with another suicide survivor to be moderately to highly helpful.

Results from this program show promise and suggest the need for fur-ther investigation, while also addressing a number of limitations. Prelimi-nary work (A. M. Mitchell, Kim, Prigerson, & Mortimer-Stephens, 2004) suggests that closely related and distantly related survivors have different reactions, and that interventions tailored toward the specific needs of these two groups bear further investigation. For example, because of the high level of complicated grief symptoms in the closely related group, we believe this is an important area to explore, especially at follow-up points (months later). Additional interventions could include expanding the bereavement crisis intervention program from a one-time intervention and increasing its number of sessions to perhaps once a week meetings over a 4-week period. This would coincide with the recovery phase (from 1 to 4 weeks) when appraisal, reappraisal, planning, narrative formation, and adjustment begin. Another possibility could involve implementing a continuing support group or working closely with existing suicide survivor bereavement support groups in the community to provide members who have participated in the program with access to an ongoing support system. Because the original Bereavement Crisis Debriefing Intervention had some marginal positive effects, we believe that with further modification, we can enhance the intensity of the intervention and increase its positive results.

☐ References

Bryant, R. A., Harvey, A. G., Dang, S., Sackville, T., & Basten, C. (1998). Treatment of acute stress disorder: A comparison of cognitive-behavioral therapy and supportive counseling. *Journal of Consulting and Clinical Psychology, 66,* 862–866.

Foa, E. B., Hearst-Ikeda, D., & Perry, K. J. (1995). Evaluation of a brief cognitive-behavioral program for the prevention of chronic PTSD in recent assault victims. *Journal of Consulting and Clinical Psychology, 63,* 948–955.

Jordan, J. (2001). Is suicide bereavement different? A reassessment of the literature. *Suicide and Life-Threatening Behavior, 31,* 91–102.

Lazarus, R. S., & Folkman, S. (1984). Coping and adaptation. In W.D. Gentry (Ed.), *The handbook of behavioral medicine* (pp. 282–325). New York, NY: Guilford.

McMenamy, J. M., Jordan, J. R., & Mitchell, A. M. (2008). What do suicide survivors tell us they need? Results of a pilot study. *Suicide and Life-Threatening Behavior, 38,* 375–389.

Mitchell, A. M., Kim, Y., Prigerson, H. G., & Mortimer-Stephens, M. (2004). Complicated grief in survivors of suicide. *Crisis: International Journal of Crisis Intervention and Suicide Prevention, 25,* 12–18.

Mitchell, J. T., & Everly, G. S. (1993). *Critical incident stress debriefing: An operation manual for the prevention of traumatic stress among emergency services and disaster workers* (1st ed.). Ellicott City, MD: Chevron Publishing Corporation.

Mitchell, J. T., & Everly, G. S. (1996). *Critical incident stress debriefing: An operation manual for the prevention of traumatic stress among emergency services and disaster workers* (2nd ed.). Ellicott City, MD: Chevron Publishing Corporation.

National Institute of Mental Health (NIMH). (2002). *Mental health and mass violence: Evidence-based early psychological intervention for victims/survivors of mass violence. A workshop to reach consensus on best practices.* NIH Publication No. 02-5138, Washington, DC: U.S. Government Printing Office.

Richards, D. (2001). A field study of critical incident stress debriefing versus critical incident stress management. *Journal of Mental Health, 10,* 351–362.

Rose, S., Bisson, J., & Wessely, S. (2002). Psychological debriefing for preventing post-traumatic stress disorder (PTSD). *Cochrane Database Syst Rev. 2002*(2), CD000560.

Slaikeu, K. A. (1994). *Crisis intervention: A handbook for practice and research* (2nd ed.). Boston, MA: Allyn and Bacon.

Van Emmerick, A. P., Kamphuis, J. H., Hulsbosch, A. M., & Emmelkamp, P. M. (2002). Single session debriefing after psychological trauma: A meta-analysis. *Lancet, 360,* 766–771.

The Tragedy Assistance Program for Survivors (TAPS)

Jill Harrington-LaMorie and Kim Ruocco

The majority of deaths in the United States Armed Forces are sudden and traumatic in nature, and involve the death of a young adult between the ages of 18 and 40 (Harrington-LaMorie, 2010). When young adults die, they often leave behind a young family. When a military service member dies, the typical demographic profile of military surviving families often includes a young adult widow, young children, young adult siblings, and adult parents (who may often be young adults themselves) (Harrington-LaMorie, 2010). Survivors affected by the death of a young adult often have a limited age-related peer group who have had a common experience and can offer support in their grief.

    The history of the self-help/peer support movement has taught us that groups whose members are disenfranchised, traumatized, stigmatized, ill, or have endured discrimination can band together to heal, advocate, and support one another while becoming stakeholders in their own care.

    Building on this tradition, a mutual-support organization, duly given the name TAPS (Tragedy Assistance Program for Survivors), emerged in the early 1990s as a peer-based emotional support program for anyone grieving the death of a person in military service to America. TAPS was founded by a military widow, Bonnie Carroll, following the death of her husband, Brigadier General Thomas Carroll, in an Army C-12 plane crash in 1992. In the face of her own trauma and grief, Bonnie Carroll turned to other military widows for support. In this mutual process of aid, she discovered the "tremendous insight for the value of peer support in a specific loss experience" (Weeks & Johnson, 2000). Turning toward other highly successful peer support programs like Concerns of Police Survivors (COPS) and Compassionate Friends, in 1994, Bonnie Carroll formed TAPS as the first nonprofit providing peer-based emotional support for survivors affected by the death of a U.S. Armed Forces member. The program was designed to provide support to all survivors, regardless of their relationship to the deceased or the circumstances or geography of the death (Weeks & Johnson, 2000). Prior to TAPS, the peer programs for survivors of military deaths were primarily for widows, with a focus on networking and on advocating for government entitlements. The long-term psychosocial support component did not exist, especially for disenfranchised groups such as siblings, parents, men, significant others, and those bereaved by military suicide (Weeks & Johnson, 2000).

One of the primary missions of TAPS was to provide an unprecedented, national survivor network of individuals who could, through peer-based programs, connect with and support one another in their grief. These programs include peer-support care groups, one-to-one mentor peer support, online support groups and chat groups, "Good Grief Camps" for children and adolescents, and regional seminars for adult survivors. Since 1994, TAPS has hosted an annual National Survivor Seminar and Good Grief Camp on Memorial Day weekend in Washington, DC, in which military service members volunteer their time to mentor children at the Good Grief Camp, and military leaders and their families attend to speak and lend support to survivors of the fallen. During the course of the weekend, survivors are invited to grief, trauma, and living-with-loss workshops; attend baseball games and other fun activities as a group; join in memorial events in the nation's capital; visit Arlington National Cemetery; and spend time with other survivors to network and support one another. The National Seminar provides an annual national commemoration, a support network, and a community of caring.

☐ Suicide in the Military

Since the United States began the wars in Afghanistan (2001) and Iraq (2003), the U.S. Department of Defense (DOD) reports that suicides in the U.S. Army among soldiers rose for the fourth year in a row in 2008, reaching the highest level in nearly three decades (DOD, 2009). The U.S. Marine Corps has also begun to bear the second largest proportional rise in suicide deaths over the past few years (DOD, 2009). Even in a peace-time nation, all branches of the military have experienced the death of service members by suicide (DOD, 2009). Although not officially recorded by the DOD, concern is increasing as well for those in the military who die as a result of self-destructive and indirect, life-threatening behavior (substance abuse, noncompliance with medical/mental health treatment, speeding, death by cop, and autoerotic asphyxiation), other-wise known as sub intentional suicide.

☐ Suicide Bereavement

"Death by suicide is not a gentle deathbed gathering; it rips apart lives and beliefs, and it sets its survivors on a prolonged and devastating journey."

Dr. Kay Redfield Jamison
Night Falls Fast: Understanding Suicide *(1999, p. 295)*

When a loved one, friend, family member, or coworker dies as a result of a sudden, traumatic event, the immediate trauma and ensuing chaos may leave survivors vulnerable to a more prolonged and com-plicated grief process (Rando, 1993). There are many faces to suicide, but more commonly, suicide is experienced as a sudden, traumatic loss, covictimizing survivors in its aftermath. For each person who loses his or her life to suicide, conservative estimates are that six persons close to the deceased are affected (American Association of Suicidology, 2009).

☐ TAPS Meets Its Mission ...

In 2005, TAPS began to see an increase in the number of survivors of military suicide seeking grief and trauma support services. The major-ity of these survivors had experienced stigma, both in the military and civilian communities, which had caused significant interference with a healthy grieving process. In many cases, the stigma of men-tal illness and suicide had cut them off from their support systems, leaving them alone to struggle with the chaos of suicide. In other instances, the suicide caused a division of the family, with family members spinning off with their own anger, guilt, blame, and sorrow. Some had reached out to their place of worship only to be told that their loved one had committed a sin and had been sent to hell. Others had found the body of their loved one and were paralyzed by the trauma. Some were fighting with investigators to obtain any bit of information that would help make sense of the tragedy. Burial honors, awards, and benefits were sometimes denied because of the circumstance of the death (leaving some young families with children in financial ruin). Some survivors had chosen not to reveal to others, including family members and children, that the death was a suicide or act of self-destruction. The common intersection of most survivors, families, friends, the military, the media, and the community was the displacement of real and perceived anger and blame. There was little, if any, common ground to heal and find support in a safe, nonstigmatizing and blame-free environment with others who had walked on this lonely path of profound loss and sorrow—a path where the memory of their loved one or friend was not permanently etched as the last few days or moments of the circumstance of their death, but rather as a life that was loved and valued and their service in the U.S. Armed Forces was appreciated.

When these survivors began to reach out to TAPS, it became evident their exposure to traumatic bereavement further complicated their grief, requiring specialized services in addition to those already offered by TAPS. With these issues and others in mind, TAPS began to build a peer-support system specifically designed for the healing process of those who had lost a loved one to suicide in the military.

☐ Peer-Based Support and Bereavement Resources

A survivor can call TAPS 24 hours a day, 7 days a week for military suicide loss-specific peer-based support. A resource and information packet is sent to survivors when they first access information and support. These packets include the latest *TAPS Magazine,* information on services available from TAPS, contact numbers for TAPS professionals, a resource list of national services, a suggested reading list, and the book *After Suicide Loss: Coping With Your Grief* (Baugher & Jordan, 2002). An individual bereavement resource packet is personally tailored with counseling referrals, as well as lists of traumatic loss child therapists, peer groups, and other specific services for suicide survivors in their own geographic area.

When a survivor contacts TAPS, a trained professional, who is also a survivor, will take an assessment of the immediate needs of the survivor. TAPS has found that suicide survivors not only want to talk to another suicide survivor, they also want to be connected to someone who has experienced the loss of a similar relationship. For example, a mother who lost a son wants to talk to another mother; a spouse/ significant other who lost a husband/partner wants to talk to a simi-lar peer; a sibling typically wants to speak with another sibling. TAPS not only matches circumstance of suicide death and relationship, but also branch of service and/or other commonalities, such as religion or region of the country. The survivor is matched with a trained peer mentor who will contact the survivor and begin a safe, nonstigmatiz-ing, judgment-free atmosphere in which a healing relationship may be established.

A case example is that of a Navy spouse who was in her twenties, 8-months pregnant with her first child, who came home from work one day to find that her husband had taken his own life. Distraught, con-fused, isolated, overwhelmed, and about to give birth, she reached out to TAPS for help with the journey ahead of her. When she called TAPS for support, TAPS connected her with another widow, who had also been in her twenties and lost her husband to suicide while pregnant and ready to give birth to their son within days of the death. Coincidently, they both lived in the same state. This peer mentor immediately called the new widow and began a relationship that fostered a unique under-standing of one another's circumstances. The peer mentor was able to act as a model of resiliency in the face of tragedy, and hope in the face of devastation. She was also able to help this new widow navigate all the complicated issues that the mentor had already painfully, yet successfully, mastered.

Web-based services are another option for military suicide-loss survivors. TAPS has a Web site (http://www.taps.org) where survivors can access many services, including a newsletter, specific grief and trauma resources, chat rooms, professional training, peer-mentor train-ing, and survivor seminar and event schedules. TAPS offers chat rooms that are based on relationship to the deceased, as well as chats specific for suicide survivors. A chat room offers a private, anonymous place where survivors can go and have complete control over how much they share and participate. Participants can listen to others, gain insight, or join in the discussion. An electronic mailing list of military suicide-loss survi-vors is also available so survivors can contact one another independent of TAPS.

☐ Suicide Survivor Seminar and Good Grief Camp for Children and Adolescents

A gathering that is the first of its kind, the TAPS Annual Suicide Survivor Seminar and Good Grief Camp is a 2-day event that is open to all those who are grieving the suicide of a member of the U.S. Armed Forces. It is specifically designed to address the complex issues associated with grieving a suicide loss. The programming takes into account that survivors are at various degrees in their grief process, and will differ in their relationship to the deceased, circumstances of suicide death, and the highly mixed emotions they experience. Participants are offered formal sessions with emphasis on peer support, education, spirituality, remembrance, and advocacy. Informally, the setting provides a safe, supportive place surrounded by peers where survivors can open up and begin the healing process.

Religion and spirituality are often important issues that need to be addressed by survivors of suicide. TAPS provides sessions that explore the confusing emotions that may be triggered by religious beliefs and teachings. These topics include anger, abandonment, blame, guilt, sin, and the afterlife. Many survivors have expressed to us that finding some resolution and peace in their spirituality allowed them to really begin on their journey of recovery.

TAPS invites experts in the field to provide educational sessions for survivors. These teaching sessions cover a variety of topics and are intended to address the most common difficulties and concerns experienced by suicide survivors. Topics include how suicide affects children; what and how to tell children; disbelief, shock, and anger; depression and when to get help; the roller coaster of emotions; and the loss of a child.

Holistic healing methods are also offered at the TAPS seminars. Participants can choose between such media as writing or art, or can utilize meditation, and visualization. These sessions offer a complementary approach to the traditional expression of emotions and seem to be very therapeutic for many.

Peer-mentor training is offered to any suicide survivor who is at least 1 year past the death and is willing to help others. New peer volunteers are assessed for their ability to provide assistance to others while managing their own grief process. The peer-mentor training is offered at the TAPS seminars as well as online. Participants learn mentoring skills such as active listening, problem solving, and how to set boundaries. Following this training and completion of their certificate, participants are able to offer peer-based comfort and care to new survivors. Peer-mentor volunteers are asked to participate in grief, trauma, and loss continuing education training workshops offered by TAPS during the course of the year.

TAPS offers opportunities for survivors who are further along in their grief process to tell their stories for the purposes of postvention and education. We have found that telling one's story is very desirable and therapeutic for many survivors of suicide. It seems to allow the survivor to do something positive with such a painful event. In addition, each time survivors tell their stories, they seem to learn something about themselves and increase understanding of this confusing type of death.

A remembrance ceremony concludes our Suicide Survivor Seminar. This ceremony includes saying the loved one's name out loud and having a physical representation of the person such as lighting a candle, tying a note to a helium balloon, or saying a prayer over a flower and tossing it into the water. At this point in the seminar, participants know each other well and are able to offer very personal comfort to one another.

☐ TAPS Staff and Volunteers

TAPS was founded and continues to operate as a nonprofit peer-based emotional support organization funded by private donations and grants. TAPS is staffed by professionals who are themselves survivors, family members of U.S. military personnel, peer survivors, and retired military. Professional mental health clinicians provide training and oversight to all peer-based programs, as well as professional, clinical casework. Peer-based support services are provided by a legion of volunteers, both nationally and internationally.

☐ Making the Difference

TAPS fills the gap in the aftercare of survivor support. Peer support provides survivors of a military death with the very sentiment and validation of their own experience. Survivors of suicide loss often struggle with stigma related to the circumstances leading up to the death, as well as the circumstance of the death itself. This may leave survivors feeling disenfranchised as they cope with a profound and confusing sense of loss, often leading them in their grief to a place of loneliness and isolation. TAPS provides a safe environment for all those affected by the suicide death of a military service member. It is a community where the commonality of grief can be shared as a universal experience secondary to the circumstance of the death. TAPS is a place where survivors are honest about the tough stuff, tough about the honest stuff, and committed to making a positive difference in the lives of those who have been touched by suicide in the military.

☐ Risk Reduction: Suicide Postvention as Prevention

Those bereaved by suicide are at higher risk for suicide (Krysinska, 2003) due to many factors, such as exposure to traumatic grief (Jordan, 2001), and the high correlation of a family history of suicide (Krysinska, 2003). One of the greatest assets TAPS has provided to both the survivor and military community is its postvention services to survivors and the impact this work has had on suicide prevention. Communal support and peer mentoring provide the benefit of "monitoring" suicide-loss survivors. Peers are able to build bridges of trusts and mutual "in the same boat" understandings, which outsiders to the community cannot do. The benefit of peers monitoring suicide-loss survivors for suicide risk is vital in prevention work. Peer groups increase social support to suicide-loss survivors, as well as simultaneously promote peer role models who can provide an understanding of this complex emotional journey for grieving survivors. The TAPS peer groups also provide calmness and structure during a time of trauma and confusion for survivors.

TAPS has presented workshops to active duty military personnel on bases, posts, and ships, and to units. Led by senior peer mentors and the survivor staff, these workshops are used to highlight and emphasize the impact a service member's suicide has on the family and where to reach out for support. TAPS suicide-loss survivor stories and the human connection between survivors and at-risk military service members have made an impact on saving lives. The TAPS community of military suicide-loss survivors is helping to teach others to heal while also helping to heal itself. It is with this power of peer support that TAPS has harnessed the strength, courage, and resiliency of survivors to "remember the love, celebrate the life, and share the journey" (TAPS Survivor Seminars Web site, http://www.taps.org/services.aspx?id=1028).

☐ References

American Association of Suicidology. (2009). *Survivors of suicide fact sheet.* Retrieved from http://www.suicidology.org/c/document_library/get_file? folderId=232&name=DLFE-160.pdf

Baugher, B., & Jordan, J. (2002). *After suicide loss: Coping with your grief.* Newcastle, WA: Authors.

Harrington-LaMorie, J. (2010). *The efficacy of peer-based emotional support in traumatically bereaved survivors of a military death* (Unpublished doctoral dissertation). University of Pennsylvania School of Social Policy and Practice, Philadelphia, PA.

Jamison, K. (1999). *Night falls fast: Understanding suicide.* New York, NY: Random House, Inc.

Jordan, J. (2001). Is suicide bereavement different? A reassessment of the literature. *Suicide and Life-Threatening Behavior, 31,* 91–102.

Krysinska, K. E. (2003). Loss by suicide: A risk factor for suicidal behavior. *Journal of Psychosocial Nursing and Mental Health Services, 41*(7), 34–41.

Rando, T. A. (1993). *Treatment of complicated mourning.* Champaign, IL: Research Press.

U.S. Department of Defense (DOD). (2009). *Procurement Reports and Data Files.* Retrieved from http://siadapp.dmdc.osd.mil/personnel/CASUALTY/Death_ Rates.pdf

Weeks, O., & Johnson, C. (Eds.). (2000). *When all friends have gone.* Amityville, NY: Baywood Publishing Company.

American Association of Suicidology and Survivors of Suicide Loss

Michelle Linn-Gust

The American Association of Suicidology (AAS) serves as an international umbrella organization for survivor services. Founded in 1968, AAS was the first national organization to offer survivor services. It was through the AAS annual conference that many of the survivor pioneers (LaRita Archibald, Iris Bolton, Betsy Ross, Adina Wrobleski, Marilyn Koenig, Karen Maxim, and Stephanie Weber) met in the 1980s. Although the first AAS conferences they attended included no workshops for survivors, by 1986, several were available. In 1989, the first Healing After Suicide (HAS) conference was held. Also in 1989, the Survivor Division was formed. The newsletter *Surviving Suicide* began publication that same year.

It was through the advocacy efforts of the survivor pioneers listed above that national survivor resources formed, and it was because of the connections forged at AAS conferences that the American Foundation for Suicide Prevention (AFSP) and the Suicide Prevention Action Network USA (SPAN USA) became realities. The AAS annual conference, held each spring, continues to be "the" place where people from all associated pillars of suicide (prevention, intervention, and postvention) meet. In conjunction with the AAS annual conference (which hosts a variety of workshops geared toward survivors and their grief and/or advocacy work), the HAS conference offers a day of healing, bonding, and remembrance for survivors worldwide. AAS has collaborated with both AFSP and SPAN USA to produce the day-long event.

Today, AAS is a national resource, highly visible on the Internet (http://www.suicidology.org), with information for survivors that includes national support group listings by state; book reviews/bibliographies of survivor-related books; suicide grief information; and booklets for purchase specifically for survivors on issues surrounding survivorship. The AAS Survivors Division (which began as the AAS Survivors Commitee) provides survivors with organization as well as a voice for survivor issues. In addition, AAS annually recognizes survivors for their contributions with a Survivor of the Year Award. *Surviving Suicide*, a newsletter filled with survivor stories, information, and other resources for survivors, also is available as part of the AAS membership. AAS offers a separate survivor membership as well.

Through the years, these resources have evolved and changed, particularly as survivor connections have expanded throughout the world (with help from the Internet), and it has become easier to find resources for suicide loss. This has allowed AAS to expand its reach to access survivors beyond the borders of the United States.

As the pioneers of the survivor movement are reaching retirement, many of them have a sense of needing to spend more time with their families. At the same time, some aspects of the movement have reached a plateau. There is a sense of, "Okay, we've accomplished all this and here we are. Now where do we need to go from here? What do we need to refine?" AAS is working to help create and offer some of those future developments and projects to meet the needs of survivors in their healing journey.

Several working projects at AAS will make their debut between 2010 and 2011. Several new booklets for survivors will be offered, including a support group guide and a booklet on helpful ways to cope with suicide. A support group guide was offered in the early days of the survivor division, but is being revamped to include helpful information and current resources for people who want to start and sustain survivor support groups. Other booklets will be offered as useful topics are selected.

In 2011, AAS aspires to launch the first national survivor bereavement talk line. It has become evident that while local support groups and the Internet fulfill a need, people still search out instant support via the telephone. Several other countries already use telephone support (Australia, the United Kingdom, and Ireland, to name a few). More details about these projects will be available at the AAS Web site (http://www.suicidology.org).

The AAS central office in Washington, DC (which currently has one staff member who is a survivor), fields phone calls and e-mails from survivors around the world, as well as from people who want to help survivors. These calls and e-mails are routed to members who are active in the organization and can be useful to those searching for help. The questions posed cover a range of needs. Some survivors are looking for the nearest support group. If they are looking for someone to talk to, they are connected with a willing individual. Others are people looking to help loved ones coping with a suicide loss. In addition to support groups, they also might be seeking resources (such as books and booklets). Those who work with survivors call asking for speaker suggestions for conferences and to see if certain resources are available (such as support group guides). Finally, individuals call and inquire about the HAS conference (as well as the AAS annual conference). Often, they simply want to make sure they will feel comfortable attending the event and wonder how it is set up and who will be in attendance.

One of the difficulties of running a national center is the constant connection that needs to take place, ensuring that resources are current and needs are being met in communities far from the central office. AAS must use central office staff as well as its membership (including the survivors who serve on the board, specifically, the Survivor Division Chair) to keep in contact with its members and to know if the organization is taking care of survivors who reside far from its home base in Washington, DC.

In many ways, AAS serves as a clearinghouse for survivor information. It also acts as a connection point, thanks to its annual conference, bringing survivors together (and uniting people involved with the other facets of suicide as well). AAS not only tries to help survivors find hope in what seems like an insurmountable loss, but also provides inspiration through ideas, demonstrating how one can give back to the community (international, national, and/or local) through advocacy or simply being there for other survivors. When the pioneers set out to begin the movement, they only wanted to help others who were similar to them and to prevent more suicides from happening. The organization has not strayed from those goals, even as programs and resources continue to evolve. Paraphrasing the words of the founding father of AAS, Ed Shneidman, postvention is prevention for the next generation (Shneidman, 1973, p. 41).

☐ Reference

Shneidman, E. S. (1973). *Deaths of man*. New York, NY: Quadrangle.

American Foundation for Suicide Prevention's Survivor Initiatives

Joanne L. Harpel

The American Foundation for Suicide Prevention (AFSP) is a national not-for-profit organization exclusively dedicated to understanding and preventing suicide through research and education, and to reaching out to people with mood disorders and those affected by suicide. AFSP is based in New York City, with over 30 affiliated chapters throughout the United States.

From its inception in 2002, the initial focus of AFSP's Survivor Initiatives Department has been to develop programs for two primary audiences: newly bereaved survivors of suicide loss (those whose loss was 5 years ago or less) and the facilitators of the more than 500 survivor support groups throughout the country. Having successfully developed an array of programs and other resources in these areas, AFSP's likely future survivor initiatives will focus on special populations of survivors and third parties who work with survivors, as well as on survivor participation in research.

AFSP's survivor programs are developed by the staff of AFSP's Survivor Initiatives Department and implemented, as appropriate, by

AFSP's field staff, local volunteers, and/or paid members of AFSP's training corps. The AFSP Survivor Council, composed of 15 long-term survivors from around the country, serves as an advisory body. Consistent
with its overall commitment to offering programs and resources based on
best practices, AFSP builds evaluation into all of its survivor programs.

Information about all of AFSP's survivor initiatives is available
at http://www.afsp.org. In addition, free e-mail updates about upcoming programs are sent to survivors and interested others through AFSP's
Survivor e-Network; registration is open to the public and is available on
AFSP's Web site.

☐ National Survivors of Suicide Day

AFSP's signature survivor program is National Survivors of Suicide Day,
developed in 1999 in response to U.S. Senate Resolution 99 (sponsored
by U.S. Senator Harry Reid [D-NV], the survivor of his father's suicide),
which declared the Saturday before Thanksgiving "National Survivors of
Suicide Day."

On National Survivors of Suicide Day each year, AFSP reaches out
to survivors through hundreds of local healing conferences held simultaneously in communities throughout the country and abroad. This unique
network of conferences connects survivors within their own communities and across the world. For many, National Survivors of Suicide Day
is the very first time they have met anyone else who has lost someone
to suicide.

The day includes a 90-minute national program (developed by
AFSP's Survivor Initiatives Department and distributed free of charge by
Web cast or DVD), during which a diverse panel of survivors are joined
by nationally recognized mental health professionals. Together, these
presenters address various aspects of suicide bereavement, including, for
example, how to explain suicide to children, how to handle the holidays,
and how to manage the unfortunate stigma that still surrounds suicide.

Individual conference sites are organized locally and independently, and sites conduct their own publicity and registration. They are
encouraged (although not required) to add their own local programming; many invite local survivors and mental health professionals to
speak or provide the opportunity for attendees to share their experiences in small breakout groups. A step-by-step guide to organizing a
site can be found at http://www.afsp.org/index.cfm?fuseaction=home.
viewPage&page_id=DDB3A46E-DBC2-D415-2F3ECA0E5A436BD0

Survivors can participate even if there is not a local conference in their
area or they find it difficult to attend in person by watching the program

online at http://www.afsp.org, and joining in an online chat afterwards. The program is also archived on AFSP's Web site for 2 years (in both English and Spanish), so survivors can watch the program free of charge at any time. Thousands access the program electronically each year.

National Survivors of Suicide Day is sponsored by AFSP as a public service. Among participating conference sites, approximately 40% are formally affiliated with an AFSP chapter. Each year, approximately 30% of sites are organized by new volunteers, reflecting how simple the program is to implement.

Funding for the national program is provided by AFSP's Out of the Darkness Overnight and Community Walks (see below), as well as private foundations and grants. AFSP does not charge participating conference sites a fee to access the program, nor does it charge individuals a fee to watch the program online. Each site is responsible for its own local expenses, if any (AFSP does not provide funding to local conference sites), and many sites charge attendees a modest registration fee or seek local sponsors to offset any local costs.

Thousands of evaluations collected annually from hundreds of Survivor Day conference sites demonstrate that approximately 70% of attendees are there for the first time, 20% are within 12 months of their loss, 60% are within 5 years of their loss, over 75% are female, and 80% are aged 35 or older. Most importantly, the evaluations reveal how deeply powerful Survivor Day is:

> I just wanted to thank you for making the Suicide Day conference available. I just watched it, and found it to be very therapeutic. I lost my brother, and Survivor Day marked 6 months since he died … I find some days much harder than others, but I think the entire experience of dealing with my brother's suicide would be so much worse if not for AFSP. So thank you. And have a Thanksgiving filled with peace.

From an initial 19 sites, the program has grown to more than 200 cities throughout the United States, and is drawing increasing interest from the international survivor community. Australia, Canada, Chile, Ghana, Guatemala, Hong Kong, India, Ireland, Italy, Japan, Kenya, Mexico, Nepal, and South Africa have all participated, and the number of international sites continues to grow annually.

☐ Survivor Outreach Program

Through AFSP's Survivor Outreach Program, trained local survivor volunteers are available to meet in person with newly bereaved survivors and their families, offer reassurance that surviving a suicide loss is possible, and provide information about local resources for support.

Outreach visits are conducted upon the request of survivor family members and/or friends. They are not intended to provide clinical or mental health services or an ongoing system of support. Typically, an outreach visit consists of one in-person visit of 1 to 2 hours in length, followed by periodic phone calls over the next several months. Visits are normally made by a team of two volunteers in a comfortable setting of the survivor's choice. Volunteers listen, offer reassurance, and provide local resource packets.

All potential outreach volunteers must be affiliated with a participating AFSP chapter, and must be:

- A survivor of the suicide of a family member or close personal friend

- At least 2 years from their own loss

- Sufficiently far along in their own healing (for example, through attendance at a support group or counseling) to be able to listen, rather than *needing* to share their own story

- Able to share their own story appropriately

- Able to accept that it is not their role to provide answers, but rather to offer their listening skills, support, and information about available resources

- Able to work well with other volunteer team members

- Willing and able to attend a mandatory 1-day training

Submitted applications are referred to the AFSP Survivor Council Outreach Committee, which conducts a phone interview with each applicant. Once approved by the Survivor Council Outreach Committee, all accepted volunteers must then attend a mandatory 1-day training session prior to conducting any visits. The trainings are offered by AFSP periodically throughout the year in various cities and are conducted by members of AFSP's Outreach Training Corps. Although the program is currently in its pilot phase, early evaluation data indicate survivors requesting visits are newly bereaved (nearly 70% were within 2 months of their loss), and are predominantly women (most often mothers and spouses). The majority of visits took place at the survivors' own home, but several also took place at restaurants, parks, offices, or by telephone.

AFSP field staff and select chapter volunteers are responsible for all aspects of program implementation, including publicizing the program to community gatekeepers, assembling local resource information, responding to requests for visits, and mandatory follow-up with volunteers after each visit.

☐ Support Group Facilitator Training Program

In 2001, AFSP surveyed approximately 350 survivor support group facilitators nationwide to determine how AFSP could be of help to them. Ninety percent of respondents said, "Train us." This was equally true of long-time and new facilitators.

In response, AFSP developed a 2-day support group facilitator training program that combines lecture, interactive discussion, and role-playing with feedback. The program is open to the public through submission of a registration form and costs $175 (limited partial scholarships are available on a good-faith, as-needed basis). It is appropriate for those interested in starting a new group, as well as those who currently facilitate a group (survivors must be a minimum of 2 years from their own loss). Although initially developed for a lay audience, the program has also found an enthusiastic reception within the mental health community. One attendee wrote, "As a clinician, I came to learn from the survivors. What a wonderful opportunity for a mental health provider to learn collaboratively."

The training is conducted by paid members of AFSP's Facilitator Training Corps and addresses a wide range of topics, including suicide bereavement 101; assessing an individual's readiness to facilitate; open vs. closed groups; structuring the meeting; protecting the process; handling silence and breaking taboos; and dealing with problematic behavior such as monopolizing, proselytizing, multiple family members, group members in crisis, and compassion fatigue. The training program was offered for the first time in March 2002, and is currently offered 4 to 6 times annually, in cities throughout the country. To date, over 700 people have attended.

In 2008, AFSP conducted an online follow-up survey of those who took the training between 2002 and 2006. Although AFSP has always solicited participants' feedback by way of an evaluation form completed immediately upon the conclusion of the program, the follow-up survey was the first attempt at documenting longer-term impact, and reflects AFSP's commitment to building evaluation into its programmatic activities.

The survey revealed that 88% of attendees are themselves survivors of suicide loss. Despite the fact that no continuing education units (CEUs) are offered, 24% of attendees are mental health professionals (14% of attendees identified themselves as both a survivor and a mental health professional). The follow-up survey confirmed that the program is clearly achieving its fundamental goal of encouraging the creation and sustenance of support groups throughout the country. Of those surveyed, 75% are currently facilitating a group, and 26% have created a new group. Of those not currently facilitating a group, over 60% said it was either because they had not had the time or they had not taken the training with the primary intent of facilitating a group (other reasons for attending included an interest in learning about survivors and suicide bereavement [72%] and getting more involved in the field generally [65%]).

Since many who are interested in group facilitation do not have the financial or logistical capacity to travel to a 2-day course, AFSP adapted the curriculum into a self-study package that directly tracks the content covered in the live program. The package contains a comprehensive 95-page guide to effective support group facilitation, *Facilitating Suicide Bereavement Support Groups: A Self-Study Manual;* and a 90-minute companion DVD, *Facilitating Suicide Bereavement Support Groups: Skill-Building and Special Challenges,* which features highly experienced facilitators in action, demonstrating specific strategies for handling difficult situations and sharing their own personal advice. The package is available for sale at http://www.afsp.org for $75.

As a further resource for *all* survivor support group facilitators nationwide (regardless of whether they have attended the training program or purchased the self-study package), AFSP also offers several free monthly drop-in calls, which are moderated by a member of AFSP's Facilitator Training Corps. These drop-in conference calls are open forums where facilitators can ask questions and learn from each other. The calls serve both as "advanced" training and as an ongoing source of support and information for facilitators.

In addition to the various training resources, AFSP also maintains an online directory of survivor support groups, accessible free of charge to the survivor community. AFSP does not run support groups under its own auspices, nor does it credential support groups or individual facilitators.

☐ Schools Postvention Project

AFSP and the Suicide Prevention Resource Center (SPRC) are collaborating to develop a free Web-based resource for use by schools in the aftermath of a suicide (or other death) in the school community.

The online toolkit is being developed in consultation with national issue experts and is expected to address key topics, including memorialization, contagion, use of new technologies, guidelines for assisting students and staff with managing emotional responses (emotional regulation), and incident command. The toolkit will be disseminated widely and free of charge, and will be posted on the Web sites of both AFSP and SPRC. It will be substantially different from currently available information on school postvention since existing materials typically emphasize detailed planning for crisis response rather than immediate, pragmatic answers to frequently asked questions such as: "Should we have a school wide assembly, or does that risk contagion?" or, "Do we plant a memorial garden?"

It is anticipated that this resource will be used widely in conjunction with local postvention efforts in school communities nationwide.

☐ Out of the Darkness Walks

In addition to programs developed specifically for survivors, AFSP also has a network of more than 30 chapters throughout the country, which provide opportunities for survivors to get involved in their local communities. Moreover, the Out of the Darkness Community Walks (local 5K walks held each year in cities throughout the country) and the Out of the Darkness Overnight Walk (an annual 20-mile national walk), also function as important healing experiences for survivors, and help to create a powerful sense of community. Information is available at http://www.outofthedarkness.org and http://www.theovernight.org.

☐ Merger With SPAN USA

In 2009, AFSP merged with the Suicide Prevention Action Network USA (SPAN USA); as a result of that merger, SPAN USA became the Public Policy Division of AFSP. Survivors of suicide loss are an essential voice in AFSP's developing focus on drawing on community engagement and grassroots advocacy to effect policy and legislative change.

AFSP reaches out to survivors with two goals in mind: to provide them with the support and information they seek, and to empower them to become active in the field. Through its successful and growing array of programs and resources for survivors, AFSP is dedicated to remaining a major national resource for survivors of suicide loss.

☐ References

American Foundation for Suicide Prevention. (2007). *Facilitating suicide bereavement support groups: A self-study manual*. New York, NY: Author.

American Foundation for Suicide Prevention. (Producer). (2007). *Facilitating suicide bereavement support groups: Skill building and special challenges* [DVD]. Available from http://www.afsp.org/index.cfm?fuseaction=home.viewPage&page_id=FEE689DA-B0E4-4F70-8149A2D3862A27D8

SECTION 4

Promising Programs of Support for Survivors
International Programs

Grief After Suicide
A Hong Kong Chinese Perspective

Amy Chow and Paul Yip

☐ Demographic Background

Among the population of 7 million in Hong Kong, around 1,000 suicide deaths occur annually, ranging from 799 in 1995 to 996 in 2006, with a peak of 1,264 in 2003. The average rate in 2005 was 14.6 suicide deaths per 100,000 individuals, which is slightly higher than the global average rate (Yip, Liu, Law, & Law, 2005; Yip & Lee, 2007). Following the suggestion proposed by Shneidman (1972) that there are 6 survivors for each suicide death, about 6,000 suicide survivors in 2005 were within Hong Kong.

In the same year, over 25.5% of suicide deaths involved individuals aged 65 or older, implying a group of aged spouses, aged siblings, adult children, and even grandchildren as survivors. A little more than one third of suicide deaths (36.8%) involved individuals between the ages of

25 and 44. The survivors of this age group would be young or middle-aged spouses, young or adolescent children, and aged parents.

Among the suicide deaths, the rate for males is roughly two times that of females. As for the methods, nearly half of the the deaths by suicide are by jumping, followed by hanging and charcoal poisoning (Hong Kong Jockey Club Centre for Suicide Research and Prevention, 2008).

Hong Kong is a cosmopolitan city that gathers people from around the world, but about 95% of the population is Chinese (Hong Kong Census and Statistics Department, 2007b). Despite the influence of Western values, the attitude toward suicide among Hong Kong citizens is highly affected by the Chinese culture.

☐ Chinese Cultural Attitude Toward Suicide

If we are to understand the cultural attitude, we should first examine the language and wording used to describe suicide. The Chinese word for suicide is *ji xei* (自殺), which literally means killing of oneself. Yet, this word is not commonly used by journalists or the general public. A few euphemisms for suicide in Chinese are more commonly used. The first consists of alternative descriptions of suicide: self-ending of one's life or one's problem (自盡、自我了斷). The second word type portrays suicide as a transition: starting of a new journey. The third word type makes a value judgment on suicide. Depreciation of the value of life (輕生), search for undesirable choice (自尋短見), doing a stupid thing (做傻事), inability to tolerate (睇唔開), and annoyance in facing one's life (厭世) are examples of this type.

The Chinese attitude toward suicide is reflected by these euphemisms. Suicide survivors are more inclined to use the first two types of euphemisms that have no value judgment toward those who attempt suicide or those who die by suicide. The second category also provides an image of the continuation of life after death. The third type induces a negative connotation toward those who attempt suicide or those who die by suicide, and is more commonly used by the general public. Though the users might not be aware of the meanings carried by the words, suicide survivors are sensitive to these wordings. They will feel guilty, as suicide seems to be preventable through the offering of support or education.

There is no universal attitude toward suicide among Chinese. Traditional Chinese beliefs suggest diversified motivations for suicide that seem to indicate a certain level of tolerance of suicide. There are four purposes identified for suicide, namely, to teach, express loyalty, express love, and pay a debt.

Suicide as a Means to Teach or Make a Point

The Chinese term *zi gan* (死諫) literally means the use of death to teach. The term was used in ancient times. For example, the Dragon Boat Festival originated from a "teaching suicide" by a minister, Qu Yuan, and falls on the anniversary of his death. He was said to be a loyal minister, but the king of his period trusted other ministers who were corrupt. Qu Yuan then died by suicide by throwing himself into a river, hoping to teach the king with his death. The people adored and respected Qu Yuan so much that they thought of a way to protect his body from attack by fish. They prepared rice dumplings, wrapped them in leaves, and threw them into the river. At the same time, they beat drums on a long, narrow boat, the dragon boat, to scare away the fish. The custom of preparing rice dumplings and racing dragon boats is still very much alive today in different parts of China and in other parts of Asia. The suicide of Qu Yuan is not condemned, but honored even now.

Today, some people kill themselves to spread their religious or political views. More commonly presented in Hong Kong are the helpless or hopeless mothers, who attempt suicide as a means to teach their children to be obedient and/or get rid of some bad habits (e.g., drugs or gambling). Generally, the public seems to be sympathetic or even approving of these acts.

Suicide as a Means to Show One's Loyalty

There are numerous stories of Chinese emperors who killed themselves, as well as their wives and daughters, before their reign was taken over by their enemies. The last emperor of the Ming Dynasty, Chong Zhen, gathered all his family members, as well as some of his followers, and ordered them to take their own lives when he anticipated the fall of his dynasty. Most of them followed the instruction to show their loyalty to the country and the family, and Chong Zhen finally hanged himself, too. One of his daughters, Princess Chang Ping, refused to join the suicide pact. The emperor cut off one of her arms out of anger. Her story was passed on through a popular Chinese opera, the *Tragedy of the Emperor's Daughter*. She was said to be offered a wedding with her beloved by the new emperor, but she killed herself by poisoning on the wedding night to show loyalty to her father and country. The truthfulness of her suicide is doubtful, as some reports indicated she died of illness 1 year after the marriage. Still, the suicides of the emperor and the family members are somewhat respected and sympathized by many people.

Some forms of suicide that express loyalty to the family can still be found in Hong Kong. There have been a few homicide-suicides, with those who die by suicide being women who have marital problems. Just like Chong Zhen, the woman perceived that her family reign was being taken away by another woman, thus she ordered the children to die, or even killed them, before her suicide. Still, this action is not accepted by the general public. Follow-up public education programs have firmly asserted the right of the children to live (Yip, Law, & Cheung, 2009).

Suicide as a Means to Show One's Love

In Chinese literature and opera, numerous stories romanticize suicide that occurs for love. For example, the legend of "butterfly lovers" is about the suicide of a young woman who dies by suicide at the grave of her deceased lover. The two then become butterflies and are reunited. A common Chinese saying, "Though we cannot be born on the same day, I hope we can die on the same day," reflects deep love, but only a very small group takes this seriously today. On the other hand, a ritual called after-life marriage saves the lives of young bereaved lovers. Though after-life marriage was originally for two deceased persons, it now includes the marriage of a deceased person with a living person. This offers an alternative to suicide for the grieving person who wants to show his or her love to the deceased.

Suicide as a Means to Pay a Debt

Traditional Chinese beliefs suggest resurrection after death. Misdeeds in previous lives are expected to be made up in the coming lives. When facing suicide, where it is difficult to comprehend the causes, survivors might view the motivation for the suicide as a means of debt clearance. This prescribed reason might relieve the survivors of the agony of searching for "whys" and reduce the self-blame. Yet sometimes, the debt is perceived as not being owed by the person who died by suicide, but by other family members, usually the older generations. The survivor who holds this belief might feel great self-blame, or alternatively may put the fault on other family members, ruining family relationships.

☐ Hong Kong Attitude Toward Suicide

The attitude toward suicide in Hong Kong is affected by not only these functional perspectives, but also by philosophical and religious beliefs. Hong Kong is currently enjoying religious freedom. A wide range of religions are practiced in Hong Kong, but most people are influenced by Confucianism and Buddhism. Both Confucianism and Buddhism condemn suicide. From the Confucian outlook, hurting one's body is a disrespectful act to one's parents. Thus, taking one's life is disapproved of even more. From the Buddhist viewpoint, whether the death is good or not is affected by the final moment. For suicidal persons, their last state of mind is usually confusion, and this might result in further suffering in future lives. Other religions practiced in Hong Kong, such as Catholicism and other forms of Christianity, also condemn suicide. However, empirical data have suggested that there are myths found in religious people about suicide deaths implying they could be reunited with their loved ones after they die (Hong Kong Jockey Club Centre for Suicide Research and Prevention, 2005).

☐ Measuring Attitudes Toward Suicide in Hong Kong Chinese

Lee, Tsang, Li, Philips, and Kleinman (2007) developed a scale that measures attitudes toward suicide among the Chinese in Hong Kong. The item pools were actually generated from focus groups carried out in Hong Kong. Nine factors were identified. Negative appraisal is the factor with the highest loading. Suicide is perceived as stupid, irresponsible, timid, a betrayal, and a selfish act. The second factor, the stigmatization of suicide, includes items of avoidance of suicide attempters and even suicide survivors. Suicide spectrum constitutes the third factor and includes items related to suicide attempts and completion. The fourth and fifth factors relate to the causes of suicide, which include fatalism and social changes, respectively. Two factors relate to positive attitudes, including support toward suicidal people and sympathy toward suicide. The last two factors are about the nature of suicide, including contagiousness and function. The identified factors reflect the diversified, and even contradictory, aspects of attitudes toward suicide in Hong Kong. On the one hand, there are negative appraisal, stigma, and perceived contagiousness. On the other hand, there is sympathy toward the person who died by suicide, and suicide is viewed as serving special functions. The fatalistic views of suicide may offer externalization of control, without blaming those who died by suicide or survivors. As with traditional views, there is no single, conclusive attitude toward suicide among Hong Kong Chinese, which makes any suicide prevention program for raising the awareness or demystifying the myth of suicide even more difficult.

☐ Observations About the Grieving Trajectory of Suicide Survivors in Hong Kong

The grief of suicide survivors is not only affected by their values and philosophical orientation, but also by contextual factors. There are unique concurrent environmental stressors that make the bereavement trajectory of survivors in Hong Kong more challenging.

There are no official guidelines governing reports of suicide in the mass media, although an effort has been made to provide recommendations about how to report suicide news more responsibly (Fu & Yip, 2008). It is not uncommon to find pictures on the front pages of newspapers of the deformed bodies of those who died by suicide. Survivors may be traumatized by reading these reports of the death of their loved one. They are also torn between the urge to read, as a sign of loyalty to the deceased, and the fear of being emotionally disturbed. In addition, relatives, friends, and neighbors can read the reports, and therefore the survivors may have no way to save face. The occasional fabricated stories about the causes of suicide that are created by reporters may also cause unnecessary stress and suspicion among family members. Furthermore, for many survivors, their psychological wounds will be further worsened when they read similar suicide stories in the future.

The method of the suicide also poses an additional stressor for survivors. The three most common methods are jumping, hanging, and charcoal burning (Yip & Lee, 2007). About 80% of these suicides happen at home or in the neighborhood of the person who died by suicide. Moreover, the bodies of those who died by suicide show a certain degree of mutilation. The survivor may be the first one to discover the suicide (Chow, 2006). The image of the body may thus be imprinted in the mind of the survivor for a long time and become an unwelcome intrusion.

Police and coroner investigations are necessary to ascertain that the death is indeed a suicide rather a homicide. Yet, this can be stressful to the survivors, too. The reporting of details around the time before death, the viewing of the body for identification, and facing a suspicious attitude by the police seeking to determine whether it is a suicide or a homicide can be tortuous for survivors, especially when they are facing acute grief about an unexpected death at the same time.

There is also a long waiting list for body disposal in Hong Kong, due to the insufficient facilities for dealing with the excess number of deaths in an aging society. On average, survivors have to wait for at least two weeks before the body of the deceased can be cremated. The wait is even longer for the survivors of suicide, since the booking can only be started after the coroner's investigation is completed.

The funeral can also be a time of heightened stress. If their religious affiliation is Christian, the survivors have to find a member of the clergy who is understanding, as suicide might be considered a sin in some conservative minds. For those who are more inclined toward Taoism, extensive and elaborate rituals are prescribed for suicide deaths. These rituals might cost a great amount of money, but survivors might irrationally carry out all of them to compensate for their guilt and self-blame, without carefully considering their affordability. In addition, there is a common Chinese saying, "Black headed is not entitled to the respect by white headed" (白頭人不送黑頭人), meaning it is not appropriate for the older generation to attend the funerals of their descendants (Chow, Koo, Koo, & Lam, 2000).

As noted earlier, a substantial number of survivors are aging parents, who may feel it is not proper to attend the funeral of their child. Since the loss of a child is a risk factor for bereavement, coupled with the sudden and preventable nature of death in suicide and the social disapproval of participation in any ritual, this group of grievers may go through a much more difficult grieving journey. There is also a growing trend toward having fewer children in Hong Kong. In 2006, the average household size was 3.0 (Hong Kong Census and Statistics Department, 2007a; Yip et al., 2009). Therefore, for some parents, the loss of one child might involve the loss of all their offspring, and with it, the loss of their entire future.

☐ Silver Linings for Suicide Survivors in Hong Kong

Although suicide survivors face all kinds of challenges, there are still hopeful and encouraging developments in the field of support for them. In the past few years, some celebrities have killed themselves (Yip et al., 2006), and there have been extensive reports by the media of these suicides, but the attitude has been shifting from condemnation to compassion, especially toward those deaths related to depression (Fu & Yip, 2007). There is also more public education about mental illnesses and mental health. This openness makes it easier for survivors to acknowledge the deaths of their loved ones by suicide. A suicide survivor in a bereavement group shared, "My son just died the same way as [the name of celebrity who died by suicide]." This helped her feel more normal and less stigmatized.

Systematic research has been carried out with suicide survivors in recent years. The Hong Kong Jockey Club Centre for Suicide Research and Prevention carried out a psychological autopsy study in 2005 (Chen et al., 2006; Wong, Chan, & Beh, 2007) that provided more information about the survivors in Hong Kong. Ng, Wong, and Fu (2006) published a book of stories from survivors in a psychological autopsy study as well.

The Centre recently received a donation to start the "Peter Lee—Care for Suicide Survivor Project" to continue research on suicide survivors. Peter Lee, a local entrepreneur and a survivor, will provide financial support for this much neglected service to survivors in Hong Kong. The proposed service study is a pilot project, based in the Centre for Suicide Research and Prevention, the University of Hong Kong (HKU CSRP), with enthusiastic support by its collaborators, the Queen Mary Hospital Mortuary (QMHM) and the Forensic Pathology Service of the Department of Health. The aims are to develop, study, and evaluate a yet-to-be-developed evidence-based program to both understand the needs and identify best practices to help survivors of suicide. Hopefully, it will eventually help to reduce the suicidal risk among survivors and the suicide rate in the general community.

Specifically, the aim of the project is to develop evidence-based and sustainable care for all newly bereaved suicide survivors in Hong Kong through five major components:

1. Provide timely informational support to the deceased family members in the mortuary, including a booklet on making arrangements after death published by the Food and Environment Hygiene Department, and a booklet on suicide bereavement published by the HKU CSRP at the Kwai Chung Public Mortuary (KCPM), Fu Shan Public Mortuary (FSPM), the Victoria Public Mortuary (VPM), and QMHM.

2. Provide timely, brief counseling for the survivors after their interviews with the forensic pathologists at the KCPM.

3. Provide short-term counseling (three to four sessions) for survivors during their grieving process.

4. Refer survivors who have developed psychiatric disturbances to community psychiatric services.

5. Disseminate the findings and acquired knowledge from this study to professionals (police, mortuary staff, coroner's office, etc.) and the general public via seminars, Web sites, and reference manuals.

The major outcome measures for this study are measuring satisfaction levels of survivors who have utilized the newly implemented service; understanding help-seeking patterns of the survivors of suicide approached by KCPM, FSPM, VPM, and QMHM; and measuring the efficacy of the short-term counseling by longitudinal follow-up with the survivors who participate in the short-term counseling service study. All families of suicides from the Chinese population who are encountered by the forensic pathologists from the four mortuaries during the study period will be invited to participate. Once a consent form is signed, the researchers in the HKU CSRP will establish contact with clients and provide the counseling support to those in need.

The development of systematic services for suicide survivors in Hong Kong is still in its infancy. Social workers of the family services center identify suicide survivors from newspaper stories. Social workers then approach the families to explore their need for services. Other referrals might be made by school teachers or other social welfare agencies to the social workers in the family service center, who are trained to take care of various problems, without a specialization in bereavement or suicide bereavement.

The Jessie and Thomas Tam Centre of the Society for the Promotion of Hospice Care, was established in 1997. It is the first community-based bereavement counseling center in Hong Kong. Suicide survivors are some of the recipients of their services. Individual counseling, group counseling, and memorial gatherings during festivals are offered to suicide survivors, along with other bereaved families (Chow & Chan, 2006). The center has organized two professionally led suicide survivor groups in the last 2 years. During the same period, the Samaritans Befrienders of Hong Kong has expanded its services beyond those with suicidal ideation to now include survivors. It currently runs an open and a closed support group for suicide survivors.

Another suicide prevention agency, Suicide Prevention Services, also received funding from the Peter Lee Care for Life Charitable Foundation, and established a center for suicide survivors in early 2008. A comprehensive service delivery model has been developed that includes individual emotional support; practical support, including emergency fund or escort services; professionally led and survivor-led support groups; and memorials and healing ritualistic activities. The goal is to address the multifaceted needs of suicide survivors. More importantly, the initiation of this service is a developmental milestone in the recognition of the unique and extensive needs of suicide survivors. It is believed that suicide survivors who have transformed their grieving experience can contribute a great deal to suicide prevention. Eventually, the hope is to enlist suicide survivors in reducing the number of suicides in Hong Kong, which would become the silver lining in the clouds of suicide.

With the research, training, and practices that are still being developed in Hong Kong, we shall be able to find a unique way to provide timely and much needed services for the survivors. The experiences in helping the survivors from the West would be useful; however, a culturally sensitive model should be developed locally to engage the survivors successfully. The survivors can then become important stakeholders in advancing the suicide prevention effort.

Acknowledgments

The authors would like to pay tribute to the survivors who contributed to our understanding of suicides, the support of the Peter Lee Care for Life Foundation, and the volunteers who provide the service and support for the survivors.

References

Chen, E. Y. H., Chan, W. S. C., Wong, P. W. C., Chan, S. S. M., Chan, C. L. W., Law, Y. W., … Yip., P. S. F. (2006). Suicide in Hong Kong: A case-control psychological autopsy study. *Psychological Medicine, 36*, 815–826.

Chow, A. Y. M. (2006). The day after: The suicide bereavement experience of Chinese in Hong Kong. In C. L. W. Chan & A. Y. M. Chow (Eds.), *Death, dying and bereavement: The Hong Kong Chinese experience.* (pp. 293–310). Hong Kong, China: Hong Kong University Press.

Chow, A. Y. M., & Chan, C. L. W. (2006). Bereavement care in Hong Kong: Past, present and future. In C. L. W. Chan & A. Y. M. Chow (Eds.), *Death, dying and bereavement: The Hong Kong Chinese experience* (pp. 253–260). Hong Kong, China: Hong Kong University Press.

Chow, A. Y. M., Koo, B. W. Z., Koo, E. W. K., & Lam, A. Y. Y. (2000). Turning grief into good separation: Bereavement services in Hong Kong. In R. Fielding & C. L. W. Chan (Eds.), *Psychosocial oncology & palliative care in Hong Kong* (pp. 233–254). Hong Kong, China: Hong Kong University Press.

Fu, K. W., & Yip, P. S. F. (2007). The long-term effect of mass media on suicide. *Journal of Epidemiology and Community Health, 61*, 540–546.

Fu, K. W., & Yip, P. S. F. (2008). Changes in reporting of suicide news after the promotion of the WHO media recommendations. *Suicide and Life-Threatening Behavior 38*, 631–636.

Hong Kong Census and Statistics Department. (2007a, February 22). *Domestic households and average domestic household size, 1996, 2001, and 2006.* Retrieved from http://www.bycensus2006.gov.hk/FileManager/EN/Content_981/d101e.xls

Hong Kong Census and Statistics Department. (2007b, February 22). *Population by ethnicity, 2001, and 2006.* Retrieved from http://www.bycensus2006.gov.hk/FileManager/EN/Content_981/a105e.xls

Hong Kong Jockey Club Centre for Suicide Research and Prevention. (2005). *Research findings into suicide and its prevention.* Hong Kong, China: Hong Kong Jockey Club Centre for Suicide Research and Prevention.

Hong Kong Jockey Club Centre for Suicide Research and Prevention. (2008). *Statistics.* Retrieved from http://csrp.hku.hk/WEB/eng/customized.asp

Lee, S., Tsang, A., Li, X. Y., Philips, M. R., & Kleinman, A. (2007). Attitudes toward suicide among Chinese people in Hong Kong. *Suicide and Life-Threatening Behavior, 37*, 565–575.

Ng, C. C., Wong, P. W. C., & Fu, K. W. (2006). *The final words for the beloved: Stories of suicide survivors* [in Chinese]. Hong Kong, China: Breakthrough Ltd.

Shneidman, E. S. (1972). Foreword. In A. C. Cain (Ed.), *Survivors of suicide* (pp. ix–xi). Springfield, IL: Charles C Thomas.

Wong, P. W. C., Chan, W. S. C., & Beh, P. S. L. (2007). What can we do to help and understand survivors of suicide in Hong Kong? *Crisis: International Journal of Crisis Intervention and Suicide Prevention, 28*, 183–189.

Yip, P. S. F., Fu, K. W., Yang, K. C., Ip, B. Y., Chan, C. L., Chen, E. Y., Lee, D. T., Law, Y. W., & Hawton, K. (2006). The effects of a celebrity suicide on suicide rates in Hong Kong. *Journal of Affective Disorders, 93*, 245–252.

Yip, P. S. F., Law, C. K., & Cheung K. (2009). Ultra-low fertility in Hong Kong: A review of related demographic transitions, social issues, and policies to encourage childbirth. In G. Jones, P. Tay-Straughan, & A. Chan (Eds.), *Ultra-low fertility in Pacific Asia: Trends, causes and policy issues* (pp. 132-159). London, England: Routledge.

Yip, P. S. F., & Lee, D. T. S. (2007). Charcoal-burning suicides and strategies for prevention. *Crisis: International Journal of Crisis Intervention and Suicide Prevention, 28*, 21–27.

Yip, P. S. F., Liu, K. Y., Law, C. K., & Law, F. Y. W. (2005). Social and economic burden of suicide in Hong Kong SAR. *Crisis: International Journal of Crisis Intervention and Suicide Prevention, 26*, 156–159.

Yip, P. S. F., Wong P. W. C., Cheung, Y. T., Chan, K. S., & Philip, S. L. (2009). An empirical study of characteristics and types of homicide-suicides in Hong Kong 1989–2005. *Journal of Affective Disorders, 112*, 184–192.

28
CHAPTER

International Perspectives on Suicide Bereavement— The Australian Example[1]

Peter Bycroft, Jill Fisher, and Susan Beaton

☐ The Australian Government Context

Australia has a long history of government and community involvement in the prevention of suicide. In 1995, the Australian Health Ministers embarked on a National Youth Suicide Prevention Strategy (Australian Health Ministers and Commonwealth Department of Human Services and Health, 1995) that culminated in an extensive literature review and report on the key issues in youth suicide nationally and internationally (National Youth Suicide Prevention Strategy, 1999).

[1] Parts of this chapter draw on research that was funded by the Australian Government Department of Health and Ageing. The views expressed in this chapter are those of the authors. They do not necessarily represent the position of the Australian government.

439

In 2000, the Australian government released the National Suicide Prevention Strategy (NSPS) (Commonwealth of Australia, 2000) and by 2006, most states and territories in Australia had adopted their own suicide prevention strategies, based largely on or adapted from the national strategy (Department of Human Services Victoria, 1997; NSW Health, 1999; Queensland Health, 2003; Department of Health and Community Services, 2003; Australian Capital Territory [ACT] Health, 2005; Department of Human Services Victoria, 2006). By 2007, the Australian government was promoting a coordinated national approach to suicide bereavement and had committed funds to a range of projects to improve community capacity to respond to the needs of those bereaved by suicide. After reviewing its national strategic framework that year, the Australian government released new action areas of focus for suicide prevention (Commonwealth of Australia, 2008a):

1. Improving the evidence base and understanding of suicide prevention

2. Building individual resilience and the capacity for self-help

3. Improving community strength, resilience, and capacity in suicide prevention

4. Taking a coordinated approach to suicide prevention

5. Providing targeted suicide prevention activities

6. Implementing standards and quality in suicide prevention.

Australian initiatives were influenced by a series of milestone events, government reports, and systematic evaluations. The most influential international reports were the World Health Organization's Report on Strategies for Reducing Suicidal Behaviours in the European Region (1990) and the United Nations' *Preventing Suicide: Guidelines for the Formulation and Implementation of National Strategies* (1996). Throughout the 1990s, a wide range of government reports and actions relating to key risk and protective factors in suicide built the foundation for Australian government initiatives in suicide prevention and postvention in the 21st century. Key themes of these reports and actions related to the deaths of Indigenous Australians in custody (Royal Commission into Aboriginal Deaths in Custody, 1991), mental health (Australian Health Ministers, 1992; Burdekin, 1993), youth suicide (Australian Health Ministers and Commonwealth Department of Human Services and Health, 1995; Mitchell, 1999, 2000), depression (beyondblue, n.d.), suicide prevention[2,3] and suicide bereavement[4,5] (Corporate Diagnostics Pty Ltd., 2006). By 2000, the Australian government's involvement in suicide prevention was focused on these themes, which are recognized as high-risk areas. As a result of these initiatives, by 2006, systemic Australian government initiatives in the areas of postvention, loss, grief, and suicide bereavement had begun.

☐ The Australian Community Context

Investing in the capacity of communities so that they are empowered to have a role in shaping their own future is recognized universally as a key strategy to achieving communities that are safe, healthy, and strong. In Australia, the prevention of suicide is recognized as a shared responsibility across all sectors, organizations, and communities.

Although the Australian government oversees the development of strategic policies and priority areas for the prevention of suicide, it is local communities who are best equipped to instigate actions and to respond to the needs of families, individuals, and groups needing support. In Australia, it is the experience and practice of local communities that informs and often drives high-level government policy. Indeed, in 2006, when the Australian government initiated a scoping study of the best approaches to suicide bereavement, it encouraged a "bottom-up" approach—built on comprehensive consultation with service providers, bereavement support groups, and people bereaved by suicide throughout Australia (Corporate Diagnostics Pty Ltd., 2006).

---

[2] In 1999, the Australian government established the National Suicide Prevention Strategy (NSPS) and an advisory committee, the National Advisory Council on Suicide Prevention (NACSP), drawn from the suicide prevention and human services sectors.

[3] In 2004, the National Advisory Council on Suicide Prevention (NACSP) convened the first National Suicide Prevention Planning Forum. As a direct result of this forum, the Australian government announced a range of initiatives and funding for suicide prevention, including support for national activities that target people bereaved by suicide.

[4] In 2005, the National Advisory Council on Suicide Prevention (NACSP) established the National Bereavement Reference Group (NBRG), an industry-representative body that was charged with overseeing the development of a nationally coordinated approach to suicide bereavement activities.

[5] In 2007, the Australian government, through NSPS funding, supported the first Australian National Suicide Postvention Conference, which initiated an ongoing forum and network linking all agencies developing, testing, or delivering suicide postvention activities.

☐ The Incidence of Suicide in Australia

In 2007, 1,881 people took their own lives in Australia (Australian Bureau of Statistics, 2009b). This is an age-standardized rate of 9 per 100,000 people (the age-standardized rate accounts for the changing age structure of the Australian population over time). This rate has been decreasing since a peak of 14.7 suicides per 100,000 people registered in 1997 (Australian Bureau of Statistics, 2008). However, a review of suicide statistics is currently underway to fully investigate the accuracy of these data, which are considered to be significantly underreported (De Leo et al., 2010; Harrison, Pointer, & Elnour, 2009).

Australia is approximately the same size as the mainland United States, but has significantly less population and arable land. Of Australia's land area, 6.55% is arable. The country has a population of 22 million people (Australian Bureau of Statistics, 2009b). The United States has around 19% of its land area as arable land and a total population of around 308 million people (Geoscience Australia, 2009; U.S. Bureau of the Census, 2009). In Australia, social isolation and a lack of locally available support services means that people bereaved by suicide are often unable to easily access the support they require.

☐ The Stigma of Suicide

Historically, religious and cultural taboos have created the potential for stigma around suicide. In contemporary Australia, this is far less the case than it was some 50 years ago, when the topic of suicide was considered taboo. It is now generally accepted that suicide is a tragedy and the people who are left behind often experience significant levels of grief and loss that may differ significantly from other forms of bereavement. Indeed, many people who have been traumatized by suicide loss feel their trusting relationship with the world has been betrayed.

People who are grieving often feel helpless, threatened, vulnerable, cheated, or disbelieving that the suicide event has happened to them. For them to rebuild their trust and a sense of safety in the world, they need increased support from their family, friends, and communities. They need to know that they are not alone; the world has not turned against them; and they have the support and security they need to cope with life's challenges. The inability to know what to do or what to say to someone who has experienced a suicide loss can make the situation worse.

There has been insufficient research on the notion of stigma linked to suicide. One recent study found that improved or helpful responses from family and friends outweighed strained or hurtful responses, in some cases by a factor of three to one (Feigelman, Gorman, & Jordan, 2009). However, despite their comparatively low incidence, behaviors typified by "a wall of silence," "the absence of a caring interest," or "unhelpful advice," (e.g., "time to move on") can have a dramatic impact on the bereaved and be perceived as stigmatization (Feigelman, Gorman, & Jordan, 2009).

Recent Australian research suggests that the stigma of suicide can often be a perception of the bereaved rather than the reality of how they are being treated—it may be a result of friends, family, neighbors, and associates withdrawing due to not knowing what to say or do, rather than deliberate efforts to stigmatize those left behind (Corporate Diagnostics Pty Ltd., 2007). The perception of stigma can often be linked to a loss of social connectedness. A comment from an anonymous focus group participant in consultations undertaken as part of the redevelopment of the Australian National Suicide Prevention Strategy (Corporate Diagnostics Pty Ltd., 2007) highlights this point:

> My biggest problem was that I just didn't know what to say to them. In the end, I decided not to say anything. Much later, I realized that I had probably caused them even more grief—not saying anything was probably the worst thing I could have done. (Commonwealth of Australia, 2008b)

☐ The Scope of Postvention Activity in Australia

In 1999, approximately 8% of youth suicide prevention activities in Australia specifically targeted postvention, and approximately 14% of youth suicide prevention activities used postvention as the main prevention activity, with the majority being based in community organizations. The youth suicide postvention interventions were primarily self-help support groups (Mitchell, 1999). In 2006, an estimated 60 self-help suicide bereavement support groups in Australia were covering a wide range of interest groups—by age, gender, religion, ethnicity, and geographical location—under the auspices of a range of agencies—not-for-profit, religious, cultural, and local government (Corporate Diagnostics Pty Ltd., 2006).

Between the mid-1990s and 2006, many initiatives were undertaken at local, state, and federal government levels to assist Australians bereaved by suicide. The primary sources of systemic support during those years were:

1. One-off initiatives (brochures, targeted counselling services, referrals to professional support) by specific medical practitioners, service providers, mental health and health agencies

2. Information or support kits distributed by the coroner's office or by not-for-profit agencies

3. Telephone counselling services

4. Community-based professional response services for people bereaved by suicide

5. Community-based self-help support groups for people bereaved by suicide

In 2006, the Australian government commissioned the study *National Activities on Suicide Bereavement* (Corporate Diagnostics Pty Ltd., 2006). That study, delivered to the Australian government in August 2006, included a scoping of suicide bereavement literature, a mapping of suicide bereavement activities across Australia, the identification of gaps in suicide bereavement research and activities, and a recommended framework and ongoing strategy for suicide bereavement activities in Australia. The 2006 study also undertook a major analysis of the role and effectiveness of the most widely used suicide bereavement support kit (see point 2, above)—an Australian adaptation of the United Kingdom initiative *Information and Support Pack for Those Bereaved by Suicide and Other Sudden Death* (Commonwealth of Australia, 2003, 2007; Hill, Hawton, Malmberg, & Simkin, 1997).

In light of this research, the 2006 round of Australian government NSPS funding included an allocation of $23.5 million for 46 community-based projects. Thirteen of the 46 community-based projects (approximately $8.5 million over 3 years) focused on building community capacity to respond to people bereaved by suicide (e.g., suicide response services, bereavement response services, enhanced training of service providers, grief and loss counselling). The 2006 round of Australian government funding also included a requirement that all projects be independently evaluated. In most cases, the 2006 funding was also made available for a 3-year period to allow effective longitudinal measurement of project impact, effectiveness, and success. Ten of the postvention projects funded in 2006 are currently being systematically evaluated—two are included as case studies later in this chapter. Summaries and contact details for the remaining eight are shown in the Appendix to this chapter.

☐ What We Have Learned—Responding to Suicide Loss, Grief, and Bereavement

The *National Activities in Suicide Bereavement: Final Report* (Corporate Diagnostics Pty Ltd., 2006) had several outputs, two of which are of specific interest in the current discussion. First, the research found that the provision of a comprehensive kit of information about suicide and suicide bereavement at or near the point of suicide was largely ineffectual. The study found that people bereaved by suicide need varying amounts of information and support at different points during their experience of grief. The concept of delivering a one-stop paper-based resource to people bereaved by suicide at the first point of contact did not reflect the wealth of evidence about the needs or the receptivity of the bereaved at this point in their grief.

The report recommended that the needs of people bereaved by suicide could best be met by a coordinated, systemic, *whole of community* approach. This approach requires a focus on face-to-face support at or near the suicide incident and an integrated community capacity to understand and respond appropriately, supported by a range of specifically targeted resources appropriate to the changing needs of the bereaved. Figure 28.1 summarizes this approach. The left-hand column in Figure 28.1 shows a typical time sequence of events that a person bereaved by suicide may experience. The right-hand text identifies the community-based and systemic processes that need to be in place if people bereaved by suicide are to be supported effectively.

☐ What We Have Learned—Indigenous and Culturally Diverse Australia

Australian research into suicide prevention and bereavement has also identified the uniquely different needs of indigenous Australians and of people from differing cultural backgrounds. Suicide among Australia's indigenous population is significantly higher than the general Australian population, with some estimates suggesting that the suicide rate for

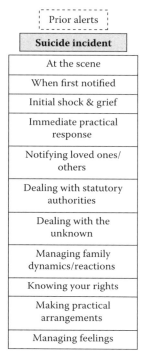

There is a major emphasis on rapid response, first-point-of-contact, face-to-face support systems.

- *There has been a broadly based **community education** campaign based on demonstrable evidence.*
- *Community awareness and understanding has been raised and there is a **ready-response capability** amongst community, family and friends.*
- *Emergency services core training protocols include basic principles of a supportive framework—"**psychological first-aid—Do no harm.**"*
- *There is a central "**one-stop**"/ "**one-call**" contact point which can direct bereaved to the most appropriate mix of products and services.*
- *Emergency services have **contact details for support**.*
- *There is a locally based 24-hour coordinated **quick-response, face-to-face support service** for people bereaved by suicide.*
- *There is an **entry under "S"** for "suicide help" in telephone directory.*
- *There is a **national help line** to direct people to locally based support.*
- *There is a **national network** of coordinated suicide response services.*
- *There is a national network of **suicide bereavement support groups**.*
- *There are appropriately trained and **accessible local counsellors**.*

Supported by a range of specifically targeted resources through several different media.

FIGURE 28.1 Establishing a systemic response capability for those bereaved by suicide.

indigenous people is 40% higher. Indigenous suicide has certainly increased dramatically over the past 30 years, with young indigenous males being the most at risk (Fremantle, 2005). This development is even more tragic when it is realized that anthropological evidence suggests that suicide was almost nonexistent in indigenous Australia prior to the 1950s.

Trauma and grief are significant problems within many displaced and/or marginalized indigenous cultures. Life expectancy for Australian indigenous males is much shorter than for nonindigenous males (56.9 years compared with 75.2 years) (De Leo, Hickey, Neulinger, & Cantor, 1999). As a cultural group, Australian Aborigines are exposed to death more frequently, especially early death, and this exposure, combined with historic experience of dispossession and cultural loss, has significant impact for grief processes "in the constant cycle, or procession, of grief" (Tatz, 1999, p. 91). Suicidal persons experience great difficulty tolerating loss, conflict, and frustration (Ellis, 2000); however, these situations are endemic to the experiences of Indigenous Australians. The most common method of suicide in Indigenous communities, hanging, has cultural and specific meanings for Aborigines and has become an institutionalized and pervasive cultural stereotype that is internalized by Indigenous Australians exposed to it (Tatz, 1999).

Despite the comparatively high incidence of suicide and the impact this has on extended families and communities, bereavement support for indigenous Australians is insufficiently understood by nonindigenous Australians and the health and mental health professions. The most effective bereavement support can vary significantly depending on the language group, the gender, and the status of the person who has died by suicide; kinship structures; the levels of cultural disintegration; and the social disadvantage of the specific indigenous community in which the suicide has occurred.

Similar difficulties arise in providing bereavement support for people from culturally and linguistically diverse (CALD) backgrounds. People from CALD backgrounds are less likely than other Australians to seek help for mental health problems or feelings of grief. They often miss out on suicide and bereavement support services because there is a lack of information available in community languages, and there may be a lack of culturally appropriate services. They may also find it difficult to use mainstream mental health services because of language and cultural barriers. People from CALD backgrounds are often unaware of the range of available services and supports, confused about how services operate, and misunderstood by health and mental health professionals.

In the 2006 round of NSPS funding, the Australian government supported several projects that specifically addressed the needs of bereaved indigenous communities (through culturally appropriate family-support programs) and bereaved cultural communities (cultural awareness training for frontline mental health workers and providing customized grief and loss workshops). There has also been a greater focus in recent Australian government funding on services that recognize a holistic understanding of health, a common belief among indigenous and CALD communities.

☐ Pathways to Care—Client-focused Interventions

People respond differently to traumatic life events and are, therefore, likely to seek different pathways to support and care. In some CALD and indigenous communities, a bereaved person is far more likely to seek support from family and the community than to approach a health or mental health professional or support service. In the case of suicide bereavement, feelings of loss, grief, and bereavement can fluctuate and be triggered by an apparently innocuous event—a song on the radio, a similar car, someone in similar clothes, or the absence at a specific event (birthdays, Christmas, weddings, anniversaries, etc.) of the person who died by suicide. People bereaved by suicide may follow a linear path to integration of or adaptation to loss, but many will follow a zigzag path—apparently coping, and then suddenly overcome by an event, a memory, or an apparently benign trigger or tipping point.

Until recently, the spectrum of health interventions developed by Mrazek and Haggerty (1994) has been the most common model for the delivery of support services in the Australian health care sector, particularly in relation to mental health and suicide prevention. Their spectrum proposes five phases of mental health interventions: prevention, early intervention, treatment, recovery, and continuing care. The intervention spectrum model, however, is supplier/service delivery focused and fails to define interventions around the needs of the consumer.

In attempting to improve the understanding of the needs of those bereaved by suicide, those traumatized by life events, or those experiencing mental health problems, a *pathways to care* model has been developed (Corporate Diagnostics Pty Ltd., 2007). This model:

1. Places the health and well-being of the individual at the center of the model

2. Respects and acknowledges the fact that individuals vary in their response to adverse life events

3. Recognizes that responses between individuals and over time for any one individual can vary substantially—each requiring a different intervention

4. Moves away from a spectrum or typology of interventions (supplier/provider focus) toward a client-centered continuum of care (consumer/patient focus)

5. Provides an integrated and coordinated range of support and care combining professional services with family and community support

6. Demedicalizes the terminology usually associated with this field, including introducing plain language specifically related to suicide prevention and postvention

7. Strengthens the role of community-based "safety net" functions between systemic interventions

8. Raises community awareness and understanding of the major issues in suicide prevention and postvention

☐ Australian Case Study 1—The StandBy Response Service

The StandBy Response Service is a community-based active postvention program that provides a 24-hour coordinated response to assist families, friends, and associates who have been bereaved through suicide. The StandBy Response Service was developed during the late 1990s in response to several suicides that occurred on the Sunshine Coast in Queensland and was formally established in 2002. The program is funded by the Australian Government Department of Health and Ageing and managed by United Synergies Ltd., a not-for-profit company committed to making a difference to the lives of others.

The Scope of StandBy's Support Service

The StandBy Response Service is available to any person who has experienced a local suicide, including an immediate loss; a suicide that occurs elsewhere but affects local people; or a previous suicide that continues to affect individuals or groups in the StandBy Response Service geographical areas. The StandBy Response Service also responds to school settings, community groups, and workplaces experiencing collective bereavement, emotional trauma, or distress following a suicide.

How the System Works

Most often, a suicide occurs in the community or a need is expressed for bereavement support following a nonlocal suicide or previous loss. Usually the first responders (police and ambulance service officers) attend a local incident and provide StandBy's contact details to the bereaved. Responders, or the bereaved themselves, contact StandBy for direct immediate outreach support or to arrange a suitable meeting time, as directed by the bereaved themselves. Local first responders have a StandBy Vehicle Visor Pack, which contains the contact details in a variety of formats (e.g., refrigerator magnet, business card, brochure). All information exchanged between the first responders and StandBy is confidential. This is a key feature of a Memorandum of Understanding between United Synergies and the state offices of the first responder organizations.

StandBy harnesses the cooperation of local services and support groups to respond to people bereaved by suicide, providing a reliable single point of contact. Linkage to local community support ensures that the bereaved do not feel alone or neglected and are less likely to be emotionally and physically overwhelmed by their loss.

StandBy is built on the principle that people bereaved by suicide are best enabled by locally resourced, timely, and respectful understanding and support. It is this philosophy which has ensured that the StandBy approach provides the right response to the right people at the right time and in the right place—an approach built around the principles outlined earlier (Figure 28.1). The service was designed through extensive consultation with bereaved people.

The StandBy Response Service Team

The StandBy Response Service is delivered by a skilled Crisis Response Team managed in each location by a StandBy coordinator. The StandBy Crisis Response Team is composed of paid professionals who have extensive experience, training, and a sound working background in crisis intervention and in responding to loss and grief. The StandBy Crisis Response Team also has extensive knowledge of the local community, available support services, and existing referral pathways to care.

The StandBy Crisis Response Team provides a crisis response based on an agreed intervention model that focuses on:

- Engaging with people bereaved by suicide by invitation only (usually following an initiative made by the bereaved as a result of information about StandBy being distributed by first responders)

- Providing a genuine, empathetic response to the bereaved

- Providing information on services and support available

- Ensuring safety of the Crisis Response Team and assessing risk of bereaved

- Building rapport, liaising with, and providing linkage to the local referral pathways

- Reporting bereavement response outcomes to the StandBy coordinator and fulfilling all reporting and documentation requirements

- Participating in regular debriefing and clinical supervision sessions

- Participating in ongoing reviews and evaluation for managing responses to bereavement by suicide

- Maintaining knowledge and skills through training and personal development opportunities

The StandBy Crisis Response Team provides 24-hour response "anytime—any place" in the community, including offering telephone support, providing face-to-face outreach and home visits, attending community locations where there has been a "whole-of-community" impact, facilitating group sessions at schools and workplaces; and offering general support on an "as required" basis.

Linking the Bereaved Into the Community

After initial bereavement care, the bereaved are linked to the StandBy Referral Pathways—a coordinated community response plan built on local community support, following an extensive program of community workshops, education, and training undertaken as part of establishing the StandBy Response Service locally. Where appropriate, the StandBy Response Service is provided in collaboration with local indigenous and cultural communities at a time and place guided and styled by the identified community leaders.

StandBy also assists in linking bereaved people to peer support via prearranged agreements with local bereavement support groups and with individuals who have themselves been bereaved.

The bereaved can make contact with StandBy at any time. However, as part of its duty of care, StandBy provides follow-up with bereaved clients 1 week, 3 months, and within 12 months after first contact as part of a customized support plan.

StandBy Goes National

The StandBy program has received many accolades for its innovative approach and its unique model of service delivery. This resulted in a high level of demand from other communities around Australia seeking to replicate the StandBy model in their local area. In 2008 and 2009, the StandBy program was tested in four Australian communities—the Sunshine Coast (regional coastal community), north Brisbane (urban city environment), Canberra (National Capital), and Cairns (regional city with a comparatively large indigenous population and multicultural communities). The trial sites were selected because they represented a diverse range of demographics and suicide patterns. In January 2009, the StandBy Response Service was expanded nationally to include Tasmania and remote indigenous regions in northern parts of Western Australia (the Kimberley and the Pilbara regions).

The StandBy trial was undertaken with financial support from the Australian Government Department of Health and Ageing to test whether the program can be easily and effectively transferred to other communities.

Evaluation of the StandBy Trial

The replication and trial of StandBy in other Australian communities were independently evaluated; independent evaluation is now a contractual condition of all projects funded under the Australian Government's National Suicide Prevention Strategy. The purpose of the evaluation was to evaluate the impact and efficacy of the implementation and provision of a StandBy Response Service in each region.

Released in August 2009, the independent evaluation found:

1. The StandBy Response Service reduces suicide ideation. This positive attitude improves over time to levels equal to or above those of the general population who have not experienced a suicide-related trauma.

2. The support and assistance of the StandBy Response Service appears to "normalize" the grief experience for people bereaved by suicide, increasing levels of happiness and vitality to levels similar to those shown by people who have experienced a recent nonsuicide trauma/loss.

3. The StandBy Response Service provides demonstrable assistance in reducing clients' feelings of sadness, tension, and grief related to their loss, thus increasing their ability to live with their loss over time.

4. Contact with the StandBy Response Service increases clients' awareness of available services and improves their ability to activate their own social networks.

5. There are very high levels of client satisfaction with the StandBy Service. This is particularly linked to the ability of the service to assist the suicide bereaved to understand their emotions and their bereavement, and to improve their knowledge of the support they need and where to access that support.

6. The StandBy Response Service reduces the incidence of adverse health and well-being outcomes, such as sadness and depression, for people bereaved by suicide. This reduction in negative health outcomes will likely improve StandBy clients' overall functioning and productivity and reduce their need for long-term treatment and support from community services.

The results of the evaluation process provide a detailed understanding of the impact the StandBy Response Service has on the community as a postvention model and provide the ability to refine and further improve the StandBy model. The evaluation process also provides valuable information to assist both federal and state governments in policy development and funding allocation in the field of suicide prevention and postvention. The StandBy evaluation has also made a significant contribution to the research field of suicide prevention/postvention, a field that has previously been lacking in evaluation and assessment.[6]

☐ Australian Case Study 2—Suicide Bereavement Support Group Standards and Practice

Another example of postvention activity in Australia is the Suicide Bereavement Support Group (SBSG) Standards and Practice project (2006–2009). A component of any coordinated "whole of community" approach to

---

[6] StandBy's external evaluation final report can be found at http://www.unitedsynergies .com.au/index.php?option=com_content&view=article&id=39&Itemid=23

postvention includes the provision of suicide bereavement support groups. As previously mentioned, the sixth action area under the NSPS framework is "implementing standards and quality in suicide prevention." As such, the SBSG Standards and Practice project undertook to investigate and reflect on the evidence of what works with support groups and develop tools to support best practice. The National Activities in Suicide Bereavement project referred to earlier in this chapter provided both a strong recommendation to pursue the development of national standards and best practice guidelines for support groups, and also a first draft of a standards framework.

Currently across Australia, there exists a diverse range of SBSGs providing much needed support to those bereaved by suicide. These groups provide invaluable support to people experiencing this most tragic loss by providing a safe and comfortable place to make connections to others who have shared a similar experience. Edwin Shneidman (1972, p. x) described postvention as "prevention ... for the next generation" and as such, support groups can be an effective means of reducing the impact of grief complications, suicidality, and enhancing psychological well-being.

Previous to this project, there were no minimum national standards or benchmarks available against which groups could guide their development or gauge how well they were performing, and few accredited training tools that facilitators could obtain to assist them in running SBSGs. Grief is a uniquely individual experience and not all those bereaved by suicide would seek to attend a support group or find a support group suitable to their needs. However, a caring community should make such a group available for those who choose to attend and ensure that the group is guided by standards and best practice and run by trained facilitators.

Lifeline Australia and a consortium of collaborative partners[7] undertook this project to address the shortfall in best practice guidelines by comprehensively reviewing the fabric of SBSG provision to fully appreciate current practices and the topography of the SBSG landscape. A broad consultation strategy was implemented to invite input from the suicide bereaved, SBSG facilitators currently running groups, and suicide bereavement service providers across Australia. An expert reference group closely guided the development phase of the project. The review led to the creation of clearly defined standards and guidelines that organizations providing SBSGs can use to support their group's development, to measure themselves against, and to evaluate their own performance and effectiveness.

---

[7] Collaborative partners included StandBy Response Service, New South Wales Department of Forensic Medicine, Compassionate Friends Victoria, Jesuit Social Services Support After Suicide Service, and the Australian Psychological Society.

These standards informed the development of a best practice handbook and a suite of training tools to assist in both the facilitation of individual SBSGs, and the training of those who facilitate them. The effectiveness of these newly developed standards and tools was tested in a series of eight trial groups undertaken across Australia in 2008, throughout which time a comprehensive external evaluation was carried out.

The project had a workforce development focus and aimed to provide training and support materials for facilitators with a view to improving the level of effectiveness they deliver and the quality of care provided to those who attend SBSGs. Eight Lifeline crisis centers were selected from six states across Australia to participate in the trial, and each sent three facilitators to be trained and then conducted a trial SBSG in their region.

Objective One—Standards and Guidelines

The standards and guidelines consist of four major standards articulated below. Each has various subsections that delineate further detail:

1. Support group establishment and maintenance

2. Support group philosophy and processes

3. Support group facilitation and management

4. Support group services

This set of standards and guidelines was developed to support those who participate in and operate SBSGs and has been disseminated broadly with rationale and encouragement to adopt this voluntary code of conduct (Lifeline Australia, 2009a). The "standards and guidelines" have been accepted onto the SPRC/AFSP Best Practices Registry for Suicide Prevention, under Section II—Expert and Consensus Statements.

Objective Two—Develop a Best Practice Handbook

A literature review was undertaken at the outset of the project alongside a review of the practice evidence derived from experienced SBSG facilitators, both nationally and internationally. A comprehensive *Practice Handbook* was developed to provide a resource for facilitators to enable more effective facilitation in the provision of SBSGs (Lifeline Australia, 2009b).

Objective Three—Develop Training Tools

The Australian Quality Training Framework (AQTF) is the national set of standards that assures nationally consistent, high-quality training and assessment services for clients of Australia's Vocational Education and Training (VET) system. For sustainability and credibility reasons, this project undertook to develop SBSG facilitator training mapped to nationally accredited competencies under the AQTF. The project participated in the Community Services and Health Industry Skills Council (CSHISC) review of the Community Services Training Package by developing two new competencies to support the training of SBSG facilitators.[8] These, along with two other existing competencies,[9] were also used to guide the development and mapping of training. A diverse, collaborative group of highly skilled, knowledgeable, and experienced trainers came together to develop and present the 3.5-day intensive experiential residential training and assessment tasks based on these competencies. Facilitators completed prereading as well as pre- and posttraining tasks. Trainees also completed the 2-day LivingWorks Applied Suicide Prevention Skills Training (ASIST) to ensure their suicide first aid preparedness and duty of care for participants.

Objective Four—Train Facilitators and Conduct Trial SBSGs

The project provided two intakes of training for trainee facilitators. Each Lifeline Centre team of three facilitators was trained and then conducted a trial SBSG guided by the standards, guidelines, *Practice Handbook*, and training. Facilitators were supported by centralized (quality assured) external group supervision (via telephone) after each SBSG meeting, and met in teleconference with all other trial facilitators in monthly "Update and Practice Issues" forums throughout the trial. The second delivery of

---

[8] Competencies are units within qualifications that sit within the Vocational Education and Training (VET) system. CHCCS426A provide support and care relating to loss and grief; CHCCS417A provide support and care relating to suicide bereavement.

[9] CCHICS405A facilitate groups for individual outcomes; CHCCOM403A use targeted communication skills to build relationships.

the training was informed by action research feedback from the first set of four trial groups.

SBSG trials were conducted in a range of geographic locations across Australia, with varying numbers of participants. Some were in metropolitan areas, but many were located in rural/regional areas where participants and facilitators had to travel considerable distances to attend.

Objective Five—External Evaluation

As previously stated in this chapter, external evaluation was a requirement of this Commonwealth project. The evaluators worked with the project from the outset to be able to provide cumulative feedback to inform the project at every step. The evaluators used the following methodologies: observation of training, evaluative survey feedback from trainee facilitators immediately after training, telephone interview after completion of trial groups, comparison of a self-rating task completed by trainees at three stages of the trial, telephone interviews with the five-person training team, telephone interviews with trial Crisis Center managers, telephone interviews with the two external group supervisors, survey feedback from SBSG participants, and survey feedback from key providers of suicide bereavement services in Australia.

Next Steps for the *Standards & Guidelines* and the *Practice Handbook*

An implementation plan is under way to disseminate the *Standards & Guidelines*, and the *Practice Handbook* to those involved with the delivery of Suicide Bereavement Support Groups. It is planned that Facilitator training will be further refined and able to be tailored for novice facilitators and more experienced facilitators. SBSG facilitators often operate in isolation, and this project has illuminated the value of creating a community of practice for facilitators to be able to network regularly, to share ideas and challenges, and to be supported by the materials that have been developed under this project and therefore enhance their skills and knowledge to be able to support those bereaved by suicide.[10]

---

[10]An executive summary and the resources produced in this project can be located at http://www.lifeline.org.au/find_help/suicide_prevention/suicide_bereavement_and_postvention

☐ Conclusion—Looking Forward

The Australian government, academics, researchers, and policymakers at all levels (federal, state, and local) have a long and commendable history of commitment to funding, improving the evidence for, and delivering quality services in the fields of suicide prevention and suicide postvention. In addition, the not-for-profit community and health sectors have a long history of providing a variety of support services for those who feel depressed or suicidal, for those with a mental illness, or for those who are bereaved by suicide.

In recent years, initiatives in the postvention sector have intensified—with the first National Postvention Conference occurring in Australia in 2007, an increase in Australian government funding to projects that focus on people bereaved by suicide, and a commitment for more proactive and targeted support identified in the new National Suicide Prevention Strategy Workplan (Roxon, 2008). There are many projects currently underway that are being independently evaluated so that the lessons learned from them can be translated to service providers nationally. There is also a wide network of suicide support groups that are now in regular contact. Standards, guidelines, and principles for these support groups are finalized, accompanied by evidence-based, accredited, facilitator training. On current indications, the prognosis is positive for this sector and for people bereaved by suicide in Australia.

APPENDIX

☐ **Summaries and Contact Information for the Remaining Eight Australian Government-Funded Postvention Projects**

The Grief & Loss—"Counselling the Bereaved" Workshops Project

Contact: Kerry McGregor—manager@yic.com.au
Web site: http://www.yic.com.au/
This project supports the Youth Initiative Council to conduct the "Living Works" Grief and Loss—'Counselling the Bereaved'" workshops in the Pilbara region of Western Australia. This region encompasses several remote indigenous communities. Aboriginal Health Services is among the project's partners. The project seeks to promote individual resilience, healing and help-seeking behaviour through collaborative community partnerships.

The SANE Australia Mental Illness Bereavement Project

Contact: Barbara Hocking—barbara.hocking@sane.org
Web site: http://www.sane.org/campaigns_content/suicide_prevention.html
This national suicide project aims to improve services and support for family and friends of people with mental illness who have died by suicide or are missing. It features three major activities:

1. Training workshops

2. Development and provision of factsheets

3. Development of bereavement policy guidelines for mental health services to provide a structured approach to responding the families after suicide

The program has external evaluation via consultation with an evaluator from the School of Population Health at Melbourne University.

Jesuit Social Services Support After Suicide Program

Contact: Louise Flynn—Louise.Flynn@jss.org.au
Web site: http://www.supportaftersuicide.org.au
Support After Suicide is a state-based program that seeks to increase the availability of timely and appropriate support to families in Victoria, especially those with young children, who are bereaved through suicide. The program also provides education, health, and welfare professionals who have the capacity to support those affected by suicide. In addition, Support After Suicide provides innovative and creative education programs to professionals working in the education, health, and welfare sectors. The program seeks to increase knowledge of issues relating to suicide bereavement and enhance the capacity of professionals to respond effectively to people bereaved by suicide.

Anglicare South Australia Living Beyond Suicide Project

Contact: Michael Hawke—mhawke@Anglicare-SA.org.au
Web site: http://www.anglicare-sa.org.au/living-beyond-suicide/
Living Beyond Suicide is a statewide service of Anglicare's Loss and Grief Center in South Australia. Living Beyond Suicide offers survivor-sensitive early support for families bereaved through suicide. Emotional and practical support are provided by appropriately skilled and trained volunteers to help families navigate service systems and access the assistance they need. Volunteer training occurs across several regional areas. The service engenders a survivor sensitivity and responsiveness within services, public authorities, and the wider community through community-based education and capacity building.

The Perth & Hills Division of General Practice "Promoting Living" Program

Web site: http://www.ppcn.com.au/site/index.cfm?display=38142

The main aim and purposes of the Promoting Living Program are to enhance community capacity in suicide prevention and postvention support in the catchment area of Perth Primary Care Network (PPCN). The program does this by encouraging and fostering partnerships of community groups, service providers, and government agencies through community-based projects and integration with other suicide prevention strategies and programs. The program has three primary objectives:

1. To build integrated pathways in the region for people at risk of suicide and their family/carers

2. To reduce the risk of suicide and self-harm associated with harmful drug and alcohol use

3. To increase early intervention and prevention of suicide

The program also plans to host training events for General Practitioners and Practice Nurses and provide a Train the Trainer program for men in the community setting.

Salvation Army Hope for Life Campaign

Contact: Alan Staines—alanstaines@optusnet.com.au
Web site: http://suicideprevention.salvos.org.au/
The national "Hope for Life" campaign includes the Living Hope QPR (Question, Persuade, Refer) online training developed by authored by Dr. Paul Quinnett to assist in suicide prevention and postvention support. The Living Hope training targets caregivers, pastoral care workers emergency services, as well as those from the health, social welfare, and education sectors. In addition, the program also hosts the national Hope Line—a 24-hour telephone support service as well as the Salvation Army's Hope for Life Web site.

Telethon Institute for Child Health Research—ARBOR

Contact: Sharon Hillman—S.Hillman@curtin.edu.au
Web site: http://www.ichr.uwa.edu.au/preventingsuicide/arbor

Inspired by the work of Dr. Frank Campbell in Louisiana, USA, the ARBOR (Active Response Bereavement Outreach) service provides an outreach service for family and friends in the Perth area of Western Australia who lose a loved one by suicide. ARBOR aims to help the newly bereaved access support, resources and assistance, as well as reduce the sense of isolation experienced by the bereaved. Short-term professional grief counselling is available and support by trained bereaved volunteers is also provided. The Ministerial Council for Suicide Prevention and the Centre for Developmental Health (Curtin University) manage the project, which also hosts support groups. The program has ongoing evaluation, with the well-being of peer supporters and clients regularly monitored.

Women's Health Care (WA) Postvention Project

Contact: info@whs.org.au
Web site: http://www.whs.org.au/services/whch/indigenous
This project seeks to address postvention issues with indigenous communities by extending the existing Intergenerational Aboriginal Grandparents Family Support Service. This service provides support to Aboriginal and Torres Strait Islander grandparents caring for their grandchildren or great-grandchildren. Based on family, social, health, and well-being principles, the program improves grandparents' access to government and other services, provision of information, advocacy, and peer support. Through activities, including self-care events, respite camps, peer support, and Aboriginal playgroups, grandparents have experienced improved health and well-being, and the confidence to assist them in maintaining strong and happy families. This service is an initiative of the Women's Health Services, Western Australia.

☐ References

Australian Capital Territory (ACT) Health. (2005). *Suicide prevention, Managing the risk of suicide 2005–2008: A suicide prevention strategy for the ACT.* Canberra, Australia: Author.

Australian Bureau of Statistics. (2008). *Causes of death, Australia, 2006.* Canberra, Australia: Commonwealth of Australia, Catalogue No. 3303.0, March.

Australian Bureau of Statistics. (2009a). *Population clock.* Retrieved from http://www.abs.gov.au/Ausstats/abs@.nsf/0/1647509ef7e25faaca2568a900154b63?OpenDocument

Australian Bureau of Statistics. (2009b). *Causes of death, Australia, 2007*. Canberra, Australia: Commonwealth of Australia, Catalogue No. 3303.0, March.

Australian Health Ministers. (1992). *National Mental Health Policy*. Canberra, Australia: Commonwealth of Australia.

Australian Health Ministers and Commonwealth Department of Human Services and Health. (1995) *The health of young Australians: A national health policy for children and young people*. Canberra, Australia: Australian Government Publishing Service.

beyondblue. (n.d.). Retrieved from http://www.beyondblue.org.au

Burdekin, B. (1993). *Human rights and mental illness: Report of the National Enquiry into Human Rights of People with Mental Illness*. Canberra, Australia: Australian Government Publishing Service.

Commonwealth of Australia. (2000). *Living is for everyone: A framework for prevention of suicide and self-harm in Australia*. Canberra, Australia: Author.

Commonwealth of Australia. (2003). *Information and support pack for those bereaved by suicide or other sudden death*. Canberra, Australia: Department of Health and Ageing.

Commonwealth of Australia. (2007). *Information and support pack for those bereaved by suicide or other sudden death* (2nd ed.). Canberra, Australia: Department of Health and Ageing.

Commonwealth of Australia. (2008a). *Living is for everyone (LIFE) framework (2007): A framework for prevention of suicide and self-harm in Australia*. Canberra, Australia: Author.

Commonwealth of Australia (2008b). Living is for everyone (LIFE) *Factsheet 22: "I don't know what to say, I don't know what to do."* Canberra, Australia: Author.

Corporate Diagnostics Pty Ltd. (2006, August). *National activities on suicide bereavement: Final report*. Unpublished presentation to the Department of Health and Ageing.

Corporate Diagnostics Pty Ltd. (2007, July). *Redevelopment of the living is for everyone (LiFE) framework project: Final report*. Presented to the Department of Health and Ageing,

De Leo, D., Hickey, A., Neulinger, K., & Cantor, C. (1999). *A hidden problem: Suicide in older men in Queensland*. A report to the Office of Ageing, Families, Youth & Community Care. Queensland. Brisbane, Australia: Australian Institute for Suicide Research and Prevention.

De Leo, D., Dudley, M., Aebersold, C., Mendoza, J., Barnes, M., Ranson, D., & Harrison, J. (2010). Achieving standardised reporting of suicide in Australia: Rationale and program for change. *Medical Journal of Australia, 192*, 452–456.

Department of Health and Community Services. (2003). *Northern Territory strategic framework for suicide prevention*. Casuarina, Australia: Author.

Department of Human Services Victoria. (1997, July). *Suicide prevention: Victorian task force report*. Melbourne, Australia: Author.

Department of Human Services Victoria. (2006). *Next steps: Victoria's suicide prevention forward action plan 2006, A public statement*. Melbourne, Australia: Author.

Ellis, T. E. (2000). *Psychotherapy with suicidal patients*. In D. Lester (Ed.), *Suicide prevention: Resources for the millennium* (pp. 129–151). Philadelphia, PA: Taylor & Francis.

Feigelman, W., Gorman B. S., & Jordan, J. R. (2009) Stigmatization and suicide bereavement. *Death Studies, 33*, 591–608.

Fremantle, J. (2005, August). *From data to detail—pathways to policy: Closing the know-do gap.* Presentation to the Australian Research Alliance for Children and Youth (ARACY) National Conference, Sydney, Australia.

Geoscience Australia. (2009). *Australia's size compared.* Retrieved from http://www.ga.gov.au/education/geoscience-basics/dimensions/aus-size-compared.jsp

Harrison, J. E., Pointer, S., & Elnour, A. A. (2009). *A review of suicide statistics in Australia.* AIHW Injury Research and Statistics Series No. 49. (Cat. No. INJCAT 121). Adelaide, Australia: AIHW.

Hill, K., Hawton, K., Malmberg, A., & Simkin, S. (1997). *Bereavement information pack: For those bereaved by suicide or other sudden death.* London, England: Royal College of Psychiatrists (Gaskell Press).

Lifeline Australia. (2009a). *Towards good practice: Standards & guidelines for suicide bereavement support groups.* Canberra: Author. Retrieved from http://www.lifeline.org.au/find_help/suicide_prevention/suicide_bereavement_and_postvention

Lifeline Australia. (2009b). *Practice handbook—Suicide bereavement support group facilitation.* Canberra. Australia: Author. Retrieved from http://www.lifeline.org.au/find_help/suicide_prevention/suicide_ bereavement_and_postvention

Mitchell, P. (1999). First national stocktake of youth suicide prevention programs: A content analysis. *Youth Suicide Prevention Bulletin, 2*, 2–7.

Mitchell, P. (2000). *Valuing young lives: Evaluation of the National Youth Suicide Prevention Strategy.* Melbourne, Australia: Australian Institute of Family Studies.

Mrazek, P. J., & Haggerty, R. J. (1994). *Reducing the risks for mental disorders: Frontiers for preventive intervention research.* Washington, DC: National Academies Press.

National Youth Suicide Prevention Strategy. (1999). *Setting the evidence-based research agenda for Australia (a literature review).* Canberra, Australia: Department of Health and Aged Care, Commonwealth of Australia.

NSW Health. (1999). *Suicide: We can all make a difference.* Sydney, Australia: Author.

Queensland Health. (2003). *Reducing suicide: The Queensland Government Suicide Prevention Strategy, 2003–2008.* Brisbane, Australia: Author.

Royal Commission into Aboriginal Deaths in Custody (RCIADIC). (1991). *National report: Overview and recommendations by Commissioner Elliott Johnston, QC.* Canberra, Australia: Australian Government Publishing Service.

Roxon, N. (2008, September 10). *World suicide prevention day—New Australian Suicide Prevention Advisory Council.* Press Release. Retrieved N from http://www.health.gov.au/internet/ministers/publishing.nsf/Content/1B4ECCC9 9DCA6F6DCA2574C00023FBE9/$File/nr122.pdf

Shneidman, E. S. (1972). Foreword. In A. C. Cain (Ed.), *Survivors of suicide* (pp. ix-xi). Springfield, IL: Charles C Thomas

SPRC/AFSP Best Practices Registry, Section II: Expert and Consensus Statements. *Towards Good Practice: Standards and Guidelines for Suicide Bereavement Support Groups.* Retrieved from http://www.sprc.org/featured%5Fresources/bpr

Tatz, C. (1999). *Aboriginal suicide is different:* A report to the Criminology Research Council on CRC Project 25/96-7. Sydney, Australia: Macquarie University.

United Nations. (1996). *Preventing suicide: Guidelines for the formulation and implementation of national strategies.* New York, NY: Author.

U.S. Bureau of the Census. (2009). *U.S. POPClock Projection.* Retrieved from http://www.census.gov/population/www/popclockus.html

World Health Organization (WHO). (1990). *Strategies for reducing suicidal behaviours in the European region, 1989, summary report.* Geneva, Switzerland: Author.

International Perspectives on Suicide Bereavement

Suicide Survivors and Postvention in Norway

Kari Dyregrov

Norway is a small, wealthy, Western country with a population of only 4.7 million people. The official death records of 2007 reported 485 annual suicides in Norway, with 149 women and 336 men dying by suicide. This implies a total rate of 10.3, and a rate of 7.7 for females, and 16.5 for males (Statistics Norway, 2009). If one estimates a minimum of 10 close bereaved persons for each suicide, this represents a total of more than 5,000 survivors of suicide every year. As in most countries worldwide, Norwegian survivors have over the years met with different forms of stigmatization on the part of society. They have experienced various forms of discrimination from religious and social institutions, and from insurance companies. However, positive changes have taken place in Norway over the last 15 years, a development that is predominantly due to increasingly flexible attitudes about other stigmatized areas of society, but also to requirements for increased tolerance in general.

☐ A Social Shift of Stigma

An important initiative for creating openness and respect for suicide and suicide survivors was led by one of Norway's former prime ministers, Dr. Gro Harlem Brundtland, when in 1992, she informed the nation of the suicide of her son. Some years later, another prime minister drew attention to and normalized the burden of psychological distress when he officially declared that he would be taking 6 weeks sick leave due to depression (Grad, Clark, Dyregrov, & Andriessen, 2004). Other politicians and prominent persons disclosed the suicides of their children and spouses in the years that followed. The openness about these situations within the media had a number of positive repercussions at different levels in Norwegian society. Survivors of suicide clearly profited from the candor of these dignitaries, and were further empowered by the establishment in 1999 of the organization Landsforeningen for etterlatte ved selvmord (LEVE; The Norwegian Association for Suicide Survivors—http://www.levenorge.no). This organization was formed as a result of the Norwegian Support and Care study that showed a need for more extensive peer support and professional help for survivors of suicide (Dyregrov, 2003).

Since 1999, this organization has conducted campaigns and arranged nationwide seminars to shed light on suicide and suicide survivors. LEVE's members have, to a broad extent, come out and given the bereaved a face, both through the media and through participation in research on the suicide survivors (Dyregrov, 2003; Dyregrov & Dyregrov, 2005). The breaking down of stigma has been accelerated by survivors telling their stories as completely ordinary families who suddenly experience the impossible and catastrophic reality that someone close to them can no longer bear to continue living. This has also contributed to the population acquiring greater insight into the fact that the survivor experience is an extremely difficult psychosocial situation, and that the support of the social network—rather than its judgment—is important (Dyregrov & Dyregrov, 2008). Further, professionals in the field have acquired new knowledge about the experience of losing a close loved one by suicide, on how the survivors wish to be met, and on what they can do to support suicide survivors. Finally, the focus has lessened the burden of stigma on survivors. This important shift, however, could not have occurred so quickly without the positive cooperation from journalists and the media. In collaboration with suicide experts, key media organizations have assumed responsibility for educating members of the media profession about the significance of openness in connection with suicide, about the accompanying side effects, and about the importance of supporting the suicide survivors. Mainly, this was a result of the Norwegian public plan of action and other suicidologists' joint efforts to make the media understand and take responsibility in the field.

☐ Attitudes Toward Suicide and Survivors Today

The fact that the suicide survivors today experience less stigma than just a few years ago is reflected in how they are met in their social networks, at the workplace, by the church, and by other public institutions. My extensive contact with suicide survivors indicates that most of them today tell close friends, family members, and their social networks that they have lost someone by suicide without experiencing judgment (Dyregrov, 2003, 2003–2004, 2006). The myths maintaining that suicide only takes place in families under a particular strain have subsequently lost much of their credence. The survivors, to an increasing extent, inform the workplace about what has happened, either by their own volition or with the help of supervisors and colleagues. The same is the case in the schools, where the special needs of surviving children and young people are attended to, such as through the arrangement of rituals following the suicide of a parent or sibling. The church arranges bereavement groups, memorial services, and church services for suicide survivors, and in so doing sends a signal that the Norwegian State Church no longer stigmatizes the survivors. Often, clergy and funeral agents encourage survivors to be open about the suicide so that they will subsequently receive the necessary support and assistance from the people in their surroundings (Dyregrov & Litlere, 2009). Another important signal indicating the breakdown of stigma on the part of the public sector is that insurance companies pay out insurance to the survivors, even when it turns out that a death has been self-inflicted.

Still, some attitudes remain reminiscent of the past—more so in some ethnic and religious subgroups than others. This statement is, however, more of an impression, due to the difficulties encountered thus far in carrying out research on suicide within such subgroups. Thus, mainstream Norwegians seem to be more open toward suicide and the people left in its wake than the minority of fundamentalist religious and ethnic groups. The reason for this may be that the latter have a "longer way to go" or have not been influenced by the suicide destigmatization campaigns of recent years. Therefore, although the church, law, and social institutions have stopped discriminating against survivors of suicide, the centuries-long stigmatization of suicide still exerts some influence in Norwegian society.

☐ Informal Support Toward Mastering Suicide

The Norwegian Support and Care study that started in 1996 has yielded much knowledge about Norwegian suicide survivors (Dyregrov, 2002, 2003, 2003–2004, 2006; Dyregrov & Dyregrov, 2005, 2008, 2010; Dyregrov, Nordanger, & Dyregrov, 2003; Dyregrov, Plyhn, & Dieserud, 2010; Grad, Clark, Dyregrov, & Andriessen, 2004). The earliest findings differ from those resulting from later projects, mainly showing a rapid development of society's willingness to assume increased responsibility for suicide survivors. Also, survivors have gradually become more self-confident and self-assertive in a positive way, demanding to be heard, understood, and to receive offers of necessary help and support.

It is difficult to claim that there is *one* typical way of dealing with suicide among survivors in Norway. However, *the* most typical survivor would be open and honest about the suicide in relation to his or her surroundings, would want and receive support from family and close friends, and would expect (but not always receive) flexible and individually adapted assistance from local professionals or the church. Last, some would seek help in acquiring contact with others who have experienced a similar type of death. As LEVE has now been extended to all of Norway's counties, more and more survivors are making connections with other survivors to find understanding, identification, hope, and encouragement. Here survivors support each other through cafés, seminars, trips, youth groups, grief groups, bereavement help lines, and so forth. The membership fee of $60 per family, charitable gifts, and a governmental subsidy of $60 per membership constitute the economic basis of LEVE. Access to its offices is free of charge. The unpaid work of members has also been an important means to run the organization. In addition, LEVE has received project grants from the government and trusts for such projects as developing and running a newsletter and a home page on the Internet, and taking responsibility for organizing World Suicide Prevention Day in Norway. A main principle for the organization is the collaboration between survivors, volunteers, and professional helpers to integrate survivor support within a national strategy for suicide postvention. In addition to the goal of supporting survivors, LEVE is helping with antistigmatization work through information and cooperation with the health services through national networks of helpers.

Friends and family are *the* most important single factor on the path to recovery. Survivors consistently point out the importance of social networks for their healing after suicide. The extensive support that many receive from family, friends, colleagues, and neighbors is greatly appreciated (Dyregrov, 2008). It is of the greatest importance, according to the survivors, that the network "cares." This implies that family and friends make contact and are available on the terms of the survivors to listen, to show empathy, and to speak with the survivors about the deceased. Flowers, visits, telephone calls, and letters are other appreciated forms of support, as is someone who steps in to help with children and the practical matters of daily life. Help to return to a more normal daily life through work and social activities is also a highly valued form of support (Dyregrov & Dyregrov, 2008).

However, in spite of all of the positive support, most survivors also experience community reactions that can sometimes be insufficient or even destructive. Some report that people from whom they expect to receive support avoid them by "crossing the street," neglect to contact them, or ignore them at times when, under normal circumstances, they would have spoken. Others state that they become hurt or angered by their networks' "good advice" or inept remarks (Dyregrov, 2003–2004). Survivors specified different self-mastering strategies as important means of coping with this. In the Support and Care study, 81% of survivors suggested that "openness" represented their most important strategy for coping with the difficult social situation following the death. For them, openness implies sincerity, honesty, and direct speech connected to the suicide. To a large extent, this was viewed as the result of giving clear signals to their surroundings. For example, when the suicide survivors write in an obituary that the deceased "could not bear to go on living" or "chose to leave us," it is a means of communicating the cause of death to their community. Survivors believe that such signals are an important means of informing others of what has happened, how they are feeling, the type of support they need, and how others can best support them. Research (Dyregrov, 2006; Dyregrov & Dyregrov, 2008) confirms that this is the kind of signal families and friends ask for to improve their support efforts for the survivors. Other coping strategies mentioned by survivors include talking/writing about the deceased, visiting the cemetery, carrying out physical exercise, spending time with close friends, and so forth (Dyregrov & Dyregrov, 2008; Dyregrov et al., 2010).

☐ Organized Professional Services—A Principle but Not Always a Praxis

Through the Support and Care study from 1998 (Dyregrov, 2003), four strategies were identified as to the manner in which Norwegian communities organized their support for suicide survivors. These strategies were prevention (early intervention), treatment (after discovery of symptoms), demedicalization (user empowerment/shift of focus away from health care professionals), and avoidance of and ignoring the matter. Thus, the quality of support and care that the survivors received after a suicide proved to vary significantly. Since then, a more consistent help strategy has been developed. In accordance with the Norwegian Act of June 23, 2000, No. 56, relating to health and social emergency preparedness, local communities shall in their health care services offer "necessary health care assistance and social services to the population during war and with crises and disasters in peacetime" (Section 1-1). Therefore, most local governments in Norway today offer some form of immediate contact with professionals after a suicide (Dyregrov, 2002). An increasing number of crisis teams today have a goal of routinely contacting all of the closest suicide survivors, which, in addition to the family, also may include close friends. Beyond providing emotional first aid and information about the suicide, the team investigates the type of professional help needed and subsequently ensures that close survivors receive the help they require. All such help is paid for by the public sector. The team also investigates whether friends and family have received information about the suicide and whether they can be of support for the survivors. If help is needed in contacting the school, public health care system, or other survivors through LEVE, the team can also take responsibility for this. The crisis teams also have a focus on the potential necessity of making practical, legal, or financial help available.

However, the ideals of the crisis teams are not always transformed into reality. As experienced by the survivors, the quality and quantity of such help varies from community to community. This is related to the type of help offered, from whom help is received, the frequency of offers, whether the support is proactively offered or must be sought out by the survivors, and the duration of the assistance. The most common type of help provided is short-term counseling, provided by clergy, physicians, or nurses. Very few of the local governments have follow-up schemes that continue beyond the first year, in spite of the fact that a large majority of the survivors seek precisely this (Dyregrov, 2002). Also, relatively few local communities focus on providing help for surviving children, the type of assistance most frequently requested, along with help from a psychologist (Dyregrov, 2009a, 2009b). In other words, the survivors want more or different types of professional help than which they receive. At the same time, they state that they are not asking to become lifetime clients in a treatment system. On the contrary, they ask for routine and rapid assistance so they can avoid becoming long-term clients. They would like help that is geared toward helping themselves get on with their lives in the best and most expedient manner possible. They ask for support with stability and continuity, qualified assistants, but at the same time, an assistance scheme that is flexible and adapted to the individual (Dyregrov & Dyregrov, 2008).

It is likely that communities will gradually address the above requests through improved routines and knowledge based on the needs of the survivors. My research group at the Norwegian Institute of Public Health has prepared an action plan/guidelines for support to survivors of suicide in the communities for the Norwegian Social and Health Directorate. Hopefully, this will be implemented in 2011 and will complement the Web site (http://www.kriser.no) that has been an important guide for professional support efforts for survivors since 2004.

☐ Support at the Workplace

Throughout the course of the last decade, workplaces in Norway have begun creating plans for psychosocial care of employees who experience crises and disasters at and outside of the workplace. Although some connect the guidelines to the existing company health service, others allow the routines to function in tandem. Others, particularly large workplaces such as the police department, also have peer support schemes. Many survivors praise colleagues for their fantastic support, while others experience disappointment in relation to colleagues and understanding at the workplace. They find that the goodwill and understanding both from management and colleagues are prerequisites to their returning to "a normal life." A constantly recurring theme among the survivors is how the workplace is either a support in the grief process, or in contrast, how insufficient attentiveness, understanding, and accommodation contribute to longer periods on sick leave and a more complicated grief process. In workplaces with psychosocial support plans, open information at the workplace paved the way for enabling colleagues to ask questions and express their own reactions and empathy in relation to the survivors through gifts of flowers and funeral attendance in collaboration with the family of the deceased (Dyregrov &

Dyregrov, 2008). When others are provided knowledge of the suicide, this creates an opportunity for the survivor to speak about and process what has happened.

☐ A Better Future

The positive changes of recent years, to a great extent, have improved the situation for most survivors of suicide in Norway. Even though the personal loss remains just as difficult as for survivors as in previous years, it has become easier for them to go on living as a result of the increased acceptance and understanding in Norwegian society, as well as improved help and support from peers, social networks, and professionals.

☐ References

Dyregrov, K. (2002). Assistance from local authorities versus survivors' needs for support after suicide. *Death Studies, 26,* 647–669.

Dyregrov, K. (2003) *The loss of child by suicide, SIDS, and accidents: Consequences, needs and provisions of help* (Doctoral dissertation). HEMIL. Faculty of Psychology, University of Bergen. ISBN 82-7669-099-8.

Dyregrov, K. (2003–2004). Micro-sociological analysis of social support following traumatic bereavement: Unhelpful and avoidant responses from the community. *Omega: Journal of Death and Dying, 48,* 23–44.

Dyregrov, K. (2006). Experiences of social networks supporting traumatically bereaved. *Omega: Journal of Death and Dying, 52,* 337–356.

Dyregrov, K. (2008). Painful, difficult and incredibly rewarding: New research delves into the support process between social networks and parents who suffer the traumatic death of a child. *Surviving Suicide* (a quarterly newsletter of the American Association of Suicidology), *20*(3), 7–8.

Dyregrov, K. (2009a). How do the young suicide survivors wish to be met by psychologists? A user study. *Omega: Journal of Death and Dying, 59,* 221–238.

Dyregrov, K. (2009b). The important role of the school following suicide. New research about the help and support wishes of the young bereaved. *Omega: Journal of Death and Dying, 59,* 147–161.

Dyregrov, K., & Dyregrov, A. (2005). Siblings after suicide—"The forgotten bereaved." *Suicide and Life-Threatening Behavior, 35,* 714–724.

Dyregrov, K., & Dyregrov, A. (2008). *Effective grief and bereavement support: The role of family, friends, colleagues, schools and support professionals.* London, England: Jessica Kingsley Publishers.

Dyregrov, K., & Dyregrov, A. (2009). Helping the family following suicide. In B. Monroe & F. Kraus (Eds.)(2nd ed.), *Brief interventions with bereaved children* (pp. 213–228). Oxford: University Press.

Dyregrov, K., & Litlere, M. (2009). "Førstehjelpernes" møte med etterlatte ved selvmord—psykososiale utfordringer (The first-responders' encounters with suicide survivors—psychosocial challenges). *Suicidologi, 14*, 21–24.

Dyregrov, K., Nordanger, D., & Dyregrov, A. (2003). Predictors of psychosocial distress after suicide, SIDS and accidents. *Death Studies, 27*, 143–165.

Dyregrov, K., Plyhn, E., & Dieserud, G. (2010). *Etterlatte ved selvmord. Veien videre.* (Survivors of suicide. The road ahead). Oslo, Norway: Abstrakt Forlag.

Grad, O. T., Clark, S., Dyregrov, K., & Andriessen, K. (2004). What helps and what hinders the process of surviving the suicide of someone close? *Crisis: International Journal of Crisis Intervention and Suicide Prevention, 25*, 134–139.

Statistics Norway. (2009). Suicide and suicide rate per 100 000 population, by sex and age. 1951–2007. Retrieved from http://www.ssb.no/dodsarsak/tab-2009- 04-07-08.html

International Perspectives on Suicide Bereavement—Slovenia

Onja Grad

Men are disturbed not by things, but by the view which they take of them.

Epictetus

☐ Cultural Attitudes Toward Suicide and Survivors

Slovenia is a small Central European country with a long-lasting problem of suicidal behavior. The suicide rate has been very high for the past 40 years (between 25 and 35 per 100,000 per year). This fact was hidden to the international public in the much lower Yugoslav rates until 1991, when Slovenia became an independent state.

At the end of the 19th century, the rate was still one of the lowest in Europe, but again hidden in the rates for the Austro-Hungarian multicultural empire (with unreliable data). It started to increase slowly after World War I and significantly after 1960. Its peak was observed in 1984, when it was 35.8 (Milčinski, 1985). Since then, it has shown slightly decreasing trends. Suicide—even though mentioned and studied extensively by Slovene scientists and artists—has so far remained predominantly in the domain of psychiatry, clinical psychology, and the medical system, which is more or less true for the care of suicide survivors as well.

When suicide is such a frequent phenomenon, every adult inhabitant of Slovenia knows one or more people who died by suicide and has their own experiences of being a survivor of some sort. This has a great influence on the individual and national attitudes toward the phenomenon, but is also reflected in the everyday language, where phrases that include insinuations about a suicidal act are quite common ("My life is so awful I should just do away with myself."). The always-present problem can produce two antonymic reactions and behaviors at the same time—suicide can be either understood and even expected under certain circumstances, or it can be condemned and persecuted.

Slovene literature (both prose and poetry) throughout the last 500 years reveals that the problem of suicide is a frequent theme (Marušič 2005). It started back in the Middle Ages in folk songs, and is well represented in written texts since the 18th century, with the explosion of writing about suicidal behavior in the 20th century literature. The reasons and explanations for the act vary: Suicide of a certain character can be an approved exit from the unbearable situation, provoked by shame and disappointment, when the main reason for suicide is described as self-blaming, which is more difficult than being blamed by society. Literature reflects real life in society and offers a good display of different reactions toward suicide survivors, which range from intimate and public blame to feelings of guilt and lower self-respect. It also describes the copycat effect and the impact it has on the survivors.

Two vignettes from two novels show how suicide of a literary character determined the survivor's potential legacy.

- In a suicide note a father writes, "Dear son, I will hide my suicide, so that you will not suffer any blaming from our stupid people, who will proclaim you as a son of a suicidal father." He shot himself abroad, out of the sight of the public eye, which was explained as a sign of the father's love. (Jurčič, 1866, in Marušič, 2005 pp. 52–54)

- "In our people there is a prevalent wish for self-destruction, more than in any other nation. We tried really hard to make life as dull as possible. Suicide, if it is picturesque enough, usually produces new suicides." (Bor, 1971, in Marušič, 2005 pp. 101–103)

Slovene literature, reflecting the attitudes of the environment in which it is written, usually explains suicide as a result of failure, insanity, or despair, and therefore is interpreted as highly sinful, and thus a non-Christian death.

General attitudes about suicide in Slovenia have ranged from taboo and stigma to a very tolerant and permissive standpoint (Kocmur, 1997; Zadravec, Grad, & Zavasnik, 2006; Arnautovska & Grad, 2010), which is true for the attitudes toward survivors as well. When survivors are asked if they have experienced any unpleasant or rude reactions from their environment, they deny any direct reactions, but they always have a feeling that people value them differently than before the suicide.

> Three adult children came for help after losing both their father and mother by suicide within a few years. Although all three were highly educated and successful, they expressed several thoughts of their lowered position in society. One of them very picturesquely said, "When I am interested in some new girlfriend, my value has dropped due to my parents' suicides. I think this is irreversible."

☐ Coping With Suicide

Slovenia is a small, predominantly monoethnic, mostly Catholic society, with a long and turbulent history of fighting against foreign aggression. The inhabitants have been producing, consuming, and abusing an abundance of alcohol, which is still the main social (national) pathology in the country. They have lived through many different political systems, had different economic developments, and gained state independence, but the very high suicide rate has remained untouched throughout all the major changes of the 20th century. These historical facts affect the value and belief system of Slovenes. Slovene national character has been described as very hard-working, perfectionistic, reliable, individualistic, but rigid and full of introjected aggression, with the need of an individual to be the best (Grad, 1995; Musek, 2005). People are demanding and intolerant toward themselves, but also strict, demanding, and critical toward their children (both as parents and as teachers). Due to a closed and rather small society, there is much social control. These characteristics also bring specific reactions to survivors when suicide occurs in the family, school, or workplace. There is a strong need to find somebody or something to be blamed, or somebody who is supposedly guilty.

> In the small, rural elementary school, two minors, aged 12 and 13, killed themselves by hanging (at 60%, the predominant method of suicide in Slovenia). The school faculty called the experts to hold a workshop and offer help for the teachers after the local newspaper had published an anathematizing article on the role of the parents and school. When working with the teachers in small groups, there was much guilt-seeking among the different teachers. Blame was pinned on to the parents and both children, but self-blame was expressed, too. Searching for reasons and blaming other groups for the suicides were obviously the way for people to cope with their own feelings of guilt.

The described *support for schools* is one of the possible ways of helping suicide survivors after a disastrous event in Slovenia. A team of experts in prevention and postvention after suicide organizes regular seminars on how to recognize and help suicidal students, with a special perspective on what to do when it does happen and how to offer help in the time of bereavement to students, parents, and faculty members (Clark, Andriessen, Dunne, & Grad, 2003; Leenaars et al., 2001).

When suicide occurs in the family, survivors usually cope with it inside the family or with the support of friends. They search for help when they deem their bereavement too intense, too long, or too painful to bear in the inner family circle. There are a few options available inside the health care system: First, since 1989, support *groups* have been offered and led by two experienced therapists. These closed groups meet eight times and consist of up to 12 members. Second, an *outpatient clinic for individual or family treatment*, especially for the survivors, is available and covered by health insurance, and so far not limited by the insurance in the number of sessions. Third, survivors with serious depressive symptoms or with suicidal thoughts can be admitted to a special crisis ward where they are treated by combining pharmacotherapy and different kinds of psychotherapy (Grad & Zavasnik, 1997b; Grad, 2006). There are some lay- and professionally staffed nongovernmental organizations (NGOs) dealing with death and dying, with groups for the bereaved after any death, also offered to suicide survivors.

Whenever suicide happens, there are people affected, very much so if they were involved with the deceased person through work obligations. Among the most frequently and deeply touched are different members of the medical staff (therapists, nurses, GPs), prison personnel, teachers, school counselors, and priests. In particular, psychiatrists and psychologists, whose work is very much rationally and emotionally connected with the life of a suicidal patient, can suffer a similar response to those of a family member (Grad, 2005; Grad & Zavasnik, 1997a, 1998; Grad, Zavasnik, & Groleger 1997).

It is particularly difficult if a patient dies by suicide in the hospital or while at home for the weekend. This act provokes many subjective and objective problems for the responsible staff. They have to respond formally for the administrative requirements, but most important, they have to deal with their own emotions. The reactions also vary due to the different personal traits of individual experts; their personal and professional experience, knowledge, understanding, and anticipation of the event; their own current emotional state and stage of life; and many other personal factors.

As all these might be too difficult for some, so that they might have some serious problems (Grad & Michel, 2005), the Slovenian Association for Suicide Prevention (SASP) and University Psychiatric Hospital published a booklet with *suggested procedures*, describing what to do in such circumstances for different groups of staff (Grad, 2009).

☐ Case Example

There are a few problems concerning suicide survivorship in Slovenia that might be different from elsewhere, especially in the United States. The example provided here illuminates some of them.

A 61-year-old father came for therapy after the suicide of his only son, who shot himself in the family house at the age of 17. The father came for help because he feared that he could not control his extensive drinking anymore. He was a director of one of the most important national companies and had thousands of workers to lead. He and his wife had a childless marriage for more than 10 years and almost gave up all hope when their son was born. The son was everything they could wish for: bright, talented, handsome, and well-behaved. A year before the suicide, he started to withdraw into his room, stopped playing in the band, and stopped socializing. His work at school degraded and he stopped talking to his parents. They thought this was normal for his age and respected his wishes for isolation. His mother, completely unprepared, found his body in the basement. She did not want to come for any help. She had a high position at her work and resumed working the day after the funeral. Her husband told the therapist that she had completely changed, and stopped talking and working in the house. As for him, he did not want to be included into a group. His reason was that he was well known to everybody and held an extremely important position in society, so it made sense to work with him individually. He recovered well.

After he finished therapy, he persuaded his wife, whose daily routine at that point consisted of work and coming home, staring at the ceiling in silence, to finally come for help. At the first session, her outfit was impeccable, while her manner was arrogant and full of denial about the possibility that she needed help. After this unpleasant introduction, she talked without a break for an hour, did not stop after the time expired, and almost had to be rudely stopped. This pattern was repeated until the fourth session, when she started crying and talking about all the horror, guilt, and devaluation she felt as a mother and a human being. She feared her crying would never stop if she started, and she would lose her mind. At the end of therapy, she claimed she felt better, but could not thank the therapist and left without saying any conclusive words.

Both parents never started anything public in the memory of their son. They could have organized many things—a network, an association, or a donation (they were wealthy)—or they could have supported the Slovene Association for Suicide Prevention (SASP). They could have gone public and shared their experiences with the public. The father remained an important public figure for many years after he became a survivor, but he did not have the strength of overcoming the narrowness of the society (and his own feelings). His appearance as a survivor would open up a new chapter for other survivors. He and his wife were never willing or capable of doing so. When SASP organized its European congress, his company was asked to sponsor or donate. As director, he declined.

This case shows the attitude, social atmosphere, taboo, denial, stigma, shame, self-blaming, and low self-esteem of Slovene survivors. This might not be universal but is illustrative.

Something similar happened when we wanted to establish a socializing place (such as a club) for all those survivors who were members of the bereavement groups. There were some beginnings, which faded quickly. No network has ever been organized, even though there are so many survivors in the community. Among them are physicians (including psychiatrists), psychologists, politicians, business people, and many capable individuals, who could be outspoken pioneers in the media and in the public.

It seems particularly interesting that in an environment such as Slovenia, where suicide is a more frequent event (even though in absolute figures still a rare event) than elsewhere, the society "protects" its members with less awareness, more permissive attitudes, more literary productions (making suicide an acceptable solution), and more taboo and stigma attached to the survivors. Thus, as of 2009, no political effort in the form of a national program has yet been accepted, even though the experts have written it already (Grad & Zavasnik, 1995). No political organization has ever expressed any interest in it, which reflects the same ambivalent atmosphere of the entire society. Further, no NGO has been organized to connect survivors to help them, as is the case with many other groups. Now, in 2010, it has finally started to change, and a national program for suicide prevention has been added to a newly prepared national program for mental health, which is currently waiting to go through the procedure in the Parliament of Republic of Slovenia. Even though the experts wanted the suicide prevention policy to be independent, as the problem of suicide is far more multilayered than the mental health field, it is better than gaining nothing.

☐ Conclusions

Slovenia is one of the countries in Europe where suicide is a long-lasting and resistant problem. Therefore, there are many suicide survivors of different kinds—relatives and friends, but also different caregivers. Some good support has been organized in terms of help inside the medical system, but very little has been done by survivors themselves or the society as a whole.

☐ References

Arnautovska, U., & Grad, O. (2010). Attitudes toward suicide in the adolescent population. *Crisis*, *31*(1), 22–29.

Clark, S. E., Andriessen, K., Dunne, E., & Grad, O. (2003). Perspectives of suicide postvention from around the world. In *Final programme and abstract book of the 22nd World Congress of the International Association for Suicide Prevention* (IASP) (p. 115, Abstract 1). Stockholm, Sweden: IASP.

Grad, O. (1995). Why is the incidence of suicide one of the highest in Europe? In O. Grad (Ed.), *How to reduce suicide in Slovenia? The proposal of the national programme for suicide prevention* (pp. 81-89). Geneva, Sweden: World Health Organization.

Grad, O. (2006). How can we help suicide survivors in clinical practice? First International Suicide Postvention Seminar. 11th European Symposium on Suicidal Behaviour. *Psychiatria Danubina 18* (Suppl.), 27.

Grad, O. (2009). Therapists as survivors of suicide loss. In D. Wasserman & K. Wasserman (Eds.), *Suicidology and suicide prevention: A Global Perspective* (pp. 609–613). Oxford, UK: Oxford University Press.

Grad, O., & Zavasnik, A. (1995). Proposal for a national programme for suicide prevention in Slovenia. In O. Grad (Ed.), *How to reduce suicide in Slovenia? The proposal of the National Programme for Suicide Prevention* (pp. 3–21). Geneva, Sweden: World Health Organization.

Grad, O. T. (2005). Suicide survivorship: An unknown journey from loss to gain. In K. Hawton (Ed.), *Prevention and treatment of suicidal behaviour: From science to practice* (pp. 351–369). Oxford, UK: Oxford University Press.

Grad O. T., & Michel, K. (2005). Therapists as client suicide survivors. In K. M. Weiner (Ed.), *Therapeutic and legal issues for therapists who have survived a client suicide* (pp. 71–81). New York, NY: Haworth Press.

Grad, O. T., & Zavasnik, A. (1997a). Postvention for the caregivers after suicide or death of their patient. Paper presented at the XIX Congress of the International Association for Suicide Prevention. Adelaide, Australia.

Grad, O. T., & Zavasnik, A. (1997b). Shame: The unbearable legacy of suicide. In D. De Leo, A. Schmidtke, & R. F. W. Diekstra (Eds.), *Suicide prevention: A holistic approach* (pp. 163–166). Boston, MA: Kluwer.

Grad O. T., & Zavasnik A. (1998). The caregiver's reactions after the suicide of a patient. In R. J. Kosky, H. S. Eshkevari, R. D. Goldney, & R. Hassan (Eds.), *Suicide prevention: The global context* (pp. 287–291). New York, NY: Plenum Press.

Grad O.T., Zavasnik, A., & Groleger, U. (1997). Suicide of a patient: Gender differences in bereavement reactions of therapists. *Suicide and Life Threatening Behavior, 27*, 379–386.

Kocmur, M. (1997). Stalisca do samomora pri Slovencih (Attitudes toward suicide in Slovenes). *Teorija in praksa, 34*, 421–432.

Leenaars, A. A., Wenckstern, S., Appleby, M., Fiske, H., Grad, O., Kalafat, J., Smith, J., Takahashi, Y. (2001). Current issues in dealing with suicide prevention in schools: Perspectives from some countries. *Journal of Educational and Psychological Consultation, 12*, 365–384.

Marušič, M. (2005). *Problem samomora v slovenski knjizevnosti* [The problem of suicide in the Slovene literature] (Final thesis). Faculty of Philosophy, University of Ljubljana, Ljubljana, Slovenia.

Milčinski, L. (1985). *Samomor in Slovenci* (Suicide and Slovenes), Ljubljana, Slovenia: Cankarjeva zalozba.

Musek, J. (2005). *Psiholoske in kognitivne studije* (Psychological and cognitive studies). Ljubljana, Slovenia: Znanstveni institut Filozofske fakultete. ISBN 86-7207-163-8. [COBISS.SI-ID 221104640]

Zadravec, T., Grad, O., & Zavasnik, A. (2006). Lay and expert explanatory models on suicidal behaviour. Eleventh European Symposium on Suicidal Behaviour. *Psychiatria Danubina 18* (Suppl.), 106.

A New Zealand Perspective on Suicide Bereavement

Margaret Nelson Agee

New Zealand, or *Aotearoa* in the Māori language, is known for its striking scenic beauty and relatively safe, "clean, green" environment. Mental health statistics, however, and the suicide rate in particular, reflect a dark side to this romantic view.

During the last 50 years of the 20th century, marked changes were evident in New Zealand suicide rates (Beautrais, 2003a). Although there were downward trends in the 45-plus age group, rates of suicide approximately doubled among those aged 25–44 years, while suicide rates among those aged 15–24 years doubled between 1950 and 1980, then doubled again between 1980 and the mid-1990s. Additionally, suicide rates for males increased from 2.5 times the female rate around 1950, to approximately four times the female rate by 2000 (Collings, Blakely, Atkinson, & Fawcett, 2005). Although there had been a 19% decrease since the peak of 16.3 suicides per 100,000 people from 1996 to 1998, deaths by suicide increased from 488 in 2004, to 502 in 2005. Thus, the official number of deaths by suicide has averaged approximately 500 per year since 1991

(Ministry of Health [MoH], 2001, 2007), in a population of approximately 3.68 million in 1996, and approximately 4.3 million by the end of 2008 (http://www.stats.govt.nz). New Zealand suicide rates are high in comparison with selected countries in the Organization for Economic Cooperation and Development (OECD) (MoH, 2008a). In our relatively small country, the effects of these trends have been particularly noticeable.

In terms of ethnicity, according to the 2006 census, approximately 73% of the New Zealand population identify as being of European/Other descent, 13% as Māori (the indigenous people of New Zealand), 8% as Asian, and 6% as Pacific Island (including Samoans, Cook Island Māori, Tongans, Niueans, Fijians, Tokelauans, and Tuvaluans as the major groups) (http://www.stats.govt.nz). Māori have the highest rate of suicide (17.9 per 100,000 in the period from 2003 to 2005, compared with the non-Māori rate of 12 per 100,000), and the majority of Māori suicides occur in those aged 15 to 35. European/Other record the second-highest rate, followed by Pacific, and then Asian. Hospitalization rates for intentional self-harm follow a similar pattern (MoH, 2008a).

☐ Youth Suicide and Community Support for Bereaved Families

Addressing youth suicide was an urgent priority by the early 1990s when it had become second only to automobile accidents as the highest cause of death among young people in the 15 to 24 age group. New Zealand had acquired the unenviable distinction among the OECD countries of having the highest or near-highest reported youth suicide rate (Ministry of Education & National Health Committee [MoE & NHC], 1998).

From 1986 onwards, in response to youth suicides, support groups were established by community organizations and by bereaved survivors of suicide in three major New Zealand cities and some provincial towns. One group, founded in 1988, also provided counseling, community education, and advocacy for some years (Calder, 1995). Currently, seven suicide bereavement support groups are active (http://www.spinz.org.nz).

☐ Suicide Prevention: The Context for Postvention

Following the release of the first official report into youth suicide (Barwick, 1992), the Department of Health commissioned the Youth

Suicide Prevention Project in 1992. Since then, extensive government-sponsored initiatives to prevent suicide have been undertaken in New Zealand. Public policies, postvention recommendations, and action plans have been developed in the context of these initiatives, with the primary aim of preventing further suicides within the vulnerable population of people bereaved by suicide. Support for those who were bereaved or affected by a suicide was identified as a key theme or goal in both the report from a government-appointed Steering Group on Youth Mental Health Prevention (MoH, 1994), and in the development and implementation of a National Youth Suicide Prevention Strategy between 1996 and 1998 (Ministry of Youth Affairs, Ministry of Health, & Te Puni Kōkiri, 1998). The role of education and training institutions was also highlighted (MoH, 1994).

Postvention in Schools

A key aspect of attaining this goal involved the development of guidelines by the Ministries of Youth Affairs and Education to assist schools in responding effectively to student suicides. In New Zealand high schools, school counselors usually have leading roles in the management of the response (Agee, 2001; Silva, 1999). Schools developed crisis response plans and procedures, assisted by both local (Taylor & Silva, 1990) and international resources (e.g., Oates, 1988). Guidelines (Rivers, 1995) were developed by the Special Education Service (SES), a government agency staffed primarily by educational psychologists who act as consultants to schools. The development of a traumatic incident response plan in schools was recommended, based on principles promulgated by the Centers for Disease Control and Prevention (CDC), to limit the risk of contagion following a serious suicide attempt or death by suicide (MoE & NHC, 1998).

Postvention in the Context of the National Suicide Prevention Strategy

Despite the almost exclusive emphasis on youth in initial suicide prevention policies, the majority of those who die by suicide in New Zealand are aged 25 to 45 (Beautrais, 2003b). The broadening of suicide prevention goals to encompass the whole community in the National Suicide

Prevention Strategy 2006–2016 (Associate Minister of Health, 2006) accommodates more inclusive acknowledgment of the needs of the bereaved, and strategies for the provision of more accessible support. Under the sixth of seven goals, *Support families, whānau,[1] friends, and others affected by a suicide or suicide attempt*, providing support for the bereaved is the first of three areas for action. Part of the action plan also involves a review of traumatic incident response resources and services provided to schools.

During 2007 and 2008, a model of postvention support was developed, delivered, and evaluated in three regions of New Zealand as part of the Suicide Postvention Support Initiative (MoH, 2008a). Contracted to deliver the program were the New Zealand Council of Victim Support Groups (Victim Support), a volunteer-based, first-responder service to victims of crime and traumatic events, and Clinical Advisory Services Aotearoa (CASA), a team of clinically trained and experienced mental health professionals. CASA staff provided training to the Victim Support workers to equip them to deliver a suicide bereavement support service. Three further aspects of the Initiative that were developed and evaluated by CASA include: Postvention Planning for Communities, a Flexible Response Team that could assist communities with the management of crises after cluster suicides had occurred, and support for families and whānau after a suicide attempt.

The evaluation of the project (Clinical Advisory Services Aotearoa [CASA], 2008) confirmed Victim Support's role in providing a first responder service of volunteer-staffed, community-based support, and recommended that specialized professional grief counseling be made available to bereaved survivors. Also recommended was the amalgamation of the Postvention Planning for Communities program and the Flexible Response Team into a single service (CASA, 2008).

CASA was funded by the Ministry of Health to implement the recommendations and establish a free specialist counseling service for those bereaved by suicide or affected by a suicide attempt in seven regional District Health Board areas, three of which are in the Auckland region. Since December 2008, the service has been accepting referrals to approved counselors and psychologists, chosen because of their relevant experience and suitability for working with suicide-bereaved survivors. CASA is providing support and professional development for the practitioners

---

[1] The nearest equivalent of *whānau* in English is probably extended family. Metge (1995) explains that originally it referred to siblings born to the same parents, but in its common usage it has referred to a large family group comprising several generations and parent-child families related by descent from a recent ancestor (p. 16).

involved, who include Pākeha (white New Zealanders), Māori, Pasifika, Chinese, and Koreans.

The first meeting with each new client takes place in the client's home. Special care is being taken to develop a model of service delivery that is culturally appropriate and accessible to Māori whānau and individuals. Whānau are offered the support of an approved Māori counselor, along with support from kaumatua and kuia (elders), and kai ātawhai (Māori community workers). Although there are large areas of the country that are not covered by this service, a separate source of funding is available to support patients with mild/moderate mental health conditions through medical centers that are Primary Health Organisations (PHOs). This may enable some others bereaved by suicide to access counseling.

☐ Meeting the Needs of Māori and Pasifika Communities

Developing effective ways of providing support to Māori is a priority in the current suicide postvention strategy. The loss of an individual's unique contribution to whakapapa (genealogy) is spiritually significant and contributes to intensifying the distress of the bereaved (MoH, 2008a). Māori leaders in mental health believe strongly that social and contextual factors, many of which are seen as associated with the effects of colonization, primarily contribute to explanations for Māori suicide. It has been suggested that suicide rates among Māori may be seen as a marker of the health of contemporary Māori society (Hirini & Collings, 2005). The circumstances that contribute to poor health outcomes for Māori may also contribute to complicating the grieving process for the bereaved in the aftermath of a suicide.

More specific emphasis on services for Māori, developed and provided by Māori, and on the involvement of Pasifika mental health services in postvention, can therefore be seen in the latest National Suicide Prevention Guidelines (MoH, 2008b). Working with whānau is particularly important, as most often they are the primary source of support after a suicide (MoH, 2008a). Acknowledgment of the collective natures of Māori and Pasifika cultures and identities is integral to effective therapeutic postvention and the provision of social support for Māori and Pacific peoples. So also is the acknowledgment of social change, and the needs of many who have multiethnic identities (Webber, 2008), and/or a more individualized lifestyle, and who may no longer be connected in a meaningful way with their *hapū*[2] and *iwi*,[3] or with their *marae*.[4] Not all Māori or Pacific people will therefore choose to seek help from culture-specific services. Postvention approaches also need to incorporate spirituality, which is integral to the world views of Māori and Pasifika people (Durie, 2001; Culbertson, Agee, & Makasiale, 2007).

Churches within Pacific communities can serve as major sources of support for Pacific families following a suicide, while there can be comfort and healing for Māori in the rituals of *tangihanga*,[5] which usually take place on the marae, though sometimes now in private homes in urban settings, over 3 days (Ministry of Youth Development, 2005). The open expression of grief and sorrow in the presence of the deceased loved one, the experience of communal support, and the cultural values of sharing and reciprocity that underpin the rituals associated with tangi, help to strengthen the bonds among the mourners, thereby supporting cultural, social, and spiritual well-being (Ngata, 2005).

Māori find the processes involved in a coroner's inquest after a suicide, including delay in the release of a body and the need for an autopsy, extremely distressing, intensifying their trauma in the aftermath of a suicide. They believe that "the deceased must be kept constantly warm and comfortable by the presence of kinfolk, in order to calm the soul and assist it on its journey to the spirit world" (Ngata, 2005, p. 33).

Although support tends to be offered to Pacific families as an entity rather than to individual family members (Henare & Erhardt, 2004), the different ages, status, and cultural identities of family members may make it difficult for all members to receive meaningful personal support in this way. The taboo against talking about suicide in some Pacific communities, as well as painful reactions such as shame, guilt, stigma, and a sense of failure to care for and support the deceased person adequately (Tiatia & Coggan, 2001), mean that both individual and collective forms of

---

[2] The *hapū* is a subdivision of a tribe; a number of hapū make up an iwi, with a paramount chief at the head (Barlow, 1991, p. 21).

[3] The *iwi* is the largest political unit in Māori society. One iwi or tribe is composed of many hapū. An *ariki* or paramount chief is the leader of the tribe (Barlow, 1991, p. 33).

[4] The *marae* is a symbol of tribal identity and solidarity. Formerly, the marae proper was designated as the open area of land directly in front of the sacred carved house. Nowadays, all the buildings associated with a community facility are collectively known as a marae. These consist of a carved meeting-house, a dining-hall, and cooking area, as well as the *marae ātea*, or sacred space, in front of the meeting-house (Barlow, 1991, p. 73).

[5] *Tangihanga* is one of the few surviving institutions in Māori culture. There are many customs and traditions associated with tangihanga, and many important concepts concerning both the physical and metaphysical world are revealed here (Barlow, 1999, p. 122).

support are needed. Within traditional hierarchical social structures, the voices of children and young people are often unheard. Assisting adults to understand and support children and young people in grief could form a valuable aspect of postvention for Pacific families. The significance of cultural rites associated with suicide for different Pacific groups also needs to be recognized in postvention support (MoH, 2008a).

In response to the disturbing rates of suicide in New Zealand and the trauma experienced by individuals and communities in the aftermath of a suicide, strong commitments have been made by government and community agencies in New Zealand to the development and evaluation of postvention services based on the best available evidence. Although still in the early stages of development, the Specialist Counselling Service is a significant recent initiative that holds great promise for providing effective therapeutic support to bereaved survivors of suicide, who so often struggle to find places of empathy, understanding, and acceptance in their journey through their intensely painful experiences of grief.

☐ References

Agee, M. R. N. (2001). *Surviving loss by suicide: Counsellors' experiences of client suicide* (Unpublished doctoral dissertation). University of Auckland, New Zealand.

Associate Minister of Health. (2006). *The New Zealand suicide prevention strategy 2006–2016*. Wellington, NZ: Ministry of Health.

Barlow, C. (1991). *Tikanga whakaaro: Key concepts in Māori culture*. South Melbourne, Australia: Oxford University Press.

Barwick, H. (1992). *Youth Suicide Prevention Project workshop report and literature review*. Wellington, NZ: Department of Health.

Beautrais, A. L. (2003a). Suicide in New Zealand I: Time trends and epidemiology. *New Zealand Medical Journal, 116* (1175). Retrieved from http://www.nzma.org.nz/journal/116-1175/461/

Beautrais, A. L. (2003b). Suicide in New Zealand II: A review of risk factors and prevention. *The New Zealand Medical Journal, 116* (1175). Retrieved from http://www.nzma.org.nz/journal/116-1175/461/

Calder, K. (1995). *Who cares? A social history of the Canterbury Bereaved by Suicide Society, 1988–1994*. Christchurch, NZ: Canterbury Bereaved by Suicide Society.

Clinical Advisory Services Aotearoa (CASA). (2008). *Postvention Support Initiative evaluation report*. Auckland, NZ: Author.

Collings, S., Blakely, T., Atkinson, J., & Fawcett, J. (2005). *Suicide trends and social factors New Zealand 1981–1999: Analyses from the New Zealand census—mortality study. Report 5: Social explanations for suicide in New Zealand*. Wellington, NZ: Ministry of Health.

Culbertson, P. L., Agee, M. N., & Makasiale, C. O. (Eds.). (2007). *Penina uliuli: Contemporary challenges in mental health for Pacific peoples.* Honolulu, HI: University of Hawai'i Press.

Durie, M. (2001). *Mauri Ora: The dynamics of Māori health.* Auckland, NZ: Oxford University Press.

Henare, K., & Ehrhardt, P. (2004). *Support for Māori, Pacific and Asian family, whānau and significant others who have been bereaved by suicide: Findings of a literature search.* Wellington, NZ: Ministry of Youth Development.

Hirini, P., & Collings, S. (2005). *Whakamomori: He whakaaro, he kōrero noa: A collection of contemporary views on Māori and suicide. Report 3: Social explanations for suicide in New Zealand.* Wellington, NZ: Ministry of Health.

Metge, J. (1995). *New growth from old: The whānau in the modern world.* Wellington, NZ: Victoria University Press.

Ministry of Education & National Health Committee (MoE & NHC). (1998). *The prevention, recognition and management of young people at risk of suicide: A guide for schools.* Wellington, NZ: Author.

Ministry of Health (MoH). (1994). *Report and recommendations of the Steering Group on Youth Mental Health and Suicide Prevention.* Wellington, NZ: Author.

Ministry of Health (MoH). (2001). *Suicide trends in New Zealand 1978–1998.* Wellington, NZ: New Zealand Health Information Service.

Ministry of Health (MoH). (2007). *Suicide facts: 2005–2006 data.* Wellington, NZ: Author.

Ministry of Health (MoH). (2008a). *New Zealand suicide prevention action plan 2008–2012: The evidence for action.* Wellington, NZ: Author.

Ministry of Health (MoH). (2008b). *New Zealand suicide prevention action plan 2008–2012: The summary for action.* Wellington, NZ: Author.

Ministry of Youth Affairs, Ministry of Health, & Te Puni Kokiri. (1998). *New Zealand youth suicide prevention strategy.* Wellington, NZ: Author.

Ministry of Youth Development. (2005). *After a suicide: Practical information for people bereaved by suicide.* Wellington, NZ: Author.

Ngata, P. (2005). Death, dying and grief. In M. Schwass (Ed.), *Last words: Approaches to death in New Zealand's cultures and faiths* (pp. 29–40). Wellington, NZ: Bridget Williams Books and The Funeral Directors Association of New Zealand.

Oates, M. D. (1988). *Death in the school community: A handbook for counselors, teachers, and administrators.* Alexandria, VA: American Counseling Association.

Rivers, L. (1995). *Young person suicide.* Wellington, NZ: Special Education Service.

Silva, V. (1999). *Helping young people survive the suicide of a school friend* (Unpublished master's dissertation). University of Auckland, New Zealand.

Taylor, B., & Silva, P. A. (1990). *In a time of crisis: Some management recommendations for schools and other institutions in the event of a death or other serious crisis.* Wellington, NZ: Ministry of Youth Affairs.

Tiatia, J., & Coggan, C. (2001). Young Pacifican suicide attempts: A review of emergency department medical records. *Pacific Health Dialogue, 8,* 124–128.

Webber, M. (2008). *Walking the space between.* Wellington, NZ: New Zealand Council for Educational Research.

Survivors After Suicide
A Comprehensive Suicide Survivor Program in Flanders, Belgium

Karl Andriessen

☐ Introduction

Belgium is one of the Western European countries where the suicide rate has increased during the past decades. The most recent data of the Flemish Region (northern part of the country, 6.1 million inhabitants) concern the year 2007, with the male suicide rate of 22.57/100,000 and the female suicide rate of 9.77/100,000. Suicide is the second-leading cause of death among those aged 15–24 years, and the first cause of death in males aged 25–49 years and in females aged 20–39 years. Half of both male and female suicides are younger than 50 years old.

The country is now largely secularized and culturally diverse, but stems from a strong Catholic tradition with typical low public and political interest in suicide prevention. Political concern increased due to the active advocacy by researchers and field workers. In 1997, the Flemish Department of Well-being, Health, and the Family asked the Community Mental Health Centres (CMHC) to give special attention to the needs of suicidal clients. Accordingly, the CMHC were allocated an extra budget to develop coordinated suicide prevention activities with other caregivers such as general practitioners, hospitals, police, school counselors, and so forth (Andriessen, Clara, & Beuckx, 2002).

However, in contrast with the development in the prevention field, the postvention field was neglected. During the 1990s, there have been no more than five support groups for suicide survivors. As in many countries, suicide survivors not only had to cope with the loss, but also suffer with a stigma that obstructs social and/or professional support, which is mostly offered in support groups (Andriessen, 2004, 2009; Andriessen, Beautrais, Grad, Brockmann, & Simkin, 2007; Andriessen, Delhaise, & Forceville, 2001; Cleiren & Diekstra, 1995; Clark, 2001; Clark & Goldney, 2000; Dyregrov, 2002; Farberow, 2001; Farberow, Gallagher-Thompson, Gilewski, & Thompson 1992; Grad, 1996, 2005; Grad, Clark, Dyregrov, & Andriessen, 2004; Krysinska, 2003; Saarinen, Viinamäki, Hintikka, Lehtonen, & Lönnqvist 1999; Saarinen, Hintikka, Lehtonen, Lönnqvist, & Viinamäki, 2002).

At the same time, support groups were available for a variety of other physical, mental, and social problems. In addition, we noticed in our neighboring country, the Netherlands, that in each province several suicide survivor support groups were available, although without national coordination. In brief, in the Belgian Flemish region, we observed both the need and the room for improvement in support for survivors after suicide.

☐ Working Group on Suicide Survivors ("Verder")

At the beginning of 2000, the Working Group on Suicide Survivors was established with 15 working members, including representatives from survivor support groups, the suicide prevention crisis line, the general help line, the victim support network, and the previously mentioned Suicide Prevention Program of the CMHC (De fauw & Andriessen, 2003). The Cera Foundation, a charity fund of a financial holding, granted a 3-year fund (2000–2002), followed by yearly grants of the Flemish Department of Well-being, Health, and the Family.

Aim and Objectives

The Working Group coordinates, supports, and initiates activities with and for suicide survivors in Flanders. The mission is to raise awareness, improve suicide-survivor support, destigmatize survivors, and increase openness in society. The Working Group integrates suicide survivors and caregivers to increase the availability and the quality of the support for survivors. Goals are to make the support groups better known, lend support to the groups, facilitate new initiatives by suicide survivors and/or by mental health or community agencies, and develop a broad community network with support groups, CMHC, and other agencies (De fauw & Andriessen, 2003).

A policy was written outlining the goals and the activities to be performed during the first 3 years (2000–2002). After evaluation by the members of the network, new objectives were included. In addition, the funding governmental department evaluates the goals and the results based on its observations and the yearly reports of the Working Group.

Activities

A directory of survivor support groups was compiled, first in a booklet, then subsequently in a database. It provides basic information on suicide bereavement and survivor support. Each group is listed with its name, contact address, and other useful information. During 5 subsequent years, an updated version was published, in total over 100,000 copies. The booklet was freely distributed among general practitioners, hospitals, CMHC, help lines, self-help groups, victim care centers, social services, and undertakers, and it is announced in the media for the general public. The Web site of the Working Group includes an updated database of the directory. Several Web sites of other organizations, such as the CMHC, the self-help umbrella, several survivor groups, and so forth, include a link to the Web site of the Working Group.

Survivor support groups can receive a Quality Label, which was developed in collaboration with survivor groups and suicidologists, when they meet a set of quality criteria. These criteria include:

• Support group leaders attend peer supervision meetings, held twice annually. The purpose is informational, educational, and supportive for group leaders.

- Group leaders are invited to attend a 3-day training program.

- Groups offer a welcome/intake procedure, and the type of group, the leadership, and the attendance fees are clearly published.

- Groups use a standardized name label to show their affiliation with the Working Group.

- Groups affiliate with a CMHC for logistic and professional support.

Most members of the Working Group have roots in or are connected with social or mental health centers. Per province, one suicide prevention officer of the CMHC has become a member of the Working Group and serves as a local contact for the group. This enables advocacy of postvention issues in social and health structures at the local and regional levels. The Working Group has an active public relations policy (e.g., outreach to journalists) and the Working Group has become well known by the press.

From the start, it was clear that each suicide-survivor group has its own style of operating, partly depending on the type of group and the background of the group leader. To give a clear view to those interested in starting a group, it was decided to publish a manual with good practices in initiating and facilitating different types of survivor groups. To this end, we obtained permission from the World Health Organization (WHO) and translated the booklet *Preventing Suicide: How to Start a Survivors' Group* (WHO, 2000–2008; Werkgroep Verder, 2005).

In May 2002, the *Charter: The Rights of Suicide Survivors* was launched. This brief document presents the basic principles and goals of the Working Group and puts forward the basic aspirations of suicide survivors. The charter invites survivors and caregivers to contact the Working Group. The goals are to widen the network, raise awareness, and promote empowerment to improve the support and the social position of suicide survivors. The charter was translated into Finnish by the Finnish Association for Mental Health in collaboration with the Suicide Survivors Association (Mäenpää, 2003). Table 32.1 presents the charter.

Flemish Suicide Survivor Day

Since 2002, the annual Flemish Suicide Survivor Day takes place on the third Saturday of November. This day aims to provide a platform where survivors, caregivers, and policymakers can listen to and learn from each other, and to sensitize the general public, caregivers, media,

TABLE 32.1. The rights of suicide survivors

The survivor has the right:
1. To mourn in his or her own way and within the time it takes
2. To know the truth about the suicide, to see the body of the deceased, and to organise the funeral with respect to one's own ideas and rituals
3. To consider suicide as the result of several interrelated causes that produced unbearable pain for the deceased
4. To respect one's own privacy as well as that of the deceased
5. To find support from relatives, friends, colleagues, and survivors, as well as from skilled professional helpers
6. To contact the clinician/caregiver (if any) who treated the deceased person
7. To be treated with respect and support, including by police and administrative offices
8. To not be reduced as being a survivor, but to be seen with vulnerabilities and strengths
9. To live, wholly, with sorrow and joy, free of stigma or judgement
10. To never be as before: there is a life before the suicide and a life afterwards

Source: Werkgroep Verder, Charter: de Rechten van Nabestaanden na Zelfdoding [Charter: The rights of suicide survivors], Werkgroep Verder, Halle, 2002–2008. Reprinted with permission.

and policymakers to issues involving suicide survivors. In the morning, plenary presentations are held, including one by the Flemish Minister of Well-being and Health. The afternoon includes a variety of support meetings and workshops, including support meetings for adult survivors, for adolescents, and for parents who have lost a child by suicide, a workshop on grief in children and adolescents, workshops for caregivers after client suicide, on rituals, on the methodology to facilitate a group, creative workshops with clay and paint, etc. The program includes short breaks with poetry or music. A cafeteria, an exhibition of a variety of social services, a "quiet room," and a peer-support room are open all day. During the preparations, communications are regularly sent to the media and stakeholders.

This day clearly meets a need of survivors. The number of participants increased from 180 at the first meeting to over 400 in 2007 and in 2008. Participants appreciate the content and the format that are offered.

The climate of the meetings is kind-hearted and offers safety and warmth. In addition, the Survivor Day and the theme of "suicide survivors" receive extensive media coverage. From the second meeting onward, the day was organized under the auspices of the International Association for Suicide Prevention (IASP) and in cooperation with World Suicide Prevention Day. In 2004, her Royal Highness Princess Astrid of Belgium attended Survivor Day.

Theater Plays

"Out of Life," a play on survivorship, was written for the Working Group. During a 2-year tour through the Flemish region, it attracted 1,000 spectators. In the play, with acting and singing, a young woman is bereaved by the suicide of her husband. Attempting to understand his suicide, and especially "why?", she searches his laptop and discovers a few secrets, such as financial debts. In addition, she is confronted with both supporting and abusive reactions from others. Given the success of the first play, a new theater project is in preparation.

Media Award for Responsible Portrayal of Suicide and Survivors

Part of the initial media policy was that every time a simplistic or sensational portrayal of suicide or survivors was published, the journalist or editor was contacted and provided with the media guidelines available from WHO, Samaritans, and so forth. However, this was time-consuming, and the results were poor. Therefore, we decided on a new strategy, an award to promote good practices of media coverage, launched during the 2003 Survivor Day (Andriessen, 2005).

The Ministry of Well-being and Health, the Working Group, and representatives of the media had developed and disseminated a set of recommendations for the media. The major recommendations are:

- To avoid sensational, simplistic, or romanticized portrayals

- To avoid pictures if not essential

- To avoid details of place and method

- To provide addresses of support services

In addition, the selection criteria of the Media Award highlight a few specific points:

- The portrayal mentions the complexity of suicide and mental problems, and the bereavement of survivors.

- The privacy of the deceased and the survivors is respected.

- Survivors have the opportunity to proofread and modify their contribution.

- The portrayal includes an expert who provides information on help-seeking.

- Support is available on the spot, when the survivor is involved.

Yearly, an independent jury, appointed by the Working Group, with a survivor as the chair, selects the recipient of the award, which is presented during the Survivor Day. Currently, both the implementation of the media recommendations and the Media Award are being evaluated.

Interactive Web Site

The Working Group has become well known and receives many inquiries. The aim of the Web site is to inform the public on the activities of the Working Group and to provide addresses and other support resources for survivors, with specific pages for children, adolescents, adults, clinicians, and journalists. Online chat forums are available (http://www.werkgroepverder.be).

Initiatives for Children and Adolescents

The Web site of the Working Group includes separate pages for children and adolescents. A series of three books were published for different age groups. The Victim Care services facilitate support groups for children. Early in 2009, we were invited to participate in a meeting of the Committee of Well-being of the Flemish Parliament. In addition, a meeting was held with young survivors and his Royal Highness Prince Filip of Belgium.

Inclusion of the Coordinated Suicides-Survivor Activities in the Flemish Suicide Prevention Action Plan

The Flemish government and the Ministry of Well-being, Health, and the Family have put forward the prevention of depression and suicide as a new health target. The subsequent Suicide Prevention Action Plan

2006–2010 sets out a series of goals, strategies, and actions; it started new pilot projects and included all currently available resources, among others, the Suicide Prevention Program of the CMHC and the Working Group on Suicide Survivors. This is an important recognition of the achievements of the Working Group and its societal value. Indeed, "suicide prevention without the involvement of survivors would be poor prevention" (Andriessen, 2009, p. 46).

☐ Conclusion

Accomplishments to Date

Looking back on the Working Group's activity since 2000, there are several results:

1. The major result is a substantial increase in the availability of suicide-survivor support from 5 to 15 groups spread equally in the Flemish region. Through the publication of the directory and the active ambassadorship of the Working Group, the support groups are better known, especially among the referring caregivers and media. The Quality Label and peer supervisions have provided the opportunity to discuss group matters and to increase the quality of group leadership. It seems that this strategy and the activities previously mentioned have decreased barriers and enabled new groups to start and sustain their operations.

2. By organizing the Suicide Survivor Day, the theater play, and the Media Award, and by distributing "The Rights of Suicide Survivors," we hope to reduce the taboo against and to generate a more supportive climate in Flemish society for suicide survivors.

3. During the years of operation, the Working Group has developed cooperation between suicide survivors, mental health and suicide prevention services, and policymakers. The strength of this network is unique in the history of mental health and suicidology in Belgium.

Looking Toward the Future

1. Activities will be continued and, if possible, new initiatives will be developed when specific questions or needs are observed. For example,

we developed a training module for railway staff who are confronted with suicide, and plan activities regarding employers/workforce survivors. In addition, the Working Group will follow up the implementation of the media guidelines.

2. The number of survivor support groups has remained stable during the last 6 years, and the quality criteria are accepted by the groups. Hence, we expect that the increased support for survivors will last.

3. Further, we expect that suicide-survivor activities and the goal of caring for their needs will be sustained in the field of suicide prevention by its inclusion in the Suicide Prevention Action Plan of the government.

☐ References

Andriessen, K. (2004). Suicide-survivor activities: An international perspective. *Suicidologi (Norwegian Journal of Suicidology), 9*(2), 26–27, 31.

Andriessen, K. (2005). A media award for responsible portrayal of suicide and survivors. *Pogled: The View, Acta Suicidologica Slovenica, 3*(1–2), 66–70.

Andriessen, K. (2009). Can postvention be prevention? *Crisis: Journal of Crisis Intervention and Suicide Prevention, 30*, 43–47.

Andriessen, K., Beautrais, A., Grad, O., Brockmann, E., & Simkin, S. (2007). Current understandings of survivor issues: Research, practice and plans. *Crisis: Journal of Crisis Intervention and Suicide Prevention, 28*, 211–213.

Andriessen, K., Clara, A., & Beuckx, K. (2002). The Suicide Prevention Policy of a Mental Health Centre. *International Journal of Mental Health Promotion, 4*(1), 20–23.

Andriessen, K., Delhaise, T., & Forceville, G. (2001). *Zorgbehoeften van nabestaanden van zelfdoding: Een exploratieve studie* [The needs of care of suicide survivors: An explorative study]: Studie in opdracht van het Ministerie van Sociale Zaken [Study on the request of the Ministry of Social Affairs, Reports in Flemish/Dutch and French]. Brussels, Belguim: Centrum ter Preventie van Zelfmoord [Suicide Prevention Centre].

Clark, S. (2001). Bereavement after suicide. How far have we come and where do we go from here? *Crisis: Journal of Crisis Intervention and Suicide Prevention, 22*, 102–108.

Clark, S., & Goldney, R. (2000). The impact of suicide on relatives and friends. In K. Hawton & K. van Heeringen (Eds.), *The international handbook of suicide and attempted suicide* (pp. 467–484). Chichester, England: Wiley & Sons.

Cleiren, M., & Diekstra, R. (1995). After the loss: Bereavement after suicide and other types of death. In B. Mishara (Ed.), *The impact of suicide* (pp. 7–39). New York, NY: Springer.

De fauw, N., & Andriessen, K. (2003). Networking to support suicide survivors. *Crisis: Journal of Crisis Intervention and Suicide Prevention, 24,* 29–31.

Dyregrov, K. (2002). Assistance from local authorities versus survivors' needs for support after suicide. *Death Studies, 26,* 647–668.

Farberow, N. (2001). Helping suicide survivors. In D. Lester (Ed.), *Suicide prevention. Resources for the millennium* (pp. 189–212). Philadelphia, PA: Brunner Routledge.

Farberow, N., Gallagher-Thompson, D., Gilewski, M., & Thompson, L. (1992). The role of social supports in the bereavement process of surviving spouses of suicide and natural deaths. *Suicide and Life-Threatening Behavior, 22,* 107–124.

Grad, O. (1996). How to survive as a survivor? *Crisis: Journal of Crisis Intervention and Suicide Prevention, 17,* 136–142.

Grad, O. (2005). Suicide survivorship: An unknown journey from loss to gain, from individual to global perspective. In K. Hawton (Ed.). *Prevention and Treatment of Suicidal Behaviour: From Science to Practice* (pp. 351–369). Oxford, England: Oxford University Press.

Grad, O., Clark, S., Dyregrov, K., & Andriessen, K. (2004). What helps and what hinders the process of surviving the suicide of somebody close? *Crisis: Journal of Crisis Intervention and Suicide Prevention, 25,* 134–139.

Krysinska, K. (2003). Loss by suicide. A risk factor for suicide. *Journal of Psychosocial Nursing and Mental Health Services, 41*(7), 34–41.

Mäenpää, E. (2003). Tukea ja oikeuksia itsemurhan tehneen läheisille [Support and rights for suicide survivors]. *Mielenterveys, 6,* 34–36.

Saarinen, P., Hintikka, J., Lehtonen, J., Lönnqvist, J., & Viinamäki, H. (2002). Mental health and social isolation among survivors 10 years after a suicide in the family: A case-control study. *Archives of Suicide Research, 6,* 221–226.

Saarinen, P., Viinamäki, H., Hintikka, J., Lehtonen, J., & Lönnqvist, J. (1999). Psychological symptoms of close relatives of suicide victims. *European Journal of Psychiatry, 13*(1), 33–39.

Werkgroep Verder (2005). *Suïcidepreventie: Het Opstarten van een Gespreksgroep voor Nabestaanden na Zelfdoding* [Suicide prevention: How to start a survivors' group]. Geneva, Switzerland: World Health Organization & Halle: Werkgroep Verder.

Werkgroep Verder. (2002–2008): *Charter: de Rechten van Nabestaanden na Zelfdoding* [Charter: The rights of suicide survivors]. Halle: Werkgroep Verder.

World Health Organization (WHO). (2000–2008). *Suicide prevention: How to start a survivors group.* Geneva, Switzerland: Author.

SECTION

5

Conclusions

Going Forward
A Research Agenda for Suicide Survivors

John L. McIntosh and John R. Jordan

As this volume demonstrates, clear strides have been made in our knowledge about the aftermath of suicide, in particular in the past 20 years. These advances notwithstanding, it also remains obvious that much must still be learned to further enhance and expand the information we need to meet the needs and assist in the grief process of those bereaved by suicide. In some cases, our present knowledge needs to be refined and sharpened by improved research methodologies; in others, the information gap represents an issue or aspect of suicide survivorship that has been neglected, ignored, or inadequately investigated. These gaps exist with respect to aspects of the grief experience of survivors, as well as the interventions that aid survivors.

☐ Research Methodology Issues

Although the number of investigations of suicide survivors has increased substantially in the past 2 decades, many of the limitations in interpretation and generalization of the findings of these studies are largely the same as those from previous times. The intent here is not to elaborate on each of these methodological issues, since that has been done by multiple authors over time (e.g., Cain, 1972; Clark, 2001; McIntosh, 1987, 1993, 1999). Instead, we provide here the primary research methodology issues of which investigators should be aware. It is hoped that awareness of and follow-through on these issues will improve the quality and quantity of research on suicide bereavement.

Control and Comparison Groups

As noted in Chapter 2, one of the most basic difficulties of early investigations involved the absence of any control or comparison groups with which the findings about suicide survivors could be contrasted and compared. As has been steadily seen in the detailed reviews over time, beginning with the effort of Calhoun, Selby, and Selby (1982) in which not a single control group study was found, research including comparison groups has increased (e.g., McIntosh, 1993, 1999; Sveen & Walby, 2008). This basic essential design feature is a minimal starting point for any quantitative empirical investigation that is to be conducted regarding suicide bereavement and intervention. An evidence-based body of knowledge must have as its core the strength and foundation associated with solid research design.

This requirement raises the crucial question of what is an appropriate control or comparison group for suicide survivors. The natural and primary answer that has emerged over time is to include groups of survivors of other modes of death with whom suicide survivors are compared. As has emerged from these investigations and been noted multiple times in this volume, these studies have often shown many similarities in grief and bereavement for suicide and other sudden and traumatic modes of death. However, some potential themes that seem to represent differences in suicide as compared to other causes of death have also been noted (see Chapter 2 for details).

In addition to these mode-of-death comparisons, which are essential in the building of the body of evidence, other types of comparison groups should also be included when feasible in suicide bereavement studies. For instance, studies that measure mental health, coping, and other reactions to suicide loss should include additional comparison groups of non-bereaved individuals to determine how those bereaved by suicide and other modes of death differ from the population that has not experienced a death. Preferably, as with comparison groups of individuals bereaved by other causes of death, the groups should be matched on variables such as relationship to the deceased (e.g., kinship or relationship to the index person), age and gender of both the bereaved and the survivor, race and ethnicity, geography, socioeconomic status, and other characteristics that may affect bereavement and reactions to a loss.

A final issue of groups in suicide bereavement research involves the use of convenience samples and the potential for associated selection bias. This refers primarily to investigations of readily available groups of individuals in research. Although this is often an understandable and sometimes unavoidable aspect of group studies dictated by economy as well as feasibility and practicality (e.g., randomized assignment to conditions used broadly in research is not possible in bereavement studies), researchers first need to identify this aspect of their design as well as potential limitations on their findings. Ethical research cannot be conducted, of course, without the use of individuals who are voluntarily participating, but it should be noted that study results might not be generalizable if the participants are not representative of the larger population to which one wishes to generalize. As we suggested in Chapter 1 of this book, the field of suicidology has not adequately defined who is a survivor. Thus, we do not know for certain if those suicide survivors who volunteer to participate in a bereavement study are representative of all survivors of such deaths. We do not know how many survivors there are, who they are, and what their characteristics are. Nor do we know what bereavement processes and issues exist for those who do not participate in studies of bereavement. Similarly, we do not know how survivors who seek out and attend survivor support groups or therapy differ from survivors of the same mode of death who do not seek out support groups or therapy. Research cannot proceed without willing volunteers, and greater efforts should be made to include broader and potentially more representative samples. One way in which this could be done would be to study consecutive cases of deaths from various causes within a community, and to contact and invite survivors from each death to participate in the investigation of bereavement, beginning first with the "obvious" survivors of immediate kin of the deceased. Then, a so-called "peer-nomination" or "snowballing" technique could be employed to ask this initial wave of survivors to "nominate" and possibly help recruit additional people who they believe have been significantly affected by the suicide. This process could be repeated with each new survivor of a given suicide who is recruited into the study so that a much more representative sample of all the persons affected in a given social network are included in the research. Such a study would almost certainly be more complex and time- and resource-consuming than a typical survivor study. However, the strength of this more robust design would allow for increased generalizability and confidence in the findings than we find in the typical convenience sample study of survivors done to date.

Sample Size and Measurement

Adequate sample size and the quality of measurement are just as basic to solid research design as the inclusion of control groups. Most studies in the suicide bereavement literature, excluding qualitative studies and individual accounts, involve relatively small numbers of participants in suicide bereaved and other groups. Although not entirely invalidating the findings, this aspect weakens the potential significance and representativeness of the investigation and its results. This effect is magnified when studies break the groups of bereaved individuals into subgroups by characteristics such as relationship to the deceased, gender, age, etc. Researchers must utilize sound research procedures regarding the determination of adequate sample size to ensure their findings attain the statistical strength required.

An issue that is certainly not unique to the study of suicide bereavement is the desirability of strong measurement of the variables of interest. This involves, whenever possible, the use or development of standardized instruments that are both reliable (i.e., measure the variable consistently) and valid (i.e., measure the variable intended). A number of instruments have been utilized to measure general bereavement in suicide research, including the Texas Revised Inventory of Grief (TRIG; Faschingbauer, 1981); the Grief Experience Inventory (GEI; Sanders, Mauger, & Strong, 1985); and the Grief Experience Questionnaire (GEQ; Barrett & Scott, 1989), the latter being the only bereavement measure specifically developed for use with suicide survivors. In addition, measures of complicated grief or prolonged grief disorder are also emerging (e.g., Inventory of Complicated Grief [Prigerson, Vanderwerker, & Maciejewski, 2008; Prigerson et al., 1995, 2009]). Measures of relevant general mental health (e.g., Beck Depression Inventory [Beck, 1978]) have also been frequently included.

At the same time, researchers have often included measures, sometimes as simple as a single question, to measure issues and variables that may not be included in other instruments. Frequently, no indication of reliability or validity (other than perhaps the unspoken "face validity" of the question itself) are provided. An example of such a question would be to ask survivors, "Did you feel guilty following the death?", and asking that the response be made on a 5-point Likert scale from "Not guilty at all" to "Extremely guilty." Given the complexity of a reaction such as guilt feelings, it is uncertain how reliable or valid such a question might be without data to indicate these properties. Such a question is almost certainly too simple to provide adequate information about the many issues associated with guilt among the suicide bereaved. (See Neimeyer, Hogan, and Laurie, 2008, for a thorough discussion of the issues involved in the measurement of grief.)

Research Designs

An important addition to the research aspects noted above is the recommendation that replication studies and investigations employing a variety of methodologies be conducted. This latter point emphasizes the need to provide a convergence of findings that provide support for what may be substantial results. Thus, one practical application of this idea would be to conduct not only quantitative but also qualitative studies of survivors utilizing well-established qualitative research methodologies. As another example, in addition to studying survivors who are part of support groups, a study of survivors that utilizes the previously mentioned "snowballing" procedure to recruit participants could be conducted.

The crucial point here is that similar or consistent findings, derived from carefully conducted research of various methodologies, would represent particularly strong research evidence. On the other hand, some findings may emerge from one type of research and not from another (e.g., qualitative vs. quantitative), and this may lead to new research with other methodologies to validate and qualify the original findings. No single form of research is the exclusive provider of useful knowledge. Information from qualitative as well as quantitative studies, including individual accounts by survivors and case histories by clinicians, all have the potential to inform our knowledge about survivors of suicide.

A special issue of research design often noted in reviews of survivor research is the tremendous need for longitudinal research designs. The majority of research has utilized a retrospective approach or a one-time measurement of grief and bereavement. By comparison, a longitudinal or follow-up study investigates the same group of individuals at several points in time, asking the same or related questions as were asked at "Time 1." This design is particularly relevant for bereavement research, as investigators (and interveners) often wish to know about the course of the grieving process and not simply take a "snapshot" at a single point in time. Few studies have appeared in the suicide bereavement literature employing even a single follow-up with survivors. One notable exception, by Farberow and colleagues (Farberow, Gallagher,

Gilewski, & Thompson, 1987; Farberow, Gallagher-Thompson, Gilewski, & Thompson, 1992a, 1992b), was highlighted in Chapter 3. The use of this type of longitudinal design may also permit the identification of high-risk periods in the grieving process. In addition, studies of grieving that begin early in the bereavement process and proceed over time are especially needed to provide information on this important initial phase of loss. Although ethical issues are raised about conducting research during this sensitive time for the suicide bereaved, carefully conducted, ethical research can be done to study this important time period (see Parkes, 1995; Stroebe, Hansson, Stroebe, & Schut, 2001; and Stroebe, Hansson, Schut, & Stroebe 2008, for research guidelines for bereavement research). Additional studies that include longitudinal designs are greatly needed and hold the promise of providing rich information with respect to the progression of suicide grief over time, including long-term or so-called "sleeper" effects (Jordan, 2001).

Time Since Death and Kinship Relations

The time that has elapsed since the death of a significant individual by suicide seems logically to be an important issue in suicide bereavement. Empirical support is growing for the observation that for most people, the trend for grief-related symptoms is to decrease with time. This is true for all types of loss (Prigerson, Vanderwerker, & Masciejewski, 2008), as well as for suicide survivors in particular (Feigelman, Jordan, & Gorman, 2009). Obviously, this does not mean that suicide bereavement follows a single, universal course over time or a single process or specific timeline is associated with grieving a loss by suicide. Rather, in this context, the issue of time since the death is raised to both highlight the importance of recognizing and controlling for this issue in research with suicide survivors, as well as to note that many studies in the present literature have not adequately recognized the possible limitations of their findings regarding this issue. For example, it is not uncommon for a survivor study to include individuals who have had a suicide loss that occurred within a few months of their participation in the study, as well as those for whom the loss was years or even decades removed (and almost any time period between these two extremes). This may be true in both general bereavement and intervention studies, since survivors may seek support or other interventions soon after their loss or at some time much later (e.g., Campbell, Cataldie, McIntosh, & Millet, 2004). This problem may be further complicated by the inclusion of comparison groups for which the time elapsed since the loss is more compressed than for the suicide group, or simply a situation in which the researchers have made no attempt to determine or control for this variable in their analyses of the findings.

Similarly, as pointed out most specifically in Chapter 3, the kinship or other relationship of the survivor to the deceased consistently produces an important effect on the individual's bereavement. Studies that combine survivors from numerous relationships to the deceased into a single group of "suicide survivors" may mask important reactions and issues among the diverse survivors. We emphasize the need to study separate groupings of survivors by kinship relation and/or to include sufficient numbers of survivors to meaningfully control for relationship in the interpretation of the findings.

Additionally, as noted in Chapter 3, only a small number of relationships have been the focus of published survivor studies, with most research investigating the bereavement of parents, spouses, and children after suicide, or combining all survivor relationships into a single grouping. To provide some indication of the variety of relationships that might meet the definition of "suicide survivor" discussed in Chapter 1, recall that Campbell (1997) noted that individuals from 28 different relationships to the deceased sought support services from the Baton Rouge Crisis Intervention Service. Research is needed to determine if and how suicide survivorship is affected by these various kinship relations to the deceased.

Finally, some effort to control for, or at least measure, the emotional closeness of the survivor to the deceased should also be included. For example, two individuals with the same kinship relation to a deceased individual (e.g., two siblings) may have had very different relationships with the deceased. Kinship alone may not always be the best indicator of the emotional bond of a survivor to the deceased.

Intervention Research

Although Chapter 34 addresses the issue of future programmatic needs with suicide survivors, some research-based aspects should be addressed here. In addition to the general need for multiple methods in bereavement research (such as qualitative methods), bereavement caregivers must ensure that the array of innovative and diverse intervention models for suicide survivors are part of the evidence-based body of knowledge. That is, we must have more research that demonstrates the efficacy of the therapies and support methods utilized (Constantino & Bricker, 1996; Constantino, Sekula, & Rubinstein, 2001; de Groot, de Keijser, Neeleman, Kerkhof, Nolen, & Burger, 2007, a randomized control study; Farberow, 1992; Jordan & McMenamy, 2004; McDaid, Trowman, Golder, Hawton, & Sowden, 2008). As noted in the sections on Promising Programs (Sections 3 and 4 of this volume), little or no assessment research has been conducted regarding these programs. This information is sorely needed to inform practice and enhance the healing process of suicide survivors. In times of limited resources (which seem to be always) and a growing emphasis on evidence-based best practices, such knowledge is needed to inform policymakers, program administrators, and individual clinicians that a particular model has evidence that justifies the devotion of time and resources. It will often be necessary for clinicians and other interveners to partner with researchers to affect these much-needed efficacy studies. As most agencies and organizations have discovered, clear methods of intervention and program assessment are needed to obtain and retain funding and support for new and ongoing services.

A special intervention issue related to time since the death is suggested by Campbell's Active Postvention Model (APM) findings (Campbell et al., 2004; Cerel & Campbell, 2008). The APM involves teams of suicide survivors who accompany the coroner to the death scene and provide immediate postvention with the survivors. The survivors are also told of the local crisis center's support group. Campbell and colleagues (2004) observed that on average, the survivors who sought support services did so 39 days after the death as compared to the approximately 4.5 year average for general suicide survivors seeking the services. In a second analysis of data, Cerel and Campbell (2008) found a less dramatic, but still clear, reduction in time before seeking services for those who received APM as compared to others who sought services (48 days vs. 97 days, respectively). With the assumption that receiving assistance sooner will lead toward more rapid or less complicated healing (an assumption that needs to be empirically verified), this might be one important issue to be systematically studied by researchers and clinicians.

☐ Research Agenda: What Do We Need to Know?

The chapters in this volume have raised and identified many questions that must be answered by sound research. A basic foundation is for future research to include the solid empirical research design elements noted above (i.e., control or comparison groups, standardized instruments or determination of psychometric properties for instruments utilized, adequate sample size, and recognition that a variety of qualitative and quantitative designs are appropriate, including clinical and anecdotal evidence). In addition, studies are needed to determine and refine our knowledge about the commonalities and distinct themes and aspects of suicide bereavement as compared to grief following other modes of death and death characteristics (e.g., expected versus unexpected). Additional considerations that are needed to move survivor research forward include the following points:

1. Clear operational definitions of "suicide survivor" as used in research should be included as part of the description of the sample, but efforts are needed to reach a standardized definition of suicide survivor (Chapter 1 of this volume suggests such a definition).

2. Basic epidemiological information is crucially needed. Sound, well-designed epidemiological research is needed to provide estimates of the number and characteristics of suicide survivors.

3. The standard demographic characteristics collected about suicide survivors who participate in research should assess for a family history of suicide and suicidal behaviors. Given existing evidence that suicide "runs in families," this information will help to address this contention, as well as possibly the oft-made statement that "Postvention is prevention for ... the next generation" (e.g., Shneidman, 1972, p. x; see also Andriessen, 2009).

4. As mentioned repeatedly, research on the complete range of kinship relations and other relationship categories is needed, as virtually nothing is known about the majority of relationship groups. This should include the circles of relationships surrounding the deceased with respect to issues such as closeness, bonding, and attachment of the survivor to the deceased, as well as impact on and distress of the individual, and duration of the distress. Additionally, investigation of the impact of suicide at various developmental periods continues to be important. Special issues often exist for survivors depending upon their own life-cycle period as well as that of the individual who took their life. This may be particularly true for child survivors of suicide (Cerel, Jordan, & Duberstein, 2008). Research focused on the effects of suicide loss on whole family systems is also needed. In addition, more research is needed on the effects of suicide on mental health and intervention providers.

5. Among the measures utilized, increased emphasis on coping mechanisms would inform intervention and logically aid healing by survivors. Both helpful and unhelpful attempts at coping would be informative to explore (e.g., which types of interactions with others following a suicide were most beneficial for survivors and which were not helpful and perhaps even hurtful). This issue includes the social support network of the individual survivor, especially, but not exclusively, that of the immediate family system. Interaction with other social networks (e.g., peers, classmates, etc.) as well as professionals (Feigelman, Gorman, & Jordan, 2009) must be understood as we build a knowledge base of the social impact of suicide.

6. A number of variables regarding suicide survivors have been absent or nearly absent from research scrutiny. These variables include cultural differences, such as differences based on race, ethnicity, and indigenous origin. Other "special populations" or factors worthy of study include clinicians as survivors, survivors of certain methods of suicide (e.g., are more violent suicides, or more public suicides more difficult), the impact of discovering the body or witnessing the suicide act, identification of those at greatest risk for poor bereavement outcome and the development of prolonged grief disorder, and the mental health problems and need for services among long-term survivors (e.g., the "sleeper effect").

7. It has been frequently noted in this volume that stigma, shame, guilt, and related emotional and feeling states are often associated with suicide survivorship and that efforts to destigmatize suicide are desirable. In this regard, attitudinal studies to monitor levels over time in these and other subjectively perceived aspects of survivorship also should be conducted. After some preliminary investigations nearly three decades ago (see, e.g., Calhoun & Allen, 1991; Calhoun & Selby 1990; Rudestam, 1987), few such studies have been conducted in recent years on attitudes toward survivors (with the exception of the Peterson, Luoma, & Dunne (2002) study of attitudes toward therapists of suicides; see also Ward & McIntosh, 2007a, 2007b). In a related issue, groups need to be identified for special attention in training and awareness-raising about suicide survivors so that biases and prejudices can be altered and better services provided.

8. Research demonstrating the effectiveness of intervention approaches is essential to advance the support and treatment of survivors in their healing journey (see e.g., McDaid, Trowman, Golder, Hawton, & Sowden, 2008). First is the general question, "Do our support

interventions generally help those who receive them?" Chapters 1 through 5 documented the many deleterious effects that may result from exposure to suicide for some people, including, most importantly, the elevation of the risk for suicide in people bereaved by suicide. We have barely begun to answer the question, "Do interventions for survivors actually prevent the development of or speed the recovery from these deleterious sequelae?" Although there is anecdotal evidence for this proposition, to the best of our knowledge, no controlled research has ever demonstrated that participation in a survivor support group actually reduces suicidal ideation, behavior, or death in people exposed to suicide. This kind of research would be invaluable in demonstrating the literally life-saving benefit of participation in postvention programs attributed to such participation by many survivors.

9. Additional intervention characteristics that must be investigated are variables such as whether the group (or other type of intervention) is facilitated by a professional or a peer-survivor leader, the format or length of the program, online support versus face-to-face intervention, whether there are subgroups of survivors for whom support or therapy may actually be detrimental, and whether all survivors either need or would benefit from an organized intervention following the suicide death of their loved one. Research on some of the variations of support groups has been surveyed (e.g., Cerel, Padgett, Conwell, & Reed, 2009; Rubey & McIntosh, 1996), but which of these variations represent "best practices" is not yet known.

10. Sections 3 and 4 of this volume on promising programs in both the United States and internationally detail specific approaches and efforts in several nations. However, there is a need to catalog others not included here to permit replication of models in new locations, as well as to provide information about the diversity of approaches that exist. Without adequate details, programs cannot be replicated elsewhere or evaluation studies conducted properly. Lifeline Australia, for example, has developed a training program for group facilitators that is exemplary in its detail and suitability for research measurement, and could serve as an excellent foundation for a manualized support group intervention study (see Chapter 28).

11. One topic of research that would provide helpful information to all future research investigations of suicide bereavement would be a study that demonstrated that no harm was being done to those who participate. Research following up with study participants to determine any detrimental, or even perhaps beneficial, effects of participating

in research may well allay concerns by institutional review boards (IRBs), which must approve investigations before they are conducted, and might also determine issues of research ethics to inform future researchers. In addition, a number of issues associated with bereavement research must be considered (e.g., Balk & Cook, 1995) and the establishment of a database of research protocols that have been approved by IRBs would help to establish both best research practices as well as assist future researchers who must navigate the sometimes seemingly daunting process of IRB approval.

12. When the term *postvention* is used more broadly to refer to the aftereffects of suicidal behavior and not exclusively that associated with fatal outcomes, a final issue of postvention concerns the effects following a nonfatal suicide attempt, both on the individual who made the attempt on his or her life as well as among the family and social network. Much remains to be explored in this neglected area, as noted in Chapter 3, regarding the effect and impact, as well as regarding interventions to assist those with relationships with the attempter to deal with the aftermath of the attempt. The nearly exclusive focus has been on therapy and intervention for the attempter, with the primary focus on preventing future suicidal behaviors. Other psychosocial effects on the attempter and their social networks have been mostly ignored.

☐ Conclusion: Including the Voices of Survivors

Careful reflection on the focus in Sections 3 and 4 of this volume on promising programs leads to an important observation. Many of the pioneering programs for survivor support in the United States, and to a lesser extent in other countries, have emerged out of the experience of survivorship itself. The passion and dedication the founders of these programs have shown have clearly been shaped by their experience as survivors of suicide loss and, in turn, have shaped the development of their programs. Notable about the programs highlighted in those sections is the general convergence in the types of services being offered to survivors. The heart of most of these services involves opportunities for peer-to-peer contact with other survivors with the same experience, typically with the help of a trained lay or professional facilitator. As we go forward, we believe strongly that the voices of survivors should continue to be heard and that survivors should become even more active in shaping the direction of research and program development in this field (Cutcliffe & Ball, 2009; Jordan & McMenamy,

2004; Myers & Fine, 2007). This "bottom-up" approach involves asking the people who are coping with the problem what they have learned from their experience, and what service providers can do that will assist with their recovery. This respectful, nonhierarchical approach recognizes fully the value of the hard-won wisdom that survivors have to offer both for the development of research ideas and interpretation, as well as for the design of intervention programs for survivors (see Chapter 34).

In conclusion, we believe that the research agenda outlined above, if pursued vigorously by researchers in cooperation with clinicians and survivors, would dramatically increase our knowledge of the aftermath of suicide for survivors. An emphasis in the research agenda must be to utilize the rich information from the diversity of research methodologies (i.e., qualitative, quantitative, clinical, and anecdotal) to bridge the gap between academic research studies and professional and lay caregivers who work directly with survivors. This information has the potential to significantly facilitate the grief and bereavement healing process for survivors and to assist them in their loss journey.

☐ References

Andriessen, K. (2009). Can postvention be prevention? *Crisis: The Journal of Crisis Intervention and Suicide Prevention, 30*, 43–47.

Balk, D. E., & Cook, A. S. (Issue Eds.). (1995). Special issue: Ethics and bereavement research. *Death Studies, 19*(2, whole issue).

Barrett, T. W., & Scott, T. B. (1989). Development of the Grief Experience Questionnaire. *Suicide and Life-Threatening Behavior, 19*, 201–215.

Beck, A. T. (1978). *Beck Depression Inventory.* San Antonio, TX: Psychological Corporation.

Cain, A. C. (1972). Introduction. In A. C. Cain (Ed.), *Survivors of suicide* (pp. 5–33). Springfield, IL: Charles C Thomas.

Calhoun, L. G., & Allen, B. G. (1991). Social reactions to the survivor of a suicide in the family: A review of the literature. *Omega: Journal of Death and Dying, 23*, 95–107.

Calhoun, L. G., & Selby, J. W. (1990). The social aftermath of a suicide in the family: Some empirical findings. In D. Lester (Ed.), *Current concepts of suicide* (pp. 214–24). Philadelphia, PA: Charles Press.

Calhoun, L. G., Selby, J. W., & Selby, L. E. (1982). The psychological aftermath of suicide: An analysis of current evidence. *Clinical Psychology Review, 2*, 409–420.

Campbell, F. R. (1997). Changing the legacy of suicide. *Suicide and Life-Threatening Behavior, 27*, 329–338.

Campbell, F. R., Cataldie, L., McIntosh, J., & Millet, K. (2004). An active postvention program. *Crisis: The Journal of Crisis Intervention and Suicide Prevention, 25*, 30–32.

Cerel, J., & Campbell, F. R. (2008). Suicide survivors seeking mental health services: A preliminary examination of the role of an Active Postvention Model. *Suicide and Life-Threatening Behavior, 38*, 30–34.

Cerel, J., Jordan, J. R., & Duberstein, P. R. (2008). The impact of suicide on the family. *Crisis: The Journal of Crisis Intervention and Suicide Prevention, 29*, 38–44.

Cerel, J., Padgett, J. H., Conwell, Y., & Reed, G. A., Jr. (2009). A call for research: The need to better understand the impact of support groups for suicide survivors. *Suicide and Life-Threatening Behavior, 39*, 269–281.

Clark, S. (2001). Bereavement after suicide: How far have we come and where do we go from here? *Crisis: The Journal of Crisis Intervention and Suicide Prevention, 22*, 102–108.

Constantino, R. E., & Bricker, P. L. (1996). Nursing postvention for spousal survivors of suicide. *Issues in Mental Health Nursing, 17*, 131–152.

Constantino, R. E., Sekula, K., & Rubinstein, E. N. (2001). Group intervention for widowed survivors of suicide. *Suicide and Life-Threatening Behavior, 31*, 428–441.

Cutcliffe, J., & Ball, P. B. (2009). Suicide survivors and the suicidology academe: Reconciliation and reciprocity. *Crisis: The Journal of Crisis Intervention and Suicide Prevention, 30*, 208–214.

de Groot, M., de Keijser, J., Neeleman, J., Kerkhof, A., Nolen, W., & Burger, H. (2007). Cognitive behaviour therapy to prevent complicated grief among relatives and spouses bereaved by suicide: Cluster randomised controlled trial. *BMJ: British Medical Journal, 334*, 994–996.

Farberow, N. L. (1992). The Los Angeles Survivors After Suicide Program: An evaluation. *Crisis, 13*, 23–34.

Farberow, N. L., Gallagher, D. E., Gilewski, M. J., & Thompson, L. W. (1987). An examination of the early impact of bereavement on psychological distress in survivors of suicide. *Gerontologist, 27*, 592–598.

Farberow, N. L., Gallagher-Thompson, D., Gilewski, M., & Thompson, L. (1992a). The role of social supports in the bereavement process of surviving spouses of suicide and natural deaths. *Suicide and Life-Threatening Behavior, 22*, 107–124.

Farberow, N. L., Gallagher-Thompson, D., Gilewski, M., & Thompson, L. (1992b). Changes in grief and mental health of bereaved spouses of older suicides. *Journal of Gerontology: Psychological Sciences, 47*, P357–P366.

Faschingbauer, T. R. (1981). *Texas Revised Inventory of Grief manual.* Houston, TX: Honeycomb Publishing Company.

Feigelman, W., Gorman, B. S., & Jordan, J. R. (2009). Stigmatization and suicide bereavement. *Death Studies, 33*, 591–608.

Feigelman, W., Jordan, J., & Gorman, B. S. (2009). How they died, time since loss, and bereavement outcomes. *Omega: Journal of Death and Dying, 58*, 251–273.

Jordan, J. (2001). Is suicide bereavement different? A reassessment of the literature. *Suicide and Life-Threatening Behavior, 31*, 91–102.

Jordan, J., & McMenamy, J. (2004). Interventions for suicide survivors: A review of the literature. *Suicide and Life-Threatening Behavior, 34*, 337–349.

McDaid, C., Trowman, R., Golder, S., Hawton, K., & Sowden, A. (2008). Interventions for people bereaved through suicide: Systematic review. *British Journal of Psychiatry, 193*, 438–443.

McIntosh, J. L. (1987). Research, therapy, and educational needs. In E. J. Dunne, J. L. McIntosh, & K. Dunne-Maxim (Eds.), *Suicide and its aftermath: Understanding and counseling the survivors* (pp. 263–277). New York, NY: W. W. Norton.

McIntosh, J. L. (1993). Control group studies of suicide survivors: A review and critique. *Suicide and Life-Threatening Behavior, 23,* 146–161.

McIntosh, J. L. (1999). Research on survivors of suicide. In Mary Stimming & Maureen Stimming (Eds.), *Before their time: Adult children's experiences of parental suicide* (pp. 157–180). Philadelphia, PA: Temple University Press.

Myers, M. F., & Fine, C. (2007). Touched by suicide: Bridging the perspectives of survivors and clinicians. *Suicide and Life-Threatening Behavior, 37,* 119–126.

Neimeyer, R. A., Hogan, N. S., & Laurie, A. (2008). The measurement of grief: Psychometric considerations in the assessment of reactions to bereavement. In M. S. Stroebe, R. O. Hansson, H. Schut, & W. Stroebe (Eds.), *Handbook of bereavement research and practice: Advances in theory and intervention* (pp. 133–161). Washington, DC: American Psychological Association.

Parkes, C. M. (1995). Guidelines for conducting ethical bereavement research. *Death Studies, 19,* 171–181.

Peterson, E. M., Luoma, J. B., & Dunne, E. (2002). Suicide survivors' perceptions of the treating clinician. *Suicide and Life-Threatening Behavior, 32,* 158–166.

Prigerson, H. G., Horowitz, M. J., Jacobs, S. C., Parkes, C. M., Aslan, M., Goodkin, K., … Maciejewski, P. K. (2009). Prolonged Grief Disorder: Psychometric validation of criteria proposed for *DSM-V* and *ICD-11.* [Electronic version]. *PLoS Med* 6(8), e1000121. doi: 10.1371/journal.pmed.1000121

Prigerson, H. G., Maciejewski, P. K., Reynolds, C. F., Bierhals, A. J., Newsom, J. T., Fasiczka, A., … Miller, M. (1995). Inventory of Complicated Grief: A scale to measure maladaptive symptoms of loss. *Psychiatry Research, 59,* 65–79.

Prigerson, H. G., Vanderwerker, L. C., & Maciejewski, P. K. (2008). A case for inclusion of prolonged grief disorder in DSM-V. In M. S. Stroebe, R. O. Hansson, H. Schut, & W. Stroebe (Eds.), *Handbook of bereavement research and practice: Advances in theory and intervention* (pp. 165–186). Washington, DC: American Psychological Association.

Rubey, C. T., & McIntosh, J. L. (1996). Suicide survivors groups: Results of a survey. *Suicide and Life-Threatening Behavior, 26,* 351–358.

Rudestam, K. E. (1987). Public perceptions of suicide survivors. In E. J. Dunne, J. L. McIntosh, & K. Dunne-Maxim (Eds.), *Suicide and its aftermath: Understanding and counseling the survivors* (pp. 31–44). New York, NY: Norton.

Sanders, C. M., Mauger, P. A., & Strong, P. N., Jr. (1985). *A manual for the Grief Experience Inventory.* Palo Alto, CA: Consulting Psychologists Press.

Shneidman, E. (1972). Foreword. In A. C. Cain (Ed.), *Survivors of suicide* (pp. ix–xi). Springfield, IL: Charles C Thomas.

Stroebe, M., Hansson, R., Stroebe, W., & Schut, H. (2001). Future directions in bereavement research. In M. Stroebe, R. Hansson, W. Stroebe, & H. Schut (Eds.), *Handbook of bereavement research* (pp. 741–766). Washington, DC: American Psychological Association.

Stroebe, M. S., Hansson, R. O., Schut, H., & Stroebe, W. (2008). Bereavement research: 21st-century prospects. In M. S. Stroebe, R. O. Hansson, H. Schut & W. Stroebe (Eds.), *Handbook of bereavement research and practice: Advances in theory and intervention* (pp. 577–603). Washington, DC: American Psychological Association.

Sveen, C.-A., & Walby, F. A. (2008). Suicide survivors' mental health and grief reactions: A systematic review of controlled studies. *Suicide and Life-Threatening Behavior, 38,* 13–29.

Ward, E. F., & McIntosh, J. L. (2007a, April 13). *Attitudes toward therapists with patient suicides.* Paper presented at the 40th annual meeting of the American Association of Suicidology, New Orleans, LA.

Ward, E. F., & McIntosh, J. L. (2007b, April 13). *Attitudes and suicide: Therapists and clients.* Paper presented at the 40th annual meeting of the American Association of Suicidology, New Orleans, LA.

34
CHAPTER

A Call to Action
Building Clinical and Programmatic
Support for Suicide Survivors

John R. Jordan, John L. McIntosh, Iris M. Bolton, Frank
R. Campbell, Joanne L. Harpel, and Michelle Linn-Gust

Historically, the stigma associated with suicide has been transferred to
the families of the deceased (Colt, 2006), along with the social isolation
that accompanies most disenfranchised grief. However, a change is happening around the world. To borrow the phrase used by the American
Foundation for Suicide Prevention, as suicide has begun to emerge from
"out of the darkness," so too have those who a.ᵒ grieving the loss of a
loved one to suicide begun to speak up, insisting on acceptance, support,
and action from their communities. Thus, the worldwide effort to recognize suicide prevention as a public health goal has had salutatory effects
on suicide survivors as well. Moreover, the political support to facilitate
this process appears to be expanding. In this chapter, we briefly review
the progress that has been made in the last decade in building societal
change and support infrastructure for survivors. We then enumerate

several goals for this "survivor movement" going forward over the next 10 years, and propose specific programmatic steps that we believe will continue this remarkable process of social change.

☐ Positive Changes

The issuance of the World Health Organization's suicide prevention document (World Health Organization [WHO], 1996), closely followed in the United States by the *Surgeon General's Call to Action* in 1999 (U.S. Public Health Service, 1999) and the *National Strategy for Suicide Prevention* in 2001 (U.S. Public Health Service, 2001), were seminal events in the movement to bring suicide out of the shadows of shame and stigma that have surrounded it for centuries. Although these documents made insufficient mention of the needs of suicide survivors, they have had the effect of calling attention to suicide as a legitimate public health concern, serving as a catalyst for the development of more organized suicide prevention efforts in the United States and around the world. They have also contributed to a change in public attitudes toward suicide survivors, along with the emergence of new support services for survivors around the world.

Several examples of the development of survivor support infrastructure are highlighted in the various chapters of this book. A review of these programs shows both a remarkable convergence of efforts that center on the value of survivor-to-survivor contact (sometimes with the assistance of mental health professionals), and the necessity of providing a sheltered setting where survivors can bear witness to their experience without judgment, criticism, or expectation to quickly "get over it." The programs also demonstrate an impressive diversity and creativity in how they accomplish this core function of providing a safe place for sharing the bereavement experience. To touch upon a few examples, the federal government in Australia has directly funded the development of evidence-based practice standards for survivor bereavement support groups and implemented the development of such groups throughout the nation. Just recently, these standards have been listed in the Best Practices Registry of the Suicide Prevention Resource Center (see Chapter 28). Additional innovative services, such as the Standby Response service for survivors and the telephone-based support program of the Salvation Army in Australia, offer new and promising avenues of support for survivors. The United States has experienced a growth in the number of new survivor groups (Harpel, 2009), an increase in the number of trained group facilitators, a dramatic expansion of participatory healing conferences such as National Survivors of Suicide Day, and the development of survivor outreach services that make early contact with new survivor families in their own homes. There are also laudable efforts to provide culturally sensitive support services for minority groups within various countries, particularly for indigenous peoples whose suicide rates have unfortunately been considerably higher than their Caucasian counterparts (e.g., the Maori in New Zealand, Aborigines in Australia, and Native Americans in the United States). The range and scope of these developments are documented in Sections 3 and 4 of this volume. Although research studies have not yet been done to provide clear empirical support for this proposition (see Chapter 33), there appears to be a reduction in the stigma surrounding survivor families. This diminution of the social condemnation and isolation of survivors can only make the seeking of support easier for traumatized and grieving survivor families. It is a most welcome development.

☐ Goals for the Next Decade

In the past, the survivor "movement" appears to have been a more or less spontaneous, but uncoordinated effort around the world. More recently, there are signs it is becoming more unified. As previously mentioned, many of the emerging programs have similar elements since survivors and postvention caregivers have converged on similar types of support services that seem to be of help to survivors. This most likely reflects the reality that the psychological experiences of survivors are more similar than dissimilar around the world, despite the cultural differences that influence the grieving process. The authors in this book hope this process of social change can be coordinated and accelerated through the dissemination of information, ideas, and exemplars of new programs that can be adopted and modified to meet the particular needs of survivors in various societies.

As we look to the development of survivor support infrastructure over the next decade, we would like to see a focus on several goals by the community of survivors and their friends, families, and coworkers, researchers, and service providers. These goals follow.

Universal Provision of Information About Resources and Multiple Pathways to Access services

Research suggests that many survivors struggle with finding services when the tragedy of suicide hits their family and community

(McMenamy, Jordan, & Mitchell, 2008). This difficulty only adds to the barriers created by the survivor's own psychological traumatization and grief, often making the search for resources a daunting and demoralizing task (Dyregrov & Dyregrov, 2008; Jordan, 2009; McMenamy et al., 2008). Perhaps understandably, the possibility of losing someone to suicide is an event for which few people prepare themselves. Many caregivers are also ill-informed about resources for survivors in their community. This should change and in 10 years we would like to see it become routine for every survivor to be given timely and relevant information about support resources in their community within a short period after the suicide.

Information about how and where to seek services should be disseminated to the general public through public service announcements, information and referral services, online databases, and so forth. In addition, after a suicide has occurred, caregivers who are likely to have initial contact with survivors (such as emergency medical personnel, funeral professionals, clergy, and mental health professionals) can play a central role in disseminating information about resources. We would like to see these early responders routinely pass on information to survivors about services that may be available. This can even include information provided "on scene" at the location of the suicide to family and friends who gather (Campbell, Cataldie, McIntosh, & Millet, 2004; see also Chapter 14). Importantly, this also includes mental health professionals who may have had contact with the deceased before the suicide (see Chapter 7 for postvention guidelines). The information should include both verbal and written information about the types of resources that might be helpful to survivors. Ideally, it should be offered not just once, but on more than one occasion since many survivors are too traumatized and stunned to retain this information or be in a position to know what they will need later in their grieving process. For example, emergency room personnel, clergy, and funeral directors could routinely follow up with survivor families in the weeks and months following the death, as clinical experience suggests that such ongoing outreach may be particularly important for traumatized families after the initial flood of social support begins to abate. Internet-based online resources, including those that help provide information and referral to services, should also become an important pathway for survivors to find resources (see Sections 3 and 4 of this volume for examples).

In addition, organizations that take responsibility for advocating for survivor needs (e.g., the American Foundation for Suicide Prevention [AFSP] and the American Association of Suicidology [AAS] in the United States) should increase their efforts to educate and train early responders about the needs and vulnerabilities of suicide survivors. We have heard many anecdotal stories from survivors who have been tremendously

professionals receive so little formal training in this area. We believe that assessment and treatment of survivors of suicide and other sudden, unexpected, violent losses should become a universal component of graduate mental health training programs, even if students do not expect to work with the issue in their careers. The data suggest that exposure to suicide is much more common than previously realized (see Chapter 1, as well as Crosby & Sacks, 2002). Thus, the reality is that during the course of their work, most professionals will encounter people who have been exposed to suicide. Interpersonal loss also underpins the development of a wide range of psychopathology (Cerel, Fristad, Verducci, Weller, & Weller, 2006; Luecken, 2008; Shapiro, 2008; Thompson, Gallagher-Thompson, Futterman, Gilewski, & Peterson, 1998). The training of mental health clinicians needs to provide them with knowledge both about suicide prevention and about the range of responses to traumatic death such as suicide. The training also needs to incorporate knowledge of the small but growing array of evidence-based treatments for complicated or prolonged grief and for traumatic loss (Bandura-Madej & Hennel-Brzozowska, 2000; Boelen, 2006; Cohen, Mannarino, & Deblinger, 2006; Cohen, Mannarino, Gibson et al., 2006; Jordan & Neimeyer, 2007; Litz, 2004; Murphy, 2006; Regehr & Sussman, 2004; K. Shear & Frank, 2006; K. Shear, Frank, Houck, & Reynolds, 2005; K. Shear, 2006; Shear, Zuckoff, Melhem, & Gorscak, 2006; Stroebe, Hansson, Schut, & Stroebe, 2008; Zuckoff et al., 2006), including interventions for suicide survivors (Jordan & McMenamy, 2004; McDaid, Trowman, Golder, Hawton, & Sowden, 2008). It is also worth noting that AFSP currently has studies underway of an intervention for suicide survivors with complicated grief (J. Harpel, personal communication, 2010).

Services for Disenfranchised Populations

There is clear evidence that certain population subgroups have elevated rates of suicide and hence are likely to leave behind higher numbers of suicide survivors from those subgroups. There are also categories of survivors for whom traditional and existing services are unlikely to be culturally appropriate or helpful. As an example of both of these problems, and as documented in Chapters 28 and 31 on postvention in Australia and New Zealand, suicide completion rates are much higher for indigenous peoples in many countries. This also is true of Native Americans in the United States (McIntosh, 2009). Comparatively little has been done to design or implement postvention services for people who may be reluctant to reach out for help because they do not have the economic wherewithal or the sense of trust in the health care system to access services. In the United States, this could include African Americans, Hispanics, and other minority and immigrant populations. We would like to see special attention given in the next 10 years to such "disenfranchised" groups of survivors for whom traditional healers, religious leaders, and community-based workers who reside in the community might be much more instrumental in offering help to suicide survivors. (See Chapter 13 for further discussion of these issues.)

Another very different group might be mental health professionals themselves who become survivors, particularly after the suicide of a client. As Chapter 5 points out, mental health professionals can be stigmatized by their own colleagues after the suicide of a client, and may be reluctant to seek services for themselves in public ways that add to their feeling of stigmatization (such as attending a general survivor support group). We would like to see the recommendations made in Chapters 5 and 7 for improved training of mental health professionals around postvention after the suicide of a client, as well as better organizational response to clinician survivors, be fully implemented in the coming decade.

A third example of a disenfranchised group of survivors might be survivors of the suicide by a member of the military (see Chapter 24). The U.S. military has traditionally stigmatized death by suicide as a dishonorable death, implicitly seeing it as coming from either weakness or dereliction of duty. This has no doubt increased the feelings of shame and isolation of military survivor families. Although traditional forms of services, such as support groups, may be effective for military family survivors, the high level of stigmatization around suicide may require extra outreach and education about the nature of suicide to make the seeking of services and the general provision of informal community support easier and more routine.

Development of Standards

The chapters on work in Australia and Belgium (Chapters 28 and 32) point to another promising development that we would hope to see accelerated in the next 10 years. Chapter 33 outlined the pressing need for more research, including research into the efficacy and effectiveness of interventions to help survivors. Beyond that, there is a need to develop evidence-based guidelines for services that can be adapted to the differing needs and service delivery realities in countries around the world. The developments mentioned previously in Chapter 28 on postvention in Australia in particular have produced a well thought-out process for training survivor support group facilitators. This detailed protocol can easily lend itself to being researched, replicated, and disseminated. We strongly encourage the development of similar efforts by other program development administrators in the coming decade.

Continuing Change in Cultural Attitudes Toward Suicide and Suicide Survivors

All of the goals previously set forth must be embedded within the context of a continuing change in societal attitudes toward suicide, and by extension, toward those who have lost a loved one to suicide. Suicide, its causes and its impact, must become an acceptable topic of public discussion in the media; in the church, synagogue, temple, or mosque; and in the schools—indeed, in all the institutions of our nations. Suicide literally must stop being an unspeakable event, and suicide survivors must move from being inappropriately stigmatized within their communities to being recognized for what they are: people grieving after the death of a loved one to a complex "perfect storm" of contributing factors. That storm typically includes deep psychological pain, hopelessness, overwhelming life problems, psychiatric disorder, and feelings of isolation from and burdensomeness to others. This change in perceptions has definitely begun around the world. In the next decade, we hope to see it progress rapidly toward a new social response of compassion, acceptance, and effective long-term support for survivors of suicide loss. When this happens, then we truly will be able to lay claim to the late Edwin Shneidman's profound observation that postvention after suicide is prevention for the next generation (Shneidman, 1972).

☐ References

Bandura-Madej, W., & Hennel-Brzozowska, A. (2000). Crisis intervention and psychotherapy in traumatic bereavement after a child's death by homicide. *Archives of Psychiatry and Psychotherapy, 2*, 61–72.

Boelen, P. A. (2006). Cognitive-behavioral therapy for complicated grief: Theoretical underpinnings and case descriptions. *Journal of Loss & Trauma, 11*, 1–30.

Campbell, F. R., Cataldie, L., McIntosh, J., & Millet, K. (2004). An active postvention program. *Crisis: The Journal of Crisis Intervention and Suicide Prevention, 25*, 30–32.

Cerel, J., & Campbell, F. R. (2008). Suicide survivors seeking mental health services: A preliminary examination of the role of an active postvention model. *Suicide and Life-Threatening Behavior, 38*, 30–34.

Cerel, J., Fristad, M. A., Verducci, J., Weller, R. A., & Weller, E. B. (2006). Childhood bereavement: Psychopathology in the 2 years postparental death. *Journal of the American Academy of Child & Adolescent Psychiatry, 45*, 681–690.

Cohen, J. A., Mannarino, A. P., & Deblinger, E. (2006). *Treating trauma and traumatic grief in children and adolescents*. New York, NY: Guilford Press.

Cohen, J. A., Mannarino, A. P., Gibson, L. E., Cozza, S. J., Brymer, M. J., & Murray, L. (2006). Interventions for children and adolescents following disasters. In E. C. Ritchie, P. J. Watson, & M. J. Friedman (Eds.), *Interventions following mass violence and disasters: Strategies for mental health practice* (pp. 227–256). New York, NY: Guilford Press.

Colt, G. H. (2006). *November of the soul: The enigma of suicide*. New York, NY: Scribner.

Crosby, A. E., & Sacks, J. J. (2002). Exposure to suicide: Incidence and association with suicidal ideation and behavior: United States, 1994. *Suicide and Life-Threatening Behavior, 32*, 321–328.

Currier, J. M., Holland, J. M., Coleman, R. A., & Neimeyer, R. A. (2008). Bereavement following violent death: An assault on life and meaning. In R. G. Stevenson & G. R. Cox (Eds.), *Perspectives on violence and violent death* (pp. 177–202). Amityville, NY: Baywood Publishing Co.

Currier, J. M., Holland, J. M., & Neimeyer, R. A. (2006). Sense-making, grief, and the experience of violent loss: Toward a mediational model. *Death Studies, 30*, 403–428.

de Groot, M. H., de Keijser, J., & Neeleman, J. (2006). Grief shortly after suicide and natural death: A comparative study among spouses and first-degree relatives. *Suicide and Life-Threatening Behavior, 36*, 418–431.

Dyregrov, K., & Dyregrov, A. (2008). *Effective grief and bereavement support: The role of family, friends, colleagues, schools, and support professionals*. Philadelphia, PA: Jessica Kingsley Publishers.

Feigelman, W., Gorman, B. S., Beal, K. C., & Jordan, J. R. (2008). Internet support groups for suicide survivors: A new mode for gaining bereavement assistance. *Omega: Journal of Death and Dying, 57*, 217–243.

Harpel, J. (2009). *AFSP support group facilitator training program: Follow-up survey of attendees 2002–2006 Executive summary*. Unpublished document prepared for the American Foundation for Suicide Prevention, New York, NY.

Jordan, J. (2009). After suicide: Clinical work with survivors. *Grief Matters: The Australian Journal of Grief and Bereavement, 12*, 4–9.

Jordan, J., & McMenamy, J. (2004). Interventions for suicide survivors: A review of the literature. *Suicide and Life-Threatening Behavior, 34*, 337–349.

Jordan, J., & Neimeyer, R. A. (2007). Historical and contemporary perspectives on assessment and intervention. In D. Balk, C. Wogrin, G. Thornton, & D. Meagher (Eds.), *Handbook of thanatology: The essential body of knowledge for the study of death, dying, and bereavement* (pp. 213–225). New York, NY: Routledge/ Taylor & Francis Group.

Litz, B. T. (2004). *Early intervention for trauma and traumatic loss*. New York, NY: Guilford Press.

Luecken, L. J. (2008). Long-term consequences of parental death in childhood: Psychological and physiological manifestations. In M. S. Stroebe, R. O. Hansson, H. Schut, & W. Stroebe (Eds.), *Handbook of bereavement research and practice: Advances in theory and intervention* (pp. 397–416). Washington, DC: American Psychological Association.

Martin, T. L., & Doka, K. J. (1999). *Men don't cry … women do: Transcending gender stereotypes of grief*. Philadelphia, PA: Brunner/Mazel.

McDaid, C., Trowman, R., Golder, S., Hawton, K., & Sowden, A. (2008). Interventions for people bereaved through suicide: Systematic review. *British Journal of Psychiatry, 193*, 438–443.

McIntosh, J. L. (2009). *U.S.A. suicide 2006: Official final data.* Washington, DC: American Association of Suicidology.

McMenamy, J. M., Jordan, J. R., & Mitchell, A. M. (2008). What do suicide survivors tell us they need? Results of a pilot study. *Suicide and Life-Threatening Behavior, 38*, 375–389.

Melhem, N. M., Moritz, G., Walker, M., Shear, M. K., & Brent, D. (2007). Phenomenology and correlates of complicated grief in children and adolescents. *Journal of the American Academy of Child & Adolescent Psychiatry, 46*, 493–499.

Murphy, S. A. (2006). Evidence-based interventions for parents following their children's violent deaths. In E. K. Rynearson (Ed.), *Violent death: Resilience and intervention beyond the crisis* (pp. 175–194). New York, NY: Routledge/Taylor & Francis Group.

Neria, Y., & Litz, B. T. (2004). Bereavement by traumatic means: The complex synergy of trauma and grief. *Journal of Loss & Trauma, 9*, 73–87.

Provini, C., Everett, J. R., & Pfeffer, C. R. (2000). Adults mourning suicide: Self-reported concerns about bereavement, needs for assistance, and help-seeking behavior. *Death Studies, 24*, 1–19.

Regehr, C., & Sussman, T. (2004). Intersections between grief and trauma: Toward an empirically based model for treating traumatic grief. *Brief Treatment and Crisis Intervention, 4*, 289–309.

Shapiro, E. R. (2008). Whose recovery, of what? Relationships and environments promoting grief and growth. *Death Studies, 32*, 40–58.

Shear, K. (2006). Adapting imaginal exposure to the treatment of complicated grief. In B. O. Rothbaum (Ed.), *Pathological anxiety: Emotional processing in etiology and treatment* (pp. 215–226). New York, NY: Guilford Press.

Shear, K., & Frank, E. (2006). Treatment of complicated grief: Integrating cognitive-behavioral methods with other treatment approaches. In V. M. Follette & J. I. Ruzek (Eds.), *Cognitive-behavioral therapies for trauma* (2nd ed.) (pp. 290–320). New York, NY: Guilford Press.

Shear, K., Frank, E., Houck, P. R., & Reynolds, C. F., III. (2005). Treatment of complicated grief: A randomized controlled trial. *Journal of the American Medical Association, 293*, 2601–2608.

Shear, M. K., Zuckoff, A., Melhem, N., & Gorscak, B. J. (2006). The syndrome of traumatic grief and its treatment. In L. A. Schein, H. I. Spitz, G. M. Burlingame, P. R. Muskin, & S. Vargo (Eds.), *Psychological effects of catastrophic disasters: Group approaches to treatment* (pp. 287–333). New York, NY: Haworth Press.

Shneidman, E. S. (1972). Foreword. In A. C. Cain (Ed.), *Survivors of suicide* (pp. ix–xi). Springfield, IL: Charles C Thomas.

Stroebe, M. S., Hansson, R. O., Schut, H., & Stroebe, W. (2008). *Handbook of bereavement research and practice: Advances in theory and intervention.* Washington, DC: American Psychological Association.

Thompson, L. W., Gallagher-Thompson, D., Futterman, A., Gilewski, M. J., & Peterson, J. (1998). The effects of late-life spousal bereavement over a thirty-month interval. In T. A. Salthouse & M. Lawton (Eds.), *Essential papers on the psychology of aging* (pp. 722–738). New York, NY: New York University Press.

U.S. Public Health Service. (1999). *The Surgeon General's call to action to prevent suicide.* Washington, DC: U.S. Department of Health and Human Services. Retrieved from http://www.surgeongeneral.gov/library/calltoaction/index.html

U.S. Public Health Service. (2001). *National strategy for suicide prevention: Goals and objectives for action.* Washington, DC: U.S. Department of Health and Human Services. Retrieved from http://www.mentalhealth.samhsa.gov/publications/allpubs/SMA01-3517/

Ursano, R. J., Cerise, F. P., Demartino, R., Reissman, D. B., & Shear, M. K. (2006). The impact of disasters and their aftermath on mental health. *Journal of Clinical Psychiatry, 67,* 7–14.

World Health Organization (WHO). (1996). *Prevention of suicide: Guidelines for the formulation and implementation of national strategies.* Geneva, Switzerland: World Health Organization.

Zuckoff, A., Shear, K., Frank, E., Daley, D. C., Seligman, K., & Silowash, R. (2006). Treating complicated grief and substance use disorders: A pilot study. *Journal of Substance Abuse Treatment, 30,* 205–211.

INDEX

Page numbers followed by f indicate figure; those followed by t indicate table.